# MASS MEDIA
# IN AMERICA

SIXTH EDITION

# MASS MEDIA IN AMERICA

**Don R. Pember**
University of Washington

MACMILLAN PUBLISHING COMPANY
New York

Editor: David Chodoff
Production Supervisor: Linda Greenberg
Production Manager: Pamela Kennedy Oborski
Text and Cover Designer: Jane Edelstein
Cover Photograph: Bill Longcore
Photo Researchers: Chris Migdol/Diane Kraut
Illustrations: Precision Graphics


This book was set in Souvenir Light by The Clarinda Co., and was printed and bound by Von Hoffmann Press, Inc. The cover was printed by Von Hoffmann Press, Inc.

Macmillan Publishing Company
866 Third Avenue, New York, New York 10022

Macmillan Publishing Company is part of the Maxwell Communication Group of Companies.

**Library of Congress Cataloging-in-Publication Data**

Pember, Don R., 1939-
    Mass Media in America / Don R. Pember.—6th ed.
        p.   cm.
    Includes bibliographical references and index.
    ISBN 0-02-393780-7 (pbk.)
    1. Mass media—United States.   I. Title.
    P92.U5P4   1992
    302.23′0973—dc20          91-11193
                              CIP

Printing:  1  2  3  4  5  6  7      Year:  2  3  4  5  6  7  8

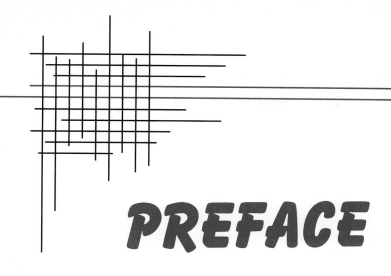

# PREFACE

Perhaps no nation in the history of mankind has enjoyed a communication system equal to the one that currently exists in the United States. It must be regarded as one of the technological marvels of the modern world. It is a multifaceted system of interpersonal and mass communication elements, and some parts of the network touch virtually everyone in the nation.

This book is about one important aspect of that communication system, the mass media—their historical and economic foundations, their organization, their strengths, and their weaknesses. The mass media in America play a vital role in maintaining civilization for a nation of 250 million people. While this book is largely descriptive, it is analytical as well, and the analysis is founded on the author's strongly held contention that in this society at least, we have a right to expect more from those who operate our system of mass communication than from those who make our automobiles or frozen TV dinners. The press—the mass media—after all, is the only enterprise mentioned in the U.S. Constitution. Those who constructed our system of government shielded the mass media from interference by the government, interference that is not uncommon in other industries or in other nations. This shield was put in place because the architects of our system of government believed that the press played a vital role in the nation, a role too important to be endangered by even a well-meaning government.

A modern society has many critical needs, including education, health care, banking, insurance, police and fire protection, a postal system, and a communications system. Yet of all institutions erected to meet these needs and many others, the mass communication system is the only one that is not operated or heavily regulated by the government. It is a system that is largely directed by private enterprise.

A communication system must meet various needs for society to survive and prosper. At the very least we need a communication system that can service our capitalistic, goods-oriented economic system; that can provide the information needed for members of the society to adjust constantly their relationship with a changing environment; that can present the members of our society and the rest of the world with a reasonable and realistic picture of the culture in which we exist; and that can provide us with the means by which we can make use of the self-governing process guaranteed to us by the Constitution. These four requirements constitute the analytical yardstick that is often applied to the mass media throughout this text.

Americans should be pleased that for the most part, the mass media in the United States are profitable and powerful institutions. It is only if they are profitable that they can reasonably be expected to service society in the ways noted above. It is only if they are powerful that they can fight any attempt by government and other interests who seek to deter them in meeting these responsibilities fairly and independently. Yet when winning profits and power becomes an end in itself, rather than a means to an end (and this is not an uncommon occurrence in the mass media today), the service we demand and need from our mass media may be seriously diminished. This is the central issue that the book attempts to explore.

This is the sixth edition of *Mass Media in America*. Several changes from previous editions need to be noted. The book has been reorganized substantially to reflect a more logical approach to the central theme. Part I outlines the basic foundations of mass media in the United States. Part II provides a detailed analysis of individual mass media: newspapers, magazines, books, radio, the recording industry, motion pictures, and television. Finally, the four chapters in Part III explore how the mass media succeed and fail in their attempt to service the economic system, provide needed information to the public, reflect our culture, and fuel our democratic political system. The sixth edition has been rewritten substantially as well. About eighty percent of the material is fresh prose that is the result of my attempts to reflect on the mass media in the eighties as well as push the reader into the nineties. The book contains new graphics: about 50 of the 100 photographs are new, and there are nearly three dozen charts and graphs, something previous editions did not contain. Finally, the sixth edition contains a clearer vision of mass communications in our society, a vision honed by my more than thirty years of work in, study of, and teaching about, the mass media in America.

There is one name on the cover of this volume, but an author never completes a book without significant assistance from scores of other persons; let me thank a few. First, I would like to thank my colleagues at the University of Washington (Jerry Baldasty, Roger Simpson, Larry Bowen, Tony Giffard, Ed Bassett, the late Bill Ames, and others), and my colleagues at other colleges and universities who offered invaluable advice (Thomas Connery, University of St. Thomas; James Hoyt, University of Wisconsin; Carolyn Johnson, California State University, Fullerton; Bill McKeen, University of Florida; Robert Ogles, Purdue University; Everett Rogers, University of Southern California; Don Singleton, Salisbury State University; and Jean Ward, University of Minnesota). I would also like to thank the editorial and production team at Macmillan, notably David Chodoff, Tony English, Chris Midgol, Diane Kraut, John Sollami, Linda Greenberg, and Pam Kennedy Oborski. I am grateful to the many students who have used this text in the past and offered their advice and inspiration. Finally, thanks as always go to the Pember clan, Diann, Alison, and Brian, for being (as usual) understanding as the author struggled to generate the sixth edition of *Mass Media in America*.

Don R. Pember
Seattle, Washington

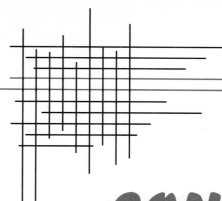

# CONTENTS

# MASS MEDIA
# IN AMERICA

PART

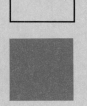

*FOUNDATIONS*

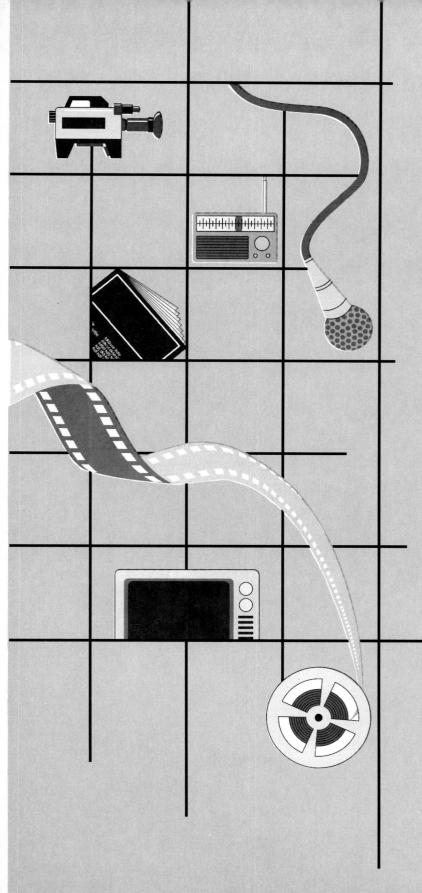

Understanding the condition of the mass media in America in the 1990s requires the student to have a foundation of other information, a foundation that Part I provides. Chapter 1 presents a brief overview of the media. Chapter 2 places them in their historical context. American mass media are surely contemporary, but they are also tradition-bound in many ways; what is done today in the world of newspapers or radio or film is often done because it has always been done.

Chapter 3 explains mass communication theory and research, which is what provides us with the information we have about the media. The study of mass communication is a social science, and like other social scientists, researchers in this field have generated techniques and methods for gathering information about their chosen subject. The information they have gathered has in turn helped them construct theories about mass communication and its relationships to various segments of our society.

Chapter 4 describes the economic structure on which the mass media are erected. In some ways this is the most important chapter in the book, for if the people who direct and create the mass media are bound by tradition, they are also most surely bound by economic concerns. This chapter explores the business of the mass media: the way the various media generate revenues and the ownership structure of the press.

# CHAPTER 1

# THE WORLD OF MASS MEDIA

**M**ass media. It's everywhere. Never has there been a society that was so saturated with systems of mass communications. Add up all the hours each day you spend with the mass media: television, radio, recorded music, motion pictures, newspapers, magazines, books. If you are like most people, you spend more time with mass media than almost anything else. Mass media are with you when you work and play, when you drive or walk. You can use mass media in the city or in the country, at a lake or in the mountains. When the astronauts are circling the earth in a space shuttle, they are usually awakened by recorded music. The crews on nuclear-powered submarines that circle the globe under the sea are entertained by motion pictures. As a patient recovers from surgery in the hospital, there is usually a television at the bedside along with a nurse and a pitcher of ice water.

Some call this the Age of Information. Maybe. Maybe not. But it surely is the Age of Mass Media. The first tool of mass communication—the printing press—was invented less than 550 years ago. Today mass communications and mass media dominate our society. Little wonder when the amount of available mass media is considered (figure 1-1). There are about 1,610 daily newspapers published each day and more than 63 million copies circulated nationwide. More than 7,600 weekly, biweekly, or triweekly newspapers publish 55 million copies. Approximately 10,000 different magazines are published every week, every other week, or monthly. Fifty thousand new book titles appear annually. More than 1,400 over-the-air television stations send their signals to television sets in 93 million American homes. Fifty-seven hundred cable systems carry television signals—including about 50 cable television networks—to 50 million homes. There are about 10,000 radio stations broadcasting to nearly 500 million radio sets in the United States. Between 400 and 500 feature films are produced and exhibited on one of the nation's 25,000 theater screens annually. Thousands more instructional and documentary and short films are produced annually as well. There are magazines distributed on computer discs, electronic data transmission systems like teletext and videotex, videocassettes, and

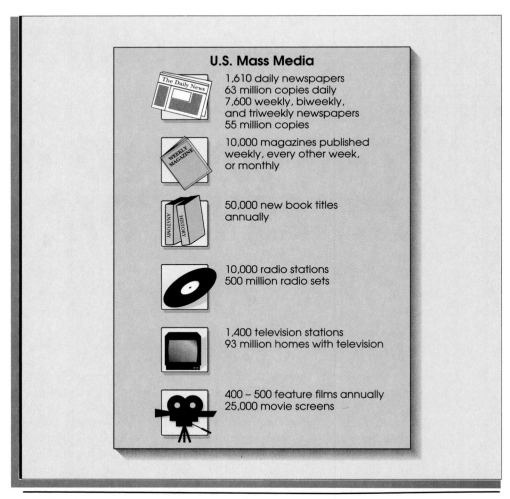

FIGURE 1-1 The enormous output and reach of the mass media reflect their importance in our society.

other emerging media forms. At times we seem in danger of collapsing from the sheer weight of it all.

The tremendous range of media forms is equalled or surpassed by the breadth of media content. From news to entertainment, ideas to helpful hints, virtually anything can be found somewhere. A contemporary American can find anything he or she wants in modern mass media. From the actions of Congress to the adventures of Calvin and Hobbes in the comic strips, from conservative philosophy in the *National Review* to liberal thought in the *Nation,* from the theater of Joseph Papp, to the energy of rap—it's all there. We may have to look for it at times, visit that out-of-the-way bookstore or obscure theater, but the mass media of no other nation contain the range of material contained in the mass media in the United States. Finally, this news and information and entertainment is something that is available to virtually everyone in this nation. Even the urban poor and persons living in extreme rural America have access to some form of mass media.

There is a wide variety of content available to persons who use the mass media. Pictured are Eric B. and Rakim, one of the earliest and most successful rap music teams in the nation. Many rap singers copied Rakim's style, and a mode of rap called "Rakimism" developed. (© 1988 UNI Records, Inc.)

# FROM CONVERSATION TO COMMUNICATION

Mass media were created to do a fairly simple thing: transmit a message from one person to other persons. This is the same thing that happens when two persons talk to each other. The same process takes place: the source of the communication sends a message through a **channel** to a **receiver**. The source usually **encodes** the message, that is, puts the thoughts into words, and speaks these words or writes them out. The receiver then **decodes** the message—translates the words into thoughts. This, of course, implies that both source and receiver know the code, or the language.

The only differences between what we call interpersonal communications—face-to-face, between two people or a small group—and mass communications are these:

1. Through mass communication the message is sent through a channel that can reach a great many people at one time—*mass* communication.
2. Mass communication generally requires the use of some kind of device interposed between the source and the receiver, some kind of medium to make massive communication possible. Hence, we talk about mass *media*.

Some people refer to the two kinds of communications as interpersonal communication and interposed communication. The interposed device is usually some kind of hardware or technological tool. It amplifies the message or allows it to be

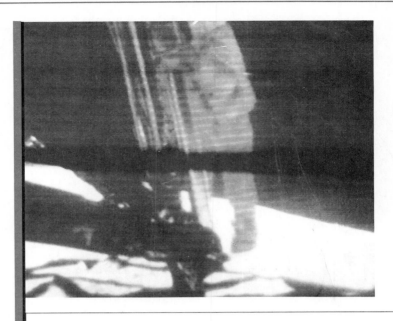

# The New York Times

"All the News That's Fit to Print"

LATE CITY EDITION
Weather: Rain, warm today; clear tonight. Sunny, pleasant tomorrow. Temp. range: today 80-66; Sunday 71-68. Temp.-Hum. Index yesterday 66. Complete U.S. report on P. 59.

VOL. CXVIII..No. 40,721                    NEW YORK, MONDAY, JULY 21, 1969                    10 CENTS

## MEN WALK ON MOON

### ASTRONAUTS LAND ON PLAIN; COLLECT ROCKS, PLANT FLAG

**Voice From Moon:**
**'Eagle Has Landed'**

EAGLE (the lunar module): Houston, Tranquility Base here. The Eagle has landed.

HOUSTON: Roger, Tranquility, we copy you on the ground. You've got a bunch of guys about to turn blue. We're breathing again. Thanks a lot.

TRANQUILITY BASE: Thank you.

HOUSTON: You're looking good here.

TRANQUILITY BASE: A very smooth touchdown.

TRANQUILITY BASE: Eagle, you are stay for T1. [The first step in the lunar operation.] Over.

TRANQUILITY BASE: Stay for T1.

HOUSTON: Roger and we see you venting the ox.

TRANQUILITY BASE: Roger.

COLUMBIA (the command and service module): How do you read that?

HOUSTON: Columbia, he has landed Tranquility Base. Eagle is at Tranquility. I read you five by. Over.

COLUMBIA: Yes, I heard the whole thing.

HOUSTON: Well, it's a good show.

COLUMBIA: Fantastic.

TRANQUILITY BASE: I'll second that.

APOLLO CONTROL: The next major stay-no stay will be for the T2 event. That is at 21 minutes 26 seconds after initiation of power descent.

COLUMBIA: Up telemetry command reset to reacquire on high gain.

HOUSTON: Copy. Out.

APOLLO CONTROL: We have an unofficial time for that touchdown of 102 hours, 45 minutes, 42 seconds and we will update that.

HOUSTON: Eagle, you loaded R2 wrong. We want 10254.

TRANQUILITY BASE: Roger. Do you want the horizontal 55 15.2?

HOUSTON: That's affirmative.

APOLLO CONTROL: We're now less than four minutes from our next stay-no stay. It will be for one complete revolution of the command module.

One of the first things that Armstrong and Aldrin will do after getting their next stay-no stay will be to remove their helmets and gloves.

HOUSTON: Eagle, you are stay for T2. Over.

Continued on Page 4, Col. 1

**VOYAGE TO THE MOON**

Neil A. Armstrong moves away from the leg of the landing craft after taking the first step on the surface of the moon

**A Powdery Surface Is Closely Explored**

By JOHN NOBLE WILFORD
Special to The New York Times

HOUSTON, Monday, July 21—Men have landed and walked on the moon.

Two Americans, astronauts of Apollo 11, steered their fragile four-legged lunar module safely and smoothly to the historic landing yesterday at 4:17:40 P.M., Eastern daylight time.

Neil A. Armstrong, the 38-year-old civilian commander, radioed to earth and the mission control room here:

"Houston, Tranquility Base here. The Eagle has landed."

The first men to reach the moon—Mr. Armstrong and his co-pilot, Col. Edwin E. Aldrin Jr. of the Air Force—brought their ship to rest on a level, rock-strewn plain near the southwestern shore of the arid Sea of Tranquility.

About six and a half hours later, Mr. Armstrong opened the landing craft's hatch, stepped slowly down the ladder and declared as he planted the first human footprint on the lunar crust:

"That's one small step for man, one giant leap for mankind."

His first step on the moon came at 10:56:20 P.M., as a television camera outside the craft transmitted his every move to an awed and excited audience of hundreds of millions of people on earth.

**Tentative Steps Test Soil**

Mr. Armstrong's initial steps were tentative tests of the lunar soil's firmness and of his ability to move about easily in his bulky white spacesuit and backpacks and under the influence of lunar gravity, which is one-sixth that of the earth.

"The surface is fine and powdery," the astronaut reported. "I can pick it up loosely with my toe. It does adhere in fine layers like powdered charcoal to the sole and sides of my boots. I only go in a small fraction of an inch, maybe an eighth of an inch. But I can see the footprints of my boots in the treads in the fine sandy particles."

After 19 minutes of Mr. Armstrong's testing, Colonel Aldrin joined him outside the craft.

The two men got busy setting up another television camera out from the lunar module, planting an American flag into the ground, scooping up soil and rock samples, deploying scientific experiments and hopping and loping about in a demonstration of their lunar agility.

They found walking and working on the moon less taxing than had been forecast. Mr. Armstrong once reported he was "very comfortable."

And people back on earth found the black-and-white television pictures of the hump-shaped lunar module and the men

Astronaut Neil Armstrong sets foot on the moon—and 500 million people watch on television. Millions then read detailed coverage in the newspaper the next day. (*Top:* Compix of United Press International)

reproduced a great many times very cheaply. Television production equipment, printing presses, stereos, radios, video recorders, satellites, all of these devices are fundamental in mass communication.

Because of the imposition of the device between the source of the message and its receiver, mass communication has some advantages over interpersonal communication. (But there are disadvantages as well.) One clear advantage is the speed with which a message can be transmitted to a large audience. Television and radio are instantaneous communication. Half a billion people saw astronaut Neil Armstrong become the first human to walk on the moon. And they saw it almost the same instant it happened; there was a few seconds time delay in transmission from the moon.

Messages that flow through the mass media tend to be more accurate than those transmitted by interpersonal communication, and this is another advantage. Why are they more accurate? Mass communicators tend to be professionals, trained to observe and relay messages accurately. Errors are certainly made in the press. And today, when broadcasters have the opportunity to go directly on the air with a news story by using sophisticated mini-cameras and transmitters, errors become even more common since the journalist does not have the opportunity to check and evaluate facts before communicating them to the community. Nevertheless, mass

Most Americans got their first close-up view of Soviet Premier Nikita Khrushchev when he was interviewed by journalists Stuart Novins and Daniel Schorr on the CBS television program "Face the Nation" in 1959. Television can bring the world into the living room.
(CBS News)

communications is usually better than interpersonal communications at relaying the correct information.

An important disadvantage of mass communications is that it is nearly always one-way communication. That is, the receiver of the message doesn't have the opportunity to talk back, to ask questions. Communication researchers call this back-talk, **feedback.** A message is frequently misunderstood when there is no opportunity for feedback during communications. A viewer can't ask Dan Rather or Tom Brokaw a question about a news report on interest rates or a Congressional debate. The broadcaster moves right along to the next topic. A newspaper will not respond no matter how many questions a persistent reader may ask. A letter to the editor can be written, but this takes time and even then the question may never be answered. Lack of feedback creates what researchers call *low message understandability*. Message understandability will always be higher when interpersonal rather than mass communications is used.

The interposition of the device between the speaker and the receiver has fostered some other important developments. It has permitted humankind to overcome two of its earliest adversaries, time and space. A written communication system made it possible for civilization to develop on this planet; it gave the human race a memory that lasted for more than a single generation. Knowledge accumulated in one era could be passed on to the next. Certainly, preliterate humans passed down stories and tales that were instructive to each new age. But a communication system tied solely to verbal skills or an oral tradition is a limited system. Written communications and later mass communications provided us with the ability to overcome time through a permanent record that permitted meaningful human development.

The swiftness of electronic communication has permitted the human race to overcome space. Until the development of the telegraph, the message and the messenger (someone delivering the mail or newspapers) arrived at the same time. There was no separation between transportation and communication, as Daniel Czitrom has noted in *Media and the American Mind*. The first telegraph dissolved the unity between the message and the messenger. In doing so it dramatically altered distance. The distance between Washington, D.C. and Baltimore, the terminal points of Samuel F. B. Morse's first telegraph line, was no greater than the distance between two city blocks, for the purposes of communicating a short message. Today mass communication has virtually obliterated the miles between almost any two points on the earth. Not only can we communicate short messages instantly, we can transmit voice and pictures as well via communications satellites. We have come to expect to know what happened in distant parts of the world almost as soon as events occur.

Finally, the development of mass media has in many ways made the simple process of communication far more complex, perhaps even complicated. Gigantic industries have developed to undertake mass communications. These large newspaper chains, television networks, publishing houses, motion picture studios, all must expend considerable energy to merely sustain themselves. Like giant animals that must graze perpetually, the giant communications corporations must work to remain alive. In some nations this work entails communicating a government message which often distorts the honest communication the medium is designed to transmit. In this nation most of our mass media must constantly publish and broadcast commercial messages to sustain themselves. Often the transmission of information and entertainment to the community is altered or harmed because of this commercial function. Commercial television, for example, can survive only if it receives support from commercial sponsors. A percentage of broadcast time is set aside for advertisements. Sponsors, however, are not philanthropists by nature and insist their messages be broadcast on programs that viewers will watch. The greater the number of viewers, of course, the higher the advertising rates the television network can charge the sponsor. There is a premium attached if the television networks can design programs that attract a large number of advertisers. Sometimes advertisers want large numbers of viewers; sometimes they want the right kinds of viewers. In either case, the wishes of the advertisers become paramount in many instances. Communication of a message, information or entertainment becomes secondary to survival (or more often success) of the television network. This is a notion that will be explored in considerable detail throughout the remainder of this book.

## WHAT THE MASS MEDIA MEAN TO US

The nation in which we live is made up of a great many systems and institutions. We have a political system, an economic system, a legal system, a governmental system. We have educational institutions, medical institutions, research institutions, social service institutions. These systems and institutions are joined together like the strands of a spider web. Pull one strand of a web, and the rest of the web collapses or sags measurably. Take away one of these systems or institutions, and our society would change measurably as well. The mass media are integrated into these systems and institutions. Our mass communications system is not like an overlay that can be withdrawn without changing the nature of our society. It is an integral part of our nation's business, education, culture, government and other systems and institutions. In other words, if by some stroke of a magic wand we could make all mass media disappear tomorrow, society would not remain intact. Without mass communications things would change dramatically.

The mass media play an essential role in serving our political and governmental systems. Democracy presumes an informed, educated electorate. In our nation the people are the governors, as old-fashioned as that sounds. As the governors we are expected to give advice to our elected representatives, and the mass media is an important ally in that endeavor. When the press covers a protest march at a courthouse, it is informing the elected representatives that some citizens don't like what is going on, some citizens want a change. The mass media have the power to amplify the message.

If we are to elect and re-elect those who choose to serve as our representatives or judges or mayors or president, we must first evaluate their qualifications and their job performance. The mass media is supposed to bring us the information that permits this evaluation. Theoretically, we could all go to Congress and watch over the shoulders of the representatives and senators. Practically, that is impossible. We are sometimes asked to vote directly on issues through referenda or initiatives. We must find out about these issues before we can vote. The press is supposed to give us this information. The political or governmental role of the press in our society is so important that we grant some special rights to persons who work as journalists. And the First Amendment to the U.S. Constitution insures that government will not interfere with the flow of information in this mass communications system.

The mass media services our capitalistic economic system. Can you imagine our economy functioning without the flow of economic information? How could competition work if buyers and sellers could not communicate? How would we know where to find the lowest prices, or the better products, or the supplies we require without mass communications? Could McDonald's exist in a world without advertising?

If mass media provide the fuel that make the political and economic systems run, they also provide the glue which holds our society together in many ways. The mass media reflects our culture. It tells us who we are, it states and helps shape our values. It is through mass media that most public opinion is formed today. The mass media have slowly chipped away at the regional distinctions in language and other aspects of culture. The mass media also divert us with entertainment. They create most of the entertainment culture we consume daily.

Finally, the mass media inform us. They tell us of our successes and failures as a people, who won last night's basketball game, what IBM closed at on the stock market, whether women's hemlines will be shorter, or men's ties wider. They have the facility to relay to us important information quickly and help us understand serious problems. And this can be done on a massive scale. But mass media also have the facility to misinform and create confusion on a massive scale.

Consider the AIDS crisis. There is no question the world would be in far greater danger from this mysterious and deadly affliction were it not for the ability of the mass media to communicate information warning people about the nature of this disease and how it is spread. And this is a good thing. But in the early coverage of the AIDS crisis the mass media also fostered confusion and misunderstanding about AIDS. There was reticence on the part of the mass media to state specifically the manner in which the disease is communicated. It wasn't until several years after the nature of the disease had been discovered that NBC reporter Robert Bazell, appearing on the "Today" show told a mass audience, "We have been squeamish—using words like intimate contact, casual contact. . . . The truth is you get this disease mainly through sexual intercourse and primarily through anal intercourse as practiced by homosexuals." Terms like *intercourse* and *anal intercourse* were not normally used in the press. So in most early stories about the disease, the press stressed the deadly aspects of AIDS but suggested to readers and viewers that it was spread through "personal contact" or "sexual contact." These kinds of stories had two effects. First, they overstated the ease with which AIDS is transmitted. This often created panic and led to schools dismissing students who tested positive for the AIDS virus, and communities discriminating against those who had contracted the disease. The second effect was just as serious. Readers and viewers were denied the critical information necessary to avoid exposing themselves to contracting the disease.

A class of junior/senior communications students at the University of Washington was recently asked to determine the importance of the mass media by imagining what life would be like without mass media. Their answers were fascinating. Many noted that it would be much quieter with no radios, televisions, or stereos. People wouldn't really know what was happening in the world, the country, even just across the state. Millions more would be out of work, since that many people are employed either directly by the mass media or in jobs that directly support the mass media, such as making newsprint. People would spend more time talking with their friends and relatives; social contact would increase.

But the loss of mass media would also affect some of the nation's basic institutions. The political system and government would probably change dramatically. Without mass media, it is doubtful we could elect a single president for this large nation; most persons would never see or hear the candidates. Our educational system would be forced to change. Without books, audiovisual materials, and other forms of mass media, students could not be expected to learn as much and as quickly. Research would also be dramatically slowed without journals to publish the results of tests and experiments. Scientists in Boston and Denver could be working on exactly the same problem and never know it unless they traveled to meet each other. Our economy would suffer. Could we operate a capitalist system so heavily involved with the production of consumer goods without advertising to both inform and promote these goods?

Americans would be forced to return to creating rather than buying most of their culture if the mass media disappeared. It would be a culture of folk arts with heavy regional and even local emphases. Society in general would likely be far less homogeneous. There would be no national role models for people to copy, no outside agencies (besides family, church, or school) to dispense acceptable social conventions. Some of the students feared they would not know what to wear to classes because of a lack of weather reports. Others said they would exercise less without aerobic dance classes (no more music) or miniature tape players to wear when jogging. Most all agreed that their grades would improve if they were not frequently distracted by television or movies. One summed up the feelings of many by saying that without the mass media, the world would be pretty "boring."

This exercise demonstrates that mass media today are far more than simple diversions. Our mass communications system is an integral part of our political system, our economy, our cultural and educational institutions, and our society in general. That is why they are worthy of analysis and criticism. Mass media—rightly or wrongly—have been vested with important responsibilities in our society. When our mass communications system malfunctions, there can be serious consequences for the nation and its people.

## SOME BASIC THEMES

In the next 12 chapters in this book an attempt is made to describe, explain, evaluate and analyze the mass media in the United States, to demonstrate how they relate to other important segments of our society, and in some instances, to compare them with mass media in other parts of the world. To accomplish this task most efficiently a foundation must first be erected. This is done in the first few chapters of this text where the history, economic and theoretical foundations of mass communications are erected. From the material on history, you will learn that in large measure the mass media are what they are because they were what they were. That is, American mass media do things today because they did them yesterday. The exploration of the economic foundation reveals a mass media system that is commercially driven. Profits are high in the mass media industry; the profit motive is very strong. From the material on theoretical considerations you will note that there is little agreement on any but the most basic theories regarding the mass media, and while we know a lot about mass communications from extensive research in that area, some fairly basic questions remain unanswered or only partially answered.

In the remainder of the book, we will devote a chapter each to newspapers, magazines and books, radio, television, and motion pictures. In other chapters we will examine in detail the media functions we talked about earlier—news and infor-

Mass media let us both explore reality, and escape it. Comic strips are still a popular part of the American newspaper, and "Calvin & Hobbes," drawn by Bill Waterson, permits readers to re-experience their childhood in all its unfettered and winsome glory. This strip frequently pokes fun at the mass media and their critics.

mation, servicing the economy through advertising, the maintenance of government and politics, and fostering of culture through entertainment.

In probably no other nation do mass media play so dominant a role in everyday living. We thrive on mass media every day—and in a way they thrive because of us. Mass media are blamed for many of our problems, decried for being vacuous, and jeered as a bane in our modern society. They are also praised for enlightening and informing us, extolled for protecting us, and lauded for uplifting us. When they are good, they can be very, very good. But when they are bad, like the little girl in the nursery rhyme, they can be horrid. In all these things, however, we must remember one central fact. Mass media are inanimate objects; boxes of wire and circuits, processed wood pulp, colored glass, and plastic. The machines are not responsible for what we do with them or how we use them. It is the human beings who direct and control mass communications in the United States that deserve both the praise and the approbation. If there is any hope for change in the mass media, change to make what is bad good, and what is good better, it is because human beings can change.

# BIBLIOGRAPHY

This is one of the materials that has been useful in the preparation of this chapter.

Czitrom, Daniel J. *Media and the American Mind.* Chapel Hill: University of North Carolina Press, 1982.

# CHAPTER 2

# HISTORICAL FOUNDATIONS

The merger of Time, Inc. and Warner Communications in 1989 was the most recent chapter in the history of two corporations that were founded in the early 1920s. In 1923, Henry Luce and Briton Hadley, two youthful Yale graduates, published *Time,* a new kind of weekly newsmagazine. Warner Communications was born about the same time in Hollywood as Warner Bros., one of the nation's earliest motion picture studios. While both corporations changed dramatically in the ensuing 66 years, both companies reflected their past as well.

Contemporary observers need to keep one eye on yesterday to understand the mass media in the 1990s. The present, as noted by historian David Shannon, is merely the cutting edge of the past. The human experience is represented by a continuum, not a series of separate or isolated parts. So even in a book about contemporary mass communications there is a need to briefly explore the histories of these industries.

Make no mistake; what follows is not a comprehensive history of the development of mass communications. A kind of narrative timeline (which corresponds to the actual timeline shown in figure 2-1) has been constructed instead. It is to function as a road map for the journey that begins several centuries ago and ends somewhere in the future. Important and/or interesting events will be noted along the way, their significance highlighted. At the end of the narrative, generalizations will be drawn that add some perspective to the trip along the timeline.

Mass communication is about 500 years old. Five hundred years—it sounds like a long time. And it is when compared with the life span of a human. But this is a short time when compared with the life span of humanity. Mass media are truly modern implements in the history of humankind. Anthropologists suggest that modern human beings—Homo sapiens with the same cranial capacity as a contemporary human being—have existed for about 40,000 years. Mechanical printing—the beginning of mass media—developed only about 450 years ago. Let's look at this in a different way. Imagine those 40,000 years of modern human history as a single calendar year. And right now it is midnight on December 31, the last day of that year. Mechanical printing first occurred on December 27, not quite five days ago. Newsbooks, the precursors of newspapers, first appeared in 1610, or about three-and-a-half days ago. Radio and motion pictures emerged as viable media in the early 1900s, about 9 o'clock this morning. And television first appeared in the United States at the end of the 1930s, or about 3 p.m. today. Despite its short existence, mass communications has come to truly dominate our lives today.

## TIMELINE

**About 1100** A.D.—Most authorities believe that by this time three of the four elements needed for mechanical printing—ink, movable type, and paper—had been developed by the Chinese. As early as the second century, printing using inked carved wood blocks was apparently undertaken. Movable type was developed in about 1050.

**1450**—Johann Gutenburg added the mechanical printing press to the movable type, ink and paper and voila—mechanical printing, the first mass medium, was born.

**1609—Newsbooks,** the precursors of the modern newspaper, first appeared on the European continent. They contained only reports of foreign events and happenings.

**1621**—Similar newsbooks appeared in England.

**1640**—The appearance of the first newspaper that reported domestic as well as foreign news, *Diurnal Occurrences,* in England. Why then and not 100 years later? This was an age in Europe that was teeming with political and religious activity and strife. The exploration of the New World was still under way. Commercial enterprise was growing. The public need for news about all these subjects and many more was apparent.

**1690**—Fifty years later, the newspaper *Publick Occurrences, Both Foreign and Domestic* appeared in Boston. This might have been the first American newspaper, but the government was displeased with the work of its publisher, Benjamin Harris, and banned subsequent editions.

**1704**—John Campbell's *Boston News-Letter* was published. It wasn't as lively as Benjamin Harris's sheet, but wasn't as controversial either. It was the first American newspaper that was published for more than one issue.

**1711**—Englishmen Richard Steele and Joseph Addison published the *Tatler* and the *Spectator,* essay papers generally regarded as the first magazines published in Great Britain.

**1741**—Printers Andrew Bradford and Benjamin Franklin vied to publish the first American magazine. Bradford's *American Magazine* beat Franklin's *General Magazine, and Historical Chronicle* off the presses by three days. But Franklin published six issues of his magazine, three more than Bradford. This experience was fairly typical for magazines in the 1700s. Several more appeared before 1800; most had a circulation of about 500 copies and lasted a year or less. Magazines of that era were generally digests of material that had been published first elsewhere, precursors of the modern *Reader's Digest.*

**1760s to the 1790s**—This is the period during which the American revolution was generated and fought, and when the new American nation was forged. The press undertook important roles during this era, roles which it more or less maintains

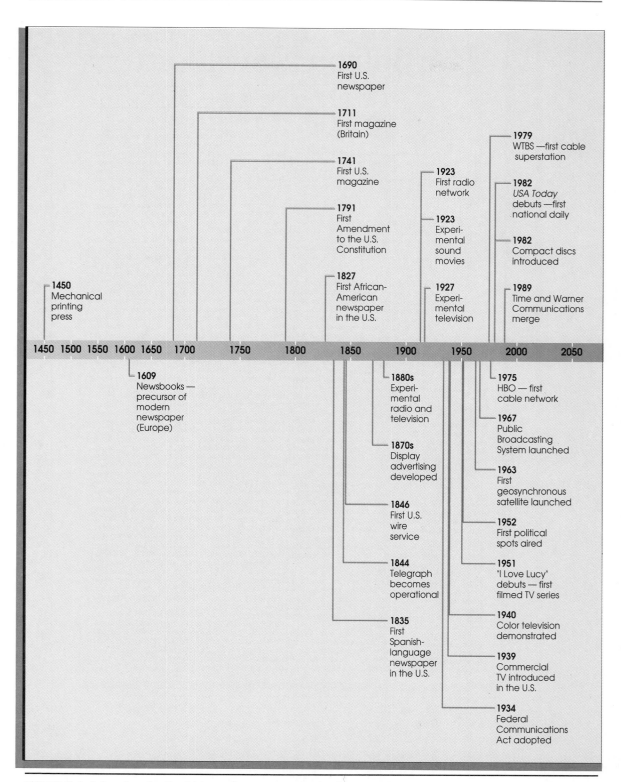

FIGURE 2-1 A timeline for the history of mass communications.

# The Boston News-Letter.

### Published by Authority.

**Numb. 1.**

From **Monday** April 17. to **Monday** April 24. 1704.

*London Flying-Post from Decemb 2d to 4th. 1703.*

Letters from *Scotland* bring us the Copy of a Sheet lately Printed there, Intituled, *A Seasonable Alarm for Scotland. In a Letter from a Gentleman in the City, to his Friend in the Country, concerning the present Danger of the Kingdom and of the Protestant Religion.*

This Letter takes Notice, That Papists swarm in that Nation, that they traffick more avowedly than formerly, & that of late many Scores of Priests and Jesuites are come thither from *France*, and gone to the North, to the Highlands & other places of the Country. That the Ministers of the Highlands and North gave in large Lists of them to the Committee of the General Assembly, to be laid before the Privy-Council.

It likewise observes, that a great Number of other ill affected persons are come over from *France*, under pretence of accepting her Majesty's Gracious Indemnity; but, in reality, to increase Divisions in the Nation, and to entertain a Correspondence with *France*. That their ill Intentions are evident from their talking big, their owning the Interest of the pretended King *James* VIII. their secret Cabals, and their buying up of Arms and Ammunition, wherever they can find them.

To this he adds the late Writings and Actings of some disaffected persons, many of whom are for that Pretender, that several of them have declar'd they had rather embrace Popery than conform to the present Government, that they refuse to pray for the Queen, but use the ambiguous word Sovereign, and some of them pray in express Words for the King and Royal Family; and the charitable and generous Prince who has shew'd them so much Kindness. He likewise takes notice of Letters not long ago found in Cypher, and directed to a Person lately come thither from St. Germains.

He says that the greatest Jacobites, who will not qualifie themselves by taking the Oaths to Her Majesty, do now with the Papists and their Companions from St. Germains set up for the Liberty of the Subject, contrary to their own Principles, but meerly to keep up a Division in the Nation. He adds, that they aggravate those things which the People complain of, as to *England's* refusing to allow them a freedom of Trade, &c. and do all they can to foment Divisions betwixt the Nations, and to obstruct a Redress of those things complain'd of.

The Jacobites, he says, do all they can to perswade the Nation that their pretended King is a Protestant in his Heart, tho' he dares not declare it while under the Power of *France*, that he is acquainted with the Mistakes of his Father's Government, will govern us more according to Law, and endear himself to his Subjects.

They magnifie the Strength of their own Party, and the Weakness and Divisions of the other, in order to facilitate and hasten their Undertaking; they argue themselves out of their Fears, and into the highest assurance of accomplishing their purpose.

From all this he infers, That they have hopes of Assistance from *France*, otherwise they would never be so impudent, and he gives Reasons for his Apprehensions that the *French* King may send Troops thither this Winter, 1. Because the *English* & *Dutch* will not then be at Sea to oppose them. 2. He can then best spare them, the Season of Action beyond Sea being over. 3. The Expectation given him of a considerable number to joyn them, may incourage him to the undertaking with fewer. Men if he can but send over a sufficient number of Officers with Arms and Ammunition.

He endeavours in the rest of his Letters to answer the foolish Pretences of the Pretender's being a Protestant, and that he will govern us according to Law. He says, that being bred up in the Religion and Politicks of *France*, he is by Education a stated Enemy to our Liberty and Religion. That the Obligations which he and his Family owe to the *French* King, must necessarily make him to be wholly at his Devotion, and to follow his Example; that if he sit upon the Throne, the three Nations; must be oblig'd to pay the Debt which he owes the *French* King for the Education of himself, and for Entertaining his supposed Father and his Family. And since the King must restore him by his Troops, if ever he be restored, he will see to secure his own Debt before those Troops leave *Britain*. The Pretender being a good Proficient in the *French* and *Romish* Schools, he will never think himself sufficiently aveng'd; but by the utter Ruine of his Protestant Subjects, both as Hereticks and Traitors. The late Queen, his pretended Mother, who in cold Blood when she was Queen of *Britain* advised to turn the West of *Scotland* into a hunting Field will be then for doing so by the greatest part of the Nation, and, no doubt, is at Pains to have her pretended Son educated to her own Mind. Therefore, he says, it were a great Madness in the Nation to take a Prince bred up in the horrid School of Ingratitude, Persecution and Cruelty, and filled with Rage and Envy. The *Jacobites*, he says, both in *Scotland* and at *St. Germains*, are impatient under their present Straits, and knowing their Circumstances cannot be much worse than they are at present, are the more incapable to the Undertaking. He adds, That the *French* King knows there cannot be a more effectual way for himself to arrive at the Universal Monarchy, and to ... the Protestant Interest, than by setting up the Pretender upon the Throne of Great Britain, he will in all probability attempt it, and tho' he should be perswaded that the Design would miscarry in the close, yet he cannot but reap some Advantage by imbroiling the three Nations.

From all this the Author concludes it to be the Interest of the Nation, to provide for Self defense; and says, that as many have already taken the Alarm, and are furnishing themselves with Arms and Ammunition, he hopes the Government will not only allow it, but encourage it, since the Nation ought all to appear as one Man in the Defence

America's first newspaper to last more than one edition, the *Boston News-Letter,* was the only newspaper in the American colonies for fifteen years. In the first issue, the editor John Campbell relied heavily on clippings from London newspapers to fill the news columns. The newspaper was not controversial, and not very interesting, either. (The Bettmann Archive, Inc.)

in the twentieth century. Through the work of publishers like Samuel Adams and writers like John Dickinson, the press helped prepare the colonies for the war of revolution. Blustery Sam Adams used his *Boston Gazette* as an important propaganda tool in generating American anger and resentment toward the British colonial government. In a public relations coup Adams transformed an albeit serious but small shooting incident into the Boston Massacre. Dickinson, on the other hand, used reason and tempered argument to persuade readers that a revolution was a necessary occurrence in a series of twelve essays that were first published in 1767 in the *Pennsylvania Chronicle*. These "Letters from a Farmer in Pennsylvania" were reprinted widely throughout the 13 colonies in the years before the war and were influential in shaping the ideas of many citizens who were unsure about the wisdom of a revolution.

During the war the press reported the plight of the military campaign and helped maintain support for the underfunded and often undermanned Continental Army. These accounts were not necessarily objective or accurate, but served to fuel the nation's sometimes flagging patriotic ardor.

With victory at hand the press assisted in the forging of the new nation. No more important material *ever* appeared in an American newspaper than the 85 essays entitled "The Federalist Papers," penned by James Madison, John Jay, and Alexander Hamilton. The essays, which contained a brilliant exposition of the planned federal republic and the newly drafted constitution, were first published in 1787 and 1788 in the *New York Independent Journal* but later appeared in newspapers in virtually every state in the Union. They played no small part in winning the approval of the new constitution by the electors in the states.

**1791**—The First Amendment to the Constitution, guaranteeing freedom of speech and press, among other things, was approved. This provision and its meaning is central to any understanding of the operation of the mass media in the United States. We will return to discuss this often throughout the book.

**1800**—A brief overview of the newspaper press at the end of the eighteenth century would reveal the following. Newspapers, both weekly and daily, could be found in most communities. They were small, often no more than four pages. The newspapers were financially supported through a small amount of commercial advertising, subscription revenues, and subsidies from political parties, the government, and other interested investors. Most newspapers had a political point of view and reported the news from that point of view. This was a political or party press, a newspaper press deeply involved in the political lifeblood of the nation. The news content was not generally as we know it today. While there were simple announcements of ship arrivals and sailings, and other community events, much of the space was devoted to essays and political commentary. Most papers had few readers, but it was not uncommon for newspapers to be read aloud at taverns and meetings and other gathering points. The readers—those to whom the newspaper was aimed, tended to be better educated, more sophisticated, more well-to-do.

**1820**—By the end of the second decade of the new century the newspaper press was firmly established in the new nation. There were over 500 newspapers being published, 24 of them daily, the rest weekly and biweekly. Circulation was still relatively small, with the largest paper selling only about 4,000 copies per edition.

**1827**—John B. Russwurm and the Reverend Samuel Cornish founded *Freedom's Journal* in New York City, what most authorities regard as the nation's first black newspaper. Like most of the 40 other black newspapers initiated before the

Civil War, *Freedom's Journal* was a newspaper dedicated to ending slavery. It was circulated nationally among both black and white intellectuals. The black press, along with the white abolitionist press, helped spread the word about the degradation and despair that resulted from slavery. It also served as a means of communication between black leaders and gave its black readers a sense of identity.

**1830s**—What might be called the nation's first technological revolution took place during this period as the power of steam was harnessed to a variety of machines. In mass communications, steam-powered presses were faster and made it possible to publish a great many more newspapers and magazines in a shorter time. Not coincidently there was a tremendous expansion in the growth of the printed press, made possible in many ways by the technological revolution but prompted by other developments as well. Substantial growth in compulsory education took place, and whether education fuels the growth of mass media, or vice versa, the number of people who could read and wanted to read rose significantly. The technological revolution resulted in meaningful advances in transportation as well. Goods could be shipped farther, faster. This meant that newspapers and magazines could be shipped farther and still be fresh upon arrival. More importantly these advances permitted the growth of regional and even national marketing of goods. In the past the cobbler made shoes for the people in his village. But new machinery permitted him to make more shoes than he could sell in his village. And railroads and canals permitted him to ship those extra shoes inexpensively to the next village and the one beyond that. But how would the people in the distant communities come to be aware of these shoes? Why not advertise them? The need for advertising increased, providing more revenues for publishers. Finally, there seemed to be a lot of folks who wanted to communicate. This decade was notable as an era for strong reform movements. Women's suffrage, prohibition, education, abolition, and many other important reform efforts were actively spurred to life. The printed press provided an important communications channel among persons who worked for these causes, and from the leaders of these movements to those not yet converted.

The singular change in the magazine industry, apart from the increase in the number of publications, was the growth of magazine genres: special interest publications. Magazine publishers began to focus upon a specific audience through selection of content. There were publications for women, those who liked to travel, persons interested in sports, young people, and many others. Today of course, virtually all magazines are aimed at a narrowly differentiated audience. And that, of course, is a striking difference between magazines and newspapers. Magazines are published for people who like to read about similar topics. There are but a handful of general interest magazines. Newspapers, on the other hand, are published for people who live in the same city or community. There are but a handful of national or regional newspapers.

**1833**—This year marked the publication of Benjamin Day's *New York Sun,* the first penny newspaper. The *Sun* cost less than other newspapers, five cents less than other newspapers. At this time five cents bought a quarter pound of bacon or a pint of whiskey. But more importantly, the *Sun* had substantially different content than its competitors. Instead of *essays* about government or foreign policy or economics, Day filled his paper with news of crime and other tragedy, sensational events, trivial but interesting tidbits of information that appealed to the undereducated audiences at which this newspaper was aimed. He was successful. In less than

Many regard James Gordon Bennett as the father of modern journalism. His employees were reporters, gatherers of news, not just writers. Bennett is shown in this old woodcut preparing the first issue of his *New York Herald* in his attic room. (The Bettmann Archive, Inc.)

six months his newspaper had a circulation of nearly 8,000, twice that of his nearest competitor. This was the genesis of the popular press.

**1835**—James Gordon Bennett, following Ben Day's formula, established the *New York Herald.* The paper cost two cents and at the outset Bennett told readers that his would not be a political newspaper. "We shall support no party—be the agent of no faction or coterie, and care nothing for any election, or any candidate from president down to constable." It is fair to say that Bennett was the father of the modern newspaper. His employees were not editors or writers who penned thoughtful essays, but newsgatherers who went out and found the news. The newspaper was spicy, aggressive, and sensational. It was aimed at the common folk. And it contained quite a lot of advertising. Significantly, the readership of these popular newspapers consisted of a broad base of people that cut through political interests. The advertisers, who had been forced to place commercial notices in a wide variety of publications to reach a mass audience, could now use Bennett's newspaper to reach most potential customers. By 1836 Bennett's newspaper had 20,000 subscribers.

North America's first Spanish-language paper, *El Crepusculo de la Libertad* (The Twilight of Liberty), was published in Taos, New Mexico in 1835. This newspaper was the beginning of a proud heritage for the Hispanic press in the United States.

**1844**—"What hath God wrought?" Samuel F.B. Morse began public operation of the telegraph in May of this year; this was the first message transmitted over the lines that hung between Washington, D.C. and Baltimore. Telegraphic news would soon become a staple in the press. The printed word had allowed humankind to overcome the barriers of time. The memory of the community was expanded beyond a single lifetime. The telegraph permitted humankind to overcome the barriers of space. For the first time, a communication or message could arrive before the messenger who carried it.

**1846**—The New York State Associated Press was formed. Newspapers in 19 upstate New York cities now shared news via the telegraph. This was the precursor to the Associated Press, which is today the largest newsgathering organization in the world.

**1861–1865**—The American press covered the Civil War as no war has been covered since. Reporters trekked across the battlefields, side by side with foot soldiers, or rode to the battles in carriages. Magazines used primitive reproduction techniques to publish sketches drawn on the battlefields by artists. It is likely that important journalistic conventions we take for granted today emerged first in this era. The use of **bylines** by reporters was established, not as a reward for a job well done, but by the order of the Union army. The generals wanted to know who was responsible for writing which stories. The inverted pyramid style of writing, in which the reporter outlines the most important facts first, gained popularity among journalists who found the telegraph unreliable. A reporter who chose to send his story in a chronological fashion might "lose the wire" before he was finished, denying his editors and readers news of the important climax of the battle.

**1870s**—At the end of the 1860s and in the early 1870s, two New York City department stores, Lord and Taylor and R.H. Macy, started to use **display advertising** (sketches, drawings, large size and decorative type faces) as opposed to the traditional textual advertising which is simply made up of lines of words. Display advertising is characteristic of most newspaper and magazine advertising today, outside of the classified ads. It was also in this era that manufacturers changed the target of their advertising messages. Previously the makers of products like flour or soap would aim their advertising directly at wholesalers or retailers, to try to encourage them to buy the goods which they would then promote to the customer. In the 1870s some manufacturers began to aim their advertising at potential retail customers—the readers of the newspapers and magazines. It was their hope that the reader would then go to the store and ask for a specific brand of flour or soap. This was the beginning of brand name advertising and the slogans and jingles that still accompany such promotion. Ivory Soap's "It floats" and "99 and 44/100 percent pure" and "Schlitz, the beer that made Milwaukee famous" are but two examples.

In addition to aiming advertising at a different target, advertisers also began to change their advertising messages as well. Up until this time most advertising was simply informative, designed to assist a potential buyer in satisfying an existing need. "You need flour? I sell flour. You need a new pair of overalls? A shipment just arrived." A new advertising strategy emerged that tried to persuade the reader that he or she had a need for something, and that this particular product could solve that need. The product might make you happier or more attractive or healthier or more popular. People lived happily on this continent for hundreds of years before advertising convinced them that they really needed deodorant or mouthwash. This strategy is at the heart of modern advertising. Early advertising was aimed at informing; modern advertising is aimed at informing and persuading.

The 1870s was a decade of change in journalism as well. It was then the craft began to move noticeably toward a standard of objective reporting, the attempt by the journalist to be fair, and keep his or her point of view out of the story. The growth of the newsgathering cooperatives like the Associated Press helped foster this change. Reporters for the cooperatives had to be impartial if their stories were to be saleable to newspapers with a variety of points of view. Also, professionalism and journalism education developed within the field. The reporter was no longer considered an itinerant writer who told readers what was taking place and what it meant, but a "craftsperson," someone skilled in observing, in interviewing, in discovering facts. And this information was to be passed along in a pristine fashion to readers who could decide for themselves what it all meant. There were protests by many that such journalism was dull, that objectivity could not be achieved, and that the journalist was in a better position than anyone to uncover meaning in news events. However, slowly but surely objectivity became the standard for the craft.

**1880s**—During the 30 years beginning in 1880 the modern print press was born. Nothing that has happened in the past 100 years is as significant as the changes wrought during this era. In addition, two new mass media, motion pictures and radio, emerged during these three decades.

Changes in newspapers and magazines were again—as in the 1830s—made possible by technological developments. Faster, larger printing presses were built. Hand-set type went by the wayside with the invention of the linotype, a machine

William Randolph Hearst founded a chain of newspapers that still exists today, a major syndicate (King Features), and a news service (INS). The Lord of San Simeon (as the castle he built in California is called) left many indelible marks on American journalism—not all of them positive.
(The Bettmann Archive, Inc.)

that did most of the typesetting work. Cheaper wood pulp paper lowered the cost of newsprint. New printing processes improved the reproduction of drawings, sketches, and even photographs. In 1850 only 750,000 newspapers were printed daily. By 1890 this number had reached 8.3 million.

The nation's urban areas swelled with new population. In 1840 only one American city had more than a quarter of a million people. Fifty years later three cities had over a million inhabitants and eight others had more than 250,000. These growing urban markets attracted the attention of manufacturers and other businesses with goods and services to sell. The amount of advertising in newspapers increased rapidly. In 1880 the typical daily paper contained 25 percent advertising; 35 years later about half the content was advertising. (Today it is between 60 and 75 percent.)

To reach the new readers, to build circulation that would be attractive to advertisers, newspapers added new kinds of content. Spreading information was only part of the new mission. Providing entertainment and diversion became essential as well. What we now call **soft news** began to fill many of the pages of the daily paper. Recipes, gossip, advice to the lovelorn, games and puzzles, news of parties and dances, the serialization of novels, comics and cartoons, and much more found its way into the newspaper. News of crime and passion and romance became the standard fare. While not all newspapers followed this formula, most of the big city dailies did. This was the era of the circulation wars in New York City between William Randolph Hearst and Joseph Pulitzer, or what some called **yellow journalism.** Newspapers used scams, hoaxes, and other circus-like attractions to draw readers. And the readers flocked to the new newspapers. This was a press for the masses.

JOSEPH PULITZER.

Joseph Pulitzer came to New York after successfully launching the *St. Louis Post-Dispatch* in the years following the Civil War. His New York *World* was the chief rival to Hearst's New York *Journal* in the Yellow Journalism wars of the 1890s. The *World* died many years ago, but Pulitzer's name lives on because of the Pulitzer Prizes, the nation's most prestigious journalism awards.
(The Bettmann Archive, Inc.)

Perhaps the least visible change in the big daily newspapers occurred inside the executive offices. For almost two centuries the publishers of American newspapers had generally been printers and journalists, persons who understood news. But at the growing newspapers in the big cities the business of newspapering became too important; most former editors didn't clearly enough understand the economics of the business. And the role of the publisher, who is the boss, changed from someone with journalistic values to someone with a business orientation. This was a slow but sure change. And it resulted in basic changes in the industry that we still see today.

Interestingly, much the same metamorphosis took place in the nation's black press as well. During the years before the Civil War, the 40 or so black newspapers were devoted to communication of information and advocacy regarding slavery. After the war, when there was the illusion that slavery was gone for good, this press lost its mission. The vigorous black press that emerged later in the century was a popular, commercial press, filled with information for the members of the community as well as many of the same features published in the white press. Like the press in general, the black press moved from the point at which someone would say, "I want to communicate information, to convince people of my ideas. I think I will start a newspaper. I can sell advertising and subscriptions to pay the costs" to the point, in

Cyrus Curtis owned both newspapers and magazines in the late nineteenth and early twentieth centuries, but he is probably best remembered as the publisher of the highly successful *Saturday Evening Post,* a remarkable weekly mass-circulation magazine that died in 1969.
(The Bettmann Archive, Inc.)

Women played an important role in the development of American magazine and newspaper journalism. The publication of Ida Tarbell's "History of the Standard Oil Company" in *McClure's* magazine in 1902 is regarded by many as the beginning of the famous muckraking movement.
(The Bettmann Archive, Inc.)

the late nineteenth century, when it was more common to hear, "I want to get into the newspaper business, to sell advertising. I can attract readers if I publish interesting information and features." The change was subtle, but very meaningful.

Magazines were reshaped by the same forces that changed the newspaper industry; new technology, growing population, the growth of advertising, competition, and the desire to reach the masses. The number of magazines grew seven-fold between 1865 (700 periodicals were published) and 1900 (5,000 different magazines

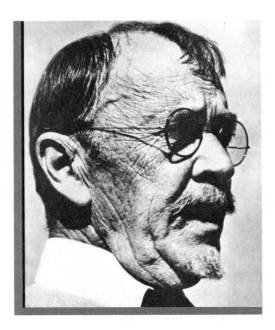

Writer and editor Lincoln Steffens is another of the several investigative journalists who were labelled "muckrakers" by President Theodore Roosevelt in the early twentieth century. Steffens's *Shame of the Cities,* published in 1904, exposed corruption in municipal government.
(The Bettmann Archive, Inc.)

were available to readers). Changes in postal laws that gave magazines and newspapers a reduced postage (the second-class mailing permit) enhanced the wider distribution of these publications. Perhaps the most important development in the periodical industry was the decision by many leading magazines to reduce their cover prices to as low as a nickel a copy and rely almost exclusively on advertising for revenues. This scheme worked for more than half a century. But when television came along in the 1950s advertisers found in many cases it was cheaper (based on the cost of reaching 1,000 readers or viewers) to use the new electronic medium. Magazines like the *Saturday Evening Post* lost substantial revenues when advertisers pulled out. Most of the mass circulation general interest magazines could not survive.

**1900–1912**—No discussion of the history of this era, no matter how brief, is complete without a reference to the **muckrakers,** a small group of highly visible journalists who for about a dozen years focused the press spotlight on the ugly underside of America. Ida Tarbell, Lincoln Steffens, and several others left an indelible mark on the craft of journalism with their exposés of big business practices, health and safety matters, government, and other heretofore unassailable institutions of our society. Their work led to significant reforms, yet by the second decade of the new century they were largely gone. The investigative journalist of the late twentieth century can find the roots of her particular craft in the work of these writers.

**1903**—Edwin Porter's *The Great Train Robbery* is produced and released. The film, our first Western movie, marked the first time a filmmaker used editing techniques to make a motion picture. Until this time motion pictures were simply

Americans today watch movies in comfortable theaters or while sitting on their living room sofas. In the late 1890s people who wanted to see a film movie watched it in front of kinetoscopes and vitascopes, peephole novelties in which the viewer would peer at the film as it was drawn across a light source. This Los Angeles phonograph and vitascope parlor was photographed in 1896. (The Bettmann Archive, Inc.)

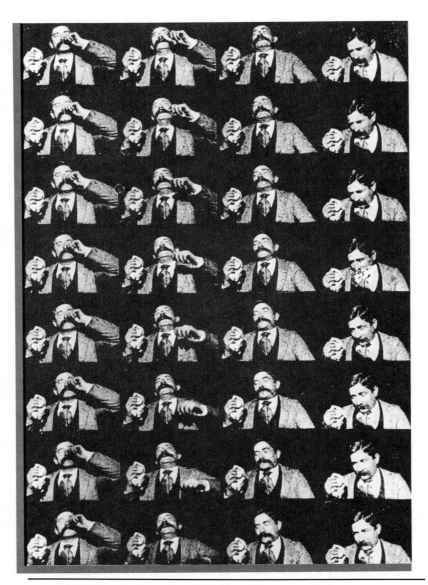

The filmstrips above comprise *Fred Ott's Sneeze.* Many regard this "production" by William Kennedy Dickson as the first movie shot in the United States. (The Bettmann Archive, Inc.)

filmed live performances; the camera started with the beginning of action and stopped when the action ended. Porter cut his raw footage into pieces, and spliced them back together in a different order to tell the story. The art of film editing was born.

**1908**—While journalism classes had been taught at colleges and universities for many years, it was in 1908 that the journalism degree was first offered. The University of Missouri in the Midwest and the University of Washington on the West Coast were the first two schools to provide the journalism major.

**1910**—Radio developed as the ideas of many men accumulated, men like James Maxwell, Heinrich Hertz, and Guglielmo Marconi. By 1910 it was possible for those few Americans with receivers to pick up occasional programs, as on January 14 when another pioneer of radio, Lee DeForest, put famed tenor Enrico Caruso on the air in a broadcast from the Metropolitan Opera. The broadcast was even reviewed by a critic for *The New York Times* who reported to readers that the "homeless songwaves kept losing their way."

**1912–1913**—The motion picture business was beginning to boom and a growing number of talented and not-so-talented individuals sought to make films. But they were often stymied by the high cost of equipment. Less expensive foreign-made filmmaking equipment existed, but Thomas Edison, one of the chief inventors of motion picture technology, had created the Motion Picture Patents Company, which used a wide variety of legal schemes to try to force the American producers and directors to use the higher-priced American equipment. Movie makers who sought to use the foreign-made equipment were forced to flee from New York and New Jersey, the centers of motion picture production at this time, to avoid constant legal hassles. They sought a place with a lot of sunshine; artificial lighting did not yet exist. And since movies were made outdoors, a warm climate was desirable as well. They settled in Hollywood, and this rural community outside Los Angeles soon became the movie capital of the world.

**1914**—About 2,600 daily newspapers were published during this year, more than ever before, more than at any time since then.

**1915**—David Wark Griffith's *The Birth of a Nation* premiered in 1915 and established motion pictures as an art form. In the three-hour Civil War epic, which

Edwin Porter's *The Great Train Robbery* was based on a popular vaudeville sketch of the era. The eight-minute film, released in 1903, introduced many film editing techniques used for the first time in American moviemaking. It is also regarded as the first Western movie.

Thomas Alva Edison was one of many U.S. and foreign inventors responsible for generating the technology that permitted the development of motion pictures. He is shown here in 1905 with one of his early motion picture machines.
(The Bettmann Archive, Inc.)

Griffith shot without a script, the filmmaker developed an itinerary of movie-making conventions that is still widely used today. Unfortunately, this sympathetic account of the rise of the Ku Klux Klan in the wake of the Civil War can only be seen by a modern viewer as a racist portrayal of American history. Nevertheless, as President Woodrow Wilson noted after seeing the movie, it was, "like writing history with lightning."

**1919**—Radio and the use of the new medium had grown rapidly during World War I. The application of the new medium by the military clearly demonstrated its potential as a communications medium, although its potential as a broadcasting medium was not yet apparent. The first commercial interest in radio came from manufacturers of radio receivers—Westinghouse, General Electric, and American Marconi. But none of the American firms held a complete set of patents needed to push ahead strongly in radio. Fearing a British monopoly, these companies, along with American Telephone and Telegraph, pooled their patents to form the Radio Corporation of America (RCA), the firm that would ultimately push the commercial development of the new broadcasting medium in the next decade.

**1922**—Radio receiver manufacturers like Westinghouse and General Electric operated radio stations to stimulate the sale of radio receivers. But AT&T manufactured radio transmitters, not receivers, and saw limited advantages in using radio broadcasting to stimulate radio sales. The telephone company saw a different use for the new medium. A customer had to pay a toll to make a telephone call. Would a customer pay a similar toll to use radio to communicate with not just one other individual, but with many? Toll broadcasting, what we now call radio advertising, was first attempted in August of 1922 over AT&T station WEAF in New York. It worked,

Probably no art form has had a single piece of work advance the state of the art so far and so fast as *Birth of a Nation* advanced filmmaking. D.W. Griffith produced this epic, which was filled with large-scale outdoor scenes like this one, without a shooting script. Prints of the film still exist, but the heavily racist theme of the film makes it difficult to watch *Birth of a Nation* comfortably today. (The Bettmann Archive. Inc.)

as a Long Island realtor paid AT&T $100 for 10 minutes of broadcast time to tell listeners about available properties. In four years WEAF was grossing $750,000 annually in advertising revenue. Other stations soon saw the advantage of this scheme, and radio advertising became commonplace.

Also in 1922, DeWitt and Lila A. Wallace, seemingly taking their cue from the early American magazine publishers who put together their magazines with clippings from other periodicals, published the first edition of *Reader's Digest.* The pocket-sized digest of condensed articles, first published in other magazines and newspapers, quickly grew to be one of the most successful magazines in the world.

**1923**—Henry Luce, like the Wallaces, said he believed that while Americans were very interested in what was going on around them, they did not have the time to read a large number of magazines and newspapers and books. Luce gave us *Time,* a compartmentalized news magazine, and the first publication of what is now one of the world's largest media conglomerates, Time-Warner, Inc. The magazine mixed editorial commentary with the news, but in the eyes of its loyal readers, satisfactorily put what was happening in the world between the 30 or so pages that were published each week.

AT&T first linked two radio stations in 1923, WEAF in New York and WNAC in Boston, and established the nation's first radio network. By 1924 WEAF had become the flagship of a six-station chain that broadcast three hours of network programming daily.

Sound movies would not be introduced to the public until 1927. But in 1923

*Nanook of the North,* made by Robert Flaherty in 1922, was the first significant documentary in the history of filmmaking. The film, which tells the intimate story of an Eskimo family and its struggle to survive in the rugged arctic wilderness, is still enjoyable to watch today. Documentary films never really received a warm reception from American moviegoers; today, documentary films are largely confined to television.
(Museum of Modern Art Film Stills Archive)

Lee De Forest, the radio pioneer, began showing short experimental films that featured the voices as well as the pictures of leading vaudeville performers.

The growing American film industry was beginning to feel a threat of state and federal censorship. To ward off these attacks from the outside it instituted a self-censorship program, first administered by Will Hays, former U.S. Postmaster General. The so-called **production code**—which became even more restrictive in the early 1930s—had strong provisions regarding sex, drugs, crime, patriotism and many other topics. Films had to be pre-screened for censors before they could be released for exhibition. Films that failed to pass muster were denied a production code seal of approval. Theater owners would not exhibit pictures that did not carry the seal. Until the 1950s, that is. Two pictures by Otto Preminger, *The Moon is Blue* (1953) and *The Man with the Golden Arm* (1955), went into the theaters without the seal, were widely exhibited, critically acclaimed, and popularly received. This broke the back of the code, which was ultimately abandoned and replaced by the movie rating system that is now used.

**1926**—AT&T decided to concentrate on telephones and get out of broadcasting. It sold its growing radio network to RCA, which had previously constructed an inferior but competing radio network. RCA now had two networks and established a new subsidiary, the National Broadcasting Company, to operate the broadcasting end of the business.

**1927**—The popularity of radio had grown beyond even the wildest dreams of its most enthusiastic supporters. By 1925 there were over 500 stations on the air. In 1912 Congress had adopted only the most minimal regulation of this new medium, requiring operators to hold a license (for which there were no real qualifications) and assigning specific kinds of broadcasts to specific frequencies. The laws of nature were far harsher, however. There is a distinct limit in the size of the broadcast spectrum (the electromagnetic waves on which the radio signals travel) and this limits the number of stations that may broadcast in any area. By the middle of the decade the growing number of stations that wanted to broadcast came face to face with the immutable laws of nature and the listeners lost. A cacophony resulted. In addition, the radio airwaves were filled with the shouts of hucksters, peddlers, con artists, and others who sought to take advantage of listeners. After intense prodding by serious broadcasters, the Secretary of Commerce (who was assigned the task of "regulating" radio), and others interested in the future of the new medium, Congress adopted comprehensive legislation in 1927 to regulate radio. Under the Radio Act of 1927 private ownership of stations would continue, but all broadcasters would have to be licensed, follow strict government technical performance standards, and use their stations to serve the public interest. An independent regulatory agency, the Federal Radio Commission, was named to supervise the control of the industry.

While television would not be offered to the public in the United States until the end of the 1930s, experimental broadcasts were already underway by 1927.

*The Jazz Singer,* widely regarded as the first sound film, was really a "singie," not a talkie. Only a couple of lines of dialogue, as well as the songs, were recorded on the film. Al Jolson played the leading role of a cantor's son going into show business, where he performed in black face. (Museum of Modern Art Film Stills Archive)

A group of independent broadcasters founded a new radio network, the Columbia Broadcasting System. But the network didn't really take on serious proportions until 1928 when William S. Paley, a cigar maker, bought the network as a means to advertise his tobacco products. Paley, who turned out to be an enlightened broadcaster, would lead CBS until the 1980s.

The major American movie studios were reaping big profits from the silent movies and were reluctant to make the large investment (both financial and creative) needed to produce sound films. Warner Bros., one of the smallest studios, released *The Jazz Singer* in 1927. The feature film had four sound musical numbers and a line of dialogue. The "talkie" (or perhaps "singie") captured the fancy of the moviegoers, and Hollywood was forced to adopt the new sound technology.

**1930s**—Radio programming became increasingly sophisticated during the 1920s and advertisers flocked to the new medium. They were given the opportunity to buy short advertising spots during programming carried on the networks and local radio stations. But many advertisers found this scheme unsatisfactory. The quality of programs varied; the content was mixed. Advertisers feared having the products they sold associated with poor programming or, even worse, programming that offended some listeners. Advertisers sought to resolve this difficulty by creating their own programs, and then buying the needed air time—an hour or thirty minutes—to broadcast them. Slowly but surely advertisers came to control the content of radio, especially network radio. At times a single advertising agency was responsible for as much as 10 percent of a network's programming schedule. This was a power that frightened even the most courageous network executives who feared losing that

George Burns (who was still performing in 1991) and his real-life and stage wife Gracie Allen, became household names among American radio listeners during the heyday of network radio. The team successfully survived the transition to television where Gracie became the new medium's first "dingbat" wife, preceding both Lucille Ball on "I Love Lucy," and Jean Stapleton as Edith Bunker on "All in the Family."

much revenue because of an angry advertiser. There was little time for public service programming, or material that was unusual, instructional, or especially controversial. Commercial interests fairly dominated the medium. It was in the backwash of these conditions that television was born a few years later.

**1934**—Congress adopted the **Communications Act of 1934,** which slightly modified the Radio Act of 1927 and created the Federal Communications Commission to replace the Federal Radio Commission. This is the law, somewhat amended, that continues to govern the operation of radio and television stations.

The boom years of the Hollywood motion picture studios began in the mid-1930s (after the successful conversion to sound) and lasted until the mid-century and the coming of television. The moguls that ran the dream factories in Southern California controlled the fantasy world of not only Americans, but of motion picture audiences around the world. The description on a motion picture, "Made in Hollywood," became a mark of distinction to most moviegoers. An elaborate system of studio production soon emerged, and the dream factories began to look a lot like other American factories which mass-produced automobiles or refrigerators. Studios controlled the entire production, distribution, and exhibition process for most films, from the initial story idea to selling tickets at the box office. Producers, directors, writers, performers, film editors, publicity agents, theater managers, and many others

Philo T. Farnsworth, a U.S. engineer, was one of several developers of modern television. Here he demonstrates a crude video system in the early 1930s. (The Bettmann Archive, Inc.)

were all under contract to a studio. Films produced by a single studio, like MGM or Columbia, tended to take on a common appearance. Although the films were made on an assembly line, many of them were very good movies. It was truly a heyday for Hollywood. There was nothing like it before; there has been nothing like it since. We today afford celebrity status to cultural icons like Tom Cruise or Madonna or Michael Jackson. But this pales in comparison to the royalty status granted to the kings and queens of Hollywood in the 1930s and 1940s. And the studios, MGM, Warner Bros., Paramount, Columbia, United Artists, and the rest, controlled the whole show.

By the end of the 1930s radio broadcasters, led by CBS News, began to gather and report the news on a regular basis. The daily newspapers, which until this time had printed logs or lists of radio programs as a service to their readers, were angered by this new competition. Many dropped their radio logs, informing local stations that they could purchase the space if they wanted their schedules printed. But the growth of radio news could not be deterred, and as the Second World War approached in Europe the radio voices of men like H.V. Kaltenborn and Edward R. Murrow were commonly heard in homes throughout the nation.

**1937**—Television sets had been on sale in Great Britain since 1930; serious attempts at telecasting began in 1937 when the coronation of King George VI was televised. Regular programming to British homes began shortly thereafter.

**1939**—Television is introduced in the United States at the New York World's

NBC's telecast of the opening of the New York World's Fair in 1939 was one of the first nonexperimental U.S. television broadcasts. In this photograph, note the television camera (arrow B) focusing on President Franklin Delano Roosevelt (arrow A). (NBC Photo)

Fair. Limited telecasting is available to the few homes with TV sets in the New York area. Why was the United States behind the British? Not for technological reasons, but for commercial reasons. The companies that controlled TV technology, RCA, CBS, and others, had a major stake in radio. They were not terribly interested in a medium that would create substantial competition to radio, which at that time was popular and very lucrative.

**1941–45**—Things slowed down dramatically during the war years, and the nation turned its eyes toward more serious matters. While the production of television sets and other television equipment was stopped because the raw materials were needed for the war effort, the advertising industry nevertheless began to prepare for the widespread acceptance of the new medium after the war. The U.S. Justice Department threatened antitrust action against NBC and forced it to sell one of its two radio networks. The network was sold to Edward J. Noble, founder and chairman of the Life Savers Corporation and in 1944 acquired the name by which we now know it, the American Broadcasting Company.

**1945**—The first regularly scheduled network news was broadcast on NBC television. Most of the video portion of the telecast was provided by independent newsreel companies, as the network did not yet have a substantial video news capability.

**1946**—The development of television technology did not slow during World War II, and the widespread introduction of color television in the immediate postwar years seemed to be a real possibility. CBS first demonstrated a color system in 1940 and in 1944 urged the FCC to accept the CBS color system as the standard for the American industry. The government agency invited CBS to demonstrate its system in 1946 and most observers were impressed. The picture was clear, the colors brilliant and stable. But the FCC found two faults with the CBS system. It was not compatible with the existing 200,000 or so television sets already in American homes. People with those sets could not receive any picture—color or black and white—if the CBS system was used. CBS color television was a mechanical rather than an electronic system, and the FCC said it was not reliable and too cumbersome. So the agency rejected the CBS technology, partly at least, on the promise of RCA to demonstrate an electronic, compatible system within six months. RCA did so, but the picture quality was unsatisfactory and the color was crude and unstable. Three years later RCA demonstrated its improved color system. The FCC was again disappointed. Finally, in 1951, RCA demonstrated an adequate color system. Two years later it was accepted by the FCC and color television sets were first produced in 1954. By then a majority of Americans had already purchased a black-and-white television set. Most would purchase a second black-and-white set before the price of the color television sets was sufficiently reduced and the color quality was sufficiently attractive. In fact, color television didn't become a reality in the lives of most Americans until the end of the 1960s. There are two important footnotes to this story. The "cumbersome" and "unreliable" mechanical CBS color system rejected by the FCC was the basis for the video system carried to the moon by the American astronauts. And in 1947, six months after he presided at the hearings in which the FCC rejected the CBS system, Federal Communications Commission Chairman Charles Denny resigned from his government post and became vice-president and general counsel of NBC, the RCA-owned broadcast network.

**1947**—More than 87 million people went to the movies each week in America, the highest box office attendance in the history of the film industry. Attendance in 1990—a good year in the recent history of the industry—was less than 22 million per week.

**1948**—Government antitrust action against the film industry culminated when the U.S. Justice Department ruled that the motion picture studios would have to sell their motion picture theaters. This was a serious blow to the studios, for the control of exhibition as well as production and distribution insured that any film Hollywood produced would get a theater showing. The previous year the federal courts had ruled that the studios had to abandon their practice of fixed admission prices and block booking. **Block booking** is a system whereby the studios provided their best movies to independent theaters only if the theaters promised to book their weakest movies as well. Films, the good and the bad, were booked as a block. These legal actions plus the coming of television foretold dark, dark days ahead for the film industry.

Unexpected technical problems in the transmission of television signals forced the FCC to stop issuing licenses for new television stations. The freeze on licensing was supposed to last for six months; it lasted three years. But during this period of time, supporters of non-commercial television were able to muster enough support to convince the FCC to set aside almost 250 channels for educational use. FCC Commissioner Freida Hennock led the fight and is credited with convincing her fellow FCC commissioners of the need for the non-commercial stations.

After World War II, strange-looking gadgets (TV antennas) began to appear on American rooftops, and a middle-aged vaudevillian became everybody's Uncle Miltie. Milton Berle was the first major entertainer to have his own television show, "The Texaco Star Theater," which first aired in June of 1948 and lasted for five years. (NBC Photo)

As television began to catch fire the networks began to lose interest in their radio programming. This was the beginning of the end for big-time, live entertainment-oriented radio. Network radio hung on until the mid-1950s, but the revenues were siphoned off for use in television. Some said it was as if network radio was presiding at its own funeral.

**1950**—A kind of cancer was infecting the political system by the middle of the century, and it spread throughout the entertainment industry. This was the era we now remember as the period of the **Red Scare.** The Cold War with the Soviet Union had reached serious proportions; a few in government and outside of government feared that the threat of Russian troops landing on our shores was unimportant compared to the danger posed by the Communists already in this country. There were charges levelled by men like Senator Joseph McCarthy of Wisconsin and others that Communists had infiltrated our State Department and our military. The mass media also became a target as investigators in Congress, in the FBI, and in scores of private vigilante organizations sought to tie leftish or liberal politics to disloyalty. People who had associated with Communist or Socialist groups in the past, in the thirties, during the war, were singled out for investigation, harassment, and even jail. A few people went to prison. But most only saw their careers ruined as their names—rightly or wrongly—appeared on what were called **black lists.** Persons who were blacklisted were simply not employed in motion pictures, television, and radio. They were suspect. And even though producers and directors and others in the business saw them as harmless, or the victims of smear campaigns, the major entertainment industries were fearful of alienating the right-wing American newspaper press, sponsors, and others in the economic community that could bring pressure to bear. In late 1950, for example, CBS required that all its employees sign a loyalty oath. While the Red Scare ended by the mid-1950s, the scars lasted far longer. Many blacklisted performers didn't find their way back into television, especially, until the 1970s. Many never did reestablish their careers. The film industry seriously hurt itself by alienating a large segment of its dwindling audience that was appalled at the manner in which the leaders of the motion picture community turned their backs on loyal employees.

**1951**—"I Love Lucy" debuted on CBS. Lucille Ball and Desi Arnez invented the situation comedy format with this show. More importantly, they invented the television rerun. Television programs were broadcast live in the early 1950s. When the show was over, it was gone forever. A crude process called Kinescope could record pictures off a television screen, but the quality of reproduction was unsatisfactory for rebroadcast in most instances. Lucille Ball wanted her show filmed before a live audience for subsequent broadcast. The network initially balked, but later consented. Film quality permitted subsequent rebroadcasts. Voila! Reruns. Other producers in the industry were quick to follow suit.

**1952**—The Golden Age of television had arrived as the networks filled many of the primetime viewing hours with original drama and comedy of a quality rarely seen since. The medium was attempting to reach those who could afford to purchase a television set, not an inexpensive item in those days. These viewers were more likely to be moved by live drama on "Playhouse 90" than situation comedies like "The Aldrich Family." Hence the sophisticated programming.

The first televised political spots were created by ad man Rosser Reeves for Dwight D. Eisenhower and his campaign for the Presidency. Democrat Adlai Stevenson, Eisenhower's opponent, refused to use TV ads, saying he didn't want to be marketed like corn flakes. Stevenson lost.

Hollywood was in the grips of economic chaos. Some of the weak studios—Republic, Mongram, Allied Artists—failed. Production was cut back; many jobs were lost. The studios sought formulas to save them. They tried new film processes (3–D, wide screen) to attract people away from the small television picture tubes. They sought to make quality, "small," black-and-white films to lure the more sophisticated film audience back to the theater. There were no successful formulas. The size of the audience continued to shrink.

**1955**—By 1955 both NBC and CBS had major studio and production facilities in Southern California. Like the film industry some 40 years before, the creative end of television moved West. But television production of another kind began in Hollywood at this time as well. It had taken nearly ten years, but the motion picture studios had come to realize that television was not a fad that would go away. The industry had to live with the new electronic medium. If the mountain wouldn't come to Mohammed, perhaps Mohammed would have to go to the mountain. Studios began to sell parts of their film libraries to television, usually films made before 1948. The new medium was hungry for any kind of content to fill up the broadcast hours and jumped at the chance to buy even old movies. Warner Bros., the film studio that had produced *The Jazz Singer,* the first widely distributed sound feature film, went a step farther. The studio began production of television programs. The first was a western series called "Cheyenne" and was telecast on ABC. It wasn't a very good program, and much of the program was made up of stock footage from old Warner

Warner Brothers was the first major film studio to begin the production of television programs. "Cheyenne," which hit the small screen in 1955, was a huge success for the studio and ABC. Clint Walker (pictured) played the prototype slow-talking, hard-fighting American cowboy. (Warner Bros. Photo)

Bros. western movies. But the fact that it was made by a Hollywood film studio caught the public's attention and it was successful. Other series from Warner Bros. followed; "77 Sunset Strip," and "Hawaiian Eye," were among the most successful. Soon, other film studios got into television production as well. This marked a resurgence of the film studios, but not the motion picture business.

Network radio was all but dead. Local stations, scrambling to fill the void left by network programming, focused most heavily on recorded music. And a new demigod of radio appeared: the disc jockey.

**1958**—The common quiz program became the most popular format on television at the end of the 1950s as a series of big money (very big money) shows caught the public fancy. Contestants on programs like "The $64,000 Question" and "Twenty-One" could win more than $100,000 for answering a series of progressively tougher questions on a selected topic. Winners were brought back week after week to try to win greater sums or defend their titles against challengers. Viewership of the programs was phenomenal; meetings were recessed, conventions adjourned so participants could gather around the television set to see if the latest video hero—just an average person—could hit the next plateau by giving the quizmaster the correct answers. The balloon popped in 1958 when revelations appeared that many of the shows had been rigged. Popular contestants had been fed the answers; others who were less popular got no help and harder questions. A Congressional investigation followed. Quiz shows disappeared from prime time, and big money shows did not reappear at any time of the day until many years later. If there was a saving aspect to the scandal it was that the networks were forced to wrest program content control away from the advertisers who had controlled these programs. The networks were held responsible for the programs; in the future they would control the programming. Sponsors could buy spots to sell their wares.

**1959**—The quiz show scandals were still under investigation in 1959 when the other shoe dropped, the **payola scandals** in the recording and radio industries. Since the turn of the century publishing houses had used song pluggers to pay performers to sing or play their songs. When radio became wed to recorded music, and when the record companies discovered the value of air play to record sales, the companies began to pay some disc jockeys to play their records. The scandal broke in 1959. Some suggest the payola became too obvious; it was bound to be noticed. Others suggest the major record labels like Columbia fomented the investigation to hurt the growing number of small independent record companies which had substantial control of rock and roll performers. The new rock music was causing economic grief for many established record companies which had failed to invest in rock performers because they believed the new music was a fad that would not last, or they found the music offensive. The scandal ruined the careers of some important American disc jockeys, including Alan Freed who was among the first to introduce the black-oriented rhythm and blues music to white teenagers in Cleveland and later in New York. And many of the independent record companies folded under the pressure of Congressional investigation and the ensuing hassles. Payola didn't end, however. Record industry executives were indicted as recently as 1990 and charged with similar crimes.

**1960**—For the first time two U.S. Presidential candidates debated on television. Congress suspended laws which had, in the past, precluded a debate between only the major party candidates. Richard Nixon and John Kennedy met three times before television cameras. The debates suggested the new power of the visual image cast by the television camera. Voters who heard the debate on radio tended to give the edge to Nixon; those who watched on television gave Kennedy the nod. Nixon, who had been ill, did not look well on the screen. He refused to use makeup. Kennedy was tanned and robust after campaigning in the sunny South. Kennedy won the election.

FM radio had been around for almost as long as AM radio, but for many years it was not taken seriously as a commercial medium. Technical problems seemed to stand in the way of its growth. The FCC even allocated a portion of the FM spectrum in the late 1930s for the transmission of television programming. The believers in the medium retained hope, however, and technical problems were solved. But the radio industry—the AM oriented industry—controlled FM as well. And it wasn't about to add competition to the field. Most FM licenses were held by AM stations, which carried the same programming (called **simulcasting**) over both frequencies. Government action in the late 1950s and 1960s gave new life to the FM format. The broadcast of FM stereo was approved. And the Federal Communications Commission ruled that stations holding both an AM and FM frequency had to limit their simulcasts to less than 50 percent of the broadcast day. Many AM licensees sold their FM frequencies rather than invest in new programming, and these stations became the foundation of the FM industry that would blossom later in the decade. The electronics industry anticipated the changes and began to commonly manufacture AM-FM radio receivers. By the early 1970s nearly one-fourth of the listening audience tuned to FM stations. Today FM captures nearly 75 percent of all listeners.

**1963**—CBS telecast the first regularly scheduled 30-minute network newscast on Labor Day. NBC offered a 30-minute evening newscast less than two weeks later. Both networks had previously aired only 15 minutes of news each evening. The expansion of the evening newscasts marked a recognition by the networks of the growing importance of television news to the nation's viewers. It took many years for advertiser interest to catch up, and television news was an expensive proposition for the networks for more than a decade. But advertisers finally realized that there was a large audience for television news, and this audience was generally in the higher economic class. News has proliferated at the networks and especially at local stations, where it is not uncommon to see as many as five hours of news programmed daily. News has become a profit center—not a drain on revenues—at most local television stations.

Syncom II, the first geosynchronous satellite, was launched and went into stationary orbit. Telstar, the first communications satellite, had been launched a year earlier, but was not in a stationary orbit. It orbited only 4 months. A geosynchronous satellite rotates around the earth at a speed that matches the earth's speed of rotation and is thus stationary above the earth. This idea was first proposed in 1945 by science fiction writer Arthur C. Clarke. Clarke estimated that with just three such satellites positioned 120 degrees apart along the equator, a television signal could be sent anywhere in the world. The communications satellites now carry nearly all television signals transmitted more than a few miles and have made possible cable television networks.

By the mid-1960s an innovative new printing technology called **offset printing** came into widespread use. Offset printing, a refinement of the older lithography process, is explained in Chapter 5, see page 148. Its importance in this decade was that it made possible the printing of newspapers and other kinds of publications at a relatively low cost, when compared with the traditional letterpress printing. The cold-type processes associated with offset were also a cheap means of preparing a newspaper for publication. It was the existence of these low-cost processes that made the so-called **underground press,** which flowered in the late 1960s and early 1970s, possible.

**1967**—The Public Broadcasting Service was launched. Following a recommendation made a year earlier with the publication of the "Carnegie Commission Report on Public Television," the nation's educational television stations are formally linked into a public television network. Congress created the Corporation for Public Broadcasting to operate and fund the new public network. Unfortunately the promise of adequate government funding was never realized.

**1974**—*People* magazine debuted. By 1974 the last of the great, mass circulation, general interest magazines like *Colliers, Saturday Evening Post, Look,* and *Life* had died. The decision made 70 years ago to rely primarily on advertising for revenue became fatal when advertisers switched to the newer and cheaper medium, television. *People* was the first successful national weekly magazine launched in 30 years. Time, Inc., the publisher, designed the magazine as a successful substitute for the scores of celebrity-oriented movie and television magazines that were on the newsracks. The magazine was sold off racks in supermarkets and convenience stores, avoiding the high cost of postal delivery. It made a profit within 18 months, spawned a host of imitators, and pushed the more staid newsmagazines toward the softer side of journalism.

**1975**—Time, Inc. launched Home Box Office, the first pay cable channel. For people all over the nation who had perfectly good television reception, cable now offered an added value: programming that could not be seen on over-the-air television.

The release of Steven Spielberg's film *Jaws,* the story of havoc caused by a man-eating shark off the Long Island coast, brought long lines back to the movie theater during the summer months. The film marks the early resurgence of the American film industry.

**1977**—The promise of *Jaws* was fulfilled by the release of George Lucas' *Star Wars,* which quickly vaulted to the position of one of the most popular films of all time. Lucas, Spielberg, and others recaptured the hearts of young filmgoers that Disney had held but lost in the sixties. The movie also pushed the industry onto a special effects roller coaster that has not yet stopped, raising the cost of movie-making to continually higher levels and pushing producers to often replace coherent stories, meaningful acting, and thoughtful dialogue with hi-tech action. Sony introduced its Betamax home video recorder. Heralded initially as a gadget, home VCRs would later change the face of both television and the motion picture industry.

**1979**—Ted Turner's "superstation," WTBS, a local Atlanta television station, found its way onto cable systems all over America via satellite. The earlier promise of richer programming from the plethora of cable channels was put into perspective with the success of the WTBS menu of reruns, movies, and mail-order advertising. Cable television revenues surpassed $1 billion.

**1981**—MTV, perhaps the boldest cable television venture since the launching of HBO, premiered on August 1. The Warner-Amex cable channel set its sights on and captured the teenage audience. By broadcasting music videos almost continuously, 24 hours each day, the new cable channel exposed American record buyers to a wide range of new musical performers, many of whom were British, and who hadn't been able to get radio airplay for their recordings. Video techniques used to produce many of the videos will come to have a serious impact on the production of television commercials and even television programs and films.

Stereo broadcasting by AM radio stations was touted in the industry as a means of bringing back AM radio, now seriously lagging in its battle with FM. But the federal government refused to select one of the five technologically feasible systems; let the marketplace decide, the FCC ruled. A listener needed a different receiver to pick up each system, so the public did not flock to buy AM stereo receivers. Stations became reluctant to select a system that might lose favor in the long run, so few adopted the technology. The idea flopped.

**1982**—The Gannett Corporation introduced *USA Today,* the nation's first national newspaper. The paper is put together in Virginia, and finished pages are transmitted electronically by satellite to printing plants (usually Gannett newspapers) around the nation. By the end of the decade the new paper still had not shown more than a "paper" profit, but its bold color, strong emphasis on graphics, and short story-good news format had influenced daily newspapers across the nation.

Compact laser discs, or CDs, and disc players, were introduced to the record-buying public. The crisp sound was attractive to music lovers, and sales were brisk. The record companies re-released their inventory of vinyl recordings on compact disc and this influx of cash assisted the major recording companies in overcoming a serious slump in sales. By 1990 CDs are pushing long-play records out of the retail stores.

**1989**—The merger of Time, Inc. and Warner Communications into the largest communications company in the world put a capstone on the decade of the 1980s, a decade in which mergers and buyouts resulted in the concentration of the ownership of the nation's mass communications enterprises into fewer and fewer hands, a cause for great concern, except among the captains of America's communications industry.

What can we learn from this brief account of the history of mass communications that will permit us to have a better understanding of the mass media? Each reader is capable of reading what he or she wants into this brief narrative. Some conclusions seem to jump out of this history; others are a bit less obvious.

In its inception the new mass medium of printing was first and foremost an instrument of mass communications. There were information and ideas that needed to be spread throughout the community, across the country. The printed press was really just a mechanical amplification of the speakers in the village square or at the town meeting or in a local tavern or church. Today mass communications is a huge enterprise, a big business, and a business that needs to use the channels of communications to generate revenues to sustain itself. And often serious conflicts arise when the use of the mass media to generate revenue collides with the use of the mass media to communicate information. In whose favor should these conflicts be resolved—the public that needs the information, or the businessperson who needs the revenue to sustain the mass medium?

Our mass communications system has become deeply integrated into our political, social, and cultural systems during the past 500 plus years. Today the mass media are more than simple amplification systems. We can see how integral the press was in supporting and sustaining the American revolution. And the important role it played in the formation of the new government. Our political process today would undoubtedly fail if the mass media were to suddenly disappear. The presidential election process in the United States has become, rightly or wrongly, a television event. Celebrities created by the mass media are our cultural icons. We decorate our clothing and automobiles with the commercial trademarks and slogans of advertisers. The content of the mass media is an important topic of conversation at all levels of our society. Could we sustain our capitalistic economic system without advertising in the mass media? Could a nation as large as ours be governed without an elaborate mass communications system?

At the same time, the mass communications system is tied to the nation and changes in the nation. Literacy grew in the 1830s; the press grew as well. Immigrants filled our cities in the 1890s; the press responded to these newcomers with a different kind of newspaper. The industrial revolution permits the development of better manufacturing and transportation systems; the mass media find new sources of advertising. The mass media are part of the national fabric. Remove the mass media and the fabric is substantially altered.

The mass media in America underwent three important technological expansions. The addition of steam power to the printing press in the 1830s was the first. Technological innovation of many shades occurred in the later part of the 1800s and early 1900s. These innovations greatly changed the manner in which the printed press was published and encompassed the early efforts to develop electronic mass communications, such as radio, motion pictures, and even television. Finally, the decades of the 1960s and 1970s saw the introduction of satellite communication, video recorders, digital audio and video recording, and many other mass communication implements.

The innovations during these three periods all led to enlarging the size of the audience for mass communications. The circulation of American newspapers and magazines grew to giant proportions in the early twentieth century. Home video recorders greatly expanded the audience for motion pictures in the 1980s. Satellite transmissions made cable television networks possible, expanding the audience for programming offered by someone other than the three national over-the-air networks. In these ways technological innovation worked for the audience as well as the communicators.

But in fact the history of mass communications in the United States also demonstrates that new technology is introduced when it is beneficial to the communications industry, not as soon as it is available or when it might benefit the audience. The introduction of sound motion pictures was forced upon the movie studios by the actions of one studio. The introduction of television was delayed to protect radio. The introduction of FM radio was stymied by those who controlled the technology and AM radio. The growth of cable television was slowed by the over-the-air television interests. Economic considerations take a higher priority than public interest or even advertiser needs. Only when the introduction of a new technology becomes profitable is it offered to the public. This is something one might expect in a system constructed upon private ownership of mass communication systems.

The entire mass communications enterprise in the United States is geared to acceptance of content by an audience, usually a mass audience. In seeking a mass audience, the urban press of the late 1800s added entertainment to the news content of the newspaper. Network television has long been dominated by the "ratings race." Today even the news is shaped by the forces of market research. The needs of the audience are rarely defined, and when they are, are served by the private forbearance of the industry only so long as it is affordable. All three major television networks made serious cutbacks in the early 1980s and 1990s in their production of news. This clearly affected the quality of network television news and was done to increase the profitability of news programming.

Our system of mass communications has emerged without the slightest nod toward rational planning, and that is perhaps the most remarkable thing about it. We rely on many institutions and systems in our society: education, health care, financial, social services. The development of all of these systems has been subjected to close supervision by the government and the society. Policies have been made; planning has taken place. But the mass media, like Topsy in *Uncle Tom's Cabin,* just grew. This lack of planning or policy has resulted in spirited competition that at times has been good for media users. But not often. More typically this lack of planning has resulted in chaos, or poor service, or unfulfilled opportunities, or additional costs to consumers. The early days of radio were chaotic. The failure of the government to select one AM stereo system retarded and ultimately doomed the development of this innovation. For many years consumers who purchased home video recorders had to choose between two formats. Ultimately the Beta format died, and millions of perfectly usable Betamax machines became obsolete. Competition rather than policy dictated what color television system would be adopted, and this delayed the adoption. In fact, for as much as we rely upon mass communications to facilitate the operation of so many things in this nation, it is remarkable that things work as well as they do.

Something that is not as apparent as it might be from the short chronology previously presented is that the history of mass communications has been marked by a struggle for the freedom to communicate. From the very beginning of printing, governments have sought to control the communication process or limit its use in one way or another. Yet the democratization of Western Europe and the New World was accompanied by the development of influential ideas regarding freedom of expression. Today, in the United States at least, government censorship, while it still exists, is not the dominant threat to freedom of expression. That threat comes from the mass communications system itself, as fewer and fewer persons control the content of more and more mass media. The phenomenal concentration of the ownership into the hands of relatively few persons is something that began to develop early this century. Its pace was steady until the 1960s when it accelerated rapidly. The growth of newspaper chains, the merger of giant media companies, appearance of more and more media monopolies, and many other developments has heralded a serious new threat to functioning of the mass media as instruments of freely flowing information and ideas.

As each new medium has developed in this century, hopes of greater freedom of communication, more diversity of ownership and use, have been dashed by the domination of the medium by large, commercially oriented interests. Many saw the introduction of radio as a means for the public, through stations controlled by labor unions and churches and schools, to compete in the marketplace of ideas with the business interests which owned the press. But it didn't work that way. Radio became even more commercially oriented than newspapers. And cable television was viewed as a means of competing with the powerful television networks and chains of local over-the-air stations. But today the ownership of cable is more concentrated than the ownership of over-the-air telecasting.

This nation has constructed the most sophisticated mass communications system in the world. It has only been in the past two decades that Japan and some nations in Western Europe have built comparable and (in a few cases) superior communications technology. And virtually all Americans are tied into this system, if only as receivers of entertainment and information. With this system of mass communications it is possible to enlighten, educate, and inform the great masses of Americans about a limitless array of topics. This is possible. Yet if the history of mass communications in the United States teaches us anything, it is that the content of the mass media, the messages that are carried, is rarely defined by what is possible. More commonly the content of the mass media is defined by what is profitable. This was determined when the American mass communications system evolved as a part of the private enterprise system as opposed to an arm of government or political parties or labor unions or whatever. This remains the most critical limitation on the institutions of our mass media.

## BIBLIOGRAPHY

These are some of the materials that have been helpful in the preparation of this chapter.

Barnouw, Erik. *A History of Broadcasting in the United States.* 3 vols. New York: Oxford University Press, 1966–71.
————. *Tube of Plenty.* New York: Oxford University Press, 1975.
Caute, David. *The Great Fear.* New York: Simon & Schuster, 1978.
Emery, Edwin, and Emery, Michael. *The Press and America: An Interpretative History of the Mass Media.* (6th ed.) Englewood Cliffs, N.J.: Prentice-Hall, 1988.
Farrar, Ronald T., and Stevens, John D. (eds.) *Mass Media and the National Experience.* New York: Harper & Row, 1971.
Harmon, Jim. *The Great Radio Heroes.* New York: Doubleday and Co., 1967.
Higham, Charles. *Hollywood at Sunset.* New York: Saturday Review Press, 1972.
Randall, Richard S. *Censorship of Movies.* Madison: University of Wisconsin Press, 1968.
Schickel, Richard. *Movies: The History of an Art.* New York: Simon & Schuster, 1963.

# CHAPTER 3

# THEORETICAL AND RESEARCH FOUNDATIONS

*Scenario One*   Imagine you are an account executive for a large advertising agency and you are preparing a new campaign for a client, Western Airlines. Working with your client you have decided to try to portray Western as an airline somewhat different from competitors, one that really cares about what passengers want in an airline. But what do passengers want in an airline? Better schedules? Tastier food? Roomier seats? More destinations? The way to answer these questions is through research; in a simple, but scientific way, ask passengers what they want in an airline.

*Scenario Two*   After laboring for ten years behind the microphone at radio stations throughout the Midwest, you have just landed your first job as program director at an FM station in a mid-sized market. The ratings for the station (which followed an adult contemporary format) have been lousy for the past two years; the station manager thinks a format change could attract more listeners. But what kind of format should the station adopt? A carefully constructed survey of people in the community could reveal what kind of programming they would like to hear, but cannot presently find on the existing radio stations. Research can't tell you what kind of format you should recommend, but it can give you a good indication of what listeners think is missing in the market.

*Scenario Three*   After spending 15 years as a reporter and subeditor at a mid-sized daily newspaper on the West Coast you are named managing editor. The first thing your publisher asks for is a 15-page report on what kind of a newspaper the company should be publishing. As you sit down and begin to prepare your report you ask yourself: Who are the people of this community? What kind of newspaper would best serve their needs? How well educated are they? How much money do they earn? What kinds of books do they read? What is their ethnic background? And their religious background? What do they do for a living? You realize that after 15 years you really don't know who the people in this community are. But these data can be generated through research. Census data can provide much of this information, along with histories of the area, economic reports, and a study of business and industry in the area. Most of this information has already been gathered by others — you just have to dig it out of the books at the library or the computer data bases.

*Scenario Four* It is the middle of the semester or the term, and that term paper you were assigned on the growth of monopoly newspapers is due next week. It is time to head to the library to look for books and articles on this topic. Maybe a visit to the local newspaper would be useful, to talk with the publisher or the business manager. You might conduct a simple poll among the people on your floor in the dormitory, asking whether they think it is better to have two newspapers or one newspaper in a community. Research again.

We know what we know about the mass media largely through research. And the people in the mass media know what they know about their clients, their audiences, their readers, their viewers, and others because of research. Research and theory are sometimes unpopular words to many undergraduates. But they shouldn't be. Learning about our environment, whether it is the physical environment, or our media environment, is an important and interesting aspect of our education. And it is through research that we know these things.

In one way or another we are all researchers. Every move we take, every decision we make, is guided by research we have conducted. Persons who work in the mass media spend a considerable portion of their time doing research. Reporters gather news. This is research. Public relations practitioners seek to discover the cause of problems in communications. This is research. Advertising and television executives try to determine the wants of consumers and viewers. This is research. The significant difference between the manner in which professionals (academics, journalists, pollsters) conduct research and the way in which we conduct research in our daily lives is the existence of rules; professionally-conducted research is guided by rules. And, if it is done properly, some kind of theory.

It is the purpose of this chapter to explain to you a little bit about how we know what we know and to outline for you some of the major points regarding mass communications research and theory. No attempt is made to teach you to be a researcher. Other courses and other books meet that need. The goal here is simply to describe the development of communications research and theory, explain how research can be conducted, talk a little bit about some theories and models of communication behavior, and examine briefly what we know about the effects of mass communications upon the members of the audience.

# UNDERSTANDING COMMUNICATIONS

Of all the social sciences, communications is the youngest discipline. Initial research on mass communications dates back to the early part of this century, World War I, when governments used mass media to both keep up the morale of the troops and those at home, and to shape public opinion, and then attempted to study the effectiveness of their efforts. Less formal research was surely conducted as well in this era. Comedians Stan Laurel and Oliver Hardy, for example, visited local motion picture theaters to watch the initial screenings of their comedies. They would watch the au-

Some of the earliest communications research was undertaken by comedians Stan Laurel and Oliver Hardy. The pair would attend screenings of their films to gauge audience reactions to the gags. Subtle editing often followed to lengthen or shorten the pauses in the film after the gag lines.

dience. If laughter after a gag went on too long and drowned out the next line of dialogue, they would have the film re-edited to extend the time before the dialogue began. Similarly, if the gag generated less than the anticipated amount of laughter, they would tighten the editing and take out the dead space. Communications research—crude perhaps, but effective.

By the late 1920s research had reached the point where "attitudes were extracted as "things" to be created or changed [by communications] and certainly to be measured by increasingly sophisticated techniques of psychology and sociology," according to Keith Stamm and John Bowes, authors of *The Mass Communication Process.* Journals like *Journalism Quarterly* (1924) and *Public Opinion Quarterly* (1937) were founded in the years between the wars to circulate the results of studies conducted by the fledgling communication scholars. By the 1930s public opinion polling was common, and radio programs were rated by services like Crossley and Hooper. By the time of the Second World War major strides had been taken and communications research was firmly established as a social science discipline.

Still, this is a young discipline. The late Wilbur Schramm, an eminent communications scholar, estimated that more than one-half of all research on human communications has been undertaken since 1952. Mass media research is likewise barely out of its adolescent stages. Many cogently argue the field has yet to develop a coherent body of research and theory that can explain the effects and other ramifications of mass media in a modern society. In fact, communications research has tended to focus upon widely disparate and often seemingly unconnected phenomena. Shearon Lowery and Melvin DeFleur argue that because mass communications researchers have come from a variety of disciplines (sociology, psychology, history, speech, political science, philosophy, and more recently communications) they have not coordinated their efforts or built upon the results of previous research. "Many investigations have been carried out simply because there was a substantial amount of money to do so and the public wanted answers to some policy questions," the two writers assert in their book, *Milestones in Mass Communication Research: Media Effects.* Many of those questions were not theoretically significant, they added. "In other words, media research did not move forward in a neat and orderly way following the ideal model of science," Lowery and DeFleur conclude. This may not be true of all communications research or even all areas of communication research. But the single outstanding aspect of communications research in the 1990s remains its relative youth and the immaturity of many of its findings. The impact of mass media on our lives remains largely undocumented, despite the fact that we direct an increasingly large proportion of our attention toward newspapers, magazines, film and the other electronic media.

# MASS COMMUNICATIONS RESEARCH

Research traditions in communications have emerged from a great many other disciplines. Certainly there are those who look primarily at the behavioral act of communications in their research. But a great deal of research is focused upon other aspects of communications. Some of the earliest research on mass communications was conducted by historians, who attempted to study the growth of the institutions of the mass media: newspapers and magazines. Historical research, undertaken by those trained in both history and communications, is common today. This research can be as simple as to focus on one individual—a biography of an editor, or one medium—the history of a newspaper. But it can also be far more elaborate. A study of the use of the telegraph by nineteenth-century newspapers, the growing influence of business on editorial decision making in the 1890s, or the manner in which the press reported the Free Speech Movement at the University of California in the 1960s are typical of the kinds of historical studies being conducted today.

The historian looks to the past for the data to write the history. Primary sources, first-hand descriptions of people and events, are the basic stuff of good history. Historians will go to personal diaries, published and unpublished personal papers, letters; to newspaper, magazine, radio and television accounts; as well as voting records, bank statements, company financial records, and other similar records to discover what they seek, and then try to weave a narrative with these materials.

Behavioral or social science research is as prevalent in communications as historical study. The communications historian initially borrowed methods from the historian. The behavioral researcher initially borrowed methods from the psychologist and the sociologist. The communications behaviorist looks at the widest range of communications problems and uses a variety of tools.

The use of a survey or interview schedule is a common form of research. Imagine you want to know whether people who subscribe to a daily newspaper know more about local government than those who don't subscribe. One way to find out is to ask both kinds of persons some questions about government. It is unlikely that you could ask everyone; instead you select a sample of persons to talk with. Sampling techniques range from asking every sixth person you meet on a street corner, an unsophisticated method, to selecting a random sample in which everyone in the community has an equal opportunity of being selected, a sophisticated method. If a proper sample is drawn, the probability is very high that the answers given by the small number of persons in the sample reflect the answers that would be given if all persons were questioned. Once a sample is drawn, those selected are questioned. It can be by mail, by telephone, or in person. The answers are then tabulated and the data are analyzed. On the basis of these answers it can be discovered who has more information about local government.

Social scientists often use **experimental research** as well. While it is often difficult to duplicate real life in an experimental setting, sometimes no other research method will work. For years social scientists have tried to determine whether extensive publicity about a criminal case can harm the right of the defendant to a fair trial by prejudicing potential jurors. The best way to study this problem would be to study real trials; measure the publicity, follow the jurors into the jury room and see if, while they deliberate about the defendant's guilt, they are influenced by the publicity in the mass media. But researchers are not permitted access to a jury room. So social scientists have generated experiments which attempt to duplicate the trial situation. In these instances persons selected as "jurors" are divided into two groups; some are given pseudo news stories that are neutral; others are given pseudo stories that contain information that is prejudicial to the defendant. The "jurors" are then asked, on the basis of what they know, if the defendant is guilty or not. In some cases classes of students are used as jurors, a setting far removed from a real trial. In other instances the subjects are actually taken to a real courtroom, exposed to a mock trial as well as various kinds of news stories, and then asked their opinions on guilt or innocence. This is closer to real life.

A **content analysis** is another common tool of the social scientist. Scholar Bernard Berelson calls content analysis a tool for the objective, systematic study of message content. Historians use content analyses too, but generally don't follow the strict rules that govern the behavioral scientist. A basic problem in a content analysis is consistency. Imagine a researcher wants to evaluate television coverage of a presidential election; did the networks favor one candidate over another? First the researcher will have to get videotape of all the TV coverage. That is not too difficult these days. Then the researcher will have to develop some kind of means to evaluate the coverage. Perhaps counting seconds of coverage is the tool. How many seconds or minutes were broadcast about George Bush? How many seconds or minutes about Michael Dukakis? A simple device, but the results would not be terribly revealing. This does not distinguish between stories that praise the candidate, are neutral, or criticize the candidate. So some means to characterize words, tone, pictures, and so on must be established. And the goal is to develop criteria that are capable of being used in the same manner by many different people. In other words, if one person (called a coder) looked at a particular story and decided it was negative towards Bush, every other coder who looked at the same story would come to the same conclusion. (When a historian uses a content analysis, he or she tends to be somewhat more subjective and is usually satisfied with merely characterizing the material in one way or another, not counting specific instances of positive or negative coverage.)

The purpose behind such a sophisticated method is to permit the researcher to reduce the results to numerical data. Behavioral scientists, as opposed to historians, deal in quantification. They want to be able to precisely, as precisely as possible, generate percentages or ratios or other kinds of numerical comparisons or measures. The data, whether it is from a survey, an experiment, a content analysis, or any number of other methods can then be subject to sophisticated analysis by computer.

Both the historian and the behavioral scientist attempt to use research to answer questions about communications and mass communications. But they tend to work from different ends of the spectrum. The historian studies individual instances, and when enough of these have been studied, will attempt to generalize this result to the whole population. If we have fifteen biographies that show that nineteenth-century editors had political ambitions, the historian feels comfortable asserting that nineteenth-century editors frequently saw the press as a means of gaining election or appointment to political office.

The behavioral researcher, on the other hand, attempts to generalize to individual cases by studying the population in general. If through a survey it is determined that magazine subscribers tend to read more books than nonsubscribers, the social scientist feels fairly comfortable asserting that Jack Jones, who subscribes to six magazines, probably reads a lot of books as well.

A great deal of communications research today focuses upon international or cross-cultural communications. Humankind has always tried to communicate across national borders. Early newsbooks in Europe only reported on the happenings in foreign lands. Today mass communication is an international concern. Multinational corporations own media throughout the world; American movies and television programs are viewed around the globe. The satellite has made the movement of information across international borders as simple as the movement of information across the street.

The study of international communications is broad-based. We have seen research on the impact of the introduction of American mass media (television, radio, magazines) on the peoples of Third World nations. Other studies have tried to track the flow of news in the world. Who tells us about what is happening in North Africa? North Africans or Americans reporting from North Africa? It makes a difference. Do advertising appeals that work in the United States work as well in Japan? What is the best predictor of high personal media usage in a nation? Political activity, education, income? And does this vary from nation to nation? Cross-culture research focuses on not only peoples of different nations, but peoples of different cultures within the same nation. What is the content of a typical newspaper or radio station aimed at an African American audience, as compared to a newspaper aimed at a broader audience? What medium is most trustworthy among Hispanics? Researchers who study international and cross-cultural communication problems use many different kinds of research tools. Sometimes they use the tools of the historian; other times the tools of the behavioral or social scientist. Research methods, especially those used in cross-cultural research, have been developed exclusively for such work. The maxim that researchers try to follow is that the problem to be solved should determine the research method that is used.

Where communications and the law intersect is the focus of a considerable amount of research as well. The study of mass communications law, like research on international communication problems, is a subcategory of the larger historial/behavioral research categories. Much of the research in this area is aimed at simply determining what the law on a specific topic—such as libel or obscenity—is at any given

Shortly after the war in the Persian Gulf began in January of 1991, popular children's television host Fred Rogers prepared special messages and used a portion of his show "Mister Rogers' Neighborhood" to try to tell children why they should not be frightened by the news of the fighting. Rogers celebrated his 35th year on television in 1989.
(Family Communications, Inc.)

moment. Much American law is based upon decisions by American courts. It is an inductive system of law, in which a contemporary legal problem is resolved by first determining how courts have resolved similar problems in the past. Court decisions are collected in books, organized by court jurisdiction and chronology. (For instance, the decisions by the Michigan State Supreme Court are collected in a single set of books and organized in a chronological fashion.) A researcher must use various indexes to locate all the cases on a particular legal issue to determine contemporary law. It is a laborious process and has led some observers in foreign nations that use a different kind of legal system to remark that the American common law is the law nobody knows. This kind of research, by the way, is the same task faced by lawyers.

Research in mass communications law also has historical dimensions as, for example, scholars attempt to determine what the members of the First Congress meant when they wrote and approved the words "Congress shall make no law abridging freedom of speech or of the press," in the First Amendment. Other researchers have used the survey method to try to determine whether changes in libel law have changed the way editors deal with controversial news stories, i.e., are they censoring themselves to avoid legal problems? Experimental settings have been employed to try to determine whether newspaper and magazine readers perceive statements printed in various parts of a publication to be statements of fact, which are subject to libel suits, or statements of opinion, which are more broadly protected against law suits. (Judges have frequently—with little basis—expressed the view that articles on the editorial page are perceived to be opinion by readers, for example.)

There are many other varieties of communications research being undertaken worldwide today. A small but growing branch of communications research called critical studies has grown from research in comparative literature. These researchers focus on the meanings that they think are contained in the content of the mass media, meanings that shape our perceptions of social or political or economic aspects of our life. They study the text of the written word, the content of popular cultural artifacts such as televised situation comedies, in an effort to discern the meaning of these messages, and the implications of this meaning.

Communications research also focuses upon specific matters involving advertising (market research, for example), broadcasting (television ratings), and public relations. Anyone who looks into the body of collected data will be impressed by its size and breadth.

# MODELS AND THEORIES

Communication research permits us to find out about mass communications, what is going on. Communication models and theories permit us to try to describe what is happening, and even explain it. Stamm and Bowes note that while the differences between models and theories are difficult to distinguish, the simplest distinction is this. A model is a comprehensive picture or map of a communication situation or phenomenon. It is a description. A theory, on the other hand, may also be a description. But it is an explanation as well. It attempts to tell us why.

There are many communication models. One of the earliest was proposed by Harold Lasswell. He attempted to describe the act of communication this way: "Who Says What in Which Channel to Whom with What Effect?" That is pretty simple, but it has the basic elements of a one-way act of communication whether it is a conversation between two friends, or a television news program. Communication research is often categorized by using the Lasswell model.

Studies focusing on the "who" look at communicators like journalists, for example. Who are journalists? How old are they? What are their political beliefs? What is the content of the messages transmitted? We spend a lot of time in this book talking about the content of messages. How is news defined? What does the motion picture industry put into films in an attempt to keep the box office busy? What kind of programming is carried on public television?

In this text considerable space is devoted to the study of the "channels" of mass communication. Who owns the mass media? How are the major motion picture studios able to maintain control over the film industry through their power of distribution? How many minorities are employed in the newspaper industry? (This could be a study of "who" as well.) "Whom" refers to the receiver of the message, the audience. The discussion of television ratings, newspaper readers, radio listeners, and other media consumers focuses upon the "whom" in Lasswell's model. Finally, "what effect" does the message have on the audience or receiver? This is a question we will deal with more closely in a few moments.

Communication researcher Wilbur Schramm offers another model of a communications situation. In the Schramm model, the "source" of the communication "encodes" the "message." The message is "decoded" at its "destination," and at this point the receiver of the message can give the source "feedback." The Lasswell model implies a one-way communication process, from the source to a passive receiver. The Schramm model implies that both the source and the receiver have to act on the message—encode or put an idea into a language, and decode or translate the words back into the concept that is being communicated. And the receiver responds in some way with a verbal message or perhaps only a nod of the head. As noted in the introduction, however, mass media does not provide an easy avenue for feedback so the Schramm model is not too useful in that regard.

Many other models have been proposed as well. Claude Shannon and Warren Weaver offered a mathematical model of communication in 1949 which added the concept of "noise" to the basic Lasswellian model. Noise is anything that is added to the message or signal by someone or something other than the source. Bruce Westley and Malcolm MacLean proposed the Westley-MacLean model to deal with journalistic communication. This complicated model includes many different communications, perceptions, objects of orientation, and so on.

Our purpose here is not to explain the meaning of a specific model, but to explain the significance of models. The entire process of communication is simplified when it is broken down into parts and then these parts are arrayed on a kind of map. This permits the researcher to focus on a single part of the process, to examine one element, and learn how this part in the process is influenced, or influences, other parts.

If models try to describe the process, theories try to explain it. The best way to explore the question of theory is to examine some basic theoretical propositions regarding the impact of mass communications upon the attitudes and behavior of the audience, the "what effects" element in Harold Lasswell's model.

## ☐ Media Effects, or the Lack Thereof

What are the effects of mass media on people? Mass media can certainly give us information about what is happening in the world, inform us of events, enlighten us regarding political campaigns, reveal to us the deeds and misdeeds of public officials and government employees. Can the mass media change our attitudes on matters? Can they lead us to like things we don't like, believe things we are reluctant to believe, accept things we have rejected, want things we really don't want? Can a favorable documentary program on the Palestinian people change our minds about the issue of resettlement of Jews on the West Bank of the Jordan River? Can a series of newspaper articles on the plight of Southeast Asian refugees lessen resentment to these persons when they take jobs from Anglo-Americans in some communities?

What about changing our behavior as well as our attitude? Can television or motion pictures affect us in such a way as to lead us to take an action we might normally not take? Does viewing television violence provoke us to behave more violently? Does viewing a pornographic film lead men to sexually abuse women? Will political spot announcements by one candidate cause us to vote for that candidate? Does an advertisement for Ivory soap cause us to buy that brand when we shop?

Surprisingly, perhaps, we don't know the answers to most of these questions. The scientific evidence that exists seems to be inconclusive or contradictory. Common sense also seems to suggest various answers to these questions. Many people who will argue—on the basis of intuition or common sense—that watching a lot of violence on television must provoke violence in the viewer will just as easily reject the idea that television commercials determine their buying habits. This is not to say that some social scientists have not established their own answers to these questions, for they have. But there is hardly a consensus in the academic community.

Melvin DeFleur and Sandra Ball-Rokeach present the dilemma that faces many students of the mass media. "A trustworthy method—science—says the media have few effects," they wrote in *Theories of Mass Communication*. "Another trustworthy method—careful study by insightful historians and other analysts of the broader picture—say that they [mass media] have sweeping effects." Who is to be believed? Yet the statements above are not necessarily contradictory. Both science and history could be correct. This historian looks at the world through a somewhat different prism than the behavioral scientist. The historian will consider the long-term changes in our life, our government, even our people, and can rationally suggest that the mass media have had a profound impact upon modern history. The introduction of printing changed the world. It broke the monopoly that the government had on the flow of information. It fostered the growth of democratic systems. It had a profound impact on religion as well, being integrally tied to the Protestant Reformation. On a less cosmic scale the introduction of television 50 years ago has profoundly changed the way people live, the manner in which we elect national and local leaders, and aided and abetted important political movements. Civil rights demonstrators in the South, antiwar protesters in the seventies, and the Arab terrorists in Lebanon all learned the power of television to help them manipulate public opinion. Researcher Joshua Meyrowitz, who attempts to evaluate the long-term impact of television in his book *No Sense of Place: The Impact of Electronic Media on Social Behavior,* argues that television has homogenized the life experiences of disparate members of our population, forcing us to become more alike. To argue that the mass media have no effect on the way we think or act is utter nonsense when the long-term impact is considered. But the behavioral scientist usually works in a much smaller arena, searching not for long-term change but more immediate reactions. Watching 60 minutes of violent television programming may produce little noticeable change in most persons; watching 60 years of such programs may cause a subtle or even significant shift in our attitudes. It is akin to some environmentally produced illnesses. Being exposed to asbestos for a single week or several weeks may not produce noticeable harm. But a lifetime of such exposure may fatally damage the human lung.

## ☐ Mass Communication Theories

Before World War II when research on communication was still in its infancy, there was little evidence to support the theory that mass communications had an impact on the audience. But that did not stop many social scientists from asserting dogmatically that mass media did in fact affect human beings. These conclusions were based upon the then current and popular stimulus–response theory. The social scientists borrowed a perfectly good physics theory—for every action there is a reaction—and tried to apply it to human behavior. For every stimulus there is a response. Examples of the accuracy of this theory abounded in the media, it was believed. Radio programs, magazine advertisements, newspaper editorials all stimulated the audience. The audience in turn responded in some manner. Contemporary researchers have dubbed this primitive idea the **hypodermic needle theory** or the **bullet theory.** These picturesque appellations pretty well describe the conventional wisdom of the time, according to Norman Felsenthal in *Mass Communications*. "Communication was seen as a magic bullet that transferred ideas or feelings or knowledge or motivations almost automatically from one mind to another," he wrote. The premier example that the bullet theory was valid took place on Halloween night in

The Mercury Theater broadcast of "War of the Worlds" in October of 1938 caused panic in many parts of America. The reaction to the Orson Welles (pictured) production of the H.G. Wells story about a Martian attack on the Earth seemed to support those communication theorists who believed in the "hypodermic needle" or "bullet" theory of mass communications. (Culver Pictures)

1938 when Orson Welles scared the devil out of many people with his "War of the Worlds" radio broadcast. Hundreds of thousands of persons panicked in fear of the invasion of the planet by slimy Martians. Welles provided the stimulus; much of the nation reacted.

Essential to the hypodermic needle theory is the idea that information flows directly from the mass media to the members of the audience. To reach the people, to change their minds, to suggest a novel idea, use the mass media. But researchers began to poke holes in that notion. Social scientists discovered that while some people got information directly from the mass media, many more got information from other people who had gotten it from the mass media. It was a two-step communication, and the theory which evolved from this research was dubbed the **two-step flow theory.** This research also cast doubts upon the power of the mass media to persuade people to change their minds or accept new ideas. The power of the mass media to persuade seriously paled in comparison to the power of a human being to persuade another human being. This fit into the two-step flow theory as well. Some people—called opinion leaders by researchers—would get their information from the mass media, develop an opinion about the issue the information focused upon, and then pass along both the information and their opinion to other people, persuading them in the process. Research programs, especially in agriculture, sought to identify these opinion leaders, provide them with important information, and attempt to use them to spread this information to others in the community.

But additional research suggested that the two-step flow theory was flawed as well. Researchers concluded in the 1950s and 1960s that only a small portion of the content of the mass media is distributed by word of mouth via the two-step flow:

usually only the most important information (there is a gas leak at a rail car that tipped over a few blocks away) and the least important (Ralph, my brother-in-law, bought a new car). Other researchers discovered that there was really only a one-step flow of information from the media to the people, but there was a two-step flow of influence on beliefs, attitudes, and behaviors. That is, a person may find out by watching television that Congress plans to ban arms shipments to South Catare, but that person's attitude on whether such a ban is good or bad will likely be shaped by discussions with other people on the subject, not by newspaper editorials or television commentary.

The one-step and the two-step flow ideas implied that mass communication was a powerful tool in generating effects in an audience. And both theories looked at the audience as a largely undifferentiated mass of people. Yes, the two-step flow did recognize that there were opinion leaders, but all opinion leaders were pretty much the same. By the mid-1950s and 1960s new ideas about the audience began to emerge. No longer was it seen as a mass, but a collection of individuals. Members of the audience had different motivations and education, different beliefs, values, needs, and opinions, different levels of persuasability. They were different ages, had different kinds of jobs, worshipped in different churches, had different levels of income. And all of these factors and many more influenced the way in which a mass-communicated message affected a member of the audience, researchers suggested. This view of the audience changed the view of the power of mass media to influence behavior or even modify attitudes. The effects of mass communications were perceived to be minimal, to be weak.

"The communicator's audience is not a passive recipient—it cannot be regarded as a lump of clay to be molded by the master propagandist," wrote W. Philips Davison in 1959. "Rather, the audience is made up of individuals who demand something from the communications to which they are exposed, and who select those that are likely to be useful to them." In 1984 Albert Gollin, associated director for research for the Newspaper Advertising Bureau, echoed Davison, when he told a public forum that media audiences are socially differentiated, self-selective, often inattentive, and in general, obstinate. "As targets they are elusive and hard to please or convince," he said. "People actively use the media for a wide variety of shared and individual purposes. People are not readily used by the media. Why is it, then, that we believe that others in the viewing or reading public are more gullible or passive than we ourselves?" he added. Given a reasonably large audience, communication varies in its impact, according to Raymond Bauer of the Harvard Business School, a specialist in public opinion research. "It affects some [people] one way, some in the opposite way, and some not at all." Bernard Berelson, a pioneer in communications research, years ago stated the same propositions somewhat differently: "Some kind of communications on some kinds of issues, brought to the attention of some kinds of people under some kinds of conditions, have some kinds of effects."

Imagine that you and ten friends watch a motion picture. All of you then sit down and write a two-paragraph summary of the story of the film. How much variation would there be in the 11 written statements? A considerable amount, if past research is a guide. And this variance would increase if you waited a week or ten days to prepare your summaries. In looking at the same picture or reading the same story, people see and remember different things. Social scientists call this phenomenon **selectivity.** The theory of selectivity was a substantial support for the "minimal media effects" school of thought. Ideas about selectivity go like this.

We all have some control over the information we receive, and most of us tend to seek out information that interests us. We are practicing *selective exposure*, according to social scientists. Felsenthall also asserts that we try to avoid those messages we consider boring, and those that conflict with what we already believe. When readers turn to the op-ed page of their local newspaper they usually have a wide array of opinion from which to choose: liberal or conservative, pro or anti, optimistic or pessimistic. The theory of selective exposure suggests that most of us will, on most issues, read those articles with which we tend to agree. It has been discovered that some people actually do read material with which they disagree, but only to help them develop counter-arguments or to reassure themselves that their position is the correct position, or to see what the opposition is saying.

When focusing upon the same communication or message, different people tend to see different things. Attempts to uncover the cause of a violent demonstration at the University of Wisconsin in the late 1960s prompted the formation of a full-scale research team, brimming with capable social scientists. Yet in the end researchers were unable to put their finger on what sparked the violence. People in the same physical location often saw totally different things happening; police saw unruly students and students saw aggressive police. This is called *selective perception*.

Reporters find selective perception an occupational hazard. People who attend an event covered by a reporter are frequently amazed at how the journalist could have so fouled-up the story. That is not at all what happened, they complain to the editor. Both the reporter and the angry reader suffer from selective perception, seeing what they want to see, what they expect to see, what their eyes and mind are prepared to see.

Finally, we tend to remember those things that support our beliefs, confirm our prejudices, and sustain our opinions. This is called *selective retention*. Ask someone to read an editorial or news article that outlines both the positive and negative aspects of a public policy. Ask that person two weeks later to recite those negative and positive points. Chances are very good that the subject of this little experiment will remember more of the positive points if they favor the policy, but more of the negative points if they oppose the policy.

The choice of the communications and messages we select to receive, what we see in those messages, and what we remember about those communications is influenced by a great many factors. The importance of the information to the receiver is a key factor, especially with regard to what is remembered. But such things as self-assurance, intelligence, sense of humor, family life, and levels of tolerance also play a factor, researchers say. Associates, family, and friends also determine to a large degree how the selectivity process works within an individual. Social scientists call these **reference groups.** Age, education, sex, marital status, and other demographic details may play a role as well.

The concept of selectivity was challenged in the 1960s by two researchers who reevaluated many of the studies that purportedly demonstrated that selective exposure operated when individuals used the mass media. J. L. Freeman and D. O. Sears reported that the data generated by these studies simply did not support the conclusions that had been drawn; there was as much evidence contradicting the hypothesis as there was supporting it. There is very little basis for saying that people consistently go out of their way to avoid information with which they disagree, they argued.

The attack on the notion of selectivity seriously undercut the foundation for the idea that mass media produces minimal effects on its audience. While researchers continued to support the theory that the audience was not a mass, but a collection of different individuals, new research was generated that began to suggest that mass communication was more powerful (not all powerful, but more powerful) than had been believed during the previous two decades. Minimal effects was out; moderate effects was in.

In 1973 researcher Elisabeth Noelle-Neumann wrote, in what many consider to be a seminal discussion of the changing ideas regarding media effects, "The thesis that mass media do not change attitudes but only reinforce them cannot be upheld under conditions of consonance and cumulation. Our data point in this direction." By consonance Noelle-Neumann meant agreement; by cumulation she meant repetition. If the same idea is repeated throughout the mass media over and over again, it can modify attitudes, despite the *tendency* humans have toward selectivity, she suggested.

New theories on the impact of mass communications reflect the notion that the mass media have moderate impact on changing our attitudes. As Everette Dennis wrote, "One thing seems certain. The press is neither the all-powerful giant imagined by the propaganda researchers nor the peripheral influence seen by the political researchers." And Stamm and Bowes have written,

> We do not feel that the new rejection of the limited effects model signals a return to the view of media as tools with unlimited power to manipulate their audiences. It reflects instead a more balanced view in which certain kinds of effects do occur but only under the right circumstances.

## New Theories

New ideas regarding the impact of mass media on an audience abound. Let's briefly look at two of them.

One of the most popular ways to view mass communications today is through the **uses and gratification theory.** Attempts to explain the impact of the mass media by determining why people use them go back almost 50 years to studies in the 1940s which attempted to explain why people listened to soap operas. The concept of the differentiated audience gave new impetus to these ideas.

Under this theory the effects of the mass media are determined by individuals in the audience. Exposure to mass media is purposeful, motivated by individual needs. The audience is perceived under this theory as active, not a passive agent upon which the communication imposes effects. Using this theory as a guide, a researcher who seeks to look at children and television would ask, "How do children use television?" and not, "What does television do to children?" Major research guided by this theory has focused upon what satisfactions people gain from using mass communications, what social/environmental circumstances lead people to turn to the mass media in the first place, and what needs are members of the audience attempting to satisfy. Uses and gratification theorists view communications as a consequence, not a cause, of behavior.

**Agenda setting** is another theoretical proposition under considerable study today. The concept is best summarized by political scientist Bernard Cohen who noted, "While the press may not be successful much of the time in telling people what to think, it is stunningly successful in telling readers what to think about." Again the idea is not necessarily a new one. Walter Lippmann suggested in his 1922 book

Big Bird listens as Aristotle, a blind Muppet, reads from a braille book on the popular "Sesame Street." The show, which is more than 20 years old, is geared toward preschoolers and is regarded by many as a model of how television can be used as a teaching tool. (Children's Television Workshop)

*Public Opinion* that the mass media dominate the creation of the pictures of public affairs that we have in our heads. The press, then, provides for us our pictures of reality. Studies by researchers like Donald Shaw, Max McCombs, David Weaver, and others have substantiated this notion. The mass media does have the ability to mentally order and organize our world for us. "People do learn from mass communication," wrote McCombs and Shaw. "Not only do they learn factual information about public affairs and what is happening in the world, they also learn how much importance to attach to an issue or topic from the emphasis placed upon it by the mass media."

Bringing an issue to public attention may not insure that the public will focus on that problem and ultimately reach a solution. The public may reject that particular agenda item. Surely this has been the case with the federal deficit and taxes. There is little doubt that nearly everyone knows that raising taxes is probably the simplest way we can materially reduce the federal debt. Yet few are rallying to that cause. On the other hand, if the public is ready to deal with an issue, or can deal with it easily, media attention can often foster public action. Hunger in northern Africa was not an issue on the public's agenda before NBC telecast those stark pictures from Ethiopia in the fall of 1984. The pictures touched a public nerve and mobilization of aid followed.

David Weaver and others have concluded that through publicity of issues and ideas the mass media can not only determine which candidate will be nominated for high political office, but may also play a critical role in determining who is elected. One wonders what would have happened if the press had ignored the attempts by the George Bush staff in 1988 to make the pledge of allegiance to the flag an issue. The Bush staff was also able to use images to convince many voters that it was Bush, not Dukakis, who was the stronger environmentalist. How many times did we see the pictures of a polluted Boston Harbor? A false image was created in this case, as a thorough study of the positions of both candidates toward the environment would reveal.

Everette Dennis reminds us that the ideas regarding media effects are not "simply a scholarly debate among social scientists in methodological tools, but a very real issue in the society at large." Mass media are so important in contemporary American society that whether and what the mass media do to us, or how we use the mass media, are central questions in the debate on most public issues. Let's examine just one issue that has been the focus of a public policy debate for almost two generations for a moment to demonstrate this point.

# VIOLENCE AND MASS MEDIA

Violence in America seems to be a growing problem, from random street shooting to serial murders to bloody fights in junior high schools. What role has the mass media played in creating this climate of violence? Violence in the mass media and its impact on human behavior has provoked more debate in the past four decades than perhaps any other issue involving the mass media. Violence in comic books became the subject of heated controversy in the late 1940s and a comic book code resulted from the controversy. For the past 20 years the impact of televised violence on members of the audience has been the subject of great concern. It has been estimated that 2,500 separate research studies have focused upon this issue. And both the Surgeon General of the United States and the National Institute of Mental Health have issued reports on the matter. More recently women's groups have focused upon erotic and pornographic films, books, and magazines and have argued that such material provokes violence against women. Attempts to get such material banned in both Minneapolis and Indianapolis have failed. And some have complained about the violence or violent settings of some music videos.

Public concern about violence on television began almost 40 years ago when studies were first undertaken to count the number of violent acts committed on television on an average evening. Results of such research appalled many persons. But the television industry failed to respond to this criticism, and violence on the small screen increased, peaking perhaps in the late 1950s and early 1960s with the broadcast of the "Untouchables," regarded as the most consistently violent television series ever aired. It was in the sixties that intensive research began in earnest on the impact of television violence on members of the audience. Such research continues today.

The response of the television industry has been cautious. Programming has changed over the past 15 years and is less violent today than at other times in the past. But this is largely the result of changes in public taste, not an effort to rid the small screen of its violent subject matter. Situation comedies are the dominant form of programming today; police shows, westerns, and private-eye dramas are not as popular. The industry has consistently denied that evidence exists to prove that television violence causes violent behavior in individuals. It has, of course, not argued that television has no impact on behavior. After all, financial support for

Television created a whole new world of nonviolent heroes and heroines for kids and adults alike when it descended on American homes in the 1950s. Some of the earliest heroes for youngsters were the characters on the popular "Howdy Doody Show." Howdy was a smiling puppet and his pal was Buffalo Bob Smith. Also featured was a zany clown named Clara-bell, played by Bob Keeshan, who later would become CBS televi-sion's "Captain Kangaroo."
(NBC Photo)

the industry is based upon the premise that some television programming—commercials in this case—have some impact on behavior, the buying habits of the audience.

Some of the difficulties of studying a question like the impact of television violence on individuals in the viewing audience seem almost insurmountable. How do you define violence? How do you differentiate between fantasy violence in a "Bugs Bunny" cartoon and real-life violence on the news and the fictional violence in "Wise Guy" or "Friday the 13th"? If the violence is justified, does this make a difference in the way it is perceived? How do you measure the full effects of watching television violence on a human being? Researchers have spent most of their time measuring the impact of television violence on the succeeding 30 minutes to an hour in an individual's life. But how do you measure the cumulative effect of watching 30 to 40 years of television violence? Where can you find a control group of persons who have not been exposed to television or television violence? And how can you determine what is cause, what is effect, or whether there is a third condition or factor that plays a part? None of these are easy questions.

Two kinds of research have been undertaken in an effort to determine what impact television violence might have on human behavior. Some researchers have used experimental research designs, an attempt to duplicate real-life behavior in a laboratory where it can be studied. Other researchers have used survey research methods, an effort to discover what is happening in the real world by asking people how they behave.

The experimenters have attempted to answer two kinds of questions: whether after viewing television the viewer will attempt to *imitate* what has been seen on television, and whether televised violence can actually *instigate* violent behavior in the subjects of the experiment. The experiments have demonstrated that the research subjects can imitate what they see on the small screen. But it is less clear whether televised violence can increase the likelihood of aggressive behavior in the viewer as well.

Surveys have been used to attempt to uncover any connection between exposure to television violence and aggressive tendencies. After viewing a television program, subjects were asked how they might respond in various situations. Responses from those who watched a violent television program were compared to responses from persons who watched a nonviolent show. The survey results tend to show a modest relationship between exposure to television violence and the selection of a violent response.

Finally, some recently completed long-term studies have suggested that there indeed seems to be a correlation between viewing violent television programming and aggressive behavior. But the ten-year study suggests that there is a blurring of effects over time. And researchers are unable to determine whether people who are normally aggressive tend to watch violent television programming, or whether violent television programs tend to make people aggressive. There could even be a kind of tautological chain—usually aggressive people tend to watch violent programming which makes them more aggressive which leads to viewing more violent programming, *ad infinitum.*

From this brief outline it is possible to see the kinds of research studies that have been undertaken over the past two decades. From these studies three general theories or hypotheses have emerged relating television violence to aggressive behavior. They are called the catharsis hypothesis, the modeling hypothesis, and the catalytic hypothesis.

The **catharsis hypothesis** is constructed on the principle of catharsis—the purging of emotions and feelings through indirect or vicarious experience. Imagine a child filled with anger who wants to strike his sister in retaliation. The child sees a police officer shoot a robber while watching a television program. This gives the child a feeling of satisfaction and reduces his desire to strike his sister. Supporters of the catharsis hypothesis—and there are not a great many—suggest that exposure to television violence will allow a viewer to purge his or her violent tendencies through fantasy. Watching violent television shows will provide a safe and harmless outlet for human frustration and hostile impulses in the same way hitting a punching bag will often make someone who is angry feel better.

Violence on television, whether in a real-life or fantasy setting, will increase aggressive behavior, harden viewers to pain and suffering, and lead viewers to accept violence as a way of life and a solution to social and personal problems, according to proponents of the **modeling hypothesis.** In attempting to "clean up" some of the violence on television, the networks have tried to sanitize it in the past two decades. When someone is shot or beaten up on television, there is often little evidence of the pain and suffering associated with such violence in real life. It is common to watch a killer point a gun and pull the trigger without being shown the victim being hit and bleeding and dying. If the modeling hypothesis is correct, television's attempt to make violence less brutal is probably a very poor idea. Viewers who may model their behavior on what they have seen on the small screen don't know what real violence is like. The sight of a real corpse, shot several times with a gun, might actually sicken a viewer and make violent behavior a less desirable alternative.

It is the **catalytic hypothesis** that garners the most support today. A catalyst is an agent that brings about a reaction or change between certain specific substances. If you mix ammonia and water, you simply dilute the ammonia. But mixing ammonia and chlorine bleach produces a deadly gas. This is a catalytic reaction; two normally safe substances create a toxic substance when mixed. The catalytic hypothesis suggests that for most people viewing television violence is like mixing ammonia and water—nothing happens, it has no effect at all. But violent television programming can trigger aggressive action by some unstable individuals. This theory really reflects the modern conception of the mass media audience, a widely differentiated collection of individuals who respond in different ways to the same content.

The film the *Deer Hunter* is about the impact of the Vietnam war on men who fought in it. There is a striking scene in the film in which a leading character is tortured by his captors who play Russian roulette with a pistol, spinning the chamber, pointing the weapon at the head of the POW, pulling the trigger. There is no record that such torture took place in Vietnam, according to Dr. Thomas Radecki, President of the National Coalition on Television and Violence. Yet at least 26 deaths have been attributed to persons playing Russian roulette after seeing the film. The movie has been seen by tens of millions of people. Yet little more than two dozen have tried to mimic the scene. The movie obviously became a catalyst for a handful of unstable people. Much of the research that has been conducted on the relationship between television violence and aggressive behavior tends to support the catalytic hypothesis.

## ☐ Federal Reports

The federal government has released two massive studies of the connection between viewing television violence and aggressive behavior. The 1972 report by the Scientific Advisory Committee on Television and Social Behavior concluded that there probably was a causal relationship between viewing violence on television and aggressive behavior. The Committee went on to suggest, however, that television violence seemed to cause aggression only in some children, those predisposed to be aggressive. The report further suggested that the relationship between violence on television and aggressive behavior appeared only in some environmental contexts. Some said the report was too tentative; others criticized it as overstating the causal relationship.

Ten years later the National Institute of Mental Health (NIMH) released the second federal report which concluded that there was now "overwhelming" evidence that viewing "excessive" violence on television leads directly to aggression and violent behavior among children and teenagers. This study was not based on any new research. Instead, it attempted to draw conclusions from the over 2,500 studies that had been previously carried out by researchers. The report concluded that the link between television viewing and violent behavior was "obvious;" yet researchers conceded that the link had not been proved conclusively by any single study. The report writers said "most television researchers look at the totality of evidence and conclude . . . that the convergence of most of the findings . . . supports the positive conclusion of a causal relationship." Critics argued that the NIMH report, in fact, focused upon only 14 studies. And the findings of one of the 14 were rejected because no evidence of lasting, long-term, increased aggression was found.

Researchers continue to debate about whether televised violence poses a seri-

Despite researchers' condemnation of violent television programs and films, the entertainment industry found Americans had a hearty appetite for such material. The murder and mayhem in *Robocop 2* exceeded even that in the original film. (© 1990 Orion Pictures Corporation)

ous likelihood of increasing violent behavior in human beings. And whether or not you believe televised violence is a problem is probably related directly to how much you believe one set of research findings rather than another set of research findings.

But doesn't this suggest that research really can't answer these important questions? That perhaps it is just so much eyewash? Certainly not. Americans don't reach such conclusions when it comes to contradictory medical research findings or contradictory biological research findings. Is moderately high blood pressure a serious medical problem for most people? Doctors are not in agreement on this. And is the warming of the planet the result of an increase of carbon dioxide in the atmosphere, the so-called greenhouse effect? There is dispute about this as well. But doctors now know that smoking tobacco can cause serious health problems. And scientists know that dumping chemicals and sewage in a river can seriously harm the fish and other animals in the water. The reason that medical researchers and biological scientists are much more certain about the findings on tobacco and pollution than they are on blood pressure and the warming of the planet is because they have studied these problems more thoroughly, over a longer period of time.

Communications research is subject to the same qualifications. Undoubtedly, some day, there will likely be highly definitive evidence on many aspects of mass communications effects, effects which are now often disputed because of disparate research findings. But this is the nature of scientific discovery; slowly building up evidence over time. This qualification governs all research. If there seems to be many unanswered questions regarding mass communications, it is perhaps because mass communications, and especially mass communications research, are relatively modern phenomena.

## BIBLIOGRAPHY

These are some of the materials that have been helpful in the preparation of this chapter.

Bettelheim, Bruno. "A Child's Garden of Fantasy," *Channels,* September/October, 1985.

Cohen, Jeremy, and Gleason, Timothy. *Social Research in Communications and the Law.* Newbury Park, Cal.: Sage Publications, 1990.

DeFleur, Melvin L., and Ball-Rokeach, Sandra. *Theories of Mass Communication.* (5th ed.) New York: Longman, 1989.

Dennis, Everette E., Ismach, Arnold H., and Gillmor, Donald. *Enduring Issues in Mass Communications.* St. Paul, Minn.: West Publishing Co., 1978.

Felsenthal, Norman. *Mass Communications.* (2nd ed.) Chicago: Science Research Associates, 1981.

Lowery, Shearon, and DeFleur, Melvin L. *Milestones in Mass Communications Research.* New York: Longman, 1983.

Meyrowitz, Joshua. *No Sense of Place: The Impact of Electronic Media on Social Behavior.* New York: Oxford University Press, 1985.

Stamm, Keith R., and Bowes, John E. *The Mass Communication Process.* Dubuque, Iowa: Kendall/Hunt Publishing Co., 1988.

# CHAPTER 4

# ECONOMIC FOUNDATIONS

*I*t was in December of 1943 during a meeting of the board of directors of the Encyclopaedia Britannica. Board member Henry Luce, the founder and publisher of *Time* magazine, was tiring of the deliberations. He scribbled a note on a scrap of paper and passed it to Robert N. Hutchins, then chancellor of the University of Chicago. What would it cost, Luce wrote, to undertake a study of the current state and future prospect of freedom of the press? Sixty thousand dollars a year, until it is completed, Hutchins replied. This exchange was the genesis of the Commission on Freedom of the Press, which in the late 1940s published a most sobering report on the status of our First Amendment freedoms. Or so the story goes.

The United States was in the midst of fighting the Second World War. We had watched the glow of freedom of expression be snuffed out in Europe as the Nazis overran the continent. Could our freedoms disappear so easily as well? This was the apparent motivation for Henry Luce's idea.

Time, Inc. donated $200,000; the Encyclopaedia Britannica added $15,000. And in March of 1944, thirteen of the nation's best thinkers (none of them associated with mass communications) began the task of making the assessment Luce had sought. Led by Hutchins, writer and scholar Archibald MacLeish, philosopher William E. Hocking, Harvard Law School professor Zechariah Chafee, and Yale political scientist Harold Lasswell, the Commission members interviewed nearly 300 persons over the next three years. The result of this work was a formal report from the Commission and a series of books written by members of the Commission.

The Commission members set out to answer the question, Is freedom of the press (and press was intended to include all mass media) in danger? The answer to the question: yes, it is in danger. But contrary to what Luce and others had seen in Europe with the growth of totalitarian fascism, the danger to the press in the United States stemmed from other seemingly more benign factors. Commission members said the freedom of the press was in danger due in part to the consequence of the economic structure of the mass media, in part to the consequence of the industrial organization of modern society, and in part as the result of the failure of the directors of the mass media to recognize the needs of a modern nation and to estimate and accept the responsibilities which those needs impose upon the mass media. What the Commission members saw was a mass communications system that was beginning to take on the configuration of the modern American economic system, a system in which larger and larger companies controlled the production of more and more goods and services, a system that was heavily commercially oriented.

The threat to freedom of the press was an economic threat. Fewer and fewer people could use the mass media as a communications system. There was less diversity of voices as business interests, and the principles upon which business is built, tended to filter the messages carried by the mass media. This meant that the vision of the nation as reflected by the mass media was skewed to one side, did not represent the great heterogeneity in our society. "The owners and managers of the press determine which persons, which facts, which versions of the facts, and which ideas shall reach the people," Commissioners wrote. And the commercial cacophony in the media tended to drown out other more serious, more important information and entertainment.

The members of the Commission said they were distressed. Freedom of the press is essential to political liberty, they noted. When men cannot freely convey their thoughts to one another, no freedom is secure. Where freedom of expression exists, the beginnings of a free society and a means for every extension of liberty are already present. Free expression, then, is therefore unique among liberties: it promotes and protects all the rest, the Commissioners wrote.

If the members of the Commission were distressed with the state of freedom of expression, many in the mass media (including Henry Luce) were distressed with the Commission, and the conclusions it had drawn. "Poppycock!" "The work of 'ivy-bound professors' or 'agents of European socialism.' " The impact of the study, except among some persons in academia and a few of the more thoughtful individuals in the media, was nil. The reports were relegated to bookshelves and have gathered more dust than readers in the past 40 years.

The conclusions drawn by the Commission remain controversial, but its vision of the changing nature of the ownership, control, and nature of mass communications was prophetic. In the past half-century all the trends noted by the Commission on Freedom of the Press have manifested themselves to a far greater extent. It can still be debated whether the press is more or less free. But there is no debate that the ownership of the mass media has been intensely concentrated into fewer and fewer hands, that more and more newspapers and broadcasting stations are controlled by newspaper and broadcast chains, that more and more communities are confronted with a monopoly newspaper, that the people who own magazines also own television stations and cable television companies and even movie studios, and that intense commercialism, the need to continually increase revenues and profits, is the governing philosophy in the mass media today, often at the expense of service to the public.

At the beginning of Chapter 2, it was noted that an understanding of the history of the mass media was essential to an understanding of why and how decisions are made today by those who work in and control mass communications in America. Equally important is an understanding of the economic environment that is the setting for the mass media today. In the remainder of this chapter, we will attempt to sketch this environment. We will focus first on where and how the mass media get the revenues to continue operating. Then, we will focus on the economic structure of the industry today.

## SOURCES OF REVENUE

The mass media in America are not operated as philanthropies. They must earn revenues in order to survive. Even nonprofit entities like *Consumer Reports* magazine or public television need to generate funds in order to keep operating. Most American mass media are profitable, quite profitable. This will be documented in the chapters ahead.

Revenue to support a mass medium can be generated in a great many ways. The government can support a mass medium. This is common throughout the rest of the world where radio and television, especially, are funded and operated by the government. Filmmaking is often subsidized by the government (i.e., the Canadian National Film Board). And in many countries newspapers are published by the government. *Izvestia,* for example, is published by the government of the Soviet Union. In the United States, our public television and radio systems are funded partially by the government. But that is really the only government economic commitment to mass communications that are domestically consumed. (The United States government does support radio and various publications aimed at listeners and readers abroad. This is called propaganda.)

Special interest groups can also support mass media. Around the world labor unions, churches, political parties and other groups sponsor newspapers and maga-

Newspapers in foreign countries often rely on the government or political parties for funding. *Pravda* was published by the Communist Party in the Soviet Union. News was reported through the filter of the philosophy of this political organization, rather than the business-oriented philosophy of most American newspapers.   (*Pravda*)

zines, and even operate broadcasting stations. These are mainstream, popular mass media, filled with news and information of general interest, and consumed by persons outside the special interest groups. *L'Ossvervatore,* for example, a widely read newspaper in Rome, is published by the Vatican and is regarded as a voice of the church.

Political parties were active in their financial support of the early American press, as we noted in Chapter 2. Today we still have such publications in the United States, but they have comparatively few readers. The Republicans and the Democrats both publish newsletters, for example. And the United Auto Workers labor union publishes a newspaper; but it is aimed largely at union members and focuses narrowly on their concerns.

There are two other means by which a medium can support itself. It can rely upon support from users, such as readers or listeners. Or it can rely upon advertisers' support. Both these schemes are used by various mass media throughout the world. These are the primary means by which mass media in the United States support themselves. And of the two, advertising is by far the most important. Let's briefly look at the various mass media and sketch out sources of revenue.

## ☐ Newspapers

There are many kinds of newspapers—weeklies, biweeklies, triweeklies, and dailies. Newspapers tend in almost all cases to have a local orientation and are circulated to people in a city or town or village. There are a handful of newspapers that are circulated nationally (i.e., *USA Today*), but they are unusual. The generalizations that follow apply to a typical, local daily newspaper.

A newspaper earns about 75 percent of its revenue from advertising, about 25 percent from subscriptions and single-copy sales. It is conceivable that a newspaper could be published that relied solely on circulation revenues. And it wouldn't necessarily cost four times what it now costs to make up for the loss of ad revenue. Without ads the paper would be much smaller, lowering both labor and material costs. Most experts estimate an adless paper would cost about two or two-and-a-half times as much as a newspaper that carries advertising.

But we are unlikely to see an adless newspaper. The difference in cost is significant, the difference between 35 cents and 90 cents. Advertising revenue tends to flow into the newspaper more steadily because advertisers have contracted in advance for the publication of their ads. And readers tend to like advertising.

The cost of placing an advertisement in a newspaper is determined by several factors. Advertising placed by local advertisers, such as a local supermarket, costs less than advertising placed by national advertisers, such as Coca-Cola or Ford. No one is able to put forth a logical reason for this cost difference. It has just always been that way.

The size of the circulation of the newspaper is a factor; the more copies sold, the higher the advertising cost. The size of the ad is another factor. A half-page ad costs more than a 10-inch, one-column ad. A color advertisement costs more than a black-and-white ad. Finally, what is called a "run-of-press" or **ROP** ad costs less than an ad placed in a preferred position. The newspaper publisher can place the ROP ad anywhere in the newspaper. The advertiser pays extra to be on the back page of a section or next to the box scores in the sports section.

Nearly 85 percent of advertising revenues come to the newspaper from local

Most American newspapers are supported by advertising, but a few depend on subscribers or political organizations to pay the bills. The *Workers World* is subsidized by the Marxist-oriented Workers World political organization. Note the nonobjective tone in the articles.
(*Worker's World*)

advertisers (figure 4-1). A little more than a third of this 85 percent (30 percent of all newspaper advertising) is generated by **classified advertising,** those small "for sale" and "help wanted" ads stacked one upon another in the back of the paper. A little less than two-thirds of this 85 percent (about 55 percent of all newspaper advertising) is called local display or **retail advertising.** These are the large, graphically interesting advertisements placed by supermarkets and department stores. The other 15 percent of the advertising revenue is collected for publishing the **national display advertising.** There is one additional source of advertising revenue. The

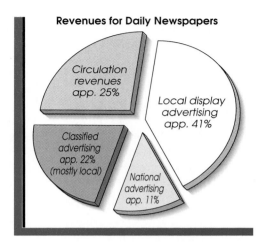

**Revenues for Daily Newspapers**

*Circulation revenues app. 25%*

*Local display advertising app. 41%*

*Classified advertising app. 22% (mostly local)*

*National advertising app. 11%*

FIGURE 4-1 Newspapers rely heavily on local advertising revenues.

newspaper is paid to deliver those colorful preprinted inserts that are stuffed in the newspaper and fall on the floor as you carry your newspaper to the front door of your favorite store. There will be much more to say about these inserts in Chapter 5.

## ☐ Magazines

Newspapers tend to be identified by locale; magazines tend to be identified by reader interest. There are local magazines, but the typical magazine is circulated nationally or regionally. Magazines also rely most heavily on advertising revenues, although some publications are increasingly counting upon circulation revenues. When the great, national weekly *Life* died in 1971, subscribers were paying about 12 cents per copy for a magazine that cost 41 cents per copy to produce. Consequently many magazine publishers sought to build stronger circulation revenues. Many publishers also have tried to build newsstand sales, rather than rely upon subscriptions. It costs less to circulate via the newsstand because postal rates have increased so dramatically in the past fifteen years. And many advertisers are encouraged by magazine buyers who actually purchase a publication at a newsstand, as opposed to those who receive it in the mail and may or may not look between the covers. *Family Circle, Woman's Day, TV Guide,* and *People* are examples of publications that rely heavily on circulation revenues.

There are adless magazines that rely totally upon readers for their revenues. *Consumer Report* is one, but is supported by the Consumers Union. A better example is *Mad* magazine, the long-standing comic-type publication that through quirks of financial fate has become a part of the largest media company in the world, the Time-Warner company. After carrying advertising for nearly 18 years, *Ms.* magazine dropped all advertising in 1990.

The cost of most magazine advertising is determined by the same criteria applied in pricing newspaper advertising. The size of the circulation of the magazine is a factor, as is the size of the ad. The demographic quality of the audience is also a factor. A magazine like *Architectural Digest,* which is distributed to a highly affluent audience, can command a higher price for its advertising than a magazine with a similar circulation that is aimed at a general audience. Color costs more than black and white, and if an advertiser wants a preferred position (back cover, inside front cover), premium rates will be charged. Frequent advertisers, and advertisers who buy a lot of space are sometimes given a discount. A discount is also offered to advertisers who buy what is called **remnant space,** advertising space that is still unsold as the magazine is about to go to press. Some advertisers have standing orders with the magazine to buy into this remaining space.

All the above factors are contained in what is called the advertising "rate card." Ad prices are determined by using the rate card. In 1987, *McCall's,* a woman's magazine, became the first major magazine to abandon the rate card to determine advertising costs. Spokespersons for the magazine said advertising prices would be negotiated with individual advertisers, a system more commonly used in television. Publishers of the magazine said they believed they could generate more revenue in this manner. Some other magazines are considering following this strategy as well.

Most advertising in magazines is display advertising, although a few magazines carry a small amount of classified advertising. Most advertising in magazines is national or regional, since most magazines are circulated nationally or regionally. Some magazines do offer local advertisers the opportunity to purchase an ad in those copies of the magazine distributed only in that specific city or metropolitan area. These are called geographic **breakouts.** This permits a bank in Minneapolis, for example, to put an ad in *Newsweek.* The bank gains the prestige of being associated with a national magazine at a very low rate; the magazine gets the additional advertising revenue. Some magazines offer demographic breakouts as well. Pockets of people at the high end of the socioeconomic scale are identified by where they live. Magazines that are delivered to these areas, as identified by ZIP code, carry advertising not contained in copies that are generally circulated. The maker of an expensive automobile, for example, may want access to persons with an annual income greater than $75,000. This advertiser can purchase an ad in a general circulation magazine, but the ad rate is determined by the number of copies circulated to the small, subgroup of readers. (See Chapter 6 for more.)

## ▢ Television

It is much harder to make generalizations about television advertising today. Television comes to us via a variety of channels in the 1990s, and revenue is generated for the medium in a variety of ways. Over-the-air television, both local stations and the television networks that service these local stations, is 100 percent advertiser-supported. Basic cable channels, ESPN, CNN, MTV, get their revenues from advertising and from subscriber fees. A local cable company pays a cable channel like MTV a few cents each month for each cable subscriber. The cable television company (the business that attaches the wire to your home) is paid largely through subscriber fees, but local cable companies are increasingly selling advertising time as well. Premium cable channels (HBO, Showtime, Disney, and so on) receive all their revenues from cable subscribers who pay extra each month to receive their premium channels. Finally, public television receives money from the government, from businesses or sponsors, and from public donations (pledge drives). We will use a network-affiliated over-the-air local television station for our extended example.

First of all, what is a network-affiliated, over-the-air television station? Over-the-air means the television signal is broadcast through the airwaves. The signal of an over-the-air station may be picked up by a local cable company and transmitted to cable subscribers via a wire. But the signal can be received with just an antenna by noncable subscribers. A **network affiliate** is a station that has a contractual relationship with one of the major television networks—ABC, CBS, NBC, or Fox. The contract states that the network will provide the local station with exclusive programming; the station agrees to telecast that programming in its particular market.

While almost one-half of the advertising carried by a network affiliate comes directly from the network (i.e., is included in network programming), this advertising provides a small percentage of the station's revenues. (As much as 10 percent for a station in a small market; only 3 to 4 percent of the revenues for a station in a large market.) For carrying this advertising, the local station is compensated by the network. Not surprisingly, this is called **network compensation.** This is how it works. NBC will sell a 30-second advertising spot on "The Cosby Show." Imagine the cost of the spot is $350,000. All that money goes to NBC. NBC must then compensate all its affiliated stations which transmit this spot to viewers across America. Compensation rates are determined by a variety of factors, but speaking generally a station is paid at a rate that equals about one-third of the amount the station could collect if it sold that 30 seconds on its own to a local or national advertiser.

In addition to getting the programming from the network, and the compensation money, the station is also given the opportunity to sell advertising time during the programming. Nine-and-a-half to ten minutes of advertising is contained in a primetime hour of television. The local station gets between 90 seconds and two minutes of that time, usually around the breaks at the hour and half hour. Selling this time, and all the other advertising contained in nonnetwork or locally originated programming, provides the television station with the bulk of its revenues. Many of these spots are sold to local advertisers, car dealers, department stores, water bed retailers and the like. But some time is sold to national advertisers like McDonald's and Chevrolet and Chevron. This is called **national spot** advertising. National advertisers frequently forego national network advertising when they want to test market a particular ad campaign or product. Or perhaps there is limited distribution of a product. Maybe they just want to tailor a message to an audience. (For example, it makes little sense for Texaco to advertise a gasoline additive that keeps your car running smoothly in below-freezing weather to people in Southern California.) To reiterate, a local television station makes most of its money by selling time to local and national advertisers.

The question of network compensation is a controversial one today. People at the networks have asked aloud whether it makes sense for the networks, which are making a little money, to make payments to their affiliates, which are making lots of money. CBS first proposed eliminating compensation for the wildly popular network features like the Super Bowl, the World Series, or highly promoted miniseries. Giving a station the opportunity to sell time in these highly rated shows is sufficient, the network declared. The network also proposed increasing compensation on the marginal shows, to try to lure more affiliated stations to carry these rating losers. (A local station can preempt network programming and telecast its own programming, selling 100 percent of the advertising time. If a station does this too often, however, the network may look for a new affiliate in that market, and loss of the affiliation can cost a local station a great deal.) The affiliated stations did not like these CBS proposals, and the issue died. More recently NBC did change its compensation formula, rewarding local stations that get high ratings for network programs with a higher rate of compensation. Local stations on which network shows get poor ratings will receive less compensation. Because NBC was the ratings leader in the late 1980s and early 1990s, it had the muscle to push this policy through the affiliates. But affiliated stations, unhappy with this policy, began preempting more NBC shows during the 1990–91 season, and NBC executives said they were reconsidering the new policy.

Rates charged for television advertising are negotiated with individual advertisers but are generally determined by several factors. The time of day the ad is telecast is important because the size of the audience varies through the various **day-parts** of a broadcast day. Advertising during prime time, 7 P.M. to 11 P.M., costs the most. The length of the advertisement is a factor as well. In the beginning, all commercials were sixty seconds long. In the sixties, 30-second commercials became popular; the longer ones cost too much. Sixty and 30-second spots remain the standard, but 15-second and even 10-second ads appear. The size of the audience that watched the advertisement or the "rating" for the program is another factor that is considered. An advertisement telecast on a **run of station** basis, that is, to be run any time the station can fit it in during a particular day-part, costs less than one in which the advertiser specifies a particular spot (i.e., in the break between "Cosby" and "A Different World" on Thursday, or just before the sports on the evening news). Advertisers can get a variety of discounts by buying early, buying a lot of time, or buying leftover or remnant space.

Public television stations operate somewhat differently, and the financing of public television is thoroughly covered on pages 360–364 in the chapter on television. Briefly, a public television station gets a percentage of its revenue from the government—federal, state, local, or even school district; a percentage of its revenue from private business and private foundations (this is called underwriting); and a percentage of its funds from us, the viewers who subscribe. The ratio of one source of funding to another varies from station to station.

## ▣ Radio

What we have said about television applies generally to radio as well, except radio networks play an insignificant role in commercial broadcasting. Virtually all revenue earned by a radio station is generated by the sale of advertising time. Most of the time is sold to local advertisers, but national sponsors buy radio time as well. Advertising rates are negotiated, but are generally determined by several factors. How many people hear the spot is the key factor. This is partially determined by the time of day the spot is carried. What is called "drive time" is prime time in radio, those early morning and late afternoon hours when motorists are stuck in their cars during the commute to and from work. This is when listenership is highest for most stations. The popularity or rating of the station at that time of day also determines the cost of an advertisement. Who is listening is important as well in radio advertising. Radio stations are capable of focusing narrowly (see pp. 222–226 for more) on a segment of the audience and programming for that group. A teenage audience is not a particularly attractive audience to most advertisers, who prefer older, employed persons with more income. Putting these factors together determines the cost of most radio advertising. For example, in the late 1980s the highest-rated Seattle radio station, KIRO, which had a news/talk format, charged about $350 per minute for advertising during the morning drive time. At the same time, the second-highest-rated station, which was a popular music station, was only charging $90 per minute. The KIRO audience was somewhat larger, but also older and wealthier. For an advertiser, it was a much more attractive audience. Radio stations also give their advertisers discounts for buying early, buying many spots, or continually buying spots, and for buying remnant time.

There are a handful of small radio stations that operate on revenues generated solely through listener subscriptions. But these are very unusual. Public radio stations gain their funding in much the same manner as public television stations. For the most part, radio in the United States is supported by advertising.

The recording, film, and book industries are supported almost exclusively by people who buy records, watch motion pictures, and read books. Funding of these industries is specifically addressed in subsequent chapters. It is important to note, however, that advertising is beginning to creep into motion pictures, both overtly as short commercials shown before the feature, or less obviously as more and more products are placed in motion pictures and film companies are paid for this placement. (See pp. 278–279.) Also, one publisher, Whittle Communications, announced in 1989 a plan to pay leading authors to write short books that would contain advertising. Other publishers said they were skeptical of the idea.

It is fair to say, then, that major American mass media are supported by the people who use them, either advertisers or readers and viewers and listeners. Advertising is predominant in newspapers, magazines, radio, and television. The next question to ask is does this affect the content of the mass media. And that answer is obvious: Yes.

## WHO PAYS THE PIPER

The maxim that "Who pays the piper calls the tune" is no less true in mass communications than in any other facet of life. Those who provide the bulk of the revenue for a mass medium are going to have something to say about what that medium carries. This is obvious in looking at the three audience-supported media—film, records, and books. In the early 1980s author Tom Clancy published a book called *The Hunt for Red October,* the story of a Soviet submarine commander who decides to defect to the United States and bring his state-of-the-art Soviet submarine with him. In the ensuing story Clancy focused heavily on the efforts of the U.S. Navy and American intelligence agencies to help the Russian. He also focused heavily on the hardware; the ships, the planes, and so on. The publishing industry has labeled this type of fiction as "techno-thriller," and while Clancy's book wasn't the first of this genre, it was a huge best-seller. It took very little time before other authors and publishers attempted to duplicate Clancy's success; techno-thrillers began popping up regularly on the book racks. And many did very well, including sequels by Clancy. The point is, the public bought the first book; the content of many future books was affected by this acceptance. The same is true in the record industry as popular music trends come (rap) and go (disco). The film industry is often even more blatant in trying to clone successful films. Look at the host of movies that tried to capitalize on the popularity of *Raiders of the Lost Ark,* the first Indiana Jones saga. We will focus more on these matters when each of these mass media is explored in greater detail.

The impact of advertising on newspapers and magazines, radio and television, is just as *evident,* but considerably more complicated. One of the complications is the fact that advertising is not supposed to affect the publication and broadcast of news.

This is a widely and rather closely held tenet in the journalism business. Entertainment is one thing, but news, well, that is something else. Let us try to carefully explore the issue of media content and advertising.

## ADVERTISING AND MEDIA CONTENT

Making generalizations about how advertising affects the content of the mass media is dangerous. Whether or not advertising influences what goes into the newspaper or what is shown on television has less to do with industry standards than with the values of individual editors, news directors, and programming chiefs. People who consider this matter usually think about the advertiser who orders the newspaper to kill a story or lose his account, or the corporation executive who tells the television network to make changes in a documentary or she will pull her spots out of the show. The impact is usually far more subtle.

First we need to make the distinction between how *advertising* influences the content of the mass media, as opposed to how *advertisers* influence the content of the mass media. The examples above represent attempts by an advertiser to affect media content. While it is not uncommon for advertisers to make such demands, it is quite uncommon for the mass media to fold under this pressure. Maybe in the future the television network will be a little more wary of the kind of documentaries it telecasts, but yielding to such pressure on the spot demonstrates an unflattering kind of cowardice frowned upon by people inside and outside the industry.

There is no question, however, that advertising, the placement of commercial messages in the mass media, does affect the content of mass communications. In the first place, the advertiser wants to use mass media that reach a specific audience, usually a large audience. To be an attractive medium to advertisers, the editor or program director is going to have to present a newspaper or television program that will attract the large audience sought by the advertiser. More people are going to watch "Cheers" than a play by Molière. That is why we have more situation comedy than seventeenth-century French comedy on television today. Perhaps an advertiser is seeking a specific audience. The mass medium will frequently try to meet the advertiser's needs by bringing the proper audience to the medium through alteration or addition of content. Many television news departments have recently developed early evening news programs that feature a female anchor, lighter stories that focus on health, fitness, fashion, and parenting. There is little news of government, very little news analysis, and few stories about problems such as the homeless, drugs, and crime. The show is constructed as a setting for advertising aimed at upscale, suburban women (pool and patio females in industry jargon) who watch the "Oprah," "Donahue," or "Sally Jesse Raphael" talk shows from 4 P.M. to 5 P.M. This kind of news is more likely to hold these viewers than the traditional newscast. Or how about the travel or real estate section in the newspaper. Realtors could put their ads on the sports pages, in the style or living sections, or even on pages containing general news. But the newspaper has created a comfortable setting for those ads, a section of the newspaper devoted to home buying and selling, home repairs, and financing tips. If the sellers of real estate were not important advertisers, there is very little likelihood that there would be a real estate section in the newspaper.

The tone of a particular medium is very important as well to most advertisers. This is especially true in television, but affects other media as well. (*USA Today* features a kind of happy talk newsplay that is unusual in print journalism. In promotional material the publishers of the newspaper claim, "*USA Today's* Positive Journalism Creates a Positive Environment for Your Advertising.") Television is primarily an entertainment medium, rather than a medium that communicates information, at least in part because it is totally supported by advertising. A business that spends $300,000 for 30 seconds to try to sell us a car or a brand of chewing gum wants us to be in a good mood when that message is telecast, not worrying about the destruction of the rain forests or polluted drinking water or famine in North Africa. For the most part, even the entertainment should be upbeat. In the early days of the medium, the so-called Golden Age, when serious dramatic anthologies were almost as common as situation comedies are today, advertisers ultimately rebelled at the often dreary (real life?) stories presented on programs like "Playhouse 90" and "Studio One." In his book, *The Sponsor,* broadcast historian Erik Barnouw recounts the difficulty many advertisers had with these dramatic shows:

The realistic but often joyless portrayals of Americans in many dramatic television programs of the 1950s were unappealing to many advertisers. Advertisers preferred the simplistic but satisfying world usually portrayed in the Western series, such as CBS's "Have Gun, Will Travel," starring Richard Boone. Eleven of the 20 top-rated shows in 1959–60 were Western series.
(CBS Photo)

Social and psychological problems seldom have neat, clean-cut solutions. The commercials featured products that solved problems of business and pleasure in a minute or less. To a writer like [Paddy] Chayefsky these same problems had social or psychological ramifications. These might be fascinating, but they often made the commercials seem fraudulent.

Chayefsky's stark drama "Marty" was telecast in 1953. It is the story of a 34-year-old Bronx butcher who fears he will never get a girl because he is unattractive. He meets a woman with similar fears at a Saturday night dance, and the two manage to stumble into romance. In between acts sponsors told viewers that if they used this brand of mouthwash or that brand of deodorant or drove a certain make of car they would be popular and loved. But this didn't work for Marty. Barnouw wrote that the lower-class settings also offended sponsors who "preferred beautiful people in mouthwatering decor to convey what it meant to climb the socioeconomic ladder . . . the drama undermined the commercial message." Interestingly, while "Marty" was critically acclaimed, it did not receive special recognition from the television industry. It was made into a film the following year, using essentially the same script, with most of the same cast and the same director. It won four Academy Awards, including best picture of the year.

What did advertisers want? The western series was the perfect vehicle for commercial messages. In the western good people are rewarded, bad people punished. "The orderly completion of a western gives the viewer a feeling of security that life itself cannot offer. The western serves the same emotional needs as consumer goods," wrote Dr. Ernest Dichter, a psychologist who advised the advertising industry on program selection. Scores of westerns proliferated in the television schedule in the late 1950s and early 1960s. Today it is situation comedy that is the basic staple of entertainment television, another perfect setting for the television commercial.

As a general rule advertisers have a far easier time getting specific content into a medium than in keeping specific content out of a medium. Newspapers and broadcasting stations receive hundreds of press releases each week. Releases from advertisers are usually read a bit more closely. Often the advertising department at the newspaper or broadcasting station will intercede on behalf of the advertiser to insure that the story is brought to the attention of the news staff. The news coverage given to the opening of a new shopping mall, for example, is to satisfy the advertisers, not the readers or viewers.

Today advertisers can buy the space for a story if they want to. Sometimes the sponsorship of the message is obvious; other times it is not. Advertisers will buy entire sections of a newspaper or several pages in a magazine. The words "Prepared by the Advertising Department" or "Advertisement" are usually, but not always, clear to readers. Or advertisers will buy an hour or thirty minutes on television (these are called **infomercials** in the industry) to show viewers their wares.

Sometimes the insertion of programming is a bit more insidious. Several companies offer to television stations prepared "news and information" features for use on newscasts. These are typically about health or medicine and are very professionally put together and paid for by a business, usually a pharmaceutical company. The sponsorship of the segment may or may not be mentioned. **Video news releases** (or VNRs) are also produced and given to stations. Key Pharmaceuticals, the manufacturer of a brand name asthma medication, paid for a two-minute spot that looked like a news report about asthma. The *The New York Times* reported that the story conveyed the message that generic drugs are less safe than brand name asthma medications, like the one manufactured by Key. The story was telecast on more than two dozen stations in the late 1980s, the newspaper reported. And no one was told that Key had paid for its preparation. Other video releases sent to television stations included one from Arm & Hammer baking soda that showed the restoration of the Statue of Liberty, in which baking soda was used as a cleaning agent; a feature on daylight savings time, which prominently featured a Timex clock, the sponsor; and a holiday gift feature, that lingered on a Spectra camera, made by Polaroid, which paid for the feature.

Some mass media are more vulnerable to pressure from advertisers than others. A large supermarket that is the major advertiser in a small weekly newspaper would have a better chance of getting its way with this newspaper than with a large daily that has many different advertisers. Small television stations, with small staffs and several hours of news programming to fill each week, are especially vulnerable to the video press release.

Even a large mass medium can be vulnerable to advertiser pressure in some circumstances. Since the 1970s researchers have demonstrated that women's magazines that tend to rely heavily on cigarette advertising have largely ignored one of the biggest health stories of this era, the dramatic increase in the incidence of lung cancer in women. By 1985 lung cancer had become the number one cancer killer for women. Lauren Kessler most recently documented this correlation in an article published in *Journalism Quarterly* in the summer of 1989. Kessler showed that smoking-related health stories were largely absent from the major women's magazines between 1983 and 1987, although other health issues were heavily reported. Only eight articles, out of a total of almost 700 health-related stories, focused upon the health risks associated with tobacco. Cigarette advertising accounts for as much as 15 percent of all advertising in some of these magazines, Kessler reported. In addition many of the tobacco companies also own subsidiaries that manufacture food and cosmetics, which are also advertised in these magazines. If a company like Phillip Morris or RJR Nabisco were to be angered, it could mean a serious loss of advertising revenue to a publication. (Recently one tobacco company dropped its longtime association with an advertising agency that had prepared a spot for Northwest Airlines announcing its no smoking on flights policy.) In a revealing article in the first "adless" edition of *Ms.* magazine entitled "Sex, Lies and Advertising," (July/August, 1990), consulting editor Gloria Steinem outlined the brutal realities of advertiser pressure on magazines.

Does advertising influence the content of the mass media? Surely. But this should not come as a revelation to any but the most idealistic. Is this a serious problem? In some instances it is. And it is probably a more serious problem now than it was 20 years ago as business becomes better and bolder at asserting its interests, and as editors and news directors become more sympathetic to the needs of these customers. This is a reflection of the intense commercialism inherent in the American mass media today. The trends in the ownership of the mass media, noted by the Commission on Freedom of the Press more than 40 years ago, have not abated. In fact, as we will note shortly, the concentration of ownership of American mass communications, has become far more pronounced. As this has happened, the financial performance of newspapers, radio and television stations, magazines, motion picture companies, and book publishers has become even more significant. Owners have always been concerned about profits and losses. Today, stockholders, financial analysts, and potential buyers must also be impressed. Many American businesses are run with a strong emphasis on the quarterly financial reports. American mass media are no exception. When this occurs, the position of the advertisers, who pay most of the bills for most of the American mass media, is greatly enhanced.

## INDUSTRIAL PROFILE

To most people the words "mass media" conjure up visions of newscasts, feature films, record albums, TV comedies, or even advertising. And there is no question that all of these represent mass media. But the mass media are also businesses. In this country they have always been businesses of one sort or another. When John Peter Zenger agreed in 1733 to publish the *New York Weekly Journal* for Lewis Morris and James Alexander, it was because he needed the business, not because he necessarily believed in what Morris and Alexander asked him to print. But today the mass media are not just businesses; frequently they are big businesses, really big businesses. In order to understand the system of mass communications that has been erected, it must be viewed as essentially a system of businesses.

American business in the past 50 years has come to be dominated by fewer and fewer, larger and larger companies. The independent grocery store has been pushed aside by the modern chain-owned supermarket. There were once more than two dozen active automakers in the United States. Three remain. Two American companies manufacture jet passenger aircraft. A handful of corporations now market most of the major brand name food items. There is no shortage of industrial corporations in the United States; nearly 360,000 according to one author. But a mere one percent of these businesses account for nearly 90 percent of all sales.

The economic structure of the mass media tends to mirror this profile quite closely. In 1983 University of California journalism professor Ben Bagdikian published a study entitled *The Media Monopoly.* At that time Bagdikian demonstrated that 50 large multinational corporations controlled the majority of the mass media in the United States. Bagdikian revised his book in 1991. Had things changed? Dramatically. At that time 23 corporations controlled the majority of mass media in the United States.

Specifically, Bagdikian says:

Fourteen corporations control more than 50 percent of the 63 million newspapers sold each day in the United States.

Three corporations earned the majority of revenues from the 11,000 or so magazines published in the United States.

Three corporations—the owners of the three major television networks—dominate the television industry when measured by either revenues earned or the audience that is reached.

Six of 25,000 book publishers earn most of the annual revenues from book sales.

Four motion picture studios control most of the revenues in that business.

If you add this up, it totals 30 corporations, not 23. That is because many corporations appear on more than one list. For example, Paramount Communications Company is a major holder of book (Simon & Schuster, Ginn and Company) properties and also owns Paramount Pictures, a major motion picture studio. Capital Cities/ABC owns both newspapers and television properties. Hearst has both newspapers and magazines.

The 1989 merger of Time, Inc. and Warner Communications was a fitting end to a decade in which the ownership of the nation's mass media seemed to collapse in a heap around the feet of a frightfully small band of businessmen and women. The new Time-Warner Inc. is the world's largest media company. (See Table 4-2 for a list of its holdings.)

Members of the Subcommittee on Economics and Commercial Law of the U.S. House of Representatives, a legislative panel which is supposed to worry about the anticompetitive impact of such mergers, applauded the $18 billion deal, saying they were happy that the largest media company in the world was a U.S. company. "The strength of this newly combined company will mean expanded and more successful overseas markets for American made films, records, cassettes, and television shows," said Rep. Carlos J. Moorhead, a California Republican.

The Time-Warner merger was the biggest deal of the decade, but certainly not the only noteworthy transaction. All three national television networks changed hands during the 1980s. Capital Cities Communications purchased the American

### TABLE 4-1 The Top 25 Leading Media Companies by 1989 Revenue

| Rank | Company | Net Revenues in Millions (1989) |
|------|---------|--------------------------------|
| 1 | Capital Cities/ABC | $4,767.0 |
| 2 | Time-Warner Inc. | 4,575.0 |
| 3 | Gannett Co. | 3,518.2 |
| 4 | General Electric | 3,392.0 |
| 5 | CBS Inc. | 2,959.9 |
| 6 | Advance Publications | 2,881.7 |
| 7 | Times Mirror Co. | 2,807.1 |
| 8 | TCI | 2,353.0 |
| 9 | Knight-Ridder | 2,261.8 |
| 10 | News Corp. | 2,203.0 |
| 11 | Tribune Co. | 2,098.8 |
| 12 | Hearst Corp. | 2,094.5 |
| 13 | New York Times Co. | 1,768.9 |
| 14 | Cox Enterprises | 1,664.0 |
| 15 | Washington Post Co. | 1,372.9 |
| 16 | Thomson Corp. | 1,327.6 |
| 17 | Viacom International | 1,198.7 |
| 18 | E.W. Scripps | 1,180.0 |
| 19 | Dow Jones & Co. | 975.2 |
| 20 | Continental Cablevision | 780.0 |
| 21 | Reed Publishing USA | 730.0 |
| 22 | Turner Broadcasting System | 728.7 |
| 23 | Ingersoll Publications Co. | 669.5 |
| 24 | Westinghouse Electric Corp. | 646.0 |
| 25 | Advo-Systems | 617.7 |

*Source: Advertising Age*

### TABLE 4-2    Major Holdings of Time-Warner, Inc. in 1991

- WEA Records—Warner, Electra, Atlantic labels and others.
- WEA Corp.—nation's largest record and home video distributor.
- Warner/Chappell Music—world's largest music publishing company.
- Warner Bros. pictures.
- Warner Bros. television.
- Warner Home Video—nation's largest producer of home videos.
- Home Box Office, Cinemax—pay cable channels.
- HBO Video—videocassette distribution.
- American Television and Communications, Warner Cable Communications—nation's 2nd and 5th largest cable companies.
- Magazines, including *Time, Sports Illustrated, People, Money, Fortune, McCall's,* and 20 others.
- Time-Life Books; Book-of-the-Month Club; Little, Brown; Warner Books; DC Comics.

Broadcasting Company for $3.5 billion. At the time of the sale ABC owned five television stations, 12 radio stations, and several magazines. Capital Cities owned seven television stations, 12 radio stations, and 17 daily and weekly newspapers. General Electric bought RCA, which owned the National Broadcasting Company, for $6.28 billion. At that time NBC owned several radio and television stations, and RCA owned both recording and book interests. CBS fought off hostile takeover bids by conservative Republican Senator Jesse Helms and Turner Broadcasting Company. The network's savior was Laurence Tisch (Loew's International) who purchased a controlling interest in the network. Tisch was named CEO and began selling off long-held CBS properties. The book division, the magazine division, and CBS records were all sold. Tisch then made what one writer has described as "draconian cuts" in broadcast operations—especially the news operations—to recoup some of the money the network lost fighting the takeover attempts.

The eighties were the decade in which Australian media magnate Rupert Murdoch invaded the United States. In 1991, in addition to his massive holdings in Australia and Great Britain, Murdoch owned newspapers in Boston and San Antonio, *TV Guide,* 20th Century Fox film studios, Fox Broadcasting, television stations in Boston, New York, Los Angeles, Chicago, Washington, Houston, and Dallas, and Harper & Row Books. During the decade he also owned and sold the *Chicago Sun-Times,* the *New York Post,* and the *Village Voice.* The foundation of the Murdoch empire began to wobble a bit in 1991 when the Australian media lord was forced to sell nine magazines to facilitate the repayment of debt he accumulated in the 1980s. Murdoch went on a buying binge during the 1980s and paid too much (including $3 billion for *TV Guide*) for several media properties.

Gannett became THE newspaper chain of the nation during the 1980s. In attempting to add luster to its huge, but generally mediocre chain of newspapers, the corporation purchased the *Des Moines Register* ($200 million), the *Detroit News* ($717 million, the deal included five television stations); and the *Louisville Courier-Journal/Louisville Times* ($300 million). Gannett currently owns approximately 90 daily newspapers, more than three dozen weeklies, *USA Today,* ten television stations, 16 radio stations, GTG Entertainment, and several smaller media-related properties.

Cable television was supposed to be the new medium that would redemocratize broadcasting; break the corporations' hold on radio and television broadcasting; power to the people. The 1980s was the decade that showed how fatuous those predictions were. The delivery of cable services came to be dominated by just a handful of businesses. Sixty percent of all cable subscribers are served by just 20 multiple service cable operators (MSOs). Perhaps even more telling, nearly one-quarter of all persons using cable are served by just two cable companies, Tele-Communications Inc., and Time-Warner Cable. Think of the power those two companies have in determining whether or not a cable channel will succeed or fail. If TCI and Time-Warner choose not to include a new cable channel in their menu for customers, failure is almost assured.

The eighties were the decade in which foreign interests, which had long coveted American media properties, made their move. Sony bought CBS Records, one of the nation's largest and oldest recording companies. Labels in this group include CBS, Columbia, and CBS Masterworks. The price was $2 billion. A year later Sony purchased Columbia Pictures Entertainment for $3.4 billion from the Coca-Cola Company. Sony is picking up a major film and television production company with 2,700 feature films, including such cultural icons as *Lawrence of Arabia,* and 260 television properties, ranging from "Jeopardy" to "Designing Women." Coca-Cola reportedly lost interest in the film business after the *Ishtar* debacle, a movie that cost Columbia mega-millions in the late 1980s. Bertelsman, a West German company and the second largest media conglomerate in the world, acquired RCA Records, including the Arista and Ariola labels, Doubleday Bantam Dell publishers, an extensive array of book clubs, including the Literary Guild and the Mystery Book Club, and *Parents, Young Miss,* and *Expecting* magazines.

MGM-UA became MGM-Pathe in late 1990 when it was sold to Italian financier Giancarlo Parretti for $1.3 billion, and Matsushita Electric Industrial Company of Japan (the folks who manufacture Panasonic, Technics, and Quasar audio and video equipment) purchased MCA/Universal for more than $6 billion a few weeks later. These sales mean that five of this nation's six largest record companies (which usually account for about 95 percent of all U.S. record/tape/CD sales) and four of the nation's seven leading motion picture studios are now foreign owned. Only Warner-Time (WEA records and Warner Bros. pictures), Disney, and Paramount are domestically controlled. Even the French got involved. Hatchette S.A., France's largest publisher, bought Grolier Inc., the publisher of the *New Book of Knowledge, The Encyclopedia Americana, American Academic Encyclopedia,* and other educational material. The publisher of the book you are now reading, Macmillan, is owned by Maxwell Communication, a British company that owns many other media properties as well.

As you may note from some of the prices quoted above, buying mass media properties is not an inexpensive endeavor. In 1979 Gannett bought the Combined Communications Corporation (billboards, newspapers, and broadcasting) for $340 million. At that time this was the largest price ever paid for a media company. Less than ten years later GE paid almost $6.3 billion for RCA. In 1988 Disney agreed to pay $320 million for a single television station, KHJ in Los Angeles. Hearst paid $375 million for the *Houston Chronicle* in 1987. Rupert Murdoch paid $3 billion for *TV Guide* in 1988. And in 1989 the McClatchy Newspapers chain bought three small daily newspapers in South Carolina for $74 million. The combined circulation of the three newspapers totaled 47,000. The total profit for the three newspapers in

1988 was $620,000. Media properties in the 1980s and early 1990s are selling for three to four times what other kinds of businesses can bring on the market. Why? Because mass media businesses are so profitable.

The selling and buying frenzy has created instant media barons. William D. Singleton did not own a single newspaper in 1983. By 1989 he owned 60 newspapers including the *Denver Post,* the *Houston Post* and the *Dallas Times-Herald.* His was the 11th largest newspaper chain in the nation at that point.

Where will it all end? The hectic buying spree of the 1980s has slowed, but most experts do not see an immediate end in sight. The big will continue to gobble up those that are smaller. Bagdikian quotes investment banker Christopher Shaw who said that by the year 2000 all the United States mass media could be in the hands of six conglomerates. British publisher Robert Maxwell said in 1984 that by 1994 there would be only ten global communication corporations. And J. Kendrick Noble, a Wall Street media analyst, has speculated that by the end of this century the largest media properties will be owned by a half-dozen huge corporations. Not a happy picture to those who believe that our democratic process and economic free enterprise rest upon diversity in the mass media.

## ☐ Reasons for Concentration

The shrinking number of owners of American mass media is a phenomenon that has been occurring for several decades. But during the 1980s, what some have called the "decade of the deal," the accumulation of media assets by a few giant corporations took on grave new proportions.

From 1984 through 1986, 10,786 business mergers or acquisitions took place according to *Money and Acquisitions* magazine. That amounts to ten per day, *every* day, for three years. And many of these involved mass media. Two things happened that fostered this rapid increase in the concentration of ownership. The first involved government policy. The Federal Communications Commission significantly reduced restrictions on the ownership of broadcast properties by a single company. The FCC also abandoned its rule that a new owner must hold a broadcast license for at least three years before selling it. More about those changes in a moment. In addition, the Cable Communications Policy Act of 1984 legislated the cable industry into a largely unregulated monopoly.

While the law enhanced the big buying spree of the 1980s, it was a development in the financial market that made it possible. Before major corporations could expand their holdings, they needed pools of capital that could be used to support their large new investments. The birth of the high yield so-called "junk bonds" provided this capital. The investment firm of Kohlberg Kravis Roberts & Co. quietly began using junk bonds for leveraged buyouts in the mid-1970s. But their business remained obscure. In 1982 Wall Street finally noticed this new financial phenomenon when an investment group led by former treasury secretary William Simon bought the Gibson Greetings Company with $1 million of their own money, and a $79 million loan underwritten by junk bonds. They sold the company 18 months later for $290 million. Junk bonds are simply high-risk, high-yield securities. Investors buy the bonds because of the extraordinary potential return. The bond seller uses the proceeds of the sale of the bonds to buy the targeted company, usually at a high price, and then uses the profits from the company, or the sale of some of the company's assets, to pay the high interest on the bonds until the business can be sold, usually at a tremendous profit. Bondholders are paid off at that point. The only thing the buyer needs to worry about is paying the interest on the bonds until the company or at least some of its divisions or subsidiaries can be sold. Initially the junk bond investors looked toward risky, developing businesses like long-distance telephone carriers, said Richard MacDonald, director of equity research at First Boston. "But soon they realized that higher returns and lower risks were available through TV stations and other media properties with a safe enough cash flow to finance the acquisitions," MacDonald added. So those who wanted to had both the legal and financial means to gobble up more and more mass media. But why mass media and not shoe factories or lawn mower manufacturers?

The simplest and best reason is money. There is an awful lot of money to be made in mass communications. The owners themselves readily admit this. It is well worth the money to buy overpriced newspapers, according to Rupert Murdoch who has massive media holdings in the United States. "You pay three times the revenue because it's a monopoly and a license to steal money forever," he noted. "I buy newspapers to make money to buy more newspapers to make more money," said publishing baron Roy Thomson before he died. "As for editorial content, that's the stuff you separate ads with." When stock analysts once asked Gannett Co. chairman Allen Neuharth whether the corporate name was pronounced *Gan*nett or Gan*nett,* he smiled and replied the correct pronunciation was MONEY.

Persons who own a newspaper chain or a broadcast group or a mixture of the two can both save money and make more money. Savings can be accumulated in many ways. Certain important business functions can be centralized and expenses can be shared among all newspapers or stations. A single attorney, for example, can advise managers or editors at several broadcast or newspaper outlets. Elaborate computer facilities can be shared among several newspapers through satellite and microwave transmissions. A newspaper or broadcast chain can share the cost of a Washington or foreign news bureau and a national advertising staff. As media stock analyst John Morton noted recently, a big company (like Gannett) buys everything from newsprint to paper clips at prices well below those paid by a single newspaper. These economies of scale can result in significant cost savings.

A chain or group of media conglomerates can also realize savings in other less obvious ways. High priced managerial talent—too expensive for a single publishing company or broadcasting station—can be employed to streamline operations in a media chain. This can save money. The chain owner also finds it's easier to borrow money at the bank, pay less interest on what is borrowed, and more easily refinance the loan when needed than would the owner of a single newspaper or radio station. Chains also find it easier to use the growing number of automated labor-saving production systems. The Booth chain of newspapers in Michigan (which was sold to the S.I. Newhouse chain) made such good use of automated editing and printing facilities that in four years the chain doubled the productivity of each employee. This is a remarkable saving in an industry that has large labor expenses. While all newspapers or broadcasting operations can use such labor-saving devices, the chains make much better use of these facilities and the savings are multiplied.

But persons and companies that own many newspapers, broadcasting stations, magazines, cable companies, and other media elements plan to do more than just save money; they plan to make money—lots of it.

We are living in what some have dubbed the "Age of Information." People have developed a growing appetite for information and entertainment. Never before have mass media commanded so much of our time or our money. At the same time consumer goods in the United States suffer from a serious lack of what marketing specialists call "product differentiation." There is hardly a dime's worth of difference between most brands of soft drinks, beer, cigarettes, automobiles, clothing, soap— you name it. Each product costs about the same for each company to manufacture; each product costs about the same to purchase. Manufacturers more and more use advertising to try to create the illusion of differences between brands to try to increase sales and develop brand loyalty among customers. The major beneficiaries of annual increases in advertising expenditures are the nation's mass media. This growth in advertising has helped make media companies more profitable than companies in most other industries. By virtually any meaningful statistical measure such as return on investment, profit margin, or whatever, newspapers, magazines, radio and television stations all do considerably better than shoe manufacturers, food processors, or virtually any other industry you can think of. This profitability makes mass media a desirable target for persons interested in getting a good return on their investments. So there is lots of buying and selling of media properties. But that is only half the story.

Companies that generate a lot of profit (like mass media companies) must decide what to do with that money. It can be paid to shareholders as dividends. Or it can be invested. If the company just keeps the money the Internal Revenue Service will tax it heavily as excess profits. Look at the typical newspaper that wants to grow, wants to become larger, wants to make bigger profits. It can invest its income in one of three ways. First, money could be invested in the existing company. New presses could be purchased, the newsroom could be remodeled, the employees could be given a lounge or cafeteria. That is fine for a short time, but what about next year's profits? Also, such an investment might result in a bit better productivity, but it won't help increase revenues that much.

The profits could be invested in another kind of company. The publisher could open a chain of ice cream parlors or buy a brewery. But the publisher doesn't know much about ice cream or beer. Also, these businesses won't give the publisher nearly the return on investment that the newspaper has provided. So the third choice is the logical option—invest in another newspaper. Virtually all communities that can support a newspaper (with the high profits the publisher is used to earning) already have a newspaper. So the publisher has but one economically logical choice—buy an existing newspaper. And that is what happens—over and over again in America with newspapers, magazines, and radio and television stations.

Why would the publisher of an existing newspaper (which earns a good profit) sell out? Perhaps the publisher is tired of newspapering. Or perhaps the publisher has died, and the family wants to sell the newspaper or has to sell the newspaper to pay the estate taxes. Perhaps the publisher simply wants to make a killing because, as can be seen by the outline of sales at the beginning of this chapter, mass media properties sell for enormous amounts.

A newspaper or broadcasting station is not simply selling its physical assets when it goes on the auction block. In fact, the building and the presses and other equipment may be the least important asset for sale. What is being sold is access to readers (or listeners or viewers in broadcasting) and the ability to make a substantial profit in the years ahead. Consequently, media properties like newspapers are often sold at a price far in excess of the apparent worth of the company. Stock analyst Morton points out that one way to measure the acquisition price of a business is to compare what a company earns in a year with its price, something called multiples of earnings. If a newspaper earned $3 million last year and is sold for $30 million, the sale multiple is ten times earnings. Most businesses, Morton notes, are sold for about ten times earnings. However, newspapers and broadcasting stations often are sold for double or triple that amount. Gannett frequently will pay as much as 50 times earnings when it buys a family-owned newspaper. Is that smart business? It certainly is for the seller, who makes a bundle of cash and is off to Kauai and a retirement condominium. But it has turned out to be smart business for many buyers as well.

Gannett has found, for example, that a family-owned paper is often poorly run, according to the chain's standards. Usually editorial staff layoffs follow a Gannett takeover; the new editor doesn't need as many reporters. Advertising rates are normally increased dramatically. Gannett immediately raised advertising rates by 42 percent when it bought the company that owned two newspapers in Salem, Oregon. Profits for the newspapers tripled in two years. Of course Gannett also can lower expenses through its ability to purchase raw materials and supplies at a lower cost than the former owners. "After two or three years of ownership, a newspaper that had been earning its former owners eight cents on the dollar starts bringing to Gannett 15 to 20 cents on every dollar," wrote John Morton in the *Washington Journalism Review.* Of course as more and more newspapers and broadcasting stations become chain-owned, the smaller number of independent operations become more valuable to persons seeking to start or expand an existing chain. Prices go even higher, giving owners an even stronger nudge to sell.

This simplified economic picture is not the only reason America has experienced such an epidemic of newspaper and broadcasting sales. But it is the most important reason. The desire and ability of many good American capitalists to make money, lots of money, has resulted in serious problems of economic concentration in the press in this nation.

While money is the primary reason small media owners want to get bigger, and big ones want to get huge, power is certainly a secondary reason. Ownership of a newspaper or broadcasting station or magazines can influence public opinion in many ways, and this surely confers certain power upon the owner. Ownership of many newspapers or broadcasting stations or magazines confers even more power upon the owner. When a newspaper publisher asks a U.S. senator to return his or her call, there is generally a quick response. But the chief executive officer of a company like Gannett which owns newspapers and broadcasting stations in a majority of the states has special access to a majority of the members of Congress.

In the past, the ownership of a newspaper or chain of newspapers was often the stepping stone to high political office. Both William Randolph Hearst and Horace Greeley used their prominence and power as publishers to foster their bids for the Presidency. In 1920, the Presidential candidates of the Democratic and Republican parties, James Cox (who lost) and Warren G. Harding (who won) were both newspaper publishers. Today, most media barons are more interested in profit margins than foreign policy. But there is no question that the owners of the mass communications industry in this nation use their power to influence legislation that will benefit their businesses, their interests, and themselves. It is through the political power that accrues to a major mass media owner that they expand their economic power.

The government has done little or nothing to retard the growth of the concentration of ownership of mass communications. In fact, current government policies actually encourage or foster such concentration. As noted, during the 1980s the Federal Communications Commission modified rules which limited the number of broadcasting properties any single individual or company could own. Under previous rules no person could own more than seven AM radio, seven FM radio, and seven television stations. Even that is a hefty chunk of mass media. In the early 1980s the agency changed its rules to permit a single licensee to own 12 of each of the above, so long as the television holdings did not reach more than 25 percent of the total U.S. viewing audience. At the time this rule was announced the FCC said it would abandon ownership regulations altogether by 1990. Congress intervened at this point and told the agency it would not permit a total abandonment of ownership rules. The 12–12–12 rule remains in force, but is not much of a limit on ownership, especially if those 36 properties owned by a licensee are in major U.S. markets. The FCC also abandoned its anti-trafficking rules that blocked the sale of a license unless the licensee held the station for three years. Three years doesn't sound like a long time, but many of the fast-buck media investors of today don't want to spend that much time in one spot. It is currently possible to sell a license after holding it for only a year.

Tax laws also have fostered the growth of broadcast and newspaper chains. In the 1940s many, perhaps most, of the newspapers and broadcasting stations in the nation were family-owned businesses. But when the founder or owner of a family-owned business dies, it is often very difficult to maintain family ownership of that property. First of all there is family pressure. If there are three heirs, one might want to keep the business, but the others may have little interest in the business and wish to sell. The Bingham family of Louisville, Ky., ultimately sold the *Courier-Journal* and its smaller sister paper, the *Louisville Times,* to Gannett in 1988 when the heirs discovered "divergent interests" which precluded retaining the newspapers. The family had owned the *Courier-Journal,* widely regarded as one of the nation's finest newspapers, for 70 years. And the family-owned King Broadcasting Co., a highly regarded media company that owned six TV stations, six radio stations, 13 cable companies, and the nation's largest mobile TV production company, was broken up and sold in 1991 because the heirs did not want to stay in the business.

But even if the heirs want to hold onto the property, U.S. tax laws often make this impossible. Estate taxes are based upon what others are willing to pay for the property, not necessarily its real value. And because chains and other media corporations are willing to pay so much for a newspaper or broadcasting station, the value of a piece of property for tax purposes is often wildly inflated. Imagine, for example, that a newspaper owner has died. The real assets (land, building, equipment) have a book value (a real value) of $5 million. But these have a market value (what a buyer is willing to pay) of $15 million. In addition the newspaper has certain intangible assets; it is a successful publication, with subscribers, management in place, a good reputation. These intangibles are valued on the market at $35 million. Total value of the property for tax purposes: $50 million. Estate tax on that amount in 1990 was $27 million. How is the heir to raise that much money without selling the newspaper? In 1990 Congress slightly amended the tax laws to permit owners of a family-run business to transfer common stock in the company to an heir before the owner dies with less serious tax penalties than were previously accrued. But this change does not come close to solving the estate tax problem.

Tax laws permitting the depreciation of property make the newspaper much more valuable to the new owner than the old owner. Property can only be depreciated for a specific number of years. When this period ends the owner of the property loses a valuable tax deduction. But the new owner can have the building and equipment reappraised on the basis of current market value and replacement cost. The depreciation cycle begins again, accruing to the new owner a huge tax savings. These laws apply to all businesses, but seem to work especially harshly against the public interest of maintaining a diversity of ownership in the mass media. Attempts have been made by members of Congress to amend the tax code to alleviate this problem, but thus far none have been successful. The Independent Local Newspaper Act was introduced in the early 1980s to permit independent newspaper owners to prepay their estate taxes by establishing a government trust. Payment would be made to the trust each year; then when a death occurred, the inheritance tax could be paid from the trust fund. Another proposal would have permitted the tax payments in installments over several years. A strong advocate of these laws has been Congressman Morris Udall, who said recently: "I'm hoping that [this kind of tax relief] will enable small publishers to resist these takeovers, but if that doesn't work I'm prepared to introduce a bill that would actually limit the number of papers any company can own." Udall's idea to limit newspaper ownership—while desirable from many standpoints—would certainly run into both political and constitutional problems. But no action has been taken on these proposals.

Finally, U.S. antitrust laws, designed to insure that there is fair competition in the marketplace, that no monopolies develop, have simply not worked with regard to the concentration of ownership in the mass media. The government has clearly not enforced these vigorously. More importantly, perhaps, the government simply does not believe that because one company owns 90 newspapers, a couple of dozen broadcasting properties, and other media holdings, that this is a monopoly. Each year dozens of newspapers change hands, almost always going from independent or small chain ownership to large chain or media conglomerate ownership. Yet there is no government action. Legal scholar Catherine Roach explains why:

> Because of the structure of the communications industry—basically a collection of local circulation and advertising markets—antitrust enforcers have encountered difficult problems of proof as to anti-competitive effects in relevant markets. As the statistics indicate, newspaper chains can usually safely skirt antitrust violations as long as they refrain from purchasing a newspaper in competition with one they already own.

In applying the antitrust laws to the problem of local monopolies, the Justice Department sometimes makes the problem of concentration worse, not better. In 1964 the Los Angeles-based Times-Mirror Company bought the *San Bernardino Sun* and *Telegraph* for $15 million. But the purchase by the *Los Angeles Times* of the two profitable dailies, located some 40 miles from Los Angeles, was challenged by the government, which asserted that ownership of the *Times,* the *Sun* and the *Telegraph* by the same company would substantially reduce competition in the Southern California region. A federal court agreed and required the Times-Mirror Company to sell the *Sun* and the *Telegraph.* Gannett bought the two newspapers. A victory for lessening economic concentration in the mass media? Hardly, when the two newspapers were simply added to the largest chain of newspapers in the nation. A victory for the people in the San Bernardino Valley? That is very questionable, since they end up with an absentee owner for their newspapers—one whose corporate headquarters is not 40 miles away in Los Angeles, but 2,000 miles away in Rochester, New York. More elusive but equally important is the qualitative differences between the two owners. The *Los Angeles Times* is one of the half-dozen best newspapers in the nation and undoubtedly some of this quality would have rubbed off on the *Sun* and the *Telegraph*. The Gannett chain, on the other hand, owns a few good newspapers. But most are clearly mediocre. More important, profitability, not excellence is the hallmark of the newspaper chain. Sale of the *Sun* and *Telegraph* to a local owner would have made more sense than the sale of the newspapers to either the small chain owned by the Times-Mirror Company or the large chain owned by Gannett. When that was impossible, the readers of the community would have likely benefited more from a sale of the newspapers to the nearby owner of a quality newspaper.

Newspaper publishers have sought exemptions from the antitrust laws, as weak as they are. In 1970 the Newspaper Preservation Act was adopted by the Congress after an intense lobbying effort by the newspaper industry. Some legislators were told by publishers to support the bill or face editorial opposition at re-election time. The Justice Department opposed the bill. Even President Richard Nixon was apparently against the measure . . . until he had a meeting with Richard Berlin, the president of the Hearst Corporation. After the meeting Nixon supported the measure, repudiating the stand taken by his own Attorney General.

This exemption to the federal antitrust laws permits two local newspapers to merge their advertising, printing, and circulation departments. Only the editorial departments remain separate and independent. This is called a joint operating agreement. Pairs of newspapers in 22 different cities had such agreements in 1969 when the Supreme Court ruled that such arrangements were a violation of federal antitrust laws. Why? Because in merging business operations the two newspapers significantly reduce their costs. The chance of a third daily newspaper succeeding in such an economic environment is nil. Hence, this is considered a restraint of trade. The adoption of the Newspaper Preservation Act reversed this Supreme Court ruling.

About 21 joint operating agreements exist in America today. Two newspapers seeking to enter such an agreement can qualify for immunity from antitrust prosecution only if the agreement is first approved by the Justice Department. The single most important criterion to qualify for a joint operating agreement is that one of the two newspapers be in danger of failing. It is reasoned that it is better to have two competing editorial voices in a community than only one. The joint operating agreement is designed to keep the failing newspaper alive. The Justice Department can require a hearing to determine whether the newspaper is indeed failing—but usually does not. The company that owns the newspaper does not need to be in danger of failing; only the particular publication must demonstrate economic difficulty. That was discovered when the plans for the *Seattle Times* and the *Seattle Post-Intelligencer* to enter a joint operating agreement were challenged. The *Times,* the dominant afternoon paper, sought to merge its noneditorial operations with the weaker morning *Post-Intelligencer*. Charges were made by opponents of the agreement (advertisers, suburban daily and weekly publishers, and *Post-Intelligencer* employees) that the *P-I* was not really in danger of failing. It was losing money, but the Hearst Corporation, its owner, was highly profitable and could afford to keep the paper printing almost indefinitely and write off a nice tax loss each year. Opponents also charged that Hearst was taking more money out of the *P-I* than it was putting in and, in the words of one newspaper analyst, "A little energy, a small amount of capital and a little faith . . . would put this paper in a tremendous position in the entire

Northwest." Even the antitrust division of the Justice Department argued that the *P-I* was not a failing newspaper in terms of the law, but was overruled by the Attorney General. A federal appeals court finally approved of the agreement in 1983.

In 1986 the *Detroit Free Press,* owned by the Knight-Ridder newspaper chain and the *Detroit News,* owned by Gannett, announced they would enter into a joint operating agreement. Many questioned how anyone could seriously contend that either paper was in danger of failing when their corporate owners were so profitable. (Gannett is the largest newspaper chain in the United States; Knight-Ridder is second.) True, both newspaper were losing money at the time. But they were in the grips of a dogged circulation war that had a serious impact upon revenues. Each paper was being sold for 15 cents a copy, half of the typical selling price. And advertising was being sold at cut-rate prices. The Justice Department recommended that a hearing be held on the need for the joint operating agreement. A hearing judge took several weeks of testimony. In December of 1987 he urged the rejection of the proposed joint operating agreement. The applicants had failed to prove, he said, that there exists in Detroit an irreversible market condition that would cause the *Free Press* to ultimately fail. "The losses incurred by the *Free Press* and the *News* are attributable to their strategies of seeking market dominance and future profitability at any cost along with the expectation that failure to achieve these goals would result in a favorable consideration of a JOA application," wrote administrative law judge Morton Needelman. The antitrust division of the U.S. Justice Department also opposed the JOA. But Attorney General Edwin Meese approved the merger, and the United States Court of Appeals upheld his decision in 1989. The Supreme Court of the United States heard a further appeal, but a four-to-four vote by the high court meant the decision of the Court of Appeals was sustained.

In 1990 two other joint operating agreements were approved by the Department of Justice. A JOA between the *York* (Pennsylvania) *Daily Record* and the *York Dispatch* was approved by Attorney General Richard Thornburgh in February of 1990, and the attorney general okayed a similar agreement between the *Las Vegas Sun* and the *Las Vegas Review-Journal* on June 1 of 1990.

There are many critics who oppose joint operating agreements and argue that at a time when the concentration in mass media ownership is reaching epidemic proportions the government should be fighting mergers, not passing laws that permit them. "This bill [Newspaper Preservation Act] tends to subvert the First Amendment by making it legal for established publishers to engage in monopolistic practices against which weekly newspapers and other potential rivals cannot compete," wrote Morton Mintz and Jerry Cohen in *America, Inc.* There is considerable testimony from the owners of smaller, competing newspapers in communities with dailies in joint operating agreements that these small papers have been seriously crippled in their efforts to compete for advertising. (Lower costs and special combination advertising rates give the dailies under joint operating agreement an edge in dealing with advertisers.) When the Newspaper Preservation Act passed the Congress in 1970, the *New Yorker* magazine pointed out another problem with the law:

> [The law] is most probably not a newspaper preservation bill as much as a publisher preservation bill. Any newspaper that has to be preserved this way might as well be preserved in formaldehyde. . . . The public is better served by a dead paper than by one mortally sick and given a semblance of health . . . by the government about which it is bound to speak the truth.

# IMPLICATIONS—GOOD AND BAD

What are the implications of this industrial profile of the mass media in America? Many argue that there are distinct advantages to such a structure. Big can be better, they argue. Some examples: Big companies have greater resources. When a large media corporation buys a struggling newspaper or broadcasting station, it can invest in improving the product. In the news business this may mean new presses for a crisper-looking newspaper. Or more experienced reporters may be hired with these additional resources. Big corporations usually have more sophisticated management skills; better managers can produce a better magazine or television broadcast. They can save money that can be put back into the medium to improve its quality.

A big corporation can better fend off an attack by the government, or protect itself from a legal action. There is no question these are important elements. Many small newspapers in America have given up on hard-hitting, investigative reporting because they cannot afford to defend themselves in the case of a lawsuit. And of course a big wealthy corporation is better able to deal with an advertiser who attempts to pressure the medium to make changes in content. When the grocery store pulls its ad out of a small weekly, this can be a catastrophe. If Ford decided to stop advertising on NBC, it would hardly be noticed.

All of the above are true. There are certain virtues to having our mass media controlled by large, powerful media conglomerates and chains. But while size and wealth may be very helpful in reaching these laudable goals, size and wealth in and of themselves do not assure the accomplishment of these ends. There are other requirements. First among these other requirements is the need for the owners to want to do these things. They must care about the products their companies produce, care about the readers and listeners and viewers. Company management must be convinced that it should use its greater resources to make a better newspaper, rather than use the newspaper to simply enhance its revenues. The sophisticated managers must apply cost-cutting measures that don't damage the quality of the news broadcast or the content of the magazine in their effort to show increased revenues and lower costs at the end of the fiscal quarter. Unless there is a will to do these things, to make better newspapers, to defend the First Amendment, it won't happen, no matter how wealthy or how big the corporate owner may be. And that seems to be the rub. Experience suggests that this will be usually lacking, that the people who own 60 newspapers rarely put out a better product than the woman who owns one or two. In many cases the large newspaper chain puts out an inferior product. There are, most will acknowledge, good things that can result from this changing profile of media ownership and control, but these good things don't happen automatically.

There are many more potential negative consequences, however. The first is obvious and has been alluded to more than once. With fewer and fewer owners, there is less diversity of ownership of the mass media. Diversity runs strongly through our public ethos in the United States. We believe that the more people who can vote, the better. Hence we have many laws that guarantee voting rights. Our free market enterprise is pegged to the idea that if someone makes a better product or sells for a lower price, this person must have access to the marketplace. Similarly, diversity is important in the development of political thought. In 1919 Justice Oliver Wendell Holmes wrote that "the best test of truth is the power of an idea to get itself accepted in the competition of the market." In 1943 an equally wise jurist, Judge

Learned Hand, wrote that the First Amendment "presupposes that the right conclusions are more likely to be gathered out of a multitude of tongues, than any kind of authoritative selection." Lack of diversity in the mass media seriously threatens the chances of an unorthodox idea even getting into the marketplace, let alone being accepted. And when 23 large corporations control most of the mass media that serve nearly 250 million people, this is hardly a multitude of tongues.

There is a clear threat of censorship of ideas and information when so few control most of the mainstream mass media in a nation. And when these few tend to share the same values, this threat is exacerbated. Few critics of American mass media suggest that the large corporate owners of the press are sinister or evil, that they wish to brainwash Americans with an alien philosophy. Surely there are instances in which corporations have sought to squelch the news. Bagdikian reports that Mark Dowie, an investigative reporter who discovered that the Ford Motor Company had knowingly produced the Pinto model automobile with a highly dangerous gas tank had a very difficult time finding a publisher for his book. Dowie documented in his book that Ford officials determined that in the long run it would be cheaper to pay off victims who were injured because of misplaced fuel tanks than to make the needed manufacturing changes. The book was offered first to Simon & Schuster, which is owned by the large corporation called Paramount Communication Co. It was turned down by the publisher, according to Bagdikian, because the story about Ford made all corporations look bad.

Of course many of the major corporations that own mass media have extensive holdings in other areas as well. In Alaska in 1989 Veco International, the company hired by Exxon to clean up the oil spill in Prince Edward Sound, was extremely unhappy over press coverage of the work it was doing. So it bought Alaska's second largest daily newspaper, the *Anchorage Times*. The company promised fair coverage of all important matters, including the oil spill cleanup. For another example: General Electric owns NBC. GE is also one of the nation's leading defense contractors. What if reporters for NBC were to discover that GE is cheating the government? Would this story be reported? More importantly, would the people believe what NBC news said about GE? A news medium must be a little like Caesar's wife; it must not only be virtuous, it must be perceived as being virtuous.

There is a greater threat of censorship, however. And this is that the commercial interests of the corporation will simply get in the way of the transmission of news and information. The corporation will put its business interests first and make decisions about the publication or broadcast of news and information based on criteria related to profit and loss and not public interest and societal good. In 1988 a group of musicians called Artists United Against Apartheid presented a concert in London to "Free Nelson Mandela," a black South African anti-apartheid leader who was jailed for life in 1964. (Mandela was released in 1990.) The concert was televised to 60 nations; the music was interspersed with political commentary by the performers about the racial injustices in South Africa. Viewers in the United States, however, did not hear most of the political commentary. The Fox Television Network and Westwood One, the companies that transmitted the concert throughout the United States, replaced the political commentary with celebrity gossip and chatter. It wasn't that these corporations didn't approve of the sentiments expressed by the musicians and wanted to censor them. They simply didn't want any serious discussion to destroy the entertainment value of the concert and reduce the size of the viewing audience.

In the frenzy of buying and selling the needs of the public are often lost. In an article in the *Gannett Center Journal* Richard McDonald, director of equity research at First Boston, describes the new media owners as either "monsters" or "builders." Builders invest in mass media to create something that will surely be profitable, but something that will last, something that will produce a useful commodity for the audience. Monsters, on the other hand, treat mass media properties simply as investments. Get in, make as much money as possible, and get out. Frank Munsey, a wealthy financier and media baron of the late nineteenth century might have been the first "monster." He bought single newspapers; he bought chains of newspapers. If they became unprofitable, he killed them. The obituaries of the *New York Star,* the *Philadelphia Evening Times,* and many others were written with Mr. Munsey's pen. He was responsible for the merger of the *New York Herald* and the *New York Tribune,* two revered publications founded in the first half of the nineteenth century. When Munsey died, Kansas editor William Allen White wrote,

> Frank Munsey contributed to the journalism of his day the talent of a meatpacker, the morals of a money changer, and the manners of an undertaker. He and his kind have succeeded in transforming a once-noble profession into an eight percent security. May he rest in trust.

The term "monster" certainly fits Australian Rupert Murdoch who has bought and sold billions of dollars worth of American mass media. He purchased and sold both the *Chicago Sun-Times* and the *New York Post,* and when he sold both papers (for considerably more than he paid) these two newspapers were in shambles. Murdoch bought *TV Guide* from Walter Annenberg for $3 billion and immediately changed the publication from one that often took a hard, close look at the television industry, warts and all, to a publication that celebrates the often vapid content of network television, including his own Fox Network.

Trafficking in media properties is harmful to the public in many ways. The quality of the newspaper or broadcasting station obviously suffers. Owners will try to increase the value of the property by making it more profitable. This is done by cutting costs and increasing advertising rates. As the cash flow increases and expenses decrease, the value of the property to the next buyer is enhanced. Murdoch bought the *Chicago Sun-Times* in 1984 for $100 million. He sold it two years later for $145 million. In the early 1980s Metromedia bought television station WCVB in Boston for $220 million. Three years later the station was sold to the Hearst Corporation for $450 million.

The credibility of newspapers and broadcasting properties that change hands often is surely hurt. And without credibility, even the best newspaper or television news operation has little chance to succeed. Quickly changing faces on the screen, different bylines in the newspapers—the public appreciates stability; they like to know who is bringing them the news.

Finally, the buyers and sellers of many of these media properties, the ones who get in quick and get out quick, have no affinity whatsoever for the communities served by their newspapers or magazines or broadcasting stations. They don't live there, their children don't go to school there. They don't serve this community well while they are media owners, and they really have no regard to whom they sell these properties. The high bidder will win almost every time. And when the high bidder wins, very often the public loses.

Ben Bagdikian, who has documented these problems better than anyone, has written that the difficulty is not one of universal evil among corporations and their leaders. There is, in the output of the corporations that control most of our mass media, a rich mixture of news and ideas, Bagdikian said. But there are also limits, limits that do not exist in other democratic countries with private media systems. "Many of the corporations claim to permit greater freedom to the journalists, producers and writers they employ. Some do grant great freedom. But when their most sensitive economic interests are at stake, the parent corporations seldom refrain from using their power over public information," Bagdikian concluded.

One way to point out some of the implications of the concentration of ownership is to look specifically at two problems endemic to the newspaper industry—chain ownership and monopoly newspapers.

## ■ Newspaper Chains

The American daily newspaper industry is dominated by chain-owned newspapers. Chains own about 75 percent of all American dailies, and, because chains tend to be more interested in medium-sized to larger newspapers, they control 85 percent of

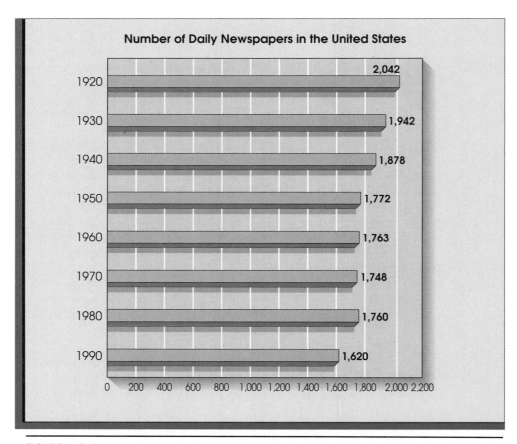

FIGURE 4-2 The number of daily newspapers in the United States has shrunk by 20 percent in the past 70 years, while the U.S. population has increased by more than 125 percent.

daily newspaper circulation. This contrasts greatly with the situation in 1900 when there were 2,042 daily newspapers and 2,022 daily newspaper owners. Gannett is the largest chain, in terms of number of newspapers owned and in terms of daily circulation. It owns about 90 newspapers (this changes frequently) and prints about 7 million of the 63 million copies of newspapers published daily. Other large chains are Knight-Ridder, Newhouse, Scripps-Howard, Thomson, Hearst, Capital Cities, and News America. (See figure 4-2.)

There are some excellent newspaper chains: those small chains operated by the New York Times Company, the Washington Post, and the Los Angeles Times-Mirror Company are just three examples. And there are some awful newspaper chains as well. Most newspaper critics would single out the chains owned by Thomson, Donrey, Lesher and News America for this dubious distinction.

Chains have the capacity to perform important services for both the newspaper industry and for newspaper readers. When a chain purchases a dying newspaper and brings it to life by infusing new money and talent into it, the chain serves both that community and the industry. A chain is capable of using its vast resources to make a better newspaper. Chain newspapers can have regional, national and even international news bureaus. They can support investigative reporting projects by spreading the costs of these expensive ventures over many newspapers. They can buy the most modern publishing equipment and thus lower costs, and these savings can be passed on to advertisers and readers. They can do all these things.

But chain ownership, regardless of the good or bad deeds of the owners, automatically has negative implications as well. Two independently owned newspapers provide greater diversity of ownership than two newspapers owned by the same chain. And diversity is an important value in our society, as we have noted. A chain owner is an absentee owner. He or she does not reside in the community in which the newspaper is published, does not face its problems, does not have to deal with the failings of its government. The children of the chain owner do not attend local schools or play in local parks. The owner of the newspaper must pay taxes in the community but does not gain the full advantage of those taxes. Hence a call by government to raise taxes is often viewed from a hostile position. Some newspaper chains give their newspaper managers or publishers extraordinary leeway, but even in those cases it is very likely that the chain owner will hire managers who share his or her values. There is usually a similarity of thinking.

Beyond those inevitable negative implications are a long list of possible problems that accrue. These are not the result of chain ownership per se. They are instead the result of the fact that chain newspaper owners tend to be more oriented toward earning a profit than public service.

Rarely is a community with a chain-owned newspaper or broadcasting station rewarded because of the strong economic position of the medium's owner. The money that is made in one town is most often invested in another community when the chain adds a new link. After studying the concentration of media ownership in Canada for more than a year, a special subcommittee of the Canadian Senate concluded:

> The general pattern, we regret to say, is of newspapers and broadcasting stations that are pulling the maximum out of their communities and giving back the minimum in return. That is what, in contemporary parlance, is called a rip-off.

A chain-owned newspaper or broadcasting station has the economic resources to bring to the community stronger news coverage and aggressive community leadership. Yet that happens rarely. Chain-owned newspapers tend to have less editorial vigor, according to a study by Ralph Thrift reported in *Journalism Quarterly*. Thrift studied the editorial pages of 24 West Coast dailies for a 15 year period, 1960 to 1975. Sixteen of these newspapers were purchased by chains during that 15 year period. Editorial page vigor—defined as the publication of argumentative editorials on controversial matters—declined in the newspapers that were bought by the chains. There was little change in the newspapers that remained independent. Thrift concluded that the chain ownership had a serious impact on the editorial quality of the newspapers he studied. "And certainly," he noted, "the impact is not helpful to readers who seek guidance on local matters when they turn to the editorial pages of their daily newspaper."

One need not look far for possible explanations for the results uncovered by Thrift. Even a chain that permits local editorial autonomy will, like Gannett, require a positive profit picture. A newspaper or broadcasting station that takes a strong stand on a controversial issue could alienate advertisers, which could result in a loss of revenue. When profitmaking is the prime motivation, it is best to publish a safe, noncontroversial product. Like food from the franchised food operations, chain-owned newspapers and broadcasting stations are rarely very spicy.

Ben Bagdikian argues that chain-owned newspapers also provide readers with less news. Studies show, the author of *Media Monopoly* asserts, that chain-owned papers give readers 7 percent less news overall and 23 percent less hard news. Again, there is a handy explanation. Profits can be increased by cutting expenses as well as increasing income. Two things normally happen when a chain buys a newspaper; advertising rates go up and the editorial staff is cut. John C. Bosterna reported in *Journalism Quarterly* in 1988 that the Gannett newspaper chain charges 55 percent more for national advertising space than comparable non-Gannett newspapers. Fewer reporters produce less news. Replacing local news are generic soft news features that have become so common today; garden columns, self-image stories, diet plans, medical oddities, and the like. The chain can buy these at a reduced cost for all its newspapers. And none of it will offend advertisers.

Those in the industry often say that the critics of newspapers chains—usually teachers and professors, journalists, and former journalists—are off base in their criticisms because they are outside the industry, or at least the business side of the industry. And that is sometimes a valid argument. The criticism that follows, however, is not from an outsider. These are the words of the late C. K. McClatchy, taken from a speech presented in January of 1988:

> Independently owned newspapers have special advantages. In most circumstances, all things being equal, I believe local ownership generally serves the local community well. A different equation exists between a newspaper and the community when it is chain owned. . . . I thought Jim Ottaway Jr., a senior vice president of Dow Jones, made some perceptive comments about the growing concentration of ownership in a speech early last year. He said the rampant buying and selling of papers has tended to "reduce the quality, slow the growth and threaten the future of many papers." He also said he sees the profit motive becoming dominant over the search for truth, editorial quality and public service. . . . To make a gross generalization, one can say that good newspapers are almost always run by good newspaper people; they are almost never run by good bankers or good accountants. . . . I fear the day when newspaper people are no longer in charge of newspapers.

C.K. McClatchy was editor and chairman of the board of the McClatchy chain of newspapers.

## Local Monopolies

In 1920 nearly 700 American cities had two or more separately owned, competitive daily newspapers. By 1953 this number had shrunk to 51. Today, only 19 cities have commercially competitive daily newspapers. All the rest have one newspaper, two newspapers owned by the same company, or two newspapers in a joint operating agreement or using shared printing facilities. Newspapers are continuing to die each year. During 1989 the nation lost a total of 20 dailies. Included among the casualties was the *Los Angeles Herald-Examiner* which just closed its doors and left the *Los Angeles Times* as the only newspaper in that city. Newspapers in Wilmington, Del.; Lewiston, Maine; Jackson, Miss.; Worchester, Mass.; Raleigh, N.C., and four other cities merged to leave these cities with just one daily newspaper. Other dailies became weeklies. In 1990 there was a net loss of nine daily newspapers. Nine new papers started, but two of these failed before the year ended. Three others, including the *St. Louis Sun,* suspended operations; eight merged with other daily newspapers; and five became weekly publications. If we look at the world capitals like London, Paris, Rome, Tokyo, and Moscow, each of these cities is served by anywhere from nine to 18 different newspapers. Washington D.C. has two, and one of the two, the *Washington Times* is owned by the Unification Church (the Moonies) and would not still exist if it had to show a profit. Ninety-eight percent of American cities have but one daily newspaper. This means the newspaper business is in bad shape, right? Wrong. The industry is very healthy, indeed vigorous.

But American daily newspapers have been dying at an alarming rate since the First World War. They have been afflicted by high labor costs in the mechanical end of publishing, not in the newsroom. Television drew away some readers. There has been a certain amount of mismanagement and greed. The quality of the product has slipped noticeably. American lifestyles have changed. All of these have contributed to the demise of daily newspapers. But interestingly, the demise of competition between newspapers is primarily the result of another force—the habits of newspaper advertisers. Let's paint a simplified picture of an urban community in 1935. Our town has three daily newspapers and a handful of community weekly newspapers to serve the 150,000 residents. It is also the home of dozens and dozens of small, independent businesses. There are 15 different independently owned hardware stores all across the town. There are similar numbers of independently owned grocery stores, drug stores, variety stores and clothing stores, each serving the section of the community in which they are located. Advertisements by these stores are placed in the daily newspaper that best serves the local neighborhood as well as the community weekly.

A big change takes place in the postwar years. Chain stores move into the community and buy up most of the hardware stores, grocery stores, drug stores, and clothing stores. Each store in the chain is intended to serve a specific neighborhood, just as the independent stores did. But all the stores in the chain sell identical merchandise, have identical sales, provide identical services. So a single advertisement can convey all information for the chain store; there is no need to have a different advertisement for each store.

The owner of the chain of stores faces a choice when deciding where to publish that ad. The owner could place the same ad in all daily and weekly papers. All the newspapers carried some advertising for the independent stores. But that doesn't make much sense for a chain of stores. There will be tremendous duplication. Almost everyone who subscribes to a weekly paper also subscribes to a daily newspaper. These readers would receive duplicate copies of the ad. So the advertisement doesn't go into the weekly newspapers. There is also probably a tremendous amount of overlap in the circulation of the three daily newspapers as well. There is strong pressure on the chain store operator—who wants to keep costs low so prices can remain low—to save money. So the chain store ad is published in only one or two of the three daily newspapers, the ones with the highest circulation. The chain store supplements this with some direct mail promotions to reach people who aren't newspaper subscribers. The advertiser reaches almost everyone in town, but at a considerable savings. This strategy first kills the community weekly press since the neighborhood stores—formerly independent, now chain-owned—represent the economic base upon which the newspaper must depend.

As the advertisers tend to favor one of the dailies over the other, this increases the revenue for that daily. The money can be used to improve the newspaper, and more readers will be attracted. As circulation goes up, the cost to the advertiser to reach 1,000 readers goes down even farther. Soon, other advertisers desert the weaker daily newspapers. At this point, the economics of publishing newspapers kicks in and causes more problems for the smaller newspaper or newspapers. As newspaper analyst John Morton points out, the cost to produce the first copy of a newspaper is usually the same for all the daily newspapers in the same market. For a newspaper of about 100,000 circulation, let's assume that cost is $50,000 for a 50-page newspaper. For a competing newspaper with a circulation of 60,000, the same $1,000 per page cost applies, $50,000 for a 50-page newspaper. If we spread the first copy costs (which include production, editorial, advertising sales, circulation sales, and distribution) over the total number of subscribers, we can see that the production costs for the larger newspaper are about 50 cents per copy, and about 83 cents per copy for the smaller newspaper. So costs, on a per-copy basis, are higher for the smaller newspaper.

But revenues are lower for the smaller newspaper as well, as Morton points out in the *Washington Journalism Review*. If the larger paper (100,000 circulation) charges an average of $1,600 per page of advertising and publishes a 50-page paper with 60 percent advertising, it will collect $48,000 per edition. Morton then adds in $15,000 in circulation revenues for a total of $63,000 in revenue per issue, or 63 cents per copy, a copy that costs 50 cents to produce. The smaller paper must charge less for advertising because it reaches fewer readers, and advertising rates are based on the cost of reaching 1,000 readers. If it matches the cost per thousand rate of the larger paper, $16, it can only charge $960 per page. This will generate only $28,800 in advertising. Add in $9,000 for circulation and the total is $37,800, or 63 cents per copy on a newspaper that costs 83 cents to produce. This is a big loss. The smaller newspaper can reduce its costs by cheapening its content, but this will undoubtedly mean a loss of more readers, since both newspapers cost the reader the same to buy. Or the smaller newspaper can increase its advertising rates, which will drive some advertisers to the larger paper, and this will not increase revenues. This is why most towns can support only one newspaper once advertisers decide to give primary support to one of the two or three daily newspapers.

In their rush to support the larger newspaper, the advertisers really act like lemmings as they push their way to be the first to fall to their death over the edge of a cliff. For when the weeklies are gone, when the other dailies are gone, the advertiser must live with a monopoly newspaper which can set its advertising rates at almost any level it chooses. No one profits but the owner of the larger newspaper when this happens. The community loses the advantages of competitive journalism; the advertisers lose the advantage of competing advertising media. And even the winning paper can suffer in the end as the advertisers—frustrated with high advertising rates—seek substitute means of reaching potential customers through hand-delivered or postal-delivered circulars. Money—the desire to make more of it—builds media empires; the desire to save as much as possible causes unhealthy monopolies.

Many people argue that the implications of a monopoly newspaper in a community are not serious. Newspaper readers have access to a wide range of newspapers in most communities, papers like the national edition of *The New York Times,* and *USA Today.* And there are radio and television stations for both news and local advertising. And of course there is the single newspaper.

Our economic system is based on the principle that competition breeds competence. In those few areas where society must tolerate a monopoly, government regulations insure public service. Newspapers are not regulated, and probably can't be considering the First Amendment. There is no assurance that the single daily will do a good job covering local news. And radio and television are not equipped to provide comprehensive local news coverage. Readers can find out what is happening in the nation and the world from the out-of-town newspapers. But there is simply no substitute for a daily newspaper for local news.

There is nothing to compel a newspaper to publish any advertisement it doesn't want to publish. Many newspapers refuse to carry advertising for adult-rated movies. In Seattle in 1990 the *Seattle Times* refused to carry advertising for a new consumer **videotex** data base system called Prodigy. The newspaper has its own fledgling service and simply did not want any competition. Radio and television do provide an advertising outlet. But television is too expensive for many small advertisers and simply does not lend itself to the kind of display advertising used by many merchants, such as grocery stores or retail record outlets. Radio audiences are so fragmented that a merchant would have to buy advertising on many stations to reach the readership of a typical daily paper. While in theory there may be no monopoly with but a single newspaper in a community, for many, in practice, there is a monopoly.

## ☐ Structural Impact

We have talked about the effect of the economic structure on the product, the content of the press. But the requirement that newspapers and magazines and television produce substantial profits to satisfy corporate boards of directors and shareholders has had an impact upon employees as well. Reporters, for example, soon learn that there are only a few publications or broadcasting stations that encourage excellence. If a journalist is lucky or clever or perhaps just restless he or she may gravitate to one of those few publications. If not, the reporter will probably stay where she or he is, growing cynical about the work and learning to live with a kind of sour professional despair. Often both overworked and underpaid, these people hardly make model employees. As one writer noted in the Canadian Senate report on the press, "Often you can see it in their faces. Most city rooms are boneyards of broken dreams. The economics of the industry and the placing of profits ahead of product have made them so. That is the tragedy of practicing journalism in a commercial culture. Unless you are very strong, or very lucky, or very good, it will murder your dreams."

The giant corporatism that has affected (or infected) the mass media is beginning to turn off the audience as well. A study conducted by E. R. Einsiedel and James P. Winter and published in *Journalism Quarterly* revealed that the public is worried about the ownership of the press. Those most concerned are those that tend to use the press the most, people with a higher education and a higher income. "The present study indicates a concern about media concentration and cross-ownership [of media] on the part of the public," the two Syracuse researchers concluded.

For some time it has been evident that people in America have begun to distrust all large impersonal institutions. *The New York Times* associate editor John Oakes noted this trend in a speech he gave recently on the media and the public:

> Although public perceptions that increased concentration of media ownership leads to a loss of diversity and conflict of interest may rest on nothing more substantial than intuition, there is grave risk of dislocation in the relationship between the public and the press, a relationship which is grounded in the constitutional guarantee of a free press. The quality of the product turned out by the conglomerates' publishing and broadcasting arms may be less important in the long run than the loss of public confidence in the press engendered by fears of 'the sinister effect of riches' upon the institution of the press.

Most instances of domestic conflicts during the past three decades—the demonstrations, the riots, the sit-ins, the hassles that generated the bulk of the social anguish in the sixties and seventies—have a single thing in common: they were concerned with people versus institutions. The press may be losing friends for the same reason that government and courts and corporations and schools and other large institutions are losing friends. They are so big they find it very difficult to know how to relate to people. They are viewed as large, impersonal, uncaring institutions.

A great many media owners today say they believe they are mere spectators to the process of social change in America. But they are not. "They control the presentation of the news, and therefore have a vast and perhaps disproportionate say in how society defines itself," one observer noted. The built-in institutional bias of the mass media that tends to favor corporate control of the news, that tends to favor other corporations over people, and relies heavily on revenues from corporate America, could be one reason for the current public disenchantment with the media.

Concentration, monopolization, conglomerization, corporatism—all are words that were really quite foreign to mass communication even 50 years ago. But today they describe a widening segment of American mass media. The view on the horizon gives one cause for some alarm. We see a situation in which there are fewer and fewer companies controlling the mass media in America. We find an economic environment that is not only hospitable to this trend, but actually encourages it. Mass communication companies are getting larger and larger and as they grow they bring to society all the problems inherent in any vast and powerful institution. Our society depends so heavily upon information to function and to govern itself. Yet there seem to be fewer places where we might speak and be heard; there is a growing sameness to what we do hear. The press, which must ultimately depend upon the people of the nation to support the constitutional right of free expression, may be alienating Americans. Are there solutions to the problem?

# REDUCING THE CONCENTRATION

There is no simple solution for reducing the concentration of ownership of the mass media or the effects of this concentration. Some people think the horse is already out of the barn, and it is too late now to close the door. But things can get worse, so efforts at making the situation better are not fruitless. Others place their hope in new technology; forget the old mass media, work toward establishing more diverse control of the mass communication systems. But each new technology is swallowed up by the same companies that owned the old technology, almost before people know it exists. Which way to turn? Here is a short summary of some suggestions offered by many thoughtful persons.

## Simple Ideas

Before a problem can be solved, people must know the problem exists. Few people in America are aware of the growing concentration of ownership of the mass media and the difficulties this concentration may entail for the nation. The press is the one agency that could widely report this matter, but thus far it has failed to cover this story. Simple disclosure of the problem by the press is an initial step that must be undertaken. While newspapers and magazines and broadcasting stations could outline the full dimensions of the concentration of ownership of the press, it is highly unlikely that will occur. But certainly it is not too much to ask for each individual publication or radio station to clearly and frequently announce the names of its owners to the community. When NBC News broadcasts a story about a GE defense contract, viewers should know that NBC is owned by GE. True, this information is available in the library to anyone willing to spend the time looking for it. But this is economic information that should be reported frequently and clearly in the medium itself. Readers and viewers and listeners can come to their own conclusions about problems when they discover that much of their local mass media is owned by corporations located in distant states.

Readers should also ask that publications and broadcasting stations report on their own financial condition a little more often. Business news is in vogue today, and the financial pages of most newspapers are bulging with stories about the profit and loss statements of national and local businesses. Why isn't there a quarterly report on the corporate earnings of the local newspaper or television station? The people who use and buy the mass media in a community should be told exactly how profitable those businesses really are. Such information might suggest to some citizens that the local media could afford to be giving readers and viewers considerably more than they often give.

One more thing newspaper and magazine readers should do—start picking up a bigger portion of the tab for the cost of these publications. Advertisers pay the biggest proportion of the bills for most magazines and for all newspapers. As long as the advertiser is doing this, the advertiser will be the primary constituent of the medium. Readers will begin to have an impact in the board rooms and editorial offices only when they begin providing the largest share of the company's revenue. The common policy of many newspapers of profit first, product second, would be doomed to failure if readers paid three-fourths of the cost of the newspaper. The publisher would be forced to put out a product that pleased the readers.

Disclosure of pertinent economic data and stronger economic support from readers are simple ideas, but they could work to foster important change in the mass media.

## Limits on Ownership

Fewer and fewer people own more and more of America's mass media. This is a theme that has run throughout this chapter. A simple solution, then, seems apparent: limit how many newspapers or broadcasting stations or magazines any one person or corporation can own.

The broadcasting industry has been controlled in this manner for 50 years. The government, through the Federal Communications Commission, has placed absolute limits on the total number of broadcasting properties an individual may own: 12 television stations, 12 AM radio stations, and 12 FM radio stations. (One individual or company can actually own 14 of each category of station if two of the television stations are the weaker UHF variety or at least 50 percent minority owned, and if two of each kind of radio station are at least 50 percent minority owned.) In addition, the government has ruled that no single broadcasting company can own stations that will reach more than 25 percent of the total television and radio audience. These numbers are too high. If the government can constitutionally limit broadcast ownership to 12 of each kind of property, it can constitutionally limit broadcast ownership to three of each kind. And it should do this. There are a great many buyers who would be happy to share the wealth of broadcast ownership, and this could significantly diversify the ownership of radio and television.

The FCC also limits ownership in other ways. No individual or company is permitted to own two television stations or two AM or FM radio stations in the same community. This is called the **duopoly rule.** In 1970 the FCC announced what is called the **one-to-a-customer** rule that prohibits a single individual from owning a TV/AM/FM combination in a broadcast market. The individual must choose between owning an AM/FM combination or a television station. The rules adopted in 1970 were all prospective—they only applied to future licensees. The FCC did not break up any existing three-media combinations, and many still exist.

The FCC also announced that in the future it would not permit newspaper owners to buy a broadcasting property in the same community, and vice-versa. In this case the Commission did dismantle 16 existing newspaper/broadcast combinations in small communities where "there appeared to be a monopoly on the expression of views on issues of public concern."

Having rules is one thing, enforcing them is another. In 1989 the FCC permitted Rupert Murdoch to retain ownership of both television station WFXT in Boston, as well as the *Boston Herald.* Murdoch had fought to keep both, and the regulatory agency supported his request when he agreed to transfer the management of the television station out of his corporate hands and into those of a trust. Murdoch still reaps the profit from the station but has lost day-to-day control. In making this decision, the commission rejected applications from two groups that sought to get the license away from Murdoch and provide a bit more diversity in media ownership in Boston. This is an FCC that still retains strong vestiges of the very pro-business orientation of the Reagan presidential administration. Remember, one of the planks in

Mr. Reagan's political platform was, "Let's get the government off the back of business."

Could similar rules that restrict ownership be applied to the print media, newspapers specifically? Could the government limit the total number of newspapers a single publisher could own? Could it prohibit the ownership of more than a single newspaper in a town by one individual? This is highly unlikely, no matter how desirable it might appear. First, a rule limiting to one the number of newspapers any company might own in a single town would have little impact. More than 95 percent of the towns in America only have one daily newspaper. A limit on the total number of newspapers that might be owned, or a limit on percentage of circulation would clearly run afoul of our contemporary interpretation of the First Amendment. (The Constitution currently treats the printed press and broadcasting quite differently. See Chapter 11.) As will be seen, the current interpretation of the First Amendment frustrates many attempts to control the economic structure of the mass media. The important words in the sentence above are "current interpretation." On its face the First Amendment would seemingly have little impact on laws that regulate the economic structure of the press. The guarantees of free expression were, after all, designed to protect the content of the media—the free flow of information and ideas. But the American press has been very effective in raising this constitutional guarantee as a bar to most attempts to regulate economic aspects of the publishing industry. Some have suggested the industry has tried, and at least partially succeeded, in turning the First Amendment into a piece of trade legislation.

Another kind of limitation on ownership has been proposed as well. Such a rule would bar owners of existing forms of mass media from owning and taking control of new media forms. A good idea perhaps, but clearly closing the barn door after the horse is gone. The heavy investors in the new media—cable, pay cable, video recordings, satellites, videotex—are the leaders in the old media. And again, the contemporary understanding we have of the guarantees of free speech and press would likely block any attempt to institute such regulations. Limits on the ownership of our mass communications systems don't promise to be effective means of restructuring the mass media in America.

More vigorous enforcement or new interpretations of the federal antitrust laws have been suggested as a means of controlling the concentration of ownership. As noted previously, the failure to strongly enforce these laws, coupled with the structural ineffectiveness of the laws, has in fact fostered the growth of concentrated media ownership. Few who are knowledgeable about antitrust laws feel the current laws are capable of controlling the spread of newspaper chains or media conglomerates. It would take a bold new interpretation of these laws by the U.S. Justice Department and American courts to make them effective. Congress could adopt new antitrust legislation, redefining the meaning of competition as it applies to mass media, focusing on the control of information and ideas as well as the concentration of economic power. But Congress could also pass laws to slash its own pay, abolish Political Action Committees (PACS), forbid lobbying, and provide universal health care, housing, and food for all American citizens. All of these things are unlikely. Right now Congress is considered by most to be part of the problem, not part of the solution. Too many members of Congress are either heavy investors in the media business themselves or owe strong political allegiance to the press in their districts, the institutions that help form public opinion. Congress has been reluctant to alter tax laws to make it easier for heirs who want to keep a newspaper or broadcasting station in the family to pay estate taxes.

## ☐ Making Media More Competitive

To this point most of the solutions that have been proposed involve the government taking some kind of action against those into whose hands the media is being concentrated. But many persons suggest a different strategy—that government should try to prevent such concentration by helping weaker newspapers and magazines and broadcasting stations.

Paying direct cash subsidies to competitively weaker newspapers, magazines, or broadcasting stations has been suggested as a means of making continued concentration of ownership less likely. Financially weak publications and broadcasting stations become easy prey for chains seeking to add to their holdings. Subsidies might provide just the margin of difference needed to keep such publications and broadcasting stations independent and alive.

This proposal sounds sinister and outrageous at first glance, especially if applied in a democracy like our own where the press is supposed to be the watchdog of government, not the beneficiary of government support. But the scheme has worked in nations in Europe for many years. Weaker daily newspapers in Scandinavia often receive direct government grants, and many papers would not be publishing today without them. And on any objective measure, the Scandinavian press is no less free than its counterpart in the United States. A law could easily be framed providing a government subsidy to a newspaper whose percentage of circulation in the market fell below 35 percent, for example. Or the law could be based on percentage of advertising revenues in the market rather than circulation. Such a subsidy could go a long way to revitalize the community weekly press which has been seriously hurt by monopoly daily newspapers and the advertising strategies of chain stores.

Government has given various indirect subsidies to the press in the United States for many years, but this money has been distributed to newspapers without regard to need and has often helped the rich get richer. Local governments are required to publish legal notices in local newspapers, and the newspaper is paid to publish such material. More often than not the newspaper selected to publish such notices is one that politically supports the government in power. And second class mailing rates for newspapers and magazines, rates far lower than the first class rate, have amounted to an indirect subsidy as well. American broadcasters used the valuable airwaves in this nation for years without paying any fee at all. Now fees for use of such frequencies are minimal. This has amounted to a subsidy.

Such indirect subsidies could be used more selectively to strengthen weaker newspapers and magazines. For example, postal rates could be lowered substantially for magazines and newspapers that carry a low percentage of advertising, but raised substantially for magazines that carry a high percentage of advertising. The financially weakest newspaper could automatically be assigned the job of publishing legal notices. Licensing fees for broadcasters could be based on station revenues; the stronger stations would pay a substantially higher fee. The levying of a progressive tax on advertising has even been suggested. That is, a newspaper that carries 75 percent advertising would not only pay more taxes because it earns more revenue than a newspaper that carries only 55 percent advertising, it would pay a higher tax rate. It would be penalized for carrying so much advertising. Such a financial penalty might force the newspaper to raise its advertising rates and that could push some of the advertising to the weaker newspaper. At least that is the theory.

Such subsidies seem almost un-American when first considered, but could have a strong impact on helping to strengthen the diversity of ownership in the American press. The alternative, continued and growing concentration of ownership of the mass media, is equally un-American, for it strikes at the foundation of our political system that permits us to function as a democracy.

## ☐ Providing Access to the Press

Many persons correctly point out that there is really no shortage of mass media in the United States; the problem is that there are too few media owners. The wide array of publications, broadcasting stations, and the like tend to be owned by the same people or the same kind of people—the wealthy, the business oriented. Diversity of ideas could be restored to the political system if all persons had the opportunity to use existing mass media to be heard and seen, to explain their ideas, to support their causes. Such a notion has the shorthand name: **access to the media.**

Law professor Jerome Barron has vigorously argued since the mid-1960s that the First Amendment was intended to protect the diversity of viewpoints and the right of all persons to speak and be heard. It was not intended as trade legislation to protect the owners of the press in America. "It is time," Barron wrote in the *Harvard Law Review,* "to focus our attention not only on the protection of ideas already published but on making sure the divergent opinions are actually able to secure expression in the first place." The press has an obligation to provide space on a nondiscriminatory basis for representative groups in the community, according to Barron.

Critics of the Barron point of view have at least two complaints. The idea is too vague, they argue. What are the representative groups? Where does the press find the space? How much space? How often should such space be allotted? Who will make certain the press lives up to its obligation? Barron replies that it is the government that must force the press to provide the space for legitimate requests. And that gives rise to the second complaint. It strikes at the heart of our concept of freedom of the press to permit the government to force any editor to publish something that he or she chooses to leave out. In 1974 the Supreme Court of the United States sided with the critics.

The *Miami Herald* challenged a Florida law that required the newspaper to provide space for a reply prepared by a political candidate whom the newspaper had attacked in an editorial. The Florida Supreme Court ruled that the law was a valid exercise of state power. The election of public officials is the basic precept upon which our democracy rests, the court said. While there is a right for the press to publish without government restraint, "we emphasize that there is a correlative responsibility that the public be fully informed," the court added. Getting important information to voters is a vital part of the democratic system. The law does not interfere with what a newspaper can publish—it merely requires that in special circumstances additional information must be published. The court added in the unsigned opinion:

> Freedom of expression was retained by the people through the First Amendment for all the people and not merely for a select few. The First Amendment did not create a privileged class which through a monopoly of instruments of the newspaper industry would be able to deny to the people the freedom of expression which the First Amendment guarantees.

But the decision of the high court of Florida was overturned by a decision of the high court of the nation. A unanimous Supreme Court ruled that "A responsible press is an undoubtedly desirable goal, but press responsibility is not mandated by the Constitution and like many other virtues it cannot be legislated." Chief Justice Warren Burger said that the Florida law did penalize the press because the publication of replies by political candidates took space and time. And this interferes with the function of editors. "The choice of the material to go into a newspaper," wrote the Chief Justice, "and the decisions made as to limitations on the size of the paper, and content and treatment of public officials—whether fair or unfair—constitutes the exercise of editorial control and judgment."

The ruling in this case, *Miami Herald* v. *Tornillo* largely ended the serious consideration of the public right of access to the press. But it did not end the debate over whether such access is needed or is desirable. And other notions of how more people might find a voice in the press have been explored; in these explorations the press has generally been a willing partner.

Press councils emerged in the sixties and seventies as mechanisms to increase the public voice in decisions made by the managers of the mass media and at the same time permit the editors and broadcast managers to discover what was on the minds of the people in the community. A typical press council is made up of citizens, editors, broadcasters, and sometimes educators. The group meets periodically to discuss problems that community members see in the local press. This enhanced communication gives interested citizens a stronger voice in the development of editorial policy. While the press council will often hear complaints against the media, it has only the power of publicity and cannot sanction the press in any way. But few press councils have been developed. A 1973 survey of 135 newspapers revealed that only 3 percent of those that responded participated in a press council. Nine percent of the remaining respondents reported that members of the newspaper's staff worked with some kind of community advisory board. This was in the heyday of press councils.

A National News Council (NNC) was formed with a large grant from the Twentieth Century Fund in the early seventies. Its purpose was to monitor the national news media such as the wire services, the news magazines, the television networks, and leading newspapers with national circulations. The NNC served primarily as a sounding board for complaints against the media, and for its 11 years of existence remained one of the best-kept secrets in the nation. A majority of print and broadcast editors opposed the idea of such a council. Members of the American Society of Newspaper Editors, for example, voted three to one against the establishment of such a body. Editors of both the *Washington Post* and *The New York Times* announced they would not cooperate with the Council. Other editors criticized their colleagues. Lester Markel, a longtime Sunday editor of *The New York Times,* asked why the press was opposed to such a body. "Because the press, pretending to believe that there is no credibility gap and asserting its near-infallibility, countenances no effective supervision of its operations; it has adopted a holier-than-thou attitude, citing the First Amendment and in addition the Ten Commandments and other less holy scripture," wrote Markel on the Op-Ed page of *The Times.*

Almost 11 years after it was founded the NNC died. During that period it had heard almost 250 complaints against the national press and determined that only about 85 had even partial merit. During its existence the reports of the NNC were published in the *Columbia Journalism Review* and later in the *Quill.* But the mainstream press in America largely ignored the Council, rarely published its findings. Hence its work, even its existence, was hidden from the public. "We were never able to build a public constituency," commented Richard Salant, former CBS news chief and the final president of the group.

Today virtually all press councils have disappeared. Only the Minnesota News Council remains actively functioning. The demise of these useful communication institutions is probably the result of media indifference to the problem and lack of public concern. The cultural environment of the sixties and seventies that spawned the consumer movement, the antiwar movement, and the civil rights movement had disappeared, replaced by a culture more concerned with personal development than societal problems. Public dissatisfaction with the press today seems to be played out more often in courtrooms with lawsuits than through press councils or other nonofficial agencies.

Most newspapers have small "letters to the editor" sections, and a handful of newspapers and broadcasting operations today permit members of the audience to speak their piece via op-ed pages, and "talkback" programs. All these vehicles provide meaningful if limited access to the press and certainly enhance the diversity of ideas in the mass media. Some newspapers employ what are called ombudsmen or reader representatives to hear complaints and make corrections if they are warranted; another limited but positive step toward permitting the audience to gain access to the eyes and ears of the community.

None of the solutions listed above, access to the press, press councils, op-ed pages, and the like, will eliminate the concentration of ownership in the mass media today. But each can reduce one serious, deleterious impact of that concentration—the lessening of the diversity of viewpoints in the press today. A small step but an important one.

The economic structure of the American mass communications industry has a distinct and deleterious impact on the content of the mass media. In its simplest form, mass communication is supposed to be an extension and amplification of the human communication process. The same messages are supposed to be transmitted, only faster and farther. The same people are supposed to be able to communicate. That is not the case. Because the mass media are imbedded in a giant industry, the content of the messages are often changed. And only a handful of persons are permitted to communicate with millions of others.

If Americans are to change this situation, if that is what they want, then action of some sort will be required. The industry will not do this on its own. And this action must begin soon. A U.S. Senate staff report noted the following in the late 1960s.

> The American people do not realize what has happened to them. They are not aware that a communications revolution has occurred. They do not appreciate the tremendous power which the new instruments and new organization of the press place in the hands of a few people. They have not yet understood how far the performance of the press falls short of the requirements of a free society in the world today.

Things are much worse now than in the sixties. But while people are undoubtedly aware that our communications systems have changed, there is little new awareness of the changing equation of power wrought by the growth in the concentration of press ownership. And the one agency that could best report that story—the press—is likely to remain silent.

## BIBLIOGRAPHY

These are some of the materials that have been helpful in the preparation of this chapter.

Alter, Jonathon. "Era of the Big Blur," *Newsweek,* May 22, 1989.

Anderson, Mary A. "JOA Law May Be a Turning Point," *presstime,* October, 1989.

———. "Ranks of Independent Newspapers Continue to Fade," *presstime,* August, 1987.

Arvidson, Cheryl. "The Price That Broke the Register," *Washington Journalism Review,* April, 1985.

Bagdikian, Ben H. *The Media Monopoly,* (3rd ed.) Boston: Beacon Press, 1991.

Barnouw, Erik. *The Sponsor.* New York: Oxford University Press, 1978.

Busterna, John C. "Daily Newspaper Chains and the Antitrust Laws," 110 *Journalism Monographs,* March, 1989.

———. "National Advertising Pricing: Chain vs. Independent Newspapers," 65 *Journalism Quarterly* 307, Summer, 1988.

Dyk, Timothy B., and Wilkins, William J. "Regulation and Ownership: Washington's Influence on Who Owns the Media," *Gannett Center Journal,* Winter, 1989.

Genovese, Margaret. "JOA," *presstime,* August, 1985.

Hershey, Robert D., Jr. "Time Merger Is Cheered by House Panel," *The New York Times,* March 14, 1989.

"Japan Goes Hollywood," *Newsweek,* October 9, 1989.

Jones, Alex S. "Sale Price Arouses Wonder Over Deal in South Carolina," *The New York Times,* October 9, 1989.

Kessler, Lauren. "Women's Magazines' Coverage of Smoking Related Hazards," 66 *Journalism Quarterly* 316, Summer, 1989.

MacDonald, Richard. " 'Monster' Entrepreneurs and 'Builder' Entrepreneurs," *Gannett Center Journal,* Winter, 1989.

McIntosh, Toby J. "Why the Government Can't Stop Press Mergers," *Columbia Journalism Review,* May/June, 1977.

"Merger Mania: What's Behind All the Sudden Activity?" *Television/Radio Age,* July 8, 1985.

Morton, John. "JOA Update," *Washington Journalism Review,* December, 1985.

———. "Newspapers Are Losing Their Grip," *Washington Journalism Review,* May, 1987.

"Murdoch's Empire," *Newsweek,* August 22, 1988.

"1991 Field Guide to the Electronic Environment," *Channels,* December 3, 1990.

Stein, M.L. "Publisher Pans Peers," *Editor and Publisher,* February 6, 1988.

Steinem, Gloria. "Sex, Lies, and Advertising," *Ms.,* July/August, 1990.

Warner, Charles. "Networks Changing Ties with Affiliates," *Washington Journalism Review,* July/August, 1989.

P A R T

# THE MASS MEDIA

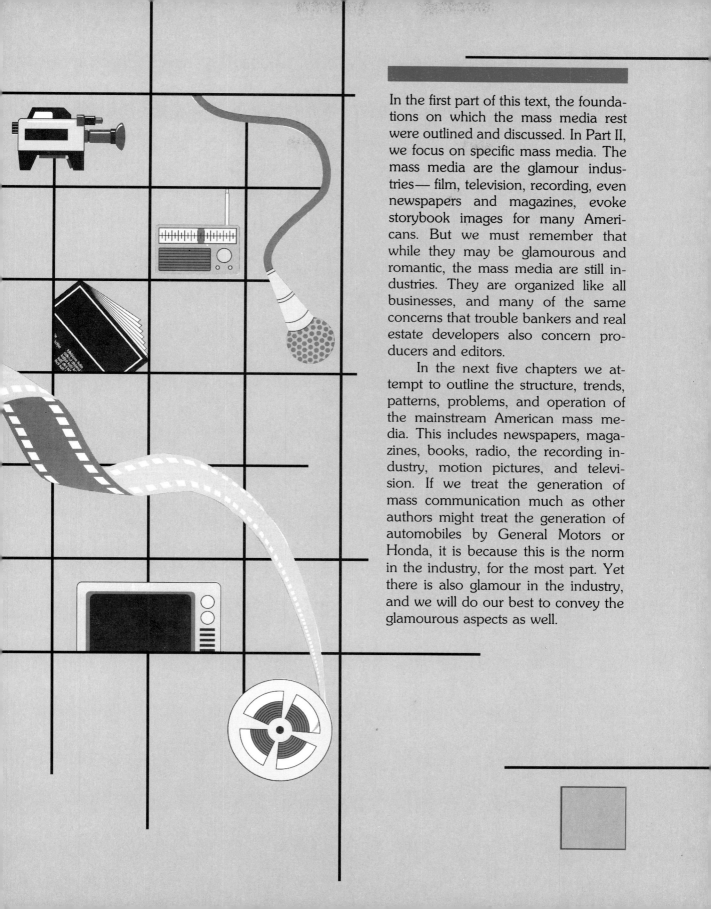

In the first part of this text, the foundations on which the mass media rest were outlined and discussed. In Part II, we focus on specific mass media. The mass media are the glamour industries— film, television, recording, even newspapers and magazines, evoke storybook images for many Americans. But we must remember that while they may be glamourous and romantic, the mass media are still industries. They are organized like all businesses, and many of the same concerns that trouble bankers and real estate developers also concern producers and editors.

In the next five chapters we attempt to outline the structure, trends, patterns, problems, and operation of the mainstream American mass media. This includes newspapers, magazines, books, radio, the recording industry, motion pictures, and television. If we treat the generation of mass communication much as other authors might treat the generation of automobiles by General Motors or Honda, it is because this is the norm in the industry, for the most part. Yet there is also glamour in the industry, and we will do our best to convey the glamourous aspects as well.

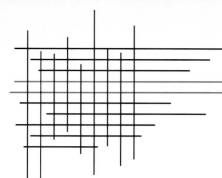

# CHAPTER 5

# NEWSPAPERS

*I*t is easy to forget the newspaper when contemplating this electronic age of mass media which has descended upon us. Printing presses have been around for five centuries; this is truly a mature technology. Newspapers are a grey phenomenon; they contain little of the sparkling living color and glitter of television, film, or even magazines. And nothing moves on the newspaper page, no one talks to the reader. The newspaper must surely appear to be a sterile object to a generation poised near the brink of the twenty-first century.

Yet newspapers today are the dominant mass medium when measured against several important criteria. Daily newspapers earn more advertising revenue than any other mass medium—almost as much as television and radio combined. Newspapers employ more persons than any other mass medium. Sixty-three million daily newspapers are sold each day; an additional 55 million weekly or semiweekly or triweekly newspapers are sold each week. Finally, newspapers, more than any other mass medium, provide the people of the nation with the news and information that is essential if we are to continue to successfully operate our representative democracy.

But the newspaper industry is not without its problems, despite its dominance in many areas. The number of daily newspapers published keeps falling each year. This means that more and more communities have but a single daily newspaper, not a good omen in a nation in which competition is presumed to serve the best interests of the consumer. The number of people who read a newspaper each year fails to keep pace with overall population growth. And there is a new battle for the advertiser's dollar in many communities, a battle that some newspapers are losing and one in which many others are barely holding their own.

So the newspaper industry presents us with a paradoxical picture: dominant, successful, and strong on the one hand; shrinking, vulnerable, and troubled on the other. This chapter will explore both the newspaper and the newspaper business. The shape and size of the industry will be outlined, circulation trends plotted, and the readers of daily newspapers will be examined. The newspaper business, and its successes and failures, will be discussed. How a newspaper is put together will be explained. The chapter will also outline the sources of the material published in a newspaper. The world of electronic publishing will be examined and the chapter will conclude with an examination of some of the more serious problems facing contemporary newspapers and, at least indirectly, newspaper readers.

# THE NEWSPAPER INDUSTRY

A newspaper is a publication that carries information on newsprint (a particularly cheap grade of paper made of wood pulp) for a general audience, and is issued daily, on Sundays, or weekly, according to author and journalism professor Ben Bagdikian. This is as good a definition as there is. There are approximately 9,250 such publications in the United States, according to the IMS Ayer Directory of Publications. About 1,610 of these are issued daily; the remainder appear once, twice, or even three times each week. There are also thousands of "newsless" publications called shoppers or throwaways that appear weekly or semiweekly, but since these periodicals do not carry news they do not qualify as newspapers.

People tend to think of a big city daily newspaper when the word newspaper is used, but actually most newspapers are not like that at all. Look at Los Angeles, for example. At the center of the media array is the 1,200,000 circulation *Los Angeles Times.* But there are four other daily newspapers published in the city: two financial publications, the San Fernando-oriented *Los Angeles Daily News,* and *La Opinion,* a Spanish-language newspaper. There are ten dailies published in Los Angeles county, and almost a dozen more in nearby Ventura, Orange, and Riverside counties. Editions of the *Wall Street Journal,* the *Christian Science Monitor,* and *USA Today* are also published locally. Finally, there are almost 300 weekly or semiweekly newspapers, including ethnic and religious publications, published in the Los Angeles area. Los Angeles is obviously not a typical American city, but the point is still valid. Most

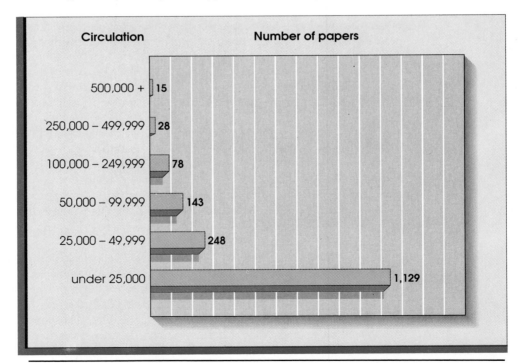

FIGURE 5-1 Number of U.S. daily newspapers arrayed by circulation. Metropolitan dailies with huge circulations are not typical of American newspapers.

newspapers are not big city dailies. Figure 5-1 presents a recent tally of American newspapers arrayed by size. As can be readily seen, most American daily newspapers are small community papers that circulate to fewer than 25,000 persons each day.

## ☐ African-American Newspapers

While by definition newspapers are generally regarded as being published for and circulated to a broad, undifferentiated audience, there are many newspapers in the United States circulated primarily to members of minority communities. There are

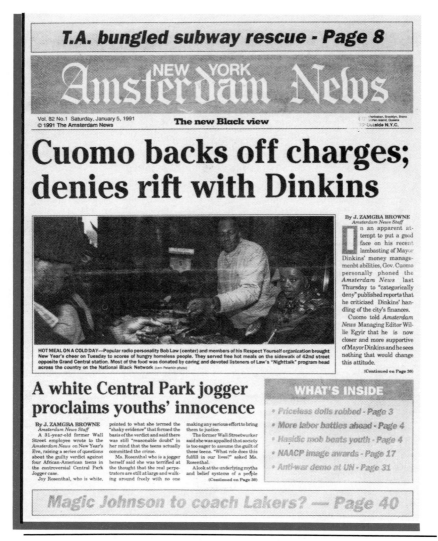

New York's *Amsterdam News* is one of many newspapers published by and for the black community. These newspapers are designed to provide news and analysis that reflect black concerns and ideals. *(Amsterdam News)*

about 300 newspapers owned by blacks and circulated predominantly in the black community. Because many black newspapers are small, and most do not have an audited circulation, it is difficult to determine exactly how many such papers exist. There are, however, 200 members of the National Newspaper Publishers Association, a trade organization that represents black newspapers in the United States. There are at least three daily papers; the rest are published weekly or biweekly. The dailies include the *Chicago Daily Defender,* the *Atlanta Daily World,* and the *New York Daily Challenge.* Many of these papers have a circulation of only a few thousand copies or less, like the *Savannah Tribune* in Savannah, Ga., with a circulation of about 1,500. Others, like the *Amsterdam News* in New York City are much larger. But no black newspaper has a circulation of more than 150,000.

The black press in America began as a cause-oriented press, fighting the war against slavery. After the Civil War, the black press tended to melt away. It emerged at the end of the century as a mirror of its white counterpart press; community-oriented, publishing the news, information, and other material sought by black readers. And this is how it remained until the fight for black civil rights erupted in mid-century. Many black newspapers took on a new militancy and attained a greater popularity. The *Black Panther* newspaper, the organ of the militant Black Panther party, once legitimately claimed a circulation of 100,000. Despite the incomplete gains of the civil rights struggle of the sixties and seventies and the racism that still infects many aspects of United States society, the black movement press has largely disappeared. And some think the black press as a whole has suffered as well. "The popularity of the black press has declined," wrote Henry G. La Brie III in 1986. "Some believe that it is obsolete, and others argue that the black press limits progress for blacks in the traditional press," La Brie added.

But others argue that the black press continues to play an important role. The weekly community press is the heart and soul of the black press in America today. These newspapers provide the routine coverage of the black community—marriage, deaths, church and school news, club and fraternal information—that the white press tends to ignore. The black press also captures the problems, the conflicts, and the concerns within the black community; stories which the white press might cover, but the black press reports from the black perspective.

A typical 20-page black community newspaper might contain two full pages of business news from the community, a full page of church news, another full page devoted to entertainment and social notes, and a generous number of pictures. The old maxim, "names make news," is an important guide to most editors of black newspapers.

## ▢ Hispanic Press

The first Hispanic newspaper published in the United States, *Crepusculo de la Libertad* was founded in 1835, and in some ways the modern history of the Spanish-language press mirrors that of the black press. The Hispanic press grew rapidly in the 1960s and 1970s during the farm workers' strikes and the growth of the Chicano movement. These papers were activist and militant. As the activity in this movement waned, however, the Spanish-language press reverted to its traditional role of community journalism.

Big or small, daily or weekly, Spanish-language newspapers offer regular sections like their English-language counterparts, according to Ana Veciana-Suarez in

*Hispanic Media, USA.* They carry sports, editorials, features, local and national news. National news is provided by the U.S. wire services, AP and UPI, as well as EFE, the Spanish newsgathering service, and Notimex from Mexico. The dailies also carry special sections—women's news or features on food—on a weekly basis. These papers also carry a good deal of community news. "These papers do not shy away from publishing the graduation portrait or the banquet picture. They do not mind running short articles about the neighbor who has excelled in college or the local garden club's annual bazaar," notes Veciana-Suarez. "Such is their lifeblood," she adds.

Spanish-language newspapers also try to relate to their readers information about the Spanish-speaking world outside this nation. Hence, papers in different parts of the United States have a different international emphasis. Those in Texas and California focus most heavily on Mexico, their readers being predominantly of Mexican origin. Papers in Florida focus on Cuba, Nicaragua, and Latin America. In New York, the Spanish-language press carries a broader range of international news, placing emphasis on Puerto Rico and other parts of Central America.

There are at least five large daily Spanish-language newspapers. *La Opinion,*

*La Opinion* is one of five daily Spanish-language newspapers published in the United States. More Spanish-language publications should be forthcoming because Hispanics are the fastest growing minority population in the nation. Many of the Spanish-language papers traditionally have been considered a service to the community; more and more, however, they are being thought of as a good business investment. *(La Opinion)*

which is located in Los Angeles and is now owned by the *Los Angeles Times,* has a circulation of over 100,000. *El Nuevo Herald,* in Miami, has a similar circulation. *Diario Las Americas* is also published in Miami. *El Diario/La Prensa,* published in New York City, until recently was owned by Gannett. It was sold in 1989 to an investor group which is about 40 percent minority owned. The fifth daily, *Noticias del Mundo,* is owned by the Unification Church (the "Moonies") and publishes daily editions in four cities, New York, Los Angeles, Chicago, and San Francisco. Each paper has a common eight-page core daily, but carries local news and advertising as well.

There are a few smaller dailies and many weekly newspapers as well, perhaps close to 100. Again, many do not have audited circulations and start and stop publication as the means exist or disappear. Hispanics make up the fastest-growing minority in the United States, and by 1990 it was estimated their population was close to 25 million, or 10 percent of the total U.S. population. There is a tremendous market for Spanish-language advertising, but much of this money is going toward radio and television, as we will note later in this book. The Spanish-language press is represented by the National Association of Hispanic Publications.

In addition to these Spanish-language newspapers many other U.S. newspapers publish bilingual news sections.

## ▣ Industry Profile

The number of daily newspapers in the United States has been declining, off and on, since about 1914 when 2,600 different papers were published. (Of the 2,600, 2,200 were English-language, general circulation newspapers.) During the 30 years between 1945 and 1975, the number of daily newspapers remained fairly constant at about 1,760. Beginning in the mid-1970s the industry began to suffer another decline in the number of dailies. The American Newspaper Publishers Association reports that only about 1,611 daily newspapers were being published at the beginning of 1991. But noting the loss of 149 newspapers between 1975 and 1991 really doesn't tell the entire story about the success and failures in the industry. Each year many newspapers die, others start publishing, and still others merge. In 1988, for example, 12 new dailies started, but 13 disappeared. Two failed outright, including the *Miami News,* ten merged with other dailies, and one daily converted to weekly publication. Net loss: one newspaper. In 1989, five new dailies started, including the *St. Louis Sun,* the first big city daily to open its doors since the Unification Church began publishing the *Washington Times* in 1982. Publisher Ralph Ingersoll already had a strong base in St. Louis, publishing almost 45 weekly and twice-weekly papers in the St. Louis area. (Seven months later, however, the *Sun* folded, suffering a $40 million loss.) Ten dailies were lost in 1989 through merger with other dailies, 14 converted to weekly publication, and the 118-year old *Los Angeles Herald-Examiner,* circulation 232,000, shut off its printing presses for good. Net loss for 1989: 20 newspapers. The industry recorded a net loss of nine newspapers in 1990.

The failure of the *Herald-Examiner* in 1989 and the *Miami News* in 1988, represents the continued pattern of the failure of big city daily newspapers. The *Chicago Daily News* died in 1978 when its circulation was 320,000. The early 1980s saw the death of the *Washington Star* (cir. 323,000), the *Philadelphia Bulletin* (cir. 400,000) and the *Cleveland Press* (cir. 300,000). The *St. Louis Globe-Democrat* closed its doors in 1986 and since then, in addition to the mergers previously noted, we have

The *St. Louis Sun* was the first metropolitan daily newspaper to begin publication in almost a decade. It lasted seven months before publisher Ralph Ingersoll closed its doors. The paper had suffered a $40 million loss, a graphic example of how it is almost impossible in the late twentieth century to start a competing daily newspaper in a U.S. city.
(*St. Louis Sun*)

seen the merger of two daily papers into one in Minneapolis, Louisville, Ky., Corpus Christi, Tex., Albany, N.Y., Willmington, Del., Jackson, Miss., and Raleigh, N.C. The failure of these large metropolitan newspapers is in no way balanced by the creation of small, community dailies. Shock waves travel throughout the industry as hundreds of persons lose their jobs with each closing.

The net loss of 149 daily newspapers in 16 years is significant and suggests an industry in financial peril. And for a few newspapers this peril is a real threat. But for most daily newspapers economic conditions are good. Not great, but surely acceptable. The economic troubles of the industry as the 1990s begin simply heralds the slight decline of the substantial profit margins most American daily newspapers have enjoyed during the past decade. Publishers will have to begin to accept profit margins of 15 to 16 percent, rather than the 18 to 20 percent the industry has averaged in the past, according to newspaper analyst John Morton. "There are lots of industries that do not see 15-percent margins in the midst of their biggest booms in history," Morton wrote. Typical successful American businesses earn a profit margin from 5 to 7 percent.

The failure of the big city dailies can be explained by the phenomenon described in Chapter 4 in which large retail chain-store advertisers in a particular community tend to favor the larger paper over the smaller, and this ultimately kills the smaller daily papers. (See pp. 101–103.) Advertising revenues were somewhat depressed in all mass media during the late 1980s and early 1990s. Advertising revenues in 1990 were flat, after growing only 4 percent in 1989, compared with 6 percent in 1988 and 9 percent in 1987. And in some major urban areas, daily newspapers suffered an actual decline in advertising lineage. Consumer retailing was in disarray in many communities as many large department store chains, victims of junk-bond supported takeovers in the 1980s, went bankrupt or suffered severe financial trauma. Department stores are major contributors to newspaper retail advertising. Banks and savings and loans also cut back in many areas, given their financial problems. Even healthy businesses began to get skittish as threats of a recession were acknowledged. Downturns in the sale of real estate and automobiles hurt classified advertising sales also. Many newspapers began increasing their per-copy sales prices in order to recoup some of this lost advertising revenue. Perhaps more ominously, many advertisers are reevaluating the daily newspaper as an advertising medium, according to analysts. "Household penetration, reading frequency, and regularity of reading have been declining significantly, particularly among baby boomers and women," according to Lisa Donneson, a newspaper analyst at County NatWest Bank in New York. Without circulation growth, it is unlikely that advertising will increase, Ms. Donneson told the American Newspaper Publishers Association in April of 1990.

But remember, newspaper advertising revenues increased by 120 percent between 1980 and 1990, while the nation's gross national product increased by only about 100 percent. And while the Dow Jones Industrial Average increased by 240 percent during the decade, the Editor and Publisher Index of Newspaper Stocks went up 464 percent. "This is one of the most profitable industries around," wrote David Eisen of the American Newspaper Guild, the newsroom union which has a vested interest in monitoring the economic performance of the industry.

Publishing costs are increasing each year, and this has exacerbated the problem of lagging advertising revenues. The price of newsprint, the basic raw material of newspapers, more than doubled between 1975 and 1990. It cost $685 per ton last year. These price increases hit big newspapers much harder than small newspapers. At a small paper the cost of newsprint accounts for between 16 and 20 percent of total costs. At a large urban daily, newsprint can account for as much as one-third of all costs.

Distribution problems continued to plague urban newspapers, especially those published in the afternoon. Just getting the newspaper from the printing plant—often located in the downtown area—to the reader's home, which tend increasingly to be in the suburbs, can be a serious problem. This is forcing some newspapers to build satellite printing plants in the suburbs—an unexpected and substantial cost. Or, in order to move the newspapers to the carriers on time, establish early morning news and publishing deadlines for afternoon newspapers, something which vexes editors and readers alike. Other newspapers have tossed in the towel and have shifted from an afternoon to an early morning delivery schedule.

Morning newspapers dominated the industry in the late nineteenth and early twentieth centuries, the early years of the mass newspaper. But as the workday shortened for most Americans, there was increased leisure time in the evenings to read an afternoon newspaper and the "P.M.s" became dominant. In 1960 there were almost 1,460 afternoon daily newspapers with a total circulation of about 35 million copies per day. The nation's 312 morning newspapers circulated only 24 million copies. Today the circulation numbers have almost been reversed. There are still more afternoon newspapers, about 1,080 of them. But the circulation for these newspapers totals only about 21 million. More than 550 A.M. newspapers circulate over 40 million copies daily. The distribution problems in urban areas have surely forced some newspapers to switch from afternoon to mornings. The almost empty streets and highways at 2 A.M. make trucking a newspaper to a distant point quite effortless. Also more and more readers seem to prefer a morning newspaper. Fewer people seem willing to spend time relaxing with a newspaper in the evening; there are too many other things to do. The United States has shifted from an industrial economy to a service-based economy, which means people are going to work later and coming home later. This means there is more time to spend with a newspaper in the morning, and less time in the afternoon. And if the evening newspaper has come off the presses at 9 A.M. that day, much of the news will be stale anyway by 6 P.M. that night.

Big city dailies are also under assault from competition. While it is rare that an urban daily has direct, day-to-day competition from another daily carrying the same city name (i.e., the *Chicago Tribune* and the *Chicago Sun-Times),* dailies or even weeklies that once served neighboring communities have entered the battle for suburban readers as the suburbs have stretched to their doorstep. In the Puget Sound region of the Pacific Northwest, for example, the suburbs of Seattle now stretch 30 miles north and south to the cities of Everett and Tacoma. Established dailies in these once "distant" communities now fight the Seattle newspapers for the lucrative readership in those suburbs. In Los Angeles, the face-to-face competition for the *Times,* (the *Herald Examiner)* died in 1989. But the *Daily News* (until recently a weekly) in the affluent suburbs of the San Fernando Valley and the *Orange County Register,* to the southeast of the city, contend strongly for both advertisers and readers in those suburban areas. The free-distribution *Weekly Tab* in the suburbs of Boston is offering stiff competition for the powerful *Boston Globe* —which until recently had claimed the suburbs as its own—and the weaker *Boston Herald.*

In addition to suburban competition, liberal alternative weekly newspapers— many in the mold of the 35-year-old *Village Voice* in New York City—are springing up in cities across America and giving younger readers, who don't tend to favor newspapers generally, a source of information about arts and entertainment, restaurants, and upscale urban news. About 100 of these tabloid-sized weeklies are now published in the U.S. and Canada, according to C. David Rambo in an article in *presstime.* Some publish as many as 180 pages weekly, and most put a premium on good writing, stylish graphics, and feature stories. Both Los Angeles and Seattle have their *Weekly.* Portland has its *Willamette Week.* In the Windy City it's the *Chicago Reader.* And, typical of the newspaper business generally, chains of these alternative weeklies are beginning to appear. *Creative Loafing* was first published in Atlanta in 1972 by Deborah Eason. Her son, Ben Eason, started a second *Loaf* in Charlotte in

TABLE 5.1   Top 20 American Daily Newspapers by Circulation

| Rank | Newspaper | Circulation |
|------|-----------|-------------|
| 1 | *Wall Street Journal* | 1,857,131 |
| 2 | *USA Today* | 1,347,450 |
| 3 | *Los Angeles Times* | 1,196,323 |
| 4 | *The New York Times* | 1,108,447 |
| 5 | *New York Daily News* | 1,097,693 |
| 6 | *Washington Post* | 780,582 |
| 7 | *Chicago Tribune* | 721,067 |
| 8 | *Newsday* | 714,128 |
| 9 | *Detroit Free Press* | 636,182 |
| 10 | *San Francisco Chronicle* | 562,887 |
| 11 | *Chicago Sun-Times* | 527,238 |
| 12 | *Boston Globe* | 521,354 |
| 13 | *Philadelphia Inquirer* | 519,895 |
| 14 | *New York Post* | 510,219 |
| 15 | *Detroit News* | 500,980 |
| 16 | *Newark Star-Ledger* | 476,257 |
| 17 | *Houston Chronicle* | 442,044 |
| 18 | *Cleveland Plain-Dealer* | 428,012 |
| 19 | *Miami Herald* | 414,646 |
| 20 | *The Baltimore Sun* | 410,293 |

All of these newspapers except the *Detroit News* publish morning editions. *Newsday,* the *Houston Chronicle,* and *The Baltimore Sun* publish evening editions as well. (American Newspaper Publishers Association)

1987, and a Tampa Bay *Loaf* in 1988. The publisher of *New Times* in Phoenix now has papers in Denver and Miami as well. And Landmark Communications, one of the nation's larger daily newspaper chains, has alternative weeklies in Norfolk/ Hampton Roads, Va.; Richmond, Va.; Greensboro/Winston-Salem, N.C.; Jacksonville, Fla.; and New Orleans.

These small papers are not serious threats to well-managed, monopoly big city newspapers. But they do draw off some affluent readers ("Basically, we're talking about yuppies," said Ben Eason) and smaller businesses such as clubs, restaurants, and boutiques that can't afford to pay the tab for an ad in a big daily newspaper.

The metropolitan newspapers are attempting to fight back, especially against their suburban competitors. "To preserve their share, big city dailies almost everywhere are relying increasingly on either zoned editions with local news and advertising, or free publications delivered to those who do not subscribe—and sometimes both," wrote Albert Scardino in *The New York Times.* A zoned edition will have a page or pages or even a section of news and advertising aimed at a small community within the larger circulation area. With multiple presses and even multiple printing plants, it is now possible for a newspaper to tailor as few as 10,000 copies out of a total circulation of hundreds of thousands to suit a geographic or demographic neighborhood. The *Miami Herald* offered zoned editions for the first time in 1977 and now produces nine zoned editions each day and 12 neighborhood sections twice a week. It also publishes a zoned shopper (a free publication) for 330,000 non-subscribers. It has 13 zoned editions.

The regional daily-within-a-daily can pay for itself over time with cut-rate ads targeted to localities that represent only a part of the daily newspaper's total press run. The *St. Petersburg Times* publishes ten of these zoned editions seven days a week. "They serve readers in different localities with the PTA, police, and pothole news they need while reclaiming the mom-and-pop advertisers driven off by the full-run ad rates," wrote Eugene Patterson, chairman and chief executive officer of the *Times*. "And these regionals make money," he added.

While the zoned editions often meet the needs of the newspaper and even some advertisers, they usually don't fulfill the need the reader has for a full-fledged newspaper. Staffing on the zoned editions is often thin; reporters are generally inexperienced and paid substantially lower wages than their downtown counterparts. It is generally the case of the press looking in from the outside on a community, its problems, its hopes, and dreams, as opposed to the publication of a newspaper by persons within the community, persons who can better feel and sense the pulse of that community.

With all that has been said about the problems facing the larger newspapers, please note that most of these businesses are quite successful. And a well-managed newspaper in a smaller community is generally especially successful. The industry presents somewhat of a paradox, with a few newspapers falling by the wayside each year, but most making a handsome annual profit.

## ☐ Daily Circulation

The number of people in the United States who buy a daily newspaper each day has vacillated between 60 and 63 million since 1965. Daily sales totaled 62.3 million in 1990, a three-tenths of a percent decrease from the previous year.

Newspaper circulation in the United States is among the lowest per 1,000 people in the developed world. Only 255 copies of a daily newspaper are sold per 1,000 people in this nation. Compare this with other nations. In Sweden 586 copies per 1,000 people are circulated. In Japan 584. Norway—540; Finland—667; Iceland—515; East Germany—413; United Kingdom—443; U.S.S.R.—374; and South Korea—265.

National rankings are for pride, but they are also a measure of civilization. Newspaper readership in the United States is actually declining, declining rapidly, when compared with the growth of our nation's population, or the number of households (figure 5-2). In 1950, 124 copies of daily newspapers were sold per 100 households. This dropped to 111 per household in 1960, 90 per household in 1970, and 79 per household in 1980. About 69 newspapers were sold per 100 households last year. Here is another way to look at the same phenomenon. The population of the United States was about 150 million in 1950. Today it stands at almost 250 million, an increase of about 66 percent. Daily newspaper circulation was about 54 million copies in 1950. Today it is about 63 million, an increase of about 17 percent.

Can we describe some characteristics of a typical newspaper reader in the United States? Research can give us a rough outline. Newspaper readers tend to be married, have a family, and probably own a home or condominium or live in an apartment. Newspaper readers tend to have some roots down in a community. The typical reader also tends to earn a little more money and is a bit more educated than the average American. Newspaper readers are more likely to be active in their communities, in politics, neighbor associations, and in the schools or other civic or cultural affairs. These people tend to be busy—but they still find time to spend with their newspaper. Studies reveal that they watch a little less television than most Americans. Since there is really no shortage of these kind of people in the country today, why are Americans reading fewer and fewer newspapers? Let's examine that dilemma for a moment.

## ☐ Disappearing Readers

Loss of readers is one of the chief concerns of the editors and publishers of U.S. daily newspapers. There are a few who believe the decline in readership has ended. Foremost among those is Gerald Stone of Memphis State University, who argues that research data demonstrates the long loss of newspaper readers has been halted, primarily because of the aging of the population. Others say it hasn't stopped, but the decline is slowing. There are even those who suggest that it is silly to worry about this loss; daily newspapers should no longer attempt to attract a mass audience. "Advertisers are telling us they like a targeted audience not simply a mass audience," Frank Bennack, Jr., president and chief executive officer of the Hearst Corporation, told a convention of newspaper advertising and marketing executives in early 1989. Still others have argued that newspapers should attempt to deliver only the most desirable demographic groups to their advertisers and stop worrying about total household penetration. But more typical of those in the industry is David Easterly, president of Cox Newspapers, who recently noted that "Readership is the most important challenge facing the newspaper industry. We've got all kinds of people everywhere who don't read."

There is no shortage of studies that attempt to explain why we are reading fewer and fewer newspapers. The reasons proposed for this decline cover a broad spectrum. A 1987 study by the American Society of Newspaper Editors ("Love Us and Leave Us") offered the following ideas:

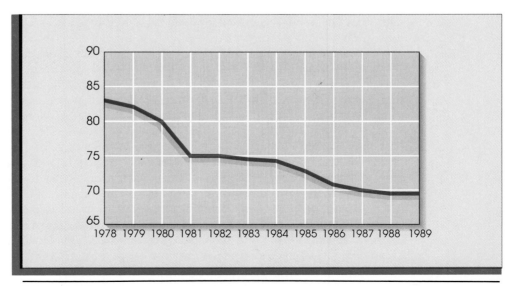

FIGURE 5-2 The number of copies of daily newspapers sold per 100 U.S. households has been steadily shrinking.

- Almost half the people surveyed told interviewers that they stopped subscribing to newspapers because they didn't have the time to read them. This is an interesting comment in an era when the work week seems to get shorter and we supposedly have an abundance of leisure time. But there is far greater competition for our leisure time today. Television and its attendant video recorders, computers, and elaborate stereo systems all compete for the time we have to spare. As does the growing interest in physical fitness. It's hard to read a newspaper when you are working out or jogging.
- Other subjects said they were frustrated by delivery and billing problems.
- Still others said they received sufficient news and information from radio and television.

The high cost of newspapers was the reason given by many nonreaders to researchers at the University of North Carolina. A daily newspaper in the U.S. typically costs 25 to 35 cents, although many big city dailies cost more. A Sunday newspaper costs anywhere from 50 cents to $1.50. On a monthly basis this can total as much as $6 to $7.50, or $90 a year. This is a budget item that takes on relatively significant proportions for many families in an era of low real income growth for most persons.

While this may be obvious, it is still worth noting. People are reading fewer newspapers because there are fewer newspapers to read. Newspapers tend to go out of business because they lose advertisers, not because they lose readers, although the two sometimes go hand in hand. When a large newspaper fails, the successors or competitors rarely manage to capture more than a small percentage of the lost readers.

Most research indicates that younger people are less likely to read the newspaper than older people. A 1990 study by the Times Mirror Center for the People and the Press revealed that younger people (persons under 30 years old) tend to read the newspaper less than older people and have less interest in news. Only 37 percent of those surveyed who were between the ages of 18 and 30 said they regularly read a daily newspaper. Nearly 50 percent of the persons between 30 and 49 said they regularly read a daily newspaper, and 64 percent of those over 50 responded that they were regular newspaper readers. There appears to be much less disparity between age groups when questions about the use of television and radio are asked. Those under 30 also show substantially less interest in news and less knowledge about current events. Will these younger people begin to read newspapers more regularly when they get older? Many undoubtedly will, but probably not enough to stop the slow decline in newspaper readership.

Some argue that newspaper readership has declined because a lot of people can't read a newspaper. In 1989 literacy expert Jonathan Kozol argued that as many as 70 million people lack the reading skill to comprehend a newspaper editorial. If people can't read, they won't read. Newspapers should forget about changing newspaper content to try to attract new readers, Kozol argues, and start focusing on one of the biggest unreported stories of the era; the failure of federal, state, and local governments to educate a substantial number of the nation's citizens.

The credibility of American newspapers is not terribly high, and some argue that people are setting their newspapers aside because they don't believe what they read anyway. Among the groups of people who have the lowest confidence in the news media, according to a 1985 study, are blacks, people in the lowest income and education groups, people who live in large communities, and young people. And these groups tend also to rank low in newspaper readership.

Reflecting the sentiments of a few that were noted earlier, many newspapers have ceased trying to reach all readers. The elderly, who have the time to read a newspaper, but who don't go out a lot or spend lavishly on consumer goods, have been generally shunned by all advertising-supported mass media, newspapers included. Advertisers don't find this group to be terribly voracious consumers, except for certain age-specific products. So the press rarely includes content that might be attractive to these readers. The same is true for the poor, especially the minority poor. (Persons making less than $15,000 per year.) A large percentage of the poor in the United States are African Americans, Hispanics, and other minorities.

"We have done a lousy job promoting readership in the minority communities," said Ron Myatt, circulation director of the *Rocky Mountain News* in Denver, and past president of the International Circulation Managers Association. There is little minority news in most newspapers, unless the minority person has in some way had an impact on the larger white community. Minority social clubs are often ignored; minority service organizations are rarely given the publicity given to their white counterparts. Because minorities tend to be substantially underrepresented in business and government, this avenue toward news coverage is often denied as well. Minority employment at newspapers and broadcasting stations is low. All of these factors, and others, make it difficult for newspapers to woo minority readers—even if the newspaper tries. But advertisers certainly don't encourage newspapers to reach out to these groups. So a newspaper can actively discourage circulation to the elderly, minorities, and others. In 1991, for example, the *Los Angeles Times* eliminated home-delivery and newsstand sales in some economically depressed parts of central California. This will lower total circulation and can account for lower penetration ratios. But the newspaper will also lower its costs, without substantially affecting its advertising rates, since advertisers are unwilling to pay to reach the members of these subgroups. Result: a bigger profit for the newspaper.

Finally, content changes within many newspapers have probably turned off some readers. In Chapter 4 (see pp. 79–80) it was suggested that at many newspapers an attempt is made to create special news sections to satisfy the needs or desires of advertisers. Examples were travel sections which provide a comfortable setting for airline, cruise ship, and travel agency advertising. Or real estate sections or business and finance sections or arts and entertainment sections. While these sections might be attractive to advertisers, they don't seem to be as popular with readers. Research conducted by Belden and Associates, a leading marketing and communications company, suggested that newspaper readers prefer news—community news, local news, state news, and national and international news. Interest in and readership of these "special" sections is substantially lower. So, in attempting to please advertisers, newspapers may have alienated many readers.

The loss of readership is of serious concern to most people in the journalism business, and attempts have been made to stem the outgoing tide. A substantial amount of research has been done to try to discover some answers to the problem, and suggestions founded upon this research abound. First, some of the research.

In 1979 the American Society of Newspaper Editors commissioned a major study of readers. The results of this study, *Changing Needs of Changing Readers*, conducted by Ruth Clark of the marketing firm of Kankelovich, Skelly and White, were widely publicized throughout the newspaper industry. The study was based on interviews with small groups of persons (focus groups) in 12 cities. Clark told the editors that this was the message readers gave to her: "Serve us and help us to cope. Don't just tell us about the world, help us understand it. Be our surrogate . . . remember we are hungry for good news—not just hard news." Editors were influenced by this report and began to offer readers a new menu of choices. There were more coping stories, more interpretation, more analysis, more graphic aids, shorter news stories, more soft news, with the emphasis on sociological or cultural news.

Five years later Ruth Clark conducted a second study for ASNE. This time a large survey was conducted; the small group interviews were not used. The message to editors from this study, entitled *Back to the Basics* was substantially different. "Give us news, hard news, real news. Facts about health, science, technology, diet, nutrition, childrearing. We will do our own coping." Clark told editors that her first study did not say, "don't do hard news." In making changes at their newspaper, however, editors had followed her advice on what to add, but failed to heed her warning not to abandon hard news. Circulation had not rebounded, even at those newspapers that closely followed the advice given in the 1979 study. Now Ruth Clark was saying that readers wanted news and information, not advice.

How can the substantial differences in the results of these two studies be explained? The attempt to answer this question reveals some of the problems inherent in research on readership.

First, it is possible that the results of both surveys are completely accurate; readers did change their minds dramatically in five years.

Or, the first study was a bad study. While the use of focus groups can be a productive research tool, there are problems as well when you attempt to elicit responses in a small group setting. Sometimes leaders among the subjects will emerge and tend to direct the flow of the responses. Others in the group have different ideas, but find it easier to follow the lead of these stronger individuals. Also, the interviewer can end up by leading the subjects to conclusions that they might not reach if left to their own devices.

It is also possible that the second study, the large-scale survey, was bad. If the right questions aren't posed, if they aren't posed in the proper order, if the right sample isn't chosen—these and many other problems can plague a survey.

Both studies might have been wrong. Or, all market research on newspapers might be bad. This is not an unlikely proposition, according to many critics of this kind of research. They point to two basic problems. First, people can't define what they want in a product as complex as a newspaper. A man can tell you what he wants in a can of shaving cream; a woman can tell you what she wants in an automobile. But a newspaper has many more parts, serves many more needs, plays many more roles.

It is also very difficult to define news and information by categories. Let's say the Pope travels to South America and a reader who is surveyed liked the stories about this visit and wants more. Was this a religious story? Or was it an international news story? Or was it a travel story? Or was it a story about the people and customs of a foreign land, a cultural story? Each of us might put this into a different category.

Critics also argue that there is no theoretical basis for this kind of readership research. These studies tend to work on a kind of referendum model. Readers look at what is currently in a newspaper and are asked if they want more or less. Readers are incapable of asking for things that they don't know are possible or that might be used in other newspapers. For example, many readers complain that they don't have enough time to read a newspaper. One device that would save time would be a comprehensive index, perhaps a full page, outlining every major story in the newspaper and telling readers where it might be found. Most newspapers don't use such a device. Advertisers don't like it; they like people to thumb through the newspaper to see what is there—ads and news. If a subject in an interview doesn't know such a scheme is possible, how can he or she ask for the newspaper to begin to use such an index?

Finally, there are many who believe that what the public wants is some leadership from the newspaper. Readers want to be told what they need to know in order to successfully exist in our complex environment. When a village sends a sentry out to stand on a hill and report if danger or unusual events occur, villagers don't expect the sentry to ask what kinds of things should be reported. The sentry is expected to report everything, or at least as much as is important to the survival, prosperity, and happiness to those in the village. Perhaps that is a message that newspaper editors need to hear. Katherine Graham, publisher of the *Washington Post,* warned newspaper editors in 1991 to "avoid the temptation to narrow our focus and move too far in the direction of customized newspapers. Are we going to produce 'infotainment' morsels or newspapers that offer a wealth of high-quality news, perspective, and opinion to a diversified audience?" she asked.

For more than a decade the newspaper industry has been looking for a formula or formulas to try to win back readers. And there has been no shortage of suggestions on what this formula might be. More and more people in the industry today are offering what is surprisingly a novel idea: put some of the profits earned back into the newspaper and improve the product. Newspaper analyst John Morton notes that managers in the press never skimped on reinvesting in their own businesses when there was a clear payoff in sight. "Where newspapers did skimp," he wrote, "was in investment that offered no clear payoff," what Morton calls strategic investment where the return is not in immediate dollars but in strengthening and enlarging a newspaper's hold on its readers. "The areas that needed strategic investment were obvious: higher pay, bigger news holes, more and better journalism, more and better market research and promotion," he noted. University of Georgia journalism professor Conrad Fink agrees with Morton, noting that the attempt by the press to win back suburban readers with zoned editions is doomed unless the quality of these editions is improved. "Zone bureaus cannot be Little Siberias for city desk castoffs or where fresh journalism school graduates are exiled for unsupervised seasoning," Fink said. Investing additional revenues to improve the newspaper will mean lower profits, but many believe such an investment is necessary. "We have found in *every* case that if we improve the quality of the product, get the papers delivered on time, and energetically promote circulation, we can improve circulation numbers," noted Seymour Topping, director of editorial development for *The New York Times.* And the profits? "Publishers will have to accept lower profits in exchange for holding their reader share," said Michael Fancher, executive editor of the *Seattle Times.* Only time will tell if the publishers are willing to strike that bargain.

## THE NEWSPAPER BUSINESS

Most of us think of newspapers as objects rather than as companies in a very large industry. There is a complicated financial structure that supports General Motors when it produces Chevrolets and Buicks, but we often forget that there is a similar structure supporting *The New York Times* and the *Tribune* in Ames, Iowa. Newspaper publishers talk about sales and profits and costs and overhead just like auto executives. The "business" side of the newspaper business is very important and deserves some recognition before looking at the newspaper product itself.

## ▣ The Local Daily

A singular characteristic of twentieth century American daily newspapers is their local nature. Newspapers in the United States are aimed at local readers. This is not true in other parts of the world. In England, Russia, Japan, and, indeed, in most other nations, national daily newspapers are common if not the norm.

There are some highly visible exceptions to the American rule of localism. Weekly newspapers like the *National Enquirer* and *National Star* are sold from racks in supermarkets and drugstores all across the nation. But these publications, whose stock in trade is sin, sex, senility, and sensation hardly qualify as general interest *news*papers. A new sports daily, the *National,* appeared in 1990 (and died in 1991), but this too aimed at a specialized audience. The *Wall Street Journal,* the widely read business daily, qualifies as kind of a national daily newspaper. The *Journal* is edited in New York, but published in printing plants across the nation for easier national distribution. The edited pages travel between New York and the regional printing centers via satellite. *The New York Times* follows a similar pattern — edited pages are transmitted to regional printing centers to assure sameday delivery of the newspaper in most parts of the United States. Only the local New York news sections are missing from this daily national edition of *The Times.*

In 1982 the Gannett Company began national distribution of *USA Today.* The five-day-a-week newspaper was to be aimed at the vast numbers of Americans that are travelling daily. It was to be sold at airports, train stations, hotels, motels, restaurants, and coffee shops — the habitat of the traveller who will likely miss the nightly national television news. *USA Today* was at least initially envisioned as a kind of substitute.

At first glance *USA Today* appears to be a newspaper with lots of color, lots of very short stories, a newspaper that carries an aura of triviality with some pride. These initial impressions are confirmed by the reader who goes deeper into the newspaper. *USA Today* is considered by some as the classic information source, if you define information (as opposed to knowledge) as random bits of data. And according to Peter Pritchard in his book about the newspaper, writers and editors are told to prepare the paper in this fashion.

Tell the story quickly and clearly; don't waste words. The readers are looking for a supplement, not a replacement for their regular newspaper. Don't worry about background information. Reporters are constantly told, according to Pritchard, that the readers are well informed. (There are those who argue this is a dubious assumption.) They don't need to be reminded who Ralph Nader or Phyllis Schlafly are, or what happened at Chernobyl, Pritchard says. *USA Today* devotes a large percentage of its news hole to the gloss of modern life, sports, entertainment, celebrities. It doesn't do a good job covering serious news — but it doesn't try to cover serious news. The philosophy of the paper, according to one observer, starts with a wink of the eye at the reader. "Come on, haven't you had enough serious news today?"

This is a happy newspaper, one whose various nicknames (McPaper, USA OK, The Nation's Nicepaper) fit quite well. It has a good news philosophy that emphasizes the positive side of the news. When the FAA found flaws in airline safety procedures, most papers noted this in their headlines. *USA Today* emphasized instead that not many flaws were found: "Airlines Get Good Marks for Safety." The newspaper saw the explosion of the space shuttle Challenger not as a preventable tragedy but as an opportunity for a new national resolve: "Perfect Isn't Possible; Future Belongs to the Brave" the newspaper proclaimed. Such things are bound to happen as men and women try to push back the boundaries of the frontier, readers were told. The newspaper initially refused to consider that human carelessness and overconfidence were responsible for the fiery explosion.

The newspaper promotes this image in brochures for advertisers, "USA Today's Positive Journalism Creates a Positive Environment for Your Advertising." The newspaper features bold graphic design and considerable color. It is a picture book newspaper. The space-age-looking racks from which it is sold even resemble a modern television set. But early distribution of the newspaper went far beyond the original targets, into city centers and even residential areas. The newspaper is edited in Rosslyn, Virginia, and transmitted by satellite to many printing plants around the nation, often the Gannett newspaper in the area. In 1991 the daily circulation for *USA Today* was 1.7 million copies, or 1.4 million copies, depending upon whom you believe. The company claims the higher circulation, but the Audit Bureau of Circulation, the nation's official auditor of newspaper circulation rejects this higher number because, ABC says, it includes bulk sales of the newspaper to hotels, airlines, and the like. These buyers then pass the publication along to readers without charge.

The impact of the Gannett national daily newspaper *USA Today* on American newspaper editors has far surpassed its impact on readers and subscribers. The graphically oriented newspaper has pushed many American dailies to mimic its layout and devotion to pictures and charts. *(Gannett News)*

The amount of advertising carried by *USA Today* has grown substantially in the past decade, but advertisers still express concerns about the newspaper, according to newspaper financial analyst John Morton. Advertisers have found it difficult to discover who is buying the paper. Because of the lightweight fare in the newspaper, most advertisers rejected out of hand an early Gannett study that suggested that the readers of *USA Today* compare favorably with the readers of *The New York Times* and the *Wall Street Journal.* A more recent study suggests the newspaper's readers are younger (between 21 and 44), upscale, eager consumers who are heavy TV viewers and fascinated with sports. But this is the audience that advertisers can reach much more cheaply through television. Advertisers also expressed concern about the stability of the *USA Today* circulation, according to Morton. "Advertisers worry whether the paper reaches substantially the same readers every day—a fact difficult to determine when 70 percent of the circulation is, in effect, single copy sales," the analyst said. A stable, loyal readership is preferred by an advertiser.

Finally, advertisers said they are concerned with what Morton calls the shelf-life or pass-along readership—the length of time each issue survives to be read. News magazines usually stay in one place for a week or more; *USA Today* is likely to end up in the trash at the end of the day.

Is *USA Today* making any money? That too is a "depends who you ask" kind of question. Between 1983 and 1987 the newspaper lost $450 million. Many observers believe it was still losing money in the early 1990s, but Gannett disputes this. The company has used several schemes in an attempt to raise revenues. Soon after it went on sale the price jumped to 50 cents per copy, higher than all but a handful of other daily newspapers. Distribution was reduced in some areas where sales were marginal. To beef up circulation Gannett attempted to force the subscribers to its Cocoa Beach, Florida, newspaper to buy *USA Today* by stripping the Cocoa Beach paper of most national and international news. The local paper was renamed *Florida Today,* and readers who wanted a full look at the news had to buy both. This experiment was stopped when the marginal circulation gains for *USA Today* were weighed against the substantial circulation losses for *Florida Today.*

The paper is written and edited to a large extent by loaners from other Gannett newspapers, and this is why many persons argue that if *USA Today* is actually showing a profit, it is a profit only because of the magic of bookkeeping. Gannett funded the inauguration of *USA Today* by cutting the news budgets at all its other newspapers by 2.4 percent. *USA Today* is being supported today through a similar system. Gannett newspapers send reporters and editors to work in Virginia to put together *USA Today.* Salaries and most expenses are paid by the home newspapers. *USA Today* gives each of these visiting employees, who stay for three to six months, a small cash allowance and free lodging in a 150-unit apartment complex owned by Gannett and dubbed the Roach Palace by employees. While publishers and editors and some local Gannett newspapers object to this arrangement, comparing it to a colonial power extracting tribute from its farflung colonies, Gannett officials argue that the local journalists get good experience working at *USA Today.*

The success of *USA Today* ultimately rests on convincing advertisers that the newspaper is a good buy. The newspaper's major competitors for these advertising dollars remain the three national news weeklies, *Time, Newsweek,* and *U.S. News and World Report.* But the contribution to contemporary journalism made by *USA Today* does not rest on whether it succeeds as a national daily newspaper. And that question has yet to be answered. Its impact on contemporary journalism is the impact its style and design has had on a vast number of other American newspapers.

For while most readers ignored *USA Today,* most editors read it closely. And this has had a major impact on the appearance of many if not most American daily newspapers. This notation is outlined more fully on pp. 148–151.

## ☐ Costs of Doing Business

The sources of revenue for newspapers were noted in chapter 4 (pp. 72–74). Remember, advertising provides about 75 percent of all revenue, circulation the rest. And more than 80 percent of advertising is local advertising. What about newspaper costs?

A newspaper has many costs, but two kinds of costs stand out over others. The newspaper industry is what is called a labor-intensive industry; a great percentage of its costs are to pay for labor. Most persons who work at a newspaper are highly skilled and often highly unionized. Editorial employees—reporters and editors—are paid reasonably good wages at large metropolitan newspapers, but far lower wages at most other newspapers. (More about this on pages 158–160.) The skilled technicians who actually produce the newspaper—the printers and others who work in the "back shop"—are well-organized and earn top level wages for so-called blue collar workers. A large staff of persons is required to handle circulation, sell and prepare the advertising. Truckers deliver the newspapers to the carriers. In sum, lots of people expect a pay check every week. And these wages amount to a substantial portion of the cost of operating a newspaper. The introduction of the electronic newsroom during the past decade has cut the labor costs substantially. More about that later in the chapter.

The next highest expense that faces a publisher is the cost of newsprint. Years ago the cost of this paper was not a big item. It cost $179 a ton in 1970. Since then the price has jumped by over 280 percent to $685 per ton, and at a large newspaper the cost of newsprint can amount to almost one-third of all business costs. Publishers have attempted to control newsprint cost by reducing the standard page size and by printing on thinner paper. Thirty-pound newsprint is the standard in the industry now, down from the 32-pound standard of 15 years ago. A new 26.75-pound paper has recently been introduced. While it costs about 8 percent more per ton than the 30-pound paper, there is about 8 percent more per ton, so it will go farther. Newspapers expect to realize a saving of about 2 percent on newsprint costs in using the new paper. That doesn't sound like a lot, but in 1990 daily newspapers used about 12 ½ million tons of newsprint at a total cost of over $8 billion dollars. Two percent of that is more than $160 million dollars. Additionally, the larger newspapers should be able to save money on labor, because fewer of the longer rolls of newspaper must be handled. And since postal rates are based on weight, the lighter weight newspapers will cost less to mail as well. The only thing that is holding up widespread adoption of the new paper is an ink problem; color inks or heavy black inks have a tendency to show through the other side of the paper. But careful printing techniques and new inks are helping, according to industry executives. In the meantime, those newspapers (like the *Wall Street Journal* ) that are using the new paper are using heavier paper for those few pages carrying color.

## ☐ The Bottom Line

Given the revenue and expense picture of the newspaper industry, how's business? That is not an easy question to answer in great detail. Most newspapers in America are not publicly owned corporations; hence, their balance sheets are private papers.

Also, the industry is now in a period of great technological transition and this makes any current assessment especially vulnerable to long-term changes. Finally, it must be recognized that a few newspapers are in awful financial shape; a handful go out of business each year. With all of this in mind, it is still possible to cite Ben Bagdikian's assessment of the health of the press as an accurate picture. "American daily newspapers," Bagdikian asserts, "are one of the most profitable of all major industries in the United States."

Newspapers employ more than 480,000 people and rank very high in the value of goods shipped annually. The newspaper still earns the largest percentage of advertising revenue spent in the mass media. Advertising revenues reached $32 billion in 1990, up from $25 billion just five years earlier. Newspaper advertising revenues have consistently grown more rapidly than the gross national product, one measure of national wealth. The GNP went up by 204 percent between 1975 and 1989; daily advertising revenues increased by 278 percent in the same time period.

What all the numbers mean is that the typical daily newspaper earns a good deal of money for its owners, more money than a spaghetti factory or a furniture manufacturer or most other kinds of businesses. Even during hard times newspapers are likely to do well. Despite competition from radio and television, a newspaper that can get its advertisements into the vast majority of homes within a specific geographical area holds great power over all enterprises attempting to do business in that area, according to Anthony Smith in his book, *Goodbye Gutenberg*. He added:

> If the paper manages its advertising and distribution shrewdly and keeps marginal competitors such as free newspapers or shoppers out of the zone—or at least keeps them to a manageable minimum of activity, it has a reliable source of income that must steadily expand so long as the economy as a whole continues to grow. Indeed in periods of sluggish growth the newspaper can decrease its size (if it is a monopoly) and reduce its losses and thus remain profitable through most forms of economic trough [depression].

Currently the industry is undergoing major technological innovation with the introduction of electronic newsrooms and electronic printing processes. In 1963 only 1 percent of the dailies used computers in their news operations; today even the smallest dailies have such equipment. Some newspapers are already installing their second or third generation of computers. These systems cost a great deal of money—as much as $6 million. But publishers claim that the systems can pay for themselves within five years. The big savings comes from eliminating jobs in the back shop where the well-paid unionized employees have been working for more than a century.

The industry is moving toward the virtual elimination of several costly mechanical or chemical processes that until 20 years ago were thought to be absolutely essential to the production of a newspaper. Both major U.S. wire services (Associated Press and United Press International) have adopted editing and processing equipment that drastically cuts typesetting costs at newspapers with compatible equipment. The old mechanical process of taking a news story from a typed page to the printed newspaper page accounted for between 15 and 20 percent of a newspaper's total costs before these new electronic devices were installed. Hence, the financial picture at most newspapers should become even brighter in the years to come. (These new technologies will be more fully explored later in this chapter.)

The immense financial strength of the American newspaper business is of great importance to readers as well: the press can afford to remain independent from government and special interest groups. At the same time the pressure applied by publishers of many newspapers to constantly increase profits could cause serious harm to the traditional values of journalism and cause serious dissatisfaction among readers. Somehow a balance must be struck between staying in business and staying in journalism.

Putting a newspaper together today is a big task. But before the process of how the newspaper is constructed is outlined, a brief discussion of who constructs the newspaper is appropriate.

Studies about journalists are legion; they may represent one of the best-studied occupational groups in the nation. The most recent research on journalists was conducted by the American Society of Newspaper Editors. Results were published in a 120-page report entitled *The Changing Face of the Newsroom*. Here are some of the findings.

Men outnumber women in the newsroom by about two-to-one (65 percent to 35 percent), but this ratio is changing (figure 5-3). Among younger journalists there is almost a 50/50 split; among older workers there are three men for every woman. As this work force ages, the disparity between the number of men and women should disappear. (Sixty percent of journalism school students are women). Only 6.6 percent of the journalism workers are minorities. (A 1991 study by the editors' group

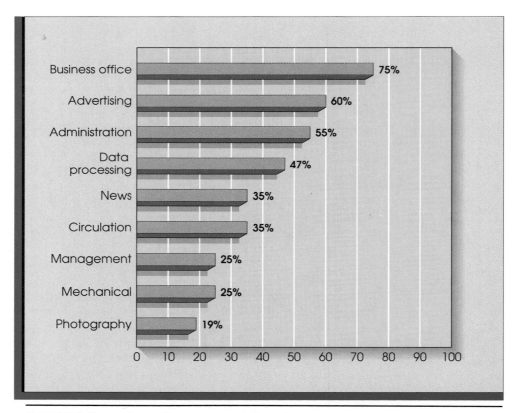

FIGURE 5-3 Percentage of newspaper staffers who are women. There are many women working at daily newspapers, but females still constitute only about one-third of the news staffs.
(American Society of Newspaper Editors)

reported that the percentage of minority employees in the newsroom had reached 8.2.) But again this number jumps to 15 percent if you only look at younger journalists, those under 25. Journalism is a young person's craft; 53 percent of all daily newspaper journalists are under 35. At smaller newspapers 62 percent are under 35.

Women and minorities fare less well when news executives are examined. Only 15 percent of the editors and subeditors are women; only 4 percent are minorities. At the beginning of the 1980s, the American press announced that the hiring of minorities and promotion of both minorities and women were an important priority. But it is apparent that much remains to be done to meet this goal.

Eighty-five percent of the journalists surveyed are college graduates and 15 percent have a graduate degree. Nearly 60 percent graduated from a journalism school. Again, if you look at only the younger journalists, those under 25, this percentage goes up. Nearly 80 percent of the young workers graduated from a college journalism or communications program. Many older journalists, including some editors, like to publicly argue that young people with degrees in political science, history, sociology, or some other related field make better journalists; a degree in journalism is not important. But the fact is these same editors are looking for trained workers when they hire new staff. And the best place to look is among journalism school graduates. That is why these graduates get most of the jobs. In addition, most good journalism degree programs require students to take most of their course work outside the journalism program, in the liberal arts, for example.

More than half of daily newspaper journalists are married, but a remarkably high percentage of them (67 percent) have no children. This is probably a function of their youthful age and the fact that 84 percent of all journalists have a spouse that works as well.

Most (62 percent) journalists say they are Democrats or liberals, or independents who lean toward the left side of the political spectrum. Only 22 percent say they are Republicans or conservatives, or independents who lean that way. Seventeen percent say they are totally independent. This should not surprise most observers of the press. A job of the journalist is one that attracts people who like to see social change, who think things can be better, who seek to work toward moving the community and its people ahead. Traditionally this tends to more closely mirror the philosophy of the Democratic Party more than the Republican Party, whose members more often value tradition and maintenance of the status quo. The values that attract a person to a career in journalism probably more closely resemble the values in social work or teaching more than the values of business or banking.

Perhaps the most interesting bit of data revealed by the ASNE survey is the finding that 40 percent of those surveyed had been employed at the newspaper for less than three years; 58 percent had been employed at the newspaper for less than five years. This speaks somewhat to the youth of the craftspeople in journalism. But it also suggests a transient nature to the work that is probably detrimental to readers, who are seeking comprehensive reporting by persons knowledgeable about a particular community. You can learn a lot about a city or town in five years; there is a lot you cannot learn as well.

How about the boss? What do we know about publishers? Not as much. A few less-than-comprehensive studies have been completed and reveal the following.

Most publishers of general-circulation daily newspapers are in their early to mid-forties. They tend to be white males. One report, by Jean Gaddy Wilson at the University of Missouri, says there are 79 female publishers of the nation's 1,611 daily newspapers. Other research reveals there are only nine minorities; six African Americans, two Hispanics, and one Asian American. A little over one-third of the publishers came into their jobs via the editorial side of the newspaper. Thirty percent came out of advertising, 11 percent out of administration, and 8 percent out of circulation. Almost 80 percent of all publishers are college graduates; 18 percent have advanced degrees. Publishers spend 15 years in the newspaper business before becoming a publisher, on the average.

# MAKING A NEWSPAPER

The motto of *The New York Times,* "All the News That's Fit to Print", is displayed each day on the newspaper's front page. Few people, even the *Times* editors, truly believe that boast today. No newspaper contains anything more than a fraction of the news that's fit to print. Still, newspapers remain the dominant news source in the nation.

A new daily newspaper is produced once or more each 24 hours. (Many newspapers publish several editions of each issue.) Each edition is a new product. This is a far cry from most manufacturing processes where the same product, say a television set or a typewriter, is reproduced continually. The editors of the *Hartford Courant,* a daily with a circulation of more than 200,000, estimates that it takes 9,876 man (and woman) hours to produce one edition of the newspaper. Newspapering is a labor-intensive industry, as noted earlier.

Putting an edition of a daily newspaper on the streets is a complicated business that is undertaken with considerable speed. News that is only being gathered at 9 in the morning is often organized, written, and published in the newspaper by noon. Close teamwork is the key to publishing a newspaper on time each day. What goes into the newspaper? Where does it come from? That is the focus of this section.

## ☐ Advertising Versus News

Most of what goes into the daily newspaper (between 60 and 75 percent) is advertising. The amount of advertising that has been sold for a particular edition normally determines the number of pages in that edition. The day before the paper is to be published the news department is given what are called dummies of the pages for the next day's edition. All the advertising is laid out on these dummies. It is up to the editors and reporters to fill in the holes on these pages with news. This space that is left over for the news is called the newshole. Of course some pages don't have any ads; the front page for example. But other pages are all advertising. The size of the daily newspaper is determined more by the shopping habits of the community and the calendar than what is happening in the world or the region. Daily newspapers have more pages on Wednesdays, Thursdays, and Fridays because people tend to shop at the end of the week and that is when the advertisers want to display their wares in print. Sunday papers are fat because advertisers know people have more time to spend with their newspapers; it is more likely the advertisement will be seen. Newspapers are also thicker around holiday seasons, when people are shopping for gifts.

The variation in the size of the newspaper, and hence the size of the newshole, is something that drives many editors just short of madness. About 50 percent of the nation's dailies have tried to establish a fixed amount of space for news each day, regardless of the amount of advertising carried. The fixed rate varies on each day of the week and is higher on traditionally heavy advertising days. The editor using such a scheme still must work around the advertising, but knows exactly how much space will be left for news on any day of the week. This permits planning an edition days, rather than hours, in advance.

There is a clear risk of overgeneralization when trying to outline the content of the newspaper beyond advertising. There are a wide variety of practices in the newspaper industry today. What is said will apply to most newspapers; not the prestige metropolitan dailies such as the *Washington Post* or the *Los Angeles Times,* but the papers most people read. An easy way to divide up the nonadvertising content of a daily paper is to separate the material a newspaper buys and what it produces itself. Let's start with the purchased material.

## ☐ Wire News

News from the major **wire services** is an important part of the content of every daily newspaper. There are many such services in the world, but five stand out from all the rest because of their size: Reuters, a British agency; Agence France Presse, a French service; TASS, the Soviet news agency; and the Associated Press and United Press International, both American wire services. These five agencies are not only the largest when measured by their news output; they distribute their news worldwide.

The Associated Press was the first American wire service founded in the midnineteenth century. It had a major impact on American journalism and American newspapers. News writing styles, the definition of news, the way news is covered; these and many more elements of journalism were at least partially shaped by the wire services. The news services are called wire services because their news was transmitted to their members or clients through telegraph wires. Even today a few newspapers receive their news through wires attached to clattering teletype machines in the newsroom. More newspapers receive their wire news electronically via microwave or satellite relay. A small disk antenna catches the news as it comes from the news service. The agencies even send their "wire photos" in this manner today. But the name wire service has stuck.

The Associated Press (AP) is different from all other wire services; it is a news cooperative association of some 1,400 daily newspapers that have agreed to supply each other with news. The AP also maintains a staff of almost 2,000 persons in nearly 200 bureaus worldwide. But each newspaper that is a member of the AP cooperative has agreed to provide other members of the cooperative with news from its locale. About one-half of all news transmitted by the giant wire service is provided by member newspapers. The AP also serves almost 6,000 broadcasting stations in the United States, plus nearly 8,500 newspaper, radio, and television outlets in other parts of the world. The AP is a very powerful agency. It can insist that all but the very large metropolitan newspapers put their news on the wire even before publishing it themselves.

The news transmitted by all the wire services has certain weaknesses which will be noted shortly. But the news carried by AP has a special weakness because the agency is a cooperative. This is the limitation of the wire. Or put another way, it is the weakness of democracy. Every member newspaper of the AP has an equal right to ask for whatever news it wants. Since there are more small papers than large ones, the smaller papers can often control what news is covered and transmitted. While new and faster transmission procedures make it easier for the AP to move more news, the file (the news transmitted by the agency) is still a synthesis of news designed to please as many members of the cooperative as possible. If a local editor, for example, wants to publish the full text of a presidential speech or a Supreme Court ruling, he or she must get a majority of those on the same circuit to agree. If the AP doesn't believe many members will use a certain story, it might not even cover that story.

Despite the fact that AP is a cooperative, it costs member newspapers a great deal to use the AP services. AP charges are based on newspaper circulation and on how many of the many AP services a newspaper takes. In 1989 it cost the *Los Angeles Times* (circulation 1.2 million) about $1.2 million for the AP services, according to *Times* writer David Shaw. The *Union,* a 20,000 circulation daily in Grass Valley, Calif., paid only $45,000.

The second major U.S. wire service is United Press International (UPI) and as this chapter was being written, it was in deep financial trouble. United Press was founded in 1907 by Edward Scripps, the owner of a large chain of afternoon newspapers. Scripps had difficulty in securing AP membership in many cities and started UP as a competitor. UP was not a cooperative, strictly an organization in the business of gathering, writing, and selling news. In 1958 United Press merged with Hearst's International News Service to become United Press International. While UPI has grown considerably from its inception, it never attained the size and strength of the Associated Press.

The Scripps Company sold UPI in 1982 and in the next eight years the news service had three different owners. At the end of 1990 the current owner, Infotechnology, was seeking to sell this journalistic institution. UPI was losing money, perhaps as much as $2 million per month. Severe staff cuts had been made; bureaus were closed. In November of 1990, employees agreed to accept a 35 percent wage reduction for three months. Infotechnology, which owned a half interest in the Financial News Network as well, sought to sell both properties because, owners contended, they were not making enough from operations to meet expenses or to cover bank loans and lease obligations. During 1990 UPI had attempted to more tightly focus its operations by concentrating more on business news and state and regional news coverage. To do this the wire service reduced its international and national news coverage.

Why is United Press International in trouble? For years it competed with AP on something other than a level playing field. AP is a nonprofit company supported by its member newspapers, who were always there to underwrite exceptional expenses. AP always had more money and more people. On a breaking national or international story one UPI reporter would often compete with a team from AP. UPI, on the other hand, had to make a profit. The company did not have the deep pockets of member newspapers to fall back upon when extra costs were incurred.

For years the two wire services had the field, tilted or not, to themselves. Today there are many smaller competitors; not only the three other international services, but numerous smaller national and regional services around the world. In addition there are many supplemental wire services in the United States. The Los Angeles Times/Washington Post service serves more than 600 clients with an average of 125 stories daily. The New York Times News Service serves about 550 clients with a similar file. Scripps Howard, Knight-Ridder, Copley, the Christian Science Monitor, Newhouse, and other companies all offer services as well. Many newspapers have found one comprehensive news service, like AP, sufficient. They supplement this with one or more of the smaller services above. While the cost for UPI isn't as high as the cost of AP, it is substantial. When the *Seattle Times* (circulation 230,000) dropped UPI in December of 1989, it was costing the newspaper $300,000 a year for the service. The newspaper was paying more than $500,000 annually for its AP service.

Most daily newspapers (excluding the large metropolitan newspapers) depend upon one or both of these wire services for nearly all their national, international, and even state news. But the wire service news is frequently flawed, in serious ways. Newspapers are no longer very interested in being the first with the news. The days of the sale of "extras" on the street corner are gone. Editors know they cannot beat radio and even television to the punch today and instead concentrate on getting more news to the reader in a more accurate fashion. But the wire services are still fond of beating one another with a story; accuracy often comes second. It was wire service reports in the wake of the Russian nuclear power plant explosion that erroneously suggested the death toll at Chernobyl was as high as 2,000. While many wire story errors are corrected before the story is ever published, others are not. This outmoded interagency rivalry does not really serve the newspaper press well.

Wire service reporters tend to focus on breaking news stories; hence the file is often heavily oriented to catastrophe-oriented news. Such events are usually easy to cover and don't require the busy wire-service correspondent to undertake a long investigation or serious research. Former *Fortune* magazine editor Max Ways described the wire services as "the least innovative, most tradition-bound of all journalistic institutions." A foreign journalist criticized the AP and UPI international coverage as being obsessed with the obvious.

Wire news can also have some undesirable impacts on the newspapers that use it. A great deal more wire news comes into a newspaper than can possibly be published. With this ready source of news copy—which has already been purchased—an editor can fill up news columns instead of hiring more reporters to write more local and regional news. Sometimes an editor will even rely on the wire service to provide coverage of a local story for the newspaper, a serious disservice to readers. Finally, the wire services provide news budgets to their clients at the beginning of every day. This is a list of what AP or UPI editors think are the top stories that day. There is a tendency for an editor to fall back on these outside experts and not make up his or her own mind on what is important for the readers to see.

Despite such valid criticisms, the wire services provide a window on the world to readers in small and medium-sized communities, often a rich supplement to the national and international news carried on television. The costs of maintaining a correspondent abroad or even in Washington, D.C., as much as $150,000 per year plus, are prohibitive for most American newspapers.

It was the clatter of the teletype machine and bells that once heralded the arrival of a wire service story in the newsroom. Today the news is transmitted electronically, via satellite. The volume of news that can be moved in such a way has vastly increased because the speed of moving the news is much more rapid.

## ☐ News Syndicates

News and feature syndicates also sell nonadvertising matter to American newspapers. The material may be transmitted electronically, or the cartoons, comics, columns, and stories may arrive at the editor's desk in the daily mail. Ansel Nash Kellogg of the *Baraboo Republic* in Wisconsin is credited with starting the first news syndicate in 1865 by Amy Hersh, who studied the development of the news services as a graduate student at the University of Missouri. But the Newspaper Enterprise Association (NEA) founded by E.W. Scripps in Cleveland in 1902 is usually regarded as the first of the modern news and feature syndicates. Syndicated material makes up a significant part of the average daily newspaper—often as much as 18 percent of the newshole. This material, which usually has a timeless quality, includes comic strips, feature columns like Ann Landers and Erma Bombeck, crossword puzzles, medical advice columns; household hints, humorous columnists like Art Buchwald and Russell Baker, "They'll Do It Every Time," and often a host of feature stories. A good deal of this material is designed as entertainment rather than news. Many subscribers do not read this soft, syndicated material; but surveys suggest that those who do read it like it very much. These readers are often intimidating to editors who seek to end one of the syndicated features, for these people will telephone and write angry letters. Former executive editor Jim King of the *Seattle Times* once remarked that it is almost impossible to stop running a comic strip featuring an animal because of the intense loyalty of a small number of readers to such a feature.

The cost of this syndicated material is generally not high, but popular features can sometimes command a princely sum. A story in the *Washington Journalism Review* revealed, for example, that the *Rocky Mountain News* agreed to pay United Features Syndicate $62,000 per year to win the rights to "Garfield," which until that time had been carried by the rival *Denver Post*. Typically a quality comic strip costs about $100 per week. There are eight or ten features syndicates including King Features Syndicate, Los Angeles Times Syndicate, Tribune Media Services, Universal Press Syndicate, and United Features.

The syndicate business is facing increasing difficulty today because of several factors in the newspaper business. The supplemental wire services compete for the same space in the daily press as the feature syndicates, and there is only so much space. There are fewer daily newspapers and even fewer competitive newspapers. It is the competitive situation (as in Denver) which causes the bidding wars that push the price for the features up higher and higher. Some progressive newspapers want more staff-written news and fewer syndicated features. And finally, with many newspapers struggling desperately to regain circulation, any decision to replace one feature or one comic strip with another is seen as very important since it could anger or please a host of readers. Hence, the managers of the feature syndicates say it takes longer and longer to get editors to make decisions on new material.

The syndicated material is fun to read, but clearly displaces both local news and local writers. An editor can buy a whole drawer full of feature material for the price of one additional reporter or one local columnist. There isn't a lot of local commentary in many daily newspapers, and the low cost of syndicated material is one reason why. A good newspaper has a mix, but shouldn't substitute "canned copy" for substantial local coverage, just to fill the paper at a lower cost.

## ◻ Local News

Local news should account for at least one-half of the newshole in a typical daily on an average day. At least that is what most responsible journalists believe. Local news can be the real strength of a daily newspaper. Readers tend to judge a newspaper by the quality of its local coverage, according to researcher Ruth Clark, who talks with subscribers about what they like and don't like in their newspapers. If the newspaper does not do a good job on local coverage the press can expect to feel "the icy chill of alienation," Clark wrote. Ben Bagdikian studied 160 newspapers that failed during the 1960s and compared them with the survivors. He found that surviving newspapers had 21 percent more local news than those that failed.

Local news should be the strength of the daily newspaper because it has little competition in this realm. Local radio and television stations simply do not have sufficient personnel to cover local news comprehensively nor the time to report it fully. A television news staff at even a large urban station might have 10 to 15 reporting teams. Even a medium-sized daily will have that many reporters in the field each day, and a large metropolitan newspaper will have 200 or more reporters. The transcript of an entire 60-minute newscast fills little more than a single newspaper page. The daily newspaper, then, simply has no peers in covering the local news. It is a tragedy in modern journalism that more time and effort is not devoted to such coverage at most newspapers. But this is costly news coverage and at many newspapers the editorial budget simply will not permit the editors and reporters to do the best job possible.

Local news is gathered by reporters who are either assigned individual stories or beats to cover each day. The reporters are guided by subeditors and editors. At large newspapers there are often scores of subeditors in charge of a multitude of departments—real estate, sports, lifestyle or women's, travel, entertainment, books, religion, maritime, automotive, food, and many others. Sometimes these departments are subdivided even farther; entertainment might include subeditors for film, music, dance, rock, art, and night-life. The bulk of the hard news is covered by reporters and editors who work in what is often called the city room, or on the city desk. But the geographical limits of these people usually range far beyond the city.

James Gordon Bennett is the father of the beat system of reporting. The city desk is divided up into various beats. At an average medium-sized daily newspaper reporters will probably cover the court beat, city hall beat, county beat, police beat, education beat, business and industry beat, political beat, and one or two others. The beat system has several advantages and disadvantages. A reporter who covers a beat has the time to learn about the beat he or she is covering, become friendly with and gain the confidence of news sources, and develop real insights into the people and the processes being reported. A good courthouse reporter, for example, will know the clerks, judges, and bailiffs; know where to look for new cases that have been filed; understand the legal jargon used so often in courtrooms; and have the ability to gather news about criminal and civil cases quickly and accurately. By being in the courthouse every day the reporter can spot trends or problems or interesting developments that can be the subject of a longer, interpretative news story. It takes many months and even some special training to become a qualified court reporter. The beat system permits this.

But there are problems. A reporter who has covered a beat for many years may begin to take too many things for granted, may not see something that would be obvious to a reporter with a fresh outlook. A beat reporter can get too comfortable with news sources, and the source can sometimes become the primary constituent for the reporter—news is written to please the source to maintain the friendly relationship and make the job easier to complete. The reporter who has a friendly relationship with the source can trust the source not to release important news to other reporters without first tipping off his friend. In turn the source can count on not being "burned" in the newspaper with a negative story—without the reporter at least talking with the source first, giving the source a chance to put the best face on the story. Such bargaining goes on between beat reporters and news sources and often facilitates the flow of information to the readers. But such "sweetheart" relationships are often harmful to readers as well, because sometimes an important story that might be embarrassing to the source simply does not get reported, or reported fully.

General assignment reporters are assigned specific stories, stories that fall between the cracks in a beat, or long-term investigative stories. The daily or weekly variety is nice for the reporter. But often the reporter has only a little more knowledge about the subject of the story than the readers, and the stories often reflect this. A general assignment reporter, for example, who is assigned to cover a story about the selection of a nuclear waste dump site is usually ill-equipped to handle such a subject. Many newspapers try to compensate by permitting reporters to specialize in a kind of reporting—broader than a traditional beat—like science or medicine or the environment. Sometimes a student will focus on such a specialty in college, before seeking work in journalism. It is unlikely, however, that a young reporter is able to work his or her specialty in the first few years on the job. Such well-prepared people often get frustrated and leave the business.

## Getting the News in Print

Reporters have been covering the news in pretty much the same way for the past 100 years or so. But a technological revolution hit the newsroom in the past decade that has drastically changed what happens to a news story from the time a reporter begins to write it until it appears in print. And things are still changing very rapidly. In the "old days" a reporter typed a story on cheap paper called newsprint. This typewritten page found its way first to the editor who checked it, then to the copy desk where it was edited and a headline added, then to a typesetter, where it began its odyssey through the mechanical processes that ultimately led it to the rotary printing presses.

Today it is a computer world. Most reporters still gather news in the old-fashioned way, by telephone or through personal interviews, but they take notes and write stories in the field on laptop computers. In the office the story is prepared on a computer terminal that looks like a personal computer. If research is needed, the reporter doesn't have to make the trip down the hall to the newspaper's library or collection of clippings (often called the morgue). There are almost 3,000 online data bases, designed mainly for the retrieval of information by reporters and other researchers who tap into a data bank through telephone lines attached to the computer terminal. "In a matter of minutes a searcher can gain access to anything printed in the *Financial Times,* say, or distributed by TASS," wrote Tim Miller in the *Columbia Journalism Review.* A reporter can call up and scan the full text of articles published by 75 daily newspapers offered by two fast-growing newspaper data bases, Knight-Ridder's Vu/Text and Oklahoma Publishing Company's Data-Times,

The modern daily newsroom is an electronic environment that in many ways bears little resemblance to the mechanically oriented newsroom of just 30 years ago; but the news is processed pretty much the same way. Pictured is the *Seattle Times* newsroom on January 16, 1991, the day allied forces began their attack on Iraq, when *The Times* published its first "Extra" in 50 years.
(Photo by Gary Settle, © 1991 *Seattle Times*)

Miller notes. Even common reference sources become far more valuable when delivered by computer. A book like *Who's Who in America* is an alphabetized reference source, organized by name. To look up Caspar Weinberger, look in the W's. "In the computerized version," Miller notes, "each word swims around in a digital soup, ready to be dipped out in accordance with almost any criterion the searcher wants to specify." Reporters at the *San Francisco Chronicle* wanted to discover the names of members of the secretive men-only Bohemian Club, so they went to the on-line version of *Who's Who*. The computer could locate the word Bohemian in every alphabetized entry, and brought up an entire list of names, including the former Secretary of Defense, Mr. Weinberger. Miller estimates that a search of this kind through the print version of *Who's Who* would have taken a reporter eight years, not counting coffee breaks.

Once the reporter's story is completed, it is stored in a central computer. It can be called up to the editor's terminal when he or she wants to see it. The story is edited on the screen by a copy editor and a headline is added. Another part of the computer will justify the story and hyphenate it where needed—that is, set the lines in the story to the specified column width used by the newspaper.

The story will be either printed on paper and laid out on dummies (mock-ups of pages) by hand, or the page will be put together electronically as well. This latter system is called **electronic pagination** and is not yet common at most newspapers. But it is coming quickly. Some smaller and mid-sized papers are now laying out pages electronically on Apple Macintosh personal computers. Once the final page is completed it is prepared for printing, typically **offset printing** today. Offset printing is different from the traditional relief-type and ink-on-paper processes. In offset printing the plates are made through a photocomposition process. After the text and photos and ads have been cemented to the layout sheets or the sheets have been produced electronically, the completed page layouts are photographed. The printing plate derived from this process is flexible and goes directly on the press. The paper that runs through the press never touches the printing plate. An ink/water mixture is put on the plate and a roller picks up the images and transfers them to the paper.

A new printing process called **flexography** is starting to emerge in the daily press. The technology, a variation of the old letter-press process, has been around for almost 60 years. Flexo ink, which has the viscosity of water, is absorbed into the paper and dries quickly. Offset ink, on the other hand, is oil-based and never really dries; it sits on the surface of the paper, is not absorbed and rubs off on anything the newspaper touches, including hands as readers scan the newspaper. The flexo process is a one-step printing process, according to Richard Leonard in a recent article in *NEWSINC*. Images are cut into the surface of a flat plate, and the negative image on the plate imprints a positive image on the paper. "The result is a much cleaner and less wasteful product with bright, consistent process color," Leonard wrote. The inks are environmentally safer and do not rub off, and the process can use a lighter-weight newsprint. Offset is still the dominant method of printing, but the newspaper industry is constantly searching for new ideas to cut costs, create a cleaner-looking newspaper, and stop the annoying problem of the transfer of ink from paper to hands and clothing, a reason cited by a growing number of people for abandoning the daily newspaper. Some newspapers, just a few, still use the old **letter-press printing** process in which hot lead is molded into type, locked in iron frames called chases, and attached to printing presses after two or three other intervening processes. But these are the dinosaurs of this era; they are doomed to extinction.

The introduction of the new production and printing processes was very costly for the newspaper business. But the cost savings that resulted from actually closing down large departments of the newspaper that were critical to the old letter-press process made the investment more than worthwhile. Newspapers were able to replace well-paid union crafts workers with semi-skilled workers in many areas. Electronics have replaced mechanics at most American newspapers and other changes still loom on the horizon.

## ☐ The Changing Newspaper

The significant changes in the way in which the newspaper is put together are hardly visible outside the newspaper building. Other changes at the newspaper, however, may be quite apparent to readers. In the past decade two content-oriented changes stand out more clearly than others.

The success of *USA Today* as a business venture for the Gannett Company remains a question; if it is showing a profit it is only doing so by riding on the back of other Gannett dailies across the nation. Less than 1.5 million people buy the news-

*The Sun,* Benjamin Day's New York daily, first published on September 3, 1833. This paper is regarded as the forerunner of the American popular press. Its front page, however, was dominated by small type and lengthy vertical columns. Its design certainly has little in common with a contemporary daily newspaper.
(The Bettmann Archive, Inc.)

paper every day, so its impact on the nation's newspaper readers is minimal as well. But clearly *USA Today* has had a major impact on American journalism, for other daily newspaper editors have studied its style and format closely, and this has resulted in significant changes in daily newspapers all across the nation. *USA Today* is being held up in the newsrooms at many newspapers as a model of what a daily should be. What kinds of changes has it fostered? Let's consider just a few.

Color is the first change. Editors had always viewed color as a problematic venture. Newspaper color is often not good color (compared to magazine color, for example), and some editors wondered what in the world color photos had to do with news. *USA Today* uses a lot of color, *every day.* And now a great many American

Many contemporary American newspapers use elaborate graphic design to help readers understand various complex issues. The *Seattle Times,* recognized in recent years for its graphic excellence, uses an almost full-page drawing by Bo Hok Cline to explain how Seattle's newest skyscraper is designed to sway slightly in the strong storm winds that often buffet the city.   (Photo © Bo Hok Cline, *Seattle Times*)

newspapers are following suit. Color adds cost to making a newspaper without substantially enhancing its value as a medium for the transmission of news and information. But editors think it attracts the reader, who is used to seeing color on television.

Graphics is another area in which the emphasis of *USA Today* has been profound. The graphics revolution, the use of more photos, charts, maps, and so on, was already under way before *USA Today* first came off the presses. But clearly the national daily enhanced this revolution. Suddenly the weather maps in newspapers got more elaborate; there were charts and tables accompanying the most mundane story. At some newspapers the graphics began pushing out the words, and reporters complained about a lack of space for their stories. Looking at the ebbing of newspaper readership and the continued strength of television viewing, editors have concluded that readers want information "quickly and concisely and in a compelling way," as one noted. Drawings and charts and tables help accomplish this, many editors argue. "In the management structure of many newspapers, the graphics editor is emerging in a key position," wrote James K. Gentry and Barbara Zang in an article in the *Washington Journalism Review.* Such editors often report directly to the executive editor, who frequently places matters regarding design on a par with the selection of news.

*USA Today* is a newspaper filled with tidbits of news, often news on the lighter side. News of celebrity, brief dollops of news from around the nation and around the world, news of the unimportant and trivial, pieces of "journalism" that are intended to make readers feel good about themselves or something else. *USA Today* professes little interest in hard news. Many daily newspapers have adopted to at least a limited extent the *USA Today* news formula as well. International and national news briefs dot the inside pages of most newspapers. Arts and entertainment sections have burgeoned. The publication of happy news, at the expense of hard news, is a common facet of U.S. journalism today.

Sports news: *USA Today* devotes one-fourth of its content to sports. Many people refer to *USA Today* as a sports section wrapped around a weather map, or vice versa. Sports coverage has increased dramatically at all newspapers. *USA Today* fills at least one page per issue with sports statistics; most other newspapers do as well. A newspaper can only afford a fixed number of reporters. When the size of the sports staff is increased, other news coverage must suffer. The ombudsman for the *Seattle Times,* Frank Wetzel, reported in 1989 that the newspaper had 23 reporters assigned to cover sports, while the paper had but a single reporter to cover 39 Superior Courts, one reporter to cover all the federal agencies and courts in the city, one reporter to cover the state capital (except when the legislature is in session) and only one reporter to cover the city and state's interests in Washington D.C.

Finally, the editors of *USA Today* eschew **jumps**; that is, starting a story on the front of a section and then printing the remaining portion of the article somewhere inside the paper. So, other newspapers are starting to avoid using jumps. The editor faces a dilemma in putting the front page of the newspaper together. The page should contain an array of stories. A high story count—the appearance of a wealth of information to dig into—is a major newspaper strength compared with other media forms. Many stories can be started on the front page and finished elsewhere. But if it is taboo to jump stories to inside pages, then only five or six stories of normal length will fit on the page, once you have placed the newspaper's nameplate, the index, a picture, and so on. That is not enough stories. To resolve this dilemma many editors shorten the stories so several can appear on the front page without having to jump them inside. This is the design tail ("we want our front page to look attractive") wagging the news dog. But this is happening to a surprisingly large number of newspapers.

*USA Today* was designed by men and women who used television as a model. Even the dispensers on the street corners look like a television set—or a microwave oven. But television has moving pictures and talks. Newspapers will never be able to lure potential readers away from television by giving them something that is supposed to look like television but is really inferior. Most critics argue that newspapers need to do something else, create a newspaper that looks like a newspaper, that contains news and information (lots of it). This will catch the attention of those who are looking for an alternative to television or a supplement to television. This may be the formula needed to bring the readers back.

A second change in newspapers may be visible only to the discerning reader, but is no less important. Throughout most of its history the newspaper has been constructed with the reader foremost in the editor's mind. Originally the newspaper was strictly a vehicle for information and ideas. Later it became a vehicle for commercial information as well, a means of bringing an audience to the advertiser. But even then, what attracted the reader to the newspaper was considered paramount.

Things have changed somewhat in the past two decades. More and more publishers (this is not surprising) and editors (this is surprising) have come to view the newspaper as a marketing tool. That is, they seek to construct the newspaper in such a way as to attract the advertiser. Since most newspapers are monopolies and since most newspapers are home delivered, getting the reader's attention has become of secondary importance. Surely the newspaper must satisfy the reader's needs or desires, but these needs or desires are soft, ill-defined. Why not work instead, in at least part of the newspaper, on satisfying the advertisers' needs and desires? In the end, the advertiser picks up the biggest part of the tab. Theoretically, at least, a newspaper can survive without readers, so long as it has advertising. But the reverse is not true.

Richard Wald, a thoughtful critic and vice-president of ABC News, noted recently in a speech on the print and broadcast media that, "We have come to accept the purpose of these mass media is to make money, not to express ideas. This is not our rhetoric, but it is our practice. We look for market niches in which to start magazines; we treat newspapers as delivery systems for advertiser-desirable printed products. . . ."

The creation of special newspaper sections is a basic example of this trend toward marketing news content to advertisers. It was noted previously that some of these sections such as the travel section and the real estate section have become regular fixtures in many newspapers. But if a newspaper is to be a record of what has happened in the world, the nation, and the community in the 24 hours since it was previously published, then rigidly setting aside large chunks of editorial space for information about buying and selling homes, exotic vacations, restaurant reviews, and similar less-than-essential data makes little sense. On days when little has happened during the past news cycle there might be room for such material. But on a busy news day, when important stories crowd shoulder-to-shoulder in the struggle for space, pushing important news aside for such minutia of daily living is absurd. But the news is left out because hard news doesn't fit in news space dedicated to advertiser interests. As noted previously these dedicated special information sections don't have a high readership when compared to news.

Newspapers put out many more **special,** special sections; one-time sections for boaters or stereo enthusiasts or recreational vehicle buffs. These are proposed by the advertising department, and often the nonadvertising material in the section is prepared by the advertising staff. This is usually so noted. The newspaper has become, in Wald's words, "a delivery system for the advertiser's" message, and little else as regards the special section.

At some newspapers, editors have gone so far as to plan general news coverage with advertisers or the advertising staff in mind. This is not a case of an advertiser influencing the content of the newspaper. This is a case of the newspaper attempting to influence the sale of advertising space. The editor cannot, he or she is told, ignore the advertising side of the business. The editor cannot ignore what persons from circulation say about who buys the newspaper and why. One expects the advertising staff to lobby hard for a publication that provides a friendly environment for advertising. But one does not expect that of the editor, whose mission should be to educate, illuminate, and inform. Advertising is a necessary evil in the newspaper; it is what makes the mare go. Without it there is no newspaper, no matter how important or well-edited the stories may be. But devoting pages of nonadvertising space to topics that please advertisers is irresponsible. It clearly strengthens short-term earnings, but it doesn't do anything for long-term quality. Publisher Eugene Patterson, who once won a Pulitzer Prize for editorials he wrote, has warned his colleagues that they must stop "mistaking money making and numbers for journalism, [stop] buying and selling instead of sowing and reaping, [stop] making like the village banker instead of the town tribune, and [stop] getting pretty complacent about what's expected of us in the way of public service in return for that constitutional shield we wear." For even though it is theoretically possible to publish a newspaper with no readers and only advertisers, practically, this is impossible.

# THE ELECTRONIC NEWSPAPER

The contemporary American newspaper is printed on cheap wood pulp paper, folded, piled on a truck, and delivered to the newspaper carrier. The carrier puts the newspapers on a bicycle or in a car and drops them off at the subscriber's doorstep. This process is age-old; the newspaper is one of the last home-delivered products in the nation. Even doctors don't make housecalls any more.

The printing and delivery process is very costly for the newspaper. Newsprint costs have soared in recent years. Printers are skilled craftsmen who command high wages. The overhead cost to maintain sophisticated printing presses is substantial. Subscription revenues are often eaten up by delivery costs. Is there some possible way to get the product—the news and advertising—to the reader without printing or human delivery?

The so-called electronic newspaper holds the promise of doing exactly that—sending the newspaper to the reader via a television signal or a telephone line. Journalists will write and edit stories as they do now. The stories will be maintained in a computer at the newspaper. When a subscriber wants it, the material will move directly to the home or business to be received on a television set or a home computer. It is necessary to understand a little bit about how these systems work before considering the possible implications of widespread adoption of this technology.

## ▢ Teletext

The simplest and least expensive (to operate) electronic data system is called teletext. Using this oneway system a sender can transmit letters and numbers and simple graphics via a normal television signal to the home receiver. The standard American television set has a screen made up of 525 lines. Not all the lines are used to carry the television picture; the teletext messages can be sent to the home receiver piggyback on the television signal, either over the airwaves or through a cable. In order to receive this information the viewer must have an adapter on the television set to extract the information from within the television signal, and a keypad of some kind to order the data. Only external adapters, costing about $300, had been available until recently, when some television manufacturers (Zenith, for example) began building this equipment into some of their higher priced television receivers. The viewer uses the keypad to select the pages he or she wants to read. Each page holds about 100 words, and about 400 pages can be transmitted by the sender. The viewer selects the page by pressing the keys on the keypad and then must wait for that page to rotate onto the screen, normally just a few seconds. The viewer can only select material that is being transmitted by the system. The viewer must pay a monthly charge for the service, no matter how much it is used. And often two lines of each data page contain advertising messages.

Teletext systems are fairly widespread throughout the nation now. Some are operated by newspapers or magazines, others by television stations, still others by businesses without other media holdings. A typical service in this country will offer subscribers news headlines, weather, stock market listings, sports scores, shopping services, classified advertising, and current events calendars.

It is in Europe that teletext has begun to make a real mark. In Britain, for example, teletext has been available for nearly 15 years to the British public on each of the four nationwide TV networks. More than a million homes are equipped to receive this electronic data; that is about five percent of all homes in Britain. The British systems, called Ceefax and Oracle, bring subscribers a wide variety of data in addition to news and market reports. Vacation information, road conditions, flight information, rail news, ferry news, and TV program guides are just some of the bits of information available to users. Another million subscribers use other teletext systems on the continent of Europe.

Teletext is a relatively simple operation. American newspapers have endeavored to use it as a supplement to their newspaper, giving readers a taste of what is coming in the newspaper to be delivered that evening or the next day. While 400 pages sounds like a lot, there is a distinct limit to the data a user can access with any teletext system. The 40,000 words contained in those pages is significantly less than the words contained in one edition of a metropolitan daily newspaper. The user must want what the sender is sending; the data base must therefore be broad with something for all subscribers. Still, as a means of transmitting small bits of changing data, teletext certainly beats printing technology. And as such, it is likely to become as popular in this country as it is in Europe.

## ☐ Videotex

Videotex is another electronic data transmission system that is being used in Europe and is seeing limited commercial operation in the United States. It is an interactive communication system normally run through telephone lines or cable television that establishes a two-way link from a viewer's television set or personal computer to a data bank. The viewer can choose from potentially a limitless number of pages of information. Services now offer between 100,000 and 250,000 pages, but the storage capacity of the computer to which the user is tied is the only factor limiting the number of pages of information. Information is selected for viewing by a user through a number code, a keypad and an index. The viewer is charged for each page of information that appears on the television or computer screen. This can be quite costly, as will be noted shortly.

It is important to understand the differences between the one-way teletext systems and the two-way videotex systems. The user can only receive that information that is being transmitted on a teletext system. Selection is made from the 400 or so pages available. Videotex users can get any information that is stored in the system; nothing is transmitted until it is requested by the user. It is fairly easy to use a teletext system because of the limited information available. Using videotex, however, can be complicated, especially for persons who are not used to using a computer. Users must learn to use the indexing system and understand what are called logic trees. In a typical interactive videotex system (the user and the computer interact) up to three lines of every page that appears on the screen contain routing information that can instruct the user how to get from one page of information to the next. These routing instructions are called **menus,** and they permit the user to move from more general information on a subject to increasingly specific information. While it does not take an advanced degree in computer sciences to use these menus, it takes considerable practice to learn to use them quickly and efficiently. The user can waste considerable time wandering through pages of irrelevant information until this skill is learned.

Once again our European cousins are significantly beyond us in the use of these interactive systems. In Britain the Prestel system already supplies tens of thousands of homes and offices with a full range of computerized information services and a data base of a quarter-of-a-million pages. Users can ask questions about horoscopes, horse races, or higher mathematics. The information comes into the home via telephone lines and appears on a television screen by virtue of a special attachment that costs the users about $200. The fees for using Prestel are added to the monthly telephone bill. In France the Minitel system is now reaching five million homes. It has become as much a household staple as French bread, offering users some 12,000 different services. It has become the world's most heavily consulted data base. Because the equipment and services are provided free, subscribers only pay for time spent on the telephone lines bringing in the information they seek.

There has been a considerable amount of experimentation with videotex in the United States and some commercial services are now available. The most elaborate thus far conceived was the Viewtron system in south Florida, funded and operated by the Knight-Ridder newspaper chain and AT&T. Subscribers to Viewtron could choose from more than 300 information services including financial news; the Associated Press and *Miami Herald* news files; education services, including a Scholastic Aptitude Test review; and many varieties of product advertising, such as the American Express products and vacation packages that subscribers can order and charge through the system. Viewtron stopped being an experiment and began as a commercial venture in 1983 and hoped to have 5,000 subscribers by mid-1984. The projection fell far short. Only 3,100 were paying to use the system by January 1985. The high cost of using the videotex system was an important deterrent to subscribers. Each subscriber paid about $30 per month, plus $600 for a keyboard terminal that hooked into the television set. Viewtron changed its policies in 1986. First it expanded beyond the south Florida area. Then it eliminated the monthly subscriber fee and charged customers only for the time they actually used the data retrieval service. Finally, it de-emphasized the use of the $600 keyboard terminals and began permitting customers to plug the system into their personal computers. Viewtron provided inexpensive (sometimes free) software to make the system operable. While the number of subscribers grew substantially when the cost of using Viewtron fell, the growth was not sufficient to save the system. On March 17, 1986, Knight-Ridder, some $50 million poorer for its efforts, announced the termination of Viewtron. Just weeks earlier, the Times-Mirror Co. ended its Gateway videotex service in Southern California.

Why did Viewtron fail where Prestel and Minitel have succeeded? Cost is one factor. The French government, for example, gave users the terminal needed for Minitel. Knight-Ridder charged customers $600 initially. The French have also allowed outside private software companies into the system. This saves Minitel and its users more money.

All videotex systems are initially difficult to use and often very slow to operate as well. As Gary Stix reported in the *Columbia Journalism Review,* Viewtron subscribers had to wade through a hierarchy of indexes and subindexes to get a desired story. This took much more time than flipping the pages of a newspaper. "My eyes can move through a section of a paper a lot quicker than they ever could through a data base," noted Charles Carlon, a former Viewtron subscriber.

T. R. Reid and Brit Hume, journalists who write a syndicated column on computers, described how long it took them to go grocery shopping using a new videotex system, Prodigy. "The real-life experience of grocery shopping by computer was so tedious that we may never do it again," they reported. It took an hour and a quarter to order $28 worth of food, hardly more than a bagful. "We could have bought them all at the store, including waiting in the check-out line, in about half the time," note these two experienced videotex users.

Perhaps the best answer to the failure of the system came from Reid Ashe, the chief executive officer of Viewdata, the Knight-Ridder subsidiary that ran Viewtron. "People just aren't sitting home feeling starved for (electronic) information—especially when they have to pay for it," he noted some two years after Viewtron died. "I guess the main thing we learned is there's just not much of a market for information services," he said.

There are still many videotex systems in use. The vast majority of them are aimed at business users. It was noted earlier (see pages 146–147) that journalists at both newspapers and broadcasting stations often rely on electronic data bases (videotex systems) for reference material and research. This has replaced the book-based library most news organizations once maintained. And there are some consumer-oriented videotex systems as well.

The *Fort Worth Star-Telegram,* for example, was serving about 4,000 subscribers with its StarText system in 1990. Computer owners paid $9.95 per month for unlimited access to the newspaper's classified advertising, news stories, Grolier's Encyclopedia, and community data. StarText began making a small profit in 1986. The *Omaha World-Herald* launched a similar system in July of 1989. And Gannett Media Services has had a good response to one of its videotex services, USA Today Sports Center. This provides up-to-the-minute sports news to subscribers.

The largest national consumer-oriented system is Compuserve Information Service, owned by H & R Block, serving more than half-a-million subscribers. It offers users news briefs, stock quotations, weather reports, and other material. The newest system (in 1990) was Prodigy, a $600-million-plus system created by IBM and Sears.

Prodigy is delivered to the user via his or her home computer terminal. Most videotex systems rely on large centrally located mainframe computers to store the data they provide users. Subscribers use long-distance telephone lines to move the data from the computer to their home or business. The charges for use of the system are based on how often and how long the subscribers use the big computers. This is expensive time, and the cost of the long-distance charges adds to this expense.

Prodigy, on the other hand, relies heavily on the computing power in the subscriber's personal computer, according to John Markoff, in an article in *The New York Times.* And instead of the subscriber drawing the data from large mainframe computers, the information comes from minicomputers in the city in which the subscriber is located. Using this approach, most of the traffic is between the user and a nearby minicomputer. The mainframe at Prodigy's White Plains, N.Y., headquarters is tapped only when the minicomputers do not have the necessary information,

The new Prodigy Interactive Personal Service offers subscribers a wide variety of services, including news and information, shopping services, stocks and market quotes, entertainment, banking services, and an encyclopedia. Some of these services are pictured on the screens in this illustration. Prodigy hopes to go where no other videotex service has gone: into the black ink of the profit columns.
(Prodigy Services)

Markoff notes. This lowers the cost to use the system. In 1990 it was less than $10 per month for unlimited use. The bulk of the work in the Prodigy system is done by the software programming running on the user's personal computer, according to Markoff. The user's computer requests the data and interprets the encoded messages for the user. Prodigy got off to a successful debut in the late 1980s, but, as Markoff noted, has a long way to go before it can convince videotex skeptics that it can turn a profit where companies like American Telephone and Telegraph, Time, Inc., Knight-Ridder, and others have lost millions. Most who see promise for videotex place their faith in the coming generations, the young people who today are making friends with computers in schools, libraries, and at home. Becoming accustomed to using interactive machines will make it more likely that when these young people become adults they will be more eager to use such systems as sources of information.

Newspapers which seek to deliver data electronically have found greater consumer acceptance with audiotex voice information systems. More than 50 newspapers today offer people an opportunity to hear a wide variety of prerecorded information which they can access by using their touch-tone telephones. Information on horoscopes, soap operas, stock quotes, weather reports, health, sports scores, classified ads, and many other subjects is available to a user who calls a central number, and then follows the instructions on a prerecorded message. The audiotex systems are far easier to use than videotex and are quite popular. In 1989 the *Atlanta Journal* and *Atlanta Constitution* received more than 5 million calls on their audiotex lines. Most of the audiotex services are advertising-supported, and a user must hear an advertisement before getting the desired information. Surprisingly, most of these services are not profitable, according to the American Newspaper Publishers Association.

Finally, since we are in the "age of fax," some newspapers have begun to offer brief (four pages or less) facsimile editions of their newspapers to subscribers. Advertising is usually stripped along the bottom of the facsimile sheets, and subscribers are charged for the service as well. *USA Today* began offering a facsimile edition in early 1990.

None of these services can ever completely replace the comprehensive news and information presented by a newspaper. But many newspapers are eager to keep their hand in the electronics business, profitable or not, so when new technology or audience acceptance makes a system like videotex a meaningful delivery option, they will be ready to push ahead.

# PROBLEMS IN THE INDUSTRY

The American newspaper industry is currently vigorous and robust, as can be seen from the overview presented in this chapter. Yet the industry is not without its problems. Failure to solve these problems could seriously endanger the health of daily newspapers. Surely the most pressing problem faced by printed press is the continuing decline of reader support. This has been noted previously in this chapter. One root cause of this problem is the deep mistrust many persons have of the American press. But this is a problem shared by television and radio as well. Declining readership may be explained in ways beyond reader mistrust, however. Two potential causes need to be examined.

## Getting the Best Resources

Many people in journalism and even in the daily press express concern that newspapers may not be getting the best talent available to produce the consistently high-quality editorial and advertising product needed to attract readers. While the failure to procure the top-notch writers and reporters may not be the primary cause of declining reader support, it certainly does not help. Why do some people believe the press is not getting the best talent? They point to at least three reasons.

Pay is at the top of the list. The low wages paid to newspaper employees (excluding the skilled union craftspersons who actually produce the newspaper) is almost legendary. Everyone who has worked as a reporter has a story about how little money they were paid when they started. Journalism school graduates from the class of 1990 were paid an average starting salary of $345 per week or $17,992 per year. Graduates who started their first job at a newspaper in a city with 500,000 people started at a higher salary. But beginning reporters at newspapers in communities with less than 20,000 people started for only $245 per week, or $12,740 per year.

Comparing these salaries with those earned by other members of the Class of 1990 reveals that journalism pays its newest workers far below the average earned by newly hired college graduates. Engineers from the Class of 1990 started at about $32,000 per year, people in the sciences at around $26,000. Even people in sales earned close to $21,500 their first year on the job. But this doesn't tell the whole story, for this accounts for only those reporters who work full-time at the main editorial offices. Metropolitan newspapers are in the process of creating a new class of journalists, called editorial trainees, suburban bureau staff members, or even stringers. These are the workers who cover the news in the suburbs and fill the news columns of the zoned editions published by the downtown dailies. Oftentimes these people aren't full-time staffers, but when they are their pay is up to 30 percent lower than that earned by a similar reporter working downtown. Publishers argue the two-tiered wage structure is needed if the big dailies are to remain competitive with the smaller suburban papers against whom they are fighting in these circulation wars. The staff at the suburban papers is usually younger and the pay is lower. Others disagree. "There is a whole subculture of reporters working on the cheap for large news organizations that can damn well afford to pay," said Joan Mitric, who spent 18 months stringing for the *Washington Post* in suburban Maryland for an average of $300 per week. And the editorial aides or trainees or stringer rarely get the job benefits of full-time, downtown workers as well. The only thing that seems to keep this system afloat is the surplus of young people who want to make their living in journalism and will take any job—at least for a while.

Many publishers will deny that salaries are low and reject the figures just cited. They instead cite the salaries paid to journalists who work for newspapers that have contracts with the American Newspaper Guild, a union which represents reporters and other newspaper employees at about 120 daily papers. And the salaries at the Guild newspapers are higher. At the two Seattle, Washington daily newspapers, for example, reporters started at over $500 per week in 1990. And a beginning reporter at *The New York Times* earned more than $45,000 annually. But the publisher's argument is flawed in two ways.

First, a reporter's starting salary even at a Guild newspaper was lower in 1990 than the average starting salary for graduates in engineering and business. And remember, newspapers on the average achieve far higher profit margins and much greater return on investments than nearly all businesses that employ engineering and business school graduates.

Second, most reporters don't start at newspapers that have contracts with the Newspaper Guild. (No one ever begins a journalism career at *The New York Times!*) These are the larger metropolitan newspapers. And this leads to the second reason why many persons believe that the daily press is losing the opportunity to hire the best people. Editors at large newspapers almost always require a young reporter to put in a two- to three-year apprenticeship at a small newspaper before they will even consider hiring them. This is a practice that probably stems from the days before schools of journalism and communication existed. A young person seeking a job in journalism rarely had any background in the craft before the first full-time job. Big city editors didn't want to waste their time training these cubs; they told them to find work first at weeklies and rural dailies where the young journalists could cut their newsgathering teeth. But a journalism graduate in the last quarter of the twentieth century is usually well-schooled in the craft before leaving college. Not only has this student taken considerable coursework in journalism, most have held part-time jobs or internships with newspapers. While seasoning is still needed, there is little training that remains to be done. But the metropolitan daily editor still rarely looks at the recent college graduate.

Good young journalists often start their careers a long way from the newspapers they have dreamed of working at, in rural communities where the pay is low and the working conditions less than desirable. These talented young people often end their careers after one or two years at the same newspapers, frustrated, disillusioned, and wondering why they spent four years at a college or university to earn wages less than an unskilled worker is often paid. The city room often becomes a graveyard of broken dreams.

Other major industries don't operate in this manner. General Motors, for example, does not require that applicants for engineering positions spend 24 months working for a small automobile parts manufacturer before they will be considered for a job. IBM does not require bright college graduates to spend three years working for a small computer manufacturer before applying for work at IBM. Successful corporations go out and recruit the best graduates on the college campuses. And that leads to the third reason many persons feel that newspapers lose out on hiring the best talent available; the failure of newspapers to recruit the best talent.

A few newspaper editors do go to college campuses to pick the cream of the senior class. Most editors sit back and wait for the youths with fire in their eyes to come to them. During the winter and spring months the college placement centers are filled with recruiters from business and industry who seek the best young engineers, business administration majors, and even liberal arts graduates. The newspaper industry operates in a far more haphazard fashion, content to let the current oversupply of journalism school graduates work in its favor. "The process of selecting reporters and editors is largely instinctive, unsystematic, without sophistication, and almost totally dependent on the attitudes and prejudices of the employing executives," reported Edward Barrett after studying how both print and broadcast news executives recruited their journalistic employees.

Only about half of the graduates of journalism schools find work in the mass media (figure 5-4). Newspapers/wire services hire about 15 percent of the graduates, the most of any medium. But more journalism graduates, more than 28 percent, go into nonmedia jobs. Three percent of the graduates go to graduate school or law school, and nearly 12 percent remain unemployed four months out of school, according to the annual Dow Jones Newspaper Fund placement study. It is not known how many of the best students, frustrated with the low pay scales and apprenticeship policies, find jobs outside the media. More critical, how many students, aware of these employment practices, never bother to study journalism but head for business programs or careers in other better paying fields?

Improvement in pay, recruitment, and employment practices will not by itself bring readers back to the daily press. But media consumers today are faced with a

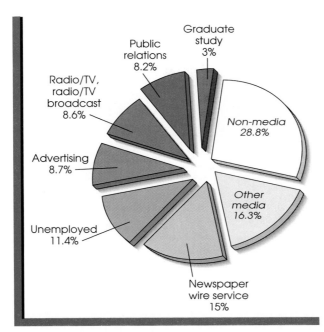

FIGURE 5-4 Just over half of all journalism/communication school graduates go to work in the mass media.
(Dow Jones Newspaper Fund, 1988)

vast array of media forms, all of which vie for their time and their money. To succeed in this competition the daily press must put forward the best possible product, and to do that it needs the best possible people.

## ◻ Minority Employees

It was noted earlier that much of the mass media, not simply newspapers, have written off that part of the audience in America's lower economic classes. Life for these people is a constant struggle for survival. Advertisers seek consumers, not mere survivors. A great percentage of the people in America's lower economic classes are minority people. The Kerner Commission documented in the late sixties that the American press—along with the country as a whole—"basked in a white world, looking out of it, if at all, with a white man's eyes and a white perspective." But the press cannot long ignore America's minorities either as consumers or readers; this segment of the population is growing faster than any other right now.

Consider these facts. Minorities—blacks, Hispanics, Asians, and Native Americans—now make up more than 20 percent of the population in the nation. By the year 2000, it is expected that minority group members will constitute 25 percent of the national population. These are potential new readers and consumers. Minorities comprise, on average, 40 percent of the population of the nation's largest cities, the bastions of daily newspaper journalism. Blacks have been mayors of major urban centers like Los Angeles, New York, Philadelphia, Detroit, Atlanta, and New Orleans. Hispanics have led cites like Denver and San Antonio. And for the first time in the nation's history a minority candidate, Jesse Jackson, received serious consideration for the presidential nomination of a major political party.

Blacks do not feel that newspapers cover them enough, according to an American Society of Newspaper Editors readership study. "Black readers complain that

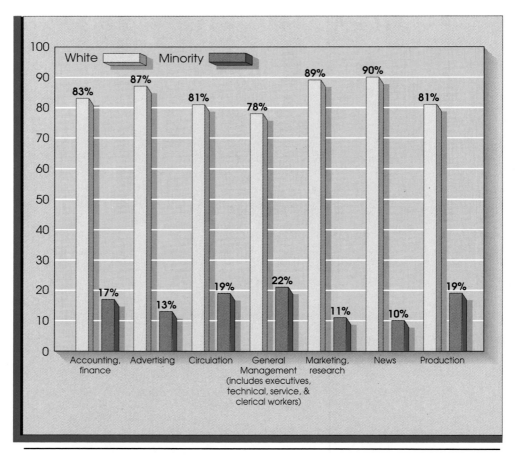

FIGURE 5-5 Percentage of white and minority employees in daily newspapers by department. (American Newspaper Publishers Association)

reporters only come around when there is trouble in the black community," researcher Ruth Clark reported. A book-length study of the Hispanic community financed by the Gannett Foundation concluded that Hispanics think news of their communities is often stereotyped or inadequate. The *Philadelphia Inquirer's* associate editor conducted a four-month study of the newspaper's coverage of the black community and found that it veered from one "flash point" to another, from "an overabundance of coverage of those blacks affected by cuts in social programs and those involved in crime" to sports heroes and "significant achievers" such as the first black mayor of Philadelphia. Because the vast majority of blacks in America fall between the cracks, receiving no coverage, Acel Moore told reporter Marcia Ruth of *presstime* magazine that "many days and some weeks there is a total white-out of news about black America."

To appeal to the minorities in America the newspaper press must provide editorial content that means something to its minority readers, and those best equipped to do that are other minorities. What is the status of minority employment in the newspaper press? Not good. In fact, it is almost as bad as it was in 1967 when rioting in the streets of American cities pushed the government to establish the National Advisory Commission on Civil Disorders, the so-called Kerner Commission, whose criticism of the press was noted above.

In 1968 minority group members held only about 5 percent of all newspaper editorial (news) jobs. In 1988 the minorities committee of the American Newspaper Publishers Association (ANPA) reported that minority group members now accounted for a little less than 10 percent of all workers in the newsroom (figure 5-5). But others dispute this statistic, saying the percentage is lower. Whatever the numbers, everyone agrees that minorities are seriously underrepresented in American journalism, despite the fact that the industry has professed a willingness to remedy this situation for almost two decades. "We have found there is a substantial amount of goodwill among broadcast and print organizations, but we have also found that there has not been a lot of progress," noted Dwayne Wickham, a columnist for the Gannett News Service who moderated a panel at a recent symposium organized by the National Association of Black Journalists.

Despite the sense of goodwill, some persons are skeptical that most newspaper publishers, who are largely white, male, and middle-aged, are prepared to make the change. "Many of you are not yet serious," said newspaper consultant Gerald S. Adolph to those attending a recent ANPA conference. And to those who are serious, Adolph added, change will come only by creating powerful incentives that would overcome the already powerful forces of racism and fear of change that exist today. Editors themselves are not happy with this record. "There is deep dissatisfaction at the highest levels of my company with the progress we've made," said Laurence G. O'Donnell of the *Wall Street Journal.* "There is the feeling we have tried, we've had the best of intentions, but we just haven't gotten the results," he added. Young minority journalists also leave newspaper careers at three times the rate of their white peers, a study by the Institute for Journalism Education revealed. Lack of opportunity was the reason cited most often by the departing minority journalist.

Why is minority employment so low in the daily press? A reason frequently mentioned is the apprenticeship requirement cited earlier, the typical journalism career path from smaller paper to larger paper. Big-city editors complain that the minority applicants they see lack reporting experience; yet the places that reporters traditionally gain experience, the smaller newspapers in the smaller communities, have the worst record in minority hiring. "With minority populations concentrated in the nation's urban centers, this employment gap is often attributed to reluctance on the part of minorities to work in largely white small communities, and on the part of editors to seek or consider minority applicants in communities where few minorities live," wrote *presstime* reporter Marcia Ruth in a special report the magazine carried.

The education system is another reason. Minority student enrollment at the predominantly white journalism schools is low. Newspapers frequently overlook recruiting (and many newspapers do undertake minority recruiting) at the historically black colleges and universities where nearly half the minority journalism students are enrolled. Why is minority enrollment low in most journalism schools? Because the mass media have a bad track record in minority hiring, bright young minority students see a journalism education as a dead end. There are also few prominent role models for the young minority students as well, especially in the printed press. The traditional low pay in journalism is also an impediment to many bright young minority students who see other industries willing to pay more for their talent.

Minority hiring at some newspapers is exemplary. The Gannett Co., for example, boasted 11.5 percent minority employees in the mid-eighties. The professional staffs at the 30 Knight-Ridder newspapers included 9.2 percent minorities in 1985, three times what it was in 1979. A few other newspapers could make similar boasts. To be able to reach out and capture a significant part of the growing minority population in this nation the newspaper press must begin to reach out to minority group readers. And to do that they will have to better integrate their own newsrooms. Most people both in and out of journalism agree that they have a long way to go in this regard.

## ■ The Struggle for Advertising

The readership of daily newspapers is not keeping pace with the growth in population, and publishers are concerned. But they are equally concerned because each year their share of the total number of dollars spent on advertising is shrinking. It wasn't that long ago that newspapers earned as much as 30 cents of each dollar advertisers spent. By 1990 daily papers received only 24.9 cents of each dollar. Who is profiting from the newspapers' loss? Direct mail advertising. In 1980 direct mail earned only 13.9 cents per dollar. In 1990 it earned 18.2 cents of each dollar. Consider one direct mail firm, the giant Advo-System, Inc. In 1980 it mailed 39 million shared-mail packages, packages in which two or more ad circulars are united as a single piece of mail. In 1987 Advo-System was mailing 2.5 billion of these packages.

American homes are being flooded with third-class (that is the postal rate at which such material is sent, not a comment on the material itself), direct mail circulars, an average of about ten per home per week, twice what was delivered just ten years ago. The amount of third-class mail delivered doubled between 1980 and 1988, and today it accounts for almost 40 percent of all material handled by the U.S. Postal Service (USPS). The direct mail industry has negotiated with the USPS for years to try to get more favorable treatment for this burgeoning industry. After postal rate increases in late 1990 for all users, including third-class mailers, persons in the direct mail industry predicted fewer pieces of advertising would be sent out in 1991. But at the same time, the industry was still negotiating with the USPS for substantial rate reductions for direct mailers who mail circulars to 75 percent of the stops on a delivery route, and who deliver the mailers to the post office in the order in which they are to be delivered.

Many mail patrons consider the receipt of this material annoying; newspaper publishers find the increase in direct mail volume threatening. The story of the growth of direct mail is a complicated one involving new advertising strategies, postal laws, and new distribution schemes with names like total market coverage and marriage mail. Here is a brief outline of that story.

For most of its history the newspaper was the only means an advertiser had of getting a printed advertisement into the hands of potential buyers. So-called shoppers, printed publications filled with advertising and little else and distributed without charge to everyone in a community, developed in the post-World War II period, but never seriously threatened the newspapers. At a time when most large cities had several newspapers and even moderate-sized communities had two, advertisers could be certain that their potential customers would see their advertising if they placed it in the local newspaper.

The growth of the large retail chains at the expense of the smaller and independently owned store began to have a serious impact upon the economic structure of the newspaper industry in the late fifties and sixties. A chain store with outlets throughout a community found it expensive to advertise in all the newspapers in an urban market and began to concentrate its advertising in newspapers with the largest circulation. This advertising decision was an important contributing element in the demise of daily newspaper competition in most urban areas.

The advertising policies of the chain stores had another impact on the newspaper industry. These large retail outlets introduced the advertising preprints mentioned previously on page 000. These preprints were initially delivered to consumers through the mail. Postal rates for junk mail went up sharply in the 1970s and merchants sought a new means to circulate these preprints. Newspapers saw the delivery of these preprinted advertisements as a new source of revenue. By just stuffing these preprints inside the newspaper and delivering them to subscribers a newspaper could earn a considerable profit. And newspaper delivery cost a retailer far less than the new postal rates. Even weekly newspapers and shoppers began distributing the preprinted advertisements.

At the same time this was occurring the percentage of people who read a daily newspaper in America began to slowly shrink, due in large part to the diminishing number of daily newspapers in the nation. When a large newspaper fails, many of its subscribers simply stop reading a newspaper; they don't subscribe to the successful competing newspaper. Other factors were also responsible for the decline in readers. There was a growing percentage of young people in our population, the so-called baby-boom bulge, and young people are traditionally not good newspaper readers. The dramatic change in lifestyles that took place in the seventies resulted in later marriages, fewer couples settling down. It is usually when a married couple buys a home and starts a family that they begin to subscribe to a newspaper regularly.

For most of the seventies the actual number of newspaper readers increased each year, but readership grew much more slowly than the nation's population. But in the late seventies the industry experienced an actual real decline of almost 2 million subscribers. This certainly concerned editors and publishers. But it terrified advertisers. Penetration of the daily press in a community had been around 100 percent in the mid-sixties. This began to drop in the seventies until in 1982 it reached 74 percent. That is, only 74 newspapers were sold for each 100 houses. The advertisers who used the newspaper for advertising—either run of press advertising or preprints—were reaching only three-fourths of their potential customers. The free circulation newspapers and shoppers that went to every home began to look like a better advertising buy and daily newspapers began to see a slight loss in the preprint business.

It was a decision by the U.S. Postal Service, however, that most seriously harmed the daily press. In the 1980s the postal service was struggling to operate in the black. In an effort to attract back many of its junk mail customers that had fled in light of the increased rates in the 1970s, the Postal Service announced it would permit a delivery strategy known as **marriage mail** or shared mail. Prior to this decision every piece of mail carried by the postal service had to carry the proper third-class postage. Preprinted advertisements from a drug store chain, a department store chain, a hardware store chain, and a supermarket chain each had to carry postage. Through marriage mail all four advertisers could put their preprints together in a single package or wrapper and pay just a single postage fee. This immediately made direct mail advertising a better buy for many advertisers than newspaper run of press or newspaper delivery of preprints.

Big retail chains began to use the postal service rather than the newspaper to deliver their advertising. K-Mart, the nation's second largest retail advertiser, was one of the first to move to marriage mail. In 1979 newspapers carried about 90 percent of K-Mart's print advertising. By 1985 that percentage had dropped to only 62 percent. Shared mail, in which two or more advertising circulars are combined into one piece of low-cost, third-class delivery, "provides about 25 percent more saturation than typical newspaper distribution," said A. Robert Stevenson, K-Mart vice-president of government and public relations. "Our customer base is everybody," he added, and "we see a response in the store level better with mail delivery than with newspaper distribution."

The 1980 U.S. Census also gave impetus to the growth of direct mail advertising. The census yielded data with which large retailers could define market demographics down to the ZIP code level. Newspapers were very slow to develop such marketing aids. A Connecticut-based firm, Advo-System Inc., began to be a major recipient of the national chains' preprint business. Advo began as a hand delivery service in 1930. Since 1950 it has used the postal system exclusively to deliver advertising. In 1980 Advo distributed 1.69 billion pieces of direct mail advertising, but only 39 million were in the marriage mail category, according to its president John A. Valentine. By 1987 it had increased its marriage mail volume to 2.5 billion pieces. By 1990 Advo-System was delivering 14 billion preprints annually—one-fifth the number carried by all U.S. daily newspapers.

Regional and local delivery firms sprang up as well, and in many communities weekly newspaper and shopper publishers banded together to offer advertisers total market coverage (TMC) with a marriage mail package. Some were even bold enough to attack the Sunday newspapers, long considered immune from such competition. In 1989 a chain of weeklies ringing St. Louis announced that the Sunday *Journal Classifieds* would be distributed to 426,000 households. The publication would be delivered free, and they would charge significantly less to distribute circulars than the *Post Dispatch,* the Sunday newspaper.

Daily newspapers began to fight back, offering advertisers their own **total market coverage** advertising packages. Some newspapers simply offer advertisers a basic marriage mail direct mail service, sending preprints daily to all nonsubscribers via third-class mail. Subscribers get their preprints in their newspapers. Other newspapers publish a weekly shopper that includes light, syndicated editorial material as well as advertising and preprints. Some newspapers offer a complete weekly marriage mail package. By 1990 nearly 90 percent of all dailies offered some kind of total market coverage options, many of which use postal delivery. While these TMC options have helped sustain advertising revenue, they have prompted lawsuits as well in many parts of the nation as competitors charge the daily paper with predatory business practices. Courts will often side with the newspaper's competitors if it can be shown that the daily is using the TMC package to hurt or destroy the competitive service, or if the newspaper is being used to unfairly subsidize its TMC service.

At first glance this fight between newspapers and direct mail advertisers may appear to have little direct impact on readers, most of whom throw out these advertisements without looking at them. (Three-fourths of such mail is typically thrown out without being read, according to a 1987 National Advertising Bureau study.) But it does have a direct impact on those who use the newspaper for news and information. Obviously, if newspapers fail to earn sufficient advertising revenues they will cut costs or ultimately fail. And this could seriously harm news coverage.

Even a standoff between direct mail and newspaper preprints is harmful to the industry, and to readers. The use of preprints by advertisers reduces the amount of run-of-press advertising in the newspaper. While the volume of advertising carried by the newspaper may remain constant, the income from that preprint advertising is substantially lower. Preprints now account for about one-third of all advertising volume, but only about 10 percent of all advertising revenues. Between 1977 and 1987 the amount of nonclassified run-of-press advertising decreased by almost 4 percent; the amount of preprint advertising tripled.

The fewer pages of run-of-press advertising, the fewer pages of news. Preprint advertising does not make up the difference and increase the size of the news hole. This means less money for the publisher, and less news for the reader. Few advertisers are sensitive to the social consequences of the spending decisions, notes industry analyst John Morton in the *Washington Journalism Review*. "They care only about getting the greatest short-run return for their advertising investment, even if this means weakening the revenue base of the major (and often only) responsible provider of important public information to the public," Morton added.

## THIRTY MEANS THE END

The newspaper press remains today what it has always been, the simplest and cheapest means of transmitting great volumes of news and information to the citizens of this nation. The production of each edition remains a kind of daily miracle. No other mass medium gives us more local news, more state and national news, and more international news. No other mass medium can provide the breadth or depth of news coverage on a daily basis. Radio may be quicker, television more colorful, and magazines more specific. But for an individual who wants to know what is happening in the community or the region or the world and wants to know reasonably soon, the daily newspaper is the place to turn. News coverage—that is the unduplicated strength of the daily press.

Perhaps the most fundamental problem in the newspaper industry today is that too many editors and publishers have forgotten that strength. Carl Lindstrom, a distinguished editor, noted in 1960 that "Newspapers today have only two major problems. One is to stay in journalism, the other is to stay in business." Many newspapers in the past 30 years have tried to prove that it is possible to stay in business without staying in journalism. And that has hurt the industry, and at least indirectly the nation. For we all depend upon the daily press to keep in touch with this rapidly changing and ever more complex world. All the signs point to the conclusion that time is running short for editors who don't take journalism more seriously. Lack of concern about the needs of the traditional newspaper readers and the tens of millions of lower economic class citizens has resulted in a failure of the industry to keep its circulation in pace with the growing population. Failure to hire and keep the best talent has led to a deteriorating editorial product which has also alienated readers. The declining percentage of readers has led to a loss of advertising revenues which has also harmed the editorial product. None of these results are irreversible. The industry is still economically healthy. But increasingly the American people find more and more diversions to compete for their time and their money. And it won't be long before all of this begins to catch up with the daily press. At that time it will likely become evident that in order to stay in business, a newspaper must stay in journalism.

## BIBLIOGRAPHY

These are some of the materials that have been helpful in the preparation of this chapter.

Anderson, Mary A. "Who Are Publishers?" *presstime,* August, 1988.

Burgon, Judee K., Burgon, Michael, and Atkin, Charles. *What Is News? Who Decides? And How?* Washington, D.C.: American Society of Newspaper Editors, 1982.

Cunningham, Linda, and Henry, Barbara. *The Changing Face of the Newsroom.* Washington, D.C.: American Society of Newspaper Editors Report, 1989.

Dizard, Wilson, Jr. *The Coming Information Age* (2nd ed.). New York: Longman, 1985.

*Facts About Newspapers '91.* Washington, D.C.: American Newspaper Publishers Association, 1991.

Fink, Conrad. "How Newspapers Should Handle Upscale/Downscale Conundrum," *presstime,* March, 1989.

Fragin, Sheryl, and Skork, Michael. "Forced Landing," *Newsinc,* September, 1990.

"The Future: Can Newspapers Serve Everybody? Should They Even Try?" *presstime,* May, 1990.

Gentry, James K., and Zang, Barbara. "The Graphics Editor Takes Charge," *Washington Journalism Review,* January/February, 1989.

Goltz, Gene. "Reviving a Romance with Readers Is the Biggest Challenge for Many Newspapers," *presstime,* February, 1988.

Gutierrez, Felix F., "The Race for Racial Inclusiveness," 6 *The Journalist* 6, April 1988.

Katz, Jon. "Hiring," *Newsinc,* March, 1990.

Kwitny, Jonathon. "The High Cost of Profits," *Washington Journalism Review,* June, 1990.

Leonard, Richard. "Flexo Is Still Fighting for Every Piece of New Turf," *Newsinc,* March, 1990.

Lindstrom, Carl. *The Fading American Newspaper.* Gloucester, Mass.: Peter Smith, 1964.

Markoff, John. "Betting on a Different Videotex Idea," *The New York Times,* July 12, 1989.

Miller, Tim. "The Database Revolution," *Columbia Journalism Review,* September/October, 1988.

Morton, John. "St. Louis Start-Up Against the Odds," *Washington Journalism Review,* June, 1989.

Patterson, Eugene. "Newspapers' Bottom-Line Mentality Threatens Vigorous Journalism," *presstime,* July, 1987.

————. "The Newspaper Future,"*Washington Journalism Review,* January/February, 1988.

"Possibility of UPI Sale Looms," *presstime,* November, 1990.

Pritchard, Peter. "The McPapering of America," *Washington Journalism Review,* October, 1987.

"Profit and Quality," *Washington Journalism Review,* July/August, 1990.

Rambo, C. David. "Alternative Newspapers Serve an Upscale Crowd." *presstime,* December, 1988.

————. "Direct Mail's Challenge," *presstime,* January, 1989.

"Recession in Some Quarters Dampens Newspaper Profits," *presstime,* December, 1990.

Rykken, Rolf. "Readership Decline Brings Newspapers to Crossroads," *presstime,* March, 1989.

————. "Supplemental Wires Vie for Clients," *presstime,* May, 1989.

Shanks, Linda C. "Information on the Line," *presstime,* September, 1988.

Shaw, David. "The AP: It's Everywhere and Powerful," *The Los Angeles Times,* April 5, 1988.

————. *Press Watch.* New York: Macmillan, 1984.

"Spanish Papers Thrive as Hispanic Market Surges," *The New York Times,* October 15, 1990.

Stix, Gary. " What Zapped the Electronic Newspaper," *Columbia Journalism Review,* May/June, 1987.

Teinowitz, Ira. "Newspapers Show Circulation Gains," *Advertising Age,* November 5, 1990.

Terrell, Pamela M. "Art," *presstime,* February, 1989.

———. "Newspapers Add Sections in Quest for Readers," *presstime,* July, 1989.

Underwood, Doug, "When MBAs Rule the Newsroom," *Columbia Journalism Review,* March/April, 1988.

Utt, Sandra, and Pasternak, Steve. "How They Look: An Updated Study of American Newspaper Front Pages," 66 *Journalism Quarterly* 621, Autumn, 1987.

Wald, Richard. "A Ride on the Truth Machine," *Gannett Center Journal,* Spring, 1987.

Weiss, Philip. " Invasion of the Gannettoids," *The New Republic,* February 2, 1987.

# CHAPTER 6

# MAGAZINES AND BOOKS

Alongside the daily and weekly press that flows in the mainstreams of American society there is a broad array of other forms of printed mass media. Magazines of various shapes and sizes, clothbound and paperback books. They constitute other tiers in the multi-level media system that services the needs and interests of the people of this nation. In this chapter we will examine these forms, where they derive their support, how they function, the roles they play. First, however, we need to examine a major fallacy about media users: the myth of the masses.

## MASSES FOR THE MEDIA

The 1930s mark the beginning of the serious study of mass media in this nation. And it was in this decade that many of our ideas about the media audience first began to form. The notion of the large, single-minded mass audience emerged at this time. There was surely recognition that tiny groups existed along either side of this huge mass, groups that displayed untypical characteristics. The poor and uneducated were on one side; the very wealthy, highly educated elite were on the other side. The primary audience, the mass, was in the middle. And a media culture or milieu was created to suit the needs and interests of this mass. There certainly was evidence to suggest that this perception of the audience was reasonably accurate. Attendance at motion picture theaters was high for the largely undifferentiated film product Hollywood was producing. Giant urban daily newspapers maintained circulations above or approaching one million. Network radio reached tens of millions of listeners each night. The broadcasts were sponsored by brand name products that attained sales never before dreamed of. The success of the general interest magazine, aimed at all readers, amazed even the publishers. Truly, these were MASS media, reaching a mass society with a mass culture.

We know now that this was probably a somewhat inaccurate picture of the audience. Nevertheless, publishers, broadcasters, and especially advertisers believed in the mass audience, and this belief became an important guiding principle for the mass media. Success in the mass media was equated with reaching as many people as possible with a program or a publication. Numbers counted. Advertising rates were established on the basis of how many persons bought the magazine or listened to the radio program.

Our cherished faith in the virtues (or existence) of the mass audience began to diminish in the post-World War II era. (See Chapter 3). Whether or not the mass audience had truly existed in an earlier era, American society began to visibly fragment by mid-century as the United States moved from an industrial society to a post-industrial society characterized by increased specialization and the growth of service industries. In such a society the populace tends to fragment into segments with various interests and various concerns—a differentiated culture, according to sociologist Richard Maisel.

Jean-Louis Servan-Schreiber suggests the same conclusions in his book, *The Power to Inform.* "Americans today find that, as a result of an era of progress from which their country benefited before any of the other industrialized nations, their immense, reputedly homogeneous society of 200 million individuals is fragmenting."

This fragmentation is the result of increased job specialization, a specialization that requires an increasing number of different publications for different fields of interest, according to Servan-Schreiber. Americans have asserted new freedoms and interests, he contends. Some of this is the result of the growth of liberal college education with its increasingly varied curriculum. By the 1990s the fragmentation of our society is evident to even the casual observer.

The United States today is a nation in which a majority of the population has more money to spend than ever before. And we have a great deal of leisure time in which to spend it. Most agree that it often seems we never have enough time to accomplish what we want to do. But compared to the ten-hour, six-day work weeks common 75 years ago, we have significantly more time to do what we want, not what we have to do simply to survive. Jobs around the home that used to take many hours have been simplified by a multitude of gadgets. We can prepare food more quickly and easily. Many of the tasks we used to do ourselves such as lawn work, cleaning, painting, and general maintenance, we pay others to do. We are better educated today; our horizons on life and its many diversions have been significantly broadened.

Americans also like to do things with other people, or at least do things that other people do. Many no longer are satisfied to identify themselves as individuals, which was a common American trait for the better part of our history. The rugged individualist has been renamed the loner, and that is not an attractive appellation. Nor do we want to consider ourselves as part of the total society. That is conformity. We seek to be something less than the mass, but more than a solitary individual. We are young, middle-aged, or elderly. New attention is paid to our individual racial or ethnic or national heritage. We are Easterners or Southerners or Westerners or Texans or Floridians or New Yorkers—and proud of it. What are sometimes derisive labels—such as **YUPPIE** for the acquisitive young, urban professional—are often worn proudly as a badge. We are environmentalists, runners, radical women, skiers, born-again Christians, sports car enthusiasts, parents-without-partners, swinging singles, gay liberationists, new wavers, or senior citizens. We collect stamps, guns, coins, comic books, antique cars, miniatures, or trading cards. We hike, walk, jog, play tennis, surf, scuba dive, camp, fish, hunt, bowl, golf, ice skate, dance, swim, and take photographs. Americans have always been and done all these things. But until the postwar era these endeavors and lifestyles and characteristics had never assumed such important proportions in our lives.

American business responded to our new interests: entire new industries developed to help us occupy our leisure time. Scores of new products were developed to consume our additional disposable income. For decades Americans had been referred to as consumers. By the seventies and eighties we began to seriously earn that title.

Fragmentation of society had deep impacts upon the mass media and the advertising industry which supports it. The search for ever-larger audiences had created media that truly reached (if not served) the masses. But the advertiser had to pay dearly for communicating with these vast numbers.

The growing fragmentation indicated not only special interests among those in the audience, but special needs as well. And many advertisers sought to reach that specific part of the audience whose needs could be satisfied with a particular product. We have noted previously how many in the newspaper industry now argue that to survive, the daily must forget trying to serve the mass audience and cater instead to a narrow, more consumption-oriented readership. And when we look at the electronic media, especially radio, it will become clear that advertisers are as interested (or even more interested) in *who* they are reaching as in how many hear or see their messages.

No mass medium is better suited to reach a specific audience than magazines, whose readership has long been defined by people with common interests rather than by people who live in a common community. And it was the magazine industry which first began to recognize that the so-called mass audience was really an elaborate quilt made up of many fragments. But this recognition took its toll.

## ◨ The End of *Life* . . .and *Post*

The giant general interest, mass circulation magazines of the 1940s and 1950s had been born in an earlier era. The *Saturday Evening Post*, the oldest of the three largest publications, was founded in 1821, but reborn as a mass magazine in 1897 when it was purchased by Cyrus Curtis. *Life* magazine began operation in 1936; *Look* magazine followed the next year. In the postwar years all three publications enjoyed tremendous popularity and by many measures were an accurate reflection of middle-American culture. Yet by the middle of the 1970s all three of these publishing phenomena were dead. Gone as well were *Colliers, American, Coronet, This Week* and the *American Weekly*. When each of these publications died, it had millions of readers. Attempts have been made to revive both the *Post* and *Life*, but neither of the new magazines represent more than a shadow of the former publications.

What happened? Three interrelated factors played a part in the demise of these publishing giants. Many of the communications functions undertaken by these magazines were taken over by other mass media. *Life* and *Look* were picture magazines and brought readers graphic, visual depictions of important events and people. *Post* and *Colliers* featured material on news and public affairs, but also provided readers with a steady diet of short stories and other fiction. Television, by the 1970s, had usurped both of these roles. The electronic wonder brought to our living rooms visual images of the news and our culture, and fiction in the form of drama and comedy shows. It was free, and all we had to do was flip a switch, sit back, and relax.

Americans continued to subscribe to the giant mass magazines, but they didn't need them anymore. Or at least that is what many advertisers believed. The sellers of commodities truly aimed at a mass audience, products like toothpaste, beer, automobiles, and life insurance, became suspicious of the effectiveness of the general interest magazines. A full-page ad in the *Post* or *Life* cost as much as or more than a minute of network television time. More important, the cost of reaching 1,000 potential customers was far less using television. The magazines began to lose many of their traditional advertisers. And those advertisers who no longer sought to reach the mass audience, the makers of motorcycles, expensive stereo and camera equipment, the airlines, and others, found the growing number of special interest magazines a better advertising buy. While these specialized magazines reached fewer people, these people were more likely to be potential customers. And the total cost of advertising was less.

The general interest, mass circulation magazines tried to fight back. They funded studies for the giant brand-name advertisers to prove that magazine advertising was effective. They attempted to lower the prices they charged for advertising by reducing their circulation, abandoning subscribers whose ZIP codes suggested they lived in less affluent areas. They tried to trim the physical size of their magazines, reducing the cost of both paper and postal delivery. Many publications began developing regional editions (called breakouts) that permitted advertisers to reach less than a national audience. (See pp. 75, 174.) But nothing really worked. Their failure was inevitable, given the economic rules that were being applied. Among the top-selling publications of the 1990s, only three might legitimately be called general interest magazines: *Reader's Digest, TV Guide,* and *People. TV Guide* does focus exclusively on television, but since nearly everyone has a television set it can be legitimately regarded as a general interest magazine.

## ☐ Growth of Special Interest Magazines

The demise of the huge circulation, general interest magazines is only half the story of magazine publishing in the postwar era. Equally as important is the story of the growth of special interest magazines.

Many of the same forces that fostered the demise of the mass circulation general interest magazines propelled the growth of the special interest magazines. Not that special interest magazines had not existed in the past; they had, and they had thrived. But the seventies especially saw an explosion of new publishing ventures. Fragmentation of the audience and greater group identity created an obvious market for magazines with a narrow focus. The seventies have been characterized as an era in which self-interest and self-improvement became dominant features on the cultural landscape. Members of the so-called "me generation" spent time and a good deal of money in pursuit of those special interests that made them feel good or look good. Special interest magazines were ready-made for such an environment. "One of the great advantages of magazines is their ability to communicate great amounts of detail about a subject and many facets of a subject," noted Roger Baron, of the advertising firm D'Arcy-McManus. Whether it was tennis, running, computers, body building, food fads, wood stoves, wine, or even chocolates, the magazine industry provided a ready source of information for interested readers.

The special interest magazines were a better advertising buy for many businesses. The point has been made, but is worth repeating. A cruise ship company that wishes to lure vacationers on board for a two-week holiday cruise in the South Pacific could use *Reader's Digest* to carry its message. It would reach nearly 17 million subscribers, but pay dearly for reaching this huge audience. Or it could pay far less and publish the same ad in *Travel and Leisure* magazine. Far fewer people will see this ad, but those who do are much more likely to be interested in cruising on the South Seas. "With their sharply defined audiences and their ability to produce detailed readership profiles through subscriber surveys, special interest magazines were perfectly positioned to take advantage of the advertiser's increased interest in getting more precision audience data," according to B. G. Yovovich in an article in *Advertising Age*.

But other developments were instrumental in the growth of specialized magazines. Refinements in offset printing techniques made it easier and cheaper to publish a small magazine. In fact, the start-up costs for a low circulation magazine are still relatively low. Computerized mailing lists became far more accessible to publishers. They were less expensive and more varied and plentiful. In 1950 it would have been difficult to get a mailing list of skiing enthusiasts, for example. Not so by 1970. Such lists abounded. Publishers found it much easier to reach potential subscribers with subscription solicitations.

Today it is possible to find a magazine for virtually any interest you might have. Certainly you can't do this if you only peruse the magazine racks at a supermarket or convenience store. Look instead at a full-fledged newsstand, or better yet in the periodical collection of a large library. Even more evidence can be obtained by skimming a publication directory such as the *IMS Ayer's Directory* or *Writer's Market*.

Even with the tremendous growth of specialization in magazines today, many publishers try to offer advertisers and readers an even narrower focus. Regional editions and demographic breakouts have been a part of the magazine industry for at least two decades. A regional edition of a nationally circulated magazine offers local or regional advertisers the opportunity to buy space in a national magazine, but the advertisement will appear only in those copies of the magazine distributed in a particular region or locale. A bank in Phoenix, for example, can buy a page of advertising in *Time*, but the ad will appear only in the copies of *Time* circulated in the Phoenix area. A demographic breakout has traditionally been constructed around ZIP codes. The demographic profile of any ZIP code area can be determined by census and other survey data. An ad in a national magazine may appear only in a limited number of copies, for example, those delivered to ZIP codes where the mean annual income is above $60,000 a year. This advertising opportunity might be attractive to a luxury car maker, whereas paying the price to have the same advertisement in all copies of the magazine would not. In both instances the publication is permitting advertisers to buy less than the full circulation of the magazine at a reduced cost.

While these schemes appear to be somewhat sophisticated they are not, compared to what publishers are capable of offering both advertisers and readers today. Magazine publishers in the 1990s, through the use of new printing and binding technologies, have the capacity to address specific content and advertising to individual subscribers.

Chances are good that the last time you subscribed or resubscribed to a magazine you received a short questionnaire from the publisher. If you filled this out, the data you provided went into a data base maintained by the magazine. This data, coupled with other data that can be easily gleaned from many public records, has given the magazine a fairly good profile of each of its subscribers. Using this data, and new technologies, the magazine can direct various kinds of content and advertisements to specific readers. *Farm Journal* began using a **selective binding** technique several years ago that permits it to create custom editions of its magazine for clusters of subscribers who share similar characteristics. Data on acreage and crops dictates which of as many as 1,000 different versions of each edition of the magazine a subscriber will receive. For example, a wheat farmer with more than 100 acres under cultivation would receive a special "Wheat Today" section as well as appropriate regional articles bound into a core edition, featuring general agricultural news. Farmers living next to one another, but raising substantially different crops, will receive substantially different issues of the magazine each month, according to Roger Randall, vice-president of marketing for the *Farm Journal. American Baby* magazine collects data from subscribers on the expected date of birth so it can send its subscribers a prenatal or postnatal edition. *American Baby* sometimes publishes as many as 100 different versions of each edition. This has permitted the magazine to woo an advertiser like Gerber Baby Foods, which will insert coupons in editions mailed only to mothers whose babies are three months old or older. In theory, at least, there are no limits to the level of specialization.

A new process called **jet-ink printing,** developed by R. R. Donnelley and Sons, America's largest printer, enables publishers and advertisers to print personalized messages on pages or cards within the magazine. The October 15, 1990 editions of *Time, Sports Illustrated,* and *People* carried the same four-page advertising insert for a computer service. Subscribers not only found their names on the ad, but also the name of the nearest store that carried the service. And the young subscribers to *Sports Illustrated for Kids* were amazed in April 1991 to see their own names mentioned in the magazine's comic strip, "Buzz Beamer." Printing and binding are done simultaneously, and the machinery developed by the company can insert a page or a card or an advertisement in one copy of a magazine and omit it in the next. That means, according to an article in *The New York Times* by Albert Scardino, that "a clothing company's advertisement can offer one reader a discount on lingerie while the next-door neighbor is invited by the same advertiser to save money on hunting jackets—and both pages can have the reader's name printed on it." When all the copies of a single issue are gathered at the end of a run, the mailing bags may contain hundreds of thousands of copies with no two exactly alike, but with every one in perfect postal sequence, ready for delivery.

Advertisers can test the effectiveness of a variety of personalized messages on cards bound into the magazine. These personalized messages frequently double the response rate from readers, according to marketing executives. "In many respects, magazine publishers have come to see their job as delivering a market to advertisers," wrote Scardino. The more tightly focused an audience the magazine can reach, the more effective the magazine becomes as a delivery vehicle. "Why not then break a single mass-market magazine into thousands of more specialized vehicles?," Scardino asks.

Some publishers remain apprehensive about this new technology. "Advertisers may migrate to only a portion of the press run," noted Steve Rees, circulation director of *InfoWorld,* a weekly magazine for computer users. In 1990 the publication offered two target editions, one for Apple Macintosh owners and one for readers interested in general computer information. If advertisers just use a portion of the press run, ad revenues could decline. Advertisers may be willing to pay more per reader to reach a select audience, but their overall advertising expenditures will be less. Publishers would still have to spend as much to sell the space to those advertisers.

The computer-generated, electronic magazine of the future offers the ultimate in specialized content. Such "publications" are built around a data base that is user-supported rather than advertiser-supported. Users can access as little or as much of the material they choose from the files. The users' interests can be as narrow and arcane as the data base permits. And as more and more computerized information systems come on line, the data bases will undoubtedly permit greater and greater specialization. Some believe that in the future we will routinely use such computerized data bases to accumulate all or most of the information we use and need in our daily lives. These will replace newspapers, magazines, and perhaps even books.

Some view this possibility in a positive light. They see it as a kind of technological Valhalla that can satisfy even the narrowest wants and needs of self-oriented people; the ultimate special interest magazine. Others, however, view this prospect—and indeed most attempts to satisfy the fragmented audience—more ominously. Dominique Wolton, a European who has studied such information systems considers them frightening. In accessing a computerized information system the user assumes the role of the newspaper or magazine editor. He or she will select the information that is now selected by trained and experienced journalists. The pre-emption of this selection task, Wolton argues, would constitute a serious break with an important tradition. "Since the eighteenth century, the press has struggled to offer the most general information possible to as wide an audience as possible," he noted. "The availability of universal information is one of the gains of the democratic era." Wolton adds:

> We all know that we learn things by coming across them unexpectedly. Reading "by chance" is one of the high roads to culture. It is also a way to communicate. This is especially so in the United States, where the newspaper has linked different ethnic and racial groups by providing them with a shared experience and a shared knowledge of their environment. What will remain of this democratic function when each person reads—or punches up on the console—only what his or her information needs require?

Wolton argues that the proliferation of diverse kinds of information is not synonymous with democracy. And he expressed a fear that the "a la carte" information systems of the future may only serve to reinforce social divisions.

The social and political isolation that could result from exposure to only narrow and specialized information is likely to make both communication and governance more difficult. The lack of shared interests, values, goals, and basic assumptions can make compromise, understanding, and ultimately political agreement impossible to reach. The result could be a system of national governance similar to the United Nations, where it is all but impossible to reach a consensus on anything but the most mundane issues. In the past the mass media have provided the people of the nation with a common body of information, ideas, and even values, out of which we have woven a national ethos. Heavy public reliance on specialized information systems could seriously undermine development or maintenance of such an ethos.

## MAGAZINES TODAY

The magazine industry of the early 1990s presents a series of contrasting pictures. Advertising revenues are growing, but slowly. In late 1990 the number of advertising pages published was down slightly when compared with a corresponding period in 1989. The average profit margin in the industry, however, reached a new high.

Costs were increasing. The price of paper was up, and there was a 22 percent postal increase in early 1991. Advertising in several important categories was down. Several magazines had failed. Optimistic publishers said things weren't as bad as they appeared. Pessimists warned that business in the 1990s wouldn't be as good as it had been in the 1980s.

There are about 11,000 periodicals published in the United States today, but the vast majority of these are trade publications, business and agricultural magazines, literary reviews, or scholarly journals. There are probably about a thousand or so consumer magazines, or magazines that accept advertising. And of this group the industry has identified 175 or so as "general consumer magazines." These are magazines that fill up the newsracks at the supermarket and the convenience store. And these 175 or so magazines accounted for 85 percent of all advertising revenue earned by the industry in 1990. It is estimated that about 10 billion copies of magazines are sold each year. *TV Guide,* with a weekly circulation of nearly 16 million, accounts for more than 8 percent of that total.

In 1990 more than 530 new magazines were started, three times as many new starts as in 1984. Nearly half of these new magazines never even publish a first issue, and only one in ten will ever show a profit. Between 1984 and 1990, 1,120 maga-

TABLE 6-1   Top 25 Magazines by 1989 Gross Revenues

| Rank | Magazine | Total Revenues (in millions) |
|---|---|---|
| 1 | *TV Guide* | $928.3 |
| 2 | *Time* | 636.5 |
| 3 | *People* | 605.6 |
| 4 | *Sports Illustrated* | 565.9 |
| 5 | *Reader's Digest* | 419.2 |
| 6 | *Newsweek* | 397.8 |
| 7 | *Parade* | 314.5 |
| 8 | *Business Week* | 298.7 |
| 9 | *Better Homes & Gardens* | 275.7 |
| 10 | *Family Circle* | 249.3 |
| 11 | *Good Housekeeping* | 245.2 |
| 12 | *U.S. News & World Report* | 244.8 |
| 13 | *National Geographic* | 226.1 |
| 14 | *National Enquirer* | 219.9 |
| 15 | *Woman's Day* | 212.8 |
| 16 | *Ladies Home Journal* | 207.2 |
| 17 | *Cosmopolitan* | 204.3 |
| 18 | *Fortune* | 202.7 |
| 19 | *Forbes* | 195.4 |
| 20 | *PC Magazine* | 182.8 |
| 21 | *Star Magazine* | 173.0 |
| 22 | *McCalls* | 167.8 |
| 23 | *Money* | 143.2 |
| 24 | *Glamour* | 141.9 |
| 25 | *Vogue* | 140.8 |

Source: *Advertising Age*

zines were started; each had the stated intention of publishing four or more issues a year. Only about 440 still exist, according to Samir Husni's *Guide to New Magazines*. The disappointing success rate is attributable to many factors: undercapitalization, misjudging a potential market, competition, and lack of skill. "Magazines are falling into the hands of people who don't know anything about magazines," noted Myron Kolatch, longtime executive editor of the *News Leader*. "The result is that you're getting an increasing number of disasters." Interestingly, many of the newer magazines, especially those that will ultimately succeed, are being financed by the sale of older magazines to major media companies. (See pp. 83–87.) As *The New York Times* writer Albert Scardino noted in late 1989, when the giants of the communications industry began buying up multiple publications, "they sprinkled fortune through much of the kingdom, making many former subjects wealthy and often eager to reenter the game with new publications." For example, Richard E. Ekstract took 23 years to build a small publishing company. In 1982 he sold a group of trade publications in the electronics field to International Thomson for between $10 and $20 million. He used this money to start new publications and today owns a group of trade publications covering many of the same subjects as before, including consumer electronics, automobile radar, and cellular phones.

Both advertising revenues and the number of advertising pages sold by the magazine industry were up in the late 1980s. In 1990 the industry earned $6.88 billion in advertising revenues. This was 3 percent higher than in 1989. And the number of advertising pages published in 1989—177,000—represented a 3.5 percent increase over 1988. Magazines continued to hold their own against other mass media, earning just over 5 cents of every dollar spent on advertising, and 17.2 percent of all money spent on national advertising. These numbers have been consistent for several years, while we have seen both newspapers and the electronic media lose shares to direct mail advertising. What kinds of businesses spend the most money in magazine advertising? The auto industry spends the most, according to the Publishers Information Bureau. Cigarettes and alcohol are second and third. Cosmetics, skin care products, fragrances, prepared food products, apparel, and financial services are among the other major advertisers.

Revenues from circulation provided nearly $7 billion in income to the industry as well. In 1975 the industry earned about two out of every three dollars from advertising. Today advertising provides a little less than 50 percent of income. This change has come about due to the conscious efforts of many in the publishing industry to force the reader to pay for a larger share of the product. Publications that do this have greater economic stability and are better protected from the ebb and flow of advertising revenues. Most publishers feel that advertising and circulation revenues are really tied together. "We have always thought that the fact a subscriber pays a fair share of the cost for the magazine helps us sell an advertiser on the idea he wants the magazine and is reading it," noted John M. Thornton, circulation director of *Forbes* magazine. The average cost of a one-year magazine subscription was nearly $28 in 1989 and persons in the industry projected that it would be $33 by 1993. Discounted subscription rates are widely available, however. Average newsstand price for a magazine in 1989? A little under $3, but expected to rise to $3.20 by 1993.

Finally, the profit margin in the industry has risen to 12 percent. While this is less than the margin earned by newspapers and broadcasting stations, it still represents a substantial accomplishment in the eyes of most American publishers.

But it was noted that the industry presented a series of contrasting pictures. And there is a downside. Publishing costs are up. In the past 20 years the Consumer Price Index has risen by a little over 225 percent. All publishing costs, except the cost of printing, have increased at a faster rate. Second-class postal rates have increased by nearly 400 percent, while the cost of paper and salaries rose 299 percent and 259 percent respectively. There is no indication costs will go down in the 1990s. If anything they will go higher. And as noted, postal rates rose 22 percent in 1991. In 1991 several national magazines (*Elle, Mirabella, Premiere, HG,* and others) down-sized or trimmed the physical size of their publications to try to reduce the cost for paper, and make the magazine lighter so it could be mailed more inexpensively. (Postal rates are based on weight.)

Advertising revenues are tied to the economy. In early 1990, magazines noted a drop in advertising in important product categories. Revenues from advertising for financial institutions (a result of the savings and loan fiasco), automobiles (lagging domestic sales), and apparel all dropped as the U.S. economy slowed. Farther down the road, but possibly more devastating, is the remote prospect that the government may ban all advertising for cigarettes. Congress has considered such a ban since the late 1980s, and while it would affect newspapers and billboards too, its impact on the magazine industry would be the strongest. Some magazines, especially women's magazines, rely on tobacco advertising for as much as 15 percent of their total advertising revenues. Some predict, however, that the number of people who smoke would decrease if tobacco advertising were banned, and this, of course, would result in substantial health benefits to the people of the nation.

Readers are a concern as well. Americans are reading more now than they did ten years ago, according to many studies. But they tend to be more directed in their reading, spending more time with publications that give them information, less time reading for relaxation or fun. Faith Baldwin, chairman of Brain-Reserve, a New York consulting firm, said that the contemporary styles of living promote a desire for more information but in short takes. Another publishing expert described the United States as a "nation of multimedia grazers and snackers." Magazines are being forced to respond to these new reader needs. Articles are shorter. Colors are bolder. "In deference to readers' short attention span, whole pages in some magazines contain nothing but one-sentence snippets of information," wrote Deirdre Carmody in *The New York Times.*

Finally, there is a concern that there are perhaps too many magazines as the industry rushes ahead into the last decade of the century. The advertising revenues were being spread among too many publications, and all were receiving a little less than before. "You can only slice up the advertising pie so much and still have a piece for everyone," said Nancy Smith, media director for advertising agency Young & Rubicam. The best thing that could happen, according to some analysts, is for a huge shakeout to occur in the industry. "Something has to give," noted Charles Elbaum, president of a consulting firm called Publishing Economics. "To survive the industry needs to wash out the most vulnerable magazines," he added. The shakeout may have started by mid-1990 as a handful of consumer magazines, including *7 Days* in New York, *Woman,* and the popular *Games* magazine folded or filed for bankruptcy.

One other dimension of the industry needs to be noted in this short profile of magazine publishing. Like all mass media in America, the magazine industry is coming under the control of fewer and fewer publishers. Ben Bagdikian reports that three publishers now get more than 50 percent of the revenues earned by the magazine industry. Of the ten magazines that earned the most advertising revenue in 1989, the giant media conglomerate Time-Warner owned four of them, including the top three, *Time, Sports Illustrated,* and *People.* Other huge conglomerate publishing companies include Hearst, which publishes 13 consumer magazines, Meredith which owns 14, and The New York Times Company which owns 15.

Ownership of the magazines by media conglomerates offers these companies unique opportunities to fashion advertising programs for clients. Time-Warner, for example, formed major alliances in 1990 with packaged goods and auto makers. News America has done the same thing with various clients. The advertiser is offered magazine, broadcast, and cable advertising opportunities as a package. "By 1994," says Edward Wax, Saatchi and Saatchi president, "every national magazine will be part of a multi-media advertising network."

The takeover of national magazines by media conglomerates which often have their eye closely fixed on the bottom line can result in some substantial changes in the publications. Rupert Murdoch's News America purchased *TV Guide* in 1988 for $3 billion, and quickly set about changing the content of the diminutive magazine that first worked its way into American living rooms almost 40 years ago. While it is perhaps an overstatement to call the pre-Murdoch *TV Guide* a critical review of the industry, the publication nevertheless on a regular basis sought to monitor the performance of American television. At least one story in each edition had a hard edge and sought to explore both good and bad industry practices. Perhaps the most famous story was its 1982 investigation of the CBS Documentary "The Uncounted Enemy: A Vietnam Deception." The *TV Guide* report, "Anatomy of a Smear," probably prompted Gen. William Westmoreland's libel suit against the network. Merrill Pannitt, one of the magazine's former executives, described the publication's pre-Murdoch mission: "We felt we had to explain to the public that television was an advertising medium and explain to the industry that it was supposed to be an art form."

Today the publication focuses on the glitz of entertainment. "They are slowly squeezing out media-monitoring stories. Murdoch thinks that's boring, sleepy journalism," noted R.C. Smith, former managing editor of *TV Guide. Washington Post* TV critic Tom Shales saw the changes more starkly. "The magazine went from a certain seriousness to an undiluted frivolousness. The whole thing is kind of swamped with gush. It's a combination of drumbeating for the industry and gushing over people who are barely stars. It's beyond lightweight." It also hasn't been lost on many observers of the new *TV Guide* that Murdoch has much to gain from hyping the television industry. After all, he owns the Fox Network and several important television stations.

## ◼ The Popular Magazine

The publishers of most of the 11,000 plus magazines published in the United States circulate a small number of copies to a readership bound together by relatively narrow special interests. Yet when most Americans think of magazines, they rarely think of these small periodicals. Instead they think of the 100 or so magazines in America that circulate more than a half-million copies of each issue. That is because it is this kind of magazine that is most readily found on the racks at neighborhood supermarkets or convenience stores, the places where most magazines are sold today.

The list of the top-selling magazines in the United States remains remarkably constant, changing little from year to year. While it is relatively simple to start a magazine in the 1990s, nurturing a publication to earn a profit, and then reaching a circulation of 500,000 plus is something else altogether. Only a handful of magazines have done that in the past 20 years, most notably *People;* the two popular supermarket pulp publications, *National Enquirer* and *Star;* and *Penthouse,* the strong competitor to *Playboy.* Probably the fastest growing magazine in recent years has been *Smithsonian.* It ranked 100th on the best-selling lists in 1973, and rests just outside the top 20 today.

Table 6-2 contains a list of the 25 American magazines with the largest circulations in 1990. The first magazine on the list, *Parade,* is a Sunday supplement that is distributed free with scores of different Sunday newspapers. *Modern Maturity,* number two on the list, is sent to all members of the American Association of Retired People. *Reader's Digest,* number three on the list, is regarded by many as America's best-selling magazine. Founded 70 years ago by DeWitt and Lila Wallace, the pocket-sized publication has remained near the top of the circulation leaders throughout most of the last half of this century. If you count its international circulation (39 editions worldwide in 15 languages), more than 28 million copies are sold

**TABLE 6.2   Top 25 Magazines by 1989 Circulations**

| Rank | Magazine | Paid Circulation (in millions) |
|------|----------|-------------------------------|
| 1 | *Parade* | 32,632,565 |
| 2 | *Modern Maturity* | 21,430,990 |
| 3 | *Reader's Digest* | 16,343,599 |
| 4 | *TV Guide* | 15,867,750 |
| 5 | *National Geographic* | 10,890,660 |
| 6 | *Better Homes & Gardens* | 8,005,311 |
| 7 | *Cable Guide* | 7,437,698 |
| 8 | *Family Circle* | 5,461,786 |
| 9 | *Good Housekeeping* | 5,152,245 |
| 10 | *McCalls* | 5,088,680 |
| 11 | *Ladies Home Journal* | 5,038,297 |
| 12 | *Woman's Day* | 4,705,288 |
| 13 | *Consumer Reports* | 4,598,804 |
| 14 | *Time* | 4,339,029 |
| 15 | *National Enquirer* | 4,100,740 |
| 16 | *Redbook* | 3,901,419 |
| 17 | *Sports Illustrated* | 3,597,891 |
| 18 | *Star Magazine* | 3,562,367 |
| 19 | *First for Women* | 3,509,688 |
| 20 | *Playboy* | 3,421,203 |
| 21 | *People* | 3,270,835 |
| 22 | *Newsweek* | 3,180,001 |
| 23 | *Prevention* | 3,134,914 |
| 24 | *Highlights for Children* | 2,800,000 |
| 25 | *Cosmopolitan* | 2,702,125 |

Source: *Advertising Age*

each month. The *Reader's Digest* legitimately claims 50.3 million readers, and was second only to "The Bill Cosby Show" (in 1990) in terms of size of an audience that a media property delivers to an advertiser. In addition to the flagship publication, the company publishes about 400 million condensed and general books each year, has a music division that sells records, tapes, and video cassettes, and recently purchased two additional magazines, *Family Handyman* and *Travel Holiday.*

A look at the best-selling magazines reveals that women's and what are called home-service magazines are dominant today. Nine of the top 25 magazines fall in these categories. A survey by the Women's Institute for Freedom of the Press listed 331 women's periodicals among American magazines, one of the largest groups of special interest publications. Two of the most successful of this category of magazines are *Family Circle,* owned by The New York Times Company, and *Woman's Day,* owned by the French media conglomerate, Hatchette S.A. Both magazines were born in the Depression and grew steadily with the development of the suburbs after World War II. Both are almost totally newsstand sold—free of the very expensive postal delivery system. The price of the magazine just about pays the cost of publication. They are heavily oriented toward the basics of life—food, shelter, money, and the family. And they specialize in editorial matter that television generally ignores. The pretty faces that make the rounds of the television talk shows don't appear on the cover of either *Woman's Day* or *Family Circle.* They are not pretty magazines. One critic noted that the graphics look as if they have been prepared with subway car spray paint. But their editorial formula has been very successful, and they have been among the top 20 selling magazines for more than a quarter of a century. A typical edition of either magazine includes thrift menus, seven new hairdos, decorating and beauty hints, advice columns, articles on family health, 16 ways to use leftover turkey, dress or clothing patterns, home craft ideas, and often some

Edward Bok ranks as one of America's greatest editors. While editing the *Ladies Home Journal* from 1889 to 1930 he introduced the idea that a magazine should serve its readers—a concept that dominates many of the women's periodicals of today. (The Bettmann Archive, Inc.)

seasonal projects. *Woman's Day* claims that almost half of its female readers hold jobs, and both magazines offer survival strategies for the economic problems of the nineties.

Practicality is another hallmark of both publications. A look at the cover of either magazine is quite revealing. While other women's magazines like *McCall's* or *Ladies' Home Journal* carry the faces of personalities, celebrities, or hot fashion models, *Woman's Day* and *Family Circle* are far more likely to feature dolls, holiday crafts, flowers, or candles.

*Woman's Day* and *Family Circle* are among what are called the seven sisters of women's magazines. *Better Homes and Gardens, McCall's, Good Housekeeping, Ladies' Home Journal,* and *Redbook* are the other five. The seven have a combined circulation of more than 37 million subscribers or buyers. Ranked below the seven sisters are a second group of women's magazines, all veterans of years of publication. Included in this group are *Cosmopolitan, Glamour, Vogue, Mademoiselle,* and *Harper's Bazaar.* Finally, there are a group of newer cousins in the family of women's magazines, *Ms., Working Woman, New Woman, Self, Elle, Lear's, Mirabella, Now, Women's World, Entrepreneurial Woman, First for Women,* and many more. Many thought that these new magazines, aimed more at the "with-it" career women of the seventies and eighties would soon outpace the more traditional seven sisters. But that has not happened. In fact many of the newer magazines have folded. Why haven't these new career-oriented magazines been more successful when more than half of the 90 million American women of working age hold jobs outside the home? Experts say that most of these women are in dead-end jobs that do not encourage career orientation. "Such women, including the vast number of female clerical workers, may be deterred by the emphasis of the magazines," according to *The New York Times* reporter Tamar Lewin. "They cannot use tips on hiring top talent or the frequent articles on networking, making use of professional and business counsel and expertise of friends and colleagues," she adds. Arthur Hettich, editor of *Family Circle,* notes that even women executives respond to traditional women's cues. "Career women cook dinner, knit sweaters, and care about their family's health, and we can help them with all of that," he said. There is no question that the newer cousins and the second tier of women's magazines are successful publications. One can't argue with the substantial circulation figures for many of these "other" women's magazines. But it appears that for now the traditional values represented by the seven sisters, values that have seemingly always been a part of women's magazines, will continue to attract the greatest number of readers.

There are two women's magazines aimed specifically at black women, the long-running *Essence* and the upstart *S'azz. Essence* was founded in 1970 and since that time maintained a black female perspective. Articles have ranged from "Sensual Black Man, Do You Love Me?" to "Telling Your Child About Race" and "Cooking the Muslim Way." The publication has also focused heavily on the achievements of black women in the arts, politics, business, education, and community service. In 1990 the magazine had a circulation of 850,000. *S'azz* was started in the spring of 1990 and has a much smaller but growing circulation. It is a glossy, upscale magazine for black women that concentrates on beauty, fashion, and travel reports.

Men's magazines exist, but certainly don't play as prominent a role in the industry as do women's magazines. As many men read magazines as women, according to James B. Kobak, a magazine consultant, but they are reading local and regional, hunting and fishing magazines, automotive magazines, and other special interest publications. Indeed, there are specific categories of magazines like automotive, out-doors, and sports that are consumed most heavily by men. And of course publications like *Playboy* and *Penthouse* still maintain substantial circulations, despite distribution setbacks in the 1980s brought on by militant efforts of pressure groups, most commonly members of fundamentalist Christian groups, to block the circulation of these publications.

The three most visible "men's" magazines in 1990 were *Esquire* (circulation of about 750,000), *GQ* (680,000), and *M* (152,000). In addition there is a popular men's magazine aimed at African Americans as well called *Players*. In the late eighties and early nineties these were joined by a half-dozen new men's magazines. *Men's Life,* a Murdoch magazine, began publication in late 1990. The magazine was aimed at men in their 30s, 40s, and 50s, according to the editor, men who have a "decent job and a decent education." The magazine is intended as "an embrace to guys saying it's O.K. to be a guy again."

*Men* magazine appeared about the same time and is aimed at "untrendy affluent suburbanites," according to its publisher Christopher Kimball. "It's the Boy Scout Handbook for the 90's for the 32-year-old man." *Details,* a magazine originally devoted to an exploration of the New York City club scene, was revamped into a men's magazine in 1990, a publication focusing upon "style, fashion, grooming, politics, adventure, music, and sex."

*Men's Health* first appeared in 1986 and was published six times a year in 1990. It focused on fitness. And *Smart,* which first appeared in 1988, began as an effort to redefine men's pop cultural magazines, according to editor Terry McDonnell. "The new ones [men's magazines] are about grooming," he said. "We're about ideas and journalism and that is all." Will these magazines succeed? Magazine consultant James Kobak told *The New York Times* reporter Deirdre Carmody that he takes the long view. "People start magazines because they think the world needs this magazine. It doesn't matter if the world needs the magazine. The question is, 'Does it want the magazine?'"

Another genre of magazines is what can only be described as the gossip periodicals. *National Enquirer, Star,* and *Globe,* three magazines that look a lot like tabloid-sized newspapers and are bought primarily off racks attached to supermarket checkout stands, have mixed sleazy celebrity gossip with simple health care stories, reports of freaks and weird events, and a heavy dose of astrology and predictive pseudoscience to sell more than 10 million copies each week. Few people seem willing to admit buying these publications, but the sales racks nevertheless empty out each week.

Data developed by the A.C. Nielsen company on the readers of the *Enquirer* probably is consistent for the other tabloids as well. Sixty-five percent of the *Enquirer* readers are women, and the typical reader is a high school graduate with a family income of about $24,000, which is at the low end of the demographic scale. Two-thirds of all readers are in the nation's 25 largest cities. "We are hardly small-town or rural," according to publisher Patrick Linskey. The vast majority of the copies are sold off the newsstand, but a few are sold through subscriptions. Most of the revenue generated by the publication comes from sales, not advertising. Efforts have been made to gain more advertising, and ad rates are substantially lower than the publication viewed by Linskey as its chief competitor, *People.*

Some critics regard *People* as simply a socially acceptable version of the supermarket tabloids. Individuals who wouldn't be caught dead buying a copy of the *Star* or *Globe* will unhesitatingly carry home a copy of *People*. Perhaps this is an unfair comparison. Regardless, *People* remains the only successful national weekly magazine launched in the last 35 years. It has spawned a host of imitators, but none have come close to its success. While it doesn't rank among the elite periodicals when measured by circulation, it ranked third in total advertising revenue earned in 1989, ahead of *TV Guide*. *People* has been described as a magazine that gave celebrity gossip a good name. Critic Edwin Diamond wrote: "*People* is a weekly celebration for the new entertainers of our post-industrial society. It is a magazine for people who don't want to read too much about the stars . . . *People* makes few demands; it can be dealt with like television." The profiles and reviews and articles in the magazine are short, usually no more than 400 words. The cover is always colorful and eyecatching; the inside of the magazine is largely black and white on low grade pulp paper. Diamond adds that "The magazine has surpassed Andy Warhol's prediction that in the future everyone would be famous for 15 minutes. The personalities of *People* live only until the page is turned."

The magazine is marketed carefully. Eight out of ten copies are sold from newsracks—generally on checkout stands in supermarkets. Precise positioning of the rack at the counter is a key to success, according to publisher Richard Durrell. "The strike zone for a sale is between the waist and eyes of the average-height woman and the closer you come to eye level the better chance you have for sales. It is really a matter of inches," he added, noting the average height of women today is 5 feet 4 inches, or 151 centimeters. *People* uses intensive television advertising to sell its weekly issues and uses market research to determine the potential popularity of stories about personalities and even cover photos.

After *People* was introduced in 1974 its publisher, Time, Inc. (now Time-Warner), the nation's largest magazine publisher, experienced a series of embarrassing failures. *TV Cable Week*, launched in the early 1980s to provide TV and cable schedules, died quickly and cost the company $47 million. *Discover* magazine, a science periodical started in 1980, was finally sold in the late 1980s after years of red ink. Time spent many months in 1985 market testing a weekly called *Picture Week* that was described as a splashy, fast-paced photo newsweekly with a minimum of text, but that publication was abandoned.

The company launched two new publications in the late 1980s and early 1990s, and while neither had succeeded when this chapter was prepared, many experts thought there was a good chance they would make a go of it. *Cooking Light*, a periodical that addressed America's obsession with healthful eating, hit the newsstands in 1989. The magazine is a bimonthly, and even if it does succeed, its revenues and profits will be quite small compared to other Time-Warner cash cows such as *People* and *Sports Illustrated*.

A more ambitious venture for the publisher was the debut of *Entertainment Weekly* in early 1990. It had a circulation goal of 600,000, made up chiefly of professional men and women with an average age of 36 and a median family income of about $42,000. (By November 1990, circulation had reached 500,000.) While the magazine publishes feature articles about the arts and entertainment industries, reviews of television programs, movies, music and video cassettes, and books take up about two-thirds of the magazine. The reviews are short and all carry a grade from A-plus to F. Observers noted the substantial potential for conflict of interest, as Time-Warner generates television programs, movies, records, videocassettes, and books, all fodder for the reviewers. But *Entertainment Weekly* editors said that their magazine would give no preference to Time-Warner productions. Yet such assurances may not be sufficient to allay the fears of critics. *Newsweek* magazine in June of 1990 asked its readers, "What responsibility does the magazine group of Time-Warner have to let its readers know that a film it praises in a news story was produced by the movie part of the corporation?" At issue was a long cover story on author Scott Turow, whose best-selling book, *Presumed Innocent*, was soon to be released as a film. *Time* was lavish in its praise for the film but did not reveal that Warner Bros. had made the movie. Officials at *Time* answered *Newsweek*'s question by saying it had no responsibility to report a corporate connection.

## ☐ Success Stories

Of the hundreds of new magazines introduced each year, only a small number go on to make a profit, and even fewer become enduring. Success in the magazine industry often reflects what is on the public's mind at any given time. After the Soviets launched Sputnik in the 1950s, science became an important topic, and while science magazines had been around for many years, the older science magazines and several new ones enjoyed an era of prosperity. Computer electronics became hot in the early 1980s, and computer magazines proliferated. Only a portion of these titles lasted into the 1990s.

A renaissance in interest in business and personal finances following the nonmaterialistic sixties and seventies spurred new interest in business publications. There are about 2,700 so-called business magazines in the nation, but the vast majority are aimed at specific business people. *Broom, Brush and Mop* or *Cosmetics and Toiletries* are two periodicals of this nature. There are many general business magazines, as well, aimed at people in any business. *Business Week, Fortune, Forbes,* and *Money* are just some of the more popular titles.

But the real growth in business magazines (and newspapers) in the eighties was in local and regional publications. In January 1985 *Newsweek* reported that nearly 100 such publications existed, five times more than in 1980. Such publications are getting stronger readership, and this is bringing in advertisers. The local publications have begun to challenge the more widely known national publications noted above and even the *Wall Street Journal.* Crain Communications, publisher of *Advertising Age,* as well as the highly successful (and highly regarded) *Crain's Chicago Business,* started *Crain's New York Business* . This is running head to head with *City Business* and other New York business publications as well as special business sections in New York daily newspapers.

Affluence again became stylish in the eighties, and many magazines were vying to catch the eye of the "rich and successful." Most of the publications which sought this "better" audience had existed for years and simply re-emphasized or redirected their editorial efforts. After immense success in the forties and fifties, *Esquire* seemed to wander in search of an editorial formula for many years. In the eighties it went after the affluent American male and made money for the first time in many years. But the desire to reach the wealthy with a publication fostered the development of many new "upscale oriented" magazines during the past decade. *Vanity Fair, Taxi, Scene, New York Woman, M, European Travel and Leisure, Elle,* Conde Nast's *Traveller,* and *Avenue* are just a few. While these magazines cover a wide variety of topics, each has aimed to attract a readership with a median family annual income in the $50,000 plus range. And most have been successful. Perhaps the most interesting story of the eighties was the story of the *New Yorker,* and how content can sometimes chase away the readers an advertiser wants to reach.

The *New Yorker* is perhaps America's greatest contribution to magazine publishing. Its distinguished history of quality is unrivaled. Over the years the magazine was the envy of the publishing industry for its financial success. Year after year the magazine ranked first or second in the number of advertising pages sold. In 1967, however, the number of advertising pages dropped seriously. In a few years the venerable publication had lost almost one-half its advertising. Profits shrank.

The cause of this precipitous drop was an important editorial decision made by the staff of the magazine. The editors at the *New Yorker* spoke out vigorously against the war in Vietnam, and in issue after issue told its readers that the United States should pull out of the war. The *New Yorker* was one of the first major periodicals to lead the nation in this direction. But it cost a lot. Readership of the magazine changed drastically, according to Ben Bagdikian in an article in the *Progressive.* In 1966 the median age of readers was 48.7—the age when executives in business were at the peak of their spending power. By 1974 the median age of readers was 34. The number had been brought down by an infusion of tens of thousands of college students into the ranks of *New Yorker* readers. These young people were buying the magazine because of its position on the war. Unfortunately, they were not the kind of readers many *New Yorker* advertisers sought, people who could afford a $10,000 watch or a $15,000 brooch.

With the end of the war the *New Yorker* began to recapture the affluent readers it had lost, and lose the younger readers that had lowered its median reader age (and income). By 1985 the magazine had more than half a million subscribers and what Karen Heller in the *Washington Journalism Review* described as 1.6 million of the right kind of readers. Median income of the readers is $92,400; net worth $622,300. About 94 percent of *New Yorker* readers own their own homes with a median value of $192,900.

If the magazines noted above hope to reach the wealthy reader, there is another small group of magazines that seek to reach the REALLY wealthy. During the eighties *HG* (formerly *House and Garden* ) battled with *Architectural Digest* to bring financially elite readers to its side. *HG* purposely cut loose 250,000 of its less economically advantaged subscribers and raised the mean average income of its readership by $40,000, close but not equal to the $114,000 annual income of the readers of *Architectural Digest.*

A handful of regional magazines have been created that also aim for the highly affluent reader. Houston real estate developer Harold Farb started *Ultra* magazine in 1981 and aimed it at the legions of status-conscious new-rich Texans. Farb mailed 60,000 copies of the first issue out to wealthy Texans whose names were culled from country club lists and the tax rolls of exclusive neighborhoods. A new magazine will often attempt to establish a circulation by giving away copies to a preselected audience. This is called controlled circulation in the industry. Advertisers can be guaranteed as to who will be reading the magazine, and the publisher does not have to generate a subscription list. The magazine, which was finely produced but had little to say, was first considered a joke by the Texas journalism establishment, according to Kaye Northcott in an article in the *Washington Journalism Review.* But soon the magazine had an impressive stable of regional and national advertisers. "Texas has such a great money image that a lot of big ticket advertisers like what *Ultra* is serving up," said J.C. Kelly, publisher of ADWEEK's southwest edition. Some prominent

Texas rich folks have happily modeled clothing and jewelry for *Ultra,* according to Northcott. And today, while Farb still sends out 50,000 free copies a month, *Ultra* boasts a paid circulation of 30,000, according to the *Washington Journalism Review* writer. Other similar magazines, such as *Goodlife* that is aimed at the rich in San Francisco, Los Angeles, San Diego, Houston, Dallas, Atlanta, Philadelphia, and Washington, D.C., have sprung up around the nation. While no threat to the *Reader's Digest* or *TV Guide,* these publications succeed in bringing together the affluent and those who wish to sell to them.

## ◻ Minority Magazines

Black magazine publishing is a thriving industry. While the circulation of most black newspapers has been steady or in decline, magazine circulation has been increasing. Today there are more than two dozen magazines aimed at blacks, including many special interest magazines such as *Black Enterprise* (business), *Essence* (women's service), and *Soul Teen* (music).

Johnson Publishing is not only the largest black-owned corporation in America, it is one of the most successful publishing companies in the U.S. The flagship magazine is *Ebony,* with a monthly circulation of nearly 1.85 million. The magazine looks a lot like *Life* and contains general interest stories that appeal to a wide readership. The stories tend to be upbeat and include profiles of successful black performers and athletes as well as "up-from-poverty" kinds of success stories. "We've always been a magazine of success and achievement, which we've redefined over the years," Johnson told *Newsweek* reporters. When the magazine started, success was defined as big cars and mink coats. "Now, it might be raising a family, overcoming a racial handicap, or sending your kids to college. We want to give great emphasis to the positive side of things," he added. *Ebony* was criticized during the heyday of the movement press for failing to take a more militant stand on social issues. But social psychologist Kenneth Clark argues that *Ebony* has a different value to the community. "*Ebony* reinforces the kind of positive middle-class aspirations and patterns that a great many blacks need," he said. In addition to *Ebony,* Johnson publishes the weekly *Jet* which has a circulation of nearly 900,000.

There is a tremendous breadth in Spanish-language magazines in the United States. Special interest magazines abound. A list of some of these include *Data Processing Digest, Mr. Te Ve* (television and entertainment), *Industria Internacional* (plant management and engineering), *Aboard* (an in-flight airline magazine), *Dinero* (business and investing), and *Fotonovela Pimientia* (adult photo magazine). *Neustro—The Magazine for Latinos* is a general interest periodical with a circulation of more than 200,000. *Cosmopolitan En Espanol* circulates more than 30,000 copies each month.

## ◻ Local Magazines

City and regional magazines have been a mainstay of the American publishing scene for a century or more. Recently, however, there has been a new burst of activity in this category of publication. And now we are seeing not only new city or state publications, but special interest magazines aimed at readers in a particular venue.

Today virtually all major cities have at least one or two speciality magazines. And while no one keeps an accurate count of such publications, it is estimated by the Magazine Publishers Association that there are about 500 publications that fall into the metropolitan, regional, or state categories. These magazines tend to reach the most affluent readers in their communities and are therefore attractive to many advertisers. Many of these publications have formed networks to attract additional national advertising, giving an advertiser a discount for publishing advertising in each magazine in the group. While some of the city magazines are little more than a megaphone for the local Chamber of Commerce, many more are thoughtful, well-written, and insightful publications that look into the best and the worst aspects of life in their communities. And many city magazines feature a depth and quality of journalism that is often lacking in the local daily press, in its rush to shorten and synthesize the news.

While the city or regional magazines are usually associated with large urban communities, in recent years such publications have been popping up in smaller cities as well. In 1989 a city magazine began publication in Athens, Ga., for example, a university town of 45,000 people. Two years earlier a retired commercial printer started a publication in Covington, Va., that now circulates almost 12,000 copies in several counties in Virginia and West Virginia. These smaller publications stand side by side with the giant circulations (100,000 plus) of periodicals like *Chicago* magazine and the *Washingtonian.*

The popularity of locally oriented magazines has spawned a growing range of local special interest publications. The capital city of Indiana not only boosts *Indianapolis Monthly,* but *Indy Sports* and *Indianapolis Business Journal.* There has been a boom in local women's magazines, led by *New York Woman,* and followed by such publications as *Boston Woman, San Diego Woman, Washington Woman,* and *Michigan Woman.* During the 1980s, 70 different local magazines for parents sprung up, including *Child's Play* in Springfield, Mass., *Pierce County Parent* in Tacoma, Wash., and *All Kids Considered* in Detroit. And there is *Albuquerque Senior Scene, Texas Architect, Jersey Jazz,* and scores of others. There is even a magazine that focuses exclusively on *Florida Real Estate.* While many of the newer publications are flashes-in-the-pan, others will endure and represent another increment in the growing specialization in the magazine publishing industry.

A final note on trends in magazine publishing. Comic books, once the refuge of pre-adolescent boys and girls, have grown up and today represent an almost half-billion dollar business. The reason: adults are buying the magazines at a growing rate. "If we had to give up every customer below the age of 15, we would survive," noted Buddy Saunders, president of Lone Star Comics, a retail chain in northern Texas. "If we had to give up everyone above the age of 17, we'd be out of business," he added. A survey commissioned by Marvel Comics and reported in *The New York Times* suggests the average comic book reader is about 20 years old and spends about $10 per week on comics, an amount most children cannot afford. Price increases in the industry have pushed the cost of the average new release to $1.25 or more. The graying of the comic book readership has not been lost on others in the mass media, as the success of the film *Batman* readily demonstrates.

Today in the United States there are about 4,500 retail stores dedicated principally to the sale of comic books, up from fewer than 100 in the mid-1970s, according to Kurt Eichenwald in a story in *The New York Times.* Marvel and DC Comics tended to dominate the industry for more than a generation. Today there are about a dozen major publishers and many more smaller ones. The turnaround in the sales success of the comic book is partially due to a significant change in distribution meth-

Comic book heroes and heroines rarely have made a successful transition to film or television. Wonder Woman, Batman, and Superman are among the exceptions. In 1990
CBS premiered the TV series "The Flash," starring John Wesly
Shipp, and hoped that the DC Comics hero would be another exception to the general rule. It was not; the series
was cancelled.    (© 1990 CBS Inc. All rights reserved.)

ods. In the past, comics were distributed like all magazines. Publishers sold the comics to independent distributors, who in turn sold them to newsstands and grocery
and convenience stores at 20 percent below the cover price. Retailers could return
any unused publications to the distributor for a refund. Comic books lacked a stable
readership, however; the sale of a particular title could vary widely from issue to issue. Independent distributors were often inundated with huge returns; hence, they
gave short shrift to comics.

Enter Phil Sueling, a former school teacher and comic book reader. "In the
1970s he negotiated an agreement with retailers and publishers to become the first
specialty distributor of comic books," according to Eichenwald. Under his arrangement, retail stores got the comic books at 50 percent of the cover price, but the
books were nonreturnable. Other specialty distributors copied this idea, and comic
books began to flow far more freely from the publishers into the retail stores. And
this encouraged new publishers, and new retailers, and with the product more easily
purchased, new readers.

Most comic books are purchased to be read as entertainment and then discarded. But there is a vigorous market for used comic books, with some Number 1

issues worth hundreds or even thousands of dollars today. Hence, many purchasers gingerly read the books, but then stash them carefully in special plastic bags for storage and future sale. Comic books became an investment, and the jargon in the trade sounds at times like a conversation between Wall Street brokers. No one knows whether this new interest in the compact and colorful story books will last, but for many adults, being able again to enjoy the adventures of Spiderman, the Avengers, Batman, or Captain America is a welcome return to a simpler time in their lives.

# THE MAKING AND MARKETING OF MAGAZINES

There is a bewildering variety of magazines among the 11,000 or so that are published in the United States. And they are put together in a variety of places, through a variety of means. The construction of a large consumer magazine might very well take place on several floors of a modern skyscraper in New York City. A small newsletter sent to the owners of Edsel automobiles might be put together in the back bedroom of a small home in Peoria, Illinois. But all magazines must have some kind of content, and consumer magazines need advertising. And they all must in some manner get from the publisher to the reader. So generalizations can be made that describe how a magazine comes to be.

About three-fourths of the editorial content of consumer magazines is nonfiction. And most of this material is written by what are called freelance writers. This is a fundamental difference between newspapers and magazines. Newspapers employ full-time reporters and writers to prepare the editorial copy. Magazines rely upon self-employed, usually part-time, writers for most of their nonadvertising material.

Being able to call yourself a freelance writer is only a little less romantic than being able to say you are a novelist. There are tens of thousands of freelancers in America today. But most experts estimate that under 500 of these writers actually make a living by freelancing. The rest do it to supplement their income from another job, to promote a cause in which they have a particular interest, or simply because they love to write. The opportunities for a freelance writer to get published are high. But as one freelancer wrote in the *Columbia Journalism Review,* the pay is lousy, the editors are worse, and making a living at writing has never been so tough.

Freelancers survive by finding out what a magazine is interested in publishing, and then writing such an article. Many freelance writers also take photographs to supplement their written work. Magazine editors spell out their needs in books like *The Writer's Market,* which list the kinds of articles the magazine is seeking (feature, inspirational, news), appropriate length, and pay. The nature of the magazine defines the subject matter—a writer wouldn't send a story on a newly created drug to *TV Guide,* for example. Successful freelance writers are always working eight months to a year in advance of magazine publication dates. Editors plan that far in advance. The time to submit a Christmas story to most magazines is in June, not December. Pay is sometimes by the word, but for larger magazines a pay rate has been established based on article length. Popular consumer magazines will pay up to $3,000 for a feature length article. Of course well-established name writers like Gay Talese or Joan Didion can command much higher pay. But usually a writer will earn under $100 for the typical article in a small, special interest magazine. Consequently, freelance writers must be working on many stories at the same time. And even then most cannot make a living wage.

While magazine editors will occasionally contact a writer and commission or suggest an article, more often the writer must contact the editor through what is called a query letter. In this letter the writer attempts to sell the article (often before it is written) to the magazine. Rejections are common simply because most magazines cannot publish more than a small number of articles in each issue. But writers are often encouraged to complete the article on a speculation basis—if the editor likes the finished product, the magazine will buy it. If not, no payment will be made to the writer. A magazine will sometimes agree to publish an article for a set price, and then change its mind. When this happens the writer will frequently get a kill fee, a sum less than the amount promised but a payment nevertheless.

Most periodicals employ some staff writers, a truly exalted position for a journalist. But magazines employ many more editors and subeditors. In fact, the entry level job at most magazines is as a subeditor, not a writer. Such jobs involve editing articles, but also checking quotes, verifying sources, making certain that the freelance author has gotten the facts straight. The pay for this sort of work is steadier than wages earned by the freelance writer, but it is not much higher. Too many young people are infatuated with the romance of the publishing business and are willing to work for low pay.

Use of freelance writers is one important reason why it is not terribly difficult or costly to start a small magazine. A small circulation biweekly special interest magazine can literally spring from the spare bedroom in someone's home. Make no mistake, when Time, Inc. or Conde Nast publish a new magazine, they spend millions of dollars on research, planning, testing, and creating this periodical. This money is spent to develop a magazine that will be of interest to hundreds of thousands of readers and scores of advertisers, one that will have a very high likelihood of lasting beyond six months or a year. A small magazine publisher working out of a spare bedroom doesn't have that assurance; that is why only one in 10 succeed for even 12 months.

It is quite simple to find a list of interested readers for a special interest magazine. Assume our publisher wants to start a chess magazine. There are hundreds of chess clubs across America; the rosters of these clubs would be a simple way to start. The publisher can act as editor and gather information of interest to chess players, information about upcoming tournaments, new books on chess, and computer programs for chess players. The publisher or friends are probably avid chess players and could generate a few articles for the first edition. After that, readers will probably submit manuscripts for consideration. Frequently with special interest magazines writers don't even expect to be paid. Actually publishing the magazine is no problem. Small printing companies exist that will print and even assist in laying out the magazine. More and more small magazines are created through the wonders of computer-generated "desktop publishing." Once printed, copies of the magazine can be distributed through the mail.

The one subject that hasn't been mentioned is money—how does the publisher pay for this publication. Money must exist to underwrite at least the first few issues. Large publishers often expect to lose money for several years before a magazine shows a profit. Small publishers usually cannot afford this. Advertising will have to be found to pay a substantial portion of the costs for this publication, unless subscription money is intended to be the only financial mainstay. Chances of success by using only subscription money are not high. It is likely that during the first few months of the magazine's existence the publisher will spend far more time attempting to sell advertising than editing or writing for the magazine. Let's examine magazine advertising for a few moments.

## ☐ Magazine Advertising

Most consumer magazines derive about 50 percent of their revenues from advertising. In the past, advertising played an even more important role. Only 20 years ago magazines earned almost 65 percent of revenues from advertising. But during the seventies, in an effort to maintain a competitive edge over broadcast media, many publishers did not raise their advertising rates as production costs increased. The readers were asked to absorb a large share of the cost of the publication. Hence, advertising revenues decreased in proportion to total revenues. At the same time, the amount of advertising in most magazines increased. The advertising/editorial ratio at the typical consumer magazine in 1970 was 45/55. Today it is more likely to be 55 percent ads, 45 percent editorial matter.

The cost of magazine advertising, as noted in Chapter 4, is tied closely to the circulation of the magazine and the size of the advertisement. Circulation is the critical variable, however. The more readers who will likely see the ad, the higher the cost. But the actual cost of the ad is only one factor advertisers consider. Another is cost per thousand (CPM) or what does it cost to reach 1,000 readers. In 1990 a full-page ad in *TV Guide* cost about $100,000. A full-page ad in *Redbook* cost about $60,000. *TV Guide* had a circulation of about 15.8 million, so the cost of reaching 1,000 *TV Guide* readers was about $6.30. *Redbook* has a substantially lower circulation, about 3.9 million. So even though the magazine only charges $60,000 for the advertisement, the cost of reaching 1,000 readers is $15.38, substantially higher than the cost of using *TV Guide*.

Isn't the magazine with the best CPM ratio always the best buy for an advertiser? Not necessarily. A low CPM ratio is the key for an advertiser selling a product purchased by a wide variety of people—toothpaste or a soft drink. But placing an ad in a women's magazine like *Redbook* is probably a better buy for a cosmetics advertiser. The total cost of the ad will be lower, and most of the readers are potential purchasers of the product.

As noted previously, some magazine publishers offer advertisers the opportunity to reach something less than the total circulation via "breakouts" or regional editions. (See pp. 174–175.) Also, some publishers will offer advertisers a totally controlled circulation. For example, the publishers of magazines aimed at physicians can offer the pharmaceutical producer a guarantee that the magazine will be seen by X number of doctors because the magazine is sent free to each and every physician. Medical societies have rosters of all doctors practicing within a state; the lists are inexpensive to buy. The so-called subscription list is built around these rosters. Large consumer magazines tend not to use such tactics; their advertisers don't require such firm assurances.

The trend in the last quarter century toward the ownership of magazine groups has provided the magazine industry with the opportunity to offer advertisers discount rates for advertisements placed in several different magazines owned by the same company. These are called "networks". Time, Inc. offers advertisers a network of *Time, Sports Illustrated, Fortune, Money,* and other publications it publishes. The advertiser can select two or three or more of the magazines. The Times-Mirror Co. has a sports-oriented network, *Outdoor Life, The Sporting News, Golf,* and *Ski* magazines. Hearst can offer a women's network through *Good Housekeeping, Cosmopolitan,* and *Harper's Bazaar.* A single company produces many of the inflight magazines for airlines; another produces many of the shipboard magazines for cruise lines. Both offer magazine networks to advertisers. The networks offer advertisers a better CPM through the group of magazines than through a single ad in one of the magazines. An advertiser seeking to saturate the female market with an advertising offer could attain almost blanket coverage by using three or four women's magazine networks.

## ☐ How Good Is Magazine Advertising?

How does magazine advertising compare to other kinds of advertising? Does it cost more or less? Is it more or less effective? Answering such questions with generalizations is dangerous. The value and effectiveness of any advertisement depends upon a wide range of factors including what you are trying to say and who you are trying to reach. But with such caveats in mind, here are a few things we can say about magazine advertising.

Advertising in consumer magazines tends to give advertisers a lower CPM than other forms of advertising except network radio and billboards. At least this is what Jack K. Sissors and Jim Surmanek contend in their book, *Advertising Media Planning.* There are even some exceptions to this rule, however. It costs only about $2.77 to reach 1,000 women through a 30-second commercial on daytime network television, but an average of $3.44 to reach 1,000 women with a full-page color ad in general interest magazines. But you can reach 1,000 readers of women's magazines for an average $2.45 cost per thousand.

Sissors and Surmanek point to some specific advantages of magazine advertising over advertising in other mass media. An advertiser has more control over selecting an audience with magazines through the use of special interest publications and zone or demographic editions. Magazines provide fine color reproduction. A magazine stays in the house for at least a week, often much longer. There are many more chances the subscriber or readers will see the ad. There is good "pass along readership" with magazines. That is, many persons may look at the same copy. But there are disadvantages as well, according to the two authors. Magazine advertisers must place their ads many weeks before they are published. The closing date (the last day to place an ad) is between 60 to 90 days for a monthly magazine, three to seven weeks for a weekly. Also, persons who subscribe to a magazine may not ever look at the publication or may not look at it for several days or weeks. Advertisements need a kind of timeless quality; it is difficult to tie a specific offer to a specific time. The reader may not get through the magazine in that time. And of course, magazine advertising cannot have the action that television and even radio advertising can feature. There is no movement, no sound effects to catch a reader's attention.

Does magazine advertising *ever* affect the editorial content of the publication? The impact of advertising on media content generally was noted in Chapter 4. It should be said, however, that magazines seem to be under more pressure from advertisers than other mass media for two reasons. First, magazines tend to rely heavily on a few categories of advertising and hence, ruffling the feathers of one kind of advertiser can cause significant harm if all the advertisers in that category pull their ads for three or six months. Tobacco advertising is a good case in point. (See pp. 82–83.) But even more important today is the growing number of magazines.

There is only so much money to be spent on magazine advertising, and this amount has not increased dramatically over the past decade. But the number of magazines scrambling for this advertising has increased dramatically. Consequently, publishers have to be willing to take a smaller share of the pie, as the ad dollars are spread around evenly, or go to new lengths to capture these dollars. Most publishers are choosing the latter, and this has resulted in some rather extraordinary happenings in the industry. *Columbia Journalism Review* Associate Editor Michael Hoyt revealed in the March/April 1990 issue, for example, the kind of impact that some advertisers can have on some publishers. The cover of the November 1989 issue of *Lear's,* for example, carried the face of what most readers might think is a model. Not so; she is the public relations director of the fragrance maker, Guerlain, and her most recent project has been the marketing of a new perfume, Samsara. Inside the front cover of the magazine is a two-page advertising spread for Samsara. On the page containing the table of contents, readers learn that the woman on the cover wears makeup by Guerlain and that her fragrance is Samsara. The magazine also reveals the name and occupation of the cover model, being totally honest with readers. Guerlain bought two-and-a-half additional pages of advertising in the November *Lear's.* "This is surely a thing of beauty from the advertiser's perspective," wrote Hoyt, "a striking advertisement supplemented by the very cover of the magazine, a new fragrance product with the essence of editorial credibility tastefully misted all over it." Frances Lear, the magazine's editor, first told Hoyt the cover was a mistake, but later said "this kind of thing is done all the time."

"Is there pressure? You bet there's pressure. There is huge pressure," said David Long, advertising director for *People* magazine. And more and more advertisers are becoming successful in applying this pressure according to Long. Hoyt quotes Stuart Ewen who describes the recent changes in the relationship between magazines and advertisers. "At one time marketers viewed magazines as a place in which they could rent space for advertising. Today they view them as real estate holdings. Once you own the real estate, you begin to think about the neighborhood, the surroundings, changing the shrubbery and so forth."

The growing trend of long special advertising sections in many magazines, sections which frequently look like editorial content, is another indicator of growing advertiser pressure and clout. Years ago magazines would refuse to accept such sections unless clearly identified as advertising matter. But some not only are designed to mirror the magazine's own design (see *Elle,* November 1989 or the January 15 *U.S. News and World Report* ), but Hoyt reports that some magazines even promote the special sections on their covers in violation of the American Society of Magazine Editors' guidelines. In a few instances a single advertiser will "buy" an entire special edition of a magazine. In 1990 *Time* published a special issue entitled "Women: The Road Ahead." Sears was the sole advertiser in the magazine. Did this affect the editorial content? There is no evidence that it did; but there is also no evidence that it did not. While Sears used its 30 pages of advertising to promote its new women's apparel lines, *Time* editors apparently approached Sears with the idea for sole sponsorship, not vice versa.

At some magazines the reverse is even true, the content affects the advertisements in a perverse kind of manner. The upscale travel magazine *Traveler* refused to accept advertising from the Keebler Cookie Company, saying the ads were not compatible with the magazine's image. The snacks were simply too ordinary to be associated with the magazine. *Mirabella,* a highbrow fashion magazine, rejects cosmetics advertising from companies such as Avon or Maybelline, which staffers believe are more associated with K-Mart shoppers than *Mirabella* readers. How can publishers be so bold as to reject such advertisers when the advertising dollars are being stretched thinner and thinner? These publishers fear offending their readers even more than losing the advertising, according to the trade publication, *Inside Media.*

## ▣ Marketing and Circulation

Creating a good magazine with lots of advertising is only half the battle. The next problem is getting that magazine into the hands of readers. Today most magazines are distributed through the mail by the U.S. Postal Service or, for a small number of publications, by independent delivery services. The remainder are sold from newsstands and from newsracks in drug stores, grocery stores, and convenience stores (figure 6-1). Single copy sales account for only about 30 percent of magazine sales, down somewhat in the past ten years. The drop in single copy sales is attributed to higher magazine cover costs and discounted subscription prices. It is difficult to make generalizations about magazines that tend to use one system more than the other. *TV Guide,* the magazine with the fourth largest circulation, sells two-thirds of its copies off the newsstand. *Reader's Digest* and *National Geographic,* three and five respectively in circulation, are largely home delivered. Magazines with large newsstand, or what are called single copy sales, tend to be the gossip tabloids—*National Enquirer,* and *Star* —and *People, Penthouse, Playboy, Playgirl, Cosmopolitan, Woman's Day,* and *Family Circle.*

There are advantages and disadvantages to both systems of delivery. Publishers must spend a considerable amount of time and money to develop and maintain a subscription list. Computers have made this easier, but it is still costly. Delivery costs are determined outside the magazine by the postal service, and these costs have been going up. Finally, advertisers are impressed with long lists of subscribers, but are even more impressed with a high percentage of single copy sales, where a reader can express a real interest in a publication by paying the full price and going to the trouble of buying it. Postal delivery, however, gives a publisher a good deal of data on subscribers and permits zoned editions. Advertisers like this as well. The postal service may at times be slow, but it is generally reliable. A few magazines have experimented with independent publication delivery systems. For a small fee such a company will distribute the issue of the magazine to subscribers in the community. Such delivery is difficult because the law prohibits these firms from using a homeowner's mailbox. The magazine is usually stuffed in a plastic bag and attached to the front door handle. Publishers claim that reliability is a key difficulty with many of the private distributors. Postal workers make good wages. Because they want to keep their jobs, they tend to do a responsible job. Private delivery services rely on low-paid, nonunion workers; that is the only way they can stay in business. Such workers are often unreliable. Subscribers don't receive their magazines and become unhappy. Advertisers become concerned. The private delivery services which at one time seemed like a meaningful alternative delivery system to many publishers appear to be far less so today.

Magazines that rely predominantly on single copy newsrack sales also face problems. Newsstand sales can vary significantly from week to week. This makes it difficult to set long-term advertising rates or even print the proper number of copies. If the June issue of the magazine is a bore, returns may be high and this costs

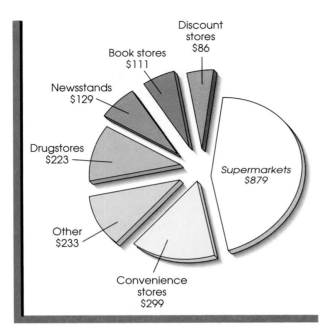

FIGURE 6-1 Most magazines are purchased in supermarkets. Convenience stores and drugstores follow in sales. (Sales are in millions of dollars.)

money. It is also often difficult to determine who is buying the magazine without further research when it is sold off the newsstand.

Getting the magazines to readers through the mail is relatively simple; the issue is delivered to the post office and the publisher is subsequently billed for mailing the issue. Getting a magazine to readers through a newsstand is a bit more complicated. The publication must pass through several levels before it reaches the waiting reader. In 1990, there were five large distributing companies that served the publishing industry. (In 1975, there were 13.) They take orders for each issue of the magazine, but never physically touch an issue. They earn from 6 percent to 8 percent of the cover price of the magazine for their work. Each issue of the publication is sent directly to one of the 450 regional magazine and book wholesalers, who have previously placed their orders through the distributors. The wholesalers then transport the magazine to the retailers. There are about 150,000 magazine retailers in the nation. The magazine wholesaler gets 20 percent of the cover price of the magazine. The retailer gets between 20 and 30 percent. Retailers return unsold copies to the wholesaler for credit. Wholesalers get credit from the publisher for returns, but shred the leftover copies rather than transporting them back to the printing plant.

Where do readers buy their magazines? Supermarkets account for most sales, almost 45 percent, according to a 1989 study by the Periodicals Institute. Convenience stories are second, accounting for 15 percent of sales. Drugstores, newsstands, bookstores, and discount stores follow in that order. But these statistics are somewhat misleading. While supermarkets and convenience stores account for 60 percent of all sales, they sell only a small spectrum of publications. Readers go to a newsstand, not Safeway, for *Scientific American, The Nation,* or *Billboard.* Newsstands carry a far broader spectrum of publications, but sell only a few copies of each. The big-volume magazines clustered in racks around the checkout counter account for most convenience store and supermarket sales. These are the same magazines noted earlier—*TV Guide, People, Family Circle, Woman's Day,* and the pulp tabloids. Competition is fierce for this prime real estate in a grocery store and generally only weekly magazines that have a high turnover qualify for these racks.

There are a few in-house distribution services: Time, Inc. deals directly with wholesalers. And a few magazines like *Family Circle* and *Woman's Day* deal directly with supermarket chains. The chains move the magazines to their stores with butter and bread and eggs. These efforts to create alternative distribution systems are the result of some unhappiness in the publishing industry with the current system. None of the 5 or so national distributors who take 6 percent to 8 percent of the magazine's retail price assume any financial risk. The wholesalers run monopoly operations and skim 20 percent of the retail price for transporting the magazines. But creating an alternate system is costly, and none but the very biggest publishers can really seriously consider such a move. Most are forced to work with the existing operators if they choose to sell the bulk of their magazines off the nation's newsracks.

Marketing a magazine is extremely important to publishers, especially those who rely heavily on single-copy sales. The magazine's cover becomes an important marketing device. Until the turn of the century the cover of a magazine was viewed largely as a protective wrapper for the contents of the publication. Some had simple illustrations; others carried a table of contents. But by 1900 publishers realized that a cover could sometimes sell the contents of the magazine. The work of many great artists—Picasso, Matisse, and Tolouse-Lautrec—as well as illustrators like Norman Rockwell became a standard feature of many magazine covers. Photographers such as Ansel Adams and Edward Steichen also created cover art for leading magazines. The 1930s became a period known for classic art on American magazine covers. But this era faded as competition in the industry became more intense. Magazine covers became billboards filled with promises, according to *Good Housekeeping* editor John Mack Carter. There are few magazines left anymore with covers that feature art, he added.

The magazine cover of the 1990s is designed to jump out at the reader from the jumble of publications on the newsstand or checkout counter racks. Publishers use market research to test covers and to test cover pictures to try to gain the maximum effect. "Cover design is not a science," said Sanae Yamazaki, art director of *People* magazine. "We frequently test covers in a simulated supermarket. We ask people what they see first on the rack, what they like and don't like about a cover," she added. Such research can produce rules or guidelines for a publisher. The rule for choosing cover subjects at *People,* according to Yamazaki is: "Young is better than old. Pretty is better than ugly. TV stars are better than music stars. Music stars are better than movie stars. Movie stars are better than sports figures. Sports figures are better than politicians."

While the cover art logically should in some way relate to editorial content, that is not always the case. *Esquire* instituted a policy in May of 1983 of putting a famous person on the cover. That first cover featured a picture of actor Roy Scheider. But readers—some quite angry—searched in vain for a feature article on the handsome actor. There was not one. Stung by criticism, the magazine revised its policy to insure that each issue would carry at least a short article on the cover subject. For years, women's magazines like *Cosmopolitan* have been featuring cover subjects—usually pretty women—who are not mentioned anywhere in the magazine. Apparently readers of *Esquire* expected something more.

Cover design cannot sell a bad magazine. But it can influence a purchasing decision by enticing a reader to pick up a periodical and thumb through it, or to convince a reader to buy *People* rather than *National Enquirer* or *Family Circle.* In the competitive world of magazine publishing, an editor will often look for any edge against a rival.

## ☐ Tomorrow

The magazines of the future? Jane Twyon, media director for Lowe Marschalk, peered into her crystal ball for the magazine *Marketing and Media Decisions* and came up with these possibilities:

Faxmags, delivered by fax machines and containing only that content ordered by the reader.

Magbags, magazines delivered in a pouch along with coupons and product samples.

Ecomags that will disintegrate after a certain period of time.

Kinder and gentler magazines for the aging population with bolder and larger type.

Idiotmags, for nonreaders, will have a voice machine that will read the magazine aloud.

Videomags, to be accessed by computer or interactive television.

VCR mags? They're already here, called "videozines," and are available to subscribers. *Set Sail* is a quarterly video magazine for boating enthusiasts. It has 5,000 subscribers and costs $19.95 per issue, or, cassette. *Travelquest* is another, and the first videozine to have its circulation audited by the Audit Bureau of Circulation. *Set Sail* carried about 10 percent advertising in 1990. The editors of *Travelquest* said they hoped to reach a 50/50 ratio of advertising to editorial in the near future. *Persona,* a monthly "videozine," is filled with celebrity profiles and interviews. It is sold in supermarkets and drugstores for $4.95 for a two-hour tape.

# THE BOOK BUSINESS

Mass media are typically thought of as a monolith, a single system serving society in a variety of ways. Indeed, the various mass media do share many common traits. But they have differences as well, differences noted in this text. It is possible by applying criteria such as immediacy of information and depth of coverage to arrange the mass media along a continuum, or on levels. Assume a momentous event has occurred—a cure for cancer or the signing of a peace treaty. Radio usually brings us the word of such an event first; it is the most immediate. But radio brings us little information. Television follows closely behind radio and adds a little more information to what we already know. Then comes the newspaper, somewhat later, but even more complete. Magazines are next, coming to us often days or weeks after the event, but with well-rounded, in-depth accounts of what has taken place. Finally, there are books, the slowest of all mass media to appear, but surely the most complete source of information.

Books are the oldest mass medium; it was a book, the Bible, that Gutenberg first printed. Books are generally the most lasting. Books tend to be the most expensive of the common mass media. Radio and television are "free." Newspapers cost a half-dollar or less, magazines usually less than $2. But books—even paperback books—usually cost more than $5 and frequently much more than that. A book can give us the greatest amount of information on a single subject, greater by far than even a long magazine article or a two-hour television documentary. Yet books offer the greatest breadth of information as well. There are magazines published on a wide variety of special interests. Books are published on *every* conceivable topic.

How many book publishers are there in America? That is a hard question to answer; even the so-called experts disagree. Virtually anyone can publish a book. It is simple. Once a manuscript is created, there are hundreds of firms that will print and bind 100, 500, or 1,000 copies of the book. Another book publisher is born. Ben Bagdikian, in his book *The Media Monopoly,* suggests there are about 2,500 book publishers. Another observer estimates that 200 new publishers join the ranks of the industry each week. Yet these numbers are deceptive in at least two ways. There is tremendous attrition in the industry. An individual starts a publishing house, issues two or three books that don't pay back the expense of publishing them, and the publisher closes up shop. A typical story in the industry. More importantly, Bagdikian asserts that only six companies, which control perhaps as many as 100 different publishing houses, control the industry, earning more than 50 percent of the revenues from book sales each year. And these six companies are heavily invested in other mass media as well. This may have implications for which books are published. The authors of a book entitled *Connections: American Business and the Mob* contend that Little, Brown and Company, which was scheduled to publish the volume, abruptly cancelled the book because sections of it reflected badly on *Time* magazine. Little, Brown is owned by Time-Warner, which also publishes *Time.* The publishers rejected this contention.

Others have contended that this ownership pattern—the major publishing houses being controlled by bottom-line oriented media conglomerates—has resulted in a new conservatism in the book industry. "The question can be raised whether they [the new corporate owners] have weakened the industry's willingness to publish controversial books," noted *New York Times* journalist Edwin McDowell, a longtime author of a publishing column in the newspaper. McDowell points out several instances in which major publishing houses have dropped book projects that have sparked controversy. Included in McDowell's list were *Personal Fouls,* a book about abuses in the North Carolina State basketball program, dropped by a subsidiary of Simon & Schuster; *Senatorial Privilege,* a book about Ted Kennedy's 1969 auto accident at Chappaquiddick, dropped by Random House; and a biography of Jacqueline Kennedy Onassis, which was published by Lyle Stuart after Simon & Schuster withdrew its offer to publish the volume.

McDowell suggests that the big publishers also seem reluctant to publish books critical of themselves or the publishing industry. No major publisher expressed any interest in Thomas Whiteside's analysis of the corporate takeover of book publishing, *The Blockbuster Complex: Conglomerates, Show Business and Book Publishing.* It was finally published by a university press. Large commercial houses similarly turned up their noses at Bagdikian's *The Media Monopoly,* which was ultimately published by Beacon Press, an arm of the Unitarian Universalist Association. "Does it not suggest something profoundly disturbing that most successful recent books of controversy had to be published by small presses, including presses operated by a church and a university?" McDowell asks. "Moreover, while the conglomerates brag that they publish more titles than *ever,* is it possible that many books on controversial subjects never get signed at all?"

## ☐ Picture of the Industry

Most of us think of two or three different kinds of books, the hardcover variety we buy at the bookstore for ourselves or for gifts, the paperback books at the drugstore and supermarket, and the textbooks we use in classes. But there is much more to the book industry than that. In that respect it resembles magazine publishing where the highly visible consumer magazines mask the much larger portion of the industry involved with newsletters, trade publications, and company magazines. The Association of American Publishers divides book publishing into 13 units—some of which have little to do with books or publishing. Let's look at these units briefly:

- Trade books—Books aimed at the general public, fiction or nonfiction, hardcover or paperback, including children's books. Trade books are generally found only in bookstores.
- Mass-market paperbacks—These fill the racks at drugstores, supermarkets, airports, and seemingly anywhere else people gather in large numbers. These tend to be fiction or very soft nonfiction.
- Religious books—Almost half the revenue generated by religious books comes from the sale of Bibles, according to book publisher Michael Crisp, but there is a wide variety of other such books published each year as well.
- Professional books—Books aimed at medical professionals, scientists, and engineers, businesspeople, and lawyers. Professional book publishing relies on selling a small number of high-priced specialized books and has grown rapidly in the past decade.
- University press—For years a press subsidized by universities and colleges published scholarly books that were of little interest to commercial publishers. Fewer subsidies today have forced university presses to balance the esoteric work with more marketable books.
- College textbooks—About 200 publishing houses specialize in both hardcover and paperback texts for use in college and university classes.
- Elementary and secondary textbooks—Books designed to be used in grades kindergarten through high school. Both college textbook publishers and the so-called "el-hi" publishers have recently started marketing computer software for use in classes.
- Book clubs—These publishers rarely generate their own material but publish book club editions of other publishers' books—usually trade books.
- Mail-order publishers—Time-Life Books, which publishes series of books on a variety of subjects, is the best-known mail-order publisher. Others exist less visibly and, like Time-Life conduct almost all their business through the mail.
- Subscription reference books—Encyclopedias, collections of classic works in special bindings, great books, and so on.
- Standardized tests—These aren't books, but many publishers generate tests for schools and businesses and market them aggressively.
- Audiovisual—Filmstrips, videotapes, films, audiotapes, records, games—again, not books, but an important part of the business for many publishers.
- Other—anything else you can think of.

It is obvious from this list we see but a small portion of the vast publishing industry when we walk in to B. Dalton's or the campus bookstore. More than 47,000 different book titles were produced in 1989 in the United States, more than in any other nation in the world. Of the 47,000 plus titles produced, only about 2,700 were hardcover fiction; another 2,250 mass market paperback fiction. Biggest category of book titles in 1989? Sociology and economics with nearly 6,000 new titles. More than 4,100 new juvenile book titles appeared as well.

## How's Business?

Book publishing has historically been an industry of ups and downs, good times and bad. But the late 1980s was a period of particular difficulty for publishers. "The American publishing industry is in turmoil," wrote Roger Cohen in *The New York Times* in the summer of 1990. Tremendous changes had taken place at many old-line publishing houses, with publishers and editors forced out by new owners. Editorial staffs were trimmed at other houses; publishing divisions within publishing houses closed down as well. Revenue was up in 1989, to $6.6 billion. And it was expected to grow to $7.2 in 1990. But book sales were flat or down. Fiction sales slumped badly. The return rate—the number of books sent back to the publisher by booksellers—surged to almost 40 percent for hardcover books after resting at about 20 percent for many years. A return rate of between 50 and 60 percent on mass market paperbacks is typical and did not change.

The economics of the book industry are fairly simple; the cost of publishing a book is fairly standard. Here is a breakdown of the typical costs of publishing a 300-page hardcover novel that is expected to sell for about $20. A press run of 10,000 copies is also assumed. (See figure 6-2.)

- $1.75 to print and bind the book.
- $1.50 for composition, typesetting, and jacket design.
- $2.65 for publisher's overhead (rent, office expenses, editorial salaries)
- $.60 for advertising and promotion
- $2 for author's royalties

This totals $8.50. The book is sold to the bookseller for about $10.50 per copy, or a little over 50 percent of list price. This means the publisher has made a profit of

FIGURE 6-2 When you spend $20 to buy a hardback novel, where does your money go? This breakdown is for a 300-page novel with a press run of 10,000 copies.

about $2 per book, or $20,000. But on the average, only about 55 percent of the books printed are sold. So this lowers the total profit to $11,000, or about $1.10 per book.

Most observers in the industry pointed to three fundamental problems as the source of the difficulties in the publishing industry in the late eighties and early nineties. The first had to do with profits and profit margins; the second concerned payments to authors; and the third focused on publishing strategies and the fickle reading public.

While revenues increased in the industry, they did not increase fast enough to satisfy the new bottom-line oriented owners of the major publishing houses. Many of these companies were servicing huge debts incurred when they acquired the publishing houses. Others had overpaid authors for recent books that failed to sell in the book stores. Some in the industry said the new owners wanted too much, too fast. The conglomerates failed to appreciate that publishing houses slowly build worth by accumulating back lists of fine books and cannot be fast-moving cash cows. Robert Bernstein, longtime president of Random House, forced out when the publishing house was purchased by Advance Publications, said that "the history of publishing shows that those interested in books do it better than those interested in money." It was the effort to increase profits that led to the cutbacks and layoffs and reshuffling of top editors in the industry. This effort also led to price increases in the industry. The longtime staple $4.95 price for a mass market paperback book was abandoned. Prices rose to $5.95 and even $6.95. And the price of hardback fiction inched above what many in the industry had regarded was a consumer price barrier, $19.95.

The other two problems are related. In recent times the strategies at some publishing houses began to resemble the strategies employed by the major film studios in Hollywood. Many shortsighted movie studio executives believe that the way to make money is to produce a megahit, a *Batman* or *Star Wars* or *Indiana Jones*. Invest as much as you have to, to get the right property or people, and if you hit the jackpot you will have a successful year. Two or three top-grossing films can subsidize a dozen or more failures and still leave the motion picture company with a healthy profit. Book publishing doesn't work that way, however. There are no equivalents of *Batman* or *Star Wars* that earn $200 million plus at the bookstores and return $60 or $80 million to the publisher. The best best-seller will rarely sell more than 3 million hardback copies, and that would return a profit of less than $6 million to the publisher.

But in an effort to publish the megahit, many publishers are offering authors extraordinary contracts. And often the promise of success that is surely anticipated when these contracts are signed is not fulfilled. In 1986 Doubleday published *Fatherhood* by Bill Cosby. The book was an immediate best seller, sold between 2.5 and 3 million hardback copies, and generated between $15 and $16 million in revenue for the publisher. Cosby had written the book with a $600,000 advance. The publisher signed Cosby to a $3 million contract for a second book. *Time Flies* was published in 1987, and while the book was the third leading nonfiction hardcover title for the year, it sold less than 500,000 copies. Doubleday earned far less on this book, but still earned a profit. For his third book Doubleday advanced Mr. Cosby $3.5 million. But *Love and Marriage* was a bomb. Of the 850,000 hardcover copies printed, only about 300,000 were sold. And Doubleday reportedly lost $1.5 million. Why did the book fail? Doubleday said Cosby refused to promote it with TV and radio interviews. Cosby says Doubleday failed to promote it. Neither would acknowledge that perhaps, with three books in three years, the public had had its fill of Cosby.

The Cosby story is not an isolated example. Random House paid $4.3 million for the rights to John Jakes' *California Gold.* Jakes is a best-selling author of 11 previous books. But the 12th failed, and Random House lost a bundle. Pete Rose got $250,000 up front for his biography, *Pete Rose: My Story.* It bombed as well. *Publishers Weekly* published a list of 24 books published in 1988 for which authors were paid big advances, sums of six and seven figures. Ten of the 24 failed to even appear on any best-seller lists. "Because you now see 1.5 million copies of a book by Tom Clancy or 1.3 million by Danielle Steel," said Morton Janklow, a literary agent, "a lot of publishers think the midlist [books that don't reach the top of the best-seller charts] should expand with it—that they should print 240,000 copies of a book that should sell 30,000 copies. Those expectations are unrealistic." Even first novelists are reaping huge advances. New American Library paid Anne Tolstoi Wallach $850,000 for her first book, *Woman's Work.*

Risks in the publishing business are inherent. But many feel that some in the industry, in an effort to generate unrealistic revenues, are taking far too many and far too costly risks. Publishing failures like those noted are hard to subsidize with successful new books and sales from the backlist, which account for as much as 30 percent of sales for some publishers.

## ◻ Success Stories

While the publishing industry in the early 1990s may be marked by the growing tendency to look for THE book, it is still sustained by continued growth and the popularity of genre books in fiction. According to a 1988 Gallup Poll on book buying, mystery and spy novels are American book buyers' favorite fiction genres. In second place are romance novels, and then action-adventure-war fiction, children's books, science fiction, humor, the occult and the supernatural, and finally westerns. The book industry has been successful in the recent past in developing new fiction genres, based usually on the success of one or two books. The success of Tom Clancy's *The Hunt for Red October* generated a number of other books by Clancy and others that fall into a category called "techno-thriller" by those in publishing. Authors like Stephen Coonts and Dale Brown have joined Clancy and others in making this new fiction genre exceedingly successful.

Fantasy is another area in which the publishing industry has succeeded in developing a fiction genre for adults, a genre that now accounts for nearly 10 percent of all fiction sales, according to William Morrow and Company consulting editor David G. Hartwell. Fantasy books have been around for decades; Lewis Carroll's *Alice's Adventures in Wonderland* is a fantasy of lasting importance. But the modern genre probably owes its lineage more directly to J.R.R. Tolkien's *Lord of the Rings* trilogy. First published in the mid-1950s, these three books remained incredibly strong sellers among adults through the sixties and into the seventies. The publisher of the trilogy, Ballantine Books, tried to duplicate the success of Tolkien's work, first by publishing classic fantasy works from the nineteenth century. But they didn't sell. Then Ballantine consulting editor Lester del Rey found a Tolkien-like manuscript by unknown author Terry Brooks entitled *The Sword of Shanara.* Using mass marketing techniques, del Rey created a best seller, attracting the same adult audience that had gobbled up Tolkien for two decades. This book became the foundation for the Del Rey fantasy imprint at Ballantine. Del Rey established the criteria for all the books to be published under this imprint, according to Hartwell. "The books would be origi-

TABLE 6-3   All-Time Bestselling Hardcover Books in the United States

| Book | Year Published | Copies Sold (in millions) |
|---|---|---|
| *Better Homes and Garden's New Cookbook* | (1930) | 23.8 |
| *Betty Crocker's Cookbook* | (1950) | 23.5 |
| *Webster's 8th New Collegiate Dictionary* | (1973) | 11.1 |
| *Joy of Cooking* | (1931) | 10 |
| *Mr. Boston Bartender Guide* | (1935) | 8.66 |
| *Tale of Peter Rabbit* | (1902) | 8.40 |
| *Gone With the Wind* | (1936) | 6.02 |
| *Prophet* | (1923) | 5.59 |
| *Guidebook of U.S. Coins* | (1947) | 4.75 |
| *Birds of North America* | (1961) | 4.70 |
| *Littlest Angel* | (1946) | 4.67 |
| *Halley's Bible Handbook* | (1924) | 4.24 |
| *Better Homes and Garden's New Baby Book* | (1943) | 3.85 |
| *Real Mother Goose* | (1916) | 3.60 |
| *Children's Bible* | (1965) | 3.27 |

The list does not include almanacs, annuals, bibles, encyclopedias, or textbooks.
(Source:*Publishers Weekly*)

nal novels set in invented worlds in which magic works. Each would have a male central character who triumphed over the forces of evil (usually associated with technical knowledge of some variety) by his innate virtue, and with the help of a tutor or tutelary spirit," Hartwell noted in an article in *The New York Times Book Review.* Del Rey then discovered another unknown writer, Stephen R. Donaldson, whose *Chronicles of Thomas Covenant, the Unbeliever* became another huge seller. The rest is history. Visit any bookstore today and note that the size of the fantasy section clearly rivals that of science fiction or even mystery. Perhaps the one distinctive feature of the fantasy genre is that most books are issued as part of a series, and readers who read the initial volume are left waiting a year or more for the next installment. Terry Brooks and author David Eddings had two different fantasy series underway in early 1990.

There was a renaissance in the late 1980s and early 1990s in the popularity of juvenile literature as well. The children of the baby boomers were in elementary school, and books were an important part of their lives. Revenues from children's books totaled slightly more than $800 million in 1985. They reached $1.5 billion in 1989 and were expected to reach $2.3 billion by 1992. In 1989 alone, ten well-established publishing houses added divisions or lines of children's books. Even children's authors, once regarded with some amusement by "real writers," were being heavily wooed by the industry. Houghton Mifflin Company paid more than $800,000 to Mark Helprin and Chris Van Allsburg for the right to publish *Swan Lake,* an elaborately illustrated version of the classic tale that retailed for $19.95. Well-known children's authors like Theodor Seuss Geisel (Dr. Seuss), Beverly

Cleary, Judy Blume, Shel Silverstein, and Maurice Sendak can just about write their own ticket, according to knowledgeable industry observers.

Children's books have built-in advantages over adult literature. It is easier for a children's book from a small or independent publishing house to make it to the best-seller charts. There is less need to heavily market such books; word-of-mouth is an effective promotional tool. Children's books stay in print and sell for many more years (usually an eight to ten year life) than adult books. Some are seemingly time-less and sell for decades. And unlike adult fiction, a children's book can actually in-crease in sales year after year. Once the initial rush is over for an adult novel, what's left goes back to the publisher to make room for something else. A popular chil-dren's book will remain on the shelf.

Books are distributed and sold in the U.S. in much the same manner as maga-zines are distributed and sold. Book publishers make use of the same 450 indepen-dent regional wholesalers that magazine publishers use. Book publishers also use many of the same retail outlets to reach the public. There are some differences, how-ever. Bookstores account for a tremendous number of sales, especially in trade books. The newsstand would be the counterpart for magazine sales, but does not do nearly the business of the active bookseller. Mass market paperback books are mer-chandised in much the same manner as magazines; they are sold from racks in su-permarkets, drugstores, and convenience stores. In fact, books can now be pur-chased off the end of most supermarket checkout counters, the same counters that are cluttered with magazine racks as well. Book clubs account for a tremendous number of book sales as well, but there is really no counterpart in magazine publish-ing. And of course textbooks are marketed in a unique fashion, not to the reader or buyer, but to the professor or teacher who will require students to read the book in a class.

There was considerable warring going on among booksellers as the 1990s be-gan, something that might be expected during a period when book sales are flat or declining in many areas. Booksellers fall into several categories. Most prominent is the independent bookseller, the corner bookstore. There are chains of bookstores as well that have grown rapidly in the 1980s. The three most prominent are Barnes and Noble, B. Dalton, and the K-mart-owned Waldenbooks. Then there are the discount chains, Crown Books being the most visible. Finally, it is even possible to buy books today in discount warehouses like Price Club, Costco, Sam's, and Pace.

The typical retail bookstore sells most books at retail price. The chains will fre-quently discount best sellers and both B. Dalton and Waldenbooks in 1990 started "preferred reader plans" which provide customers who take advantage of them with a 10 percent discount on all purchases. These schemes were an attempt to lure book buyers away from both the book clubs and the discount bookstores. Discount chains like Crown Books offer discount prices of as much as 40 percent on all books, but the discounts are sometimes not as substantial as one can get at the big discount warehouse stores. In a comparison made in June of 1990, the price of Robert Lud-lum's best-selling *The Bourne Ultimatum* was listed as follows: List price, $21.95; B. Dalton, $18.65; Crown Books, $13.17, and Price Club, $12.29. The discount ware-houses, which sell everything from baby bottles to pretzels, sell a great number of a very few books. They rarely stock more than 150 different titles at any given time.

The dispute among booksellers was between the independents and the chains. Chains buy the mass market paperback books at 56 percent of the cover price; the independent bookseller pays 60 percent of the cover price. And by virtue of their size and sales volume, chain stores also apparently get a discount on hardcover books as well. Bernard Rath, executive director of the American Booksellers Association, states that the price paid by booksellers for hardback books is set as follows: Stores that buy 1 to 9 copies pay 75 percent of the list price; 10 to 99 copies, 60 percent of list price; 100 to 499 copies, 59 percent of list price; 500 to 2,499 copies, 58 percent; and more than 2,500 copies, 56 percent of list. This means a chain can get a discount even though it stocks only a small number of copies in each of its hundreds of stores. The independent booksellers argue that this is unfair and asked the Federal Trade Commission to intervene. The FTC did issue a complaint against six publishers in 1989, but this failed to resolve the issue.

## ▣ The Paperback Phenomenon

Many persons incorrectly believe that paperback publishing began in the post-World War II years. In fact, paperback books were published in this country as long ago as the middle of the nineteenth century. The so-called "dime novel" is a direct ancestor of the contemporary paperback book. But their popularity, which was never great, waned around the turn of the century. Modern paperback publishing began in 1939 when Robert de Graff issued the first ten titles in his Pocket Books series of paperback books. *Lost Horizon* by James Hilton, *Bambi* by Felix Slaten, and works by Emily Bronte and Agatha Christie were included in this first list. It was a fantastic success. Ten thousand copies of the 25-cent books were sold in a week. One-and-a-half million books had been sold by the end of that year. The books were sold, as now, at newsstands, drugstores, and variety stores. Sears even included them in its annual catalog.

In two years de Graff had his first serious competition. Avon Books, then Dell, both spinoffs from magazines, hit the book racks. In 1945 Bantam Books was born. Fawcett began issuing original books under its Gold Medal imprint in 1949. By 1955 nearly one-third of all paperback titles were original material. By the early 1960s paperback houses were luring top-selling authors away from established hardcover publishers. Harold Robbins left Alfred Knopf in 1961 for a contract with Pocket Books. The paperback company had created its own hardcover imprint, Trident, to help lure Robbins into its stable. "Today," according to Thomas L. Bohn in *Undercover,* a history of mass market paperback books, "most paperback houses have under contract a profitable stable of best-selling writers and compete with hardcover houses for fresh writing talent."

In fact, there is a distinct blurring of the lines between paperback publishers and hardcover publishers. Many hardcover publishers have their own paperback subsidiaries. Doubleday, a respected hardcover company, also publishes Dell and Anchor paperback books. Or, both the hardcover and the paperback publishers are owned by a third company. Paramount Communications, Inc. owns Simon & Schuster and Pocket Books. And many publishers put out several different lines of both hardcover and paperback books. Times-Mirror Co. owns the New American Library, which publishes several paperback imprints: Signet, Signet Classics, Mentor, Plume, Meridian, and NAL Books.

Paperback books have become big business, representing 50 percent of all books shipped. But these little four-and-a-quarter by seven-inch books have had an impact on considerably more than just the publishing industry. As Bohn notes, "Paperback book publishing's influence on the mass media is directly related to its product, the marketing of its product, and the adaptation of its product by the other media.

There are many varieties of paperback books, but the two most common are the mass market paperbacks, the small four-and-a-quarter by seven-inch books, usually fiction, that can be found just about everywhere, and the trade paperback. Trade paperbacks are larger. This is the format most publishers use to publish the majority of their nonfiction backlist books: histories, diet books, reference books, cookbooks, and others that were first published in hardback 12 months or so earlier. Recently, however, some publishing houses are releasing quality first-publication fiction in trade paperback form. *Newsweek* described them as "large paperbacks with bold jacket designs that make them look like rock albums." Penguin first used this publishing idea in 1979 with its Contemporary American Fiction line, but it wasn't until 1984, when Vintage published Jay McInerney's novel, *Bright Lights, Big City,* that this new trade paperback phenomenon took off. *Bright Lights* sold more than 300,000 copies, and became the foundation for the Vintage line. By 1990 most major publishing houses had launched quality fiction lines in large-format paperback. Some publishers were issuing the same book in both the trade paperback and mass market formats, the former at $8.95 a copy, the latter selling for $5.95.

## ▣ Bits and Pieces

As America and Americans get older, the book industry is attempting to respond in a variety of ways. The sale of large-print books (with type about one-third larger than regular type) is growing each year. Sales were up by 30 percent in 1989, and as more and more books are released in this format, even more will be sold. Books on audio cassettes continue to proliferate as well. By 1990 Random House had some 250 titles on audiotape and often sold as many as 25,000 copies of a popular work. Other publishers have had similar success.

And in early 1990 Sony, the company that gave us the Walkman, gave us the Data Discman, the portable electronic book. The Discman fits in the palm of a human hand and uses a three-inch CD-ROM disc, a close cousin of the compact disc. The small disc can hold up to 1,000 pages of data that is displayed on a small screen. The Discman was initially viewed as a business or research tool, a means of storing financial data or retrieving notes. But it doesn't take much imagination to envision the day when we can stroll out to the park, sit down under a shady oak tree, whip out our Discman, and get lost in the latest adventures of our favorite fictional heroes or heroines.

## *BIBLIOGRAPHY*

These are some of the materials that have been helpful in the preparation of this chapter.

Anderson, Mary A. "City Magazines Compete for Elite," *presstime,* July, 1989.

Bonn, Thomas L. *Undercover.* New York: Penguin Books, 1982.

Carmody, Deirdre. "Entertainment Weekly Gains in the Mainstream," *The New York Times,* November 12, 1990.

————. "In Magazines It's a Man's World Once Again," *The New York Times,* March 26, 1990.

————. "In Magazine Publishing, Gloom But Not Doom," *The New York Times,* April 30, 1990.

————. "Magazine Publishers Re-energizing in Arizona," *The New York Times,* October 8, 1990.

————. "Newsstands Dwindle But Some Still Thrive," *The New York Times,* October 29, 1990.

Cohen, Roger. "Discount Warehouses Get a New Best Seller: Books," *The New York Times,* May 7, 1990.

————. "Industry Acts Aggressively to Increase Prices of Books," *The New York Times,* October 29, 1990.

————. "Killed Book is Haunting Time-Warner," *The New York Times,* April 16, 1990.

————. "Too Many Books Are Coming Back Unsold," *The New York Times,* April 14, 1990.

Compaine, Benjamin. *The Business of Consumer Magazines.* White Plains, N.Y.: Knowledge Industry Publications, 1982.

Eichenwald, Kurt. "Grown-Ups Gather at the Comic Book Stand," *The New York Times,* September 30, 1987.

Foltz, Kim. "Magazine Industry Bracing for Shakeout as Ads Drop," *The New York Times,* April 30, 1990.

Givens, Ron. "Prestige and Profits," *Newsweek,* November 12, 1988.

Hammer, Joshua. "Not Such a Happy Ending," *Newsweek,* January 15, 1990.

Hartwell, David G. "Dollars and Dragons: The Truth About Fantasy," *The New York Times Book Review,* April 29, 1990.

McDowell, Edwin. "Aggressive Discounting Pays Off for Crown Books," *The New York Times,* June 25, 1990.

————. "Juvenile Book Publishing Becomes the Goose That Lays the Golden Egg," *The New York Times,* October 20, 1989.

————. "Publishers Experiment with Lower Prices," *The New York Times,* May 8, 1989.

————. "Waldenbooks to Begin Challenging Book Clubs," *The New York Times,* February 27, 1990.

Scardino, Albert. "Donnelley Develops a Way for Magazines to Get Personal," *The New York Times,* November 20, 1989.

————. "Magazines Raise Reliance on Circulation," *The New York Times,* May 8, 1989.

Seelye, Katherine. "TV Guide: The Shake-Up," *Columbia Journalism Review,* November/December, 1989.

Servan-Schreiber, Jean-Louis. *The Power to Inform.* New York: McGraw-Hill, 1974.

Veronis, Christine R. "Black Press Comeback?" *presstime,* July, 1989.

Winkelman, Michael. "Magazine World 1990," *Adweek,* February 12, 1990.

# CHAPTER 7

# RADIO AND THE RECORDING INDUSTRY

It seems to be just about anywhere you can go. It's in the background at the supermarket as you push the cart along an aisle. You can hear it as you lay on a sandy beach on a sunny day. It comes from the car next to yours as you wait at a stoplight. It leaks out of the headphones worn by the person sitting in front of you on the bus. You can usually hear it in your kitchen, your living room, your bedroom, even your bathroom. Sometimes when you think you are all alone in the middle of a remote forest, you can still hear it. The sound of radio and recorded music can be heard everywhere today. It has become as common as the ubiquitous torn styrofoam paper cups and aluminum cans that litter our landscape. And almost always that sound is in the background, behind what else is happening.

Radio, and its sound companion, recorded music, are certainly not dominant mass media in the last decade of the twentieth century. Yet both are an ever present part of our modern culture. Gone are the days when the family would gather in the living room each evening to listen to the great network radio shows like "The Shadow" or "Lux Hollywood Theater" or "The Fred Allen Show." In those days radio was a foreground medium. People stopped what they were doing to attend to the particular broadcast. Sometimes they sat and simply stared at the glowing dial on the Motorola radio console, comfortable in the imaginary world created by the many wizards of the airwaves.

When we listen to the radio today we are usually doing something else like driving or cooking or cleaning or studying. That is why radio is called a background medium. And what we listen to is usually music interspersed with a multitude of sales pitches and the happy patter of the disc jockey. We attend to television. We attend to movies. We attend to newspapers and magazines and books. Radio and recorded music just seems to follow us along, a quiet friend who is always there but never gets in the way.

To say that radio and recorded music are not dominant mass media is not to say that these are not large and important industries. Nor is it to say that radio and recorded music are not important in the lives of many people. Minority people, especially blacks, consume more radio than many other forms of mass media. And recorded music, whether on LP, tape, or CD, is an important part of the lives of young people, both here and abroad.

Of all American mass media, radio has probably changed the most in the past 30 years. In 1960 most American radio stations, like most American daily newspapers, television stations, and even many magazines, were mass media in the truest sense of the word. The broadcasters attempted to reach as many persons as possible with their entertainment, news, sports, and advertising. Today most radio stations use a different strategy to survive and even prosper. While in the strictest sense radio stations are still mass media (a single voice speaking through a mediated channel to a large audience), in the 1990s most broadcasters have chosen to communicate with only a small segment of that mass audience. **Narrowcasting,** if you will, is the dominant concept. Select a particular segment of the audience, sell time to advertisers who wish to reach those particular persons, and then develop a broadcasting format (the kind of programming that is broadcast) to reach that audience. A small radio station can be relatively inexpensive to operate. If a broadcaster can find even a small niche in which to locate a particular format, it is possible to survive in most large markets with as little as a 2 share, or 2 percent of all radio listeners.

In this chapter we focus upon both radio and recorded music because the two have been wedded closely for the past 40 years. Most radio stations depend upon recorded music for the bulk of their programming, and the record-tape-CD industry depends upon radio as a key element in its marketing strategy. We will talk a bit about the size and shape of the radio industry, identify some popular and emerging formats, and look at vocational opportunities in the radio industry. We will further explore the relationship between radio and the recording industry as well as outline the impact of MTV on the recording business. Finally, a short history of pop music will be offered.

## THE RADIO INDUSTRY

There are about 9,300 commercial radio stations in the United States today. In addition, there are about 1,400 noncommercial FM stations. This latter group includes public stations affiliated with National Public Radio, college and high school radio stations, religious stations, and a small number of subscriber-supported community stations. Americans listen to these stations on their approximately 520 million radio receivers. This, by the way, is about half of all radio receivers in the world. In the United States there are two radio sets for each man, woman, and child, or about five in the average household. This seems like a lot until you remember all the portable radios, clock radios, and even radios in automobiles. Americans tend to turn to their radio for music—unless there is an emergency or a major news event. Then they look to radio for the news they normally get from newspapers and television. When Mt. St. Helens in Washington state erupted suddenly on Sunday, May 18, 1980, the number of listeners tuned to Seattle radio station KIRO—an all news and information station—jumped by 335 percent. Radio stations with strong news components noted a sharp increase in listenership during the Gulf War in early 1991. When people want to know what is happening, radio is the most immediate mass communications medium. Ninety-six percent of all people over 12 years old hear radio during any week. The average person has a radio on about 25 hours per week. Radio is also portable and can tag along on a trip to the beach or the mountains or the ball park. Joggers can listen to small radios as they circle the city park; bikers can carry them as well. The radio industry truly lives up to its long-time slogan, "Wherever you go, there's radio."

At one time network radio was king; many if not most radio stations were tied to one radio network or another. These networks provided a considerable portion of the broadcast programming for the radio station. Today that is not true. In fact, radio networks almost died in the 1970s when there were as few as four companies providing network radio service. But network radio is back, albeit in a somewhat different form. The development of the communications satellite, the device that engendered the growth of cable television networks, breathed new life into network radio as well. The movement of radio signals via a satellite from one edge of the United States to the other side of the continent became remarkably inexpensive and now even a small radio station can afford to buy some kind of network service.

Radio networks in the 1990s vary from full-time programming services to smaller enterprises which offer bits and pieces of a station's programming. Transtar and the Satellite Music Network both offer 24-hour-a-day programming services for local radio stations. Each service offers a variety of formats from which to choose. An announcer at the local station reads stations breaks, local weather, commercials, and perhaps even a bit of news. The remainder of the programming is provided by a disc jockey in New York or Los Angeles. The cost to the station for a full day of programming is remarkably small.

A wide range of radio networks provide news, sports, features, and special programming to local stations which use this service. Capital Cities/ABC offers a variety of network services that are designed to fit a station's music format. There is ABC Contemporary, ABC Entertainment, Rock Radio, ABC Directions, and ABC Talk Radio. Take your choice, based on the audience you seek to attract. Westwood One, a Los Angeles-based newcomer in the network radio business, offers a similar array of services. In 1985 Westwood bought the popular and successful Mutual Broadcasting System, which featured the Larry King Show. Two years later Westwood bought the four NBC radio networks. The oldest of the networks is the CBS Radio Network which served more than 400 stations in the early 1990s. The AP (Associated Press) Network served over 1,000 clients with primarily news and news features. These part-time networks usually offer an hourly news summary, live coverage of major events, business and sports reports, and other similar features.

Perhaps the most visible radio network in the United States is National Public Radio, which serves the 300 plus public radio stations in the nation. Its long-form news programs, "Morning Edition" and "All Things Considered" are two of the most popular network programs on radio with large, faithful audiences. Other networks include the Sheridan Broadcasting Network and The National Black Network, both serving radio stations programmed for black listeners. And the Caballero Network offers a variety of features for Hispanic-programmed radio stations.

Most stations can (and many do) survive nicely without network programming. But the use of such material offers smaller radio stations an inexpensive way to give listeners a far wider window on the world.

## ◻ How's Business?

It is as difficult to generalize about the economic success of radio stations as it is about the economic success of any other mass medium. There are radio stations that go out of business every year because they cannot make a profit. Some manage to hang on with the barest possible grip. Still others make truly fabulous profits. And success or failure can strike suddenly. The fortunes of radio stations with popular music formats sail along on the everchanging seas of tastes in popular music. And whether listeners enjoy or have grown weary of the antics of a musical host often determines the so-called bottom line at many broadcasting stations.

We must remember (see Chapter 4) that a typical radio station earns the largest percentage of its revenues (about 75 percent) from local advertising. And the prices charged for this advertising are determined primarily by the size and quality of the audience the advertiser is buying. The price of a radio spot may vary from as high as $1,000 on a top-rated station in a place like New York, to a few dollars at a tiny station in Moses Lake, Washington.

Costs at a radio station are divided among a variety of items. About 25 cents out of each dollar pays for the programming. A third is expended upon administrative and general costs (rent, the light bill, paper clips) and another third pays for sales expenses and promotions, according to the National Association of Broadcasters. Less than 10 cents is spent on technical and engineering expenses.

A well-run radio station in virtually any size market can generally make a nice profit. Industry revenues climbed from $3.7 billion in 1980 to over $10 billion in 1990. That is about a 270 percent increase in ten years. There are many more radio stations broadcasting today than in 1980, and this surely accounts for some of the increase in revenues. But each radio station is attracting more advertising as well. "Probably because the other media have become more expensive, advertisers are looking for more efficient ways to get the word out and they're using radio to do that," said Joan Voukides, an executive with the Radio Advertising Bureau. The price of television advertising, and the growing clutter of TV spots have alienated many national advertisers who now see national spot radio advertising (see pages 76–78) as a better alternative.

Finally, if we look at national averages, the average FM station makes a larger profit than the average AM station. This can be explained in two ways. First, FM radio captures seven out of ten radio listeners today. In addition, most all FM stations feature a low-cost, music-oriented format with little local news or sports or other features. While some AM stations still feature a music format, many have invested in high-cost, talk-oriented formats which quickly devour revenues. The costly operations of these stations tend to skew the average profitability numbers against the AM stations.

## ◻ Radio Around the World

Radio plays a far less important role in our nation than it does in the rest of the world. On the two-thirds of the planet that is economically and socially underdeveloped, radio is a vital part of the communications and information process. It can transcend the physical distances wrought by mountains and jungles and deserts as well as the intellectual distances shaped by illiteracy. In recent years social scientists wrote of the "transistor revolution" that is taking place in the economic Third World, the use of radio (along with government agricultural and health and social services agents) to educate people in rural, depressed areas. Much of the underdeveloped part of the world is still without electricity, making the use of television more difficult. Small transistor radios are cheap to distribute and operate. In these nations the government controls all or most of the radio stations, and these stations are used largely for utilitarian purposes rather than exclusively for entertainment as is normally the case in the United States.

The government also has a stronger hand in radio broadcasting in most of the developed world than it does in the United States. In Western Europe, Japan, Canada, and other places government ownership of most or some radio stations is typical. There are privately owned stations as well. But the decision was made many years ago in these countries that radio broadcasting was far too important to be left solely to the whims of the private broadcasters. Hence, while you can find rock radio stations in all nations in Western Europe, for example, you will also find many more stations than we have in the United States that devote their programming to more educational or informational functions. Programming on these stations tends to mirror what is broadcast on American public or educational radio stations. While it is not true to say that American radio is unique, it is fair to say that it is different from what is found in most of the rest of the world.

## THE RADIO DIAL

Radio sets normally have two standard broadcast bands, an AM (amplitude modulation) band and a FM (frequency modulation) band. Signals on the AM band tend to travel farther and are less likely to be disrupted by hills and buildings because the broadcast signals are aimed high into the air. FM signals are broadcast line-of-sight and more easily disrupted, but FM broadcasts have better fidelity, less static, and little fading or overlapping background noise. In the beginning, in commercial radio in the United States, there was only AM. FM was not developed until the late 1940s and was not utilized as a serious broadcast frequency until the next decade. Because of this running start, AM stations dominated the broadcasting industry. Most radios could not even receive FM signals. But FM radio began to take off in the sixties, for reasons to be outlined in a moment. By the early seventies FM stations garnered more than a quarter of the listeners. Today more than seven out of ten people listen to FM stations (figure 7-1). This listening pattern exists despite the fact that there are more AM than FM stations on the air: 4,980 AM to 4,280 FM stations. Why has the popularity of FM radio grown so rapidly?

For many years the broadcast industry did not give FM a fair chance. When licenses became available existing AM stations gobbled up the good ones and then simulcast their AM programming over the FM frequency. The government forced an end to this practice at the end of the 1950s. AM station owners were forced to air different programming on their FM frequencies at least half of the time. This brought about heightened listener interest in FM, which resulted in an increase in the marketing and sale of FM receivers. Also, by the 1960s the AM radio dial was jammed. Stations were often too close together on the radio dial and this increased the static on many AM broadcasts.

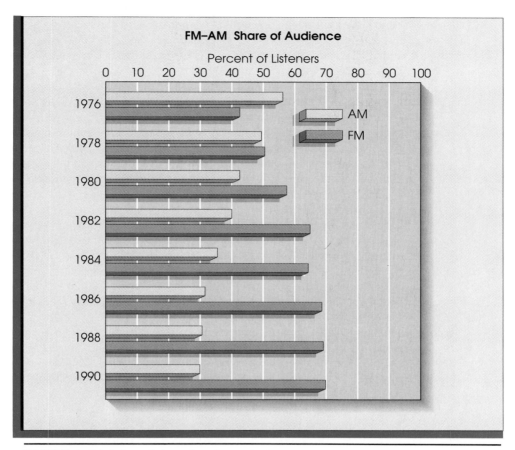

FIGURE 7-1 FM stations first captured a majority of radio listeners in the late 1970s. Today, FM dominates the market.

The crowding of the dial and the fact that AM signals travel much farther at night than they do in daylight forced many stations to shut down altogether or reduce power after sunset. The urban stations were often unable to follow their listeners as they moved to more distant suburbs. Programming on the AM dial was culturally stagnant. Stations tried to reach as many people as possible; their programming became bland and most AM stations sounded alike. This made these stations prime victims for the cultural fragmentation that hit during the 1960s. The young people of that era were the first to find FM. As they have grown older they have stayed with that band and new young listeners have joined them.

Faced with the prospect of serving less than a third of the market, the AM stations have begun to try to fight back. In many markets the AM stations have given up the young audience and are working with new formats in an attempt to attract the older listeners. In a speech to the California broadcasters, Ben Hoberman, the president of ABC radio, suggested four strategies for AM broadcasters to survive if not prosper. The ABC executive told the radio station owners to examine the news/talk format for their AM stations. "AM radio is increasingly becoming the information band," he said. Develop exciting, engaging, and provocative personalities, Hoberman asserted as his second suggestion. Explore sports—play-by-play broadcasts sound the same on AM or FM. Finally, be creative in developing new formats. Don't be afraid to take chances, he urged.

Hoberman's suggestions mirror what has been happening at successful AM stations in many markets. KIRO radio in Seattle, Washington, for example, has been the top rated station in that Pacific Northwest city for many years. The station has a strong all-news format during the drive time hours and news/information programming during the remainder of the day. The station has created several well-identified personalities, including Wayne Cody, an engaging and often provocative sports personality who broadcasts a call-in sports radio show each evening. Cody is also the sports anchor for KIRO's sister television station. The radio station at one point held the broadcast rights to the city's three professional sport teams, the American League Mariners, the NBA Sonics, and the NFL Seahawks, and University of Washington sports. Arbitron semiannual ratings reveal that the station regularly reaches 10 percent of the listeners in the market, which has more than 50 other radio stations. Successful AM stations in other markets have adopted similar formats.

All-news radio is even growing in popularity in France. But the news/talk format is not the only direction taken by AM radio stations. WWNN radio in Pompano Beach, Fla., featured a self-help format called "Winners Radio." All day long listeners could hear advice from experts such as Zig Ziglar, Tom Peters, and Leo Buscaglia about how they could improve their lives, their marriages, their businesses, and their health. "Instead of playing hit records, we play hit ideas," the programming director proclaimed. "The Motivation Station" became profitable quickly using this format.

In the late 1980s there were several "All Elvis" stations. One, WCVG in Covington, Ky., built its new format around 652 single records and 90 albums, all recorded by "The King." The station played old tapes of Elvis Presley talking about a wide variety of topics and called these memorable radio moments, "Elvis Him Selvis" features. And K-PAL in Little Rock, Ark., tried to win listeners with an all-kids format that featured storytelling and music, a joke and riddle call-in program, and news reports from their eight elementary school kid reporters.

The popularity of sports has resulted in a growing number of hours devoted to athletics on many radio stations. Some stations, like WFAN-AM in New York, WIP-AM in Philadelphia, XTRA-AM in San Diego and Tiajuana, Mexico, and KYBG-AM in Denver, have devoted all or most of their broadcast day to sports, including live coverage of games and press conferences and drafts, celebrity interviews, and call-in shows.

America's growing interest in business, as indicated by the growth of newspaper business sections and television programs and cable channels focusing upon business, prompted some radio stations to attempt all-business programming. KMNY-AM in Los Angeles was one of the first stations to construct such a format. The morning programming was aimed at people in business and was oriented toward stock market updates, news and interviews on business subjects, and reports from business analysts. In the afternoons the station focused on information for investors and consumers. Many other stations have followed similar formats, and there are several business news networks that provide news and features to radio stations across America.

Not all new formats have succeeded. An all-game show format at a station in

San Francisco died in six months. An all-weather and traffic format in Los Angeles incurred a similar fate. (What is there to report? It is sunny and smoggy and the freeways are jammed.) An all-women's station in Flint, Michigan also failed.

Surely the most controversial of the new AM radio formats is "talk radio." At lots of radio stations, announcers, news hosts, DJs, and others talk on the air. But **talk radio** is really a term of art for a particular radio format, a format built around controversial, outspoken radio hosts who interview guests and interact with listeners via the telephone, a kind of open-forum concept. This style of talk show first appeared in the late 1960s and early 1970s in many cities as the nation fairly bubbled in political and social ferment. But it largely disappeared until the mid-1980s.

The talk radio host usually selects a controversial topic as the focus of a program, and doesn't hesitate to let listeners know where he or she stands on the matter. Telephone calls follow. Some hosts try to use the program as a platform to push for political or ideological action. Talk radio hosts across America mobilized listeners in the late 1980s in a successful attempt to block a proposed Congressional pay raise. Envelopes containing tea and tea bags filled Congressional mail boxes as some citizens tried to remind their elected representatives of what had happened in 1773 when colonists protested an unpopular tax. These same talk radio hosts energized a protest against Exxon after the 1989 oil spill in Alaska. There are those who express concern that many of these talk radio hosts were DJs playing rock and roll records six months earlier, before the station changed its format. They suggest these hosts may lack both the knowledge and the common sense to be leading public opinion on important public issues.

Are these programs a new form of town meeting? A true open forum? Possibly in some cases, but research shows that only about 10 percent of the people in a community ever listen to these shows and a substantially fewer number call in. The programs can become a forum for inflammatory rhetoric in which callers make unchallenged, unqualified accusations. And misinformation usually abounds in such programs as callers, but sometimes hosts as well, make untruthful assertions which are never challenged or corrected. There is some question whether radio should be used in this fashion. But the format has been successful in many communities, and questions like this often fall on deaf ears while the money is flowing into the cash register.

Some AM stations attempted to lure back the music-oriented young listener by adopting stereo broadcast techniques common in FM radio. Stereo broadcasting was long a feature of FM radio and was another factor in the shift of the music oriented listening audience—used to hearing music in stereo through phonographs and tapes—from AM to FM. Serious technical problems plagued the development of AM stereo but by the late 1970s such broadcasts were feasible. In fact, five incompatible AM stereo broadcasting systems were developed. In the 1940s, when competing and incompatible color television systems were developed by CBS and NBC (see p. 37) the Federal Communications Commission picked one of the two for commercial development so television viewers would not have to buy two different TV sets to receive all the programs they wanted to see. It was expected that the FCC would do the same thing with regard to AM stereo, pick one of the five competing systems for commercial development. But the agency chose not to do this, opting instead for a "marketplace" solution. In the early eighties some AM stations converted to stereo broadcasting, selecting one of the five systems. Listeners were forced to buy a separate receiver to hear each of the five different formats. By 1990 only two incompatible competing systems still remained, with the Motorola C-Quam system emerging as the apparent standard within the industry. But confusion wrought by these multiple systems turned off both listeners and those in the industry. Only about 10 percent of all AM radio stations have converted to stereo broadcasting, despite its enhanced sound quality.

## ◻ Tomorrow's Technology

Two new broadcast technologies appear on the horizon, one already in reach, the other more distant. A new method of broadcasting on FM radio called **FMX** improves the quality of the stereo reception and increases a station's service area. By 1990 about 50 stations were already using the technology, and another 50 had announced they would soon adopt this system. Existing FM receivers will still work with the new system, but in order to realize the enhanced stereo reception, a listener will have to purchase an FMX receiver. FM stereo transmissions contain two channels that create the right and left signal. An FMX signal contains a third channel. This channel is compressed before it is broadcast, and then reconstucted or expanded within the receiver. The system's inventors say this reduces the amount of background noise and interference. But the system is somewhat controversial. Some audio engineers reject the notion that FMX enhances sound quality. With some stations already using the technology, listeners will have the final word on whether FMX works or not.

Digital technology has already been developed in the recording industry with the introduction of compact discs and digital audio tape. (See pp. 233–235 for a discussion of digital technology.) **Digital audio broadcasting** (DAB) has yet to be adopted, despite the fact it holds tremendous promise for the broadcasting industry. In a 1990 report to the National Association of Broadcasters, Dr. John Abel, the organization's vice-president of operations, outlined the advantages of DAB. Digital audio broadcasting provides noticeably higher quality than FM stereo (or FMX). The listener will experience far less interference in the broadcast. DAB requires very low power to broadcast. A digital radio station transmitting with a power of only 1,000 watts would be able to cover the same area as an FM station transmitting with 50,000 watts. Digital broadcasting is four times as spectrum-efficient as FM, which means there could be many more radio stations broadcasting in any given market than is now possible. (The digital signal actually takes up more space than a typical FM signal, but the digital broadcast signals can be much closer together and hence, more will fit on the same amount of spectrum space.) All DAB stereo stations could share a single tower and transmit at the same power. That is all to the good. Most experts believe that the major roadblock to DAB is that its use would require new space on the broadcast spectrum because it is incompatible with the current analog system of broadcasting. In order to find this spectrum space, it will have to be taken away from some other current use, such as cellular phones, television, military, or short wave, and so on. Or, the space currently dedicated to FM broadcasting could be used—if all FM stations adopted the DAB technology at the same time. And of course this would result in all current FM receivers becoming useless overnight. Don't expect to see DAB in the near future. Experiments were underway in 1990 at two Boston stations, and at least three companies were beginning to offer digital radio services via cable television lines. The customers said they liked it very much.

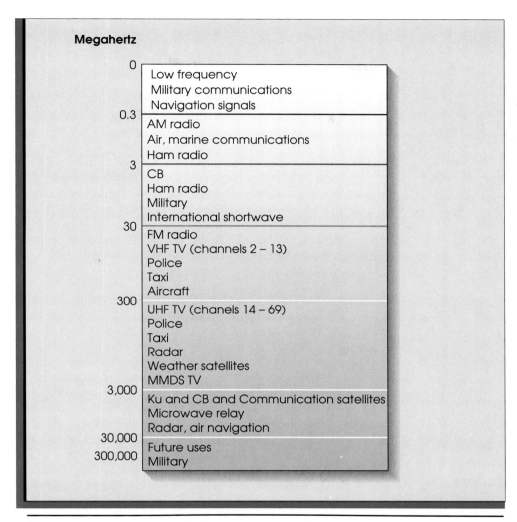

**Megahertz**

| MHz | |
|---|---|
| 0 | Low frequency<br>Military communications<br>Navigation signals |
| 0.3 | AM radio<br>Air, marine communications<br>Ham radio |
| 3 | CB<br>Ham radio<br>Military<br>International shortwave |
| 30 | FM radio<br>VHF TV (channels 2 – 13)<br>Police<br>Taxi<br>Aircraft |
| 300 | UHF TV (chanels 14 – 69)<br>Police<br>Taxi<br>Radar<br>Weather satellites<br>MMDS TV |
| 3,000 | Ku and CB and Communication satellites<br>Microwave relay<br>Radar, air navigation |
| 30,000<br>300,000 | Future uses<br>Military |

The electromagnetic broadcast spectrum is like a busy highway, shared by a wide range of communications interests.

# RADIO AND RECORDING

Joining radio and recorded music in the same chapter in this book is not an accident of organization. Today the two naturally belong together. The recording industry relies heavily on radio stations to interest record buyers in new recordings. (See p. 229 for more on this.) And the vast majority of radio stations broadcast recorded music most of the day. It hasn't always been this way. When a few radio stations began playing phonograph records over the air in the early 1920s, this was criticized as a waste of valuable airtime by many persons, including Secretary of Commerce Herbert Hoover, the man charged with the regulation of the broadcast industry. (Hoover said he found radio commercials even more distasteful.)

Legal impediments as well blocked the development of recorded music formats at radio stations. The Federal Communications Commission, the agency established in 1934 to regulate the broadcasting industry, insisted that each time a phonograph record was played over the air it had to be identified as recorded music. Ostensibly the rule was to protect the public from being deceived into believing they were hearing a live music broadcast. (Such live music programs were common in that era.) It was more likely, however, that the rule was an attempt to discourage radio stations from broadcasting prerecorded music.

Recording artists and musicians placed warnings on their records, "NOT LICENSED FOR RADIO BROADCAST," because they feared the broadcast of their recordings would hurt record sales. Many artists also had exclusive radio contracts with radio networks and were fearful that the broadcast of their recorded music by rival network stations would damage their contractual agreements. In 1940 a United States Court of Appeals ruled that the "NOT LICENSED FOR RADIO BROADCAST" prohibition was invalid; record purchasers could do anything they want with recordings, including broadcast them.

Martin Block was the first "record introducer" (the term *disc jockey* had yet to be coined) who gained prominence in America. His "Make Believe Ballroom" first broadcast in 1935 on WNEW in New York created for the audience the illusion that they were listening to live performances of popular musicians. The "Ballroom" was highly successful and caught the attention of radio programmers throughout the nation. During the 1940s the broadcast of recorded music was accepted by many in the audience and scores of radio stations used this format. It was the demise of network radio, however, that gave the greatest impetus to both recorded music formats and the elevation of the disc jockey to the status of modern folk hero.

As the forties ended the great radio networks began to cut back (and ultimately almost abandon) the broadcast of live programming through their thousands of affiliated stations throughout the nation. The local stations were left with huge holes in their programming schedules. The local broadcasters simply did not have the resources to produce the live dramas, comedy, and variety shows that had been the staple of radio. Such programming cost far too much. The broadcast of recorded music was viewed as an acceptable and inexpensive substitute. The only on-air talent needed was someone to introduce the records and to read the commercials. A small news staff complemented this announcer at many stations. In no time at all the record introducer was dubbed the disc jockey and became the most identifiable feature of American radio broadcasting.

The skills needed by even a successful disc jockey were limited. A good air voice—preferably deep and resonant—was the first requirement. A friendly and sincere sounding stream of patter was needed to attract an audience and make the radio commercials sound believable. The agility to run an audio board, including two or three turntables (and a cassette deck or CD player today) was also deemed important. Finally, and initially almost as an afterthought, the successful disc jockey needed what might be called a common ear. That is, the DJ needed the skill to pick records to play that lots of people enjoyed hearing. A disc jockey who was musically avant garde or seriously lagging behind the audience in popular taste didn't last very long.

Until the late 1950s, disc jockeys selected the records they broadcast each day. The DJ would come to the station early to answer the mail, meet with sponsors, and program his or her four to five hours on the air. At times, record stores were called to see what was selling; but most of the time these radio personalities used their own judgment to pick, from the scores of new records coming to the station, the handful that would ever by played over the air.

The power that the disc jockeys had to expose new records to the buying audience was not lost on the recording industry. By the early fifties, record manufacturers realized that air play did not hurt record sales; in fact, air play was essential if a record was going to sell. Record promoters, salaried employees of the recording companies, began calling on disc jockeys to extol the virtues of the company's newest releases.

The growing promotion of records accompanied the growth in the radio industry of what are called tight **playlists**. Competition among radio stations became intense as rock music burst on the scene and the potential to advertise millions of dollars in products to young people was seen for the first time. A top 40 (and even top 20) mania swept through most radio stations as the broadcasters played only the most popular records (plus a handful of new songs) to insure that the fickle teenage audience would stay tuned. Before a record could ever make the top 40, it had to be among that handful of new songs broadcast. Competition to crack the radio station playlists became intense. By the middle of the decade many record promoters brought not only their newest recordings to the radio station; they also plied the disc jockeys with expensive gifts and even cash. The payments violated federal regulations which required broadcasters to disclose when they had received something of value in return for air play.

These gifts and cash are called "payola." Public discovery of these illegal practices resulted in a congressional investigation of the recording and radio industries and the interruption or even the end of the careers of several popular disc jockeys. The payola scandal also resulted in a fundamental change in the manner in which radio stations selected the music to be broadcast. The DJs were stripped of the authority to pick the records they placed. Instead, some radio station managers hired program directors or music directors to make these selections, believing that someone closer to management would be less subject to temptation. The entire staff— DJs, program directors, and others—constructed the playlists at other stations. This reduced the power of a single disc jockey to that of a committee member. Finally, some radio stations hired outside consulting firms to advise them on new records and prepare the playlists.

These record programming consultants have been highly influential in the radio industry, almost a force unto themselves. Nearly 50 such services exist in the early 1990s. Often these consultants simply provide stations with weekly reports or tip sheets around which a playlist is developed. Sometimes the consultants are asked to go much farther and design the total programming for a radio station. This can include selecting the station's format (see p. 222 for more on formats), preparing the jingles and station promos, establishing the time for news and weather and sports reports (20 minutes after the hour or 5 minutes before the hour), and determining what records will be played, in what order, and when. There is often little left for the DJs or others to do except follow this heavily programmed format, read local commercials, give a time check now and then, and read an occasional station break. (Some stations have gone even one step beyond this and bring in the entire program—music, disc jockey, and all—via a satellite for local broadcast. Local announcers read local spots, and give weather reports and station breaks.)

Taking the choice of records out of the hands of the individual disc jockey permitted station owners to produce a narrower and more clearly defined sound for a station. But reducing the DJ's power to select the records to be played did not necessarily end the payola problems. Since the mid-1970s investigations have revealed that payola continues to flow in the radio-recording industries. Numerous record company executives and independent record promoters have been indicted, charged, and convicted of illegal activities. Payments of cash, clothing, money orders, airline tickets, and drugs have been made to program directors and others in exchange for the air play of records. Four radio stations which were mentioned in federal indictments were warned by FCC Chairman Al Sikes in late 1989 that their licenses could be revoked if allegations about payola were substantiated. Some news reports on CBS and NBC even tied the use of payola to organized crime. In 1990 the government filed a 57-count indictment against Joseph Isgro, who was head of promotions at Motown and EMI Records before becoming an independent record promoter. The government charged Isgro with making illegal payments to radio stations in California and Texas in return for their playing certain records on the air. He was also charged with giving cocaine to program directors at several radio stations. But the trial ended in a bust for the government in September 1990, when a federal judge dismissed all charges against Isgro after federal prosecutors had withheld from defense lawyers a key piece of evidence. Because of what the judge called the government misconduct in the case, the judge dismissed the charges "with prejudice," making it almost impossible for the government to refile these charges against Isgro. The government attorneys said they planned to appeal.

Regardless of these charges and others, there are those in both the radio and recording industries who deny the existence of payola. But most knowledgeable insiders found the denials hard to swallow. The industry is simply too big, there is too much money to be made, there is too much competition, and there are too many people who are greedy, according to one recording company executive.

## Formats

The end of network radio programming marked the beginning of subtle but important changes in American radio. Broadcasting stations from the twenties through the forties generally sought to capture a broad, undifferentiated audience with their programming. The entertainment programs were intended to appeal to the young and old, rich and poor, student and scholar. Today this is called a **horizontal programming strategy,** a programming strategy intended to reach from end to end of the audience spectrum. The growth of recorded music as the predominant radio content, however, permitted individual broadcasters to appeal to a narrower audience, less than the full spectrum of potential listeners. Programming—usually music—could be broadcast that would attract only a segment of the audience. Such a scheme is called a vertical programming strategy.

Most American radio stations today use a **vertical programming strategy.** A segment of the audience is selected and a kind of programming is defined that station owners hope will appeal to the selected listeners. This defined programming is called a **format.** Virtually every radio station has a format; even stations using a horizontal programming appeal can be said to have a format designed to appeal to a broad audience.

A format permits the station to have a personality, an identity. Thirty-five years ago there were but a handful of formats. Listeners in the fifties could listen to rock and roll stations, stations that played music for adults, country music stations, or a handful of stations that broadcast classical music. But in the past three decades, especially the past ten years, station formats have proliferated greatly. Music is the dominant component of most station formats, but as will be noted shortly, listeners have other options as well today.

The narrow variations between and among radio station formats today undoubtedly seem arcane or even silly to many persons outside the industry. The differences between all news and news/talk or easy listening and soft contemporary appear inconsequential. But the differences are real to the radio station executive trying to carve out a niche in an urban audience. So let's consider these various formats briefly.

The most popular radio format in the early 1990s is called adult contemporary, or AC. This is perhaps the broadest format and usually features a mix of mellow contemporary rock, ballads, and even softer oldies. The emphasis is on the melody, songs that people can remember or even hum. This format appeals to an adult audience, especially women in the 25 to 49 age group. This is an attractive audience for advertisers. AC stations often provide listeners with a healthy dose of news, weather, and sports, and this format is found on both AM and FM stations. Some AC stations emphasize familiar older songs over other kinds of music.

Top-40 radio, christened "contemporary hit radio" in the mid-1980s, is another common radio format, especially on FM. This is radio for young people, people who buy most of the records and tapes. Contemporary hit radio is the home of the personality DJ or DJs, as it is common for these radio personalities to work in teams. Music is the mainstay, but the DJs often bombard the listener with silly or tasteless jokes, outrageous spoofs of TV programs, games, features, and promotion contests. It is radio only an adolescent could love when carried to its furthest extremes. The chart—the top rock records—is at the heart of the the contemporary hit radio (CHR) format. All the songs are in a rotation level, heavy to light, and it is not uncommon to play the most popular songs six to eight times a day. A CHR station may have as few as 30 songs on its playlist. If there is any news, it is an afterthought. In 1990 CHR was the home of Madonna, Michael Jackson, Aerosmith, and other pop stars.

Easy listening, country, and album-oriented rock stations follow the two formats outlined above in popularity. The easy listening format—dubbed elevator music by its detractors—features soft instrumentals and vocals, usually homogenized versions of popular songs. The subdued and unobtrusive disc jockeys offer listeners a minimum of chatter. The music and the voice remain subtly in the background.

Country music stations are still popular in the United States, especially in the South and Southwest. But they are not as popular today as they were 15 years ago when country and western music literally swept the nation. In some parts of America, country and western music has been a staple of the culture for decades. And the country formats still attract many, many followers. It was the growth of the popularity of country music in the urban centers of the North and East that caused the tremendous increase in stations using a country format in the seventies. And it is in these urban areas that the popularity of the format sank in the mid-eighties.

The album-oriented rock stations are considered by some the dinosaurs of popular radio formats in the eighties. Album-oriented rock became an important format in the seventies when many stations—especially FM stations—tossed out the normally heavily commercial Top 40 format and began to play long cuts from rock albums. These stations mirrored twin trends in the music business; the growth in popularity of albums over singles, and the attempt by many rock performers to eschew commercialism and seek a kind of musical purity. But commercialism is back in the 1990s. The popularity of the album-oriented rock station faded slightly. These remain a haven of "serious" popular music fans who like their disc jockeys to know a little bit more about a musical performer than the dates and destinations of an upcoming concert tour.

News/talk and all news formats—when combined—rank high in popularity as well. The news-oriented station can only survive in a reasonably large radio market—a big city. It is not unusual, however, that such stations are ratings leaders in these markets.

There are slight differences in the all-news and the news/talk formats. An all-news station broadcasts news all day long. What is called "the news wheel" is at the center of the format. News summaries are given every 15 to 30 minutes. In between these five minute summaries, the station broadcasts news features, short documentaries, remote broadcasts, weather, sports, and other public affairs features. Virtually the same news summaries—with updates—are the main spokes of the wheel. It is this constantly revolving and repetitious wheel that many listeners find boring.

Stations with a news/talk format normally use the all news format during drive times—6 A.M. to 9:30 A.M. and 3:30 P.M. to 7 P.M. In between, however, announcers or "hosts" conduct interviews with authors, scientists, business leaders—virtually anyone who is in town who might have something to say on a subject of interest. Phone interviews with subjects in other cities—even other nations—also are a part of the programming. Topics of the interviews range from books to social problems to upcoming events to environmental concerns.

The all-news and news/talk formats are expensive to operate. A large news and production staff is essential. Equipment costs can be high as well since many of these

Larry King is the host of one of a handful of nationally broadcast radio call-in shows. These programs tend to be broadcast at night or on the weekends and attract a large and varied audience. King's program is heard on more than 150 stations. (Mutual Broadcasting)

stations have introduced a computerized newsroom similar to that found in a modern daily newspaper. A visitor at the station will find video display terminals around the newsroom and in the announcing booths and a central storage computer in a closet or behind a table. Reporters compose their stories on the terminals and the material is stored until it is needed by an announcer or host, who can bring up the story on his or her screen at the push of a button. Wire stories, weather reports, sports scores, stock market tables are all fed directly into the computer from outside sources. Multiple tape decks are used to play commercials and news interviews called "actualities." The new electronic equipment significantly cuts down the flow of paper through the studio and those who have worked with it call the system a wonder—except when it is down.

Classical music stations are the prototype of the vertically programmed broadcast operation. Classical music was once very important on American radio. Many hours of live classical music were broadcast each week; the National Broadcasting Company even had its own renowned symphony orchestra. Today usually one or two classical music stations survive in only the larger radio markets, providing listeners with full-length compositions by Bach, Beethoven, Brahms, Mozart, and scores of other master composers. While many of these stations do well in attracting listeners (KING-FM in Seattle often ranks among the top ten rated stations), it is the quality of the audience that is the key. Classical music listeners tend to be at the top end of the demographic charts, and sought after by foreign car dealers, exclusive clothing boutiques, wine shops, bookstores, and even brokerage houses. The announcers are serious and knowledgeable about the music they play. Today many of the classical stations are public radio stations, although there are private stations that program classical music as well.

Nostalgia is still big business in radio, and stations that play exclusively oldies are popular as well. There are at least two kinds of nostalgia formats. One has a rock music base and plays "newer" oldies, music from the late fifties on. Songs by Elvis, the Beatles, the Beach Boys, the Four Seasons, the Supremes, and many others fill the playlist. Another oldie format features popular (translated, that means nonrock) music from the forties, fifties, and sixties. Big bands, Sinatra, Crosby, Patti Page, Doris Day, the Four Aces, the McGuire Sisters, and others are featured on these stations.

There is a mix of different kinds of music that fits under a variety of similar formats called urban contemporary, rhythm and blues, or simply black. These stations play a mix of music such as soul (Aretha Franklin), R & B (Chuck Berry et al.) and rap (L.L. Cool J. or Tone Loc). There are more than 200 of these stations aimed primarily at the black urban audience. Yet less than half of these stations are owned or even operated by blacks. Black-oriented radio stations have existed for decades.

Spanish-language radio stations have a shorter history than black-oriented stations. The first Hispanic station, KCOR in San Antonio, began broadcasting in 1946. But since that time the influx of Hispanic people into the United States has spurred the popularity and growth of Spanish-language radio. Today there are nearly 200 stations that broadcast programming in Spanish, and many other stations include Spanish-language programs in their English-language formats. Nearly all Spanish-language stations program music, but there is a variety of music formats for the Hispanic listeners, just as there is a variety of formats among Anglo stations. Ranchera music, Mexican music similar to American country music, is the most popular format. Nortena is American cowboy-type music from northern Mexico, and Tex-Mex is a

Texas and Mexican combination country style. Some stations program contemporary or modern Spanish music, others play predominantly salsa, lively Caribbean music with a fast beat.

Competition is severe among Hispanic broadcasters who find they must diversify their programming to offer different kinds of Latin music and features to appeal to Hispanic people of different nationalities and age groups.

Religious (usually Christian) stations have a small, but extremely loyal following. Churches were some of the earliest holders of broadcast licenses in the nation. A fundamentalist Christian revival that began late in the 1970s as the world approached the millennium (the year 2000) spurred the growth of the Christian format. Religiously oriented music—even rock—is the heart of a format that also features ample segments of news, information, and religious messages.

New-age music formats appeared on stations in a few cities. KMET in Los Angeles was one of the first stations to exclusively program the soft rock, light jazz, heavily synthesized mood music. The adoption of this format at the station, which had been a pioneer album rock station, led *Newsweek* to announce the change in this manner: "Pod People Take Over KMET, Turn it into KTWV, Replace Rock and Roll with Brain-Numbing White Noise." A Seattle station adopted a similar format but a large number of the uninitiated members of the community somehow equated the new-age phenomenon with Satanism and the black arts and their protests prompted the station to quietly modify its format to soft rock/adult contemporary.

Finally, there are a small group of stations that program what they call "alternative music," a mixture of music on the fringe of a variety of musical categories. Such stations usually feature a wide range of specialty shows which feature such music as rap, reggae, dance, and house music (a hybrid of music that first emerged in Chicago in the late 1980s, influenced not only by the 1970s disco and funky dance tracks, but by people like Issac Hayes and by Italian disco imports), avant garde rock, jazz, and blues. Alternative music stations, and these are usually noncommercial college radio stations, might be considered the testing ground for the music of tomorrow. Record companies like to service these stations because the music that becomes popular on these alternative radio stations often later becomes popular among the wider general audience. U2 and REM, two of today's most popular groups, first gained prominence on college radio stations.

## ▪ Public Broadcasting and Community/Nonprofit Stations

There are only about 300 public broadcasting stations in the United States today, but their listeners are among the most devoted radio listeners in the nation. A survey conducted in 1988 revealed that each week, over 4 million listeners make a public radio station their favorite station by listening to it more than any other radio service available. Over the course of a year, about 12 percent of all adults listen to public radio. In many ways the public stations mirror the eclecticism of the college alternative music stations. Their formats are a mix of talk and music, of arts and news. Public radio stations sound a lot like radio stations used to sound before commercial radio discovered the disc jockey and recorded music in the 1950s.

The public stations are linked by National Public Radio, a vibrant network that features some of the best listening opportunities in the nation. NPR is anchored by two long-form news programs, "Morning Edition" and "All Things Considered." The network carries a variety of syndicated music shows including "Music from the Heart of Space," a new-age music show, "New Sounds," a program featuring innovative

Since its inception in 1970, National Public Radio has developed a small but highly loyal audience. It also has given public exposure to some of the most talented national correspondents in broadcast journalism, including Nina Tottenberg (who covers the Supreme Court for NPR), and congressional correspondent Cokie Roberts. Roberts is pictured here with pets Abner (on the floor) and Tabasco in her home office.
(National Public Radio)

music, "Blues Stage," and "Afropop." Public stations also provide for local broadcast of shows syndicated by American Public Radio, including Garrison Keillor's "Prairie Home Companion." Keillor's popular program ended several years ago, but was still being broadcast in reruns in 1990. Keillor's new program, "Good Evening," a mix of music and variety, debuted in September of 1989.

National Public Radio almost folded in 1983 because of a serious budget crisis that was exacerbated by Ronald Reagan's policy of reducing government subsidies for both public radio and public television. But the network weathered the storm by seeking other sources of funding, generally placing the largest burden of revenue raising upon its member stations. The network today also generates funds by leasing the excess capacity of a satellite system it owns to other broadcasting networks.

Public radio stations fill in the blank spots around the network programming with a wide variety of content. Classical music and jazz are the staples at many stations. But numerous public radio stations have tried to follow the success of the college alternative music formats and have been successful. Some public stations play avant garde rock; others, "world music," music from a variety of nations. There are local interview shows, live music, radio drama, the reading of popular works of fiction, and live broadcasts from arts festivals. Government—federal, state and local—was supposed to fund these noncommercial stations. But government has been reluctant to meet this responsibility so local stations have sought support from the corporate community, and, most importantly, listeners. Pledge drives occur with the regularity of the changing of the seasons on most public stations, but the listeners, who devour the public programming, don't seem to mind.

There are lots of nonprofit community stations, and it is harder to describe their formats than those used in public radio. The most visible nonprofit stations are probably those operated by the Pacifica Foundation, a nonprofit corporation based in California. The five Pacifica stations hold a unique position in American broadcasting. They have been censured by the Federal Communications Commission for broadcasting obscenities. The transmitter for the station in Houston was destroyed by two separate bombings later linked to the Ku Klux Klan. The liberal-to-left-wing programming has raised the ire of the conservative right and resulted in harassment from congressional committees hunting for Communists. To say the stations are nontraditional is akin to calling Wolfgang Mozart a songwriter.

Listeners to the five stations in New York, Houston, Washington D.C., Berkeley, and Los Angeles are as dedicated as the NPR supporters. On any given night—since schedules often tend to be rather eclectic—a listener might hear explicit sex counseling, radio drama, a documentary on Marxism in the Caribbean, a discussion of the Paris Commune of 1886, or a reading of poetry. A broadcast in 1973 of a monologue by George Carlin on "seven dirty words" in the English language resulted in a lawsuit against the station that ended up before the Supreme Court of the United States and sustained the power of the Federal Communications Commission to prohibit the broadcast of indecent language. In 1984 Pacifica challenged a government prohibition against editorialization by public broadcasting stations and on this occasion won a victory in the Supreme Court.

News coverage is also part of the Pacifica programming format, and the tiny network broadcasts some of the hardest hitting documentaries on radio. The hallmark of the Pacifica stations is that they don't often pull their punches. While national public radio is inevitably polite and comparatively balanced in its approach, Pacifica is often rude and polemical, noted one writer in the *Washington Journalism Review*. The stations are supported primarily by donations from more than 60,000 subscriber/listeners. Pacifica also receives small grants from the Corporation for Public Broadcasting. It manages to live on a meager budget because many programs are produced with volunteer labor. Other subscription radio stations with equally unusual formats exist in the nation. Pacifica is most noteworthy but certainly does not stand alone.

A radio station defines itself with its format. As in life itself, there are diverse identities in radio broadcasting.

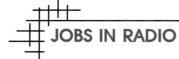

# JOBS IN RADIO

Many jobs in radio are easy to come by for a person with a little education and the willingness to work hard at many different tasks. But these jobs generally don't pay well. The attractive jobs in radio broadcasting are much harder to find and generally require education plus considerable experience as prime qualifications. Jobs in radio can be divided into two categories: off-air jobs and on-air jobs. Many people who work at a radio station never utter a word over the air. Engineers—who need technical training and a license from the government—keep the station on the air. Producers create the programming that is aired. Writers and editors prepare the news and other information that announcers read. These and many other kinds of jobs are available to people who want to work in radio but do not have the single natural requisite needed for on-air work—a good radio voice.

On-air jobs include disc jockeys, news and sports broadcasters, and announcers. College or university training is not mandatory for any of these jobs. But individuals with a college education—in communications or anything else—are far more likely to move ahead into jobs that have more responsibility; news director vs. reporter, or program director vs. disc jockey.

The pay at radio stations varies dramatically, usually based upon where the station is located. Someone beginning as a newsperson or announcer at a small, rural station may work for as little as $5 per hour. In larger cities radio reporters may start at $14,000 to $17,000 per year. Beginners at metropolitan radio stations start at a much higher salary—but usually these jobs require several years of experience at smaller radio stations. The average radio reporter earned about $14,000 in 1990.

The pay for disc jockeys is much the same. A top DJ in a big city like Chicago or Philadelphia could easily make more than $100,000 a year. As the size of the market decreases so does the salary. In smaller communities it is not unusual for the DJ to sell advertising for his or her own program—and the salary may depend on how many spots are sold.

Most beginners in radio are expected to do many jobs, both on and off the air. Experience is probably more important in getting on the air in broadcasting than it is in other mass media. Often young broadcasters start by working at high school or college radio stations—without pay—to gain the poise needed to perform at an acceptable professional level.

The radio industry suffers from some of the same problems as the newspaper industry in regard to hiring women and blacks. Vernon Stone reported in the late 1980s that only one in three radio news directors were women, and only 9 percent were minorities. When looking at management, Stone reported that his survey revealed that 72 percent of all news directors were male, and 94 percent were white.

# THE RECORDING INDUSTRY

The interdependence between the recording industry and the radio industry seems both one-sided and illogical at first glance. Recorded music is the predominant format at most American radio stations. Without records, these radio stations would have to find something else to fill up the broadcast day. But why do the record companies need radio stations? And, since both radio stations and record companies market the same product, recorded music, shouldn't they be considered competitors, not cohorts?

Record producers and artists are often more aware of the interdependence between the two industries than broadcasters. "The bulk of radio is irrevocably wedded to the music industry," notes Jac Holtzman, the former president of Elektra Records. "We need each other desperately. We both have a story to tell. We both tell our story with the aid of the other," Holzman added. The story the recording industry has to tell is the story of its new releases.

The recording and film industries are unlike any other mass medium in an important way—the continuity of product. Newspapers and magazines have subscribers, television and radio have regular listeners. Each day's newspaper or each day's broadcast is pretty much the same as the next day's newspaper or the next day's broadcast. There is a continuity of product. But in the recording and film industries there is no such continuity. One recording is likely to be substantially different from the next; even recordings by the same artist are not necessarily similar. Each new record must be sold to record buyers as a new product. Consequently the record company must bring that recording to the attention of the public. Advertising plays a role, a tiny role, in this process. Broadcast of the recording by a radio station is the most effective way to expose the release to potential buyers. Consequently, the record companies need the radio stations to play the records, to give them the exposure needed to bring them to the public's attention.

In a sense, the relationship between a recording company and a radio station is almost circular. Remember, radio stations are in the business of making money, not playing music. "The music that is played on a commercial radio station is designed to attract audiences that contribute to ratings that are attractive to advertisers," noted Eric Rothenbuhler in a recent article in James Lull's book *Popular Music and Communication.* But when stations choose to play one record rather than another, this has an impact on the recording industry. "Since songs need radio exposure to become popular, record company decision makers will try to anticipate what radio station decision makers want to play when they are producing and releasing records," Rothenbuhler adds. Since radio stations work within formats, this forces the record companies to work within formats as well. Music that falls outside or between the popular formats will rarely get air exposure, and hence will not become popular. And since it is not popular, it will never get airplay. How radio stations pick the records they will play is even more circular. First of all, there are many more records released than can even be considered for airplay. In a ten-week period at a single radio station 487 albums were received by the station, according to Rothenbuhler. Only 81, or 17 percent, received serious consideration for airplay, and only 35 ever received airplay. How did the radio stations decide which ones to play? The radio stations rely quite heavily on the promotional representatives from the record companies, who visit frequently to tout new releases. These agents are often shockingly honest, telling station program directors or music directors which songs they think will work, and which ones won't. These promoters rarely push more than a small percentage of the recordings released by their company. How do the promoters know what songs will go and what songs won't? Intuition and experience help. But they also listen to what others in the radio business are saying; which songs are getting airplay in other cities. What is written in the trade papers is also important, but the trade papers tend to report what is being said by record company promoters and music directors at radio stations. The irony of this system is, then, that the record promoters listen to what the program directors have to say, but the program directors tend to only repeat what they have heard from the record promoters, and they both read the trade papers, which report what is being said by program directors and record promoters. And this results in a tiny percentage of recorded music that *ever* gets played on the radio. Imagine a simple kitchen funnel. Hundreds of recordings each month move toward the mouth of this funnel, hoping to reach the record-buying public on the other side. The radio station represents the neck of that funnel, and only a few of these recordings ever get through that neck.

The public can be exposed to new recordings without them being played over the radio, but this is a rare occurrence. In the 1970s groups like Black Sabbath and Grand Funk sold millions of records without significant airplay. These groups used concert tours to promote their music. The growing popularity of club DJs and mobile **DJs** who play for dances provides another opportunity for certain kinds of music to get public exposure without airplay. But for most recordings and recording artists, radio air play is considered essential. "A record can never be a financial success if it lies outside a radio format, and today, with radio's more limited playlist, it's increasingly difficult to get on the air," wrote David DeVoss in *Sound Magazine*. The return of popularity of the Top 40 station (contemporary hit radio) has not been viewed with favor by the recording industry.

Over 80 percent of all single records released don't even earn back their production costs, let alone make money for the artists. The statistics on album success are not much different. There are a great many talented performers making records whom the public will never discover because their recordings will not get the airplay needed to succeed. Elvis Presley, Carole King, Barry Manilow, the Beatles, Madonna, and others all made records that no one heard of before they were discovered, before one or two songs started to get airplay.

## ■ The Music Business

The recording industry spent the 1980s on a roller coaster ride, up and down, up and down. The industry hadn't experienced an economic slump for 25 years, from about the time Elvis Presley released his first single on RCA ("Heartbreak Hotel"). But starting in 1979 the proverbial bottom fell out of the industry. By 1982 the recording business was "sick," according to producer Richard Perry. Record sales were off by as much as 50 percent at some companies. The number of million-selling albums was down sharply. And the top-selling albums (John Cougar's "American Fool" and Asia's "First Album") only sold 3 million copies. A few years earlier the Eagles led the charts when "Hotel California" sold 14 million copies in one year. While the major labels continued to show a profit, many smaller companies did not. Some died.

A combination of many factors was responsible for the slump.

- An increase in the cost of petroleum, a basic element in making a vinyl record, pushed the cost of an LP up from about $6 to almost $9. Many customers resisted this price increase and people who only a few years earlier would walk into a record store to buy one album and take home three, were buying just the one LP they originally sought.
- Recording companies were spending too much money on promotion and hype, and investing too much in new, untested rock groups. Too much was invested in costly concert tours, tee shirts, elaborate silk jackets ("The 'Nobody's' 1981 Know Nothing Tour").
- Established performers, noting the flow of big bucks to new groups, began to demand higher payments for their services. Some performers earned a royalty rate as high as 20 percent of the retail price of the album, far above the normal 10 to 15 percent.

- The advent of the low-priced audiocassette recorder permitted many persons to tape entire LPs they had borrowed or that were broadcast on FM radio. As the sale of LPs declined, the sale of blank audiotapes rose rapidly. The record industry asked Congress to affect a 10 percent surtax on the sale of the blank tapes. The monies collected would be distributed among the record companies, songwriters, and performers who lost money from the declining record sales. Congress did not act upon the request.
- Perhaps as much as anything, however, record sales declined because the music that was being recorded wasn't very interesting. Radio stations were fighting harder than ever for listeners and became even more conservative. The playlists became shorter and shorter, with stations broadcasting only sure winners, established groups. The nation had just barely survived the disco fad which lasted only a few years. In passing, disco left few major performers (Donna Summer was one of the few) and little that might be called a musical legacy. Disco did not build on earlier music; it was an abberation. The sameness of the disco sound bored many young music fans. Disco died not because something better came along; it died because people tired of it. And when it died there was nothing in America that could quickly take its place and stimulate record sales. New music was being created, but overseas, not in the United States. It would take a video innovation— MTV—to foster the importation of these new sounds. More about that later.

## ☐ Getting It Back Together

Prosperity began to return to the recording industry by mid-decade. Cost cutting at the recording studios began in earnest. Promotion staffs were cut back drastically or eliminated. The industry began to rely heavily on independent record promoters. While this saved money initially, it caused problems later. The industry lost control of promotion techniques, and when the independent promoters became the target of numerous payola investigations later in the 1980s, the publicity stained the recording companies as well. Several major labels rebuilt their promotional staffs later in the decade to regain control over the manner in which their recordings were promoted.

Fewer new bands were signed, and when they were signed they received far less in their contracts. While the traditional royalty rates stayed the same, groups were asked to pay more toward the production costs of their albums. The number of concert tours were cut, and many groups discovered the thrill of travelling on tour by bus, rather than Lear jet. And performers were expected to pay for part or all of the costs of these tours out of proceeds from record sales. Groups whose record sales failed to live up to expectations often owed their record companies substantial amounts of money when their three-year contracts expired.

The recording companies also established new relationships with record sellers. Discounts on new releases, intended to boost sales, were abandoned. Refund policies that gave a dealer his or her money back for unsold records were also modified in favor of the record companies.

Before continuing it is important to note a couple of points about the American recording industry. First, it is not really an American industry anymore. And second, it is dominated by only six companies. The six companies are:

- Time-Warner, whose WEA labels are the dominant American labels today.
- CBS (now Sony Music Entertainment) was at one time the largest U.S. recording

company. CBS records was purchased by Sony, the Japanese corporation, for $2 billion in 1988.

- The British Thorn-EMI, represented in this country by the Capitol label.
- BMG, or the German Bertelsmann Music Group, which includes the RCA and Arista labels.
- N.V. Phillips of the Netherlands, which includes the Polygram label.
- MCA, which is owned by Matsushita Electric Co., a Japanese company.

The last major independent recording companies were gobbled up in the late 1980s. MCA bought Geffen Records and Motown. Polygram (Phillips) purchased A & M and Island. Labels owned by the six majors accounted for 93 percent of all record sales in 1990.

The major companies have come to dominate the recording industry for two important reasons. They have more money to sign, record, and promote performers. More importantly, they have their own record distribution systems. In order to be successful, a record company must be able to get the product to the customers. Major label distributors can get more records into more record stores, more quickly. Independent labels, which might put out one or a dozen recordings a year, work through an informal network of regional distributors, and by mail order, or another parcel delivery service. Their releases may be accessible in major cities, and they may be available in specialty stores. But they have a harder time getting into the big record stores in the shopping malls, where much of the business is conducted in the 1990s.

An independent label can ask a major label to distribute their records, and many frequently do. But the independent company gets a lower percentage on each sale when this is done. And while they get into more stores, they still find themselves at somewhat of a disadvantage. Through what can only be described as a Byzantine pricing formula, record dealers usually make more profit off the sale of a major-label recording than the sale of an independent-label recording. Consequently, record dealers tend to promote the major-label recordings more heavily.

Cost cutting certainly proved to be helpful to the industry in rebuilding its economic strength. But two other developments were more important. This was the generation of new recording technology, and the popularity of the brash new cable television channel, MTV.

## ☐ New Technology

Compact disc or CD players began to appear in stereo stores in 1982. The high price of the recorders, as much as $1,000 for early models, put off some buyers. But the technology was startling, seemingly out of a Star Wars fantasy; recorded music had never sounded so clean or crisp. The technology—though sophisticated—is simple. A tiny semiconductor laser beam replaces the phonograph needle. Music is recorded on a shiny disc as a series of microscopic pits, a digital code. As the laser tracks around the disc, it reads this code. The beam is reflected back off the polished surface, but when it strikes a pit, it scatters rather than being reflected. The machine translates this on/off pattern of light pulses into music. There is no surface noise when a disc is played since nothing touches the surface of the disc. The disc will seemingly last forever, although engineers say a small amount of deterioration will occur over time. The laser can be cued to play only certain tracks on the disc, to skip a selection, to play a selection twice or over and over again. The discs can also hold more music (74 minutes worth) than a standard LP. (Why 74 minutes? The Japanese engineers who developed this technology enjoy classical music and wanted a format on which they could record and play back Beethoven's entire Ninth Symphony.)

The recording industry loved this new technology. While it didn't solve the problem of home taping of LPs on audiocassettes, it substantially reduced it. When an LP was taped and then replayed on a cassette, it sounded about as good as it sounded when it was played on a turntable. But much of the audio fidelity of a CD was lost when it was taped.

More importantly, the record companies found a gold mine in their record libraries that could be extracted using the CDs. Recording companies could rerelease their entire record catalogs on compact discs and expect substantial sales. When these old LPs were rereleased as CDs, the record companies only incurred pressing and promotion costs. Artists still got their royalties, but a majority were paid their percentage based on the price of an album, $8 or $9, not a percentage of the price of a CD, $14 or $15 dollars. The sale of the CDs provided an immediate flow of cash into the company coffers.

The success of the CDs has resulted in the death of the vinyl recording. The smaller single 45 rpm records had disappeared by mid-1990, and the 12-inch LPs had all but disappeared by mid-1991. Most classical music was released only on CD and audiotape, and even many popular albums were being released only on CD. The major labels changed their return policy on LPs in mid-1989, giving dealers only 15 percent of what they had paid on returned LPs that had not sold. Dealers could get nearly 100 percent on CDs and cassettes. Many dealers began to bury the LPs or stop stocking them altogether. A major chain, Wherehouse Records, stopped selling LPs (except by special order) in October of 1989 when the vinyl albums amounted to less than 10 percent of their business. The sale of CDs passed the sale of vinyl LPs in 1988. By 1989 the number of LPs shipped to retailers totaled only 17.5 million, 60 percent less than in 1990. More cassettes (211 million) were shipped than anything else, but nearly 100 million CDs were shipped as well. (See figure 7-2.)

By 1990 the recording industry was still reissuing its older material on CDs, but most of the catalog had already been released. The sharp rise in CD sales had slowed substantially, primarily because of the continued high price of the discs, according to many industry analysts. Profits on CDs were still good, though. The cost of the disc itself dropped from $3 in 1984 to about $1 in 1990, and the industry was not passing that savings along to the customers. However, performers, seeing the business healthy again, began to demand that their royalty percentages be computed at the price of CDs, not LPs.

The industry also hoped to save money by changing the method of packaging the CD, abandoning the large 6-by-12-inch "longbox" in favor of a smaller, more ecologically friendly package. Not only are the longboxes about twice as large as they need to be to package the CD, but buyers throw them away immediately after opening the package. In late 1990, a "Ban the Box" movement was generated that included many performers (Sting, Peter Gabriel, U2, REM) who demanded that their CDs be distributed in a different package. Two alternatives now exist. Some persons in the industry want CDs to be distributed in the jewel box, the hard, plastic storage shells CD buyers find when they rip open the long box. Others support a newer

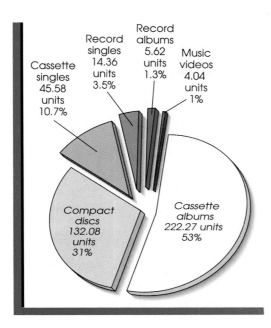

FIGURE 7-2 Music sales by format in 1990. Numbers represent units (i.e. 1 CD or 1 LP) shipped to retail stores in millions. (Recording Industry Association of America)

package called DigiTrak, which measures 5-by-11 inches and is made entirely of paperboard. The package, which can be made completely of recycled material, folds to the size of a jewel box and can be used to store the CD.

The major impediment to changing the packaging format is the record retailers, who cite three reasons why they want the longbox format retained. A package smaller than a longbox has a greater susceptibility to theft. A change in the package would require record stores to redesign the store fixtures that hold the CDs for display, a cost that could easily run to $250 million for all stores in the nation. A smaller package also lacks the visual impact of the longbox, retailers argue. Other alternatives are being considered as the pressure on record retailers by both the recording industry and an increasing number of performers continues to mount.

The CD technology was embraced by the recording industry because the industry saw that CDs could give the business a much-needed shot in the arm. The industry was less willing to embrace the next technological breakthrough, DAT.

## ☐ What's DAT?

**Digital audiotape** or DAT is regarded by many as the "best home recording system ever." Digital audiotapes have the same fidelity as a compact disc. They are based on the same technology. The tape players are about two-thirds the size of a standard cassette player and the cassettes, which are also smaller than a standard audiocassette, hold two hours worth of music. A portable playback unit is the size of a cigarette package. But the greatest advantage DAT has over other current formats is that a DAT player can record as well as play back. An individual with a DAT system has the same crisp, clean audio fidelity found in a CD and can record CDs or whatever for playback.

DAT had existed for several years before players and cassettes began to appear in quantity in American retail stores in the autumn of 1990. Why did it take so long

Digital audio tape technology was available to the public in early 1990. DAT players like the one in this photograph give listeners the same sound quality found in compact discs. This Walkman from Sony also has a record capability as well, something not usually found in portable tape players.
(Sony Corporation of America)

to get here? The DAT hardware was developed by the Japanese, who wanted to import it into the United States beginning in the mid-1980s. But the software manufacturers, the record companies who would produce and market the tapes, didn't want the DAT equipment brought to this country. Compact discs were very popular, and the industry was concerned about confusing customers with a new format. (But remember how slow the radio industry in this country was to introduce television to compete with its successful radio technology.) Retailers weren't excited about adding digital tapes to their inventory of LPs, cassettes, and CDs. But the biggest problem was DAT's greatest virtue—its ability to record as well as play back.

While the introduction of CDs did not kill the home taping of records, it slowed it. No matter how good the tape or the tape recorder, a taped version of a CD simply was not as good as the original. However a digital audiotape recording of a CD will be a perfect copy, and the recording industry envisioned another sales slump similar to the one in the late 1970s. When the Japanese attempted to import DAT hardware, the recording industry went to Congress and asked that the government block the imports, or at least require the Japanese to install safeguards in the DAT recorders to make it impossible to use them to copy the music from CDs. A small computer chip could be built into the machines that would sense an inaudible code that had been recorded on the CD. When the chip received this code, it would shut down the DAT recorder. The Japanese opposed this, arguing that it would deprive DAT users of a major use of the machinery. They also argued that the computer chips could hurt the overall sound quality of the DAT recording, and would often malfunction, shutting down the system by mistake when something other than a CD was being recorded.

The issue was not resolved until 1989. By that time the largest U.S. record company, CBS Records, had been bought by Sony, a Japanese company. Fifteen potential DAT hardware manufacturers agreed to install circuitry in their machines which would prevent a DAT recorder from making a copy of a DAT copy. The machines could copy original DATs, CDs, or anything else. Record companies and DAT makers agreed; songwriters and music publishers did not. A lawsuit followed. In 1991 all sides asked Congress to pass the Audio Home Recording Act that enacted into law the earlier agreement and established a special tax on blank tapes and DAT hardware to pay royalties to performers, songwriters, and recording companies.

The future of DAT remains in doubt. The machines introduced in 1990 cost a great deal, about $1,000. Music retailers are still not enthusiastic about the new format, so an obvious shortage of prerecorded DAT tapes is inevitable. Makers of the standard audiocassette decks recently introduced a new Dolby-S noise reduction system for cassette recorders. While Dolby-S does not match the clarity of the digital recording systems, it is far superior to Dolby-C, the first widely used system. And it offers two distinct advantages over digital tape systems. To use either DAT or Dolby-S, the listener will have to buy a new tape deck. But the Dolby-S deck will be considerably less expensive. Also, a user can continue to play Dolby-C tapes in a Dolby-S machine; they cannot be used in a digital recorder. While the DAT technology has been available in Japan for several years, the Japanese themselves have been slow to adopt it. Perhaps this is a good idea whose time has simply not yet arrived. But given the gadget-mania and audio-obsessions of most Americans, that is not likely.

## MUSIC TELEVISION

The debut of MTV in the early 1980s was directly responsible for much of the rejuvenation of the recording industry. It provided another pathway through which the recording artist could reach the record buyer, a pathway that, initially at least, was not constricted by the conventions and tight playlists of contemporary radio.

MTV was started by Warner-Amex Satellite Entertainment Co. on August 1, 1981. (Warner-Amex sold MTV and other cable properties to Viacom International for a reported $667.5 million in the summer of 1985.) In less than five years the satellite transmitted cable channel could be seen in 27.3 million homes via almost 3,100 cable systems. Today it is available to almost twice that many cable subscribers. It was the fastest growing TV channel in history. Its growth was due in part to good fortune, but was certainly no accident. MTV was the most thoroughly researched cable channel ever to travel via a coaxial cable. Hundreds of potential viewers (persons 14 to 34) were interviewed about their interest in a cable channel that telecast music videos. They were also asked about artists they would like to see on the channel, what the VJs (video jockeys) should wear, what the set should look like, etc. Robert Pittman, the then 28-year-old president of MTV, solicited opinions about the channel from advertising agencies, cable operators, and record companies. The advertisers especially liked the idea and saw the channel as a means of reaching the volatile but consuming conscious younger audience. "Our core audience is the television babies who grew up on TV and rock and roll," Pittman said. "The strongest appeal you can make [to this group] is emotional. If you can get their emotions going, make them forget their logic, you've got them." These words are like music to an advertiser.

The early success of MTV was striking. In March 1983, 68 percent of 2,000 viewers surveyed by the A.C. Nielsen Co. said that MTV was very important or important in making record album purchasing decisions. The cable channel is attrib-

Duran Duran was one of the first British bands to score with American teenagers because of exposure on MTV. Band members were attractive and the music was fresh. The
group produced a series of hit records in the early to mid-1980s before fracturing into
several disparate parts.
(EMI Records)

uted with directly furthering the careers of musical groups like Men at Work, Flock of
Seagulls, Culture Club, Stray Cats, Adam Ant, the Human League, and others. In
Houston where only one-half of the city was wired for cable, sales of an early Duran
Duran album skyrocketed in that part of the city where young people could view the
group's videos on MTV but languished in the rest of the community. Make a tactical
map of the country, one critic noted, and darken the MTV areas. You will see the
sales of certain records increasing in those areas. Kids are asking for records that
have never been played before on local radio.

And that, of course, is how MTV has helped the recording industry. It widened
the neck of the funnel between the performing artist and the record buyer. No
longer did radio stations control the exposure of recorded music to the listening public. Young people could see and hear new songs by new bands on MTV. The prime
beneficiaries of this new exposure were, at first, the British bands who were ready
when music television offered the opportunity to be seen as well as heard. Greg
Geller of RCA Records noted that the English groups are younger and they sound
new.

> The English scene has always encouraged innovation—in fashion as well as music. At a
> time when radio here had become stagnant along came MTV. . . . For the first time you
> could see a lot of these groups, and the network had a crying need for groups that were
> worth looking at. It was a great opportunity for the English.

Many British bands became very popular in the wake of their exposure on MTV, including the Eurythmics, U-2, Clash, Wham, Police, the aforementioned Duran Duran, and others. Some of the new music was surely ephemeral and would have little impact on the development of rock. But the best of it added important substance to contemporary rock at a time when American music had seriously stagnated.

MTV not only sold records and popularized new artists; it made money for Warner-Amex, and later Viacom. The network earned more than $30 million in profit in 1989 through selling advertising spots and through subscriber revenues. Cable companies must pay MTV about 15 cents per month per subscriber to carry the channel.

The success of MTV spawned a host of imitators. "NBC Friday Night Videos," "ABC Rocks," "Night Tracks" on WTBS, and the USA Network's "Night Flight" were some of the more popular. Music video shows popped up on local television channels as well, especially in those communities as yet not wired for cable. MTV even launched a second channel, VH-1 (Video Hits-1), aimed at an older audience and featuring more jazz, soul, and middle-of-the-road music.

By the early 1990s, MTV had few competitors left at the network level. The fickle audience had started to turn its back on music videos in the late 1980s. The cost of videos had escalated dramatically in the 1980s, and record companies cut back sharply on the number they released. The audiences seemed to tire of the video music (or perhaps just the music) as well. (Interestingly, however, the sale of music videos such as tapes of concerts or compilations of music videos by a single artist, grew substantially in 1990.) Ratings for MTV were flat, or even dropped slightly, according to A.C. Nielsen. (MTV disputed this claim.) And advertisers, stinging from the remote-control phenomenon known as "grazing" (viewers constantly switching channels while they watch TV) viewed each 3-to-4 minute video as an individual program that viewers would abandon if they didn't like it. MTV was forced to retool. In 1990 it dramatically changed its program content. The policy of showing videos 24 hours a day, one after another, ended. The network built its programming around a series of 30-minute or one-hour shows, and some of these programs, like a game show called "Remote Control," had very little to do with music videos. "MTV News," a film review program called "The Big Picture," and a dozen or so other features complemented the telecast of music videos. The playlist was changed as well. MTV emphasized more heavy metal music and added rap to its menu. There was less rhythm and blues, less soul, and fewer new artists. Breaking the broadcast day into 30- and 60-minute units was an effort to please advertisers who like to identify with particular program content, and to get the MTV schedule into the *TV Guide* listings. As long as the network just played videos, there were no listings.

Ratings rose for the network, but not sufficiently. In the spring of 1991, the network revamped its programming again. MTV cut back on most of its non-music programming. Network officials said the only two non-music shows that would remain (besides music news) were "Half-Hour Comedy Hour" and "The Big Picture." "We want to put the focus back on music, and back on new music. We'll be going back to the roots of early MTV," said MTV Networks chairman Tom Freston. MTV hired new VJs, planned to feature more alternative and new music, and explore new music genres. Freston said the network also planned to use experimental video art pieces between shows and segments of shows.

The impact of music videos on television programming and film should be briefly noted, before leaving this subject. The video artists who created the music videos were usually given "carte blanche" to develop the pictures that went along with the music. And the conventions of music videos developed by these artists—quick cuts, atmospheric images, and others—clearly have had an impact on television (especially TV commercials) and even some films. New ideas and new terms, associated first with the music videos, are commonly seen on television today. "Pushing" or "blowing out," which is adding a grainy quality to film, can be seen commonly in commercials today, but was first used in videos. "Matting," the process which allows the film editor to float a person or object on the screen with changeable backgrounds, was first used in the videos. A great many of the computer graphic tricks now seen in television commercials were first tried in the videos.

As important as anything, however, is the realignment of the thinking in the advertising industry about the time needed to present a commercial message. The music videos "have educated people—especially young people—to accept lots of information in a short time period," wrote Phillip B. Dusenberry, chairman and CEO of BBDO advertising agency in New York, whose accounts include Pepsi and Apple Computers. If you have the opportunity, compare a television commercial prepared in the early 1980s with one prepared today. Note the vast differences in the film editing, especially the length of the cuts, and the image emphasis. You can see some of these same changes in some action-oriented television programs and even theatrical motion pictures. MTV, then, left its mark on far more than the music industry.

## THE CHALLENGE OF CENSORSHIP

By the early 1990s the recording industry had recovered from its early-eighties slump. But it faced a new challenge that held the potential of bringing additional woes to the industry, the spectre of censorship and its attendant problems.

First, there is no question that music enjoys First Amendment protection. In four separate rulings in the 1970s and 1980s U.S. Courts of Appeals sustained this argument and blocked attempts to censor music and concert performances. But the constitutional guarantees of freedom of speech and press only protect publishers and writers and artists from censorship by the government, not from censorship by pressure groups or retailers or recording companies.

MTV had raised the visibility of rock music considerably during the 1980s. As long as the music was something kids listened to in their rooms or on their Walkmen, it was fairly invisible to adult view. But when it could be watched and heard 24 hours a day on television, it attracted much more attention. Many adults found some of the music tasteless, offensive, and even pornographic. Some claimed that rock glorified drug and alcohol use, promoted the occult (even Satanism), and that many of the videos degraded women and promoted violence. There is little doubt that a tiny portion of rock music is guilty of at least some of these charges. The industry suddenly came under closer scrutiny.

The PTA in 1984 fired the first shot, decrying what they called "porn rock," and asking for a record rating system, similar to the one used for films (P, PG, PG-13, R, and NC-17). (See pp. 289–291.) But this crusade was short-lived. A year later, a group calling itself the Parents Music Resource Committee (PMRC) picked up where the PTA left off. Leaders of this group included the wives of U.S. senators and congressmen, and they quickly caught the ear of the Congress. Congressional hearings were held on the issue, and persons both for and against a record rating system and music censorship testified. No legislation emerged from these hearings, but the industry was clearly under pressure. After all, at this time the record industry was attempting to convince the Congress to levy a surtax on blank audiotape to pay royalties to the record companies who complained they were losing money from home taping of records. Also, the industry sought the help of the lawmakers to block the importation of DAT.

Negotiations between the Record Industry Association of America (RIAA) and the PMRC continued. A settlement of sorts was reached in the fall of 1985; the industry agreed to place a PG label on the outside of a record with questionable lyrics, or print the lyrics on the outside of the record jacket. But of the 7500 albums released between January of 1986 and August of 1989, only 49 bore a warning label. In the meantime, legislatures in 19 states began to consider legislation that would force the labeling of records sold in those states. Fearing the chaos that would be caused by 19 different labeling laws and reluctant to fight the matter in the courts, the industry agreed in the spring of 1990 to a more comprehensive labeling system. The new label, a black-and-white sticker that is placed on the lower right-hand corner of cassettes, LPs, and compact discs, contains four words, "Parental Advisory—Explicit Lyrics." The record companies use their own discretion in applying the label, but are mindful that the way in which they use this discretion is closely monitored by those who would still prefer a mandatory system. The proposals for mandatory labeling had been dropped in 16 of the 19 states by mid-1990.

Why is a rating system a problem? Isn't it just a courtesy to advise customers of the contents of the recording they are buying? In the best of all possible worlds, that in fact might be all that happens. But the United States in the late 20th century is not the best of all possible worlds. The warning label is supposed to distinguish what is acceptable for children, and what is acceptable for adults. But for many people, it distinguishes between what is clean and what is dirty, what is good and what is bad. Pressure was put on record retailers not to sell recordings that are labelled. At least one large retail record chain and several smaller stores had already announced by mid-1990 that they would not carry labelled records. Record stores in large shopping malls, the family playgrounds of the late twentieth century, are especially vulnerable to such pressure. It may be difficult to advertise such records. Many newspapers already refuse to carry ads for adult-rated films.

The rating system is inherently subjective. Employees of the record companies will be forced to interpret the meaning of song lyrics, which often mean different things to different people. Most recording company executives will probably choose to err on the side of more rather than less censorship. And of course a problem with just one song on a cassette or CD will cause the entire album to be labelled.

Because they will be less accessible, such records will not sell as well as they might. Low sales will reinforce the recording industry's normal tendency toward conservatism. Groups that record songs with adult lyrics will find it harder to make such records. In the end, we will have far less access to music that is fully protected under the First Amendment, music that the government would find it impossible to censor, music that the artist has a right to express and we have a right to hear.

The dust had not yet settled in the record labelling controversy when authorities in Florida arrested the members of the rap group 2 Live Crew and a record store owner on charges of obscenity. A federal judge had ruled that the group's album "As Nasty as I Wanna Be" was obscene. Members of the group were arrested after they performed selections from the album at an adults-only concert. Record store owner Charles Freeman was arrested when he sold copies of the album. Freeman was convicted by a jury for selling an obscene recording, but a jury from the same community acquitted the rap group, ruling that the material on the album was not obscene. Freeman's conviction was being appealed as this was written.

The Florida prosecutions were the result of pressure brought on law enforcement officers from a crusading antipornography lawyer named Jack Thomson, who had lost in a bid to be elected the state's attorney general, and a former FBI agent named William Kelly. A West Coast conservative Christian activist organization called Focus on the Family also worked behind the scenes to stop the sale and airing of the rap album. Other actions in the South against rap groups featuring black performers also developed. While there is no question that some of the lyrics in the rap songs were raw, some of the lyrics were also anti-white and anti-establishment. Many observers saw the attacks on 2 Live Crew, Public Enemy, and other groups as at least partially racially motivated. Interestingly, the rap groups are really the first black musical performers who have succeeded in maintaining control over the publishing rights to their songs, as well as the production and distribution of their records. This has provided them with financial success usually denied earlier black artists who were generally controlled by white producers and record company owners. Luther Campbell, for example, the leader of 2 Live Crew, runs three record labels that grossed about $17 million in 1990.

## MUSIC IN AMERICA

Popular music is an important strand in the fabric of American culture. As has been noted above, it is also an economic institution with which to reckon. In the brief section that follows we will attempt to outline the development of modern rock music, the form most closely associated with both radio and the younger generation.

Most people like music. Of all our cultural or artistic forms, music is the one most people are involved in, either as performers or patrons. Theories abound that attempt to explain why people like music, and specifically why people like popular music. Some say popular music touches on actual human needs and concerns. Songs that become popular play on a deeply felt need all of us have for a feeling of community with other people. Although we may be alone when listening to a song, we nevertheless have the assurance that the isolated and individual feelings we experience through the music are in fact experienced by many others as well. Sociologist David Riesman, author of *The Lonely Crowd,* suggests we actually listen to popular music in a context of imaginary others. Our listening is a reaching out, an attempt to find some connection with other people.

But no two people ever hear the same song in the same way or connect it with the same things, according to writer-critic Greil Marcus. Still a kind of communication exists. The song holds all the truth of the moment for both listeners. They both know it, Marcus said; they both accept the validity of the metaphor.

The reason we like popular music could be far simpler than either of these theories suggest. It may be only a pleasant emotional sensation; it may make us feel good or at least feel alive.

Popular music went through an important revolution in the 1950s with the birth of what we now call rock, or what was called rock and roll in those days. Birth is perhaps the wrong word; evolution is really more accurate. Rock had in fact existed for some time as rhythm and blues in the black ghettos of the urban centers. What

Bo Diddley, one of the earliest rhythm and blues performers to cross over into the pop charts, featured a kind of bump and grind shuffle beat that was very popular in the 1950s. His artistic influence on performers like Elvis Presley was probably more important than his own recordings, which met with only limited success.

emerged from the black musicians who played this music was a potent strain of the urban blues that had swept the nation 20 years earlier. Recordings of this music were produced by small record companies and were known as race records. Many whites had long appreciated the original contributions of black musicians to American music and would visit black clubs to hear these performers. But the recordings made by the blacks were rarely aired on white-owned, white-controlled radio stations. Music historians note that a disc jockey named Gene Nobles on station WLAC in Nashville was probably the first to play the so-called "race records" over the air. But it was the airing of these records by Alan Freed in 1954 over a Cleveland radio station that first created a widespread appreciation of the music by white teenagers. Other DJs followed Freed's lead and soon some of these recordings by black artists began to edge onto the Top-40 pop charts in *Variety* and *Billboard*. Major record companies sought to capitalize on the popularity of the music, but not the artists. White performers recorded bowdlerized versions of the black hits like "Sincerely," "Earth Angel," and "Sh-Boom." The emotional raw edge was stripped away from the black music; the material was polished to be more acceptable to the ears of mainstream middle Americans.

But the black bands held their own. Their music was electric—both emotionally and musically. The groups employed heavily amplified rhythm and bass guitars, piano, and drums, all pushing a heavy and very danceable beat. Soloists and backup singers worked in front of the band, over the beat, with strong, gutsy vocals. Young people loved it and black performers like Chuck Berry, Bo Diddley, and Little Richard became popular stars. Freed was the person who dubbed this new music rock and roll.

The first white man to add significantly to the development of this new music was Elvis Presley. To the urban music Presley brought the traditions of gospel, the country sounds of the deep South, and the delta blues. The broad popular success of his first recordings for RCA ("Heartbreak Hotel," "Hound Dog," and "All Shook Up") demonstrated that rock and roll—theoretically a fusion of country, pop, and rhythm and blues—could appeal simultaneously to audiences of all three. Presley's appearances on such main stream television programs as the Jackie Gleason and Ed Sullivan shows added a sheen of respectability to rock and roll. Mom and Dad no longer had to tap their toes in secret while the radio was being played. Presley's success for RCA also convinced other major recording companies there was considerable money to be made from this fresh, new music.

Buddy Holly was one of the first important technical innovators in rock. With his group called the Crickets, Holly had a tremendous string of hit recordings that included "Peggy Sue," "Maybe Baby," "Rave-On," and "That'll Be the Day." He was

Buddy Holly was one of the most original and creative early rock and roll artists. He was among the first singers to write most of his own material, and his songs were tied closely to his musical interpretation and recordings of them. He had a profound influence on many later performers, including the Beatles.

among the first performers who also wrote his own material, arranged the song, and produced the recording. Holly used his voice and song lyrics to create an entire musical package—the words complemented the music and vice versa. In fact, Holly conceived of all his songs as records. He had no intention to sell the songs as sheet music for someone to play on an upright piano in the recreation room. On the recordings there was little distinct separation of the words, the singer, and the music. This was a revolutionary idea in 1957. Holly's career was bright but brief; he died in an airplane crash on February 9, 1959.

By the early 1960s rock music was already beginning to suffer from musical formulas which often emerge when an art form becomes highly commercial. Rock and roll began to fragment as well into categories of music so common today. The very commercial sounds of a group called The Four Seasons swept the nation. Dancing in clubs and at parties became very popular and hit songs memorialized the current dance fads like the Twist, the Pony, the Fly, and the Limbo. Dick Clark's "American Bandstand," beginning a long run on national television, popularized an East Coast or Philadelphia sound in rock music. The Beach Boys did the same thing for the West. Of more lasting significance than either was the growth in popularity of the less frenetic rhythm and blues music dubbed "soul" by Berry Gordy of Motown Records in Detroit. Motown music would leave a deep imprint on American music, visible even in the 1980s through the work of performers such as Michael Jackson, Lionel

Elvis Presley was the first performer to make rock and roll music economically self sufficient. His tremendous popularity led the way for a great many other performers to gain access to major record labels and a more mainstream audience. He remains an enigma after death, and contemporary "Elvis sightings" fill the pages of supermarket tabloids.

Richie, Stevie Wonder, and Tina Turner. Despite the growth of these regional sounds, many contended American music had grown stale. Enter the Beatles, the most important group in the short history of rock music.

It is truly difficult to overestimate the impact that Paul McCartney, John Lennon, George Harrison, and Ringo Starr had on popular music and, indirectly, popular culture. The group literally burst upon the American pop scene in 1964. In March they had the top five records in the nation. In little more than seven years the Beatles sold more than 100 million singles and 100 million albums.

The Beatles brought more than music to America. The group helped foster a youth culture, constructed in large part on drugs, long hair, and music. They also generated an intense interest in music and inspired many young people to begin playing musical instruments.

It was their music, however, for which they will be best remembered. The early Beatles succeeded in consolidating many diverse aspects of music popular in the late 1950s. "In encompassing so many diversified forms of music [pop, love songs, ballads, novelty songs, folk, country and western, rhythm and blues] within the basic rock and roll format," noted Brock Helander in *Rock Who's Who,* "the Beatles revitalized rock and roll." Their early music was simple, fresh, and clean. As they matured as musicians the music matured as well. Each album seemed to mark a new

This photograph of the Beatles was taken in 1964, shortly after the band enjoyed its initial success in the United States. Their clothes and hairstyles had almost as much impact in this country as their music.

milestone. Songwriters Lennon and McCartney brought an unprecedented sophistication in lyrics to rock music. Their songs reflected the social and political period and frequently contained sharp social commentary. Musical innovation reached a peak in the album "Revolver," which many consider to be the most novel album ever made. Uncommon instrumental combinations and unusual vocal harmonies were a Beatles hallmark. With the aid of producer George Martin the group often explored innovative and elaborate production techniques. The album "Sgt. Pepper's Lonely Hearts Club Band" was the first true "concept" album where an artist presented a suite of related songs in a specific order. The record container or album cover was an essential part of the music package. Building on Buddy Holly as a model, Lennon and McCartney set the standard for groups creating and performing original material rather than songs written by professional song writers. Finally, as Helander notes, the musical and songwriting advances pioneered by the Beatles "led critics to view rock music in an unprecedented light, considering it as a valid art form in and of itself."

The Beatles matured as individuals as well, and by 1970 were working apart more than together. By the end of that year all four had issued solo albums. In early 1971 Paul McCartney sued for the dissolution of the partnership which was practically dead. Hopes for a reunion or a new album by the four were dashed for good when John Lennon was murdered in 1980.

The Beatles made a lasting mark on rock music, indeed on all popular music. You can still hear Beatles songs played across the radio dial today; the oldies, new rock versions, even instrumental recordings on beautiful music stations.

Since the early seventies rock music has fragmented into a dozen or more heavily stylized forms. Without a center, which was provided by the Beatles, rock moved in many different directions. Serious rock musicians, turned off by what they viewed as a growing commercialism in rock, turned inward to musical technique and form. In doing so, they turned off much of their audience and opened the door for several musical fads which emerged during the last dozen years.

Rock courted country music for several years in the seventies. Country and western music predated rock by several decades and had its own small but loyal audience of followers. Bob Dylan and a group called the Byrds ventured to Nashville to make records with a country sound. More important, young country artists saw that by taking some of the twang out of their recordings they would sell to a far wider audience. The two musical traditions were mixed, but failed to blend most of the time. Yet for a while Nashville became the recording center of the nation for rock as well as country, and the Billboard Top 100 pop and country charts frequently mirrored each other. Old timers in country didn't approve when Olivia Newton John, an Australian pop singer, was named the Country Music Association's female vocalist of the year. Rock artists resented having to add a steel guitar to the instruments in the band. Yet many successful groups developed, groups like Credence Clearwater Revival and later the Eagles, who produced memorable albums during the decade. Today there is still cross-over between the two musical forms, but not nearly so much as in the recent past. Rock survived its romance with country with little harm done to either.

Disco, as previously noted, took its toll on the recording industry and seriously set back the music business as well. Disco was really a dance club craze that featured swinging rock music characterized by the thump, thump, thump of a heavily amplified 128 beats per minute. In a sense, disco was a reaction against the introspective and serious rock of the seventies. Disco patrons didn't want to take the music seri-

The "punk" music of groups like the Sex Pistols was angry and political, and provided a stark counterpoint to the glitzy disco music of the late seventies. The roots of what is called "new wave" and other styles can be traced to the raucous sounds of punk.   (© Bob Gruen, Fotofolio)

ously; they wanted to dress up, dance, and have fun. Live music was out; DJs in laminated booths decorated with colored lights played recordings for the dancers. The heavy emphasis on the beat made most disco songs sound alike. Donna Summer emerged as the one true disco star to survive when the fad passed away. But other groups, notably the *Bee Gees*, sold millions of records with a disco sound. By 1982 it was difficult to buy a disco record anywhere in the nation, the clubs had replaced the booths with bandstands, and rock bands were back playing for casually dressed customers. Rock survived disco, but barely.

The eighties brought still another rock variation; punk, which then spawned new wave. If disco appeared to be a reaction to serious rock, punk was certainly a reaction to disco. The music was simple, often stark—a sharp contrast to the elaborate instrumentation in disco and even rock. Music critic James Barszcz called it "scaled-down music." Punk was highly danceable, almost infectious, but dances too were simple, scaled-down, compared to the intricate dancing associated with disco. Led by the flamboyant and infamous Sex Pistols, punk turned the music business on its head. Punks thought the music of the seventies was putrid. They thought punk was putrid. They hated the establishment. They hated themselves. They hated everything. And teenagers loved them. In England, for the first time ever, a recording that no radio station would broadcast topped the pop charts. This was the Sex Pistols' "Anarchy in the U.K."

Out of punk grew what came to be known in Great Britain as "post-punk," music from groups that shared the punk artists' attitudes on the world, but which had a far more substantial musical base; groups that saw punk bands and said, "Hey, I can do that." The post-punk era's most important performers included Echo and the Bunnymen, the Cure, Siouxsie and the Banshees, and Joy Division, which, after lead singer Ian Curtis' suicide in 1980, became one of the music industry's most innovative bands, New Order.

David Byrne's (center) Talking Heads is a group that came out of the New York new wave music scene in the early 1980s. This eclectic band generated music based on a wide variety of musical traditions. Byrne has stretched beyond the music business to make the highly unusual but entertaining film, *True Stories*.
(© Hugh Brown, Island Alive Releasing/Cinecom International Films)

Punk had an impact in New York as well as in England. David Byrne's Talking Heads borrowed punk's "anything goes" sensibility and created music and images that were influenced by African music and rhythms. Blondie, a group that first emerged in 1975 as part of the New York new wave music scene, prospered at the end of that decade with a popular music sound spiced with the aggression so commonly associated with punk. And in Los Angeles post-punk spawned such groups as Wall of Voodoo, Oingo Boingo, and the Go Go's, one of the first female bands in which all the performers played their own instruments and wrote their own songs.

If there was anything consistent about the styles of music during the late eighties, it was that there wasn't any consistency. Rarely had record buyers seen such an explosion of musical variations. "Ska" and "Mod" groups like Madness and The Jam reflected fifties rhythm and blues. Elvis Costello, one of the most talented singer/songwriters in the industry today, emerged at this time. Electronic music also emerged from Great Britain, with groups like Depeche Mode, Soft Cell, Blancmange, and OMD making a mark on the best seller charts.

As noted previously, the debut of MTV gave instant U.S. exposure to many of the bands noted above and many others as well, including Duran Duran and Culture Club. MTV also gave exposure to a pop invasion from "down under," with Australian groups like Men at Work, INXS, and later Crowded House. Many other visually exciting bands and performers found that exposure to record buyers through MTV was profitable. These included Madonna, the Eurythmics, and the Stray Cats. Mainstream rock in America continued to draw a strong following with even greater success for performers like Bruce Springsteen, Michael Jackson, and Prince.

Two important musical trends to be noted as the eighties closed and the nineties began were rap music and the reappearance of popular music that carried a political message, a mixture last seen 25 years ago. Rap is a musical form that developed on

The immense success of performers like Michael Jackson and Prince (pictured here) reflects an important change in the music/recording industry. Black performers found great musical success previously, but in most instances the financial rewards that were generated flowed into the hands of white businessmen and women who controlled the artists' careers.

the streets of urban America. It has a heavy beat and features lyrics that are rapped, or spoken in a sing-song fashion rather than sung. It is controversial and viewed by many as provocative, largely because it vividly speaks of the frustrations and ambitions of those who live in the ghetto. Rap groups like Public Enemy experienced intense criticism from a few critics who consider some of their statements and song lyrics to be anti-Semitic. (Interestingly, fewer have criticized more traditional rock groups like Guns n' Roses for racist references in their songs.) And other rap groups like 2 Live Crew have been criticized for song lyrics that some argue are obscene.

Regardless of the controversy, rap was a refreshingly new musical sound, "the most exciting development in pop," according to *Seattle Times* music critic Patrick McDonald. "It holds a mirror up to conditions in the ghetto—gangs, drugs, poverty and despair—and encourages black pride and independence. It has sparked new

Many whites feel threatened by the often angry messages contained in songs by rap groups like Public Enemy, pictured here. But these groups are expressing the prevailing feelings of many inner-city blacks. Public Enemy gained national prominence when music by the group was featured in Spike Lee's film, *Do the Right Thing.*
(© Jules Allen, © 1990 CBS Records, Inc.)

ways of shaking it [dancing], showing once again that dance is one of the driving tastes of pop creativity," McDonald wrote. By 1990 rap music was appearing on the best-selling charts. Tone Loc's "Loc'ed After Dark" sold more than two million copies, and albums by scores of other performers, most of whom were unknown 12 months earlier (Heavy D and the Boys, LL Cool J, Young MC, and others) were passing the million sales mark.

Also noteworthy was the rise in popularity in the late 1980s of songs which carried a political message. Punk rock revived this tradition, but it has been bands like U-2, UB-40, and Living Colour that have seized upon subjects such as racial and sexual intolerance, pacificism, glittery socialism, and apartheid in their popular music. Musicians in England held concerts to raise money for the hungry in Ethiopia but also raised the consciousness of some young people about this worldwide problem. Since then we have seen concerts to fight apartheid (Sun City) and help the American farmers (Farm Aid). Some criticized these efforts as faddish, or opportunistic. Most, however, saw it as a breath of fresh air in an entertainment industry often marked by conspicuous wealth and triviality. Indeed, some in the industry noted that the efforts to censor songs emerged at about the same time rock music was regaining its political voice. "Right now it is sex and violence; before long it'll be, 'That's just too political,' " noted singer/songwriter John Cougar Mellencamp.

Where is rock going? Who knows? Rock music today is like a tapestry made up of scores of different threads, threads of a variety of colors and textures. It is highly unlikely that rock will ever again be defined by a single artist (i.e., Elvis) or group (i.e., The Beatles). It is a melange of music, with some styles within rock as different from one another as pop music is different from classical. The best rock music has always reflected the energy of the people who create it and who are tied to it as listeners or dancers. As the 1990s unfold new musical sounds appeared to gain strength: the "Athens" sound of a group of bands associated with Athens, Georgia, such as REM; a reemergence of soul by artists like Roachford, who label their music

U2 is one of the most successful bands of the 1980s and 90s, and one of the first rock groups in recent years to include pointed political messages in its songs. Group members include (left to right) drummer Larry Mullen, Jr., bassist Adam Clayton, guitarist and pianist The Edge, and lead singer and guitarist Bono.
(© Colm Henry, © 1988 Principle Management Ltd.)

"retronuevo"; and the highly danceable house music which is constructed upon remnants of disco and other funky dance music. In the case of the latter, DJs in laminated booths with sophisticated mixing and production equipment are again appearing in clubs, spinning records for eager dancers. What goes around, comes around.

## SERMONETTE

Many critics point out that American radio is not what it once was or what it might be. They remember that in its heyday radio was a family medium, one that developed as an art to quicken all the senses. "Radio once allowed the listener to participate," Robert Paul Dye wrote. The theater of the mind, they called it. Radio historian Jim Harmon notes that radio had a soul in the thirties and forties, one we would call cornball today. Moral absolutes like fair play, justice, kindness, patriotism, and honor ran through most scripts on dramatic radio. Radio rarely moralizes anymore; it spoofs instead. Its audience is rarely shocked into moral consciousness or fired by moral consideration. Instead, it tries to entertain. Sometimes it has the tendency to mire its audience in ambivalence. Others attack radio for not being what it might be. These people point to the BBC or to national radio services in other nations as models. Radio in America does not spend enough time informing people, teaching people, raising the cultural consciousness.

The commercial nature of American radio defines what it is and what it might become. Its heavy dependence upon advertising dictates relatively narrow parameters in which it must operate. And so to be fair, we must evaluate or criticize radio for what it is or what it can be. Radio today is an inexpensive way for nearly everyone to find musical entertainment. It is often the first source of important news in the community. When we want to know who is winning the ball game, whether it will rain tomorrow, or if the freeway is tied up by a traffic accident we turn on the radio. Radio is called the constant companion; the industry brags, wherever you go there's radio. Both statements are true and represent virtues of the modern system. Radio is far from perfect, but it probably gives most of us what we want. It has found its niche between newspapers and television and is doing very well.

## BIBLIOGRAPHY

These are some of the materials that have been helpful in the preparation of this chapter.

"Airwave Wars," *Business Week,* July 23, 1990.

*Audience 88: A Comprehensive Analysis of Public Radio Listeners.* Corporation for Public Broadcasting, 1988.

Barrett, Todd. "Start of CD Backlash?" *Newsweek,* July 16, 1990.

*Billboard,* various issues.

*Broadcasting,* various issues.

Chapple, Steve, and Garofalo, Reebee. *Rock and Roll Is Here to Pay.* Chicago: Nelson-Hall, 1977.

Costello, Mary, and Wallace, David Foster. *Signifying Rappers: Rap and Race in the Urban Present.* New York: Ecco Press, 1990.

Dannen, Fredic. *Hit Men.* New York: Times Books, 1990.

Eisen, Jonathan (ed.). *The Age of Rock.* New York: Vintage Books, 1969.

Eliot, Marc. *Rockonomics.* New York: Franklin Watts, 1989.

Fabrikant, Geraldine. "New Products Help to Bolster Music Sales," *The New York Times,* October 22, 1990.

Farrace, Mike. "Vinylwatch: The LP is Dying," *Pulse,* March, 1990.

Gillett, Charlie. *The Sound of the City.* New York: Outerbridge and Dienstfrey, 1970.

Goldberg, Michael. "Inside the Payola Scandal," *Rolling Stone,* January 14, 1988.

Laing, Dave. *The Sound of Our Time.* Chicago: Quadrangle, 1970.

Lull, James (ed.) *Popular Music and Communication.* Newbury Park, Cal.: Sage Publications, 1987.

Nelson, Robert. "The Golden Age of Public Radio," *The Seattle Times,* January 17, 1988.

Oulette, Don. "National Public Radio," *Pulse,* October, 1989.

Pareles, Jon. "Companies to Label Explicit Records," *The New York Times,* March 29, 1990.

———. "When Music Really Means Business," *The New York Times,* March 19, 1990.

Passman, Arnold. *The Deejays.* New York: Macmillan, 1971.

Pollack, Andrew. "Next, Digital Radio for a Superior Sound," *The New York Times,* July 11, 1990.

"Radio's Wacky Road to Profit," *Newsweek,* March 12, 1985.

Rohter, Larry. "Payola Case Dismissed, Judge Faults Prosecutor," *The New York Times,* September 5, 1990.

Schmidt, William. "Black Talk Radio: A Vital Force Is Emerging to Mobilize Opinion," *The New York Times,* March 31, 1990.

Sims, Calvin. "New FM System Is Challenged," *The New York Times,* February 22, 1989.

"The Sound of Money," *Newsweek,* October 5, 1987.

Stout, Gene. "The Sound of Music," *Seattle Post-Intelligencer,* January 22, 1989.

"Unusual, But Not Crazy," *Newsweek,* December 19, 1988.

Zimmerman, Kevin. "Rock 'n Roll in the 80s; High Tech, Low Excitement," *Variety,* January 24, 1990.

Zorn, Eric. "Radio News: Alive and Struggling," *Washington Journalism Review,* December, 1987.

# CHAPTER 8

# MOTION PICTURES

**S**aturday matinees, Milk Duds for a nickel, half-a-dozen cartoons, Chapter 10 of *Flash Gordon and the Intruders from Zeon,* cowboy movies with Hoot Gibson or Ken Maynard or Gene Autry, fresh popcorn at ten cents a box, laughing during the mushy parts, and the long walk home, reliving what you saw that day on the screen. When you talk to someone over 45, these are some of the things they will remember about the movies. All week long kids waited for Saturday afternoon and the sanctuary of the darkened theater. Film critic Pauline Kael remembers the anonymity and impersonality of just sitting in the darkened movie house, "enjoying ourselves, not having to be responsible, not having to be good."

The chances are very good that most of you who are reading this text never experienced the Saturday matinee, which died when the neighborhood theater began to perish in the mid-fifties. You probably don't even remember drive-in movie theaters—except as a place to go to a swap meet. The motion picture business has changed dramatically in the past four decades. The industry has been on an economic roller coaster, plunging through hard times to recovery to more hard times and back again to prosperity. In the early 1970s *Newsweek* magazine began a cover story on the film industry with this gloomy portrait: "The great Hollywood empire that ruled American tastes for more than half a century lies in dust, its tyrannical moguls dead or deposed, its back lots empty, its sound stages still, its ranks diminished and in disarray." Between 1967 and 1971 the industry lost over $400 million.

A visit to Hollywood today would reveal a somewhat different picture. While no motion picture empire exists to rule American tastes, the film industry continues to leave deep cultural impressions on American society. The tyrannical moguls are dead and deposed, but other moguls have taken their place; the corporate bosses who run Sony and Time-Warner, and media barons like Michael Eisner and Rupert Murdoch. The back lots that remain are not empty; the sound stages are alive. A visitor to the Universal Studios, for example, the largest motion picture factory remaining in Hollywood, will see activity reminiscent of the thirties and forties. Of course television production takes up much of the space today. To put it briefly the American film community, located primarily in Hollywood, has drastically retooled in the past two decades. And today the industry enjoys new prosperity. Movies may not be better than ever, as the studios like to advertise, but the film industry is doing very well, thank you.

# THE MOVIE BUSINESS

Making motion pictures in the United States, despite its romantic aura, is a business, a big business. It is dominated, like most powerful American industries, by a handful of companies. There are some smaller competitors, and hundreds of little companies that support the major producers. But in the early 1990s the industry was dominated by seven major companies that earned the lion's share of filmmaking revenues and controlled the industry through their substantial distribution networks. More about that later. The seven major companies are:

Columbia Pictures, until the late 1980s owned by Coca-Cola, but now owned by Sony, the Japanese electronics giant. Before it was purchased for $3.4 billion by Sony, Columbia had swallowed up Tri-Star, one of the leading smaller motion picture companies.

Warner Bros., which is now owned by Time-Warner. Warner Bros. recently consumed Lorimar Pictures, another important smaller filmmaker.

Disney/Touchstone, owned by the Disney Company.

Paramount, owned by Paramount Communications Company, which until recently had been called Gulf and Western.

20th Century Fox, owned by the News America Corp., Rupert Murdoch's media conglomerate.

Universal/MCA, owned by the giant Japanese electronics firm Matsushita, which manufactures Panasonic, Technics, and Quasar television sets, CD players, VCRs, and other mass communications hardware.

MGM/United Artists, owned by Pathé Communications Company, an Italian corporation, that in 1989 bought Cannon Group, a large independent U.S. film company.

There are other smaller, but important companies like New Line Cinema, Miramax, Carolco, and Orion. But the major studios dominate the business.

Box office attendance and industry revenues were up as the 1980s ended and the 1990s began. U.S. movies earned $5.02 billion in domestic box office receipts in 1990, about what they earned in 1989. This was almost 15 percent more than was earned in domestic rentals in 1988, however. Slightly more than 1 billion people bought motion picture tickets in 1990, down slightly from 1989. While attendance was a long way from the 4 billion admission tickets purchased in 1946, it was certainly better than the 870 million tickets sold in 1971. One other number increased at the end of the 1980s: ticket prices. In some cities in 1991 it cost as much as $7.50 for an adult to see a movie. The average ticket price nationwide was about $4.75.

But box office revenues aren't the only source of revenue for the film industry in the 1990s. Consumers spent $14.9 billion on videocassettes in 1990 ($11.2 billion on renting, $3.7 billion on buying). This figure was up by more than 15 percent from 1989. More than 230 million videocassettes were purchased at an average cost of $16.14, and more than $4.13 billion of videocassettes were rented at the average price of $2.70. The film industry earned almost 30 percent of its total revenues from the sale of the cassettes to VCR owners (these are called **sell throughs**) and video rental stores.

The number of films released each year tends to run in about a five-year up-

When *Back to the Future* hit the top of the box office charts in 1985, the producers decided a sequel would be a good idea. In fact, two sequels *(Back to the Future II* and *III)* were produced at the same time and then released one year apart. Pictured are stars Christopher LLoyd and Michael J. Fox (right) in *Back to the Future III.*
(© Ralph Nelson, © 1990 Universal City Studios, Inc.)

and-down cycle, and 1990 was the low year in this most recent cycle. Only 417 films were released in the United States in 1990, 29 less than in 1989 and down from the five-year high of 515 in 1987. Remember, however, that only about ten years ago fewer than 300 films were released annually in the United States. The major studios released 164 pictures in 1990, five more than in 1989; independent distributors accounted for the other 253, 34 less than the previous year. Many independent film-makers suffered at the end of the 1980s, a topic that will be explored in the next section of this chapter. One final set of statistics: about 73 percent of the pictures released in the United States were made by U.S. companies. The rest were made by foreign filmmakers with English soundtracks (about 11 percent) or English subtitles (16 percent).

While the industry as a whole has been doing well of late, individual film companies have their good years and their bad years, often on the basis of as little as two or three blockbuster movies. What were the big pictures of 1990? Here is a list of the top ten films, based on their domestic box office earnings. The number to the right of the name of the film is the amount of money earned in domestic **film rentals,** the 50 percent or so of the box office receipts that leave the theater. Many publications now carry lists of the most popular movies, accompanied by the "box office gross." The **gross** represents the total amount of money earned at the box office. The theater owner keeps about one-half of that, so the gross is usually twice the film rental. Why two sets of numbers? The gross can be tabulated quickly, as soon as the money at the box office is counted. It is a fast test of a film's success or failure. It is also the number used by the theater owner and the film distributor to see who earns what percentage of what. (See pages 271–272.) Film rental amounts are more important to the production companies, since that is the only money that they are likely to see, and this amount is often not determined until the completion of a motion picture's theatrical run. In any case, here are the 1990 winners:

1. *Ghost* (Warner Bros.)                          $94,000,000
2. *Pretty Woman* (Disney)                         $81,900,000
3. *Home Alone* (20th Century Fox)                 $80,000,000
4. *Die Hard II* (20th Century Fox)                $66,500,000
5. *Total Recall* (Tri-Star)                       $65,000,000
6. *Teenage Mutant Ninja Turtles* (New             $62,000,000
   Line)
7. *Dick Tracy* (Disney)                           $59,526,000
8. *Hunt for Red October* (Paramount)              $58,500,000
9. *Driving Miss Daisy* (Warner Bros.)             $49,500,000
10. *Back to the Future III* (Universal)           $48,951,000

Five studios, (Disney, Paramount, Universal, Fox, and Warner Bros.), accounted for about 70 percent of all box office receipts in 1990. These studios had eight of the top ten revenue-producing films of the year. Columbia and MGM/UA, on the other hand, did not have any big winners in 1990, and together ended up with less than 7 percent of the revenue pie. The message in these numbers is simple. All the major studios tend to put out about the same number of films each year, from 15 to 20. The overwhelming popularity of one or two of these pictures, so-called blockbusters, means the difference between a very good year and an okay or bad year.

If these films were the big winners of 1990, what were the big losers? A film that has a strong U.S. box office is very likely to earn high amounts in video release, from pay television contracts, and even through foreign box office. So a winner remains a winner. But a loser at the U.S. box office can sometimes succeed as a video release, or at theaters overseas. For example, films starring Mickey Rourke (*9 ½ Weeks, Angel Heart, Johnny Handsome,* and so on) tend to bomb in the United States, but are big hits overseas. Other kinds of films have similar success. What follows is a list compiled by *Variety* of the 10 all-time biggest Hollywood bombs, the movies that lost the most money. The year the film was released follows the name of the movie, and to the right of that is the amount of money the producers apparently lost on the film.

1. *Adventures of Baron Munchausen* (1989)        $48.1 million
2. *Inchon* (1982)                                $44 million
3. *Ishtar* (1987)                                $37.3 million
4. *Heaven's Gate* (1980)                         $34.5 million
5. *Cotton Club* (1984)                           $31 million
6. *Pirates* (1986)                               $30.3 million
7. *Rambo III* (1988)                             $30 million
8. *Santa Claus* (1985)                           $29 million
9. *Lion of the Desert* (1981)                    $28.5 million
10. *Once Upon a Time in America* (1984)          $27.5 million

A few of these are awful movies (i.e. *Inchon*), but some are quite good *(Once*

*Upon a Time in America)* and others did very well at the box office *(Rambo III).* Whether a film is going to earn a profit or not is dependent upon two numbers: what it earns and what it costs to make. In 1989 *The Abyss* earned $29 million, a sum many producers would be thrilled to get. But the film cost $45 million to make. The rule of thumb in Hollywood is that a movie must earn about three times as much as it costs to produce in order to show a profit. This is because theater owners take about half the gross box office receipts, and there are many other additional costs (promotion and advertising, for example) beyond the costs of actually making the movie. It cost $52 million just to produce *The Adventures of Baron Munchausen.* The film will have to earn more than $155 million from box office receipts, video and TV sales, and other sources before it has a chance of even breaking even. Bookkeeping by the studios in Hollywood is such that only a handful of pictures show a profit each year.

Those outside the industry got to see how a major studio keeps its books as a result of columnist Art Buchwald's lawsuit against Paramount Pictures. Buchwald contended, and a federal court agreed, that the film *Coming to America* was based on an idea he submitted to the studio, and that because of this Paramount owed him, by virtue of a contract, a percentage of the film's net profits. Paramount claimed the picture, the second-most popular film of 1988, and high on the list of all-time moneymakers, never earned a profit. This is the story told by the film studio. The film had earned a total of $275 million in revenues by early 1990. Of that amount, only $125 million came back to the studio, which produced and distributed the motion picture. As we noted earlier, a big chunk of the revenues stay with the theater owners.

The film cost $58.5 million to make, according to Paramount. About $40 million was spent on actual filmmaking. Both Eddie Murphy and director John Landis had what is called a **gross profit participation** deal, which means they got a percentage of the film's earnings or a flat amount of the gross revenues. Gross revenues are total earnings, before costs have been deducted. Murphy got $10 million; Landis got $1 million. (Buchwald's deal was for a percentage of *net* profits; what is left after expenses are paid.) The gross profit deals are standard today for the industry's biggest stars, directors, and producers. In *Batman,* for example, Jack Nicholson had a gross profit deal and earned a substantial sum right off the top of the revenues. Michael Keaton could not command such a deal. What these deals mean is that the participants in a gross profit arrangement are going to make money, whether or not the film makes money. While *Ghostbusters II* earned more than $60 million in domestic rentals and cost only about $20 million to make, it still showed a staggering loss on the basis of U.S. box office earnings because of gross profit deals engineered by Dan Ackroyd and Bill Murray, neither of whom were apparently terribly interested in making the film in the first place.

Because *Coming to America* was shot at Paramount Studios, the company charged $8 million in overhead fees, a standard 15 percent of production costs. This is a charge made for the use of the studio facilities, offices, wear and tear on the buildings, and so on. Total film costs: $58.5 million.

Because Paramount distributed the movie, it earned a $42 million distribution fee. Add to this another $36 million in distribution costs, advertising, making prints, and so forth. Finally, because the studio put up the money to make the picture in the first place, it was paid interest on this advance: $6.4 million. This totals about $143 million, or $18 million more than the $125 million Paramount earned on the movie.

While American film audiences tend to prefer slam-bang action thrillers like *Die Hard II,* in recent years they also have begun to respond to thoughtful, well-made movies like *Dances with Wolves.* The popularity of this film, which stars Kevin Costner, is a demonstration that older Americans are returning to movie theaters.   (© Ben Glass, © 1990 Orion Pictures Corporation)

There are no net profits because the film lost $18 million, the studio argued. Experts say *Coming to America* will continue to generate revenues, but under this accounting system the picture will never show a profit. Buchwald will get 1.5 percent of nothing. The judge in the Buchwald trial ruled in mid-1991 that the Paramount bookkeeping process was unfair, and ordered the studio to provide the columnist with some compensation.

## ☐ Making Movies One by One

Imagine a manufacturing business that produces no two products that are the same, and each product is produced by a different group of employees. The first item off the assembly line on Monday morning might be a toaster; then a bedspread, then a lawnmower, and a bird cage. How long could such a business last? But this description closely resembles the film industry, and this makes it substantially different from other mass media enterprises. Each edition of *The New York Times* contains different news stories, but there is more the same about each edition than there is different. And this month's edition of *Fortune* looks pretty much like last month's edition. It should; it was published by essentially the same people. Tonight's episode of "Murphy Brown" will have a different story than last week's episode, but the same characters will be on hand, and the show will look pretty much the same. But each movie is different, made by a different mix of people. And each film must be sold on its own merits. That is one of the reasons the film industry is so volatile; success today can be followed by failure tomorrow.

Another reason for the industry's volatility is that only relatively few films are made each year by each company, and each one costs a great deal. The industry reported in 1990 that the average cost of making a movie in the United States had risen to $23.5 million. Throw in another $9 million for marketing and distribution. That is a great deal of money riding on each throw of the dice. In the last few years of the 1980s while the Consumer Price Index was increasing by about 14 percent, the cost of moviemaking was increased by over 65 percent. Why? High labor costs is one reason. Moviemaking takes skilled people who are usually unionized. And these people command high wages. Many films are made today outside of Hollywood not only to take advantage of locations, but because "local" technicians are cheaper to hire. Canada, which looks a lot like the United States, is a popular venue for producers today. Even more important are salaries paid to performers. "We've got a lot of stars who are making $3 million to $7 million a picture, and they will normally be attached to a director who's making at least $2 million," said Gary Lucchesi, president of production at Paramount. (Eddie Murphy got between $9 million and $10 million for *Another 48 Hours;* Arnold Schwarzenegger earned about the same amount for *Total Recall.*) Add in the cost of a screenplay and a producer, and the casting of second leads, "you may be looking at $18 million before you even start shooting," Lucchesi adds. *National Lampoon's Christmas Vacation* cost $25 million. Five years ago the picture could have probably been made for $10 million less. But Chevy Chase got $6 million and writer/co-producer John Hughes received almost $2 million. There tends to be an axiom in the industry that any movie that costs less than $15 million has to rely on material (story, special effects, and so on) rather than star power.

And the high cost of special effects is another problem that skews the mean cost of filmmaking to the high end of the scale. When George Lucas released *Star Wars,* he not only enthralled millions of moviegoers, he substantially raised the level of special effects techniques that American moviegoers expect. And each subsequent film in that series, and all the other films that rely on special effects, have had to meet or exceed this level. Many observers blame the almost total failure of *Dune,* another science fiction epic, on its cheesy special effects and set design. All the thrilling action sequences, the incredible special effects, all of these cost money and have pushed the price of filmmaking ever higher.

There is no question that one can make an excellent film at a low cost. In 1991 MGM-Pathé's *Thelma and Louise* was a genuine hit, and only cost about $18 million to make, well below the national average. Oliver Stone made *Platoon* for $6 million. The intensity of the story and the ensemble acting so engages the viewer that the fact that Stone did not spend a great deal on hardware and a big name cast is forgotten. The same might be said for other successful films like *A Room with a*

Director Robert Townsend on location in Los Angeles during the filming of his first feature film, *Hollywood Shuffle.* Townsend ran out of money during the filming of this spoof of Hollywood moviemaking, and finished the picture by charging expenses on Mastercard and Visa credit cards he had received from banks across the nation.
(© Paul Slaughter, 1987 The Samuel Goldwyn Co.)

*View* or *Do the Right Thing.* John Sayles made a fine film called *The Brother from Another Planet* in 1984 for about $400,000. And Robert Townsend completed his 1987 spoof of filmmaking, *Hollywood Shuffle,* for less than $100,000, financing production on the last half of the film using Visa and Mastercard credit cards. But it becomes increasingly difficult for independent filmmakers to produce such small-budget gems because the cost of moviemaking is going up for them as well as *everyone else.*

So, three factors account for the volatility in the industry: each company makes only a few films each year; films cost more to make than ever before; and each film must stand on its own merit. There are no regular subscribers or sustaining audience. One additional factor can be noted. The filmmaker must appeal to a fairly small segment of the total audience. *Premiere* magazine reports that 75 percent of the American people see fewer than five films a year.

Most of the people who go to the theater to see a movie are young, generally under 30. Look at the list (p. 258) of the most popular films of 1990. The age of the audience explains their popularity as much as anything. The film audience has tended to be a young audience for many years. Until recently, 20 percent of the population bought 80 percent of the movie tickets. But things appear to be changing, slightly at least. While it cannot be described as "the greying of the movie audience," more and more people over 40 are going back to the theaters. (They were there in the thirties and forties.) In 1985 only 15 percent of the total film audience was over 40 years of age. In 1987 it was 20 percent. By 1990 the percentage had risen to more than 23 percent. Why?

"Older people have been re-exposed to movies on video cassettes and cable, and now are going out to see new movies," said Barry Lyndon, president of marketing and distribution at Paramount. When moviemakers began to see a somewhat older audience, they began to make pictures to attract that audience. Surely they still make *Bill and Ted's Excellent Adventure,* but they also make *Dances with Wolves* and *The Grifters.* Moviegoing became a lot simpler with the advent of the suburban multiplex theaters. Middle-aged and older people don't want to go downtown after work. They don't want to hunt for a parking spot and walk several blocks to a theater. Convenience is important.

## ☐ Keeping Them Coming to the Box Office

Early moviemakers were among the first to realize that because each new film is a "new product," there is a problem of continuing audience support. And once the novelty of watching movies wore off, filmgoers began exercising judgments that would often leave a producer with one failure after another. This was when the star system was born. Players in the movies, who initially had been anonymous, were named and even publicized. Mary Pickford was one of the first. "If you loved her in her last movie, you'll love this movie even more."

The star system carried the film industry through World War II and into the second half of the century. For all intents and purposes, it is dead today. Fonda and DeNiro could not sustain *Stanley and Iris.* Beatty and Hoffman could not resuscitate *Ishtar.* At the peak of his popularity, Bill Cosby's name did not fill the seats for *Ghost Dad.* And Bruce Willis died as *Hudson Hawk.* While many moviegoers have favorite performers and will try to see all new films featuring these performers, even this loy-

The star system generated a movie audience for at least four decades in the United States. People would go see a film when all they knew about it was that it was the "new Humphrey Bogart picture," or the "new Marilyn Monroe picture." Not any more. For example, the fact that Robert Redford starred in *Havana,* a movie set in pre-Castro Cuba, failed to move ticket buyers into the theater.
(© Elliott Marks, © 1990 Universal City Studios)

Few successful novels have been turned into satisfying or successful movies in the past twenty years. Warner Bros.'s *The Bonfire of the Vanities,* starring Tom Hanks (left) and Bruce Willis, was not an exception to that rule. It was likely impossible to translate the richness and depth of Tom Wolfe's satirical novel about New York City in the 1980s to the screen.
(© 1990 Warner Bros.)

alty usually fails to sustain a weak or unpopular film. As the nineties opened, only two performers seemed to be able to consistently draw an audience, regardless of the vehicle: Tom Cruise and Eddie Murphy. But most expected their influence to be short-lived.

For many years the industry drew on other literary and artistic properties in an effort to try to build success into a film project. Popular novels were often made into successful films. Remember *Gone With the Wind;* yes, it was a book first. But in the eighties, filming a best-selling novel was no guarantee of success. *Mosquito Coast, Gorky Park,* and *The Bonfire of the Vanities* all failed to attract long lines at the box office. What about motion pictures based on cartoon or comic strip characters? *Batman* was boffo, as they like to say in *Variety. Dick Tracy* was less so. And *Howard the Duck* laid an egg. *Oklahoma, South Pacific,* and *West Side Story* all made a successful transition from the Broadway stage to the silver screen, and the audience followed. But movie theaters were largely empty when *A Chorus Line,* the longest-running Broadway musical ever, was projected on the screen. There is no assurance that something that is successful in one medium will be as successful as a film.

Filmgoers in the sixties and seventies even flirted with giving their moviegoing allegiance to directors and producers. The fact that Francis Ford Coppola or Steven Spielberg or George Lucas had something to do with a movie was attractive and brought in an audience (table 8-1). But this was a short-lived phenomenon. Spielberg directed *E.T.,* but he also directed *1941.* And while Lucas made *Star Wars,* he

TABLE 8-1    Top Ten All-Time Money-Making Films Based
on Theatrical Release in the United States
and Canada

|  | Domestic Rentals (in millions) |
|---|---|
| 1. *E.T.—The Extra Terrestrial* | $226,618,839 |
| 2. *Star Wars* | $193,500,000 |
| 3. *Return of the Jedi* | $168,002,414 |
| 4. *Batman* | $150,500,000 |
| 5. *The Empire Strikes Back* | $141,000,000 |
| 6. *Ghostbusters* | $132,700,000 |
| 7. *Jaws* | $129,549,325 |
| 8. *Raiders of the Lost Ark* | $115,598,000 |
| 9. *Indiana Jones and the Last Crusade* | $115,500,000 |
| 10. *Indiana Jones and the Temple of Doom* | $109,000,000 |

*Steven Spielberg or George Lucas produced or directed all of these films but *Batman* and *Ghostbusters*. (*Variety.*)

Rarely does a sequel stand up to the quality of the original film, but each succeeding film in *The Godfather* trilogy was as strong as the first movie. Pictured is Al Pacino as Michael Corleone in *The Godfather Part III*. Together the three films represent American director Francis Ford Coppola's most important body of work.
(© Emillo Lari, © Paramount Pictures)

was also responsible for *Howard the Duck*. Coppola directed *The Godfather;* he also directed *The Cotton Club*. The name over the title was no assurance of success.

The closest Hollywood has come to a successful formula is the sequel/series formula. That is, producing a continuing series of films with much the same cast, just like a situation comedy or dramatic series on network television. Film sequels and series are not new. In the thirties there were several popular film series, including the Dr. Kildare films, Andy Hardy films, and even Ma and Pa Kettle and their brood. But these weren't the first-line Hollywood products.

Today the sequels and series pictures often are the first-line films, the movies with the greatest promise of financial success, the films that cost the most to make. Sequels are not always successful. *Godfather III* and *Rocky V* were flops. But they seem to many in Hollywood to present the best insurance policy that there is against failure. Seven of the top 25 box office hits of 1990 were sequels or part of a series. No fewer than 27 of the movies released in 1990 were sequels or part of a film series, including *Robocop 2, Die Hard II, Another 48 Hours, Rocky V, Back to the Future III, Gremlins 2,* and *Three Men and a Little Lady.* At various stages of development in the spring of 1991 were *Aliens III, Batman II, Beverly Hills Cop III, Dirty Dancing II, Gone With the Wind II, Good Morning Vietnam II, Honey, I Shrunk the Kids II, Jagged Edge II, Lethal Weapon III, Major League II, Mary Poppins II, Mystic Pizza II, Naked Gun II, Parenthood II, Robocop 3, Rambo IV, Saturday Night Fever III, Short Circuit II, Star Trek VI, Terminator II* and *Who Framed Roger Rabbit II.* How many of these projects might ever see the light of day remains to be seen, but it is clear evidence of the current mindset in Hollywood; if one was good, two will be better, and three will be great. While original ideas aren't necessarily scarce in Hollywood, the willingness to invest money in them is often in very short supply.

## ▣ Independent Filmmaking

Independent film producers have always been an important part of Hollywood. Indeed, the industry really started with independent producers. But by the 1920s the major studios, the dream factories, had established themselves, and these huge production companies have tended to dominate the industry ever since. One of the interesting stories of the last decade is the emergence of the independent filmmakers to positions of new power in the industry, the collapse of these independent production companies, and then their slow reemergence in the early 1990s. It is a classic Hollywood story.

Independent production companies tended to sustain themselves over the past 10 to 15 years by producing low-budget, "B" quality movies that were aimed at a very specific audience. New Line Pictures, for example, netted a nifty $23 million in profits (not revenues, but profits) on the first four *Nightmare on Elm Street* pictures, which together cost only about $16 million to produce. Other companies followed similar patterns. Independent producers did often attempt to produce bigger budget, mainstream films, but rarely with much success. They simply couldn't compete with the major studios on an even playing field with it came to production costs and promotion budgets. But in the mid-1980s some of the smaller studios, companies like Hemdale, Island Pictures, Cinecom Entertainment Group, New World, and DEG, produced some of the most critically acclaimed and financially rewarding pictures of the era. Films like *The Trip to Bountiful, A Room with a View, Platoon,* and *Kiss of the Spiderwoman* made a strong mark on the industry. With modest budgets, these companies made script- and character-driven films with little action, few gimmicks, and no top stars. And they were successful. Most observers now agree that the independents were the first to note the aging of the film audience, and they were rewarded when the pictures they produced appealed to these older moviegoers. For whatever reason, these were the salad days for the small filmmakers.

By the late 1980s the bubble had burst, and many of these smaller companies were on the rocks, or in a nose dive. Many of the smaller companies, finding success with low-budget films, decided to invest greater sums of money in hopes of earning greater profits. Productions that cost between $3 and $6 million were replaced by ones that cost between $9 and $12 million. And many of these films failed. The small producers, generally undercapitalized, could not absorb the losses. "Studio guys can afford to sit around and scratch their heads for a couple of years, waiting for a hit," noted Jonathan M. Damon, of the Atlantic Entertainment Group. "Independents don't have that luxury."

Other reasons have been cited as well. There were too many films being released, 513 in 1988 alone. That is almost ten per week. Theater owners did not have the time or the space to exhibit the smaller, independent productions, to give them time to draw an audience. Without massive advertising, word of mouth and critical reviews are the only means with which filmgoers can discover these movies. But that requires time.

In addition, by the end of the decade, most of the theaters in the United States had been gobbled up by theater chains, whose strategy is "move 'em in quickly, move 'em out quickly." Again, small, unadvertised productions usually need time to succeed. The Seven Gables Theaters in Seattle, for example, the creation of an inveterate film lover named Randy Finley, provided long runs for several smaller pictures that later became nationally successful after enjoying success in Seattle. *Stunt Man* and Francis Ford Coppola's *Black Stallion* are just two pictures that Finley rescued from oblivion by giving them the time to develop an audience. Their success in the Pacific Northwest made them attractive to theater owners in other cities. But Seven Gables was purchased recently by a national film chain, and its owners have neither the patience nor inclination to "baby" smaller films into success. Other independent theaters and theater chains have followed the same path.

By 1988 many of the major studios, noting the success of the adult-oriented pictures released by the smaller production companies, began to emulate the independents. Warner Bros. produced *Crossing Delancey,* MGM made *Moonstruck.* Five years earlier neither picture would have interested a major studio, and if made at all, the films would have been produced by an independent producer.

The independent producers have always been behind the majors in distribution and marketing pictures. The major studios maintain successful distribution arms (see pp. 280–281) that have the budgets and wherewithal to mount successful promotional efforts to publicize new films. Independent distributors can't do this; they don't have the means. As long as the independent producers were making movies that other studios were not, publicity was not that important. But when the major studios sought to grasp the same, older adult audience, advertising and promotion became important.

Finally, the video money "well" was beginning to dry up. The rapid expansion in the sale and rental of videocassettes during the mid-1980s slowed dramatically near the end of the decade. One means for an undercapitalized independent producer to raise the cash to make a film is to presell the video rights. That is, go to a

Warner Bros. released *Crossing Delancey* starring Amy Irving and Peter Riegert in 1988. The film was typical of those independent producers had been succeeding with earlier in the decade, and its release by a major studio marked the beginning of the move by majors to get involved with smaller, more personal films.
(© 1988 Warner Bros.)

video distribution company, and give it the rights to distribute the video, in exchange for cash to make the film. This money was much harder to get as the decade closed. So the combination of an intensely competitive film and theatrical market, higher film budgets, and vanishing video dollars added up to a major cash squeeze for many of the independent producers.

Some declared the "indies" dead in 1989, bested by the bigger major studios. But this obituary was premature. For as the 1990s opened, independent producers once again surged forward. *Driving Miss Daisy,* a 1989 film that won the Academy Award for Best Picture, was produced by The Zanuck Company, with the backing of Warner Bros. The film was almost not produced because major studios were not interested. The film's initial budget was $12.5 million, about half the cost of the average U.S. film. But this was too high for many backers. Producers Lili and Richard Zanuck cut the shooting schedule by one-third, traded location preparation like painting and carpentry for screen credits, and pared the shooting costs to $7.5 million. Warner Bros. agreed to support the project at this point. By mid-1991 the film had grossed more than $100 million in North American box office receipts.

Three of the top-grossing pictures of 1989 were produced by independents with the backing of major studios; *Look Who's Talking, Parenthood,* and *When Harry Met Sally.* Carolco Pictures had one of the biggest moneymakers of 1990 in *Total Recall* with Arnold Schwarzenegger. And New Line Pictures had a main line hit with

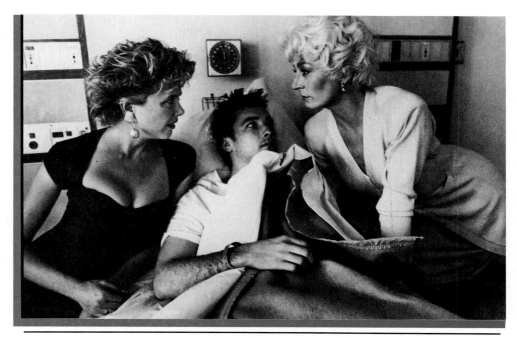

Big budget blockbusters abound in moviemaking today, but the industry has also shown a new appreciation for smaller, less costly pictures. In 1991 Miramax Films released *The Grifters,* the story of three small-time con artists, based on a 1963 novel by Jim Thompson. The film stars (left to right) Annette Bening, John Cusack, and Angelica Huston. (© Suzanne Hanover, Miramax Films)

*Teenage Mutant Ninja Turtles.* In 1990 Miramax released *The Grifters.* And Morgan Creek produced *Pacific Heights* in 1990 and *Robin Hood, Prince of Thieves* in 1991 with Kevin Costner playing the title role. What sustained this recovery of the indies?

Many of the smaller production companies have reluctantly agreed to use the major studios both for financial backing and distribution. Spike Lee normally uses major studio money to make his movies. This robs the producer of some creative control of both the film and the marketing strategies for the film and denies them some of the profits as well. But it nevertheless gives their pictures a far greater chance to succeed. Many of the smaller companies are seeking additional capitalization to permit them to absorb losses without failing as businesses. These companies are gaining these resources from foreign investors like the Japanese, who have funneled over $100 million into Morgan Creek pictures. Others have found this money in American companies like Westinghouse, which recently invested $50 million in Castle Rock Pictures. Some are even going to the major studios for help. Columbia now owns 34 percent of Castle Rock, which produced *When Harry Met Sally;* Universal owns 20 percent of Imagine, which made *Dream Team* and *Parenthood.* And many of these companies are seeking funding for individual films by selling foreign distribution rights, as they once sold video rights. The European film industry was suffering greatly in 1990. But filmgoers throughout the continent were standing in long lines to see American-made movies. Foreign distribution revenues were developing into an important source of income for American film companies. Using these and other schemes, the independent producers seemed to be regaining their footing as the last decade of the twentieth century began.

## Expenses and Income

The typical movie must earn in box office receipts about three times what it costs to make the film before the producer shows a profit. The average cost of making a movie in 1991 was $23.5 million (figure 8-1). So the average movie must gross about $75 million to be profitable to the producer. The role of the large studios has changed dramatically in the past 30 years from being primarily movie-making companies to becoming funding and distribution companies. The studios still produce movies, but it is just as likely that they will provide financial resources to an independent producer who wants to make a film. The major role of the film studios today, however, is distributing movies to theaters. But more about this later.

All the studios have budget departments that will work with producers to determine the probable cost of making a film. Costs are divided into two parts, what are called **above-the-line costs,** and **below-the-line costs.** Above-the-line cost is the money spent on the purely creative end of the film, money spent even before the production starts. Included are script costs, salaries and fees for actors and directors, and similar expenses. These are easy to establish. Below-the-line cost is the money spent actually producing the film: sets, travel to locations, film, props, rental of equipment, salaries for the crew, and similar items. These items are much harder

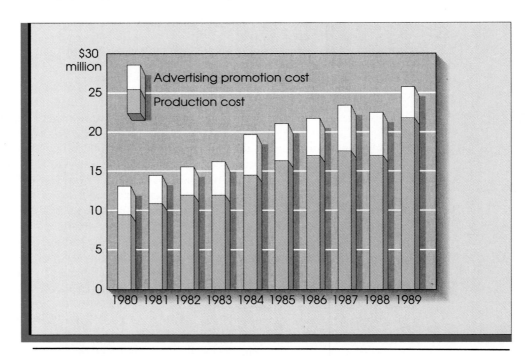

FIGURE 8-1 The cost of making and marketing movies has escalated greatly in recent years. This graph indicates the average cost of filmmaking/marketing since 1980. (Motion Picture Association of America)

to estimate. When Michael Cimino began making *Heaven's Gate,* a movie that ultimately cost $45 million, the cost of the movie was estimated at $10 million. This was based on the established above-the-line costs and the estimate of what it would take to actually produce the film.

But Cimino is a perfectionist and spent millions of dollars trying to recreate to the smallest detail a late nineteenth century Wyoming community. He shot scene after scene after scene over and over and over to get just the perfect action. Costs skyrocketed. To control the below-the-line costs the studio must tightly control the producer and the director of the film. United Artists did not, in this case, and *Heaven's Gate* virtually bankrupted the studio. A total budget for any film, then, is actually just a good guess. Some producers and directors are legendary for their ability to bring in a film on time and on budget. Others, like Cimino and Francis Ford Coppola, are also legendary for their inability to do this. A studio can often predict with some degree of accuracy what a potential film will earn and will approve a project based on a comparison of the potential earnings and the budget. When the budget goes out of whack, this frequently throws what might have been a money-making motion picture into the loser list.

## ☐ Making Money

Twenty years ago what a movie earned at the box office was all the revenue a producer could expect. Things have changed dramatically, however, in recent years. Nowadays a film can earn money in many different ways, and often a film that loses out at the box office can still make money by collecting other kinds of revenue. The industry refers to these revenue-producing opportunities as "windows." When a film is released, a window is opened and remains open until the maximum amount of money is earned. Then another window opens. Let's look at these windows and a couple of additional money-making schemes as well (figure 8-2).

## ☐ Theatrical Release

The first revenue-producing window that opens for a film is the domestic theatrical release window. The dollars that are generated by ticket sales at the theater represent a substantial part of the total revenue earned by a particular film. The first thing to note, however, is that the theater owner gets his or her share of this revenue first.

The total box office receipts earned by a film is called "the gross." From this sum the theater owner deducts the cost of operating the theater, his or her expenses. For some reason this is called **"the nut."** These expenses include salaries for employees, maintenance of the theater, electric, water, and heat bills, and so forth.

After the nut is subtracted, the theater owner then takes a percentage of what is left. How big a percentage? There is no standard figure. Theater owners usually bid for the right to show films, and the percentage they expect is a part of this bid. Oftentimes the percentage varies. The theater owner may agree to take a smaller percentage during the first two weeks of the film's run, then a larger percentage for the remainder of the run. This is all very complicated and determined by a great many factors, not the least of which is the size of the audience the film is expected to generate.

A theater owner may bid low in order to exhibit a so-called blockbuster film that is expected to generate a huge crowd. The low bid would be justified simply to gain

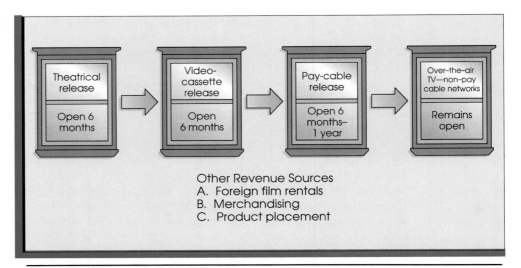

FIGURE 8-2 Revenue windows for a typical American motion picture.

the right to exhibit such a film. But also, a bigger crowd will generate more sales at the refreshment counter, and it is often through the sale of refreshments that the theater owner earns the greatest percentage of his or her revenues. Not only is the mark-up on the candy, soft drinks, and popcorn extraordinarily high, the normal business expenses (except buying the products) of selling these goodies are covered by the nut. To you and me the snack bar may look like a counter filled with candy; to the theater owner it looks a lot more like a gold mine. In some instances the theater owner has agreed to show a film without taking a percentage, simply to reap the benefits of refreshment sales. Movies that attract thousands and thousands of children who buy lots and lots of treats fall into this category.

After the theater owner has taken out the nut and a percentage of what is left, the money goes to the film's distributor who subtracts the cost of distributing and marketing the films. This is often a substantial expense, with the promotion costs of the average film estimated at about $9 million in 1991. The cost of making the prints of the film that are shown in the theaters is also subtracted. The money that is left after distribution expenses are paid is used to pay for the cost of producing the film, paying performers with gross profit deals, and other filmmaking expenses. If there is anything left after that, it is profit. In 95 out of 100 instances, there is no profit based on U.S. box office receipts alone.

To generalize a bit more, for each $1 you spend for a theater admission, the theater owner keeps about 50 cents, the distributor takes about 25 cents, and about 25 cents goes to the cost of making the film. Were it just for U.S. box office revenues, most Hollywood filmmakers would be selling used cars instead of making movies.

## ☐ Videocassette Revenues

About six months after a movie is released in the theaters, the second revenue window is opened. This is the release of the film in videocassettes. The six-month delay is standard, but not universal. Some films that are expected to fail at the box office go immediately to videocassette, where the audience is expected to be less discriminating, and the price of seeing the film is only a dollar or two rather than $4 or $5. However, *Batman* was released in videocassette only about four months after it appeared in the theaters to take advantage of the "Batmania" the film had generated.

Other films take years to appear in video. Disney still holds back several of the classic feature-length cartoons for rerelease in theaters every seven years or so. Steven Spielberg refused to release *Raiders of the Lost Ark* for two and one-half years, or until he was convinced its release in video could help promote the release of *Indiana Jones and the Temple of Doom* in the theaters. Copyright problems sometimes delay or block the release of films into video. Who owns the rights to the film? Not the studios, in many cases, even though they produced or distributed the pictures. Some of the Bob Hope/Bing Crosby "Road" movies were not on videocassette in 1990 because Paramount Pictures wasn't sure who owned them. Getting music rights can be equally difficult, especially for films with a sound track featuring a variety of artists. Singer Peggy Lee, who wrote six of the songs and provided voices for four characters in the 1955 animated film *Lady and the Tramp,* sued the Walt Disney Co. for releasing the film on video in 1987 without her permission. A court awarded Lee $2.3 million in 1991. Difficulty in gaining music rights delayed the video release of *Picnic* and *Five Easy Pieces.* And *The Last Picture Show,* in theatrical release in 1974, didn't appear in video until the spring of 1991, six months after its sequel *Texasville* was exhibited in theaters.

Money from cassette sales is very important to the film industry. VCR penetration reached 70 percent in 1990 as millions of people rented and bought films. The pricing of videocassettes by the industry is probably one of the most unusual aspects of the mass media. Imagine you went into a grocery store to buy some bread. There on the bread shelf was one brand of bread that cost $1 a loaf. Right next to it was another brand of the same style of bread that cost $25 a loaf. That's crazy, you'd say. Visit your local video store and you will find that exact pricing pattern. It costs about $100 to buy a copy of the hit movie *The Hunt for Red October.* But it costs less than $20 to purchase a copy of the hit movie *Ghost.* Why? It has nothing to do with the cost of the movie. The price is predicated on a guess made by the video distributor, a guess whether the movie is one people will more likely want to buy, or one people will more likely want to rent. A movie that has a high rental but low sell-through potential is priced higher. The company will sell many fewer copies of the video, almost exclusively to video rental stores. The high price compensates for the low sales. But the video distributor will price a movie with a high sell-through potential lower, because while it earns much less on each copy it sells, it will sell more copies. In a sense the guess on whether a movie will be bought or rented becomes a self-fulfilling prophecy, as people are much less likely to buy and more likely to rent a high priced cassette, and more likely to buy a low priced video. Only those special films—Disney classics, *The Wizard of Oz, E.T.,* and the like—seem to sell many copies, no matter what the price.

The producer of the film often receives an advance from a video distributor, sometimes before the film is even made. But ultimately the revenues the producer receives are based on a percentage of the sale of the cassettes. Usually 20 to 30 percent of the wholesale price of the cassette (which is about 50 to 60 percent of the retail price for a normally priced cassette) goes to the producer.

Video money is becoming so important that many producers employ video advisors who work on the set with the director. Showing a film on video is different

Money from the sale of motion picture videos to both rental store owners and movie buffs provide a substantial portion of the revenue earned by motion picture makers. The popularity of the cassette movies took Hollywood, the television industry, and most mass media "experts" by surprise.
(Richmond Beach Video, Seattle, Wa.)

than showing a film in the theaters. The video advisor will remind the director about lighting. A dark scene may show up fine in a darkened auditorium, but will disappear in a lighted living room when the film is shown on a home television set. And the video advisor will also remind the director to keep the action in the center of the screen. Theater screens are rectangular; TV screens tend to be square. Action on the edges of the frame, perceivable on a theater screen, can disappear on a TV screen. Some directors who resist these moves insist that their film be released on video in the **letterbox** format, which retains the full rectangular picture by stripping black borders along the bottom and top of the picture.

The video market in the 1990s is changing. The sale of VCRs has slowed. In 1989 sales dropped by almost 6 percent from 1988. And some surveys indicate that a majority of persons who bought a VCR in 1989 were buying their second recorder; they were not first-time buyers. The rental market is changing as well. Small video dealers are being pressed heavily by big video rental chains such as Blockbuster and West Coast Video. *Newsweek* reported in late 1990 that the video rental chains control about 75 percent of the market. There were 25,000 video dealers in 1990, but some experts predict that there may be as few as 15,000 by 1995. The ones that will disappear are the mom and pop stores that are at a distinct disadvantage at buying and renting videos when confronted by competition from a chain

## TABLE 8-2   Top Ten All-Time Video Rentals

1. *Top Gun*
2. *Crocodile Dundee*
3. *Dirty Dancing*
4. *Three Men and a Baby*
5. *Platoon*
6. *The Color Purple*
7. *Robocop*
8. *Die Hard*
9. *Fatal Attraction*
10. *Lethal Weapon*

*1991 — Alexander and Associates.

store which may stock 80 or 90 copies of a popular film and stock several thousand movies as opposed to a few hundred.

The film industry itself is attempting to squeeze the video market in several ways, trying to earn every penny possible through this window. One of the ways they do this is by attempting to force retailers to buy a great many copies of popular new releases so customers who want to see the film can find a copy. Pressure is applied by discounting multiple copy sales, selling cassettes in two-packs (a dealer must buy two copies to get one) and by TV blitz advertising, which will drive customers to the video store to look for new films, and then complain when there are no copies available. The cost of the cassettes to the dealers has also dramatically increased. The list price for *The Hunt for Red October* was $99, the highest ever. Dealers paid almost $70 for a copy of the cassette. (See table 8-2.)

These strategies tend to bode ill for serious video buffs. A video dealer has a budget each month to purchase new cassettes. If the industry can force the dealer to spend 80 percent of that budget on multiple copies of blockbuster movies, only 20 percent of the budget remains for smaller, less-promoted new films, foreign films, and older movies just released on cassette. If the dealer can divide his budget, spending only 50 percent on copies of the mega-movies like *Lethal Weapon II*, money remains to offer customers a broader range of titles from which to choose.

The video distributors are also trying to squeeze a few extra bucks out of the cassette market by putting advertising messages in front of the videos, and developing tie-in advertising for new videos with everyone from pizza parlor owners to clothing manufacturers. Interestingly, while the video distributors find it "just good business" to insert an ad for a soft drink or candy bar before the FBI copyright warning, they were less than pleased when a few retail video dealers tried to do the same thing. In a few locations, video dealers sold advertising time to local advertisers and placed the short spots on the leader, the blank part of the tape that precedes everything on the movie. The film industry said this was a violation of copyright and took these dealers to court. Video distributors also substantially shortened the leaders on the tapes to make it impossible to place an advertisement before the film.

Look for vending machines that dispense videocassettes for rent in the future. The Video Corporation of America said it was considering "Vidirobots" for placement in apartment lobbies, convenience stores, and workplaces. The machines will hold up to 100 tapes, and when the proper amount of money is inserted, will dispense a video to an eager viewer.

Two or three weeks after a film goes into video release, it is made available for showing on pay-per-view television systems, where customers pay a specific fee, usually $5 or so, to see the telecast of a recent movie. Pay-per-view revenues currently represent a tiny portion of industry earnings, and little more will be said about this. The realities of prospects of pay-per-view television are outlined in Chapter 9, pp. 317–318.

## ◼ Pay Cable

A year after theatrical release, six months after video release, films begin to appear on **pay cable** television channels, such as HBO, Showtime, Cinemax, the Movie Channel. The networks pay the film producers a flat fee for the right to show the film a certain number of times. Frequently the films are bought in packages; the cable channels buy the rights to the popular films and get some not-so-popular films thrown in as well. This is similar to the block booking schemes outlawed by the U.S. government in the late 1940s. (See p. 38.)

Ten years ago the major pay cable channels all showed the same films. HBO might have a movie before Showtime, but Showtime viewers would still see the film. Or vice versa. Lately, however, the cable channels have been signing exclusive agreements with producers for the rights to these films. What appears on HBO might not appear on Showtime, at least not for some time. And the cable channels have even made agreements to buy all the films produced by a particular studio during 1992 through 1994, for example.

But the pay cable channels are not that healthy today. And revenues from pay cable, while not insubstantial, are not nearly as important to the film industry as they were prior to the growth of the videocassette market. In 1989 CBS outbid the pay cable giants and bought the rights to ten films for exhibition on over-the-air network television before they will be available to the pay cable channels. Included in the package was *Batman,* for which the network reportedly paid $20 million. CBS termed this persistent report on the cost of *Batman* to be "just silly."

## ◼ Over-the-Air Television

The sale of movies to over-the-air television was once a lucrative market for the film industry. But today, before a movie gets to over-the-air television, either a network or local station, most people who want to see it have already seen it at the theater, on video, or through pay cable television. Blockbuster movies no longer draw the vast audiences like *Jaws* did when it was first shown on free television in 1979 and won a 39 rating, or 57 percent of all persons who were watching television that night. Several years later, when *Star Wars* was first shown on free television it only earned a 25 rating, or 35 percent of the viewing audience, and was beaten in its time slot by a third-rate made-for-TV movie called *Lace.* Conventional wisdom in the industry recently has been that made-for-television movies, being shown for the first time anywhere, will always do better than theatrical films. But this philosophy may be changing. With network television in the doldrums, the networks (notably CBS) are beginning to again get interested in theatrical movies. This is what prompted the Columbia Broadcasting System to outbid the pay cable networks for the *Batman* package noted above.

Movies are licensed to over-the-air television as they are to pay cable. The television network pays a fee for the right to show the film a specified number of times. Some consortiums of local stations are also bidding to show movies first on over-the-air television, so the "free TV premieres" of some theatrical films are occurring on local television stations.

## Other Revenue Sources

The exhibition of American films overseas has become much more important to the American film industry (figure 8-3). American films have always been shown abroad, but usually months or even years after they have played in this country. And the film industry has for years made a number of third-rate junk films exclusively for foreign distribution. Today, however, American films are growing in popularity, especially in Europe. They are opening soon after they first appear in U.S. theaters, and in a few instances they have opened concurrently in Europe and the United States. Foreign box office revenues sometimes exceed U.S. box office receipts. *Rambo III* earned twice as much overseas as it did in the United States. In 1989 the seven major film studios earned 43 percent of total box office revenues overseas, notably in Japan,

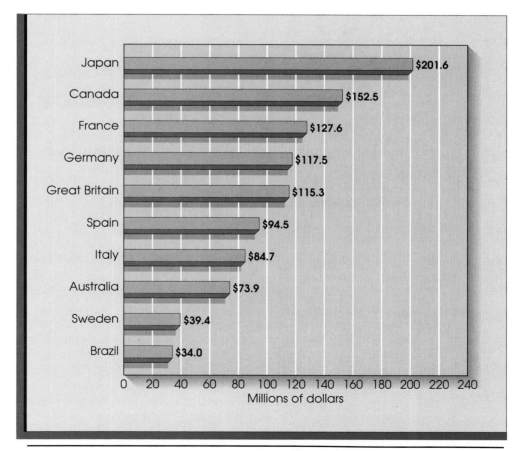

FIGURE 8-3 U.S. films are popular in other countries. Here is a list of the leading importers of American movies in 1989. ·
*(Variety)*

Canada, and Western Europe. "Before going ahead with a project, studios are increasingly considering how movie scripts and the actors they envision for the main roles will play not only in Peoria, but in Pisa, Perth and, now, Prague," wrote *The New York Times* reporter Geraldine Fabrikant in 1990. And the preferences of audiences overseas sometimes don't mirror U.S. tastes. John Candy and Tom Hanks don't do as well overseas as do Arnold Schwarzenegger and Mel Gibson. And action films do much better than comedies or dramas, where the language barrier presents a bigger problem. The Europeans, whose own film industry is suffering, are concerned, and in mid-1990 announced they wanted to negotiate a limit on the number of U.S. films that would come into their countries.

Revenues are also generated by the film industry through merchandising schemes. This can be direct merchandising, such as selling toys or plastic figures that represent the characters in a film. Or it can be indirect, such as selling tee shirts or drinking glasses or pajamas imprinted with the likenesses of movie heroes and heroines. In the summer of 1989 fans could have purchased a Batman jacket with the bat logo in rhinestones. Price: $499.95. Or an Indiana Jones watch for $150. In 1990 it was Dick Tracy paraphernalia and *Total Recall* tee shirts.

Those who seek to sell such merchandise must normally pay a licensing fee to the owners of the film, usually $100,000 or more. Mattel reportedly paid the producers of *Hook* $3 million to get the license to make toy figures of the characters in this live action retelling of the Peter Pan story. And then the film owners earn royalties on the sale of the merchandise, often as much as 10 percent of the retail price. This can add up. The *Star Wars* trilogy generated $1.2 billion in box office revenue. But the sale of "Star Wars" merchandise generated $2.6 billion in revenue, of which Lucas and company earned about 10 percent.

And then there is **product placement,** not a new idea, but one that is being used with new abandon by film production companies obsessed with the bottom line. Twenty-five years ago when a character in a film went to the refrigerator and took out a can of beer the brand was not distinguishable. In fact there was no brand; it was a generic can. When the same character grabs a beer today, the brand is clearly visible, and for good measure the character probably will say, "I think I'll have a Bud." Budweiser has paid to have that can of beer used in the film. "More and more companies now recognize that movies are an alternative advertising and promotion medium," noted one advertising executive. And some of those companies are film companies.

Disney's Buena Vista Pictures unit sent letters to large consumer-products companies soliciting product placement for a Disney film entitled *Mr. Destiny,* according to film critic Mark C. Miller. For $20,000 the company's product will be seen in the film; for $40,000 an actor will mention the product; and for $60,000 the character will actually use the product. The Disney studio is not alone in making such solicitations.

Some films are shamelessly filled with plugs via products, billboards, store fronts, and so on. The use of real products can obviously enhance the realism of some movies, make the characters and the story seem more natural. But most placement is deliberately anti-realistic, according to Miller. "Its sole purpose is to enhance the product by meticulously placing it within the sort of idealized display that occurs nowhere in real life, but everywhere in advertising," he adds. Some films have become a showcase for dozens of products. The *Back to the Future* series was filled with both historical (the fifties) and futuristic product plugs for major sellers of con-

The *Star Wars* trilogy generated about $1.2 billion in box office revenues. But the sale of *Star Wars* merchandise, including toy replicas of C3-PO and R2-D2, generated more than twice as much money. Ten percent of this money normally goes back to the licensing entity, usually the producer of the film.
(20th Century Fox)

sumer goods. And the plugs don't come cheap. Philip Morris paid $350,000 to have James Bond smoke a Lark cigarette in *Licence to Kill,* a promotion that was so overt that the filmmakers put a Surgeon General's warning about smoking hazards at the conclusion of the film. The producers said they thought it was a "nice" thing to do. Congressman Thomas Luken, chairman of the U.S. House subcommittee that oversees cigarette advertising, suggested a more pragmatic explanation. "It's a declared admission on their part that this is an advertisement and does require a Surgeon General's warning." In 1990, Congress was considering a measure to outlaw cigarette product placement in films. Both the Federal Trade Commission and Congress held hearings in 1991 on proposals that would declare product placement an unfair business practice and require disclosure (on screen) of all products "advertised" (placed) in a motion picture.

These and a few other minor revenue sources help fill the coffers of the film studios in the 1990s. The success or failure of a film at the box office is still a critical element in the financial success of that particular movie. But it surely is not as critical as it once was.

## MAKING A MOVIE

Every movie begins with a story. That does not mean the movie ends with the same story, for rewrites, script changes, character deletions, and scene restructuring is common. A television script often goes through some of the same kinds of changes, but usually for different reasons. Television scripts tend to be altered for commercial reasons—we need more auto chases to keep the audience—or by network censors. The production of a movie involves many creative people: a producer, director, scriptwriter, and performers, all of whom usually have a "better idea" of how to write a scene. Often the bosses, the people who have put up the money, insist upon changes but usually only to lower a budget.

About 8,000 motion picture scripts are registered with the Writers Guild each year, according to David Lees and Stan Berkowitz in the book, *The Movie Business*. Scripts emerge as original works, as derivations from novels, as adaptations from plays or short stories, and as rewrites from other scripts.

Financing usually comes second, but sometimes a producer has some money with which to make a film and actually is looking for the right story. Estimating how much money will be needed to make a film is very difficult. Each 737 jet that the Boeing Company manufacturers costs about the same amount of money. But the cost of making a movie varies dramatically. Even television programs have a fairly standard budget. The producer of a one-hour television show usually has a budget of $1.2 million or so to work with. But one two-hour movie (like John Sayles' *The Brother from Another Planet*) may cost $400,000. A second film (like *Licence to Kill*) may cost $45 million. Money for making movies usually comes from one of three sources. The producer will often put up the money needed to make a film. Successful producers like George Lucas and Steven Spielberg can always finance their next film from the revenues earned on their previous movies. The motion picture studios often finance films. They usually insist upon considerable control in making the movie and also demand the right to control distribution. Usually the producer and the studio hammer out these matters in a contract. Finally, outsiders often invest in movies. There are big investors, and sometimes there are lots of little investors. All are hoping for a blockbuster hit and a big return on their investment.

Preproduction work begins when the script is set, and the money is in the bank. Preproduction includes budgeting, casting, set design and construction, locating props, and location scouting. There are independent companies in Hollywood who will—for a fee—handle every one of these chores, according to Berkowitz and Lees. Studios also will handle these chores.

Actual production of the film follows and may take two months or two years. Postproduction work—some of which may take place while the film is still being shot—includes editing the film, sound work (dubbing voices, adding sound effects, and mixing), composing, arranging, and recording music for the movie, and finally making prints to be shown in the theaters.

The final task is distribution of the movie and many insist that from a business standpoint, this is the most important aspect of movie making today. A good film can die without proper distribution. But a bad film can often earn back its costs, unless they are very high, with slick marketing and good distribution. So let's look at the distribution of a movie.

## ☐ Distribution

Many people call distribution—getting the goods to the customer—the heart of the movie business. And the studios have a real lock on this end of the business. Forty years ago the studios made virtually all the movies and controlled the industry in that way. Many other people make movies today, but because the studios dominate the distribution business they still have significant control of the industry.

The studios can control distribution because they are so good at it. They have been doing it for decades and have established large and well-run distribution organizations across the nation. They also have a continual supply of films to offer theater owners, and this gives a studio leverage in getting what it wants from theater owners. An independent agency distributes one film at a time. Often these distributors must hire subdistributors in some regions to help get the movie to the theaters. Independent distributors may be cheaper, but if the film is not distributed properly, put into the right theaters at the right time, it can cost the producer considerably more than can be saved with the lower independent distribution fee.

The studios distribute all the films they produce. They also get the rights to distribute films they finance. Independent producers also often use the studios to distribute films they have produced and financed on their own. But there are some problems with the studio distribution system. A serious one is the so-called **hostage film.**

A hostage film is a movie that a studio has the right to distribute, but refuses to distribute. Imagine that a movie studio has financed the production of a film and hence holds the right of distribution. The studio has already put $7 million into the movie, but is extremely unhappy with the film when it is completed. The cost of distribution and marketing a movie is very high. From the studio's standpoint it seems foolish to invest more money—$2 or $3 million—in the distribution of a film that will not be popular. So the movie goes on the shelf, the studio eats the $7 million loss, and the public never gets to see the film. Sometimes these films are ultimately released. An independent will try to distribute the movie, or a theater owner will ask permission to show the film. Movies like *The Stunt Man, Cutter's Way, Prince of the City, The Great Santini,* and *Health* were all hostage films. The first four were ultimately freed and were released to very good reviews and some popularity in the theaters. *Health* was sold to television. But other films are never released. Steve McQueen's last movie, *The Enemy of the People,* has never gotten into general distribution. Terry Gilliam's *Brazil* was doing strong box office business in London and Paris, but Universal was reluctant to release it in the United States because, studio bosses said, 25 percent of the test audiences who saw the picture had a hard time understanding it. The picture ends with an enormous quiet from the audience, Gilliam said, and that really bothered Universal. They wanted the audience to leave the theater smiling. Universal finally turned around on the film and released it when it won the Los Angeles Film Critics' Award after a limited showing in that city.

## ▢ Selecting the Theater

The key to successful distribution is matching the movie with the movie theater. Should the film play one large downtown theater or open in several suburban theaters? Should it go to a so-called "art house," the home of more serious movies, or should it go to the multiplex theaters in the shopping malls? A good distributor knows where the movie should open.

There are several kinds of openings for films, but two are more common than all others. The first is the **wide release,** opening a movie in 800 to 1,600 theaters at the same time. The advantage of this is that for a successful film, ticket revenues roll in quickly and the distributor gets back more money, more quickly. The percent of the gross returned to the distributor and producer is usually higher in the first few weeks of a film's life. But wide release has disadvantages as well. It is very expensive. The cost of each print is about $1,400. If a film opens in 1,600 theaters print costs alone total more than $2 million. Costs of promoting a film in wide release are higher also and usually involve heavy television advertising because it is important to get people into the hundreds of theaters. Two kinds of movies generally go into wide release. The best and most popular films like *Total Recall* go into wide release because the producers know they will be successful and want to earn their money back quickly. *Total Recall* earned almost $70 million in its first month in the theaters. But sometimes very bad films also go into wide release. The producers and distributors want to try to make as much money as possible before the critics and word of mouth kill the picture.

**Platforming** is another common distribution scheme, generally reserved for smaller or more serious films, motion pictures that will attract an older audience that closely reads critical reviews. A platformed film may open in as few as two or three theaters. There is generally a minimal advertising campaign. The distributor hopes that word of mouth and critical reviews will work to bring people to the theater, and as the popularity of the film grows, it is put into more and more theaters.

Warner Bros. used the platform distribution scheme when it released *Dangerous Liaisons* in December of 1988. The company considered the movie a "tough sell," according to writer Richard Gold in an article in *Variety*. The play on which the film had been based had not been a financial success on Broadway. Marketing and promotion strategists believed the film had two pluses, and several minuses. Two of the three leads were not widely recognized box office draws in late 1988. Neither Michelle Pfieffer nor John Malkovich were widely known. Director Stephen Frears had made three consecutive art house hits, including *My Beautiful Laundrette* and *Sammy and Rosie Get Laid.* But his following wasn't large either. But the third leading player, Glenn Close, had just enjoyed a considerable success in *Fatal Attraction,* and her name had sure marquee value. The second plus was the character played by Close in the movie, a "wily bodice bursting character with a come-hither sexiness," according to Gold.

The film opened on December 22 in just three theaters, one each in New York, Los Angeles, and San Francisco. It got an excellent review in *Newsweek* by critic David Ansen, who inadvertently provided Warner Bros. publicists with a slogan for the picture. The initial advertising campaign was simply a picture of the three stars in costume and three words from Ansen's review in large type: "nasty, decadent fun." By February 1 the film had gone into 60 theaters, and ten days later was running in almost 350 theaters. When *Dangerous Liaisons* picked up Oscar nominations on February 15, an additional 300 theaters were added. And so it went.

The studios have the power to tie up the best theaters for the best dates, summertime and holidays, especially Christmas, and this gives them additional power as distributors. They can usually get as long a run as they want. An independent distributor often must take a less desirable theater for a shorter run. Finally, the studios have exceptional clout in dealing with theater chains, which are the heart of the exhibition business. Some chains control nearly 1,000 screens. A single meeting or telephone call can get a film into 600 or 700 theaters. This is why the theater chains also get the best movies. Which is simplest for the distributor—calling one chain and booking the movie into 600 theaters or calling 600 independent owners and booking the movie into 600 theaters? The answer is obvious. As we will note later in this chapter, the one part of the film industry that is in sharp decline is the independent theater owners.

## ◻ Marketing Movies

"Hype" has always been synonymous with Hollywood. Making a movie and getting it into the theaters has just been half the battle to many in the film industry. The legendary promotional campaigns for films like *Gone With the Wind* are a substantial part of the lore of American movie making. But if hype has always been a part of Hollywood, it has never been as big a part of the filmmaking industry as it is in the 1990s. "In recent years the major studios have looked to the techniques used by the sellers of detergents, toothpastes and beer and have been applying them in varying degrees to everything from the selection of scenes for advance previews to the process of deciding which movies to make and how to best make them," wrote *Wall Street Journal* staff reporter John Koten. While most people in the industry believe that sales tactics and marketing schemes can account for no more than 20 percent of a film's box office gross, that can be a substantial amount. And for many films it may be the difference between financial success or financial failure.

Advertising has always been a part of selling films to the potential audience. But in the 1990s the advertising is driven far more by market research and is most often carried by television. The hype for major movies begins early. The industry likes to get trailers (or previews) into the theaters as early as six months before a film will be released. Sometimes the movie hasn't even been shot yet. For *Total Recall,* a big-budget science fiction film released in 1990, the early trailers for the film simply showed an ominous, impressionistic rendering of the planet Mars and star Arnold Schwarzenegger, backed by a dark voice that asks, "How would you know if someone stole your mind?" And Paramount created a $7 million "teaser" campaign for *The Hunt for Red October* using billboards, posters, an ad in the *Sports Illustrated* swimsuit issue ("Invisible. Silent. Stolen."), and a TV preview 10 minutes before the Super Bowl.

On the average, studios spend about $6 million promoting the premiere of a major release. (Disney spent $10 million hyping *Dick Tracy* before it was released in 1990, and a total of $50 million marketing and advertising the film.) About 60 percent of the pre-opening advertising budget is spent on television advertising, a substantial change from just six or seven years ago when only 30 percent was spent on the electronic medium. The money has been taken away from newspaper advertising.

In the past it was the intuition of the advertising agency that shaped the advertising message. ("If you see only one movie this summer, see. . . .") Today extensive research is done before an advertising campaign is launched. Find out what the public likes, then emphasize that in the advertising. Paramount discovered in its prerelease research for *The Hunt for Red October* that the target audience for the movie, men over 25 years old, was largely uninterested in the political aspects of this Cold War tale, but intrigued by the suspense in the film. The advertising followed this line; no hammers or sickles appeared in the ads. And prerelease promotion for *Ghost* was aimed at 18–34-year-old women, when it was determined this would be the target audience for the film. Fox marketed two major films in the summer of 1988, *Big* with Tom Hanks, and *Die Hard* with Bruce Willis. There had been a series of so-called body changing movies released prior to *Big,* in which Hanks gets his wish and physically goes from adolescence to manhood in one night. Research revealed the audience was confused; had they seen this film already? So advertising only lightly touched on the story line and instead focused on the comedy elements in the film and on Hanks, a popular performer. With *Die Hard,* research revealed that a significant share of the audience had a strongly negative reaction to the star, Bruce Willis. So advertising focused on the adventure story and barely mentioned Willis's name.

Advertising can even be shaped for segments of the audience, hoping to lure different kinds of people into the theater with different kinds of promotions for the same film. Universal used this technique in marketing *Gorillas in the Mist,* a complex story based on the life of Dian Fossey, a woman who spent many years of her life (before she was murdered) living with the great apes in Africa, studying them and trying to save them from poachers and other human ravages. Research revealed that the greatest appeal of this film, which starred Sigourney Weaver, was to women over 25. A variety of television commercials were developed. One set of TV spots focused on the romantic angle in the movie and was telecast heavily during daytime soap operas. Another set emphasized the African location, the exotic wildlife, and was telecast during the ABC, CBS, and NBC early morning news and entertainment programs ("Today," et al.). A third set of commercials focused on the limited amount of action in the film and was telecast during sporting events, such as the 1988 Olympic games.

The film industry has discovered it can get additional exposure for its advertising dollars by tie-ins with other companies and products and by clever product merchandising. Animated films are naturals for tie-ins with fast food restaurants and large department stores that sell children's clothing and bedding and other items. Disney has a continuing relationship with both McDonald's and Sears. Children's films released by the studio for the Christmas holidays are usually promoted months in advance in Sears stores and in the Sears Christmas catalog, which is usually published in September.

Few films in history were hyped to the extent that Disney hyped *Dick Tracy* in 1990. More than 600 different Tracy products were sold. The Tracy character was

The Disney studio spent almost $50 million (an amount that was more than the cost of making the film) to advertise and promote its 1990 blockbuster *Dick Tracy.* This is an example of the extent to which marketing motion pictures has come to dominate elements of the industry. Pictured is Al Pacino as character "Big Boy Caprice."
(© Peter Sorel, © Touchstone Pictures. All rights reserved.)

highly visible at the Disney theme parks in musical stage shows and stores that sold nothing but Tracy merchandise. There were Tracy hats, towels, jackets, coffee mugs, pins, and key chains. Disney engineered a major tie-in with McDonald's featuring a game with $40 million in prizes. About half the McDonald's ads during the period the film was being hyped promoted not only burgers and fries, but the Tracy movie as well. Paramount teamed up with both Chevrolet and Exxon to promote the 1990 stock car racing saga *Days of Thunder*. General Motor's ads showed clips from the film and reminded viewers that the Chevy Luminas driven by Tom Cruise in the film were available from their Chevrolet dealers. Tee shirts and other paraphernalia are common today, and many movies generate game cartridges for Nintendo and other video games. And all of this works toward promoting the film.

While this movie hype is sometimes deafening, especially for the major summer releases, and while it certainly pushes many serious, well-made films deeply into the background, few find serious fault with these promotional juggernauts. Advertising is America's most popular spectator sport in the 1990s, and many of us eagerly participate in the game by decorating our clothes, cars, carry-alls, and shoes with brand names and advertising slogans. But the market research that is used to shape the promotional campaigns for the movies produced by the Hollywood studios is sometimes used by the industry for more than advertising. Some production companies use market research to shape the films before they are released, or even to select "filmable" concepts. In 1990 the Walt Disney Company was the only major production company that rigorously market-tested movie ideas for audience approval before committing themselves financially to a project. Producers, stars, and directors have vigorously fought this idea. But most studios market-test the film before it is

Paramount used tie-in advertising with Chevrolet and Exxon in an attempt to bring audiences to the theater to watch the stock-car racing film *Days of Thunder*. While the film, starring Tom Cruise and Nicole Kidman, generated substantial revenues, it wasn't the box office hit Paramount needed to offset its high cost. (© Stephen Vaughan, Paramount Pictures)

released, in an effort to gauge audience reaction. And if problems are discovered with the audience response, changes can be made in the motion picture. When the film *Fatal Attraction* was market-tested, a majority of the audience said that the vixen-like character portrayed by Glenn Close was not punished sufficiently at the end of the film. So the ending was reshot, and Close's character punished more severely. Lorimar tested and retested a film called *Made in Heaven,* a story about a man played by Timothy Hutton and a woman played by Kelly McGillis who meet in heaven, but cannot fulfill their romance unless they can rediscover each other on earth. Researchers told director Alan Rudolph that some people in the audience were confused by the picture. "Remember, you have to reach every dummy in the audience," one researcher said. "Why don't you get a smarter audience," Rudolph replied. The film was re-edited several times after additional market tests. When it was finally released, Rudolph said he could barely recognize the film and seriously considered asking that his name be removed. (In fact, the Director's Guild has provided directors who do not want their names in the screen credits with a way out. Alan Smithee, a non-existent person, is credited with directing the movie. See the credits for *A Shrimp on the Barbie* as a recent example of this.)

Such audience testing has been done for years in television, but it has been only in the past six to eight years that it has become common for motion pictures. Critics cite serious problems with the practice. The persons used for such tests are hardly representative, many argue. Many persons are drawn from shopping malls in Southern California and surely represent a slice of Americana, but a narrow one at best. And even if they do represent the American population at large, this population is not representative of the American film audience. Remember, 20 percent of the people in the nation buy 80 percent of movie tickets. If a film tests poorly it may not be released by the studio, or if it is released, it is pushed to the back burner and given little publicity or backing.

But there is a more fundamental criticism. Testing can reduce movies to a formula through which the studio may eliminate the artistic judgments and intuition of the people who actually make the film. Filmmaking is a creative process, much like writing or painting. The creative process depends on individual genius. Great books and great art are not market tested. Van Gogh didn't take his paintings around to the markets of Paris or Provence asking shoppers if they understood them, or whether he should use more red or orange. Neither did Hemingway prowl the bookstalls, asking for recommendations from buyers on the length or the amount of dialogue in a story. And both men at times failed. But failure too is part of the creative process. Unfortunately this is an aspect of creativity that Hollywood seems more and more unwilling to accept.

## MOVIE CENSORSHIP

Motion pictures have been censored, almost from the beginning of their development. In some eras they were the most heavily censored mass medium. But television is more visible today because it is in almost every home; hence it is the most heavily censored medium of the 1990s. Americans have always tended to censor most the medium that seems the most powerful at the time.

More than 70 years ago the Supreme Court first ruled that film censorship was permissible. Justice Joseph McKenna and a majority of the high court declared that the censorship of movies by the Ohio film board did not violate the First Amendment's guarantee of freedom of speech and press. The movies are a business, not part of the press nor organs of public opinion, McKenna wrote. Exhibition of films is originated and conducted for profit. True, he added, motion pictures may be mediums of thought. But so are circuses, he noted, and the greatest show on earth does not enjoy the protection of the First Amendment.

This tacit approval of prior censorship by the Supreme Court gave the green light to local censors throughout the nation. For nearly 40 years, city and state censorship boards worked diligently to purify the motion pictures shown in their jurisdictions. It was not until 1952 that the Supreme Court reversed the position it took in 1915 and started to put the brakes on the local censors. New York State denied a license to exhibit the film *The Miracle,* a simple religious story that the censors believed was sacrilegious. The Supreme Court struck down this action and ruled that motion pictures were indeed within the range of speech protected by the First Amendment. "It cannot be doubted that motion pictures are a significant medium for a communication of ideas," wrote Justice Tom Clark in the case of Burstyn v. Wilson. Seven years later, in Kingsley International Pictures v. New York, the Supreme Court affirmed its stand when it again reversed New York censors who had refused to license a film the censors claimed "portrayed acts of sexual immorality as desirable." "What New York has done," wrote Justice Potter Stewart, "is to prevent the exhibition of a motion picture because that picture advocates an idea—that adultery under [certain] circumstances may be proper behavior. Yet the First Amendment's basic guarantee is of freedom to advocate ideas."

In 1961 film exhibitors and distributors challenged the basic concept of prior censorship of motion pictures. Should a city or state have the right to preview *every* film before it is shown and demand changes or ban it from exhibition? they asked. The Supreme Court said yes, local censors do have that right. There is no absolute freedom to exhibit, even once, any and every kind of motion picture.

Today, while censors may block the showing of a film which meets the legal definition of obscenity, most film censorship boards have gone out of business. Local communities across America have attempted to control the problem of obscene movies by establishing zoning rules which either isolate the theaters that show these films in one part of town away from residential neighborhoods, or separate such theaters so no cluster of businesses dealing in pornographic wares can develop. Such laws are constitutional, so long as the zoning rules don't completely exclude such theaters from the community. While some local prosecutors, largely in the South and rural Midwest, still pursue the X-rated theater operator, in most communities this is not an issue. Groups which find such films offensive are far more interested in attacking cable television and videocassette dealers today. And the Supreme Court has erected exceedingly rigid procedural safeguards for theater owners which must be followed when a community attempts to censor films. It is not easy for a government to censor films in the 1990s.

## ◻ Political Censorship

Political censorship has also been common in the film industry in the past. Political censorship is the attempt by the government—usually the federal government—to control the content of movies through pressure on the industry. Any producer who needs the cooperation of the army or the navy or any branch of the federal govern-

The blacklisting that resulted from the Communist witch-hunts of the late 1940s and early 1950s seriously harmed many in the film business and damaged the industry as well. This is a photograph of the House Un-American Activities Committee (HUAC) as it opened its investigation into alleged subversive activities in the film industry. On the witness stand is Jack Warner, of Warner Bros. Note the committee member second from the right, Republican Congressman Richard M. Nixon, an aggressive Red hunter in 1947.
(United Press International Picture)

ment can be certain the movie's script will be closely scrutinized by the government agency before it agrees to cooperate. And almost always script changes are requested in exchange for cooperation. When Universal Pictures made the film *The Ugly American* many years ago the State Department simply refused to give the studio any aid because it did not like the script, which was critical of American foreign policy. A threat was levied against the studio that if it insisted on continuing to make the film, Universal might find it difficult to collect its foreign box office receipts.

A producer often must make a choice when shooting a film that involves the U.S. government. The realism of the film will be greatly enhanced if real U.S. Army helicopters and other official heavy equipment are used during a battle scene. And realism is important today. But the Army will insist upon some script control. The Department of Defense in 1986 refused to assist Clint Eastwood with the making of *Heartbreak Ridge*, until a scene in which a sergeant "showed excessive brutality to a trainee" was taken out of the film. The Pentagon also said the movie could not show an incident which actually occurred during the invasion of Grenada. A Marine, who was in the attack force on the island, had to use his credit card to call his headquarters in the States to get some information to help coordinate part of the operation.

For the producer who refuses to cooperate, the alternatives are not attractive. Stock footage and miniatures can be used to simulate a battle scene. Or the scene can be cut. Or the producer can build his or her own army, as Francis Ford Coppola did in *Apocalypse Now* when he rented aircraft and other equipment from the Philippine army. And the budget goes out of sight. The government can wield a powerful hand in such cases.

Political censorship assumed perhaps its ugliest form in the late forties and early fifties when Congress and several right-wing hate groups conducted a massive witch hunt in the entertainment industry for "Communists" and others on the political left, a story recounted in Chapter 3. Hollywood suffered greatly in this era, but much of the suffering was a result of the shortsighted leaders in the industry.

## Self-Censorship

The film industry has always been fearful of censorship. In the early 1920s a growing film industry attempted to test the moral limits of American film audiences with a series of pictures that, while they might be considered mild today, scandalized many who watched the industry closely. In addition, unseemly offstage behavior by some in the film community further increased public wrath. Many states began to adopt strict film censorship laws. Without clear First Amendment protection to help them fight these laws, the industry had to take some other kind of action or face a crazy quilt of state laws limiting what could be shown on the silver screen. To try to head off the censorship, the industry formed the Motion Picture Producers and Distributors Association of America (MPPDAA) to act as a kind of in-house censor for motion pictures.

Will Hays, a former Presbyterian elder and postmaster in the Warren G. Harding administration, was named to head the association. Censorship by Hays was informal at best, nonexistent at worst, according to critics of the industry. Local censorship efforts continued to grow. So the MPPDAA developed a Motion Picture Production Code that outlawed most of the kinds of sex and immorality that had been portrayed by the industry for the past 25 years. The code was strict, having been drafted by a Catholic publisher and a Jesuit priest. It was designed not only to eliminate sexual or suggestive material from the movies but to safeguard the nation's patriotic and religious morals as well.

Industry censors previewed all films before their release to the public, and only motion pictures which met code standards were given a seal of approval. Films that did not meet the standards were re-edited or shelved. No one dared release a film without a seal for fear of industry and public condemnation. But American morals were changing in the 1950s. Otto Preminger, an Austrian/American director, made two pictures that were released without production code seals. *The Moon Is Blue,* a mildly amusing comedy released in 1953 failed to win a production code seal because it contained words like "mistress" and "virgin." Three years later Preminger released *The Man with the Golden Arm,* an impressionistic melodrama about a Chicago poker dealer/drug addict who tries to kick the habit by going cold turkey. (Frank Sinatra got an Academy Award nomination for his portrayal of the addict.) Drug use was taboo under the code as well, and the movie was refused a seal. Both films were exhibited successfully without the seal, however. This revealed to others in the film industry that the production code was a paper tiger, and films that did not receive the seal could still be successful. This broke the back of the MPPDAA Code.

But the industry was fearful of permitting filmmakers to have total freedom, so another system was instituted, one in which technically nothing is censored, but under which the content of a film is labelled as being suitable for children or adults. (The word "technically" is important because self-censorship does take place when a studio insists that scenes be changed in order to win a PG-13 or R rating for a film.) The Motion Picture Association of America (MPAA) adopted a rating system which has been modified three times. Currently a movie rating board screens all films before their release and applies a rating to each one. There are five categories of film:

G—general audience, all ages admitted.

PG—parental guidance suggested; some material may not be suitable for children.

PG-13—parents strongly cautioned. Some material may be inappropriate for children under 13.

R—restricted. No person under 17 admitted unless accompanied by a parent or adult guardian.

NC-17—no children under 17 admitted, regardless of who accompanies them.

The NC-17 category replaced the X rating in mid-1990. The film industry had copyrighted all the rating labels but X, believing that no filmmaker would want to

Pedro Almodovar's 1990 *Tie Me Up! Tie Me Down!* was one of the movies that sparked a controversy over the film rating system. Almodovar challenged the rating system in court when his film was threatened with an X rating. As a result of this challenge and others, the MPAA abandoned the X rating, which was associated with sleazy films, and substituted the NC-17 for adult movies. Victoria Abril was featured in the film. (© Mimmo Cattarinich, Miramax Films)

attach an X-rating label to a motion picture. But the porno-film industry confounded the MPAA and began labeling erotic films X, XX, and even XXX to attract the audience looking for so-called adult movies. Serious films aimed at serious adult filmgoers were tainted by having to carry the X rating. In addition, many newspapers refused to accept advertising for X-rated movies. In 1990 four well-made, serious films (*The Cook, the Thief, His Wife and Her Lover; Henry: Portrait of a Serial Killer; Tie Me Up! Tie Me Down!;* and *Henry and June*) all faced carrying an X rating unless substantial content modifications were made. The producers of the first three released them to the theaters unrated rather than carry the stigma of an X. *Henry and June,* a major production released by Universal/MCA carried the X in its early distribution. In September of that year, the MPAA abolished the X rating and substituted the NC-17, which it copyrighted to preclude its use by the pornographic filmmakers. In the end the success or failure of this rating system is determined by how rigorously it is enforced by theater owners. Some critics contend that if theaters would closely monitor attendance at R-rated films, few if any films would have been rated X, and the need to change the rating categories could have been avoided.

## THE THEATER BUSINESS

The movie theater business was good in the early 1990s. More people were going to movie theaters than had gone in a long time. And rising admission prices did not seem to deter many in the audience. Many in the industry credit the introduction of home videocassette players with the resurgence of theater attendance. Surely some people watch movies at home rather than go to the theater, and this deprives the theater owner of some ticket sales. But the use of VCRs to watch movies at home has also greatly revitalized the film business. And this is good for theater owners.

Probably more Americans are interested in movies today than at any time since the heyday of the studios 40 years ago. Look at the tremendous growth in television programs about movies and the film industry as evidence of this. There are at least half-a-dozen movie review programs syndicated nationally. MTV has a film-oriented program ("The Big Picture") and all three networks offer movie reviews on their morning shows. Local television stations frequently have movie reviews as a part of their news programming. The more people are interested in movies, the more they will visit their local movie theater. Also the revenues from the sale of videocassettes have greatly increased the flow of money into the industry. More and more movies are being made because of this. And when there are more movies to see, the theaters can expect increased attendance.

There were almost 24,000 theater screens in the United States in 1990. That's right, screens. With the advent of the multiplex theater, it is far more accurate to talk of screens than theaters. And the vast majority of these screens are owned by theater chains. In the middle of 1990, United Artists Theater Circuit was the largest chain, with 2,700 screens. American Multi Cinema was second with 1650 screens. Cineplex Odeon was third with 1550 screens. (But this chain was in economic trouble and slowly selling off some of its theater holdings.) General Cinema was fourth with 1450. Even the studios, barred from owning theaters by Justice Department action in the late 1940s, were once again buying theaters. While the legal decrees that made the studios divest themselves of their theaters 40 years ago are still in effect, the U.S. Department of Justice quietly informed the movie makers that it would no longer enforce these decrees. So by mid-1990 Universal (MCA) owned 49 percent of Cineplex Odeon. Columbia owned the old Loews theater chain, about 840 screens. And Paramount/Time-Warner owned the 470-screen Cineamerica chain.

## ▢ Multiple Movie Screens

In the heyday of Hollywood, movie theaters that showed first-run films were located in the downtown area of urban centers. So-called neighborhood theaters existed, but were relegated to showing double features of films that had already been shown in the large, often palatial, downtown theaters. In the early fifties when the film industry fell on hard times, the neighborhood theaters were among the first casualties. The number of films Hollywood made dropped dramatically; first-run theaters booked movies for many weeks and by the time they reached the neighborhood, few persons who wanted to see the film had not already viewed it at a downtown theater. In the late fifties and sixties, the urban centers in America visibly began to decay as the flight to the suburbs reached high gear. The neighborhood theaters were gone, converted to supermarkets or thrift shops. But many people were reluctant to trek downtown to see a movie. Parking costs were high, traffic was bad, and the question of personal safety also arose. Attendance at the movies hit rock bottom by 1971.

Theater owners finally decided to follow the audience to the suburbs, and in the mid-seventies a massive theater rebuilding project began. American film exhibitors looked abroad and saw the growth and success of the multiscreen theaters in Europe, and this is the model that was used in this country. In shopping centers across America new multiplex theaters began to spring up. Some existing suburban theaters were divided into several auditoriums. The obvious advantage of the multiplex theater with four screens compared with single screen theaters is the substantial reduction in theater overhead. A multiplex theater needs only one snack bar, one set of rest rooms, one projectionist, and one set of ticket sellers, ticket takers, ushers, and snack bar clerks. Four separate theaters need four of everything listed above, plus four sets of exterior walls.

Americans were interested in the multiplex theaters. They were close to home. There was little traffic. Parking was free. And because exhibitors began to book first-run films into the suburban theaters, the movies were fresh. But while American theater owners used the European theaters as a model, most did not bother to emulate European craftsmanship in constructing the new auditoriums. Walls were often thin, permitting a moviegoer to hear two films for the price of one. The holding area or lobby was often small and cramped. Auditoriums were also small, especially where an existing theater had been divided into three or more auditoriums. Critics called them bowling alleys. Finally, little was usually invested in either the projection equipment or the sound system. The novelty of the inadequate multiplex theaters soon wore off for many filmgoers.

By the mid-1980s most theater owners had gotten their act together and begun building superior auditoriums with solid, double-thick, soundproof walls. Lobbies are comfortable if not attractive. Auditoriums in the multiplex theaters come in several sizes and always include one large theater with 70 mm screen capacity, a superior Dolby or THX sound system, and rocking chair seats. Even the popular special effects films suffer little in such a setting. The downtown theaters were slowly closing at the same time the suburban multiplexes were improving. Urban dwellers found themselves going to the suburbs to see first-run movies. Theater owners even added to the traditional snack bar fare of popcorn, soda, and familiar candy treats, by offering gourmet ice creams and coffee, fancy sandwiches, and other expensive delights favored by the urban professionals who attend many movies. "We are building better theaters, no more bowling alleys," said Richard Fox, president of Fox Theaters. Many of the newer multiplex operations have as many as 10 or 12 screens. The theater owners contend, according to an article by Geraldine Fabrikant in *The New York Times,* that if they build large, technically sophisticated theaters, which make moviegoing a dramatically different experience from home viewing, audiences will respond.

Theater owners have discovered that the obvious advantage of the multiplex theater—lower operational cost—is not the only benefit of the multiple screen theaters. Such a setting gives a theater owner far more flexibility. If a theater books a movie that turns out to be a bomb, it can be exhibited in a small auditorium. A film that begins to take off after it has opened in a small auditorium can be moved to a larger room to accommodate the crowds. Moviegoers who arrive at the theater to find the film they hoped to see sold out, now see what else is playing and often buy a ticket for another picture rather than going elsewhere. And parents can let their kids enjoy a G-rated film playing in one theater while they view an R-rated movie in an adjoining auditorium.

As the theater business heated up, many owners found the increased revenues from the box office and concession stand to be sufficient; others sought to squeeze out a few more dollars from moviegoers. By late 1990, advertisements for soft drinks, automobiles, credit cards, and cameras appeared on 30 percent of the nation's theater screens. Screenvision Cinema Network, one of the largest agencies for the in-theater spots, typically charged clients (in 1990) $800,000 (not including production costs) for creating and running a one-minute ad for 28 days on 6,000 screens. Screenvision split its profits with the theater owners.

By early 1990, the ads had become controversial. The Disney studio announced it would no longer book films into theaters that showed advertising. Backed by a survey it paid to have conducted, the studio said 90 percent of the moviegoing audience said they do not want to see advertisements when they go to the movies. Warner Bros. praised the stance taken by Disney, and then revealed it had had a no-advertising stipulation in its booking contracts since the release of *Superman* in 1978. And in Oregon, the state legislature considered passing a law in June of 1991 that would require theaters that showed advertising to reveal this in all advertising for the theater.

People in the advertising industry said they were shocked by the stand taken by the two studios, that their research showed that moviegoers actually liked the commercials. And they pointed out that commercials are common in European theaters, where 15 minutes of commercials may precede a feature film. Of course European viewers are not bombarded with hundreds of commercials on TV as Americans are.

The controversy sizzled in the summer of 1991, and most observers agreed that if one or two other major studios joined Disney and Warner Bros. in the boycott, advertising would likely disappear from the silver screen. Until then, those who judged the ads offensive found they had a couple of extra minutes to spend in the restroom or at the snack bar.

There is a negative note to these few paragraphs on the theater business. The smaller, independent theater owner, the single-screen operator is hurting. Such exhibitors have a hard time booking good films, at least early in their runs. A single theater has higher overhead. These theaters have been hurt by the popularity of videocassette films, for they often cannot book a film until it has already been released on videotape. Various schemes are being tried by these small businesspersons. Some try to attract the true movie devotee by exhibiting mini-film festivals, a series of Bogart films one week, Gable films the next. Others are changing films daily, showing a different double feature every day. Usually these are older films that still have popularity. Still others try to compete with price, charging $1 per person to see a recent film. This is often less than it costs to rent a videocassette. But prospects are not good. Most experts say that the last single screen theater has already been built in America, and it is only a matter of time before the independent single-screen theater owners go the way of the old neighborhood movie house of 40 years ago.

# THE FUTURE OF MOVIES

The film industry is a very volatile business, as has been noted, and that makes it especially difficult to look down the road and speculate on what lies ahead. The film industry also may be affected by evolving communication technology, such as direct broadcast satellite and pay-per-view television systems. This complicates the problem. Still, some trends appear important and can be noted.

Production costs of movies continue to rise and must, in some way, be brought under control if Hollywood is to continue to prosper. Filmmaking is labor intensive. But it is also "hype-intensive," and the cost of marketing and advertising movies seems to be rising even faster than production costs. It is still possible to make a good movie for under $1 million; every year a handful of producers prove this. But the push to make blockbuster films that will gross $100 million-plus in eight weeks forces producers and directors to pour more and more money into special effects, exotic locations, realistic action scenes, and other items that cost an incredible amount of money. If costs are not brought under control, this will surely mean that ticket prices will have to increase, something that has already started to happen in some parts of the nation. But producers will also have to charge more to videocassette distributors who may have to raise rental fees. All of this could result in dampening the public's interest in seeing movies, which will reduce revenues and could hurt the industry.

The recent history of the American film industry has been marked by an industry fear of evolving communication technologies. In the sixties, filmmakers and theater owners believed that pay television—what we now call the premium cable channels—would kill the movie industry. Videocassettes were the next problem that kept the movie moguls awake at night. And of course the growth in popularity of the videocassette recorder has actually helped the film industry. But many people speculate that the development of a workable pay-per-view television system, something that may or may not be (depending upon whom you believe) on the horizon could be a tremendous boon to the film industry. Why?

Imagine there are 30 million subscribers for a **pay-per-view television** system (see p. 317 for an explanation of PPV). A studio decides to exhibit a film on a first run basis via pay-per-view. The movie, which cost $20 million to make, is shown in 15 million homes over the span of seven showings. Each subscribing home pays $5 to see the film. The gross earnings for these showings is $45 million. The

Orson Welles's 1941 *Citizen Kane* is regarded by many film historians as the best film of all time. The motion picture was filled with cinematic tricks that at the time obscured the story of a journalist's quest for the truth after newspaper magnate Kane's death. French film director Francois Truffaut argued that *Citizen Kane* was the film that started the largest number of young film makers on their careers.
(Museum of Modern Art Film Stills Archive)

PPV system operator takes $5 million; the studio takes $40. The movie has earned more than twice its negative cost in a week. The rule of thumb is that a theater-released film must earn a gross of three times its cost to make money. But by using pay-per-view, the studio gets back a much larger share of the gross; remember the theater owner normally takes 50 percent. And the distribution costs would be fractional compared to normal distribution costs. Only one print of the film would be needed, for example. The film would likely show a substantial profit based on the earnings outlined above.

Will people actually pay $5 to see a movie on television? Some might, especially older people who are reluctant to go out to a movie. And parents, who can save the price of a baby-sitter and show a movie to the whole family for $5 might also use the system. But to most young adults, the heart of the moviegoing audience, seeing a film at a theater is as much a social experience as an evening of entertainment. Going out is the key. These people will probably still want to go to the theater. The social activity related to attending a movie is one reason why television didn't kill the film industry in the 1950s.

And some films won't play very well on the home screen, even the larger rear-projection television sets that are just beginning to become popular. The special effects films—*Star Wars* and the like—lose something vital on the small screen. Audio systems in most television sets, while improving, still have a long way to go before they can properly reproduce the sound so vital to a film like *Amadeus*. So the increased use of television by the film industry to distribute its films may still remain a long way down the road, or may never develop extensively.

Some have speculated that the industry may someday try to reduce its distribution costs by using satellites to beam first-run films to theaters equipped with giant, **high definition television** screens. This would cut printmaking costs dramatically and reduce the expenses associated with shipping and handling the large reels of film. But this remains a dream as well for the time being.

The marketing and promotion tail will probably increasingly wag the creative dog in filmmaking in the years to come; a dismal prospect for sure. The bottom-line orientation of American production companies will continue to exert pressure to produce simple comedies or action pictures, films that will appeal to an increasingly broad audience. In other words, the movies will grow to look more and more like network television. And this bodes ill for serious or even occasional moviegoers.

But it probably is not a healthy trend for the film industry either. In the first place the film industry cannot duplicate television, in which the audience has a continuing relationship with the medium. About the same number of people watch television on any given night, regardless of what is on. But each movie must win a new audience, convince it to come to the theater. And this is a significant difference. Newspapers that have attempted to mimic television with more color, shorter stories,

Unlike their counterparts in Europe, American film directors rarely generate a loyal following. Woody Allen is one exception. Here he is shown directing Martin Landau in a scene from *Crimes and Misdemeanors*.

and a less serious tone have found that this has not significantly increased readership. A newspaper is not a television program. And neither is a film. Just as important, network television is not doing well today. Why would the film industry attempt to copy a medium that has already lost substantial favor with the American public? Only the studio bosses can answer that.

Certainly movies have to be sold. And yes, films need to be entertaining as well as moving and meaningful. People who go to the movie theater expect to be entertained, to sometimes escape from the reality that binds them daily. But our culture increasingly shapes our view of important elements of our world. And filmmakers need to recognize this as well, and provide substance as well as fluff.

American film does not have the tradition of "art" often associated with foreign filmmaking. And that is not what most filmgoers expect from Hollywood today. Surely there have been artistic films—for example, the early work of Griffith, Chaplin, or Hitchcock. And look at *Citizen Kane.* But it is not accurate to compare 95 percent of the American filmmakers with an artist, the celluloid being the canvas, the director wielding the deft hand of the painter. American filmmakers might more accurately be compared to commercial artists who design advertisements or posters or signs.

Still, commercial films can be well made and fun and meaningful. Competent filmmakers can do just that if the front office doesn't confuse making movies with manufacturing disposable consumer products. Film critic John Simon noted the difference between art and entertainment several years ago in a thoughtful article in *New York* magazine. His thoughts point to what filmmakers must be permitted to do if the industry is going to continue to prosper. He said:

> For the difference between art and entertainment is, finally, one not so much of direction as of degree: though all entertainment is not art, all art must include entertainment. "Entertaining" means interest-holding, and what bores and fails to involve has no real artistic value. Granted, art makes demands; it entertains those who are willing and able to feel, perceive, and think more deeply and arduously—more courageously if you will—rather than those who always want to leave their thoughts behind, most likely because thought has abandoned them. I insist on the always; for on occasion everyone appreciates a well-made piece of fluff. A film that gives the large public exactly what it expects, i.e. sheer entertainment, is not to be ipso facto rejected. . . as long as it does it well, like *Jaws* [or *The Hunt for Red October* in 1990], rather than badly, like *Rollerball* [or *Predator 2* ].

## BIBLIOGRAPHY

These are some of the materials that have been helpful in the preparation of this chapter.

"Advertising in the Dark," *Newsweek,* April 9, 1990.
"The Blockbuster Game," *Newsweek,* June 25, 1990.
"Commercials Break into Movies," *Television/Radio Age,* September 16, 1985.
"Doing the Controversial Thing," *U.S. News & World Report,* February 6, 1989.
Fabrikant, Geraldine. "The Hole in Hollywood's Pocket," *The New York Times,* December 9, 1990.
———."How Major Studios Missed a Hit," *The New York Times,* March 6, 1990.
———."Studios Look to Foreign Markets," *The New York Times,* March 7, 1990.
Frook, John. "Paramount Owes Damages to Buchwald, Judge Says," *Los Angeles Daily News,* December 12, 1990.

298      *The Mass Media*

Goldman, Debra. "Indie Boom Turns Bust," *Premiere,* May, 1989.

Harmetz, Aljean. "Movie Merchandise: The Rush Is On," *The New York Times,* June 13, 1989.

————."The Sequel Becomes the New Bankable Star," *The New York Times,* August 8, 1985.

————."Where Movie Ticket Income Goes," *The New York Times,* January 28, 1987.

————."With Salaries Soaring, It's Fade-Out for Films Made on the Cheap," *The New York Times,* December 6, 1989.

Hartl, John. "Hollywood Horror: Big-Budget Disasters on the Rise," *The Seattle Times,* April 17, 1988.

Hlavacek, Peter. "New Indies on a (Bank) Roll," *Variety,* January 24, 1990.

Jowett, Garth, and Linton, J. M. *Movies as Mass Communication.* Beverly Hills, Cal.: Sage Publications, 1980.

Kauffman, Stanley. *A World on Film.* New York: Harper & Row, 1966.

Koten, John. "How Marketers Perform a Vital Role in Movies' Success," *Wall Street Journal,* January 6, 1985.

Lees, David, and Berkowitz, Stan. *The Movie Business.* New York: Vintage Books, 1981.

Lev, Michael. "Do People Mind Theater Commercials?" *The New York Times,* April 24, 1990.

Miller, Mark Crispin. "Hollywood: The Ad," *The Atlantic Monthly,* April, 1990.

Nichols, Peter M. "Pricing Videos: A Rental-or-Sales Gamble," *The New York Times,* January 29, 1991.

"Oscar Looks Abroad," *Newsweek,* March 12, 1990.

Parisi, Paula. "Video Revenues Up 15 Percent in 1990 to $15 Billion," *The Hollywood Reporter,* February 10, 1990.

Polskin, Howard. "Saturday Night Letdown," *TV Guide,* April 23, 1988.

*Premiere,* various issues.

Putzer, Gerald. "Ghost Grabs Ring in Year of Surprises," *Variety,* December 31, 1990.

"The Return of Hollywood," *The Economist,* October 29, 1988.

Rohter, Larry. "A 'No Children' Category to Replace the 'X' Rating," *The New York Times,* September 26, 1990.

Rothenberg, Randall. "The Trouble with Mall Interviewing," *The New York Times,* August 16, 1989.

————."Updating Promotion of Movies," *The New York Times,* February 23, 1990.

"Small Is Beautiful," *Newsweek,* November 26, 1990.

Stevenson, Richard. "Hollywood Entices the Japanese," *The New York Times,* October 3, 1988.

————."Tinsel Magic: 'Hit' Loses Millions," *The New York Times,* April 13, 1990.

"They're Putting Glitz Back into Movie Houses," *U.S. News & World Report,* January 25, 1988.

*Variety,* various issues.

Zacks, Richard. "Picture Windows," *Channels,* May, 1986.

# CHAPTER 9

# TELEVISION

*A*merican television celebrated its fiftieth birthday in 1989; a half-century of broadcasting that officially began on April 30, 1939 with the telecast of the opening ceremonies of the New York World's Fair. A great deal has changed in those five decades. But remarkably, much has remained the same. Today the United States is still lagging behind other nations of the world in the development of television—just as it was at the end of the 1930s. The British had regularly scheduled broadcasts long before they began in the United States. Today this nation is struggling to catch up in the development of high-definition television, the television of tomorrow, and in other technical areas. In 1939 RCA-NBC scrambled to fill the limited broadcast day and often ended up telecasting virtually anything that moved. A run through the 28 channels of broadcasting available to most Americans currently reveals that the medium is still searching desperately for material to fill up the broadcast day. Television, perhaps the greatest communications tool yet invented, was viewed largely as an entertainment device in the late 1930s. And so it is in present-day America.

Yet television has changed as well in 50-plus years. It was a novelty in 1939; now it fairly dominates our culture, if not our lives. TV was a small part of a large electronics company a half-century ago. Today it is a vast industry. The medium was technically crude 50 years ago: fuzzy, unstable black-and-white pictures carried over a single channel to small screens. At present, the medium is vastly superior (although not as good as it could be): fairly sharp pictures with stereo sound carried over more than a thousand television stations and networks to elaborate home entertainment centers with wall-sized screens.

In this chapter we will attempt to sketch a picture of the contemporary television industry—and it is an industry. An outline of the varied components of this communications system will be drawn. We will discuss as well some of the problems faced by the medium. A discussion of the news and public affairs arms of this entertainment industry will precede our attempt to describe and analyze the nation's public television system. Finally, a brief nod toward the future. This is a big task; books could and have been written about any single element of the short outline above. And television entertainment programming will not be covered; we reserve our discussion of this to a later chapter on American mass media and culture.

The student who hopes to fully understand what is outlined in the pages ahead needs to first digest a single fact; in the 1990s television is a business consumed by the desire to make money. Parts of the industry are suffering economically and need increased revenues to survive. Other parts are already generating substantial revenues, but want to generate more. No part of the industry is untouched by this imperative: it has an impact on entertainment and news, on over-the-air television and cable, on television producers and distributors, on commercial television, and on noncommercial television. Virtually everything that those in the industry do, want to do, or don't do is in some way governed by economics. This is not necessarily sinister or evil, but it is a fact of life. And if you are to understand television, you must grasp that simple truth.

# ORGANIZATION OF THE INDUSTRY

The organization of television is pretty much like the organization of any other large American industry. There are manufacturers, distributors and wholesalers, retailers, and customers. This is the way it has always been, although in the past the structure was somewhat simpler. If we look at television in 1950, for example, a time by which the industry had truly entered the national consciousness, we can see a fairly primitive organizational structure. The manufacturers of programming 40 years ago were the wholesalers or distributors as well. The over-the-air television networks (NBC, CBS, and others) produced most of the programming in the early fifties and distributed it to the retailers, the local television stations. And we sat at home enjoying Red Skelton, Sid Caesar, Imogene Coca, Ed Sullivan and "Time for Beany," an ingenious children's puppet show that featured a seasickness-prone sea dragon named Cecil. In 1950 there were four television networks, ABC, CBS, NBC, and DuMont, and 98 VHF television stations. Less than 10 percent of all homes had television sets.

Today the situation is a great deal more complicated. There are scores of companies that manufacture television programs today, including the once-great Hollywood film studios. The three major over-the-air television networks, ABC, CBS, NBC, produce very little programming today, outside of sports and public affairs. The networks have become instead important wholesalers, sending the programs to the 1200 or so local stations, the retailers. But the manufacturers of television programming also sell their products to other wholesalers or distributors. These include the nearly 50 cable television networks and a large number of program syndication companies which market these wares directly to local television stations. Then there are the local cable television companies which act as retail outlets for programs distributed by the cable television networks (HBO, MTV). Local cable companies also transmit programs telecast by local television stations to customers in various communities. Finally there are the customers, about 93 million American households, or nearly 99 percent of all homes in the nation. To understand this organization is to understand a good deal about television. So let's consider this structure, one element at a time.

## ◼ Customers—The Audience

There are about 93 million television households in the United States, or 93 million homes using television; **HUTs,** as they are called in the industry. This is 99 percent of all homes. More people have television in their homes than have telephones or indoor plumbing. Ten years ago there were just slightly over 75 million HUTs.

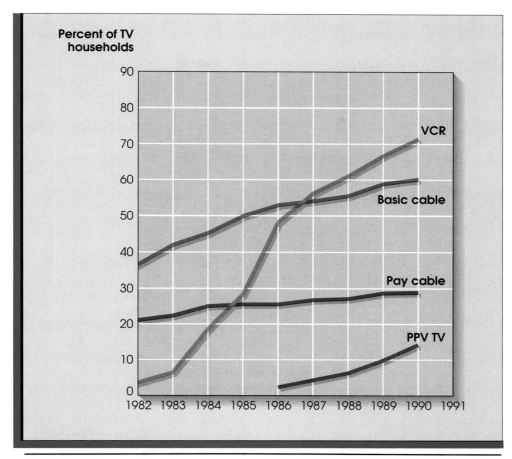

FIGURE 9-1 Homes with videocassette recorders, cable, pay-cable, and pay-per-view television.

Nearly two-thirds of all HUTs have two or more television sets. About 58 percent of Americans receive their television via cable. That is up from about 22 percent ten years ago. And about 30 percent of all HUTs receive at least one pay television channel, such as HBO, Disney, or Showtime. Only about 20 percent did ten years ago.

In 1990, 28 different channels were available on the average American television set. More than 70 percent of all homes had videocassette recorders, and nearly three-fourths of all viewers used remote controls (figure 9-1). These latter two items, VCRs and remote controls, may seem unimportant when related to television. But that is a mistaken impression, for they have fundamentally affected the industry.

The television set was on in the average American home for a little over 7 hours each day in 1990. This is substantially more than the 6 and one-half hours per day we watched TV in 1980, but less than the 7 hours and 10 minutes the set was on in 1986, the year of the highest amount of television viewing. The people of the Dallas-Ft. Worth and Detroit metropolitan areas watch more television than people in any other American cities, 56 hours and 45 minutes per week, according to an A. C.

Nielsen study. Viewers in Houston, Atlanta, and Philadelphia follow closely. Viewers in San Diego watch the least amount of television, only 37 hours and 45 minutes per week. Phoenix is next lowest, at 40 hours and 15 minutes per week. Why the variance? Do people in Dallas-Ft. Worth like television more? Probably not. A further investigation of these numbers would probably reveal that viewers in cities with high viewing times have access to more channels of programming. Residents of Dallas, for example, can pick from over 60 cable channels. More programs, more opportunities for viewing. The television set is on almost two hours per day more in homes that have both basic and pay cable service, than in homes without cable television. A comprehensive study by the A. C. Nielsen Co. revealed that the TV was on in black households almost 92 hours per week, or nearly fifty percent more than in the average American household.

Who watches the most television? The elderly, by and large. Women over 55 years of age watch more television than any other group. (While women overall watch slightly more TV than men, network research findings reported in February of 1991 show that women watch a good deal more primetime TV than men.) Those who make more than $40,000 annually watch less television than those who earn less than $15,000 annually. Television viewing is heaviest in January, lightest in July. Sunday is the night with the heaviest amount of viewing; that is why most miniseries begin on a Sunday night. Friday evening commands the fewest viewers.

The data on how much television Americans watch (almost 50 hours a week) are generated by A. C. Nielsen, the giant television rating company that actually measures how many hours each day the set is turned on in a sample of American homes. Interestingly, when Americans are asked by researchers to tell them how much television they watch each week, that amount is usually far below the 50 hours each week reported by Nielsen. Why the discrepancy?

Several explanations are plausible. When questioned about their viewing habits, some people lie. Ever since television became popular in the 1950s, it has had a reputation among many intellectuals as being an "idiot box." Watching the grass grow would be more intellectually stimulating than watching television, according to them. Consequently some people are embarrassed by how much television they watch. Television viewing has also become such a common part of everyday life that people actually don't realize how much they watch.

A. C. Nielsen measures how many hours each day the set is on; if it is viewed by several different members of the family at different times it may in fact be on 7 hours plus each day, but no single family member watches for that long. Also, the television set may be on, but no one is paying much attention to it. It has become a "talking lamp" in many homes. Nielsen counts it as viewing if someone is sitting in front of the set when it is turned on. But the viewer may be talking on the telephone, reading, sewing, eating, doing a crossword puzzle, or any number of other things and would not count this time as "television viewing." We know from studies by advertisers of the ability of viewers to recall advertising messages that many people watch television in an almost unconscious fashion. (Less than 10 percent of persons who are watching television when they are called, can remember the product mentioned in the last ad they viewed on the set.)

Finally, Americans have dramatically changed the manner in which they view television, and this certainly adds to the difficulty a person faces when asked to remember how much viewing they did during the past day or week. "Grazing" is a seven-letter word that throws fear into the hearts of television advertisers across the country. Twenty years ago when Americans watched television they turned on the set, selected the channel, and then sat down to watch the program that had been selected. A viewer who wanted to watch a different program had to get up, walk across the room, change the channel, and then sit down again. Then came the remote control, something available in the late 1970s, but something that did not become a dominant feature on television sets until the mid-1980s. Today the television viewer can (ping!) turn on the television set, (ping! ping!) change the channel, (ping!) mute the sound, and (ping!) do any number of other things without leaving the sofa or chair. So there is a lot more channel changing. Nearly half of all persons questioned in a national study said they "graze" (flick from one channel to another during a program, or when an ad comes on) while watching television. Men tend to do more grazing than women, younger people (18–24) do considerably more grazing than those over 65 years of age. The survey conducted by *Channels* magazine revealed that 30 percent of those questioned regularly tried to watch two or more programs at the same time. No wonder people forget how much television they watch.

Do we like what we see on television? When asked, "Are there more good programs to watch today compared with five years ago?" 52 percent of the people said there were fewer good shows now, 30 percent said more good shows. Younger people tend to be less critical of television; older people tend to be more critical. Seventy percent say that even with 25 or 30 channels to watch, it is not always easy to find something good on television. About two-thirds of all those questioned said they regarded television as a positive influence in their lives; 22 percent said we would all probably be better off without TV.

What would viewers like to see more of on television? According to a 1990 *TV Guide* poll, 80 percent of the viewers said they wanted more culture and educational shows; 76 percent said they wanted more movies. More than 60 percent of the viewers surveyed said they wanted more national and local news. At the bottom of the list were police dramas, sports events, and westerns.

Given all the statistics about who watches and when, one important point should not be forgotten. On any given evening, at any given time, during any given month, no matter what is being telecast, about the same number of people are watching television. The variances noted above are minor compared with the consistency of the 100 million people or so who are watching television at 9 P.M. on almost any night of the year. This tells us one important thing; Americans tend to watch *television*, not television programs. Few in the audience carefully go through the television listings each night and weigh what they might see on television against reading a book, going to a movie, bowling, showing a movie on the VCR, or listening to a new compact disc. In the vast majority of homes the television comes on after dinner, and the occupants choose what they view from what is broadcast that evening. They simply watch television.

This is one factor, but certainly not the only factor, that determines the quality of programs that are telecast. The broadcasters realize their programs do not have to compete for the attention of the viewer with best-selling books, plays, movies, magazines, CDs, or other leisure time activities. All they must do is compete with other television programs broadcast at the same time. The broadcaster does not have to produce and telecast the best; only something that is (as one programmer has said) less objectionable than the other programs being telecast. Les Brown, a former editor of *Channels* magazine, has noted that these are the simple rules of television. "While it is true that some surprisingly good shows have been produced under these conditions, it seems a terrible climate for creating quality programming."

These are the customers. Next, let's take a look at the manufacturers, the people who created the programs.

## ☐ Manufacturers—or Producers

An unusually small number of program factories produce most of the television that Americans view. This is especially remarkable considering the tens of thousands of hours of programming that are telecast each week over the almost 60 television networks (cable and over-the-air) and 1,200 local television stations. The biggest producers in 1990 were Walt Disney ("Golden Girls," "Empty Nest," "The Magical World of Disney," "Win, Lose or Draw," "Siskel and Ebert"); Warner Bros. ("Growing Pains," "Murphy Brown," "Love Connection," "People's Court," "Full House," "Perfect Strangers," "Midnight Caller"); Paramount ("Dear John," "Cheers," "The Arsenio Hall Show," "Entertainment Tonight," "Star Trek: The Next Generation"); and Columbia ("Married . . . with Children," "Who's the Boss?," "Designing Women," "Wheel of Fortune," "Jeopardy"). Other major producers are Viacom International, Fox Inc., New World, MCA Inc., Group W Productions, and Stephen J. Cannell Productions.

The production of television programs can be a very expensive matter. While the costs associated with producing a game show or a talk show are low and the profits can be great, the production of dramatic or comedy series and made-for-television movies is very costly. Typically, for all but the most popular series, the production company loses money for each episode of a drama or situation comedy it produces. The licensing fees paid by the networks to telecast the program simply do not cover the costs of making the programs. Generally, a two-hour television movie costs $2.8 million to $3.5 million. The networks are willing to pay between $2.5 million and $3 million. A single episode of a 60-minute dramatic program can cost as much as $1.5 million, and the producer can lose as much as $500,000 per episode when the program is licensed for network viewing. Why is production so costly? And why do the production companies keep on making programs if they are losing money?

American television has very high production values. It may not be as dramatically substantive as European television, but it is generally technically superior. As someone said, American television may be garbage, but it is the best-made garbage in the world. Wages for the skilled union craftspersons who put together the show are very high. In 1988 in Southern California camera operators earned almost $30 per hour, sound technicians $24 per hour, set painters $25 per hour, and make-up artists $24 per hour. During the production cycle of a program a 40-hour week is unusual, not normal. Overtime is common. The performers themselves earn substantial salaries. In dramas, location shooting rather than studio shooting, is common. Action sequences are very costly. When it was on the air, "Miami Vice" was one of the most expensive weekly series ever produced for television. The producers were losing so much money on it they threatened to move the production from Miami to California to save money. NBC increased its payment to the producers, but this did not significantly reduce the deficit.

The high cost of programming is one of the reasons there are so many situation

Gifted writer/producer Diane English is credited with bringing "Murphy Brown" to American homes. The program, starring Candice Bergen, presents one of those rare occasions when both critics (through reviews) and viewers (through ratings) support a television show. More and more women are gaining prominent roles in both television and film production.
(CBS Television)

comedies and reality programs ("Unsolved Mysteries") on television today. They are far cheaper to make than an action/adventure show like "Star Trek: The Next Generation." Even at that, producers usually lose money on situation comedies as well.

Producers have sought to cut costs in a variety of ways. During the first two seasons of the 60-minute action/adventure "Airwolf," MCA Universal lost $12 million. CBS canceled the show after 58 episodes, but the producers continued to make episodes in hopes of getting the program into **syndication** (see p. 306). They cut the production cost per episode from $1.2 million to $400,000. How? The two leading players, Ernest Borgnine and Jan Michael-Vincent, were replaced with less well-known performers. They shot the program in Canada, where production costs are lower. And they didn't shoot any more action scenes featuring the star of the series, an elaborate high-tech helicopter. When they needed action, producers simply used film clips from earlier episodes.

Shooting away from Southern California is one way to lower costs. Union rates for technicians are often significantly lower. This is especially true in Canada. Cannell Productions was shooting three separate programs in Vancouver, British Columbia in 1989–90, "Wiseguy," "21 Jump Street," and "Booker," all 60-minute dramatic series. Production costs are as much as 20 percent lower. Producers have also tried to use nonunion employees. These workers are often paid about as much as union technicians, but the producers realize savings in eased work rules, fewer restrictions on what jobs each crew member can do, and in fringe benefits. A fringe benefit payment to a union employee represents about 17 percent of the worker's gross pay, according to producer Richard Melcombe. All of this is saved by using nonunion help. The high cost of production and the reluctance of the networks to pay licensing fees large enough to cover these costs had just about killed one-hour dramatic television shows by the spring of 1991. "L.A. Law" was the only 60-minute dramatic series with a substantial audience. (In 1985 eight of the top ten rated shows were 60-minute dramas.) There just aren't many hour-long shows on TV any more. Also, producers of some successful series, like "The Cosby Show" and "Cheers" were vowing to stop production of these top-rated programs unless the networks vastly increased their licensing payments.

The second question raised about why do producers continue to make shows on which they lose money is a little more difficult to answer. First, most of the big production companies produce many kinds of programs. Paramount may lose money on each episode of "Star Trek" or "Dear John," but it makes a bundle on the low-cost "Entertainment Tonight."

More important for the producer of a series, however, is the prospect of completing a sufficient number of episodes (usually about 100) to put the show into reruns on local television stations or cable networks. The producers own these programs. When they are first broadcast on NBC or CBS, the network only pays for the right to show these programs two or three times. The producers can then sell the rights to others to show the program. Both local television stations and some cable networks thrive on showing these "off network" reruns. Instead of showing a single episode each week, as the networks do during the first run of the program, they show a different episode each day. This is called **stripping**. The producers (or the distributors with whom they work) sell the rights to strip these reruns to each individual station or cable network. The price an individual station may pay to strip reruns of a program like "Head of the Class" may not be high, but if 250 or 300 stations each pay for this right, the total amount of revenue that goes to the producer can be staggering. "Head of the Class," for example, is believed to have earned almost $1 million per episode for the first run of its syndicated life. If the rights to 100 episodes are sold, that's $100 million. These rerun contracts usually run two—three years, so when they expire, the producer can resell the rights again, sometimes for even more if the show has been particularly successful in reruns.

Remember, while the producer lost money when the program was originally licensed for network airing, most of the production costs were paid for by the original network licensing payment. So the revenues from reruns are substantially gravy, additional money, over and above what it cost to make the show originally. Performers and others associated with the program all get a small piece of these revenues. But putting a show into reruns is for a producer akin to finding a gold mine. (When the "Cosby Show" went into reruns in 1988, producers earned $4.8 million per show, the highest amount ever earned, and likely the highest amount that will ever be earned.)

Most prospectors don't find gold or gems. But enough do, and when they do, they earn enough money to keep other miners in the fields looking for treasure. Most series don't go into reruns. But enough do, and when they do, they earn

"The Bill Cosby Show" earned the highest amount of revenue (about $4.8 million per episode) of any program when it entered off-network syndication in 1989. But in many markets the show failed to generate the advertising support needed to pay for the cost of its acquisition. Syndication prices dropped sharply in the wake of this. (NBC Photo)

enough money to keep other producers making programs, even though they lose money when they license these shows for network viewing.

In the 1990s many production companies are looking abroad for foreign partners to help produce costly television films and other programs. In 1990 Disney was working with RAI Television, an Italian state-owned company that produces and distributes television programming, on the production of a potential TV series called "Plymouth." And "A Season of Giants," a miniseries about the lives of Michelango, Raphael, and Leonardo da Vinci, was coproduced by both European interests and Turner Broadcasting.

There are two advantages to looking overseas. The first is money. Bringing in European partners is a means of offsetting the high cost of producing programs by sharing expenses with European investors. Just as important, however, the American production companies want to insure the continued sale of their work to European television networks. In 1989 and 1990 many in Europe were insisting on levying quotas on the amount of U.S. television that could be shown on European channels. In 1989, the European Community adopted nonbinding regulations that stipulate that at least one-half of air time on European channels must be devoted to home-grown programming. Europeans will be more likely to look favorably upon American programming that is subsidized at least in part by European money.

Finally, many production companies are working to bolster their economic footing by building vertical integration within the television industry. A vertically integrated business is one with a variety of interests, but interests that all relate to a single product. In television this means that companies are seeking to produce programming, distribute programming, and even own television outlets. Fox is a good example. The company is a major production center, but also owns a television network and a collection of lucrative television stations in a handful of large cities. Programming produced by Fox can be carried by the Fox Network and telecast by Fox-owned television stations. This is one way to insure a program will get to the audience, regardless of its merit. Turner Broadcasting began as a local station operation, evolved into a cable superstation, then a network, and now a production company. These schemes certainly don't enhance the diversity of ownership and interests that many seek in the mass media. And such schemes put many others (such as producers) at a distinct disadvantage. The Fox Network certainly broadcasts programming that others produce, but it is natural for the network to show partiality to its own programming.

## ☐ Over-the-Air Networks

Ask most people what comes to mind when they hear the word television and they will respond with a reference to a network program; "Cosby," "Roseanne," "Dan Rather," "Johnny Carson." For many years ABC, CBS, and NBC essentially were American television. And while the three major broadcast networks no longer dominate American television, people still think of the medium in those terms. These networks are the primary wholesalers or distributors of programming to the nation's local television stations. The networks produce some of their own programming, news, sports, talk shows, and some entertainment programs. They buy the rights to distribute other programs from production companies. Using satellites, the networks beam this programming to their affiliated stations across the nation. (See pp. 75–76 for a description of this network-affiliation relationship.) The affiliates then push the programming on into the viewers' homes.

Today we really need to refer to the "four" major over-the-air television networks with the success of the Fox Network in the past three years. Since the demise of the DuMont Network in the late 1950s several attempts have been made to erect a fourth national television network. (The Federal Communications Commission defines a network as any service airing at least 15 hours of programming per week.) All failed—until Fox. The vast resources of Rupert Murdoch's media conglomerate, plus the ownership of television stations in key cities (which give Fox automatic access to 21 percent of the nation's TV viewers) gave Fox the edge that meant the difference between survival and failure. The company began modestly enough with programming on Sunday nights, and then slowly expanded night-by-night until the 1990–91 season when Fox was broadcasting 18.5 hours per week, five nights each week, plus kids' programming on Saturday morning.

Fox programming has been quite successful, even winning the rating share race for particular time slots. Both "The Simpsons" and "Married . . . with Children" broadcast on Sunday evenings in the 1989–90 season gave the other networks fits. Fox had such faith in "The Simpsons" that it began to telecast it against NBC's "The Bill Cosby Show" at 8 P.M. on Thursdays in the fall of 1990. The program did not beat "Cosby" in the national ratings, but won higher ratings in selected cities at

Taking chances on unusual programming has helped bring
success to the Fox Network. The
wacky comedy "In Living Color,"
(featuring [top] Keenan Ivory
Wayans, James Carey, Wayans's
sister Kim and brother Damon)
was considered too offbeat for
the traditional networks. It lured
a loyal following to the fourth
network on Sunday evenings.
(Kelly Television Co.)

times. The Fox broadcasts were carried on only 133 affiliated stations; NBC has
more than 200 affiliates, so its programming is available to more viewers. But Fox
sought to solve part of this problem by signing an agreement in September 1990
with Tele-Communications Inc., the nation's largest cable system operator, to carry
Fox programming into cable markets where it was not already available. This gave
Fox coverage of 91 percent of the nation's television homes, compared with 99 percent for each of the other three networks. The Fox Network began broadcasting
short news summaries in 1989. Fox Television Network turned its first profit in July
of 1989, and while its annual revenues are still small compared to those earned by
each of the other three networks, Fox's staff and overhead costs are smaller too.
Fox, like the other networks, lost viewers in the 1990–91 season. But the average
age of Fox viewers is 28, compared to 41, 35, and 44 for NBC, ABC, and CBS
respectively. And many advertisers appreciate a younger audience.

The percentage of people who watch television programs carried by ABC, CBS,
and NBC has been steadily shrinking during the past ten years. Persons watching
television in the evening during the 1978–79 season spent 91 percent of their viewing time watching programs broadcast by ABC, CBS, or NBC. The three networks

"The Simpsons" won such strong ratings on Sunday nights that the Fox Network shifted the program to run against "The Bill Cosby Show" on Thursdays. While it didn't beat the NBC program nationally (Fox does not have enough affiliates to win a national ratings contest) the program did well and beat "Cosby" in some cities.
(Kelly Television Co.)

had a 91 percent share of the viewer's time. This share had dropped to below 65 percent for the 1990–91 season. (It dipped to as low as 53 percent during the summer of 1990.) See figure 9-2.

Why are the networks losing viewers? This isn't an easy question to answer satisfactorily. First, all television is losing viewers. Americans have found there is something else they can do with their television sets—watch videocassettes with their VCRs. Given the assumption that viewers have only so much time to spend watching anything on television, the hours and minutes spent using the VCR must be subtracted from traditional television viewing.

There are certainly more programming choices for viewers today. Not only is the Fox Network draining viewers from ABC, CBS, and NBC, but a growth in independent (not affiliated with a network) local television stations has given viewers new options. The number of persons who have cable television is slowly creeping upward, and even basic cable provides a viewer with a great many more options.

Finally there are those outside (and a few inside) the industry who believe the networks have created much of this woe themselves. The broadcast television networks are completely advertiser supported. Advertiser-supported television tends to be the most conservative, the least innovative. The networks tend to rely on formulas that have worked in the past. They stress situation comedy over all other kinds of

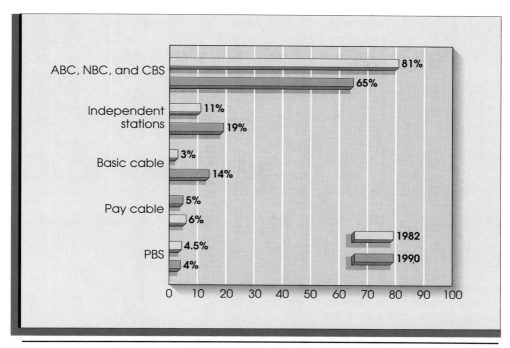

FIGURE 9-2 Percentage of viewing time during primetime, 1982 and 1990, for various television channels. (May total more than 100 percent because some households have more than one television set.)
(A.C. Nielsen)

programming. The fact that sit-coms seem to score best in the ratings each year is at least partially because there is not much else on the networks these days. As the networks saw their share of the audience begin to slip away, they became even more conservative in program selection. Fox gave America a brash cartoon in prime time, presented an openly raunchy (for television) sit-com on Sunday nights, explored a different kind of comedy with Tracy Ullman. And viewers responded.

An indication of how conservative network television had become was the national response to ABC's presentation of David Lynch's unusual and moody "Twin Peaks" in the spring of 1990. As a dramatic exposition, "Twin Peaks" was hardly bizarre or even far "off the beaten path." As a network television show, it stood out like a peacock in a chicken yard. The show earned cover stories in newsmagazines, adulation from talk show hosts, and became a quirky part of American culture a short time after it premiered. Many argue that if the networks want to attract more viewers and regain some of their lost share, they should reevaluate the programming they present and try to move it into the mode of the late twentieth century.

The loss of their share of viewers has hurt the networks' advertising revenues as much as their pride. While ad revenues continue to climb annually, the rise is very slow and much below the rise in ad revenues earned by other players in the television world. Total television advertising revenues amounted to almost $30 billion in 1990, and the broadcast networks earned about a third of that amount, nearly $10 billion. But note the chart below that shows percentage of increase in advertising spending during the past five years for all television.

Broadcast network advertising—up 19 percent

National spot advertising—up 29 percent

Local spot advertising—up 41 percent

Cable network advertising—up 177 percent

National syndication advertising—up 197 percent

Local cable advertising—up 377 percent

While the broadcast networks still have the biggest share of the pie, their share is growing at a snail's pace. Whereas in 1983 the networks earned 40.1 cents of every dollar spent on television advertising; in 1990 they earned only 32.9 cents. Ad revenues for the networks in 1990 increased by only 5 percent, a rate level with inflation.

The broadcast networks remain highly profitable, however, because of other factors. Chief among these is the fact that the three networks all own local stations (called **owned and operated stations**) in major urban centers. These are all cash cows, earning hundreds of millions of dollars each year for the parent company.

In addition, the networks are exploring new ideas to generate additional revenues in the future. Both NBC and CBS are pushing into more production ventures, producing a few of the programs they carry in their primetime schedule. At the beginning of the 1989–90 television season, 11 of the 66 hours of prime television were produced by production companies affiliated with the networks, including shows produced by their news and sports divisions. Should the government rules limiting the networks' participation in such ventures change, all three companies will be ready to move vigorously into that market.

The networks are also investing in the competition, cable television. ABC owns most of ESPN, the sports network, and a share of both the Lifetime Channel and the Arts and Entertainment Channel. NBC also owns a share of Arts and Entertainment, and has recently ventured forth with Cablevision to start a 24-hour-per-day consumer-oriented news and information network called the Consumer News and Business Channel. In May of 1991 the network bought the ailing Financial News Network and merged it with CNBC. (NBC is also co-owner with Cablevision of Sportschannel America, Bravo, and American Movie Channel.) No one will even venture an educated guess as to whether the networks' days as major elements in the organization of television are numbered. But if they are, movement into cable and production will certainly cushion that blow.

In 1991 the Federal Communications Commission tried to resolve a dispute among the networks, television producers, and the government over the financial interest and syndication rules **(fin-syn)**. Since the early 1970s the government has barred each of the broadcast networks from producing more than 5 hours of primetime programming per week, from investing money in primetime shows created by independent producers, and from profiting from the domestic syndication of primetime programs. The networks were powers with which to reckon 20 years ago. And they allegedly used this power to prey on independent producers. It was easier for a producer to get a show telecast on the networks if the network had a chance to buy a share of that program, or so many producers reported. The initial network exposure of a television show to a national audience made it possible to later syndicate the show to local stations and reap important financial rewards. It was alleged that

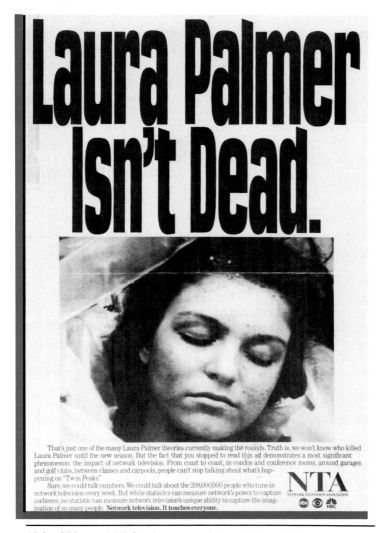

# Laura Palmer Isn't Dead.

That's just one of the many Laura Palmer theories currently making the rounds. Truth is, we won't know who killed Laura Palmer until the new season. But the fact that you stopped to read this ad demonstrates a most significant phenomenon: the impact of network television. From coast to coast, in condos and conference rooms, around garages and golf clubs, between classes and carpools, people can't stop talking about what's happening on "Twin Peaks."

Sure, we could talk numbers. We could talk about the 208,000,000 people who tune in network television every week. But while statistics can measure network's power to capture audience, no statistic can measure network television's unique ability to capture the imagination of so many people. **Network television. It touches everyone.**

**NTA**
NETWORK TELEVISION ASSOCIATION

ABC, CBS, and NBC—long considered the fiercest of rivals—joined forces to try to ward off the raids on their viewers by Fox, cable channels, and independent stations. This ad, published by the Network Television Association, is intended to remind advertisers of the still considerable strength of the three networks.
(© 1990 Network Television Association)

the networks would favor the shows they owned when planning a primetime schedule, so their programs could become popular and later be syndicated. The FCC dictated the new rules in the early 1970s; the networks agreed to abide by them. But the term of these agreements ended in 1990. And the networks fought attempts to keep them in effect.

The FCC in April of 1991 voted to relax but not eliminate these rules, permitting the networks to produce and acquire full resale rights to shows accounting for as much as 40 percent of their prime-time schedules. But the rules continue to prevent the networks from becoming distributors of shows produced exclusively for the syndication market—shows like "Jeopardy," "Wheel of Fortune," "Donahue," and "Oprah Winfrey," which are sold directly to local television stations. The networks can, however, distribute such programs overseas. The rules are extremely complex and will have little to do with what viewers see on their television screens. They are important, however, to the financial health of a variety of interests in the industry, and the revised fin-syn regulations really failed to please any of these interests completely. All parties said they would appeal the FCC ruling. The television networks, however, do gain something from this change, and this should at least slightly strengthen the networks economically in the years to come.

The other group of program wholesalers and distributors is the cable television networks. Let's consider this element in the organization for a few moments.

## ◻ Cable Networks

In 1950 there were four television networks. All four were broadcast networks. Today there are close to 60 television networks. Four are broadcast networks; the rest are cable networks.

Cable television networks became practicable with the launching of the first geosynchronous satellite in the mid-1970s. Time, Inc. showed with Home Box Office how simple it was to beam programming from Earth to a transponder on the satellite and then back down to receiving stations at local cable systems. Voila, cable networks were on their way. Today there are somewhere between 45 and 50 basic cable networks, five pay networks, seven superstations, and a handful of pay-per-view cable networks.

A package of **basic cable** networks is provided to cable subscribers for a flat monthly fee. The networks earn money by selling advertising (almost $1.2 billion worth in 1990) and from collecting subscription revenues. The cable television system operator pays the cable network a small per-subscribe fee, 15 or 20 cents per subscriber per month. The cable networks rent time on satellites to transmit their programming from coast to coast. Not all of the basic cable networks are successful; in fact, most of them are losing money. In 1988 12 of the top (most heavily viewed) channels earned a profit, and many in the industry saw this as a watershed.

The ten largest basic cable networks, in terms of the number of subscribers served, are as follows:

| | |
|---|---|
| ESPN | 61 million |
| Cable News Network | 56 million |
| USA Network | 53.8 million |
| Discovery Channel | 52.9 million |
| Nickelodeon | 52.9 million |
| Nick at Night | 52.9 million |
| MTV | 52.4 million |
| Family Channel | 51.8 million |
| The Nashville Network | 51 million |
| C-Span | 51 million |

ESPN ranks as the most successful of the cable networks. From clearly modest beginnings in 1979 with the broadcast of a slow-pitch softball game between the Kentucky Brewers and the Milwaukee Schlitzes, the all-sports network has reached the point where it is a full participant in network sports television, carrying NFL football, major league baseball, and NCAA basketball and football. Capital Cities/ABC owns 80 percent of ESPN; RJR Nabisco owns the rest. The sports network lost substantial amounts of money during its first five years of operation. It began to show a profit in 1985 and in 1989 showed a $100 million profit. This has permitted the network to compete for the cream of American sports. ESPN paid the NFL $450 million dollars for the rights to televise 37 regular season football games during the 1990–1993 seasons, plus the Pro Bowl Games, and three preseason games each of those four years. The network paid major league baseball $400 million for the rights to televise six games each week during the 1990–93 seasons. These are big league contracts.

Cable News Network, owned by Turner Broadcasting, in second place, brings 24 hours a day of news programming to American homes. The channel has not only been successful (in spite of predictions by many at the broadcast networks that such a feat was impossible), it has forced the three major broadcast networks to strengthen their own news operations. Because it is transmitted by satellite, CNN is accessible worldwide. When the American troops moved to the Persian Gulf in 1990, not only were the U.S. servicemen and women able to see summaries of these events over CNN broadcasts, but the leaders of many Middle East nations (including President Saddam Hussein of Iraq) could view U.S. news coverage of the crisis via CNN telecasts. CNN coverage of the ensuing war won plaudits, and the network sharply raised its advertising rates to take advantage of its newfound popularity.

USA Network and the Family Channel program reruns, movies, and a small amount of original programming. USA also features some sports telecasts. Nickelodeon is a highly praised channel for children, featuring animated cartoons, puppets and educational programs, game shows, music, and even some reruns. After dark, when the kids are in bed, "Nick at Night" uses the channel to offer viewers reruns. MTV features rock videos and a variety of other music oriented programming. The Nashville Network offers the same range of music programming, but with a country twang instead of rock beat. C-Span, one of the most widely watched channels, lets viewers watch the processes of government at work. Live broadcasts from the U.S. House of Representatives and Senate, congressional committee hearings, press conferences, and a wide range of other governmental functions are the staple of this oft-times heavily viewed channel. Finally, the Discovery Channel offers viewers a mix of science, travelogue, and nature in a wide variety of programming.

In addition to these ten, other widely viewed channels are the Lifetime Channel, Arts and Entertainment, the Weather Channel, CNN Headline News, Turner Network Television, American Movie Classics, and Black Entertainment Television (BET).

BET is aimed at African American viewers. In the ten years of its existence, it has grown from a two-hour slice of old movies and music videos to a profitable, 24-hour-a-day, seven-day-a-week service, available to 29.1 million homes. In its early years BET's concentration on music videos filled a need. MTV had a restricted playlist that clearly excluded jazz and rhythm and blues, and even limited air time for popular black rock artists. The majority owner of BET is Robert Johnson, a black entrepreneur who founded the network with a $15,000 loan. Minority share owners include HBO and Great American Broadcasting. Today the channel features reruns of programs like "Sanford and Son" "Frank's Place" and music-oriented programming. But it is also attempting to bring more original programs to the screen with political programs like "For the Record", featuring black members of Congress; "Teen Summit", a talk show for teenagers; "On Stage," one-act plays written and performed by blacks; and "Our Voices," a daily talk show. BET is so successful that in 1991 the company announced it was beginning a magazine venture aimed at black readers.

There are three television programming services aimed at Spanish-speaking viewers. All three are small broadcast networks, but two are cable networks as well. Univision is the largest service, available to viewers via ten broadcast stations it owns, 21 affiliated stations, and about 400 cable systems. It is headquartered in Kansas City and is owned primarily by the Hallmark Card Company. It features broad-based Spanish-language programming, and attempts to appeal to Hispanics throughout the nation with its news and other features. Telemundo is available only over broadcast channels. The Telemundo group owns six stations and services another 22 affiliates. Its headquarters are in New York. The most aggressive of these three, and the smallest at this point, is Galavision, which reaches Hispanic homes via both broadcast channels (10 in 1990) and cable systems. Galavision is focusing its programming on Mexican and Central American immigrants who account for about 75 percent of the 20 million Hispanics in the United States. Network officials say they are not trying to serve Hispanic residents of New York (largely of Caribbean origin) or Miami (largely of Cuban background). All of Galavision's news, sports, and entertainment programming is produced in Mexico City by Televisa, the Mexican communications conglomerate. Both Univision and Telemundo are heavily leveraged (they owe a lot of money), according to an article in *The New York Times* by George Volsky, and many observers doubt whether the advertising exists to support three Spanish-language television services. Only time will tell.

Cable networks come, usually with great fanfare, and go, quietly, in the night. Turner Network Television, TNT, is the most widely publicized of the recent entrants. The channel went on the air in the autumn of 1988 with access to 32.8 million subscribers, making it at birth the 16th largest cable network in the nation. (It had 50 million subscribers in 1991.) The core of programming for the new network is the MGM film library, which Turner kept when he bought, and then sold, the MGM film studio. Turner has promised one original drama or documentary each month, and early on he has kept this promise. As leverage to push his new channel into cable systems, Turner spent $450 million for the rights to broadcast some NFL games during 1990 to 1993. Football fans will push their cable systems to add TNT to get access to these games, or at least such are the hopes of Ted Turner. The NBC news and business channel, CNBC, premiered in the spring of 1989, and Sports Channel America, another venture in which NBC has an interest, came on line a few months earlier. In 1990 still another sports channel was supposed to premier, Sports News Network. Also, the Cowboy Channel, featuring old Western movies and television series, and the Sci Fi channel were expected to begin telecasting.

There has been a substantial fallout of pay cable channels. To receive such channels the subscriber must pay the cable company a fee in addition to the charge for basic cable. The cable company splits this fee with the pay channel, which does not carry advertising. There were 11 pay channels transmitted in 1985. Today there are five: HBO, Showtime, The Movie Channel, Cinemax, and the Disney Channel. American Theater Classics, the Home Theater Network, and Festival all went out of business. The Nostalgia Channel and Bravo went basic cable. The Playboy Channel became Playboy at Night, a pay-per-view channel.

The largest of the remaining group, HBO, with 17.3 million subscribers, is the only one of the channels that is making money. Showtime, with 7.3 million subscribers, Cinemax with 6.3 million subscribers, Disney with 5.2 million subscribers, and The Movie Channel with 2.7 million subscribers are all financially marginal, or losing money. These are primarily movie channels, bringing films into the viewers' homes about a year after they appear in the theater, six months after they come out in videocassette. When HBO first began telecasting, film-hungry Americans lapped up the idea of seeing relatively new movies, uncut, and uninterrupted by commercials. But the introduction of the VCR has changed all that. Film buffs who don't catch a movie in the theater have almost certainly watched it on video before it gets to a premium pay channel. So the premium pay channels are scrambling to find original programming such as concerts, original made-for-pay television movies, and sports programming to attract and hold subscribers. HBO and Showtime, in a competitive move, probably hastened the downturn in their fortunes by cutting deals with the movie studios for exclusive rights to feature films. Years ago a subscriber to either Showtime or HBO could see most of the popular feature films. But now the two services divide these motion pictures, so a movie fan needs to subscribe to more than one service to see most of the best and most popular films. That costs about $30 per month on most cable systems. A movie can be rented for $2.50 in most places, and a quality VCR can be purchased for less than $400. Total cost of the machine and 100 movie rentals is less than the cost of two years worth of HBO and Showtime. To try to hold onto viewers, HBO announced in mid-1991 that it would test a system whereby it added two channels each to HBO and Cinemax. Company officials said the six channels would rotate the same menu of films and features, and the company would not charge any more for the new service, which would give viewers a greater variety of times to see the programming.

Superstations are another kind of cable network. Seven different local television stations are beamed nationwide via satellite to cable companies for home distribution. The first, and by far the biggest, is WTBS in Atlanta, a property of Turner Broadcasting. This station has access to more than 55 million subscribers, or as many as all but two of the basic cable networks. Two superstations in New York City, and stations in Chicago, Los Angeles, Boston, and Dallas/Ft. Worth, complete this entourage. These are nonnetwork affiliated television stations that usually program reruns, old movies, sports, game shows, and a variety of other kinds of syndicated programming. Who would have believed that people in Seattle would be so hard-pressed for television that they would watch old sit-coms (which they could see on local stations) telecast on a television station in Atlanta, Ga.? But it happened. When it first started operations, WTBS even carried local Atlanta commercials for car dealers and appliance stores. These have been replaced by national spot advertising, largely of the "Slim Whitman's Greatest Hits" variety. But WTBS is showing a profit, and so are some of the other superstations.

Finally, we must consider pay-per-view channels. A viewer who subscribes to a cable television service pays a monthly fee for the service. For this fee, the subscriber gets all local stations and a selection from the basic cable channels and superstations. For an additional monthly fee, the subscriber can receive one or more of the pay channels. Subscribers to pay-per-view channels don't pay a monthly fee; they pay only for the programs they watch. Ideally, the cable industry would like all of us to pay for each program we watch. But such a system was technically impossible when cable television was first developed, and since we have become used to the monthly pay plan, it is going to be difficult to wean us from that system.

In 1990 there were seven pay-per-view systems. There were Viewer's Choice I and II, Request Television I & II, Playboy at Night, SPICE, Drive-In Cinema, Cable Video Store, and Action Pay-Per-View. The largest of the half-dozen, Viewer's Choice, had 9.3 million subscribers. In 1991 Tele-Communications Inc., the nation's largest cable company, inaugurated a movie pay-per-view channel called Encore.

Two serious technical problems slowed, and still slow, the growth of pay-per-view. The first is addressability. This is the capacity of the cable company to send a particular program to one home, and not to the home next door, without each time making an adjustment on the wire leading from the cable to the subscriber's home. Only advanced cable systems have such a capability, and it is essential to the operation of pay-per-view. The cable operator must be able to select the programming a subscriber receives from its offices; the programs must be addressable to specific subscribers. In 1991 only 15 million cable homes were addressable.

The other problem is devising a means for the subscriber to order the pay-per-view program. At this point it is usually done by telephone; the subscriber calls the cable company and tells an operator that he/she wants to see the Madonna concert. Unfortunately, too many subscribers wait until the last minute to make this decision; the telephone lines going into the cable company get jammed; orders don't get through; subscribers are unhappy, and so is the cable operator. The industry has worked to correct this difficulty. A person who subscribes to pay-per-view has a converter attached to the TV set, and in 1990 about 10 percent of these converters featured what is called impulse technology. With this device a subscriber can push two buttons on the converter, to tell the cable operator to send the program to this television set. The telephone company has also developed systems using the telephone that permits a cable company to take orders far more quickly than if the ordering is done manually.

The fare on pay-per-view at present is movies, sports, and concerts. Subscribers pay anywhere from $4.95 to view a movie to as much as $35 to see a concert or a sporting event. Pay-per-view TV telecasts movies a few weeks *after* they appear in video cassette. The pay-per-view industry would like to get them prior to video release, but the film industry has not shown any interest in this scheme. As far as sports go, wrestling and boxing are the main events. The most popular pay-per-view programs have been Wrestlemania IV, V, and so on. They drew nearly a million subscribers, and Wrestlemania V earned $23 million for promoters. Boxing is also popular. The Buster Douglas/Evander Holyfield fight in 1990 grossed $35 million.

At present pay-per-view television is small potatoes, relative to television generally. The 1990 Rolling Stones Steel Wheels Tour concert was carried on pay-per-view television after the tour. About 265,000 subscribers tuned in at $25 each, and this earned $6.6 million. The concert was viewed in less than 2.5 percent of accessible homes.

But many want pay-per-view to succeed; and not only those in the pay-per-view business. Sporting promoters, film studios, concert tour managers—all would like to see the day when a single event or performance, carried on pay-per-view, and bought by tens of millions of persons, realizes huge profits. The potential earnings could be staggering. CBS carried the 1990 Super Bowl and reportedly earned $60 million for the 36 minutes of advertising (at as much as $1.5 million per minute) it carried. The rating for the game was 25; it was viewed in 23 million homes. If the game had been viewed on a pay-per-view basis and was seen in the same number of homes for the modest price of $10, the network would have earned $230 million. But you say, many wouldn't pay $10 to see the Super Bowl. Alright, let's say pay-per-view scares away half these viewers. The network still earns $115 million, about twice what it earned via broadcast television.

Many people argue that as soon as pay-per-view becomes a feasible alternative, the big television events like the Super Bowl, the World Series, the NBA finals, NCAA Final Four, the Oscar and Emmy Awards, and others, will leave free television and go to pay-per-view. And these same people argue that this will hurt the very people who tend to use television the most, lower income Americans. Is this the wave of the future? Note this. In 1992 NBC will telecast 760 hours of summer Olympics coverage. One-hundred-and-sixty hours will be carried on the broadcast network. The remaining 600 commercial-free hours will be sold to viewers on a pay-per-view basis. Cablevision Systems Corporation is offering the 600-hour package to viewers for $150. If this scheme is successful, the network and its Cablevision partner could realize as much as $375 million in revenues. Oh yes, it's coming.

## ☐ Local Broadcasting Stations

Local broadcasting stations and cable companies are the retail operators in the organization of television. There are about 1350 over-the-air VHF (Very High Frequency) or UHF (Ultra High Frequency) television stations in the nation. In addition there are nearly 1,000 low-power television stations. More about these later. About 300 of the UHF-VHF stations are noncommercial broadcasting stations, public or educational television stations. Most of the commercial stations are owned by broadcasting chains, as noted in Chapter 4. In August of 1990 only 17 of these stations were controlled by companies owned by blacks, according to the National Association of Black Broadcasters, a trade group. While there are a great many commercial television stations dedicated to Spanish-language telecasting, the ownership of these stations is not necessarily Hispanic, or at least U.S. Hispanic. Latin American businesses have heavy interests, although indirectly, in many of these stations. Others are owned by white Americans.

Of the 1,000 or so commercial television stations, between 650 and 700 are affiliated with one of the major broadcasting networks, ABC, CBS, or NBC. The remaining stations are affiliated with Fox or are independent. Owning any television station is a usually lucrative proposition, but owning an affiliated station is much more lucrative than owning an independent.

In any year, a comparison of the total revenues and profits earned by affiliated stations and independent stations in the same sized markets reveals the difference in the economic strength of the two kinds of stations. In 1990, for example, the average affiliated station in the top ten television markets earned $86 million in revenues, and a profit of $33 million. The average independent station in the same sized market earned less than half as much revenue, $38 million, and a far smaller profit, only $5 million. Comparisons of stations in mid-sized markets and smaller markets turn out the same.

Why the differences? It costs about the same to run an affiliated station as it does to operate an independent one. But the affiliated station earns far more revenue; hence, a much larger profit. Why does an affiliated station earn more revenue? There are several reasons.

The affiliated station must buy or create some programming, but it is paid by the network to carry network programming. (See pp. 75–76 for an explanation of this.) The independent must buy or create all its programming. The network-affiliated stations have stronger broadcast signals, as a general rule. Not all channel positions are equal. The signals generated by stations on channels 2 through 6 are superior to those generated by stations on channels 7 through 13 on the VHF band and channels 14 through 69 on the UHF band. The reason for this has to do with the electromagnetic spectrum. The higher on the spectrum it is located, the stronger the signal must be to transmit crisp, clear pictures. Also, sensitive transmitting and receiving equipment becomes more critical as a station ascends the spectrum ladder. It would seem, looking at the channel numbers, that the portion of the broadcast spectrum allocated to television is a single, continuous portion of this electromagnetic field. That is not true. There is a large gap between channels 6 and 7 that includes space for FM radio, aircraft-control tower communication, amateur radio operators, and other business and government uses. There is even a bigger gap between channels 13 and 14 that is reserved for government communications. Stations broadcasting on channels 2 through 6 can achieve excellent signal coverage with only 100 kilowatts of power. Stations on channels 7 through 13 need as much as 316 kilowatts, and require somewhat more sophisticated transmitting equipment. Stations on channels 14 through 69 need power up to 5,000 kilowatts, sophisticated transmitters, and the receivers need a special antenna, that little round one attached to the back or the top of a television set.

The affiliated stations tend to have the better dial positions, because they were the first stations to be established and took the better channels. Independent stations tend to be on the upper end of the VHF band, or the UHF band. The stronger broadcast signals by the affiliates gives them greater coverage, and permits them to charge higher advertising rates.

The network-affiliated stations also tend to have a higher visibility in the community. They carry the higher rated network programs, they are identified in network advertising in newspapers and magazines, and they tend to have full-fledged news operations and news programming. Studies have revealed that viewers tend to identify with stations most readily through their local newscasts. In many markets independents are attempting to heighten their visibility by aggressively building news departments.

Finally local affiliated stations tend to be more profitable because they do broadcast news. Until the mid-1970s most television stations broadcast local news because they had to; public service was something required of all licensees. But television stations discovered in the 1970s that news could be profitable. And a station could enhance these profits significantly if it increased the number of hours each day in which news was broadcast. A station attempting to do a creditable job covering the news in a community needs a certain number of reporters. If the station broadcasts 90 minutes of news each day, the cost of the news operation must be covered by the commercials broadcast in that 90 minutes. A station can, however, broadcast four hours of news each day with only a slight increase in costs. It is not covering more news; it is merely reporting the news it has covered more often. Now the station can sell the commercial minutes contained in four hours, rather than 90 minutes, to recoup the cost of its news operation. And recoup they do. A television station in a large- to mid-sized market generally earns $2 for each $1 it spends on news. News has become a profit center at many stations. And this adds to the revenues earned by the affiliated stations. Independent stations, because of the costs involved, tend to devote much less time (if they broadcast any at all) to local news.

News is just one part of the programming that fills up the broadcast day on a local network affiliated station. A substantial portion of the programming, often more than 50 percent, comes from the network with which the station is affiliated. These stations also often produce local talk shows, children's programming, public interest programs, and originate sports broadcasts. Finally, the affiliated stations buy a limited amount of programming directly from the producers, so-called syndicated programming. This kind of programming will be discussed more thoroughly when nonaffiliated stations are outlined in the next section.

## ☐ The Independents

The independent, nonaffiliated television station was, during the developmental years of television, considered the poor cousin in the family. Denied a network affiliation and the rich entertainment, news, and sports programming that accompanied it, the independent was forced to struggle along with old movies, reruns, and poorly produced, inexpensive syndicated programming. In 1980 there were only 138 such stations.

But the decade of the 1980s was a period of substantial growth for the independent stations. By 1990 there were 339 such stations; of these 265 are classified as general entertainment stations, meaning they are not Hispanic-oriented, religious, or home shopping channels. But the decade was not without problems as well, for the growth spurt in the middle years was quickly followed by a sharp decline in the fortunes of the independent stations in the late 1980s. By 1990 things stabilized and while they are not as successful as they were in 1985–86, the independents are in a far stronger position than they were 15 years ago. Let's examine what happened to these nonaffiliated stations during this roller coaster decade.

The growth of the independents hinged on two factors, the growth of cable television and an increase in the popularity and quality of syndicated programming. As cable television systems expanded in the early 1980s, and more and more homes received their telecasts via cable, the disparities between the signal strength and signal quality of the affiliated television stations on the low end of the spectrum and the independents on the high end of the spectrum dissipated. The picture quality of a UHF station on channel 22 is largely the same as the quality of a VHF station on channel 3 when both are sent to the home via cable. So cable helped solve some of the technical problems that hurt the independent stations.

But the programming carried on these enhanced signals was also important. Some Americans had always enjoyed reruns of popular old programs. But the popularity of these shows seemed to peak in the early 1980s. Independents have the capability to strip these off-network reruns, five nights a week, in the late afternoon and early evening hours when the affiliated stations are telecasting the news. This is **counter-programming** in its baldest form, and it worked in many cities. (Using a counter-programming strategy, a television station or a network will telecast a program that is intended to appeal to viewers who are likely repelled by programming on competing stations or networks. For example, the popularity of CBS's "Sixty Minutes" to news-oriented adults has pushed NBC and ABC to telecast so-called family fare, or programs that will appeal to young people or children at 7 P.M. on Sunday nights.) While the affiliated stations battled amongst themselves for the news-oriented audience, the independents gobbled up those viewers who didn't want to watch the news. And as news programming expanded to two and two-and-a-half hours in the period from 5 P.M. to 8 P.M., the independent stations were able to capitalize on this audience.

In addition to syndicated reruns, the independents took advantage of first-run syndicated programming. This is programming that is produced by many of the same companies that produce primetime programming for the networks. But it is not shown on the networks. Instead, the producers and distributors sell the rights to broadcast such programming to individual television stations in cities across the nation. Affiliated stations can and do buy this programming. But they have less time in which to telecast it, given their locally produced programming and their schedule of network programs. So the local independent stations are often able to take advantage of the popular game shows (in 1990 "Wheel of Fortune" and "Jeopardy" were the two most popular shows in first-run syndication), talk shows (like "Donahue" or "Oprah"), reality shows ("A Current Affair," "Reporters," "Hard Copy") and even big-budget drama and adventure. Producer Gene Roddenberry had been so soured by his previous experience with NBC that when he decided to produce a new series of Star Trek programs ("Star Trek: The Next Generation"), he didn't consider offering the show for network telecast. He went directly into first-run syndication. The show, probably the most expensive syndicated program ever produced at $1.3 million per episode in 1990, has become a substantial success and often wins its time period in the ratings against network programming. (In 1991 the 80th episode of the new show was telecast—surpassing the 79 episodes of the original show.) The show is a gold mine for the stations that carry it. Paramount, which produces and distributes the program, sells about half the advertising time to national advertisers. The local stations sell the other spots and keep all the money. This is far more lucrative than the network compensation system under which the affiliated stations operate. Groups of independent stations have worked together to fund miniseries, and buy the rights to show feature films before they are telecast on network television. And some programs killed by the networks have extended their lives through first-run syndication on independent stations. The producers continue making episodes of these shows in hopes of reaching the magic 100 number which will offer them the opportunity to put the program in reruns. And some of these shows do better in first-run syndication than they did on the networks. Some programs have a strong regional popularity, and this can sustain them on stations in that region. Others fared poorly on the networks because they were in weak time slots. The NBC show "Fame" was cancelled in 1983 because it had low ratings. But the program was against "Magnum P.I.," a ratings leader at the time. Local stations have the flexibility to find a more comfortable time slot for such shows and they often attract a substantial audience. "Fame" did just that and was shown on 165 stations in first-run syndication after it was cancelled by the networks. So the improvement in signal quality brought on by the growth of cable and the growth in the popularity and quality of programming helped the independent stations gain substantial numbers of new viewers in the early 1980s. This success story fueled the growth in the number of such stations in the early 1980s. But then in 1986–87 the bottom fell out of the independent business.

There is no single reason that explains the sharp downturn in fortunes of independent stations. Three interrelated factors all played important parts: increased costs of programming, drop in advertising revenues, and loss of viewers. When the popularity of the off-network reruns increased in the 1980s, the cost of licensing these programs for the station operators increased as well. To win the rights to show these programs a station often has to bid against other stations in the market. As the popularity of the programming increased, and as the number of independent stations increased, there were more stations bidding bigger sums of money. The cost of showing the programs rose. In 1975 when the "Brady Bunch" became available for off-network stripping, the producers of the show earned about $125,000 per episode when the program was syndicated. That is, when the money paid by each station in the nation to show a single episode of the program was totaled, it amounted to $125,000. In 1979 " M*A*S*H" went out for about $250,00 per episode. Four years later "Three's Company" earned $850,000 per episode. In 1987 the producers of " Family Ties" earned $1.4 million per program. The peak was hit in 1988 when "The Bill Cosby Show" earned $4.8 million per episode (figure 9-3).

The cost to stations of buying "The Bill Cosby Show" set records. Unfortunately, the show didn't do as well for these stations as many program directors had expected. Some stations even lost money when they telecast the program. Advertis-

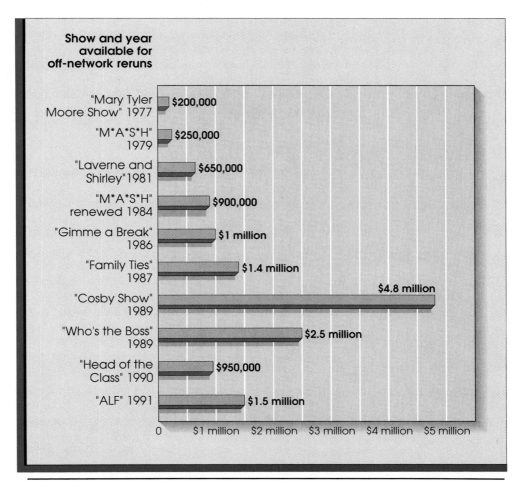

FIGURE 9-3 Prices paid per episode for television shows going into off-network syndication.

ers simply would not pay the steep rates needed to pay for the extraordinarily high cost of buying the rights to the show. With Cosby leading the way, the cost of buying the rights to older series being syndicated for the third and fourth time went up as well. Between 1980 and 1985 the costs of syndicated programming at the average independent station went up 25 percent. Programming costs ate up as much as 47 percent of the total operating budget at some stations. WCIX in Miami had been showing reruns of "M*A*S*H" profitably. When the station rebid for the rights to show the series in 1987, it had to pay $13 million for the rights to reshow 225 episodes. Advertisers would not pay enough to cover these costs. So for WCIX, showing reruns of "M*A*S*H" went from being profitable in 1982 to a losing proposition in 1987.

Interestingly, it wasn't simply bidding from other broadcasting stations that raised the ante in the fight to win the rights to air their shows. Many of the cable networks also got in the bidding and frequently won exclusive rights to air these off-network series in reruns. This was especially true for the 60-minute programs, which are not as popular with local stations. Both "Murder She Wrote" and "Miami Vice" began their lives in reruns on cable networks, not on local television stations.

Increased costs are only one part of the picture, however. The independent stations began to show a loss in viewers as well. The growth of cable television, which had helped the independent stations by enhancing their weaker signals, gave subscribers more programming choices. And this drained viewers away from the local television stations. The growth in popularity of VCRs hurt all those involved in television, including the independent stations. And of course, whereas communities had a single independent station in 1980, many had two or three by 1987. Again, more options for viewers.

The loss of viewers, coupled with the growth of competition, made it more difficult to sell advertising. The amount of money spent on television advertising has not increased rapidly enough to offset the sharp increase in the number of television operations seeking those dollars. The local independent broadcast has to compete against other independent stations, affiliated stations and even cable companies for local advertising. And the plethora of cable networks compete with local stations for national advertising. It is a much tougher sell today than it was only ten years ago.

The independent local stations seem to be on a kind of plateau. Advertising was up slightly in the early 1990s. The ratings stopped their decline. And programming costs seemed leveled off. Several stations failed in the late 1980s, and a few still on the air are vulnerable, according to experts. The nation seems to be able to sustain the 265 plus general entertainment independent stations; the worst seems to be over.

Before terminating the discussion of local broadcasting stations, the new low-power television stations must be briefly considered.

Low-power television was authorized by the Federal Communications Commission in the late 1970s. These stations differ little in concept from full-power stations, appearing both on the VHF and UHF bands. But while full-power stations transmit millions of watts and reach as far as 70 miles, the low-power stations emit only a few thousand watts and rarely reach more than 25 miles. By the mid-1980s there were fewer than 300 low-power stations on the air in the nation. By 1990 there were nearly 1,000. They feature a diversity of programming in many instances; in others, the programming has a very narrow focus. There is an all-rural station in Omaha, and an all-silent station in Los Angeles which offers captioned television shows for the deaf. Many stations produce their own programming, which is sometimes crudely fashioned. On the other hand, there is at least one network, Channel America, that serves 42 affiliated low-power stations with programming of a high quality. Paid religious networks, Spanish-language services, home shopping networks, and music channels now regularly license their satellite feeds to LPTV stations.

It costs anywhere from $50,000 to $500,000 to start a low-power station, considerably less than the millions needed for a full-power station. Advertising on a station may cost as little as $50 for a 30-second spot, to $200 for an ad on Channel America.

Some applaud the growth in low-power television but complain that its original purpose is being destroyed. Low-power television was seen by many as neighborhood television: neighbor and community news, broadcasts of community meetings, telecasts of Little League baseball or high school football, an electronic voice for the people in the community. Some stations are just that, but more look like traditional broadcasting stations operated by amateurs. These stations duplicate programming the viewer can find on full-power stations. "This is the antithesis of what low-power is intended to be," said Samuel Simon, the director of Citizen Television System in Washington. This is a nonprofit group, headed by Ralph Nader. Permits for more than 1,000 more low-power television stations have been granted by the government, and experts expect as many as 4,000 on the air by the year 2,000. What kind of stations these will be remains to be seen.

## ◻ Local Cable Systems

In 1990 about six out of every ten Americans had their television programming delivered to their home through a wire rather than through the airwaves (figure 9-4). Cable television penetration had reached almost 60 percent.

From the primitive community antenna television systems of the early 1950s, cable television has come a long way. Today it not only retransmits programming aired by local stations, it brings viewers a virtual cornucopia of programming options. Local cable companies even generate a small percentage of their own programming, and sell time for local advertising, almost half-a-billion dollars worth in 1990.

Subscribers must pay for cable television service, and the average monthly bill in 1990 was about $30. The typical subscriber takes the basic service and one premium channel. Rates for basic cable have risen steadily since 1987 when Congress restricted the power of local and state governments to approve basic cable rates. This provision was a part of the Cable Communications Policy Act of 1984. Only in those communities in which there was no effective competition for the cable system would local government retain the power to set cable rates. The FCC ruled that there was effective competition for a cable system if three over-the-air television broadcast signals were available to viewers. In nearly all American cities, then, the cable operators were free to set the basic rates as high as they pleased. Rates averaged $13.70 a month in 1987. They averaged $15.41 a month just two years later. In June of 1991 the FCC redefined "effective competition," stating a community could regulate rates if there were less than six (rather than three) over-the-air signals available. Many observers suggested this redefinition by the FCC (which does not favor such regulation) was an attempt to stave off more stringent regulation proposed in Congress, regulation that was opposed by both the industry and by the Bush administration. The average rates for premium services actually fell between

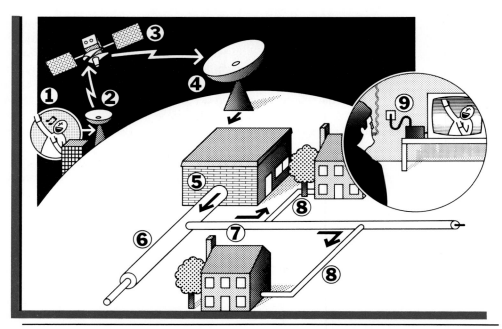

FIGURE 9-4 This diagram illustrates how cable television programming reaches a subscriber. Programs originate in a production facility (1) and are transmitted (2) to a communications satellite some 22,000 miles above the earth (3). The satellite amplifies the signal and beams it back to a receiving station on earth (4) where it is sent to the cable system's "head-end" (5). The signal is then sent via cables (6, 7, and 8) to the subscriber's home for viewing (9).
(Home Box Office)

1987 ($10.15) and 1989 ($9.66). This reflected lagging interest in the movie-oriented premium channels.

While a nearly 60 percent penetration rate for cable is impressive, it is not anything like the industry hoped for. For the past twenty years visionaries in the television industry have predicted that 80 to 90 percent of Americans would "soon" receive their television via cable. That hasn't happened. The number of people signing up for cable has actually slowed quite dramatically in the past five years. Growth in recent years has come in mature systems. There is little new wiring taking place at this time.

Extending cable service to new communities or to unwired portions of communities that are partially wired is very expensive today. Cable systems wired the least expensive parts of the nation first: suburbs, small towns near urban areas, and dense, newer parts of big cities. What is left to wire is much more costly: isolated rural areas and poorer sections of inner cities. *Channels* magazine reported in 1989 that significantly less than 50 percent of the population in many major American cities subscribed to cable. Only 43 percent subscribe in New York; 40 percent in Los Angeles; 38 percent in Chicago; 44 percent in Detroit and Houston; 40 percent in Dallas/Ft. Worth and Washington, D.C. Many of the nonsubscribers choose not to pay for cable. But in many instances they have no access to cable; their neighborhoods have not been wired. The prospect for new wiring in the poor inner cities is the bleakest. Wiring costs are very high, and the likelihood of the cable company acquiring large numbers of new subscribers is very low.

The ownership of cable systems is still collapsing into fewer and fewer hands. While deals aren't being made as rapidly in the 1990s as they were in the late 1980s (455 cable systems changed hands in 1988 in deals worth $14 billion), cable systems are still being scooped up by the large multisystem operators or MSOs. In 1990 cable systems were being bought and sold at the average price of $2,348 per subscriber, according to the *New York Times*. That is, if the cable system had 10,000 subscribers, the buyer would pay $2,348,000 for the system.

TCI or Tele-Communications Inc., is the largest MSO in the nation with 9.5 million subscribers, or approximately 53 million cable customers in the nation. That is about 18 percent of all subscribers. Time-Warner is the second largest MSO with 5.9 million subscribers; Continental has 2.5 million; Comcast has 2.5 million. Storer, Cox, and Cablevision Systems each serve 1.5 million subscribers. The top ten cable companies serve about 53 percent of all cable subscribers. The top five serve more than 35 percent of the subscribers.

The power of the MSOs is extraordinary. Two or three of the top companies can truly determine the fate of a cable network or cable channel. If TCI, Time-Warner, and two or three other MSOs decide not to carry a new cable channel, the chances of its succeeding are very slight. The MSOs exercised this very real muscle several years ago when they refused to carry CBS Cable and RCA Entertainment Cable. The CBS venture lost $30 million; RCA lost $34 million. Some argue this was the cable industry's payback to broadcasters for working for decades to stifle the growth of cable by fighting the industry every step of the way as it sought to grow. Who knows?

The cost of new wiring is one reason why cable is not growing more rapidly. But there are other reasons as well. It must be repeated, the introduction of VCRs hurt television viewing at every level. Many people who enjoyed watching movies became cable subscribers simply to gain access to the premium movie channels, HBO, or Showtime. These people now satisfy their movie cravings with rental cassettes.

Just as important is the slow realization by many Americans that while cable television has greatly multiplied the number of channels coming into the home, it has not greatly enriched the fare carried on those channels. There are some outstanding exceptions in specific areas. The amount of cultural programming is greater with cable's A & E and Bravo networks. There is much greater access to sports. Science and nature are taken more seriously on networks like the Discovery Channel. And there is much more news and information about business available via cable. But the quality and variety of basic entertainment has not been greatly enhanced. Many Americans consider it a bad buy to pay for 36 channels of mediocre programming, when they can get 8 or 9 channels of mediocre programming for nothing with over-the-air broadcasts.

In the early 1990s local cable television systems remain largely relay stations, shipping out programming they have caught on their antennas. Some original programming is produced, but very little. The industry is apparently not very interested in creating much more than 30- and 60-second spots for local advertisers. Most cable operators prefer to simply pass along what others have created, and collect the money for their deliveries.

Cable is complimented by other exotic local delivery systems. MMDS, or multi-channel multipoint distribution service, is one such system. MMDS is wireless cable. The system operator transmits television signals via the microwave band to subscribers who use a small, dish-type, roof antenna to pick up the signals, and a small converter to put them through the standard television set. In 1983 the FCC decided to allocate 8 microwave channels per market for commercial use. Today, wireless cable is available in a number of major markets, including New York City, Detroit, Washington, D.C., Denver, Cleveland, Oklahoma City, Philadelphia. It is also available in a few smaller markets as well. Nationwide, however, there are but 350,000 subscribers to MMDS. These systems are most popular for use in large apartment and office buildings. The building owner can place a single antenna and converter system on the roof of the building, and then feed the signals to the subscriber's office or apartment via coaxial cable. The slow growth of MMDS is generally attributed to a lack of attractive programming. While a few systems carry some of the popular cable channels, most do not. Some have suggested that because the owners of many of the cable channels (like Time-Warner) also own cable systems, they are reluctant to contribute to the possible success of competitors.

# THE TELEVISION BUSINESS

A story told by former Federal Communications Commissioner Nicholas Johnson reveals a good deal about the television industry. Johnson said he was plagued by a dream during the years he served on the FCC, a dream about America's last day. The bombs and rockets have fallen. The last American television station is running its 39th rerun of "I Love Lucy" when the station manager scurries across the studio floor, heading for the control room. To interrupt the program for a news bulletin? To say goodbye to the world? No, to put that last commercial on the air and into the accounts receivable before the antenna tower finally melts and falls to the ground.

American television has always been an unabashedly commercial medium and is proud of it. Critic Paul Goodman once observed that "The only part of television which has fulfilled its promise at all is the commercial." Commercials provide all the revenue for station owners, and a substantial portion of the revenue for television performers. Historian Erik Barnouw has observed that members of the Screen Actors Guild, the performers union, earn more from appearances in commercials than from appearances in theatrical films and television programs combined.

The cost of a typical 30-second network television commercial had risen to $150,000 by the 1990–91 season. A similar spot on a high rated program, like "The Bill Cosby Show," costs as much as $300,000. And advertisers paid $750,000 for 30 seconds of advertising time during the 1991 Super Bowl. The medium that gave us the "Six-Million Dollar Man" also produced the million-dollar-plus minute. The high cost of advertising on America's most visible mass medium has had the positive result of reducing sponsor power over television programming. In the early days of the medium advertisers tended to sponsor entire programs, much as they had in radio. Chevrolet brought "Bonanza" to America a full year at a time. And Ford presented "The FBI." "Alcoa Theater," "Kraft Theater," "Armstrong Circle Theater," and "Goodyear Playhouse" are just some of the other names that come quickly to mind. A sponsor who paid all the bills could exercise tight control over content, or at least try to. The infamous network quiz show scandals of the 1950s resulted in government pressure on the networks to take firmer control of their programming. Slowly the networks began to wrest control of programming away from sponsors. By the mid-sixties the increasing cost of television time had made the sponsorship of an entire program by a single sponsor simply too costly. Networks offered advertisers the opportunity to buy commercials in a wide variety of programs, an idea that many advertisers found appealing.

Sponsorship of a single program for an entire television season, in the early days 39 episodes plus 13 weeks of reruns, was a risky as well as costly venture. The sponsor of a hit show was happy, but for every hit there were many more misses. Also, even the sponsor of a hit show ended up showing his or her commercials to the same admittedly large audience each week. Scattering commercials across a wide range of programs offers advertisers several advantages. They no longer have to put all their eggs in one basket; they can put commercials on many different programs—some hits, some misses. A wider audience will see the spots. Advertisers can choose the kind of people they seek to reach—and advertise on programs that appeal to that group. (The A. C. Nielsen Co. and other rating services work with the television networks to provide advertisers with detailed demographic data on viewers of specific programs.) Finally, advertisers can plan their advertising expenditures more precisely. Sponsorship of a single program means advertising every week, 52 weeks a year. A sponsor who scatters advertising across many programs can advertise more heavily some times of the year, and forego advertising at other times. Today, networks sell their advertising time in two ways. Between 55 and 75 percent of commercial time during a television season is sold during the spring and summer before the next TV season. This is called the upfront market. Advertisers can get on the shows that were popular during the previous season, and try to pick the hits among the new shows in the coming season. The remainder of the time is sold during the television season in the so-called scatter market. Prices are often lower in this market since weaker programs are often not sold out and the network frequently offers time on these programs at bargain prices. It is true that a handful of companies (IBM, Kraft, Hallmark) continue to sponsor an entire program, a two-hour television drama three times a year for example. But such companies are rare. Sponsorship of regular series network television programs is unheard of in the early 1990s.

The typical unit of television time has changed over the past three decades as well. The 60-second spot was the standard in the industry until the mid-sixties. By 1970 less than 20 percent of all network commercials were 60 seconds long. The standard in the industry became the "piggyback 30," or two 30-second commercials from the same advertiser. (The Campbell Soup Company might piggyback a 30-second spot for Franco American Spaghetti on a 30-second spot for Swanson's Frozen Dinners.) By 1985 the rule in the industry was the "independent 30," a single 30-second commercial by a single advertiser. Nearly 80 percent of all network commercials were independent 30s, yet they were always telecast in pairs or groups of four advertisements. Advertising industry spokespersons suggested recently that independent 15-second commercials would soon become a popular if not dominant form. Many advertising people said they believed they could convey about as much information in 15 seconds as in 30 seconds, and the shorter commercials would cost less to telecast. The primary objection to the shorter commercials comes from the advertising industry itself, however. It is not uncommon to find as many as 16 different commercial messages in the few minutes between the end of one television program and the real beginning of another. This is called "clutter" and many sponsors are worried that their message will get lost in the morass of multiple commercials. (See pp. 331 and 385 for more on this.)

Television is a very profitable business. In 1990 total advertising revenues for the year approached $30 billion dollars. This was nearly 40 percent higher than they were in 1985 when the industry earned $20.6 billion from advertising sales. The companies that owned all three major television networks earned a substantial profit, although only a small share of that profit came from actual network operations. More, much more, was earned from their owned and operated television stations. Local television stations, those with network affiliations, and especially those in large markets, have a very high profit margin.

Data revealed during the merger between ABC and Capital Cities Communications show that three stations owned by the two organizations had profit margins in 1984 of 58 percent, 41 percent, and 35 percent. WTNH-TV in Hartford, Connecticut had revenues totaling $24.9 million in 1984, and expenses of only $10.4 million. In the five years previous to the merger, the station's margin of profit never fell below 58 percent and went as high as 62 percent. While the profit margins at these three stations were clearly above average, they were not that much above average. A typical television station in one of the nation's top ten markets sells about $35 million in commercial time each year, has expenses of about $24.5 million each year, for a pretax profit of $10.5 million or 30 percent, according to Luke Cornelius in a *TV Guide* article. Even stations in the smallest markets have about an eight percent profit margin. As a standard of comparison, a 5 to 6 percent profit margin is considered very good in most American industries.

Another measure of the profitability of local television stations is the price they bring on the open market. Remember, the buyer of a television station gets a large building filled with broadcasting equipment, a transmitter, a tower, and some talent. Yet a typical television station in one of the top 25 markets will usually sell for more than $150 million. In 1983 KTLA, an independent station in Los Angeles, was sold for $245 million. In 1985 the same station sold for $510 million. That same year Hearst bought WCVB television in Boston from Metromedia for $450 million. In 1988 Disney purchased KHJ in Southern California, a nonnetwork-affiliated independent station, for $320 million. When the British finally permitted the private ownership of television in the 1960s, British press lord Roy Thomson compared getting a television license with getting a license to print money. He wasn't far off the mark.

## ☐ Squeezing in Spots

Television stations are profitable because television time is a finite commodity; hence, there is a limit on the number of minutes available for commercials. The price of television time is high and gets higher all the time as there are more and more advertisers scrambling to get this valuable and limited resource. Although there are no legal limits on the number of commercial minutes a broadcaster may telecast each hour, there are a number of factors that actually restrict the number of advertising messages any station or network will carry.

Television stations are licensed by the U.S. government and are expected to serve the public interest. Stations that telecast an excessive number could be accused of serving their own commercial interests and not the public interest. Their license renewal could be placed in jeopardy. Realistically, license renewal has become pro forma in the past decade. And the Federal Communications Commission has instituted a program of deregulation which has diluted to a great extent any examination of a station's performance that might be done during the license renewal process. Hence, only the broadcaster who grossly inflates the number of commercials telecast is in danger of suffering a penalty.

For many years most large television stations and the three television networks subscribed to the Code of Good Practices of the National Association of Broadcasters which established limits on the number of commercial minutes that could be telecast each hour. The limits were voluntary but widely followed. Nine-and-a-half minutes of commercials were permitted during prime time under the NAB guidelines; higher amounts of commercials were permitted during other times of the night and day. But the NAB guidelines were ruled to be in violation of Federal antitrust laws in 1982, and the NAB code authority office closed its doors. In the immediate aftermath of the closure most television executives said they would continue to subscribe to the guidelines. But it wasn't long before first ABC and then CBS and NBC announced they would add an additional minute of advertising during prime time. Local television stations weren't far behind.

Certainly viewer displeasure concerns broadcasters who contemplate adding commercial minutes to broadcast hours. But viewers represent an admittedly powerful, but badly unorganized pressure group. It is rare that viewer wishes can be articulated in such a way as to be meaningful. Most people see commercials as the price they pay for "free" television. Viewer pressure would likely only materialize if television executives went completely overboard in programming commercials.

It is the advertiser, in reality, who is most likely to be offended by an increase in the number of commercials telecast. And the advertiser has more power than anyone else to do something about it—stop advertising. The growing clutter in television advertising is of serious concern, as previously noted. There is a limit to how many commercial minutes can be crammed into any hour without completely burying individual commercial spots, and many advertisers indicate they think the limit may have been reached. Consequently, broadcasters have been forced to be creative in their pursuit of the commercial dollar, finding ways of adding advertising revenues without necessarily adding commercials, or at least obvious commercials. Let's look at some of these schemes.

## Newsbriefs

The addition in 1978 of a 30-second "newsbreak" or "newsbrief" around 9 P.M. had all the appearances of a public service effort by the television networks. The more news the better, right? But the newsbreaks were created by the network advertising department as a means of adding a 10-second commercial, which didn't (when it was introduced) count as part of the NAB Code limited nine-and-a-half minutes of advertising. During the year the newsbreaks were introduced, the three networks added $30 million in revenues from the nightly 10-second spots. Local stations have since followed the networks' lead.

## Padding Programming

Additional minutes of advertising are normally added when the networks broadcast long motion pictures and miniseries. Time is very tight in a 30- or 60-minute episode of a television series and there is no time to add commercial minutes. Films and miniseries offer more flexibility. In many instances the networks will extend the length of a theatrical film by adding minutes not included in the original cut of the motion picture. This creates a longer film, providing an additional setting for commercials. For example, when NBC bought the rights to show *Airport 1977* from Universal, it insisted that the studio add 70 minutes to the 113-minute movie. How can this be done after the picture is completed? The studio used some of the footage it had originally edited out of the film, but that was not enough. So it added new footage. The cast couldn't be brought together again, so the new footage consisted of long shots, airport crowd scenes, and so forth—in the vernacular, junk. NBC took the 183-minute movie (three hours and three minutes), added 57 minutes of commercials and promotional material (about 14 minutes per hour) and telecast the movie over two nights in two-hour segments.

CBS used a similar technique when it bought the right to rerun the television series "Police Story." "Police Story" first appeared on television as either a one or two-hour show. The network sought to fill two and a half hours of late night programming time with two one-hour episodes or one two-hour episode plus commercials. A one-hour show ran 48 minutes; a two-hour program 96 minutes. Even with lots of commercials, that was considerably short of the 150 minutes needed. The network added additional junk footage, many public service announcements, and two and three minute long programming trailers. That still wasn't enough material. To fill out the time slot the network used what *TV Guide* called "a rare postproduction technique" called time expansion. CBS technicians slowed the running time of the program down by six percent during the transfer of the film to videotape. This added seven minutes to the running time of each two hour episode and this filled out the two-and-a-half hours of broadcast time. Experts say the six-percent reduction in speed can rarely be detected by the untrained eye, but there is noticeable distortion in the musical background.

## Product Plugs

Anyone who has watched the long credits at the end of a television game show knows that the prizes awarded on the program are given to the program producers for what is called consideration. That means the company that provides the free automobile or the airline that flies the winner to Bermuda or the refrigerator manufacturer is promoted on the program, usually when the prize is described. ("And Bill, the winners will fly to their dream vacation in Bermuda via the friendly skies of United Airlines; United Airlines serving every one of the United States and 16 foreign countries.") But so what; nobody takes the game shows seriously anyway. But the producers of television comedy and dramatic programs have long given less obvious plugs to commercial sponsors who pay to have their products used during a program. It was no accident, for example, that once every other week during the long run of the series "Hawaii Five-O" a United Airlines jet was pictured landing at the Honolulu International Airport sometime during the show. United paid for that plug. Or, the producer will simply get free use of something expensive for subtly picturing the product. Auto companies have provided free cars (usually only for the good guys) for television programs for years. It probably all started with the Corvette provided by Chevrolet for Martin Milner and George Maharis in "Route 66." The producers of the CBS-TV television movie *The Sky's the Limit* accepted free travel from Eastern Airlines and the use of a plane and airport space needed for the production.

Producers of local and national talk shows today rely on promoters of books, gadgets, food products, and personal care items to fill the time during these daily programs. These commercial plugs are labelled entertainment or information. When comic genius Ernie Kovacs hosted a similar program in the 1950s, a cash register would ring loudly anytime a guest came close to making a commercial plug.
(NBC Photo)

It would have cost the company about $200,000 to buy the tickets and rent the airplane and airport space. In return the producers included brief shots of an Eastern 757 gliding through the sky, and one of the characters in the film carrying an Eastern flight bag. Networks rarely have to seek these "donations." Advertisers are eager to provide such services and usually contact both the networks and the production companies. (See Chapter 8 to see how similar product placement schemes are used in the movies.)

## Plugola

Talk shows are a thriving institution on television, both at the network and local level. Some of these programs, especially at the local level, could not exist if producers could not call on the services of all manner of people seeking to promote a product or a service or themselves to fill up the air time. People in the industry call this plugola. The comic genius Ernie Kovacs had a cash register ring off camera each time a guest on his program gave even the hint of a plug for a product or service. But today producers with a small production budget and 60 or 90 minutes of air time to fill, often welcome the commercial spokespersons with open arms. Home economists from a variety of food companies or trade associations are always ready to share recipes (that use their products) with viewers. The product is often never named. It sits on the counter, label facing the camera, during the entire demonstration. Camera companies will send photographers who demonstrate the manufacturer's brand; do-it-yourself specialists invade the studios to quietly promote an adhesive or paint or solvent. Years ago the Duncan Yo-Yo Man invaded elementary school playgrounds across America each spring to amaze children with yo-yo tricks and provide solid arguments why this year's model was infinitely superior to last year's yo-yo that sat at home in the drawer. But the new breed of huckster makes the yo-yo man look like a piker. "Each day, millions of loyal talk show viewers are being exposed to and sold products and services through these subliminal forms of advertising," wrote Terry Ann Knopf in the *Columbia Journalism Review.* One public relations firm even sent a singing dog on the road to promote Solo Dog Food. The company's product was never mentioned during the act—but the dog sang "O Solo Mio" each time it performed.

Squeezing in extra commercial minutes was fine, but in the late 1980s and early 1990s, it was not enough. Greed had always been a dimension in the national ethos of the capitalistic United States, but it was not something that most Americans subscribed to or applauded. But in the energized eighties, being greedy not only became OK to many in the nation, greed was *good.* It ceased being immoral; it was regarded as a virtue by many in industry. Television reflected some of the worst in this regard, as some at the networks and at local stations seemed ready to sell advertisers anything, even the potted plants in the lobby, to make an extra buck. These tendencies can be seen in three distinct areas of programming: sports, program-length commercials, and the home shopping channels.

## ▨ Television and Sports—The Money Connection

The tremendous growth in the popularity of spectator sports in the last 30 years can be attributed almost directly to television. Without television the National Football League would likely be a cottage industry in eight to ten American cities and the term Super Bowl would be a brand name for a company that makes plumbing fixtures. Television has also vastly increased the visibility of and revenues for the owners and players of professional basketball, tennis and golf, and college football and basketball. But the marriage of TV and sports has been a good one for television as well. Sports broadcasting has long been a cash cow for the industry.

In the early 1990s the industry was investing more money than ever before in long-term television contracts with both professional and college organizations. NBC paid $600 million for the rights to televise National Basketball Association games for four years. The previous NBA contract with CBS cost the network only $176 million for four years. CBS will pay the NCAA a billion dollars for the rights to broadcast the national collegiate basketball tournament from 1991 to 1998. ESPN anted up $400 million to show 175 major league baseball games each season for the next four years. CBS paid out $1.1 billion for the rights to the major leagues playoffs, All-Star Game, and the World Series, 1990–1993. And the NFL will earn $3.6 billion from NBC, CBS, ESPN, and Turner Broadcasting during the next four years. The irony in these huge contracts is that the ratings for sports programming have been perceptibly slipping in the past two years. The ratings for the 1990 World Series were especially weak, for example. And when the Cincinnati Reds swept the series in four games, this meant CBS lost the opportunity to sell commercial time in three games of what could have been a seven game series.

Because the ratings have slipped, and the prices the networks have paid to air these events has dramatically increased, the networks have to do something to make up the difference. The first step is to raise advertising prices, even though the ratings are down. NBC, for example, doubled the price for commercial time in NBA games in the 1990–91 season, after it won the right to telecast the games away from CBS. Many advertisers (beer, wine, cars, and others) find the demographic profile of the television sports fan (usually upper income) simply too good to pass up, even at a high price.

Next, cut costs. A network sports budget has three categories of expenses. Rights and fees (the money the network pays to the NFL or NCAA for permission to telecast the games) amounts to between 75–80 percent of dollars spent. Nonproduction costs and salaries constitute another 5 percent. The remaining 15 to 20 percent covers the costs of production. The network has no control (once the deal has been made) over rights and fees, and it is unlikely that the broadcasting executives (nonproduction salaries and costs) are going to take a cut in pay. The only place to save money is to cut production costs. And that has been and is being done. All three networks in 1989 cut their staff in sports programming. ABC cut as many as 50 people. Some big names were let go. The networks also cut back the number of cameras and replay machines they allotted for football and basketball games. Telecasting a sports event live is costly. Today many peripheral sporting events are shown on videotape, rather than live. It costs less and is easier to package. For major sporting events like the Pan Am Games and the Olympics, the networks are buying much more of the coverage than they have in the past. In the 1987 Pan Am Games, for example, only one network crew was dispatched for 26 hours of coverage of 27

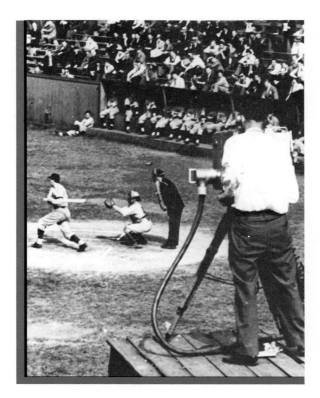

It is not uncommon for six to eight television cameras to be used to telecast a contemporary baseball game. NBC used only a single camera—the one pictured—to telecast the very first televised baseball game (between Columbia and Princeton universities). When a runner started to steal second base, who did the camera focus on? The catcher? The runner? The second baseman?
(NBC Photo)

sports. The network purchased the rest of the coverage from local videotape operators, and the critics argued the quality of the coverage suffered. There were substantial cuts in coverage of both the Winter and Summer Olympic Games in 1988, not
so much in telecasting the big name events, but in the portion of the telecasts that in
the past had attempted to set the scene or give viewers a close-up of the competitors. American athletes may be profiled, but it costs too much to send a crew to Africa to produce a 5-minute profile of a Kenyan distance runner.

Crews that are covering professional sports are being forced to set up their
equipment and take it down more quickly than ever before. Crews for an ABC baseball game were given only two hours to get the operations ready to go; they were
still soldering wires 5 minutes before game time. Communication between the production truck and the video replay truck wasn't established until the 4th inning.

But cutting costs can only save so much money. So the networks sought other
means to generate revenue. What has emerged in the past five years is an entrepreneurial attitude that has resulted in the networks telecasting sporting events—with
little regard for their intrinsic merit—that someone will sponsor. Beatrice Foods
came to CBS and asked the network to cover the Chicago Marathon. A deal was
made and the network presented a 90-minute edited version of the race. Beatrice
picked up the tab. Alpo wanted the network to reinstate its coverage of the Iditarod
Dog Sled Races. When the dog food maker agreed to buy one-quarter of the spots
on the telecast, CBS reinstated the program.

In 1986 CBS vice-president for sports programming, Neal Pilsm, told a seminar
sponsored by the International Events Group, that sponsors should bring events to
the network. If a sponsor is willing to buy between 25 and 50 percent of the advertising time, the network will carry it and put the sponsor's name on the event as well.
That is why we have had the Mercedes Horse Jumping Championships, the Pizza
Hut All-Star Classics softball tournament, McDonald's High School All-American
Basketball game, the Sunkist Fiesta Bowl, the AT&T Tennis Challenge.

In addition to filling valuable network time with low-significance sporting events,
the sponsors carry additional clout. In May of 1987, ABC ran three minutes beyond
its scheduled coverage (and into the local affiliates' time) when it covered the Shearson-Lehman Brothers Tennis Tournament. The extended coverage was not the result of the network's attempt to bring viewers an exciting conclusion to the match, a
laudable move. The match was over; the sponsor insisted the network stay on the air
so a Shearson-Lehman vice-president could be televised giving the winner an oversized check.

In many instances sponsorship has become more important than ratings in determining what is telecast and what is not. The telecasts of golf matches have always
been ratings losers, but the executives at major companies enjoy watching these telecasts and haven't hesitated to sponsor them. At the same time, important international events—formerly telecast—have been dropped at times for lack of a sponsor.
World track competitions, the world bobsled championships, the world speed skating
championships are just three such events. In 1990 Turner Broadcasting sponsored a
world sporting competition, the Goodwill Games, and beamed hours and hours of
programming around the world. Among the highlight events was men's basketball,
which got primetime coverage for several evenings. Yet the very next month none of
the networks telecast the World Basketball Championships, certainly a more prestigious event, but one without a sponsor.

The ultimate extension of the philosophy is to create pseudo sporting events for television, ones that would not exist without sponsorship, such as the Subaru NFL Fastest Man contest, Minolta Presents the Stakes Games Tennis, and so on.

A serious question looms as television gets more and more involved in the coverage of sports. That is, as *Sports Illustrated* magazine has noted, the problem of indistinguishable interests. Sports are more than games in the 1990s. They involve business, big business. Labor disputes are not uncommon. Television approaches these phenomena in a neutral pose. Yet can it truly be neutral, when the interests of the team owners are so closely tied to the interests of television? Take the National Football League strike in 1987 when, for a month, most of the players in the league refused to perform. After a week's delay, the league fielded teams with pickup players and the scheduled games were held—and more importantly, televised. This broke the strike. What if television had refused to carry these games? By telecasting these contests the networks sided with the owners in the dispute. It was business as usual. Refusal to telecast these games would have hurt both the owners and the networks, but it clearly would have strengthened the hand of the striking players. When the interests of the television industry and the sports industry become indistinguishable, there can be no neutrality.

## Commercials as Programs

The ultimate in using television to make money is to turn the programming into one long commercial. Television has recently done this in two ways, with home shopping channels and with program length commercials.

Home shopping via television hit America like a whirlwind in 1986. Soon there were more than 30 stations and several networks all vying for the attention of the bored viewer with an active credit card. The Home Shopping Network, the most visible of the bunch, at one time was capable of reaching 55 million American homes. Through the use of 800-numbers that gave customers free long-distance dialing and the ubiquitous credit cards, the HSN was shipping out between 25,000 and 30,000 items each day. Six hundred operators were standing by to take your telephone order for what was usually closeout, liquidated, or overstock goods that HSN latched onto for close to nothing. In 1988 total revenues for the home shopping networks and channels totaled $1.8 billion. And then, for a reason yet to be determined, the bottom fell out.

By 1990 there were only three networks left, the Home Shopping Network, the Quality Value Channel, and J. C. Penney—Shop Television Network. The J. C. Penney channel is really a video version of the store catalog and really doesn't resemble the other channels. Revenues fluttered below the $2 billion mark. That sounds like a lot, but total U.S. retail sales in 1989 were $1.6 trillion.

The Council of Better Business Bureaus evaluated the TV shopping services in 1988 and reported that these companies did a good job in filling orders—most customers got what they ordered. The agency called the discounted prices "fanciful." The claimed low retail prices were actually higher than the prices in the stores for the limited amount of merchandise that could even be found in the stores. The Better Business Bureau reported that more than 85 percent of the material was unavailable in stores. Researchers discovered that between 10 and 20 percent of the audience for these programs purchase products; in fact, a few people buy a lot, most don't buy anything.

Dedicating entire channels to selling products, 24-hours-per-day is certainly not sinful or evil. But it certainly demonstrates that the so-called obligation of television to serve the public interest, to meet community needs, to be what it is—the most incredible communications tool yet invented—is an obligation that many in the industry regard rather lightly.

Program-length commercials (PLCs)—or infomercials as they are called in the industry—are not a new phenomenon. What is new, however, is their blatant proliferation throughout the industry, due at least in part to a ruling by the Federal Communication Commission. Under this ruling a local television station with exclusive rights to a syndicated television program (say "Family Ties," for example) may bar cable companies in its area from showing the same program when it is carried on distant stations imported by the cable system or superstations. So if the cable companies can't telecast "Family Ties," then why not substitute Brenda Vaccaro's "Light His Fire" course in that time slot. The infomercials often are telecast on local television stations as well.

These shows frequently have the appearance of a real television show. In "TV Insiders With Investigator Vince Inneo" the program opens with a man in a trench coat boarding a small airplane, apparently off to take on a dark enemy in some distant venue. But Vince Inneo's mission is a bit more mundane; it is to sell bee pollen, portrayed on the program as a cure-all and sexual tonic. Other programs look like talk shows, interview shows, self-help programs, even documentary news broadcasts. Producers and stations are required to identify these programs as advertisements only once, at the beginning of the broadcast.

A researcher at the University of Wisconsin, Rader Hayes, reported that the number of such PLCs shown in her region reached 12,665 in 1988, six times more than in 1985. Revenues to the producers of such shows were expected to reach $750 million in 1990, a substantial increase over the $450 million earned in 1989. Critics of the programs say that viewers are often misled into thinking these are real programs; the normal defenses they erect when watching advertising messages are let down. "Even if you know it's a commercial," said Hayes, "you are getting all the messages that it is a show." Stations should be forced to identify these as commercials several times during the broadcast, these critics assert.

Other critics find a deeper flaw; they decry the use of valuable broadcast time by a merchant to hawk wares. This is hardly serving the public interest; this is hardly the best way to use these powerful communication channels. But broadcasting is a business. As long as the broadcaster needs a program to attract an audience to the commercial message, the program will be telecast. But if viewers are willing to come along only to watch the commercial, well, so much the better for the broadcaster. They can simply sell the entire 30 minutes to the sponsor rather than four-and-a-half or five minutes. And viewers can watch Barbi Benton teach them to "Play the Piano Overnight," or Dick Clark talk about "Is There Love After Marriage?" or E. G. Marshall extol "A Stop Smoking Breakthrough." An industry poll revealed that 90 percent of the nation's commercial stations ran infomercials. In the top ten TV markets (the largest cities), a station can earn as much as $15,000 for running a 30-minute PLC on a weekend afternoon.

While technically not program-length commercials, the dozens of children's programs featuring toys are a very close cousin. Prior to 1984 the FCC had a strict limit on the number of commercial minutes that could be broadcast on children's television. Children's television was the only kind of television where the government mandated strict commercial limits. Twelve minutes of commercials per hour were

In 1984 the government lifted its ban on the telecast of cartoon programs (like "The Smurfs") that had obvious merchandise tie-ins. Before Congress ordered the Federal Communications Commission to re-evaluate its decision in 1990, more than 75 such shows had turned up on television, most subsidized directly by toymakers.

permitted on weekdays; 9-and-one-half minutes on weekends. But in 1984 the FCC lifted this limit. The marketplace (i.e., viewers) would determine how many commercial messages should properly be carried in kids' programming.

But nobody asked the viewers, and the toy industry in a burst of energy began generating 30-minute cheaply animated programs featuring the denizens of toy departments: He Man and Masters of the Universe, GI Joe, Jem, The Transformers, She Ra, Care Bears, Pound Puppies, and others. Toy manufacturers have not tried to hide the fact that programs are subsidized by money from their marketing budgets. The shows are not expected to make money. As one Hasbro executive said, "The shows are part of the overall marketing effort . . . they're not designed to produce revenues." Broadcasting stations can acquire these programs at a very low price. Some companies even provide stations with a percentage of the income generated in their market by the sale of the particular toy. The programs are heavily promoted by the stations and the toy companies. This makes them popular and builds ratings for the stations. Quality children's programming, which does exist, is much more expensive for the station to purchase. The station gets no kickbacks, and there is rarely heavy promotion. The good shows must fight an uphill battle against the super heroes to even get on the air.

In late 1990 Congress passed legislation which reimposed limits on the number of commercial minutes that could be telecast during children's programming: 12 minutes per hour on weekdays, 10 and-one-half minutes on weekends. The legislation also instructed the Federal Communications Commission to carefully consider how a broadcaster served the needs of youthful viewers before granting a license renewal to a television station. Finally, Congress ordered the FCC to undertake an investigation of the 30-minute toy commercials that paraded as children's programs. President George Bush said he didn't like the legislation but let it become law without his signature. The FCC investigated the programs as instructed by Congress, and in 1991 ruled that the 30-minute animated toy-related cartoons would only be considered program-length commercials if the shows included paid advertisements for the same toy (i.e. GI Joe toys are advertised on the GI Joe Show).

## ■ HUTS, PUTS, and WUTS

It's not as if the television networks don't have enough problems. Costs of making television programs are going up; the network audience is dwindling; critics charge that broadcasters are turning the once proud edifices of network television into a shopping mall. Then, in 1990, the networks' primary constituency, the advertisers, lower the boom. They don't think the networks are being aboveboard in charging for the commercial minutes they sell; not nearly as many people are watching these commercials as the networks claim. The cry of foul echoed through the dark canyons of Madison Avenue. Network officials responded like many other corporate officials would respond to such a charge; they blamed someone else—in this case, A. C. Nielsen, the company which counts the heads of all those who watch television each evening.

Both the advertisers and the networks had been unhappy about the ratings for some time. This will be discussed in a moment. But in the late spring of 1990 unhappiness could no longer truly describe the mood. The networks were about to open their "upfront" selling season, when advertisers were expected to plunk down upwards of $4 billion to buy time on programs for the 1990–91 season. Selling prices are supposedly determined by projecting potential audience size for specific programs based on current or past ratings. But in reality, the advertisers have no idea what they are buying. But that's okay, because the networks have no idea of what they are selling either. "With more than $4 billion on the table, it might be logical to think that somebody would have a better grasp of what is going on than a tourist playing three-card monte or shell games in Times Square," noted a *New York Times* writer. "But the network television business is increasingly taking the shape of a floating game with all but indecipherable rules," the journalist added.

It was in the spring of 1990 that the A. C. Nielsen Co. announced that network television viewing had dropped by 4 percent since mid-January, the most precipitous decline in the history of the medium if the report was accurate. Sponsors suddenly cried whoa, and the networks were faced with losing as much as $360 million before the presale of 1990–91 time was completed. All three then turned on A. C. Nielsen, claiming that the ratings were inaccurate, that they didn't jibe with other data the networks had gathered. The rating system was flawed, the networks argued. People in the rating sample weren't properly participating and so on. In a fit of anger in June of 1990, all three television networks announced they would use a new system for estimating the number of viewers who watched their programs, ending complete reliance on the Nielsen data. But by the following year, all three networks had dropped this new system, which was very unpopular with advertisers who complained that ABC, CBS and NBC were inflating their audience levels. The networks went back to Nielsen, but hinted they would seek a competitor for the Nielsen Company, which enjoys a virtual monopoly in this field. Few took this latter threat seriously. CBS had tried this before and it proved to be a costly failure.

The seller, in this case the networks, must establish a fair price for its goods, the audience it brings to their television sets daily. The buyer, in this case the advertiser, will pay a fair price, if he/she is assured that there is a fair count. No shopper would buy a bag of apples at 59 cents a pound if the store owner first refused to weigh the fruit. Advertisers will complain until they are assured that they are getting a fair count; when the network reports that 30 million HUTs are tuned in to "L.A. Law," there are in fact 30 million homes tuned in. Unfortunately measuring the size of the audience is not a precise science. Some in the industry don't regard it as a science at all, rather as a black art. Let's take a look at the ratings for a minute, for they too explain a little bit more about why we see what we see on television.

## ◻ The Ratings

Broadcast ratings are almost as old as broadcasting. Radio programs had ratings as early as the 1930s. But the ratings were probably never more important to advertisers and to the broadcasting industry as they are today. The ratings determine how much the advertisers must pay when their commercials are telecast, and with the price of television time at an all-time high, advertisers are more concerned than ever that they get their money's worth.

While the ratings are really a business tool used by the television industry and advertisers, there is a certain amount of public curiosity about them as well. Many newspapers now carry the list of the highest rated shows each week. *TV Guide* annually publishes the ratings for most network shows. But these lists of top rated programs tend to be somewhat misleading. The television show that has the highest rating each week is not necessarily the most popular. The ratings — even if they are 100 percent accurate — only measure how many people watched a particular show on a particular night. Popularity certainly plays a part in a show's rating. But the number of people watching television on a given night is also a factor. And the other programs that are being telecast at the same time is also important. A program's rating is really only an indication of the popularity of a particular program, compared with other program options that existed at the same time. A particular program might win high ratings when it is broadcast at 10 P.M. on Wednesday nights because the other programs on at the same time are not at all interesting to most viewers. The same show might earn significantly lower ratings if it were broadcast at a different time, when more popular programs are on the other channels. For many years *Gidget Goes Hawaiian* was one of the highest rated movies ever shown on television. This was because the film was broadcast at the same time as two very low rated public affairs programs on the other network channels. Remember what was said earlier; the size of the television audience on any given evening is remarkably stable. And it is the network's goal to capture the largest share of that audience with the least objectionable program.

Two large companies, A. C. Nielsen and the American Research Bureau (ARB) conduct most of the ratings for American television today. The Nielsen company has a lock on the national television ratings, and its National Television Index or NTI is the standard for the industry. But both ARB and Nielsen serve local television stations as well. The rating services sell their data to the networks, advertising agencies, production companies, syndicators, advertisers, and television stations. A major advertising agency might pay as much as $750,000 to $1 million per year for a complete collection of Nielsen numbers. The TV networks pay considerably more. The rating services generate substantial amounts and kinds of data. The two most widely touted numbers, however, are the **rating** number and the **share**. The rating number is based on the total number of HUTs in the United States, about 93 million in 1991. The rating a program receives is a percentage of that number. A program with a rating of 20, then, was watched in 18.6 million homes. The share is a percentage of the viewing audience on that particular night, at that particular time, that watched a show. Imagine that viewing is taking place in 60 million HUTs. TV sets in 15 million of those homes are tuned to "Empty Nest." The program earns a 25 share, or 25 percent of all sets turned on at that time.

These numbers demonstrate one of the most serious problems faced by the men and women who make television programs. The lowest rated show in any given season usually earns at least a rating of 9. That means that viewers in more than 8 million homes watch that show each week. That could reasonably be as many as 15 or 20 million people. Yet the show is a failure; it is the lowest rated program on television. A novel can be a best seller if it sells 500,000 copies. Few record albums sell more than a million copies. A play that fills a 1,000 seat theater every night for three years is seen by just a few more than 1 million people. If 10 million people see a movie, it is considered a success. But a television program can draw as many as 20 million viewers each week and still be a monumental failure. It is a strange world, the world of television.

Network television is constantly rated, day in and day out. The ratings for the programs aired the previous day are released to Nielsen customers early the next morning. By mid-1990 local television stations in the 24 largest markets also had access to overnight ratings. But local television generally is rated only four times a year during what are called **sweeps**. Sweep months are November, February, May, and July. During these months Johnny Carson (Jay Leno starting in 1992) works each night of the week, no reruns, no guest hosts. These are the months when the networks unleash their blockbuster movies and miniseries. This is a time when both local stations and the networks bring out their best to entice viewers into their corner. Ratings gleaned during these months set advertising rates for the local stations for the next three months.

Both Nielsen and ARB represent local stations during the sweeps. Diaries are used to gather the data. Each company mails out 200,000 diaries during sweep months, according to *Wall Street Journal* reporter Bill Abrams. They hope to get half of them back. That means, notes Abrams, that diaries sent to between 200 and 1,500 homes determine the ratings in a given city. Survey participants receive a token payment for their cooperation. Networks program aggressively during this period to please the affiliates. It is also true that a strong affiliate can help network programming in the long run. Most people agree that the sweeps are an abomination, blitzing the audience with better programming for 30 days, only to be followed by the traditional drivel for two succeeding months. But local stations cannot afford the $400,000 to $750,000 needed for year-round ratings, according to Pierre Mergoz, Arbitron vice-president. As it is, larger stations must pay up to $100,000 a year for the quarterly data.

The Nielsen NTI is constructed upon a national sample of 4,000 homes, whose occupants supposedly represent the viewing habits of the remainder of the people in the 93 million plus American homes using television—HUTs. Until the fall of 1987 the Nielsen company gathered its data in two ways. First, a tiny audimeter was attached to the television set in some of the homes in the sample. This audimeter recorded when the set was on and what channel was being watched. Additionally, Nielsen asked families in another segment of the sample to fill out diaries each week that listed the programs they watched. The diaries were supposed to provide the rating company with demographic data on what kinds of people (men vs. women, rich vs. poor) watch what kinds of programs.

There were two flaws in this system. The audimeters recorded when the set was on, but could not tell if anyone was watching the program being telecast. And the diaries were notoriously inaccurate. People were supposed to fill them out as they watched television, but most waited until the end of the week and by that time often forgot what they had watched. People often thought they watched heavily promoted shows because of the promotion, not because they watched the program. Others were embarrassed to note they watched some shows. The elderly and teenagers took the diaries far more seriously and did a better job of filling them out. The results were skewed toward those groups. All in all, few were happy with the results.

Then Nielsen introduced the people meters, a ratings device that had actually been pioneered by a competing company, AGB of Great Britain. In each Nielsen household a meter about the size of a stereo tuner is wired to the television set. The meter automatically records when the set is turned on, and the channel that is being viewed. In addition to the meter, however, is a small remote control key pad that resembles a pocket calculator. Each member of the household is assigned a number, from one to eight. When a household member begins watching television, he or she presses his or her assigned number button on the key pad. This is called logging into the meter. When the individual stops viewing, he or she logs out by pushing the numbered button again. While the viewing takes place, every 9 or 10 minutes, a

Television networks and advertisers today are as interested in who is watching as how many viewers are tuned to a particular show. The people meter used by A.C. Nielsen, the giant research company, permits the various members of sample families to log-in or tell the computer who is watching the set by pushing a button on a small box.
(A.C. Nielsen)

light flashes on the meter, or words appear briefly on the screen, reminding people to log in, in case they have forgotten. The meter collects data all day long, and then at night, the data is relayed from the collector box in the meter to the company's main computer via telephone lines. The people meter, then, combines the properties of the audimeter, which automatically records when the set is on, and the diaries, which generated demographic data.

But the system is not without its flaws, some of which were common to the old data-gathering methods as well. First, there is a sample bias; that is, the 4,000 households probably don't accurately mirror the total viewing audience. To get into the Nielsen sample an individual must be a regular television viewer. There are lots of Americans who view television quite selectively. But it would not do the rating service much good to fill its sample with people who don't watch much television. Immediately the mirror image the sample purports to represent is distorted. There is a 50 percent turn-down rate by persons asked to be in the sample as well; this bothers statisticians who claim it is unusually high. Because of these two factors alone the demographic profile of the persons in the sample is awry. The Nielsen sample tends to over-represent older people, and under-represent the poor, minorities, teenagers, younger men and women, and the wealthy.

Only about 85 percent of the 4,000 sample members are actually in the sample at any given time. There are equipment failures, people out of town, people who quit and haven't been replaced. There is a substantial turnover annually; 1,300 persons wanted out of the sample after the first year the people meters were in place. The Nielsen sample does not take into account out-of-home viewing. The networks and Nielsen became concerned about this in 1988. CBS and ABC commissioned a study which revealed that millions of persons watch television each week in taverns, hotels and motels, residence halls, nursing homes and hospitals, prisons, military bases, and several other venues that are not included in the Nielsen head count. Nielsen itself reported in May of 1990 that its rating service may miss as many as 6 percent of the people viewing television at any given time. ABC's Monday Night Football may have as many as 5 million more viewers each week than are counted by the NTI because of the heavy out-of-home viewing of this contest.

Finally, many question the reliability of the sample when the participants are asked to play such an active and continuing role in the data-gathering process. Is an individual who is willing to log in and log out each time they view television representative of the broader American public?

For all the sophistication involved in the data-gathering process, the ratings of television programs developed by Nielsen and ARB often differ substantially, often by as much as 2 to 3 points. Three points is almost 3 million homes—6 to 7 million viewers. For a program with ratings problems, two to three points can often mean the difference between renewal and cancellation.

The new rating system has one additional flaw that seriously worries advertisers. It doesn't reveal much about those who watch programs they have taped with their VCRs. The people meters can tell when a program is recorded, but they cannot tell when a program is played back. Research into this problem has revealed some interesting findings that give the advertisers cause for concern.

Studies have revealed that three-fourths of all programs that are recorded are not being watched when they are recorded. Of this three-fourths, 80 percent are played back at some point. But half the time when a program is played back, the viewer fast forwards through the commercials. This is called **zapping** the commercials. Let's put these percentages into perspective. Imagine that 100 television shows are recorded. The advertisers pay for people watching these shows. But we know that no one is watching when 75 of these programs are recorded. Of these 75 programs, 80 percent, or 60 shows, are played back. When these 60 are played back, the viewer fast forwards through the commercials during 30 of these programs. So, while the advertisers have paid for 100 shows, the commercials are only seen on 55 of these shows, the 25 that were viewed when they were recorded, and the other 30 that are not zapped when they are played back. From the advertiser's standpoint, that is not such a good deal. And at present Nielsen has no way to determine whether or not the results of this rather extensive study are duplicated every night in the United States.

The networks would like some changes in the rating system provided by Nielsen. They argue that the rating company should improve its technique in approaching people to be in the sample to reduce the turndown rate. The participating households should be replaced more frequently than every two years, the current standard. Families tire of using the meter, network officials contend, and this causes them to fail to fully and diligently participate. There is only slight monetary compensation to the family or individual who is included in the sample. To pay people to be in the survey would undermine the reliability of the sample, Nielsen contends. The keypads should be easier to use so children will be more likely to use them, the networks argue. And Nielsen should do more research to determine the veracity of the ratings. Nielsen promised to study possible improvements.

Many in the industry would like to see a passive metering system developed. Now the participant must actively log in when viewing begins. With a passive system each family member would wear a bracelet or lapel pin which emits an electronic code to the meter. The meter can then automatically record who is watching, and when they get up and leave.

There are systems that are more sophisticated than the people meters used by Nielsen and others. Scan America operates a service for advertisers that ties television viewing to shopping. Television viewing is recorded with a standard people metering system. But attached to the meter is a wand that can read the universal product codes printed on most goods today. When participants return from shopping, they pass the wand over the UPCs on the products they have purchased. This data is also recorded by the meter. The advertiser can then correlate the viewing of television with purchasing decisions. Scan American expected to have 5,000 sample homes by 1992 in a dozen or more markets. Even more elaborate market research is done in a handful of communities where families selected for the sample are asked to screen special commercials from time to time for real products. The purchases made by the family are recorded at the supermarkets where they shop when they go through specially designated check-out lanes with price scanners tied to the researcher's computer.

Critics of this research are concerned about the kinds of persons who are willing to play guinea pig. Typically, the tired adult who picks up a few bags of groceries on the way home from work is not going to find scanning the UPCs with a wand as the goods are put away something enjoyable or even tolerable. And if the folks who are willing to play these games are substantially different from the general population, the data that are generated by this research are suspect at best.

# NEWS AND PUBLIC AFFAIRS

News and public affairs programming came to television a bit too late. The medium was conceived in terms of entertainment; its journalistic role has been and remains subordinated in the eyes of the people who control the medium. Only since the late 1970s, when news was first perceived as a money making venture, have news departments at local stations been given the time needed to telecast even a minimal amount of news. Unfortunately other station dicta have frequently deprived the broadcast journalists of the opportunity to approach the coverage of news in a serious fashion during these expanded newscasts. Network newsmen and newswomen still are tied to 30 minutes of evening news, and hard news inserts in the morning talk and interview programs like "The Today Show."

When television news is permitted to do its best nothing can equal its power in telling many stories and mobilizing public sentiment toward an issue. For months the *Washington Post,* one of the nation's leading newspapers, published long reports describing the Watergate controversy and cover-up. But it barely made a dent in public opinion on the matter. It was *Post* assistant managing editor Harry Rosenfeld who noted that the Watergate story did not finally gain the necessary national attention until Walter Cronkite and the "CBS Evening News" presented a lengthy report on the matter. It was television documentaries that generated instant awareness of the problems of the migrant workers ("The Harvest of Shame" and "Migrant"), malnutrition ("Hunger in America"), pollution ("Silent Spring"), and Pentagon public information practices ("The Selling of the Pentagon"). Each of the issues had been thoughtfully and widely discussed in the printed press.

The power of global television was demonstrated in August of 1991 during an attempted coup in Russia. Anti-totalitarian forces were aided in repelling the plotters by a vast constituency assembled electronically inside and outside the Soviet Union. Earlier this power was seen when Tom Brokaw and the "NBC Nightly News" telecast a story on the starving people of Ethiopia. The story had been told in print for months; the famine was years old. But the pictures of a three-year-old child dying from hunger in the arms of his mother stirred the nation and generated the outpouring of aid from this and other nations. President Bush's speech announcing war with Iraq was viewed in almost 75 million homes in 1991, and became a potent element in mobilizing public opinion to support the war.

Public affairs programming can also educate, as we dramatically saw when the Public Broadcasting Service telecast the BBC's "Civilisation" series more than 20 years ago. Other documentary series like this (i.e., "The Living Planet" and "The Smithsonian") have caught the imagination of millions of viewers and generated heretofore untapped curiosity about the world around us. And television's ability to take the viewer where the news is being made is unparalleled. The 200 million Americans who had paid for his ticket accompanied Neil Armstrong via television as he stepped onto the surface of the moon. Viewers were also at Cape Canaveral on January 28, 1986 as the space shuttle Challenger exploded into an angry fireball just moments after launch.

Yet today broadcast journalism is beset by a series of complex and seemingly contradictory problems, most of which stem from the same concern for rating points that bedevils entertainment television. Documentaries and other primetime public affairs programs have all but disappeared from the three commercial networks. The

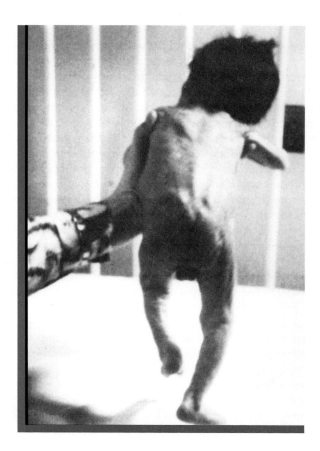

The sixty-minute, single-subject, prime-time documentaries have almost disappeared from commercial television. But in the 1960s programs such as "Hunger in America," (which revealed that millions of Americans, especially children, were starving to death in this land of plenty) were telecast frequently, and had a major impact on public policy decisions.
(CBS News)

blurring of news and entertainment has seriously devalued the quality of the news at many local stations and in network magazine format programs. And the personalization of the news product through the growing power and importance of the "news anchor" suggests to some that the medium is getting in the way of the message. Let's explore broadcast journalism briefly and attempt to better understand its great strengths and serious weaknesses.

## ▢ The Documentary

If there was a golden age of television documentaries it was in the 1960s. Former CBS producer Burton Benjamin recalled in 1989 that within the span of a few weeks in 1960 CBS broadcast "Harvest of Shame," NBC broadcast "The U-2 Affair," and ABC broadcast "Yanki No," all in prime time. Each of these programs would be on a television critic's list of the "ten best shows of the year" in the 1990s. In 1963 NBC cleared its entire prime-time schedule one night for "The Negro Revolution." The network gave the same amount of time for an exploration of American foreign policy. ABC carried a four-hour program on Africa. These were all important television programs, and like many other documentaries that could be named from that era, they had an important impact on both viewers and public policy.

"Today's television newsmen are largely without influence; they cause nothing to happen and nothing to change," noted Lawrence Grossman, former president of NBC News, in early 1990. "There have been no serious, in-depth prime documentaries televised in recent months on my former network," he added. Nor on the other commercial networks, it should be noted.

The long form, single topic, primetime documentary was the victim of several forces. Many persons in the industry consider it an article of faith that any entertainment program—even the lowest rated television series—can get stronger ratings than a documentary. To a certain extent they are right, but for the wrong reasons. Entertainment programs will often do better because they are regularly scheduled which permits the viewers to follow them. Documentaries are simply dropped into the television schedule, frequently in a time slot that the network already conceded to its competitors who have scheduled strong programs. Richard Salant, for years the head of CBS News, accuses the networks of trying to hide the documentary programs. "They put them in places where they'll do the least damage. You want to see where the competition is going to run the Oscars [the presentation program] and you put them there. If you had regularity, so people will know they're coming, once a week, and it's a habit, and you know sufficiently in advance so you can publicize them, advertise them. Sometimes we're not even told [when they will be broadcast] in time to get a listing [in the newspaper or *TV Guide*]," Salant said.

But documentary programs can win big ratings, as well as prestige. When CBS presented "The Defense of the United States" for one primetime hour on five successive nights during a week in June the program drew a huge audience. But the network invested heavily in the five-night presentation, strongly promoting the programs. In addition to winning a big audience, the show got rave reviews and captured several awards. Similarly ABC's three-hour documentary on the nuclear age, "The Fire Unleashed," also garnered a large audience. Again, the program was highly visible and widely promoted.

Even a documentary that doesn't reach a huge audience may be a good buy for an advertiser. "We get a serious, well-educated audience—the *Harper's* and *Atlantic* audience—and the impact is greater than the numbers," noted Les Midgley of NBC News. Many advertisers desire to reach such an audience and if the networks would play it a bit straighter with their bookkeeping practices, many primetime documentary programs could easily show a profit. Network programmers often justify their decision to abandon the long-form documentary by pointing to the accounting ledgers. Documentaries don't make money for the network. At one time that didn't worry network officials. Former CBS News president Salant said that 20 years ago the network's "bottom-liners" did not expect the network news divisions to turn a profit. He said at a 1990 conference on broadcast journalism that he took pride in being known at CBS as "the executive in charge of losing money." Since the sitcoms were prospering, news programs and documentaries could be written off as prestigious loss leaders.

That is not the case today. And bookkeeping practices at the networks make it difficult for even a documentary that attracts a large audience to make money. "I can make any given news show profitable or unprofitable, depending on bookkeeping," noted a top network news executive quoted by media analyst Jeff Greenfield. "For example, who gets charged for studio and crew costs on a news program? The news division? Or the network division? What about compensation costs we pay affiliates for the time when a network news program runs?" If it is charged to the news program, the show may lose money. If it is charged to the network, the show might end up in the black, he added.

Even a network documentary program that ostensibly shows a profit when costs are subtracted from revenues might be deemed a loser by the network accountants, who will argue that an entertainment program could have generated a bigger profit if it, rather than the public affairs special, had been shown.

But economics were not the only force that knocked out the primetime documentaries. The success of the magazine format shows (especially CBS's "60 Minutes") also helped close the door on this chapter of American television. The magazine format show is considered more attractive by network officials because by offering reports on three or four topics, it has the potential to draw a much larger audience. Also, the program can offer a mix of weekly topics, from the serious (the burning of the Amazon rain forests) to the sexy (Miami police clamp down on porno parlors) to the frivolous (an interview with Tom Cruise). But even with these advantages, it is doubtful that the magazine format would have become the dominant primetime public affairs format if "60 Minutes" had not been so successful.

The show began in a traditional primetime slot—10 P.M. on Tuesdays—more than 20 years ago and floundered. The ratings were barely better than "CBS Reports," the documentary hour that had previously occupied this time slot. The show was moved to 6 P.M. on Sundays where it captured a larger audience and finally to 7 P.M. that same evening. Since then the show has ranked as one of the most popular on television. In 1987 "60 Minutes" was the network's most profitable program, earning a profit of $70 million a year, according to its producer Don Hewitt. Its success continues into the 1990s.

The program was successful for reasons beyond its magazine format. The program appealed to an adult audience, while both ABC and NBC featured "family" or children's programming in that time slot. Its relentless prosecutorial tone created weekly morality plays, the good guys (Mike Wallace, Harry Reasoner, Morley Safer, Ed Bradley, Diane Sawyer, et al.) against the bad guys (thieves, rip-off artists, dishonest politicians, corporations involved in dirty dealings, labor unions, and so on). In corporate America the announcement to a chief executive that "there's a '60 Minutes' crew outside to interview you" carries a vision of doom comparable to the declaration, "a man from the Internal Revenue Service is waiting to see you." But the program has rarely tackled tough, complicated issues like arms control or the budget deficit or rising Third World nationalism. Former CBS producer Benjamin calls the show a western, the white hats against the black hats. And while he says he admires the accomplishments of the "60 Minutes" team, he is bothered by producer Don Hewitt's proclamation that there is "no story you can do in an hour documentary that we couldn't do in a '60 Minutes' segment." "Fine," Benjamin said. "So we will do 'Harvest of Shame,' 'The Selling of the Pentagon,' 'The Defense of the United States,' and 'Justice Black and the Bill of Rights' on the head of a pin." Benjamin said the current wisdom in television is that people have neither the patience nor intellectual capacity to deal with anything longer than 20 minutes. "I do not believe that is true. If it is, it is a pity and we have lost something valuable. We can, for openers, strike the verb 'to contemplate' from the language," he said.

ABC copied the "60 Minutes" format with some success in "20/20." NBC tried several different shows; all failed. Even CBS has been unable to come close to succeeding with similar magazine shows like "Magazine," "30 Minutes," and "57th Street." Regardless, network executives have seen the bottom-line potential of such shows and have shifted their public affairs resources to this arena.

The one other element that has worked against the documentary format is the cult of personality currently in vogue at the networks. What is said is not nearly so important as who is saying it. It started with Barbara Walters's celebrity interviews and moved in recent years to "Saturday Night with Connie Chung," and "Prime Time Live" with Sam Donaldson and Diane Sawyer. Again, the thought is that more people will tune in to see someone they admire or like talk about almost anything than will tune in to watch a program on an important topic. The ratings have not sustained the faith in this notion, but the idea dies hard at the networks.

## ☐ Television News

News came late to television, much as it did to radio. Twenty years after the medium was first introduced to the nation the three networks still offered only 15 minutes of news each day, and local stations rarely presented more than 30 minutes of such programming. Presentation of the news was considered a public service; nothing less, nothing more. It was not expected to generate serious revenues for the company.

By the 1970s, however, this conception of news had changed. The American public developed an increasing appetite for television news. At the networks this meant increased ratings for the early evening news shows. Network news shows began to break even, or even show a small profit. Local television stations also found that news could be profitable. Just as important, news programs provided stations with local identity, a means of bonding with the members of the community. This was an important advantage in selling advertising time for all parts of the day and night.

But network television news hit hard times in the mid-to late 1980s. ABC, CBS, and NBC had all changed owners, and the new owners had borrowed heavily to buy these properties. "What all three networks now had in common," wrote Jeff Greenfield, "was a greatly increased debt-to-equity ratio, and new owners with no link to the old tradition that tended to shield network news from the accountant and cost manager." These owners began asking questions about why news cost so much, why the news divisions didn't generate profits or more profits. Serious cost cutting took place at all three networks. Many longtime network correspondents (with big salaries) were let go in favor of younger, less experienced, and less expensive talent. Some foreign and domestic bureaus were closed or reduced in size. Investigative reporting diminished. A softening of the news package, to try to lure more viewers and increase ratings, was evident. "Increasingly the pressure is on to tailor a product to affect a wider audience as opposed to tailoring a product that meets its chief responsibility—to offer the most comprehensive look around the world," noted Hodding Carter, a former newspaper publisher and state department spokesman, who analyzed the press on a PBS program entitled "Inside Story." The television news business is increasingly run by folks who would just as soon make widgets, Carter added, "but they're stuck with news, so they run news the same way they run widget making."

At the start of the 1990s, network television news seemed to be regaining a solid economic footing when the conflict in the Persian Gulf began. The all-out coverage of the military build-up and the war cost the networks tens of millions of dollars. NBC executives reported that the network spent nearly $50 million on its coverage. While the costs of news coverage were going up, many advertisers shrank away from buying commercial minutes during the war, fearful of alienating viewers. So revenues shrank. In the late spring of 1991, executives at all three networks said that news budgets and news staffs would likely be cut to try to recoup these losses.

Today each of the networks offer a solid 30-minute news program each evening, weekends included. "Given the 22 minutes a night the producers have to work with, their packaging and pacing is consistently professional and sometimes illuminating," noted *New York Times* television critic, Walter Goodman. "The reporters generally know what they are about and the viewer who relies on them can count on at least finding out what's going on and sometimes why," he added. The networks also offer late, late night newscasts, early, early morning newscasts, and news on their wakeup programs, "Today," "This Morning," and "Good Morning America." These three programs at one time were bastions of hard news and inter-

PBS's 60-minute "MacNeil-Lehrer Report" is generally regarded as the best (most complete and most helpful) evening newscast on television. After a brief rundown of the headlines of the day, the program features three-to-four long stories each night. Robert MacNeil and Jim Lehrer, who have hosted the program for more than 15 years, are joined by Charlayne Hunter-Gault, Judy Woodruff, and Roger Mudd.
(© Christopher Little, MacNeil-Lehrer Productions)

views, but increasingly they have become the captives of the networks' entertainment divisions. ABC also offers Ted Koppel's "Nightline" each evening. This program started with the Iran hostage-taking crisis in the late 1970s and has continued to play an important journalistic role on television ever since. CBS added a 30-minute late-night news show to its schedule in late 1990. The show, anchored by Charles Kuralt and Lesley Stahl, was broadcast at 11:30 P.M. in New York.

A seriously disquieting network trend in the early 1990s is the cult of the anchor, the tendency to glorify the individual who reads the news each evening. Anchors are useful in bringing in the audiences, many argue. "A familiar face is all that distinguishes the networks from the competition," noted ABC anchor Ted Koppel. But today the trend is to send the anchor to where the news is happening to give the viewer a greater sense of assurance that Dan Rather or Tom Brokaw can tell them what is really going on. "The cult of personality is being raised to new depths," noted Richard Salant at a Columbia University conference on network news. Noting that "the Berlin wall doesn't go down unless the anchor is there," Salant said he wondered whatever happened to the reporters on the beat? Both Dan Rather and Tom Brokaw visited the Persian Gulf region several times during the United States-Iraq conflict in 1990–91. And this reflects a basic truism about network news. The challenge for the three networks is not covering the big stories; that, viewers can take for granted. It is coverage of what former NBC news executive Les Crystal calls the "non-sexy" stories that is of concern. How often, he asked, will the networks go back to Panama (or the Persian Gulf) once the American troops are gone?

Interestingly, while the networks faced cutbacks in the late 1980s, they were facing an increasing challenge to their dominance in television news from an upstart news network called CNN, or the Cable News Network. Ted Turner started the 24-hour-per-day Cable News Network in 1980. Today it is accessible to 52 million cable subscribers, the second most popular cable network. It couldn't be done, critics said. It will cost too much. There isn't enough happening. People won't watch. But CNN has proven them all wrong.

CNN coverage during the Persian Gulf war was regarded by most knowledgeable observers as being superior to that provided by ABC, CBS, or NBC. For many days only CNN had a correspondent in Baghdad. In the midst of the Romanian revolution, when reformers sought to shape a new government, they took over a television station and began to hammer out a new political future for their nation in front of video cameras. The pictures broadcast from that station were transmitted by a Soviet satellite. CNN picked up the signal and broadcast, virtually nonstop, these history-making hours around the globe. When U.S. forces invaded Panama, and the members of the U.S. press pool were stymied in their attempts to gain access to the battle, CNN carried live broadcasts of descriptions of the fighting communicated by persons in the battle zone. The network ran a telephone number under its pictures and urged residents of Panama to call in with eyewitness accounts. More than 2,000 calls were logged in at the network.

CNN has become a major player in the world coverage of news, for not only citizens of this country, but for television viewers around the world. "We have . . . managed to blanket the world with a signal," said Ed Turner, CNN's executive vice-president for newsgathering. The network services nations in the Pacific Rim, Europe and the United Kingdom, Latin America, and the Soviet Union. The word "foreign" is banned at the network to underline the world posture the network has taken.

Several factors give CNN a strong edge in covering breaking news. It telecasts

Viewers became almost intimately acquainted with formerly anonymous television reporters when the war in the Persian Gulf began in January of 1991. CNN provided almost 24-hour-a-day coverage of the war for many months, and reporters like Charles Jaco became as familiar to viewers as their neighbors.

24 hours a day and frequently uses live coverage. When the commercial networks resumed normal programming after the Persian Gulf war started, CNN carried continuous reports on the conflict. This often makes the other network evening newscasts seem stale, even if they are but a few hours old. ABC, CBS, and NBC also have the technical capability to go live. But to do so they have to interrupt the network's daytime or primetime schedules, something that is not permitted by network officials in any situation short of a national emergency. Interruption of regularly scheduled programs angers (1) entertainment divisions, which lose money; (2) the affiliates, who see their own time eaten away by network broadcasts; and (3) many tunnel-visioned viewers who believe what happens in the fantasy world of soap operas or sit-coms is more important than what happens in real life.

Finally, CNN frequently uses indigenous personnel to report international stories. News from Africa is often reported by Africans, rather than U.S. reporters who have flown to Africa to report the news for a few days. "Capitalizing on these advantages, CNN's global network has made the global village a reality," wrote Nicols Fox in the *Washington Journalism Review.* "In fact, it's out of fashion to have a war or a revolution these days without it," Fox adds.

A serious problem for all television news is a lack of African American, Hispanic, and Asian American reporters. "The fact is," wrote Ed Planer, formerly a vice-president of NBC news, "white men, white women, black men, and black women, all get to sit in the anchor seat, but when it comes to the troops in the field, the stories are done mostly by white males." Planer points out that Hispanics are the fastest growing ethnic group in the nation, yet there are very, very few Hispanic correspondents or anchors on the networks. Both ABC and CBS have (in 1990) an Hispanic correspondent based in Miami and they are sent to Latin America when a story calls. And CBS, among all networks, had seven black correspondents in the field. But overall, the networks show a poor record in minority on-air employment. Planer blames this not on racism, but on an unwitting acceptance of things as they are and as they have always been. "It is, at bottom, a failure to recognize that an increasingly multihued society requires diversity amongst those who report it," he said. It is not enough for the networks to trot out the usual statistics on the numbers of minorities who have important positions behind the scenes. "What's out front also counts."

## ☐ Local News

Local television news presents a paradoxical picture in the early 1990s. It has never been more technically sophisticated. Use of electronic newsgathering equipment, satellite transmissions, and computer graphics have given the local news team capabilities that were only dreamed of 20 years ago. More hours of local news are being telecast each day than ever before. Most stations in major to mid-sized markets feature long local news segments in the morning, at noon, and as much as two hours in the dinner-hour day-part. And then there is late night news, followed by a replay of the early evening news in the wee hours of the morning. At the same time, however, many critics say that local news is failing to meet its responsibilities to the community. Advertisers have too much clout in determining the content of news programming, "infotainment" too often replaces hard news, local stations are wasting valuable resources in attempting to duplicate network coverage, and pictures rather than importance dictate what is selected for telecast in too many cases.

The electronic newsgathering gear **(ENG)** is now the standard at virtually all stations. The videotape minicams are taken into the field to record the news on videotape for later editing and telecast. But today at many stations the news crew doesn't need to return to the station. It can broadcast the news live from the scene via their satellite news vehicles, or **SNVs**. "SNV is the new rage, replacing copters and minicams," writes Bert Briller, a former ABC vice-president and media analyst. Technicians can send the television signal from the SNV to a microwave receiving and transmitting station and then back to the station. Or, it can send the signal from virtually anywhere in the United States directly to a satellite and back to the station for storage or live broadcast. The SNVs contain full edit facilities, telephones, and even computers. Development of the Ku-Band frequency, an improved signal transmission system that is much simpler for the broadcaster to use, has made it possible for these small SNVs to transmit reliable signals, free of static and breakup. The Ku-Ban is replacing the old C-Band frequency.

Local broadcasters have used this technology in ways that enhance community coverage. But they have also used the technology to extend their news coverage to stories that are breaking nationally and even internationally. The parking lots at the 1988 national political conventions were filled with satellite news vehicles as local reporters brought news of these media events to the local viewers. More than 4,100 television news people (including producers and technicians) from 338 local TV stations covered the Democratic convention. Local reporters went to Germany when the Berlin Wall came down, and to Panama after the invasion, and to the Middle East during the crisis in the Persian Gulf. Using satellite transmissions, local reporters are now capable of giving a national or international story increased local focus.

The "SNV," or satellite news vehicle, is a common fixture at television stations in larger markets. The truck contains a mini-production studio with transmission facilities. The dish on the van can bounce live or recorded signals off a satellite for relay down back to the station for instant transmission.
(Gary Harper, King Television)

The increasing coverage of national and world events by local television stations has fundamentally changed the relationship between the local stations and the networks. National and international news coverage is one of the most important advantages a network affiliated station has, but today both affiliated and independent stations can generate their own worldwide news coverage.

But these developments have generated controversy as well. Almost all agree that sending a local reporter to cover a national or international story permits the development of a local angle or allows the station to emphasize a part of the story of special interest to local viewers. Television stations in communities with a strong Eastern European ethnic population devoted additional coverage to the destruction of the Iron Curtain and to the democratization of Poland or Yugoslavia.

But critics argue that viewers are often ill served when a local television station sends its reporters abroad. The local coverage often duplicates the network coverage more than it enhances it. The money spent to send a reporter to a political convention or to cover a war could be better spent on enhancing local coverage. Critics also argue that local reporters are often ill prepared to cover national and international stories. Expecting a reporter who has spent the past six years in Baltimore to understand a civil war in El Salvador or a political revolution in the Soviet Union is not realistic; even the network correspondents who are stationed in such faraway places often lack the education or background to provide completely knowledgeable reports on such situations. Finally, the critics argue that using exotic satellite transmissions to permit local anchors and reporters to cover national and international stories is often simply a promotional ploy, not a serious journalistic exercise, another example of television news doing what is technically feasible, not what is journalistically essential.

The exotic new telecasting equipment has only reinforced the broadcast news maxim that any story with pictures is better than any story without pictures. And more than ever, television news, especially at the local level, is defined by what can be photographed.

News producers believe that a story worth telling on television must have pictures, even though some of the most important news of the day does not lend itself to visual explanation. How can you film, for example, the cost-of-living index moving up or down each month? This is certainly news. How can you film the pollution of the forests by acid rain? It is difficult to film a Supreme Court decision or film work on a cure for cancer. Television journalists surely do attempt to cover stories beyond those that can be filmed but visual effects dominate their thinking. Sir Robin Day, a newsman with the BBC, argues that television is designed to strike a viewer's emotions rather than his intellect. The medium concentrates on action rather than thought, on happenings rather than issues, on shock rather than on explanations, on personalities rather than ideas, Day said. "Television does not always take sufficient trouble to ask 'who is responsible?,' 'why is it happening?,' or 'what is the alternative?' " Former NBC chairman of the board Walter Scott noted that "because television is a visual medium, it may scan the background and significance of events to focus on the outward appearance—the comings and goings of heads of state instead of the issues that confront them." Reporter Edwin Newman echoed the ideas of both Day and Scott. "What makes up news programs should be determined by what has happened and not by where you happen to have your cameras on any given day or by the amount of film that's available to illustrate a particular story."

Dependence upon pictures is usually a more serious problem at local television stations. If the news director sends out a camera team to cover a news event and it turns out nothing very important happens, chances are good that the story will be broadcast anyway. The station has an investment in the tape and time and cannot abandon the story. When pictures are available, a story that might deserve 25 seconds when read by the news anchor might be stretched to a minute or 90 seconds. This is a waste of time in a news medium where there is never enough time. Because television equipment is often bulky and must be set up, television is a sucker for the planned story—the news conference, the ribbon cutting, the parade, the public hearing. At times all of these events may be worthy of coverage. But a print journalist, with pad and pencil, is far more flexible than a television camera crew and doesn't have a built-in bias toward news that is planned and easier to cover. This is especially true in the coverage of international news, where a print reporter can often slip into a foreign nation unnoticed. A television crew of four persons and 20 boxes of equipment can hardly act nonchalant as they try to clear customs. Sir Robin notes: "By reasons of its own operational needs, television is incapable of giving fair and balanced reporting of a very large part of the world today. The cameras will go where they're welcome—regardless of where the most important story is."

Back at the studio, electronic devices proliferate as well. Computers will generate virtually any kind of picture conceivable on the screen behind the anchor. At some stations there is no news set; the background (the city at dusk, a view out of a window) is completely computer generated. Charts and pictures enlarge and shrink, zoom in and out, appear as though they are coming out of the screen into the viewer's home. The background for weather forecasters is filled with moving cold fronts and high pressure systems on maps that sparkle. Long gone are the days when the forecaster drew pictures of smiley suns or gloomy clouds on an acetate mapboard to help viewers understand tomorrow's forecast. Bert Briller reported in 1988 that these new "technology toys" are expensive: between $300,000 and $500,000 for an SNV van; $100,000 to $400,000 for a news computer system; $80,000 to $200,000 for a graphics generator; and $20,000 for weather graphics equipment.

Many news departments at local television stations faced serious economic problems in the late 1980s. There was a tremendous spate of buying and selling television stations in the 1980s as FCC limits on the number of stations an individual might own were relaxed. The FCC also abandoned rules requiring a new owner to hold a broadcasting property for three years before selling it. Investors paid top dollar for local stations. These new owners faced problems retiring the debt they incurred for these purchases, as well as the problems of a softening advertising market. The results were tighter budgets. The cost cutting did not hit the gadget mania that infected the stations, nor the promotion-oriented national and world reporting by local reporters. It hit in other ways.

A survey by Vernon Stone at the University of Missouri revealed fairly deep staff reductions in news departments at major markets in the late 1980s. This meant less thorough coverage on some stories, and fewer stories being covered, according to Neal Rosenau in an article in *The Columbia Journalism Review*. Investigative reporting units were abandoned. There were fewer "special projects."

Station management, normally distant from the dirty-hands business of news, suddenly became more interested in their news departments. News director Reagan Ramsey at KGW in Portland, Ore. told Rosenau that "They never come and say, 'How many tenths of a rating point have you changed?' They say, 'What are the things that you've done that really affect your viewing area, and what have you got planned for this next quarter and next year?' "

Many stations were looking for ways in which to increase revenues and found advertisers had some interesting ideas about this. "Advertisers are beginning to decide what kinds of news segments or information programs they want created as vehicles for their messages, and advertising is encroaching directly into news content," wrote Gary Cummings of Northwestern's Medill School of Journalism and a former general manager for WBBM-TV in Chicago. More and more news segments and information broadcasts are being produced primarily for the advertiser, not the viewer, he said. Of course this is akin to what has happened at many daily newspapers.

Cummings also points to segmentation—building a newscast for a particular kind of viewer, the affluent suburban woman (the "pool and patio" set), or the elderly (the "bed pan and walker" set), for example. WLS-TV in Chicago hired several older reporters for their program aimed at the elderly.

Billboards are another device the advertisers asked for and stations, after many years of refusing, agreed to it. These are onscreen graphics that feature the name of the news program and the advertising logo together (Channel 6 Eyewitness News brought to you by Atlee Oil). Stations also agreed to telecast information segments that were developed or generated by the sales department. These first appeared on the network ABC's "Good Morning America," which really isn't a news show. But local stations use these segments in their news shows as well; fashion segments generated by manufacturers like Revlon and J.C. Penney, health segments by Bristol Myers and American Home Products. These segments consume time that might be devoted to real news. "Television news cannot add pages or sections. Television is a zero sum game. For every added feature or segment something must be dropped. A broadcast packed with stories about pools and patios will inevitably 'bump' stories about unemployment, the homeless and the city budget," wrote Cummings.

Finally, more and more stations began to use video news releases to fill out their broadcast time and save some money. VNRs are taped news releases, prepared by a public relations company, and sent to stations with the hopes they will be used on the news. Pharmaceutical companies often disseminate information about new drugs in 90-second releases that look like real news reports. Hundreds of companies pay for the preparation of VNRs and a remarkably large number of them are used by stations, usually those in the smaller markets. Eugene Secunda, a marketing professor at Baruch College and an expert on VNRs notes that many of these video releases were produced by former network TV show professionals, and they are often of better quality than a local broadcasting station could produce. The VNRs are distributed to the stations via satellite. There are now companies that specialize in distribution of VNRs. Medialink, founded in 1986, and now one of the largest, has grown from 425 VNR transmissions in 1987 to more than 1,500 in 1989. It is estimated that as many as 15,000 different VNRs are distributed each year. There is nothing sinister about making such productions. The problems occur when television news programs use them, unidentified, to flesh out an otherwise barren news show, or to save the costs of hiring sufficient reporters. It should also be noted that politicians, including members of the U.S. Congress, will provide VNRs to television stations as well.

Management has even used television news programs to hype entertainment shows. When NBC aired "Billionaire Boys Club," based on a real incident, KNBC-TV in Los Angeles hyped the program by integrating dramatic clips from the two-part miniseries with news footage of the actual participants. And when ABC's "Twin Peaks" became popular in the spring of 1990, the Seattle ABC affiliate, KOMO, devoted several segments to hyping the program that was filmed in a small community near Puget Sound. The networks push this hype of their entertainment schedules. NBC sent a memo to its affiliates in April of 1991 urging local news staffs to prepare stories on transsexuals in the community, stories that would tie in nicely with an April 25 episode of "L.A. Law" that focused on transsexuals.

People say they depend on television, more than any other medium, to get the news. Those claims, made by the television industry, are subject to challenge on various grounds. Regardless, a substantial number of Americans do rely on television to find out what is happening in the world and in their community. Television news has the capacity to meet the needs of these individuals. But as the public affairs arm of what is essentially an entertainment medium, it sometimes lacks the will.

# PUBLIC TELEVISION

By all rights any discussion of public television belongs near the beginning of this chapter when network and local television are discussed. But the public telecasting system in the United States is so unlike the commercial system, and unlike other state-operated systems, that it must be considered by itself.

It is difficult to attempt to try to describe the public system because, after more than 20 years of existence, it remains an adolescent whose life is in disarray, tugged upon from this force and that, perpetually short of cash, with hopes and dreams it may never realize. Commercial television, for all its faults, knows what it wants to be and how to get there. Despite the problems of diminishing audience, rising production costs, and increasing competition for the advertiser's money, all hands on board the commercial ship seem to be working toward the same goal. Within the public broadcasting system, however, there is lack of agreement on even a goal. And the system is wracked by a multiplicity of constantly changing alliances among players in a competition for money and air time. Educators find themselves pitted against cultural broadcasters, documentarians against those who support drama, rural stations against urban stations, regional production centers against the Public Broadcasting Service, and coalitions of independent producers against the Corporation for Public Broadcasting. CBS correspondent Charles Kuralt once called public television a system that almost works. His description remains apt today. First, let's take a look at how we got here.

Noncommercial television is not a new idea. Forty years ago educational television stations dotted the nation, a collection of isolated and unjoined stations, telecasting educational fare: classes, seminars, discussions, and small bits of news and information. Stations were directly supported by school districts, colleges, and universities. Early attempts were made in the mid-1960s to tie these stations together. National Educational Television, or NET, developed from grants from the Ford Foundation and others to create a small menu of national programming.

In 1967, after a lengthy if not completely satisfactory survey of noncommercial television in the United States by the Carnegie Commission on Educational Television, the U.S. Congress created the Corporation for Public Broadcasting, a federal agency whose mission was to spearhead and manage the growth of public television. The CPB in turn spawned the Public Broadcasting Service, a network of 285 noncommercial stations that were ultimately joined together, as well as various television production units, such as the Children's Television Workshop. The presumption was that the government, primarily the federal government, would fund the system. This would be a television system insulated from the pressures of the commercial world, one in which the needs of the viewers and the creativity of the artists rather than exigencies of corporate America would determine the content of the programming. From its inception, however, the national public television system was not given sufficient federal funds to meet the stated goals. A second Carnegie Commission study was undertaken in the late 1970s and gave the public television low marks. "What public broadcasting tried to invent was a truly radical idea; an instrument of mass communication that simultaneously respects the artistry of the individuals to create the programs, the needs of the public that form the audience, and the forces of political power that supply the resources," the report said. The invention did not work, the study concluded, or at least not very well.

The second Carnegie Commission called for a massive infusion of federal money into the system. It urged that most of the money should be spent on programming, not on technological improvements, as was common, especially at local television stations. The recommendations were politely applauded by everyone associated with public broadcasting but were largely unheeded. The system today still suffers from most of the same problems noted in the second Carnegie Commission report.

Public television is accessible in 98 percent of all television homes in America. And a vast number of people watch programs on the public network. But very few

The Civil War is undoubtedly the most written about event in U.S. history so perhaps it should not have been a surprise that ratings for PBS's 11-hour documentary "The Civil War" were among the highest in the network's history. The program won critical acclaim as well for its poignant and often haunting portrait of a nation torn asunder by war. Pictured are Generals Grant and Lee.     (PBS)

people watch the same programs. So while the network can rightfully boast that more than half of all U.S. television viewers watch public television at least once a week, the overall monthly primetime ratings for public television rest at 2.5, or about 2.3 million homes using television. At times particular PBS programs can attract a substantial audience, programs like Kenneth Clark's "Civilisation," or Carl Sagan's "Cosmos." This happens less often today, although PBS scored one of its biggest ratings ever when it broadcast the Ken Burns documentary "The Civil War" over five nights in late 1990. The opening episode won nearly a 10 rating and a 14 share, a phenomenal achievement for the public network. Still, the loss of audience suffered by the commercial networks prompted by the growth in popularity of the cable networks and VCRs has hit public television as well. Audience loss in cable-served television homes that have pay cable as well has been even higher, according to John Fuller, director of research for PBS.

## ☐ Funding

Stanley Karnow, the journalist and filmmaker who produced one of public television's most memorable series, "Vietnam: A Television History," said that producing a series for PBS reminded him of a line used by a character in the comic strip Popeye. "Wimpy used to say, 'I'm inviting you over for a duck dinner; you bring the duck.' That's public television."

From the day PBS was born money has been a serious and debilitating problem. Not only isn't there enough to go around, but how the little that exists will be distributed is the primary cause of much of the fighting among those who work in the system. We aren't talking about peanuts; public television revenues were more than $1 billion in 1989. But remember that advertising revenues for the three commercial television networks alone that year were almost $10 billion.

Determining who pays for what expenses in public television is not simple. Some sources quote total public television expenditures, which include the operation of local stations, fund-raising costs, and programming. Other sources simply refer to the costs of programming. Let's focus on these latter numbers, since they seem to be most widely available and consistent.

Corporations, and corporate foundations, provide about 30 percent of all dollars spent on programming for public television. These organizations are the single largest contributors. Public broadcasting has always relied on the largess of American business for some of its expenses, but never more than it does today. Tight budgets for public broadcasting was the hallmark during the eight years of the Reagan administration. It was a mandate of this administration for public broadcasters to wean themselves from feeding at the public trough. To assist both PBS and local public stations in winning corporate revenues, the Corporation for Public Broadcasting granted far greater leeway in recognizing corporate donations over the air. In the past, rules prohibited all but a nod to corporate sponsors. "Funding for this program was made possible by the Blodgett Bathtub Company." The "enhanced underwriting rules," as they are called, permit the station to use a corporate logo, a corporate slogan, and display as many as three different corporate products. The little 15-second messages look a lot like ads; that is because they are ads. "Funding for this program was made possible by the Blodgett Bathtub Company, serving America with quality shower stalls, bathtubs, and spas since 1936. At Blodgett we help you start the day the clean way."

Are there implications to the fact that corporations pay for so much of the programming on public television? Certainly. The corporations will only pay for what they like. And by deciding what shows they will fund, corporations also indirectly decide what shows will not be telecast, according to Fred Friendly, longtime CBS news producer and former head of the Ford Foundation, which has given more than $100 million to public television. "By funding those programs—the Met [New York Metropolitan Opera], drama—that are harmless, so far as controversy goes, they are structuring the program schedule of public television," Friendly said. Corporate officials disagree, arguing that they will sponsor any good program, and that those that are not funded are simply not very good. The facts, however, tend to support Friendly. In 1988 PBS indexed all subjects addressed in its public affairs programs. There were 169 entries under the business category; only 29 entries for labor.

PBS has consistently rejected union funding for many projects, arguing that the unions are not disinterested donors. The network has for years sought funding for a multimillion dollar history of American labor, "Made in the USA," but has rejected labor funding. Yet the network had no difficulty with accepting funding from corporate America for "Free to Choose," a glorification of the free enterprise system. "Business is much broader than labor is," according to one PBS official. "Corporations put their profits into a wide variety of things. Labor unions are only going to put money into something in which they have a vested interest." But filmmaker Gordon Quinn takes a different view. "When you make your pitch to a corporation, they want something very specific for their money. Often you can appeal to unions on the basis of larger social concern—say, America's industrial future or social security. And you can get complete editorial control."

Beating the bush for corporate funding at the local level can be even more treacherous. Each year the station manager scours the community for companies that want to donate money in exchange for these commercial plugs. This already onerous task is made even more difficult if the station has undertaken any hard-hitting public affairs programming that has offended the local business community. In addition, members of the local community's business establishment are often even on the station's board of directors, which makes policy for the station.

Business support for public television will undoubtedly continue to grow. Corporate sponsors can certainly enhance their reputations by associating themselves with prestigious programming. The audience for public television may be small, but its viewers are marked by high incomes and high education. Viewers are often opinion leaders in the community. And corporate money goes much farther through the sponsorship of public television programming than through advertising on commercial television. Mobil Oil "sponsored" the entire 13-week PBS series "Ascent of Man" for under $400,000. At the time, a 30-second ad on a program like "60 Minutes" cost nearly half that much. And in addition to the underwriting plugs given to Mobil during the program, the company's logo was featured in promotional advertising for the show. This is called gaining prestige by association.

The second largest source of funding for PBS programming comes from viewers—almost 25 percent nationally. (At some stations, where management is especially good at passing the hat during the quarterly fund drives, viewers contribute as much as 40 or 45 percent of programming dollars.) How much influence do contributors have over programming? Plenty, says Lawrence Daressa, who chairs the National Coalition of Independent Public Broadcast Producers. "Public television isn't in fact, public. Stations are controlled by their members," he said. "If they like it, they'll pay for it." While this sounds democratic, it really isn't. Some people in the nation are far better able to spend the $50 to $100 a year for a membership at a local station. Those people with a low income, who, as a group, use television more than others because they can't afford other kinds of leisure activities, contribute a very small amount to public television. And their voices are rarely heard when it comes to programming decisions. Major donors, those who contribute hundreds of dollars each year to a station, are given special attention. This fact has a good deal to do with the programming, national as well as local, seen on most public television. There is a heavy emphasis on cultural programming, culture with a capital C. Some of this is excellent, but often irrelevant to the needs of a contemporary audience. Public affairs programming, with some exceptions, tends to be limited to safe topics. The documentary series "Frontline" is an exception, often presenting hard-hitting explorations of vital, contemporary issues. But many more public affairs segments focus on history, the history of wars, the history of race relations. This is often excellent history. "The Civil War" and "Eyes on the Prize" (about the civil rights movement) are extraordinary examples of such programming. But an historical documentary focuses upon what happened yesterday, usually a safe topic. Programming that focuses on what is happening now, or what will or should happen tomorrow is generally more relevant and more controversial. And public television cannot afford to anger either its local supporters, or members of Congress and the administration

Public affairs programming on PBS tries to avoid serious controversies that could endanger funding, so history has become a staple of the public network. "Vietnam: A Television History" was one of the most popular historical explorations undertaken by the network. (© Bill Herod)

which preside over the distribution of federal monies. Nothing better signifies the generally safe tone of the programming on public television than the plethora of nature series and programs that are telecast. These are especially appealing to older, educated, and wealthier viewers.

As a final note, the median age of the audience is of great concern to many in public television. It is not a coincidence that when pledge drive time arrives the stations telecast big band reunions, folk music concerts, old movies, and the like. The audience for public television is graying, and the network has not been able to attract many younger viewers. To do that the stations would have to put on programs that appeal to this age group, and many of these would offend or bore the older, staunch supporters. This is a dilemma that the public stations will have to face in the 1990s.

The remainder of programming dollars comes from governments — state, local, and federal. This is a diminishing share. The federal government continues to try to cut back on its contributions, especially at a time of budget deficits and fears of a slowing economy. State and local governments and schools have also found increased demands on their limited resources in recent years. Supporting a public television station each year looks more and more like a luxury, not a necessity, when compared with the need for funds for social services, police and courts, repairing the roads and public buildings, and such. More and more local stations seek independence from traditional constraints imposed by the schools and universities that support them, and several of these stations have abandoned such support in exchange for a "public" status.

The public system has generated some of its own resources through creative means. The Public Broadcasting Service controls six transponders (see page 42) on the Westar communications satellite and leases the unused capacity to a variety of users. And some local public broadcasting stations, which are often well-equipped broadcasting facilities, have begun to produce programming for commercial television.

## ☐ Programming Public TV

Remember what you read earlier in this chapter about how network programming gets to the local station? Well, forget all that, because that is not the manner in which the public system operates. Programming on public television stations is a mix of local, regional, and national efforts. Local programming is generally dismal at all but the largest stations because of the lack of funding. The larger stations often attempt to produce innovative news programs, sophisticated documentary programs, and even the popular magazine-format public affairs shows. Some produce their own children's shows, hobby and craft shows, and even do remote broadcasts of important public events. But these are the stations with the larger budgets, stations that hope to sell these programs to other stations in the region.

Regional programming is something that is relatively new and offers great promise. Groups of stations, by pooling their limited production funds, can often accomplish what a single station can only dream about. Extensive coverage of a state legislative session might be prohibitive for one station, but several stations can pool their efforts and make such coverage a reality. Regional production of documentary films and other specialized programming is not uncommon.

About half of all programming carried by public television stations comes from the Public Broadcasting Service, the national network that interconnects all 285 stations. Unlike commercial broadcasting, where the local affiliate is paid by the network to carry the network programs, the local public television station must pay for the network programs it carries. The richer stations can afford to buy more programming than the poor stations. Again, economics plays a large part in programming decisions. Stations use the money received from the Corporation for Public Broadcasting, from corporate donors, from local government and schools, and from members or subscribers to the station to purchase the network shows. A bigger station pays more for a network program than a small station, but via the **Station Programming Cooperative** each station has a voice in the programming PBS will produce or transmit.

Each spring local public broadcasting stations are given a catalog listing scores of shows; old shows, new shows, proposed shows—each with an estimated price tag for the station. The station programming personnel study these lists. Sometimes they invite comments from viewers or members, or even allow members to vote on the initial program selection. With its budget as its guide, the station selects the programs it would like to buy for the following year. But the "game" doesn't end after the initial selections are made in the Station Program Cooperative. Before any station can buy a program for next season, a minimum number of stations must buy the show. If not enough stations select a program in the initial round, the show is dropped from the catalog. And if only a bare minimum of stations select a program, it is likely the estimated cost to each station will rise. This, of course, might force some stations to reconsider their selection of the program. Once the catalog is revised, a second round of bidding takes place and the final schedule is determined. Not all stations carry all shows. Because of the flexibility in the PBS satellite feeds, the network can send out several different programs simultaneously and stations can transmit or tape and store the programs they have purchased.

This pure form of programming democracy has its problems. For example, the one station, one vote standard often denies a majority of the population the opportunity to see a program rejected by a majority of the stations, stations that serve a small portion of the total population. Stations tend to select shows that have always been popular in the past, certain winners like "Sesame Street," "Mister Rogers," and "Washington Week in Review." Newer shows are at a disadvantage. Stations tend to avoid controversial programs, so few public affairs shows have found their way onto the public schedule in recent years. Stations will often seek less expensive programs, so viewers will see more programs featuring "talking heads," interview shows, how to do it programs, and so on. Finally, the programming cooperative has a devastating impact on innovative or experimental programming. No station wants to risk its precious dollars on a program that viewers "might" like, but also "might" reject.

A serious crisis facing public television in the 1990s is the increased competition from other broadcasting interests, especially cable networks, for programming, especially British programming. For example, after having aired "Planet Earth" and "Life on Earth," the first two parts of David Attenborough's trilogy, PBS lost the third part, "Trials of Life" to Ted Turner's TNT. "Frontiers," a BBC documentary series on life at the common borders of nations in Africa and Asia, went to the The Discovery Channel. Arts and Entertainment is now the BBC's largest U.S. customer, and the TNT Network, which Ted Turner has said will feature quality programming, is just now entering the bidding game.

As an indication of how quickly things have changed, consider this. Lionheart Television, the television distribution arm of the British Broadcasting Corporation, picked up less than 10 percent of its revenues from U.S. cable television in 1986. In 1990 it was earning 55 percent of its revenues from U.S. cable. Similarly, in 1986, 85 percent of Lionheart's U.S. sales were to the Public Broadcasting Service or to local public television stations. In 1990 the total was 45 percent (figure 9-5).

Prices for BBC and other British-made programs have increased by almost 50 percent in the last three years. Cable channels are willing to pay $125,000 to

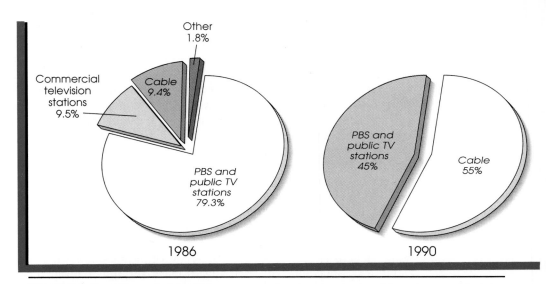

FIGURE 9-5  The U.S. market for BBC programming, long a staple of American public television, has changed dramatically during the past five years.
(The New York Times)

$150,000 more than Mobil Oil for drama suitable for Masterpiece Theater. When PBS was the only U.S. buyer of television programming made in Great Britain, the British had to deal with the network. But they never liked it, according to *Channels* magazine editor Les Brown. The Americans were incredibly slow about making deals, often taking more than a year to decide whether to buy a series. PBS would propose the series, the local stations would have to vote on it, and then the money to purchase the programming would have to be found. "The process is excruciating," Brown commented. Cable networks operate much more quickly. The very real prospect exists that in the coming decade the cable networks will skim off the best of what the British have to offer, and public television will become the buyer of last resort for producers in the United Kingdom.

This bodes ill for public television, many argue. But others say this could be the best thing that has happened to the system in many years. This could force PBS into becoming its own main source for programming. The system could begin to lose its clearly British cast, and this could increase its popularity with many American viewers who believe contemporary American problems are more suitable than mid-nineteenth century British problems as the basis for drama on U.S. public television.

Efforts were being made in 1990 to take other actions to strengthen the public system. In June of 1990 leaders of the public network unveiled a plan to station and programming executives that would streamline PBS programming. It would vastly increase the power of PBS programming executives to create a national program schedule. Programming chief Jennifer Lawson would be assisted by a 17 person committee that would include local programming officials. The plan would also place at her disposal $105 million in program and promotion funds from a variety sources. This centralization, according to supporters of the plan, would permit the quicker development of new programming. A common primetime schedule at all public stations would make it easier to promote PBS programming, and build an audience for it. It was PBS's insistence that all member stations telecast "The Civil War" at the same time that won high ratings for the series, many people argued.

But before the plan can be put into place, it must be ratified by the local public stations. And that is the fly in the ointment. Many local public stations stand to lose plenty through this centralization of power. First, they will lose some production monies. Many local stations have attempted to become regional production centers for public programming, and in the process they have developed bloated internal bureaucracies that act as fund-raising arms. A good share of the $105 million in production funds that would go to PBS would have gone to these local stations in the past. These stations will have to get smaller, as they become more like local commercial stations—the distributors of programming others produce. This will be unpopular among many at these stations. Loss of control of the primetime program schedule will make it harder for local stations to play to their local viewers, whom they deem so important for fund raising. If the network is showing a drama or documentary at 8 P.M. on Tuesday night instead of the weekly hour of nature programming, many local viewers will howl, and this may hurt the stations when the pledge drives come around. The fact that the station may gain new viewers with a national schedule is a possibility, but many stations are fearful, regarding the nature lovers as a sure thing. The move to centralize control of the network's programming is a bold move by PBS, but other bold moves in the past have been stymied by provincialism and egos at local public stations. The proposal was being vigorously debated in mid-1991.

## THE FUTURE OF TELEVISION

Anyone who attempts to write in 1992 about what television will be like in even five years is either foolhardy or stupid, or both. Failed predictions litter the path to the future of the electronic media. Futurists take note. The introduction of the videocassette recorder, the Sony Betamax, in 1975 was greeted by the television industry with a yawn. It was seen as an expensive toy. If there was to be a new video playback technology, it would be videodiscs. At that time television futurists had their eyes focused instead skyward, toward direct broadcast (DBS) satellites that they said would soon be arrayed around the globe. DBS television was the wave of the future.

What has happened since then? Today, there are VCRs in more than 70 percent of all American homes with television. The VCR has revolutionized America's use of television, the way we watch it, and what we watch on it. VCRs have provided a phenomenal boost to the nation's film industry and have seriously fouled up the rating services which attempt to count the number of viewers who watch American television programs. The VCR undoubtedly has had a greater impact on American television viewing than any other device in the past 40 years.

Videodiscs were dead in 1984, only to be resurrected in the late 1980s for video gourmets. While they will never compete with tape systems, the discs offer playback possibilities that truly enrich the video field. And as such, disc players and stores that sell discs began to slowly proliferate in 1990.

DBS was dead as well in 1986. At first companies had lined up to get permission from the FCC to go online with the satellite systems that would transmit programming from an Earth station to a satellite and then directly into the home. But by the mid-1980s the DBS saga seemed ended. All three major U.S. players in the DBS game had dropped out. Western Union, CBS, and RCA all gave up, saying there just didn't seem to be a market for DBS. But by 1990 DBS was back. Two powerful consortiums were competing to see which could offer service first. Sky Cable, headed by Rupert Murdoch, and including NBC, Hughes Aircraft, and Cablevision Systems Corporation, announced a $1 billion venture to bring 108 channels of programming via satellite to Americans by 1993. Home owners will simply have to invest in a small (12 inch by 8 inch) dish antenna for the home that will cost about $300, and pay a monthly fee to have the signals decoded. A rival group, Rival K Prime Partners, made up of Time-Warner Inc, Telecommunications Inc., and General Electric announced plans for a more modest service (10 channels) that was to start transmitting by the end of 1990. More channels would be quickly added, they promised. While these two media giants were fighting it out, a Seattle, Washington company called SkyPix Corporation said it planned to offer pay-per-view movies via DBS telecasts using the Ku-band for signal transmission. Development of DBS was proceeding rapidly in Europe. So, DBS is back. Probably.

The purpose of this little recitation is not to confuse the reader, but to demonstrate that it is very difficult to predict the future of television. The development of any new broadcasting system is only limited by what is technically possible. The growth and use of such a system is governed by what is economically possible. And the acceptance of such a system is determined by what members of the audience think they need and want. A great many technical innovations have been stymied because they did not generate the interest of people or businesses that could finance their development. But even many of those that have been developed have failed because the public was not ready to accept this new technology. DBS could be dead again in the United States unless enough Americans can be convinced that the system offers distinct advantages over systems currently in place.

Realistically, the most likely major change in American television in the near future is the refinement of the television picture itself. The television sets in American homes today are a substantial improvement over the ones that came on the market in the early post-World War II years. But the basic components of the television picture, 525 horizontal lines with a 4 to 3 width to height ratio, have stayed the same. European television is superior to U.S. TV because the picture has 625 lines and provides more definition. (That is why videotapes recorded on European TV will not work on American television sets, and viceversa.)

The introduction of high definition television will change this. HDTV telecasts are made up of many more lines. The system developed by the Japanese uses 1125 lines, and provides a picture with the quality of a 35 mm slide. The height to width ratio is 5 to 3, rather than 4 to 3, more typical of movie screens in a modern theater. The color system has improved clarity and stability. In 1991 HDTV was still in the development stages. Both the Japanese and the European Economic Community were ahead of the United States in bringing an affordable, practical, HDTV system to the market. But in late 1990, U.S. researchers achieved a remarkable technological advance that may in the end make the foreign HDTV systems outmoded. Both the Japanese and the European HDTV systems transmit only by satellite, which is unwieldy for local broadcasts. American technicians have developed a system that can be transmitted over ordinary broadcast frequencies. In addition, American researchers achieved a second, more important breakthrough, by developing a technique for transmitting HDTV programming entirely in digital computer code. Digital transmission makes it much easier to eliminate such interference as ghosts and static, just as compact discs eliminate scratches and hissing associated with vinyl phonography records.

It will be some time before HDTV becomes practical for use in American homes. The cost of the equipment is currently prohibitive. (An HDTV receiver cost $34,000 in Japan in 1990.) Additionally, the FCC or some other agency must determine how a transition from standard broadcast to HDTV will be made.

Three options have been put forth. The first is called the simulcast approach. Under this option each station would continue to telecast on its current channel, but then be given an additional channel, probably a UHF channel, for the HDTV telecast. Persons with regular television sets would continue to see regular programming; those with HDTV would see a better picture by receiving the second channel. This system seems to be favored by the FCC, which explains that when all homes have finally gotten HDTVs, the broadcasting of conventional television signals could be ended, and that part of the broadcast spectrum could be used for other purposes.

A second proposal is called the augmentation system. Under this system, television stations would continue to telecast conventional signals on their existing channels and would use a second channel to transmit the extra details needed for HDTV. The HDTV sets would take the information from the two signals and combine it into one picture. This option is considered possible but technically difficult.

A final option would be to introduce HDTV in two stages. First, what is called Advanced Compatible Television would be introduced using conventional channels. The ACTV pictures would be 30 percent sharper than current pictures, carry digital stereo sound, and have a function that automatically cancels ghost images. ACTV could be introduced soon, by 1993. It would not involve using new channel space. High definition pictures could come later, if demand warranted. By then, a system may have been developed to cram the HDTV signal into the 6 megahertz band width.

While the FCC likes the first option, there are several powerful reasons why the third may be the option of choice. And most of these revolve around money. A local television station could be converted to send ACTV signals for about $250,000. It will cost between $3 to $4 million for a station in a large television market to convert to HDTV. It is estimated that the cost of a set to receive the ACTV signals will be about $1,000, about twice the cost of a large screen set today. HDTV sets will likely cost in the $3,000 to $4,000 range by the mid-1990s. It is likely that a digital HDTV signal may be transmitted by cable into American homes before it is broadcast via the airwaves.

And in the end, what does the viewer get? A better picture? Sure. But the content of television won't be affected one whit by the new system. Are Americans so video hungry that they are willing to spend that kind of money to see, with new clarity, reruns of "I Love Lucy," or "People's Court," or the "Super Bowl?" That is the catch, and that is why predicting the future of television is almost impossible.

In 1991 there was renewed interest as well in interactive television, a system through which a viewer can electronically talk to the people who are telecasting the program. This will permit viewers to play along with game shows, construct their own news programs from a list of stories presented by a local station, select a workout program to meet their fitness needs from an array of several being telecast simultaneously, vote on mini-referenda, and even order goods and services via the television. The concept is not new. Warner-Amex introduced such a system (called Qube) in the late 1970s in several American cities and it bombed. But promoters of this system, including the FCC, argue that the Qube system failed because the technology was too hard to use, and it cost too much. Qube did cost a lot to use, and it was somewhat difficult to learn to use. But more neutral observers note that what ultimately killed this original interactive system was the fact that people didn't want to interact with their television sets. They just liked to sit and watch. Time will tell whether Americans have changed their mind about this matter.

## BIBLIOGRAPHY

These are some of the materials that have been helpful in the preparation of this chapter.

Ainslie, Peter. "The New TV Viewer," *Channels,* September, 1988.

Andrews, Edmund L. "TV Rerun Ownership in Review," *The New York Times,* September 30, 1990.

Aufderheide, Pat. "The Corporatization of Public TV," *Extra,* November/December, 1988.

Barnouw, Erik. *The Sponsor.* New York: Oxford University Press, 1978.

Benjamin, Burton. *The Documentary: An Endangered Species.* New York: Gannett Center for Media Studies, 1987.

Block, Alex B. "Hollywood's Labor Pains," *Channels,* July/August, 1988.

Briller, Bert. "Local News: Leaner and Meaner," *Washington Journalism Review,* March, 1988.

Broad, William J. "U.S. Counts on Computer Edge in the Race for Advanced TV," *The New York Times,* November 28, 1989.

*Broadcasting,* various issues.

Brown, Les. *Television: The Business Behind the Box.* New York: Harcourt Brace Jovanovich, 1971.

"Cable TV's Fresh Pitch," *U.S. News & World Report,* January 30, 1989.

Capuzzi, Cecelia. "The ABC's of Making News Profits," *Washington Journalism Review,* March, 1989.

Carnegie Commission on Educational Television. *Public Television: A Program for Action.* New York: Bantam Books, 1967.

Carnegie Commission on the Future of Public Broadcasting. *A Public Trust.* New York: Bantam Books, 1979.

Carter, Bill. "NBC Alters Its Count of Viewers," *The New York Times,* June 13, 1990.

————. "NBC Tightens Grip on Lead, But Networks Lose Viewers," *The New York Times,* April 19, 1989.

————. "NBC to Offer 600 Hours of Olympics at a Price," *The New York Times,* February 13, 1990.

————. "Very Weak Ad Sales Trouble TV Networks," *The New York Times,* October 15, 1990.

————. "With Cable as Partner Fox Dances in Ratings," *The New York Times,* September 10, 1990.

*Channels,* various issues.

Chester, Jeffrey, and Montgomery, Kathryn. "Counterfeiting the News," *Columbia Journalism Review,* May/June, 1988.

Cornelius, Luke. "Wanna Make Big Money in TV? Buy a Station," *TV Guide,* January 19, 1985.

Cummings, Gary. "The Elephant in the Parking Lot," *Washington Journalism Review,* January/ February, 1987.

————. "The Watershed in Local TV News," *Gannett Center Journal,* Spring, 1987.

————. "When Advertisers Call the Shots," *Washington Journalism Review,* December, 1986.

Diamond, Edwin, and Mahony, Alan. "Once It Was Harvest of Shame—Now We Get Scared Sexless," *TV Guide,* August 27, 1988.

Emerson, Steven. "The System That Brought You Days of Rage," *Columbia Journalism Review,* November/December, 1989.

"A Finer Grind from the Ratings Mill," *Channels,* December, 1988.

Flander, Judy. "Public Television Hits a Midlife Crisis," *Washington Journalism Review,* July/August, 1989.

Galloway, Stephen. "Some Handwringing at PBS as Power Base Shifts," *TV Guide,* September 29, 1990.

Gamarekian, Barbara. "Ads Aimed at Children Restricted," *The New York Times,* October 17, 1990.

Gerard, Jeremy. "A Plan to Improve Public Television," *The New York Times,* November 20, 1989.

———. "Public TV May Centralize Programs," *The New York Times,* June 21, 1990.

———. "TV Networks Want Nielsen to Change Rating Method," *The New York Times,* December 12, 1989.

Gitlin, Todd. *Inside Prime Time,* New York: Pantheon Books, 1983.

Goodman, Walter. "Is Network News Pushing to Do Less?" *The New York Times,* January 8, 1990.

Greenfield, Jeff. "Making TV News Pay," *Gannett Center Journal,* Spring, 1987.

Grossman, Lawrence K. "TV News: The Need for a New Spirit," *Columbia Journalism Review,* July/August, 1990.

Hammer, Joshua. "Betting Billions on TV Sports," *Newsweek,* December 11, 1989.

Hickey, Neil. "Decade of Change, Decade of Choice," *TV Guide,* December 9, 1989.

———. "The Verdict So Far on People Meters," *TV Guide,* August 5, 1989.

Holder, Dennis. "Local Coverage on the KU Band," *Washington Journalism Review,* October, 1985.

"In Search of TV's Lost Viewers," *TV Guide,* May 19, 1990.

Joyce, Ed. "Is Network News Getting Better—Or Worse?" *TV Guide,* May 13, 1989.

Kalter, Joanmarie, and Marion, Jan. "The Big Stories TV News Is Missing—and Why," *TV Guide,* July 22, 1989.

Koza, Patricia. "Tight Federal Purse Leaves PBS Scrambling," *The Seattle Times,* August 1, 1982.

Leiser, Ernest. "See It Now—The Decline of Network News," *Washington Journalism Review,* January/February, 1988.

Lipton, Michael. "What You Want to See in the Next Decade," *TV Guide,* January 22, 1990.

"Low Power TV Going Strong," *The New York Times,* May 14, 1990.

"Making a Leap in TV Technology," *U.S. News & World Report,* January 23, 1989.

Mandese, Joe. "Dear Diary: I'm Confused," *Channels,* October, 1988.

Marash, David. "There's More to Local News Than Fender-Benders," *The New York Times,* July 2, 1989.

*Media Economics and Sports Coverage.* New York: Gannett Center for Media Studies, 1988.

Meier, Barry. "Commercial TV Is Living Up to Its Name," *Seattle Post-Intelligencer,* February 20, 1990.

"The New Voice of America," *Newsweek,* June 12, 1989.

"The 1991 Field Guide," *Channels,* December 3, 1990.

"Paid Ads on Public Television," *The New York Times,* August 8, 1985.

Planer, Ed. "Network Faces: White and Male," *Washington Journalism Review,* June, 1990.

Pollack, Andrew. "Format Emerging for Advanced TV," *The New York Times,* March 23, 1990.

*Public Attitudes Toward Television and Other Media in a Time of Change.* New York: Television Information Office, 1985.

"Rating Problems? Let Satan Help," *Washington Journalism Review,* July/August, 1989.

"Ready for Prime Time," *Newsweek,* December 25, 1989.

Rosenau, Neal. "After the Cutbacks: What's the Damage to Local TV News?" *Columbia Journalism Review,* September/October, 1988.

Rothenberg, Randall. "Black Hole in Television," *The New York Times,* October 9, 1990.

Salmans, Sandra. "Masters of the Morning Show," *Marketing and Media Decisions,* October, 1987.

Sanger, David E. "Public TV Joins Venture to Send Finance Data to Computer Users," *The New York Times,* January 2, 1985.

Stevenson, Richard W. "Networks Plan More Moonlighting," *The New York Times,* January 30, 1989

Swift, Al. "Crisis in Communications," vol. 23 *Television Quarterly* 13, No. 2, 1988.

Taffe, William. "It's Bottom Line Time," *Sports Illustrated,* October 12, 1987.

Tunstall, Jeremy, and Walker, David. *Media Made in California.* New York: Oxford University Press, 1981.

*Variety,* various issues.

Veciana-Suarez, Ana. *Hispanic Media USA.* Washington, D.C.: The Media Institute, 1987.

"Viewing Trends: From 50s to 80s," *Television/Radio Age,* July 22, 1985.

Waters, Harry F., and Huck, Janet. "Networking Women," *Newsweek,* March 13, 1989.

Weisman, John. "Public TV in Crisis, Parts I and II," *TV Guide,* August 1 and August 8, 1987.

Woletz, Bob. "On to 1990: Can the Next Fin-Syn War Be Averted?" *Channels,* February, 1988.

P A R T

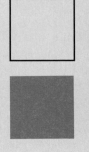

*MEDIA FUNCTIONS*

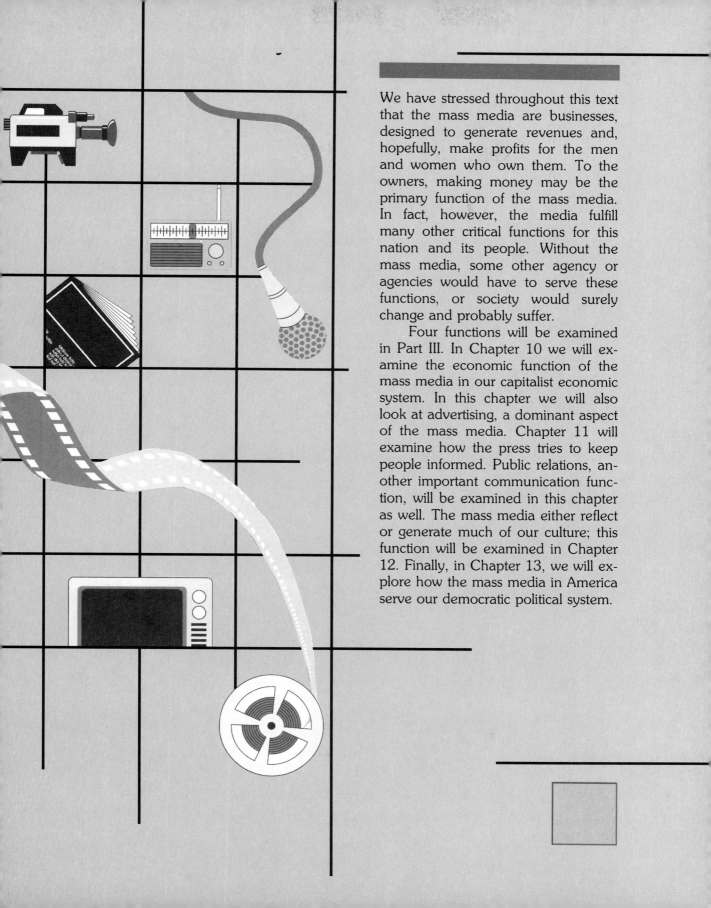

We have stressed throughout this text that the mass media are businesses, designed to generate revenues and, hopefully, make profits for the men and women who own them. To the owners, making money may be the primary function of the mass media. In fact, however, the media fulfill many other critical functions for this nation and its people. Without the mass media, some other agency or agencies would have to serve these functions, or society would surely change and probably suffer.

Four functions will be examined in Part III. In Chapter 10 we will examine the economic function of the mass media in our capitalist economic system. In this chapter we will also look at advertising, a dominant aspect of the mass media. Chapter 11 will examine how the press tries to keep people informed. Public relations, another important communication function, will be examined in this chapter as well. The mass media either reflect or generate much of our culture; this function will be examined in Chapter 12. Finally, in Chapter 13, we will explore how the mass media in America serve our democratic political system.

# CHAPTER 10

# THE ECONOMIC FUNCTION: ADVERTISING AND ECONOMIC INFORMATION

*I*n a capitalistic system where the mass production of consumer goods is needed to sustain the economy, create employment, generate tax revenues, and so forth, a means must exist to bring the sellers and the buyers of these goods together and to stimulate consumption and investment. Advertising plays an indispensable role in this regard in the United States. "There can be little doubt," wrote Paul Baran and Paul Sweezy more than 25 years ago, "that the chronic underutilization of resources that has plagued the United States for more than a generation now would have been a good deal more severe if it had not been for the spectacular growth of advertising during this period." In this article, first published in *Science and Society* in 1964 and which can hardly be called pro-advertising, the authors conclude that "the elimination of advertising as we know it today would require the elimination of capitalism." Some would disagree with this and argue that capitalism could exist nicely without advertising, or perhaps as much advertising. And that may be true, but it probably would not be the kind of capitalism we know today.

There is no intent to resolve such a debate in this chapter, only to point out that advertising plays an important role in the society we have created. And because the mass media are the messengers that carry advertising messages, this function of the mass media requires an examination. We have previously discussed the impact of advertising on the content of the media. In this chapter the focus is on advertising itself: its history, how it operates, and its impact on other parts of society.

# A BRIEF HISTORY OF ADVERTISING

It is not really accurate to say that advertising dates back to ancient times, even though tradespeople and merchants have hawked their wares for many centuries. Advertising is a relatively modern phenomenon associated with the market economies of the modern world. The arrival of capitalism really heralds the beginning of advertising. A handbill printed in 1478 by William Caxton, which advertises a book, is generally credited with being the first printed advertisement. Newsbooks or newspapers began carrying advertising in 1625 when *Mercurius Britannicus* carried an advertisement for a book on February 1. The first food advertisement—a printed message for coffee—appeared in 1657. By the beginning of the 1700s, newspaper advertising was well established. Advertising notices were carried in the earliest papers printed on this continent. These advertisements were small, generally only text, and usually announced that a retailer had goods of some kind to sell. The ads rarely changed or carried any illustrations. They were generally a single column wide and resembled the legal notices carried in the classified pages of modern newspapers.

The 1830s brought the industrial revolution to the nation and with it, the growth of modern advertising. "The institutional aspects of advertising are to be found in its performance of the function of supplying market information," according to University of Illinois communications scholar James Carey. It was not until the nineteenth century that this market information became a vital part of our economic system. Carey notes:

> Mass production generally means centralized production and decentralized distribution, i.e., mass marketing. However, another concomitant requirement of mass production is mass communication. As production became increasingly centralized market power became more concentrated, branded merchandise developed, and the old interpersonal relationships in the marketplace became displaced by relationships mediated by mass communications facilities.

The industrial revolution gave manufacturers the ability to make more goods than they could sell locally. Supply began to outstrip demand. Producers needed to enlarge their markets and saw advertising as a way to communicate with a far greater number of potential buyers. As companies got larger, sold more goods, and made more money, they could afford to buy even more advertising. It was this change in the American marketing system, brought about by the industrial revolution, that provided the impetus for the rapid growth of advertising.

Display advertising—the kind we are used to seeing in newspapers and magazines—was almost unheard of until the second half of the nineteenth century. Lord and Taylor and R. H. Macy, two New York department stores, used the first display advertising in the late 1860s and 1870s. Other important changes in advertising occurred in this era as well. Up to then, most manufacturers would advertise their goods directly to distributors or retailers, and the store owners would then hawk the wares to the public. But in the second half of the nineteenth century, manufacturers began to aim advertising directly at the readers, and brand-name products began to appear. Manufacturers believed that advertising could create a consumer demand for a product, and consumers would then request the retailers to sell the brand-name goods. Three soaps—Sapolio's, Pear's, and Ivory—and Royal Baking Powder were the most prominent early brand-name advertisers. Slogans and jingles and trademarks appeared shortly. Ivory soap's "It floats" and "99 44/100 percent pure," Prudential's "The Prudential has the strength of Gibralter," and Schlitz's "The Beer that made Milwaukee famous" were early popular slogans.

Development of brand-name advertising marked an important and long-lasting change in the basic purpose of advertising. Initially, advertising was used by manufacturers to couple existing market demand for a product to their own supply. "You need flour; I sell flour." But with brand-name advertising, the manufacturers began attempting to create a demand for a product. Historian David Potter noted: "Since the function of advertising had become one of exerting influence rather than one of providing information, the older factual, prosy notice which focused upon the specifications of the commodity now gave way to a more lyrical type of appeal which focused on the desires of the consumer." In 1905 the trade publication *Printer's Ink* proclaimed: "Everywhere . . . there are dozens of mongrel, unknown, unacknowledged makes of fabric, a dress essential, a food, with a standard trade-marked brand, backed by the national advertising that in itself has come to be a guarantee of worth to the public."

By the mid-twentieth century the major thrust of advertising had been refocused. The science of marketing had heavily influenced the industry. Instead of trying to create a consumer need for a product through persuasive communications, advertisers sought to discover those needs consumers already had that weren't being completely filled. The aim of marketing is to know and understand the customer so well that the product or service fits the customer and sells itself, wrote business guru Peter Drucker. Researchers may discover, for example, that consumers seek a specific product. In the late 1980s consumers seemed to indicate they wanted a beverage that tasted like beer but did not contain alcohol. The increased marketing of "nonalcoholic" beer in the early 1990s followed. But researchers also are aware of other needs in people—the need to be loved or wanted, the need to be successful, the need to have fun, the need to relax, the need to be popular. Products can be offered as the means of attaining these ends. A man or woman who feels the need to be loved may accept the argument that a hair dye or cosmetic or an aftershave can give them an added ability to gain that love from someone close to them. Success is a relative value, but the man or woman who drives a $40,000 European sedan or wears a $3,500 watch or buys a $30-per-bottle, single-malt scotch whiskey at least appears to others to be successful. We all seek security. When the stock market dived in the late 1980s and brokerage houses had little else to sell, the Dean Witter brokerage began to sell the security of the family in its advertising. It pictured a grandfather, father, and son, all fishing on a tranquil lake. Is there a scene that suggests more security to a male than being surrounded by these relatives, all there to help if needed, their strong presence to be relied upon?

The changing marketplace in the past 100 years has placed new emphasis upon advertising as a business tool. This is especially true in the selling of consumer goods and services, the industries which generate the bulk of advertising today. In a capitalist system, businesses compete against each other to win customers. This competition may be based on several factors. To a consumer the most important factors are the nature of the goods or services themselves and the price. If one particular brand of canned soup is superior to all others, it is likely to be the best seller in an equitable marketplace. Or, if the products tend to be similar in quality, the one which costs the least will usually win the most customers.

Since the last quarter of the nineteenth century, the American marketplace has

TABLE 10-1    The Top 25 Advertisers in the United States Ranked by the Amount Spent on Advertising in 1989. (These companies also represent the top sellers of consumer goods.)

| Rank | Advertiser | Total U.S. Ad Spending in Millions |
|------|-----------|-----------------------------------|
| 1 | Philip Morris Cos. | $2,072.0 |
| 2 | Procter & Gamble Co. | 1,779.3 |
| 3 | Sears, Roebuck & Co. | 1,432.1 |
| 4 | General Motors Corp. | 1,363.8 |
| 5 | Grand Metropolitan (London) | 823.3 |
| 6 | Pepsico | 786.1 |
| 7 | McDonald's Corp. | 774.4 |
| 8 | Eastman Kodak | 718.8 |
| 9 | RJR Nabisco | 703.5 |
| 10 | Kellogg Co. | 611.6 |
| 11 | Nestle SA. | 608.4 |
| 12 | Unilever NV (London) | 604.1 |
| 13 | Ford Motor Co. | 602.1 |
| 14 | Anheuser-Busch Cos. | 591.5 |
| 15 | Warner-Lambert Co. | 585.9 |
| 16 | AT&T Co. | 567.7 |
| 17 | Time-Warner | 567.5 |
| 18 | K-Mart Corp. | 561.4 |
| 19 | Chrysler Corp. | 532.5 |
| 20 | Johnson & Johnson | 487.1 |
| 21 | General Mills | 471.0 |
| 22 | American Home Products Corp. | 456.1 |
| 23 | Bristol-Myers Squibb Co. | 451.6 |
| 24 | Ralston Purina Co. | 429.5 |
| 25 | Toyota Motor Corp. | 417.6 |

*(Advertising Age.)*

changed from one in which a great many small companies compete (the original vision of capitalism) to a market in which fewer and fewer large companies account for most of the sales. There are 360,000 industrial corporations in the United States, according to journalist and media critic Ben Bagdikian. But of this number 500, or less than one-tenth of one percent, control 87 percent of all sales. In most areas of business we have what economists call an **oligopoly,** a market condition in which there are but a few sellers of a particular kind of product or service. These sellers have important power to influence price and other market factors.

Price competition is generally avoided under oligopolist conditions, and there is little of that today in the sale of consumer goods. A new mid-sized Chevrolet costs about the same as a mid-sized Ford. A six-pack of Pepsi is priced about the same as a six-pack of Coke. With consumer goods, we have reached the point where qualitative differences are minimal as well. Most consumers have brand loyalties, but the differences between Budweiser and Miller's beer, between Kodak and Fuji film, between Goodyear and Firestone tires are fairly insignificant.

With little difference in quality and price, what is the basis for competition in the 1990s? Advertising. It has replaced both price and quality, and today is a primary tool used by one company to differentiate itself from other companies in the same field. Therefore, advertising has become an important undertaking for all businesses today. Most people in business truly believe the slogan heralded by the advertising industry: "What happens if you don't advertise? NOTHING!"

The amount of money spent annually on advertising has increased at a surprisingly fast pace over the past century. In 1890 only $76 million was spent on advertising in U.S. newspapers and periodicals. Advertising passed the billion-dollar-a-year mark in 1929 when $1.1 billion was spent. Thirty-five years later nearly $15 billion was spent on advertising in the mass media. In 1984 this total was $50 billion. In 1990 the total amount spent on advertising in the United States passed $125 billion, an amount greater than the annual budget for all but the largest states in the nation.

## THE INDUSTRY

Advertising is defined as "the presentation of controlled, identifiable information and persuasion by means of mass communication," according to Wright, Winter, and Ziegler in their text, *Advertising*. The industry is very large, employing as many as 400,000 people in all its phases. There are about 7,000 advertising agencies which employ almost 80,000 people. Agencies are the most visible (to lay persons) aspect of advertising. The advertising agency executive has been the lead character in a number of novels and films and at least a couple of television series. But most large companies and retail stores have their own advertising departments. And the mass media—newspapers, magazines, radio, and television—also employ tens of thousands of persons who sell, prepare, and schedule advertising.

While advertising is an international phenomenon, it nevertheless has become closely identified with the United States, for good or for ill. And American companies dominated the industry for decades. Today, foreign-owned companies, especially the British, are pushing energetically into the world spotlight. In the late 1980s WPP Group P.L.C, a British firm headed by 44-year-old financier Martin Sorrell, consumed J. Walter Thompson Company and Ogilvy and Mather, two of the oldest and most respected U.S. advertising agencies. WPP is now regarded as the world's largest advertising enterprise. The company already controlled Hill and Knowlton, the world's largest public relations company. Saatchi & Saatchi P.L.C is also a British company and the chief competitor of WPP. Together these two companies control almost 10 percent of the $350 billion spent annually around the world on advertising and marketing.

Advertising is used for many purposes, such as introducing a new product, reestablishing customer loyalty to an older product, promoting a public cause like protecting the forests from fires, and acquainting the electorate with a candidate for public office. Consumer product advertising is seen as an aid to the salesperson or a substitute for a salesperson. Many years ago James Webb Young, considered by many to be one of the founding fathers of the business, said that advertising works in these five ways:

1. By making the product or service familiar to the people.
2. By reminding people about the product or service.
3. By spreading news about the product or service to the people.
4. By overcoming inertia in potential customers.
5. By adding value to a product that is not in the product. (A sleek new sports car

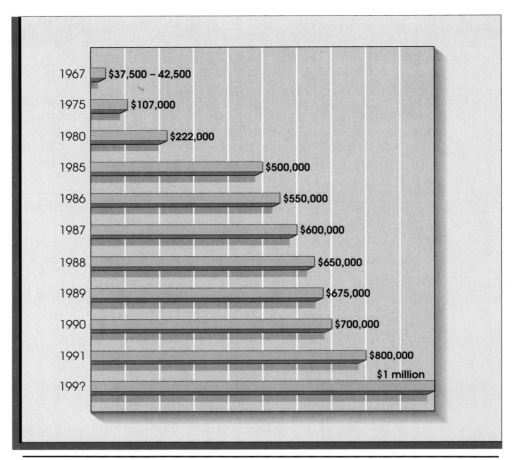

FIGURE 10-1 TV's most expensive minutes, and the nation's most expensive advertise-ments: spots aired during the Super Bowl. The first Super Bowl was played in 1967: a 30-second advertisement during that game cost less than $50,000. The same 30-second spot cost about 20 times as much in 1991.
*(TV Guide)*

is not sexy in and of itself. But advertising messages can give buyers the feeling that they will feel and look sexy when they drive this car, thus adding a value to the product.)

Advertising comes in all shapes and sizes; some of it is very expensive, some of it very cheap. It can cost as much as $800,000 for a 30-second television spot on a program like the Super Bowl (figure 10-1). You can buy a 25-word classified ad in your local newspaper for a few dollars. A full-page four-color advertisement in *Reader's Digest,* which may reach 50 million readers each month, costs more than $110,000. But a 60-second ad on a small rural radio station may cost only $5.

## ▢ Preparing the Advertisement

It is a long and complex project to prepare a major national advertising campaign. It must be remembered that advertising is only one part of what is called the **marketing mix** used to sell goods and services. Marketing is a system of business activities designed to plan, price, promote, and distribute something of value to potential customers and users, according to William J. Shannon, author of *Fundamentals of Marketing*. Sales, sales promotion, packaging, and distribution are other aspects of the marketing mix.

Many businesses invest heavily in sales promotion and spend much more money on the salaries and commissions earned by sales representatives in the field than they spend on advertising for their products. Advertising may be directed toward specifically helping these sales people do their job. A particular advertising campaign may be designed in part to excite sales representatives about the product or service, to make them more enthusiastic about what they are selling. Or the advertisements may be used to bring the product or service to the attention of wholesale or retail buyers who are then more likely to be receptive to sales representatives.

Sales promotion involves many things including free samples, coupons, sweepstakes, and other kinds of contests. Food manufacturers usually spend more money on cents-off-coupons for their products than they spend on advertising. Sales promotion also includes what is called point of sale promotion—displays, racks, banners, signs, and other hoopla installed where the product is sold. Sometimes sales promotion devices are used to stimulate the salespeople rather than the consumer. Sales contests, with winners receiving free trips or expensive merchandise, are considered sales promotion.

A great deal of money is often invested in packaging a product so that it stands out from competitors and catches the consumer's eye. And of course, no product can be sold if it is not delivered to the dealers. Distribution is a very important part of marketing.

Advertising constitutes about 20 percent of selling cost for the average consumer product. Sometimes a considerably higher percentage of selling costs is devoted to advertising. Nearly 60 percent of the money spent on selling over-the-counter drugs is spent on advertising. The sale of cosmetics, liquor, breakfast foods, pet foods, magazines, and cigarettes also depends heavily on advertising. Other products and product lines often use little or no advertising. It has been estimated that large bakeries spend as little as 5 percent of sales costs on advertising their bread and other baked goods. Hershey's chocolates did no advertising at all until 1970 when it was forced to fight off attacks on its market share by rivals Nestle's and Mars. Founder Milton Hershey claimed that a good product, well distributed, sells itself. Of course Hershey's chocolate bars were widely distributed in the rations given to soldiers and sailors during the Second World War. To many people of that generation, a chocolate bar is a Hershey bar. Volkswagen did little advertising in the United States prior to 1959. The car was sold largely by word of mouth, the testimony of satisfied owners and the praise of auto experts.

The advertising for a product or service is designed and used in connection with all other aspects of the marketing strategy. Research usually precedes every other step if the marketing process is carried out properly. The product itself is studied; what are its features, its advantages, its strong points? Researchers also examine the potential market for the product—to whom do we hope to sell this item? And finally, it is useful to study the competition as well.

Market research generally has a bad name. Critics often charge that the research is carried out to help the marketer manipulate the consumer, to develop what Vance Packard called "the hidden persuaders." But researchers defend their work, claiming they are only seeking to discover what the consumer really wants. But that is only partially true, according to sociologist Michael Schudson, author of *Advertis-*

*ing, the Uneasy Persuasion.* What market researchers actually seek, Schudson wrote, is to find out what consumers want from among commercially viable choices. Marketers keep the consumer in mind only to the degree that the consumer defines his or her own prospects in terms agreeable to the marketers. What marketing research is really designed to produce is data that will allow the seller to successfully "position" his or her product or service in the marketplace. That is, offer a product that meets a perceived consumer need—no matter how narrow—revealed by the research. Research findings like these can sometimes influence the development of a product. Research findings in the early eighties undoubtedly revealed that many cola drinkers, concerned about the effects of caffeine in their soft drinks, were turning to other kinds of soda. Industry response was the development of caffeine-free colas. Other times, research will merely suggest the manner in which a product might be advertised or promoted. The Miller Brewing Co. discovered through research that most beer is consumed at the end of the day, after work. The "Miller Time" advertising campaign resulted, suggesting that people enjoy a Miller High Life beer when they finish work in the late afternoon. Regardless of how research is used, it is the important first step in all advertising and marketing campaigns.

A budget for advertising is prepared once a basic marketing strategy is determined. The budget really defines the amount and kind of advertising that will be prepared. Then several different things take place, usually simultaneously. The actual advertisements are prepared. This is the creative or communicative aspect of advertising; to many people, the romantic part of the business. But it is only a small part of advertising. Copywriters and artists work to prepare the words and pictures that will carry the advertising message to the audience. A production staff works to actually produce the final advertisements that will be published in newspapers and magazines or broadcast on radio or television.

At about the same time, media planning is underway. Media planners determine the best route to reach the target audience for the advertising. The seller of an acne medicine seeks to aim the advertising at teenagers. What are the best media to reach this audience? A daily newspaper would reach some teenagers—many more non-teenagers. The same would be true for an episode of "Golden Girls." A better media selection would include radio spots on a popular rock station, music television broadcasts, and perhaps magazines like *Seventeen.* Media planners must also consider the advertising budget when selecting media. Reaching the correct audience at the lowest possible cost per thousand readers or viewers is usually the target. Once the media plan is developed, media planners and media buyers place insertion orders with publications and buy radio and television time.

More research is desirable after the advertising has been published or broadcast. How well was the message communicated? Did the proper audience see or hear the message? If the product failed to grab consumers was this because the advertising failed or because the product failed?

## ☐ Advertising in the 1990s

Changes are taking place in the marketplace in the 1990s, and some of these changes are not good for advertising. The marketing of consumer goods is becoming more and more difficult in some ways, and manufacturers are seeking new devices to attract buyers to their products.

For example, new products have proliferated into supermarkets at a rate never experienced in the past. There were 84 different cereal brands on the shelves in 1979; 150 in 1989. A typical supermarket stocked 10 different brands of toothpaste in 1979; 31 brands were on the shelves in 1989. "As brands proliferate, they become more alike," noted marketing consultant William M. Weilbacher. "Advertising cannot serve to differentiate these brands," he added. Producers are using more point of sale promotions, discounts and cents-off coupons to lure customers to try these new products.

Knowledge of customer wants and needs has always been regarded as power in the sales business, and at one time, because of their research capabilities, advertising agencies often knew more than anyone else about what the customer wanted and was buying. The introduction of the check-out scanners at supermarkets has changed that. Today, the stores know more about what they are selling and who is buying what product than at any time in the past. It is now difficult for a manufacturer to try to convince a buyer for a supermarket chain that its new cereal is selling and in great demand when the buyer has accurate data on her desk that reveals that the chain has sold less than 100 cases of the breakfast food in the past three weeks.

Supermarkets have started renting shelf space to manufacturers who want them to stock particular products. These "slotting allowances," as they are called, can cost as much as $4,000 per product per store. Slotting allowances come out of advertising budgets, and hence there is less money to spend on advertising and other marketing schemes. Most manufacturers claim they can get a better response to a new product by slotting it into supermarkets and distributing cents-off coupons for the product than by mounting elaborate advertising campaigns that try to extoll differences that probably really don't exist between the new product and existing products.

Product clutter is only one problem. Advertising clutter, especially on television, is another equally serious problem for advertisers. According to reliable estimates, about 2,600 commercials were telecast on national television each week in 1971. Now, about 6,100 are telecast each week. The number of ads shown on network television increased by 14 percent between 1988 and 1989, according to *Newsweek*, while studies suggest that viewer recall of TV commercials has begun to drop significantly. "The television medium is cluttered with increasingly more complicated ads," according to Roger Flechsig, vice-president of SAMI/Burke, a marketing research company. "There is only so much people can absorb."

The total amount of time devoted to commercials on national television has not increased substantially. The increase in advertising messages is largely the result of shorter commercials. The 60-second spot was the norm 20 years ago. Today it is the 30-second spot, with a great many 15s thrown in as well. From the real ending of a primetime show (the break before the closing credits) until the real beginning of the next program (after the break following the opening credits), it is not uncommon to find 15 different commercial messages. This is what the industry calls "clutter." A 30-second television commercial, that costs on the average of $185,000 to produce and another $250,000 to show, is buried amongst an avalanche of other advertising messages. Success in advertising in the 1990s involves finding ways to distinguish your messages from the others that are shown and published. Several strategies have been used.

## ▣ Celebrity Identification

Testimonial advertising is not a new idea but, in the 1980s and 1990s, identifying products with celebrities through endorsements and other means is an important part of consumer goods advertising. The "Cola Wars" provide a good case in point. In 1989, according to the *New York Times,* Coca-Cola employed singers Kim Carnes, George Michael, Whitney Houston, Elton John, and Robert Plant; vocal groups Earth, Wind & Fire, Manhattan Transfer, the Pointer Sisters, and Run DMC; actors Art Carney and Don Johnson; model Elle McPherson; NHL hockey star Wayne Gretzky; and cartoon character Roger Rabbit to sell Coke. Not to be out-done, Pepsi-Cola employed singers David Bowie, Ray Charles, Madonna, Robert Palmer, Michael Jackson, and Tina Turner; songwriter/record producer Lionel Richie; performers Billy Crystal, Michael J. Fox, and Patrick Swayze; sports stars Dwight Gooden, Catfish Hunter, and Joe Montana; vocal group Menudo, and former Congresswoman and vice-presidential candidate Geraldine Ferraro to sell Pepsi.

"Coke and Pepsi aren't in the product business anymore," said Clive Chajet, chairman of Lippincott & Marguiles, a corporate identity firm. " They're in the image business, in show business. There is almost no differentiation between Coke and Pepsi, so they have run out of things to say about their products. They have to do it via images," he added.

This can be a very lucrative business for the celebrities involved. Contracts be-tween Pepsi and Michael Jackson, Madonna, and Lionel Richie reportedly totalled $5 million each. James Garner's work for Polaroid earned him $3 million. (Interest-ingly, lots of viewers remembered the camera ads done by James Garner and Mari-ette Hartley, but about one-third of those interviewed remembered them as ads for Kodak, not Polaroid.) Bill Cosby has had million dollar plus contracts with Coca-Cola, General Foods (Jell-O), and Kodak. Experts say that the quarterback on the winning Super Bowl team can earn between $500,000 and $1 million in endorse-ments, including a sizable sum for walking across the field when the game ends and answering on camera the question: "Now that you've won the Super Bowl, Joe Blow, what are you going to do?" Answer: "I'm going to Disneyland!"

Even the dead give celebrity endorsements. James Dean sells Levi jeans and Converse shoes; Charlie Chaplin sells IBM computers. There are at least two major American companies who license the likenesses of the dead for use in commercials. Curtis Management Group represents more than 50 dead celebrities. The Roger Richman Agency, with 30 deceased celebrities in its stable, is Curtis's major compet-itor. The legal liability an advertiser may incur from using the likeness of a dead ce-lebrity varies from state to state, with some states like California strongly protecting the rights of the dead celebrities and their families. Other states, like New York, largely reject the concept that the dead have legal rights to their likenesses. Advertis-ers normally use companies like Curtis and Richman to protect themselves from law-suits for using the dead to endorse or promote products.

A celebrity endorsement or promotion can certainly push a particular product ahead of the competition. But these endorsements can also backfire. Pepsi had to pull its widely publicized "Make a wish" ad with Madonna when many viewers con-fused the TV spot with a racier and more sexually suggestive music video Madonna released at the same time. Faced with a growing controversy over religious imagery and the threat of a consumer boycott, the soft drink maker pulled the spot at a re-

The use of celebrities in endorsements and advertisements is one of the hallmarks of modern advertising. Even dead celebrities are used. James Dean, pictured here with Natalie Wood in the film *Rebel Without a Cause,* is one of the most widely used of the dead celebrities; agents control the use of his likeness in advertising. (Photofest)

ported cost of $10 million. James Garner's ads for the beef industry suffered when the actor underwent coronary bypass surgery. And Bruce Willis's partying habits, which received wide publicity in the tabloid press, forced Seagram's to take his ads for their wine cooler off the air. Still, there seems little let-up in the rush to sign the latest popular celebrity to endorse this or that product. Advertisers believe this is one way to distinguish their advertising from that of their competitors.

Another way to distinguish your advertisements from the others is to get your advertising into the news. This inadvertently happened for Pepsi-Cola in 1984 when Michael Jackson's hair caught fire while he was filming a multimillion-dollar song and dance extravaganza for a commercial. Certainly Pepsi and its advertising agency, BBDO, had not planned this near-tragic accident. But they had planned and worked toward getting media coverage of the filming of the unusual commercial.

But there was nothing inadvertent when an advertisement for the cold remedy Drixoral made headlines in late 1989. Dozens of local, network, and syndicated television news programs, including "NBC Nightly News" and ABC's "Nightline," carried the story that two of the commercial television networks had refused to carry an ad for the cold medication because the commercial included footage of both President George Bush and Soviet President Mikhail Gorbachev without their permission. Most of the television reports included the complete 15-second commercial.

A public relations agency sent out copies of the ad to several journalists before the commercial was released, with a suggestion in writing that there might be a story in this commercial because previous U.S. administrations had not looked kindly on such exploitation of presidents. The hope, of course, was to get some news coverage for the commercial. Dan Klores, who works for Howard J. Rubenstein Associates, later revealed, "I planted the idea of calling the White House to make a better news story. I was hoping for an 'Isn't that funny' or a 'You shouldn't do that.' " But when the networks refused to show the spot, the story got even bigger. "What a great stroke of luck," Klores said. "Now it goes from being a column to being a full-blown two- or three-day news story."

This strategy, of course, is one that is mined heavily in political advertising. In 1988 two of George Bush's campaign ads (the Willie Horton prisoner-furlough spot and the dirty Boston Harbor commercial) became so controversial that they were repeatedly played on news programs when reporters wanted to explain to viewers what the controversy was all about.

Both Pepsi-Cola and Coca-Cola have successfully pushed their commercials into the news; Pepsi with its tearing down of the Berlin Wall advertising, and Coke by the reshooting with original cast and families of the "I'd Like to Teach the World a Song" spot. The increase in the amount of time devoted to news, especially on the local level, and the need for news directors to fill this time, substantially increases the likelihood of the use of these well-produced video news releases about commercials and a host of other advertiser-related subject matter.

## Seeking the Masses

Not all advertisers seek to reach a mass audience with their messages, but those who do could, until recently, turn to the traditional television networks (ABC, CBS, and NBC) as vehicles to reach nearly all the people in the country. No longer. The audience share for the networks is down substantially to the 65 percent level. (See pages 309–310.) And many advertisers are finding it hard to get the saturation coverage they seek. Comprehensive, multimedia campaigns are now being used by some advertisers to try to gain the massive coverage network television once provided. A K-Mart campaign in 1989 is a good example.

The retailer worked with *Family Circle* magazine to produce several articles on the renovation of a home, written by Martha Stewart, an interior designer and home entertainment writer. K-Mart purchased all the advertising space around the stories in each issue of the magazine. Stewart, who is a paid K-Mart consultant, used products sold by the giant retailer as she renovated the dwelling. She also appeared in television advertising which tied the home renovation and the K-Mart products together. Some observers questioned whether the magazine had sold its news space to K-Mart to get the advertising. Putting that matter aside, however, the campaign generated considerable visibility for K-Mart and reached an audience that was much larger than television alone could have reached.

## Using Bookends

One of the most visible and widely discussed advertising campaigns of the late 1980s featured an improbable star: a bright pink bunny, wearing Ray-Ban sunglasses and blue thongs, banging a big bass drum as it strutted around the set. The Eveready

The Eveready Energizer Bunny was one of the most visible and popular commercial systems of the early 1990s. Advertisements featuring the pink bunny with shades and blue thongs were perhaps the most successful example of book-end–style television commercials.
(The Eveready Battery Company, Inc.)

Energizer bunny immediately caught the attention of not only the advertising world but of television viewers across the nation.

The campaign was generated by the Eveready Battery Co. in an effort to maintain its dominance in the alkaline battery market. Duracell had been steadily cutting into Eveready's share of this high-volume business. The mechanical bunny, powered by an Energizer battery, runs amok in the studio during the advertisement and marches out the door. Commercial over; roll the next spot—an ad for coffee or nasal spray. In the midst of the next spot, which looks exactly like a commercial for coffee or nasal spray, the bunny marches in, knocking over props. It just keeps on running. Startled viewers are left wondering where the feisty bunny will pop up next.

"Consumers see so much advertising that they are bored with the average commercial and we thought the best way to catch their attention was to have the Energizer bunny seem to be popping up in other people's commercials," said Tony Wright, vice-president and management supervisor at Chiat/Day/Mojo, the agency that created the commercial.

The device used in this commercial was a variation of a new television advertising technique called **bookends.** A bookend is a commercial that is split into two parts, separated by commercials from other advertisers. The first segment creates a problem; the second segment solves it. For example, a headache sets in during the first spot and Excedrin tablets are consumed for relief. In the second segment, telecast 15 or 30 seconds later, the headache is gone. Excedrin did it again.

"Bookends are intriguing to people because they set up a scenario in which the viewer has to keep watching to get the rest of the story," said Richard Costyra, director of media for J. Walter Thompson. "By arousing curiosity, the advertiser has a better chance of his message being heard. It's the element of surprise that makes these ads effective," he added. The surprise of the Energizer bunny popping into various commercials was apparently effective. The company noted an increase in Energizer sales after the ads were telecast.

# ISSUES IN ADVERTISING

There is no shortage of issues in advertising, but a couple seem to come to the fore more often than any others. Is advertising truthful? Does it work, and succeed in getting consumers to buy things they don't need or want? We will focus on each of these matters briefly.

## ◻ Is Advertising Truthful?

Anyone who tries to answer the question, Is advertising truthful? is looking for trouble. It is a question that can only be partially answered at best. What does "truthful" mean? That's easy: can the claims made by an advertiser for a product be proved? But most contemporary advertisements for consumer goods don't make any claims. An ad will show a group of healthy, happy, attractive young people drinking soda or beer, eating burgers or pizza, playing football or basketball, taking a vacation or discussing a work-related problem. And then the ad will attempt in some way to tie the very existence of these people to the product that is offered for sale. Is that truthful? Can that be proved? Of course not. If a realtor offers to sell you a three-bedroom, 2,400 square foot home on a 100 foot by 100 foot lot for $250,000, each of these promises can be proved truthful or false. But if the realtor offers to give you the serenity of a summer sunset, the warmth of a cozy fireplace, the security of a family dinner, or the joy of home gardening if you buy a home in Pleasant Valley subdivision, none of these claims are subject to a meaningful test of truth. And this is the sum and substance of most advertising in America today. Truth, then, is an elusive concept.

Product claims made by advertisers do have to meet certain standards. Advertising messages are subject to scrutiny by bodies within the industry itself and by various government agencies. Advertising is protected by the First Amendment to the United States Constitution. The government may ban false or misleading advertising or advertising for illegal products and services. But truthful advertising cannot be censored unless the government can demonstrate there is a substantial governmental or public interest that will be served by such censorship, and censoring the ad will in fact serve this government interest.

Regulation of advertising by the industry itself is a relatively new phenomenon. (Actually, all regulation of advertising is a relatively new idea, dating back only to the beginning of this century.) Advertising departments at television and radio stations and at newspapers do some screening of advertising before publishing or broadcasting these messages. The national television networks, for example, have rather rigid guidelines about comparative advertising, spots in which the advertiser compares his or her product to a competitor's. Ads that don't meet these guidelines are simply not accepted.

Two agencies within the Better Business Bureau, the National Advertising Division (NAD) and the National Advertising Review Board (NARB), have been established by the industry to regulate national advertising for consumer goods and services. The services of these organizations are open only to advertisers; that is, the purpose of the NAD and the NARB is not to protect consumers from false advertising claims, although that is in fact a result of their activity. Their purpose is to protect one advertiser from the false advertising claims made by a competing company. The agencies are attempting to insure honesty in competition, not necessarily honesty in advertising.

This is a subtle but important point, for it involves once again that elusive concept "truth." Consumers hope advertising is 100 percent truthful. But the maker of Bufferin is only interested in insuring that the maker of Tylenol not be permitted to make a claim that Bufferin cannot make. An analgesic can relieve headache pain, not cure the cause of the headache. The maker of Bufferin would complain if the manufacturer of Tylenol began to claim that this product could cure the cause of a headache. But nearly all brand-name over-the-counter headache remedies strongly suggest that their brand-name remedy will work better at relieving pain than generic aspirin or acetaminophen, which is much cheaper. This is not true. Yet none of the brand-name advertisers will complain about this because they all are permitted to make the same claim. It is the consumer who loses out in this case, not the competing advertiser.

The NAD and the NARB will examine the claims made by an advertiser when a complaint is issued. If the claims are found to be untruthful or unproven, the agencies will ask for a modification in the ad or that the ad be discontinued. The NAD and the NARB have no power to enforce these orders, but the mass media will not publish or broadcast advertising that has been cited by the NAD or the NARB. So while there is no punishment of the advertiser, the untruthful advertisement disappears from view.

In the 1980s advertisers began to sue one another under a federal unfair trade practices statute for false advertising claims. Lawsuits under section 43(a) of the Lanham Act had been permitted for many years, but it has only been recently that federal court money judgments in these cases have made the lawsuits worthwhile to most advertisers. In the late 1980s U-Haul won $40 million in damages from competitor Jartran in a false advertising action. This has generated new interest in this remedy among many advertisers. Regardless of the damage awards, however, some advertisers will sue competitors simply because the stakes in the selling of some consumer products are so high. American Homes Products, the makers of Anacin and Advil, and Johnson and Johnson, the makers of Tylenol, have been in federal court, almost continuously, since 1976, regarding conflicting claims over the relative merits of their brand-name pain relievers. Half-a-dozen suits have already been tried, and many more await trial. To distinguish among the trials, lawyers use Roman numerals: Tylenol I, Anacin II. The federal judge hearing these cases has publicly expressed his fears that he is doomed to spend the rest of his days as a judge as "the czar of over-the-counter drug advertising."

Government regulation of advertising is inconsistent. There are federal regulations, state regulations, and even city and county advertising regulations (usually called consumer protection laws). But the enforcement of these laws generally depends upon the aggressiveness of those with the power to regulate. Some state attorneys general feel such enforcement is important and diligently pursue false advertising complaints. Others do not. Local prosecutors, usually overburdened with cases involving violent crime, usually put matters like false advertising on the back burner, unless strong community pressure arises. The Federal Trade Commission has the responsibility to enforce federal law. This is an independent regulatory agency whose five members are nominated by the president and approved by the Senate. The agency has a huge staff but is also given the responsibility to enforce a host of other federal laws, including the antitrust statutes. In the fifties and early sixties the agency had the nickname, "The Little Gray Lady of Pennsylvania Avenue," because it was so timid in enforcing U.S. trade statutes. The FTC became energized in the late sixties and seventies and vigorously prosecuted several big-name advertisers. New remedies were devised by the FTC, and Congress gave the agency some broad new powers as well. But President Ronald Reagan promised to get government off the back of business when he was elected in 1980, and with the support of a more conservative Congress, he managed to hobble the FTC by appointing commissioners who were prone to inaction. The agency did not languish, but it was certainly not an aggressive friend of the consumer.

The FTC has spent many years attempting to define false and misleading advertising. Its latest test has three parts:

1. There must be a representation, omission, or practice that is likely to mislead the consumer. A claim by a drug maker that its nasal spray will cure a cold is a lie, and as such would be a misrepresentation. Omissions can be important as well. Beneficial Finance Corporation was ordered to stop advertising its "instant tax refund" to consumers because it failed to disclose that the instant refund was actually a loan, for which the consumer had to apply.
2. The act or practice must be considered from the perspective of a consumer who is acting reasonably. The FTC does take special care to protect some groups of consumers, such as children or the terminally ill. But the so-called "reasonable consumer" is considered the benchmark for the agency. And a reasonable consumer, for example, would not expect that baked goods sold as Danish pastry were actually made in Denmark.
3. The representation, omission, or practice must be material. A Chevron gasoline commercial for a new fuel additive featured a no-nonsense spokesman "standing here in front of the Chevron research labs." In fact the announcer was standing in front of a courthouse in California, the research labs being somewhat less picturesque. Claims were made that the advertisement was deceptive, but the FTC ruled that consumers did not buy the gasoline on the basis of what the research labs looked like. The claim was false but was irrelevant.

The FTC has several means to attempt to corral false and misleading statements. In most instances the advertiser agrees to stop making the claim by signing what is called a consent agreement. In this document the advertiser promises never to make a specific advertising claim for a particular product, but does not admit having made the false claim in the first place. Advertisers who are unwilling to sign such an agreement can face court orders to stop the advertisements. In a few instances advertisers have been forced to admit to consumers that previous advertising was not totally truthful. But this latter sanction is rarely used.

The constant exposure to commercials, which is inherent when living in an advertising-driven society such as ours, has probably helped most Americans to develop their own detection systems for false and misleading advertising. Some people, cynical, battle-scarred veterans of consumer wars, tend to believe very few, if any, advertising claims. These tend to be older people, since it is known that younger persons are more susceptible to advertising messages. Other people, those who really expect to find the pot of gold at the end of the rainbow, tend to take most advertising claims at face value. In the end, the most important test of truth in advertising probably lies in the mind of the beholder.

## ☐ Does It Work

Whether or not advertising works as it is supposed to, that is, whether it convinces us to buy the goods and services promoted in the advertisements, is also an unanswerable question for the most part. That may sound strange, considering that nearly $125 billion was spent on advertising last year. If there is no real proof that it works, why spend the money?

Michael Schudson points out that advertising agencies and the mass media can argue the point either way. "If they are trying to convince an advertiser to increase its media budget, they can cite examples of devastatingly successful advertising campaigns. But if they are defending themselves before the FTC or a civic organization decrying television advertising for children, they trot out their data that demonstrate advertising has slight or no effect on product sales."

Critics of the industry argue intuitively that of course advertising works, that it propels us to buy goods we don't need and probably don't want. Look in the medicine cabinet, they argue. Look at all the bottles and jars and boxes of over-the-counter pharmaceuticals that people really don't need to be healthy. Or look in the laundry room at all the soaps and bleaches and softeners. This is prima facie evidence that advertising is successful in peddling unneeded goods to consumers.

The marketplace offers fewer examples today of ultra-successful advertising campaigns than it did in the early days of television. The Revlon factory couldn't turn out cosmetics fast enough to satisfy the demand when the company sponsored the popular "$64,000 Question" television program in the 1950s. And advertising made Alberto Culver Company's VO-5 hair grooming products into household words. Hyundai's $25 million advertising budget in 1986 helped push the sale of this Korean import car beyond even the company's expectations. Hyundai hoped it would sell 100,000 cars in the U.S. in 1986. It sold almost twice that many. By the end of 1987 its Excel model was the best-selling import car in the nation. And advertising by the Australian Tourist Council prompted 1.5 million Americans to call an 800 telephone number to get a free Aussie Holiday Book and made Paul Hogan, the affable Australian spokesman, an American movie star. American tourism to Australia doubled within a year.

The evidence that advertising works is apparent on a smaller scale as well, many in the business note. If you buy a classified ad to sell an automobile, and the car is sold to someone who reads the ad, that is evidence that advertising works. Or, visit the linen department of a local department store the morning the advertised white sale begins. The crowds are more evidence that advertising works.

Longtime advertising professional Rosser Reeves of the Ted Bates agency takes a different point of view. "If the product does not meet some existing need or desire of the consumer, the advertising will ultimately fail," he said. Others agree. The preeminent example of the failure of advertising to sell an unwanted product is Ford Motor Company's Edsel. The highly touted car of the late 1950s and early 1960s

## Somewhere West of Laramie

SOMEWHERE west of Laramie there's a broncho-busting, steer-roping girl who knows what I'm talking about.

She can tell what a sassy pony, that's a cross between greased lightning and the place where it hits, can do with eleven hundred pounds of steel and action when he's going high, wide and handsome.

The truth is—the Playboy was built for her.

Built for the lass whose face is brown with the sun when the day is done of revel and romp and race.

She loves the cross of the wild and the tame.

There's a savor of links about that car—of laughter and lilt and light—a hint of old loves—and saddle and quirt. It's a brawny thing—yet a graceful thing for the sweep o' the Avenue.

Step into the Playboy when the hour grows dull with things gone dead and stale.

Then start for the land of real living with the spirit of the lass who rides, lean and rangy, into the red horizon of a Wyoming twilight.

### JORDAN

JORDAN MOTOR CAR COMPANY, Inc. Cleveland, Ohio

The dominant and identifying advertising trend of the 1920s was the increasing use of psychology, "the deepening appeal to the secret emotions that motivated people to buy," as one author noted. The ad that epitomizes this better than any other is Ned Jordan's 173-word classic, "Somewhere West of Laramie," first published in *The Saturday Evening Post.*
(The Bettmann Archive, Inc.)

simply died, despite huge investments in marketing and advertising. The public was simply not in the market for another mid-sized car, the experts said.

More recent research tends to support Reeves as well. Some 250 volunteers in Eau Claire, Wis., have participated in what is probably the most intensive study ever made of the power of advertising and the sale of consumer goods. Researchers monitored all the commercial advertisements, print and broadcast, that the families saw. Special commercials were often beamed to the families for new products. Subjects in the study shopped at selected supermarkets where computerized checkout equipment recorded all their purchases. Comparing the data on the commercials and the coupons and the purchases, researchers were able to discern the impact of advertising and other promotional devices.

Researcher Gerard Tellis, who evaluated the data, concluded after a year that television advertising has almost no effect on consumer buying habits. Tellis, who is on the faculty of the University of Iowa, said that in the case of laundry detergents, lowering the price of the product through sales or coupons resulted in a large boost in sales, whereas television advertising had only minimal effects.

Esther Thorson, a researcher at the University of Wisconsin, says advertisers have mistakenly assumed that consumers evaluate products and make purchasing decisions in a rational way. With this theory, good advertising should increase sales. But Thorson argues that most people have very little conscious involvement with the things they buy. She argues that consumers are more often swayed by an emotional rather than an intellectual appeal in advertising. "Making consumers feel something is much more important than convincing them that a product is better," she said. And advertisers are taking this advice. Recent advertising for a cake mix, for example, does not speak of the ease of baking a prepared cake mix or the wonderful, moist taste. Instead, Betty Crocker tries to move consumers by showing them how baking a cake can express love for one's family.

When advertisers try to hit emotions with their ads, they are attempting to somehow touch feelings and ideas that the consumer already has. This is what many authorities agree is the prime function of advertising, to reinforce socially or biologically determined wants and preferences, according to Paul Baran and Paul Sweezy. Most materialistic desires stem from the general climate prevailing in society. Advertising can reinforce these desires, "intensify these propensities and facilitate their gratification," Baran and Sweezy noted. Some have called advertising an alarm clock for America's sleeping desires. So advertising does not succeed because it changes people's attitudes, but because the advertiser is able to find, through research and other means, a way of linking a product or service with an existing attitude, emotionally bonding with a consumer. Michael Schudson put this idea a bit differently when he wrote, "Advertising does not so much invent social values or ideals of its own as it borrows, usurps, or exploits what advertising takes to be the prevailing social values. It then reminds us of beautiful moments in our own lives or it pictures magical moments we would like to experience."

Is advertising essential to the sale of a product? The most successful consumer products in the mass market in the past three decades have been illegal drugs: marijuana, cocaine, heroin, and so on. They have succeeded with absolutely no advertising. This supports the notion that product sales depend upon a great many factors—social factors, demographic factors, economic factors, even time factors.

## ☐ Is Advertising Bad or Good for Us?

In the end the debate comes down to, Is advertising good or bad for us? Much advertising does inform us about products and prices and other facts of life in the marketplace. Even the strongest critic of advertising can find value in classified ads, for example. Some argue that advertising stimulates the economy by publicizing material and cultural incentives. This helps motivate increased productive efforts by both workers and management. Margaret Mead, the noted anthropologist, wrote: "Ours is an economy that is geared to a rising standard of living. We are geared to a notion that we could live better than we do—so no one has settled down very comfortably

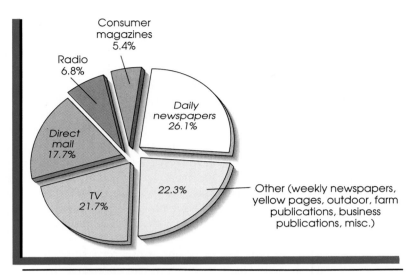

FIGURE 10-2 Distribution of advertising expenditures in 1989 among various mass media.
(American Newspaper Publishers Association)

and is satisfied with the way he lives." We work to buy, then. Many think this is an unsatisfactory reason for working. But these critics are essentially challenging the basis of our economic system. If we are going to live in the kind of system we have created, then advertising plays an important and positive role. If we want to create and live in a different kind of system, then advertising may become unneeded, superfluous. (See figure 10-2.)

But even its staunchest supporters don't find advertising without its warts. Advertising is often offensive, insulting, and stupid. Even advertisers support the notion that there is too much advertising in the mass media. (Ideally an advertiser would like but a single ad in a newspaper or during an evening of television, its own ad.) While advertising does increase the visibility of consumer goods, it also increases the cost of many goods. This is a tricky equation, for some will argue that without the mass production made possible by mass demand, which is partly the result of advertising, prices for many goods would be higher, not lower. Possibly. But there is absolutely no question that the cost of advertising goods and services is passed on to consumers in the form of higher prices, and for some kinds of goods (cosmetics, for example) this cost far exceeds the cost of creating the product in the first place. Advertising can also be used to promote dangerous or potentially dangerous products. This is the argument used by those seeking to ban the advertising of alcohol and tobacco. And certainly advertising does promote the use of these products. But many observers will argue that dangerous products should not be in the marketplace in the first place. Banning advertising for tobacco and alcohol products makes no sense, many argue, as long as the manufacturer of these products continues to be subsidized by the government. (The U.S. subsidizes the cost of growing both tobacco and grain, the raw materials for cigarettes and alcoholic beverages.) If the government's farm policy was changed, the cost of both of these commodities would rise, increasing the cost of the products in the marketplace. A price increase probably would have a greater impact on reducing demand than a ban on advertising.

Baran and Sweezy make an argument against advertising that many would agree with, even many in the field. They argue that the biggest problem with advertising is the belief that it doesn't do any harm because no one believes it anyway.

> The greatest damage done by advertising is precisely that it incessantly demonstrates the prostitution of men and women who lend their intellects, their voices, their artistic skills to purposes in which they themselves do not believe and that it teaches the essential meaninglessness of all creations of the mind; words, images and ideas. The real danger from advertising is that it helps to shatter and ultimately destroy our most precious non-material possessions: the confidence in the existence of meaningful purposes of human activity and respect for the integrity of man.

This is a strong indictment of a craft whose purposes seem little more than to tickle our mind to draw attention to a product or service. Yet there is an essential truth as well in what the authors say; advertising does represent a cheapening of the human spirit by its predominant and incessant focus on commercialism, buying and selling, materialism. But this is a criticism that today could be applied to a vast portion of American commerce. Advertising is simply the most visible portion of this aspect of our culture.

## CAREERS IN ADVERTISING

Jobs in advertising span a wide range of activities. Unfortunately, most young people who are interested in advertising see themselves working for an advertising agency. While there are many agency jobs available, they tend to be located in a handful of cities (New York, Chicago, San Francisco, Los Angeles, Houston, and a few more), and landing such a job tends to be quite competitive.

Even within advertising agencies there are a myriad of tasks that need to be performed. So-called full service advertising agencies will offer their clients a complete range of services, including research, creative work, media planning, and even public relations services. All of these at a fairly reasonable cost to a client. Traditionally agencies earned most of their income from collecting a commission—usually 15 percent—from the mass media that carry the advertising placed by the agency. Imagine that Stem Root Beer decides to spend $500,000 on television advertising. The advertising agency will prepare and place the spots and collect $500,000 from Stem. But the television network will only charge the agency $425,000 for the television time, leaving the advertising agency with a $75,000 commission for its work on the campaign. The advertising agency will bill the client directly for costs associated with producing the advertisements—talent, film, studio rental, and so forth. To this they will add a small service charge. In recent years the commission system has been slowly replaced by straight cost-plus billing at some agencies and pay for performance contracts at others. If the ads work, the agency earns a large fee. If not, the fee is smaller. Not all advertising agencies offer full service to clients. Such agencies, often called boutiques, focus exclusively upon the creative end of advertising. The client must employ others to do the other chores.

Work in an advertising agency might involve any number of jobs. Agencies hire copy writers, art directors, artists, media planners, media buyers, production technicians, researchers, and individuals called account executives who supervise the client's account in the agency. Journalism and communication schools usually offer programs that prepare people for most agency jobs, excluding creative art positions. The skills of an artist are best learned in an art school.

There is a considerable amount of advertising work outside the agencies. Most large companies have their own advertising departments. Newspapers, magazines, and broadcasting stations employ people who sell advertising space or time and even prepare advertising for smaller advertisers.

Most jobs in advertising are to be found in large cities. It is estimated that as many as half of all people who work in advertising work in New York, Chicago, or Los Angeles. Salaries for beginners are not high, but tend to rise rapidly. Persons successful in advertising can make a comfortable living and earn far more than persons with comparable jobs in newspapers or even broadcast journalism. (This, of course does not include the broadcast news superstar anchorpeople.) Yet it takes an individual with a special type of personality to stick with a career in advertising, according to Larry Bowen of the University of Washington's School of Communications. The pressures to produce quality work under often impossible deadlines make advertising a 24-hour-a-day fixation. Work stays with the advertising practioner night and day, ulcers and heart attacks create more vacancies than the industry will admit, Bowen said. The average age of the advertising professional is 43; it tends to be a young person's industry.

## BIBLIOGRAPHY

These are some of the materials that have been helpful in the preparation of this chapter.

Baran, Paul, and Sweezy, Paul. "Theses on Advertising," *Science and Society,* Winter, 1964.

Barnouw, Erik. *The Sponsor.* New York: Oxford University Press, 1978.

Behrens, Steve. "How Well Does TV Sell?" *Channels,* July/August, 1988.

Callahan, Jean. "Even in Death Big Names Keep On Working," *Seattle Post-Intelligencer,* August 18, 1989.

Couzens, Michael. "Political Quick Step," *Channels,* March, 1989.

Engel, Jack. *Advertising: The Process and Practice.* New York: McGraw-Hill, 1980.

Foltz, Kim. "TV Ad Clutter Grows, So Rabbit Runs Wild," *The New York Times,* October 23, 1989.

Kleinfield, N. R. "Spread of TV Ad Networks Brings Concern About Glut," *The New York Times,* February 10, 1989.

McGill, Douglas. "Star Wars in Cola Advertising," *The New York Times,* March 27, 1989.

Monkman, Carol S. "Consumer Cynics Aren't Fooled by Ritzy, Glitzy Ads," *Seattle Post-Intelligencer,* September 15, 1989.

Pope, Daniel. *The Making of Modern Advertising.* New York: Basic Books, 1983.

Rothenberg, Randall. "Ad Research Shifts from Products to People," *The New York Times,* April 6, 1989.

———. "Brits Buy Up the Ad Business," *The New York Times Magazine,* July 2, 1989.

———. "Change in Consumer Markets Hurting Advertising Industry," *The New York Times,* October 3, 1989.

———. "Surveys Proliferate, But Answers Dwindle," *The New York Times,* October 5, 1990.

Sandage, Charles H., and Fryburger, Vernon. *The Role of Advertising.* Homewood, Ill.: Irwin, 1960.

Schudson, Michael. *Advertising: The Uneasy Persuasion.* New York: Basic Books, 1984.

"Science 1, Advertisers 0," *U.S. News & World Report,* May 1, 1989.

Tolley, Stuart B. "TV Advertisers Should Take a Closer Look at Viewers' Ability to Remember Commercials," *presstime,* November, 1990.

"Tuning Out TV Ads," *Newsweek,* April 17, 1989.

# CHAPTER 11

# THE INFORMING FUNCTION: PUBLIC RELATIONS AND NEWS

*V*irtually all who have studied the mass media and attempted to explain their functions or roles in society have included an informing function. The flow of information in a society is critical to the well-being of the members of the society. It was cultural historian William Irwin Thompson who once described the gathering of information as the individual's means of storing energy to help control his or her relationship with the environment.

There are scores of agencies and organizations within a complex society that perform an informing function. The government is one. In addition to the political functions of government (making laws, and so forth), agencies at all levels of government generate huge amounts of information that is often invaluable to the people who live in our society. This information ranges from tips on how to safely can fruits and vegetables to suggested questions potential homeowners should ask mortgage lenders to the safety record or gas mileage of various automobiles. The governments, federal, state, and local, circulate this material through libraries, the mass media, or directly to interested citizens.

Universities and colleges generate information as well. Some of this is disseminated by teachers in classrooms; some of it is provided directly to members of the community through bulletins and booklets; still more is disseminated by researchers via scholarly journals aimed primarily at other researchers. Information is also generated by public interest research groups, business and industry, public utilities, and many other institutions that exist in a modern society.

In the United States today, the mass media play an important role in the dissemination of information. Some of this information is generated by reporters and editors who work for newspapers and magazines, radio and television. But much

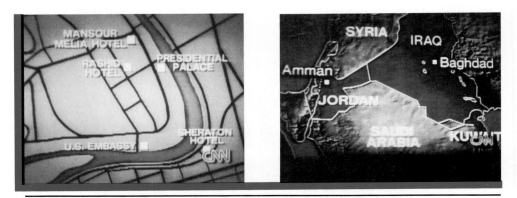

In times of grave crises, Americans turn to the mass media for information. As the war broke out in the Persian Gulf in January of 1991, television viewing skyrocketed—even though broadcast reporters in the Middle East could often show us little more than maps of the region.
(CNN)

more of this information is generated by persons outside the mass media and is communicated to the general public by the press.

Americans rely heavily on the press for information. We rely upon the mass media to tell us not only what has happened of importance in the world and the nation and the region, but to tell us who won last night's basketball game, whether it will rain or snow today, the winning numbers in the state lottery, which store has the best buy on dress shirts, the closing Dow Jones average, whether the new Mel Gibson movie is worth seeing, and hundreds and hundreds of other items of information.

But the press cannot tell us everything that has happened, everything that is important. That would surely be impossible. Choices must be made, and that is what editors and news directors are paid to do—decide what information to pass along immediately, what information to pass along later, and what information to discard. On what basis are these decisions made? That is a critical question and one to which the consumers of the mass media should know the answer. Often times it is as important to know what is left out of a news broadcast or a newspaper as it is to know what is published or broadcast. While a reader or viewer cannot always find out what news hasn't been published or telecast, if the criteria used to select the news is understood, they can often gain a sufficient understanding of what kinds of news is missing to protect themselves.

One of the most important factors consumers of news must understand is that most information that comes to us in the press was generated by someone outside the press who wants us to know that information. In many instances the source of this information is benign: the press officer at the Supreme Court of the United States who passes out opinions by the high court so reporters may tell readers and viewers about these decisions. In other instances the source of information has a baser motive: a public relations spokesperson for the tobacco industry assuring people that there is no evidence linking smoking cigarettes and health problems. An entire industry or craft has developed whose central function is to insure the flow of information about a particular business, government agency, trade association, university, or whatever. This is called public relations. An understanding of this largely misunderstood undertaking is essential to any comprehension of the flow of information in our society.

# PUBLIC RELATIONS

What is public relations? Public relations are actions of a corporation, store, government, or industry in promoting good will between itself and the public, the community, employees, customers, and so forth, according to *The Random House Dictionary of the English Language.* Scott Cutlip and Allen Center in *Effective Public Relations,* define the public relations function as a "planned effort to influence and maintain favorable opinion through acceptable performance, honestly presented, and with reliance on two-way communications."

The definitions make clear that public relations involves a total communication effort, an understanding of both public attitudes and the policies of the client. The public relations specialist through various devices, including the use of the news columns and news broadcasts of the mass media, attempts to integrate corporate (or government or social service agency) needs and societal needs and develop strategies that serve both sets of interests. Listening is as important as speaking or writing to a public relations professional. Understanding the needs of all parties concerned is an important element in developing successful policies.

Although public relations is frequently associated with big business, a wide range of organizations and institutions use public relations techniques today, including trade associations, schools, government agencies, civic organizations, universities, the military, social service agencies, and churches. In business top public relations managers are in the highest echelons of the corporate structure. In government the nation's most visible publicist is the president's press secretary, or media advisor.

## ☐ The Development of the Craft

When public relations is defined as the two-way communication system outlined above, its history is rather short. When it is defined loosely to include all attempts to publicize and sway public opinion on a matter, the craft is almost as old as civilization. Greeks and Romans used public relations to foster their cultures. Grecian poets were commissioned by the government to write poetry that would manipulate public opinion. Virgil's "Georgics," a poem that extolls the virtues of country living, was ordered by the Roman government, which sought to convince the citizens of Rome to move out of the overcrowded city. In this nation the most visible publicist of the colonial period was Samuel Adams, who utilized the colonial press to foment a revolutionary spirit in the citizens of New England. Through intensive propaganda Adams turned a mob action against British troops in which five citizens were killed into the much-heralded Boston Massacre. To enhance public understanding and create resentment of British import duties, Adams staged the Boston Tea Party in 1773. Frederick Whitney wrote:

> . . . a group of thugs dressed as Indians in Boston where an Indian hadn't been seen for 150 years, dumping tea into the harbor and calling it a tea party had a certain amount of pizzazz, bore telling and retelling with a chuckle. It had drama and propaganda value in generating word-of-mouth transmission.

Ivy Ledbetter Lee is regarded by most as the father of modern public relations. His early work is still studied today.
(The Bettmann Archive, Inc.)

Practices we have described as true public relations did not emerge until the early years of the current century. The vast industrial growth in the latter decades of the nineteenth century had produced a popular distrust of modern business. The revelations of the muckrakers, the investigative journalists of the late nineteenth and early twentieth centuries, cast an even darker shadow over American economic enterprises. Such an atmosphere of distrust and suspicion proved challenging to an individual who sought to deal in the truth, a man like Ivy Ledbetter Lee, regarded by many as the father of modern public relations. Lee had been a journalist with *The New York Times* and the *New York Journal.* He proclaimed himself "a press agent who dealt in the truth" in 1908 and sent his declaration of principles to all editors with whom he corresponded. He told newspeople that "this is not a secret press bureau. All our work is done in the open. We aim to supply news . . . Our matter is accurate." Editors who distrusted his releases were urged to check them independently. "Our plan is," he wrote, "to supply to the press and the public of the United States prompt and accurate information concerning subjects which it is of value and interest to the public to know about. . . ."

A serious train derailment on the Pennsylvania Railroad lines helped make Lee a famous man. Company officials proposed to hush up the accident, which took several lives. Lee instead provided the press with full and accurate accounts of what had taken place. Journalists were sped to the scene of the tragedy in special trains, arranged by Lee, to see for themselves what had happened. Lee convinced Pennsylvania Railroad officials to survey the rail beds throughout the system to help avoid future derailments. The railroad line, Lee announced, would provide financial aid to the families of persons killed or injured in the accident. Ivy Ledbetter Lee turned the derailment tragedy into a public relations triumph for the Pennsylvania Railroad, noted one author.

The government followed private industry in seeing that effective public relations was important to gain public trust and support. During World War I, President Woodrow Wilson organized the Committee on Public Information to help the nation understand the war and build support for the government effort. Edward L. Bernays, a member of the Committee, emerged in the 1920s as another founding father of modern PR. Bernays practiced public relations in New York City, taught classes on the subject at New York University, and has been credited with creating the concept of the "public relations counselor," a professional who works for various commercial and noncommercial clients. In his book, *Crystallizing Public Opinion,* Bernays wrote:

> Perhaps the chief contribution of the public relations counsel to the public and to his client is his ability to understand and analyze obscure tendencies of the public mind. . . . It is his capacity for crystallizing the obscure tendencies of the public mind before they have reached definite expression, which makes him so valuable.

Bernays, like others in the field, began to take advantage of the growing body of literature on public opinion theory. The literature was being generated by a growing number of persons interested in communications research—although it was not called that in those days. By the 1950s public relations specialists were working very closely with communication researchers to study the formation and changing of public attitudes.

The bloom on the rose of public relations began to fade in the 1940s. Press agents and others whose sole purpose was to get publicity for someone or something became highly visible, especially in the entertainment industry. "I don't care what you say about me as long as you spell my name right" became the maxim of high-powered Hollywood press agents. The term "flack" became a popular derogatory synonym for the high flying press agents of publicists. Serious public relations practitioners, dismayed by the growing public condemnation of the field, formed the Public Relations Society of America to put as much distance as possible between true public relations and the rampant press agentry. PRSA sought to establish standards for the practice of public relations. In 1969 the organization went a step further and established mandatory accreditation procedures for all members of the national society. A practitioner must have a minimum of five years experience in public relations before becoming eligible to join PRSA. Actual membership hinges on passing an eight-hour written and oral examination administered by members of PRSA. These standards succeeded in separating the men from the boys, so to speak. Today only about 10 percent of all the people who claim to be doing public relations work are members of PRSA.

There are many kinds of public relations work. PRSA has identified eight major job classifications which include: writing, editing, placement (working with the mass media), promotion (planning, preparing special events), speaking, production, programming (counseling, advising, long-range communications efforts), and institutional advertising. Someone looking for work in public relations is in somewhat of a conundrum—there are lots of jobs available, but a lot of the jobs that are available don't pay any wages. Scores of community service agencies, citizens' groups, and other community organizations seek help from volunteers on public relations projects. Experience for the willing hand along with a hearty thanks and a recommendation for a job well done is often the only reward. Most available paying jobs in PR exist in small nonprofit service agencies that function in all communities. As one PR instructor noted, these jobs produce lots of work, minimal supervision, considerable frustration, and often plenty of personal satisfaction. The pay is usually low. There are some entry-level jobs in both corporate and government public relations, most dealing with specialities such as editing a company newsletter or media relations. These are good training positions that pay reasonably well (corporate jobs pay better than government jobs), permit the worker to learn more about the craft, and offer the possibility for upward mobility. At the top of the entry level job list are positions with public relations agencies. Most agency jobs—which pay anywhere from $20,000 to $25,000 to start, require some previous experience. Work for an agency, where a practitioner may balance up to a dozen clients and their needs—is exciting, but produces early burnout.

Most of the people entering public relations today still do so via other jobs in the mass media. Most public relations practitioners have worked, earlier in their career, for newspapers, magazines, or broadcasting stations—normally the news side. When these persons join a company or agency as a public relations specialist, they already have a considerable number of contacts in the mass media who can assist them in doing their job. Many schools of communication and journalism today offer programs in public relations and it is likely that in the future more and more entry-level jobs in public relations will be taken by graduates of these programs, rather than journalism or broadcast journalism graduates who have worked in the mass media.

## PR . . . or Not PR

A wide variety of communication efforts that are called public relations are not true public relations. And practitioners are quick to point that out. Press agentry is not public relations. The function of the press agent is simply to get media attention for his client. Press agents are not concerned with creating understanding. Product publicity—attempting to build confidence in both a product and its manufacturer —is another kind of work that really falls outside the spectrum of public relations. These kind of publicists try to gain as much publicity for their clients as possible, and one way to see the fruits of their labor is by opening up the food section of your daily newspaper and noting the recipes featuring certain brands or varieties of food. Nonproduct publicity is commonly (and incorrectly) thought of as public relations. The goal of nonproduct publicity is to build a favorable image for a business or a government agency or an institution like a university. People with these sorts of jobs are generally referred to as information specialists or public affairs specialists and concentrate upon reporting to the mass media the day-to-day activities of their employers. (Ruplesten Mattress Co. just set a new sales record! The Department of Labor regional office is holding a seminar on job discrimination.) This is an important function, but again not truly public relations.

Lobbyists also conduct many communications activities that resemble public relations work. These include informing government officials of the needs and desires of their clients, promoting legislative interests, and getting government cooperation in publicity efforts. When the governor declares the week of April 5 as Auto Safety Week, you can bet a lobbyist has been hard at work. Many corporations today have vice-presidents of public affairs or public affairs officers. Sometimes this is a euphemism for public relations, but sometimes the job is quite distinctive. Such individuals usually supervise a broad spectrum of corporate/public/government activities that could include political education for employees, civic service by employees, and corporate participation in civic, social, and political affairs.

All of the tasks just described differ from complete public relations service because they do not include the broad range of listening, counseling, planning, and communication skills that are integral to a total public relations function. Carl Byoir and Associates, public relations counselors, have described their functions in these terms:

1. Analysis—of policies and objectives of the client . . . of relationships with various publics, including employees, customers, dealers, shareholders, the financial community, government, and the press. Continuing research keeps the analysis of these relationships up-to-date.
2. Planning and programming—of specific undertakings and projects in which public relations techniques can be employed to help attain the objectives through effective communication between the client and its publics.
3. Implementation—of the programs and projects by maximum and effective use of all avenues of communication, internal and external, to create understanding and stimulate action.

Only when such a total range of activity is undertaken are complete public relations practiced, suggest many persons who are in the field.

## PR, Media, and Society

The activities of persons working in public relations provide important support for the American mass media. Journalists would be hard-pressed to bring to the public the high volume of news we are used to without the assistance of information officers in government and elsewhere. Also, any individual, whether in the press or in public relations, who can help the public better understand either business or government is to be valued. Still, valid criticism of public relations still exists.

A considerable amount of the material generated by people who call themselves public relations specialists is simply self-serving publicity for a client or an agency, regardless of the fight that goes on within the field about what is true public relations, what is press agentry. True public relations is supposed to have a dimension of public or social responsibility, according to authors Cutlip and Center. "Satisfying the public interest to the mutual advantage of all parties in conflict is a prerequisite to profitable public relations," they note. In the late 1930s Harwood Childs, author of a book entitled *Introduction to Public Opinion,* said that public relations was simply a name for activities which have a social significance. "Our problem in each corporation or industry is to find out what these activities are, what social effects they have, and if they are contrary to the public interest, to find ways and means for modifying them so that they will serve the public interest," Childs wrote.

But this is not a universally held view. Author Raymond Simon *(Public Relations: Concepts and Practices)* quotes economist Milton Friedman who argues: "There is one and only one social responsibility of business—to use its resources and engage in activities designed to increase its profits so long as it stays within the rules of the game, which is to say, engages in open and free competition without deception or fraud." This is the more prevalent philosophy in business today. Consequently much of the work of corporate public relations departments seems directed toward protecting the company from anything that might harm its ability to make a profit, or enhancing the company image for the same purpose. Government public relations officers often follow a similar pattern, misusing their power to distort information or shape information rather than inform the public of what is truly happening. This kind of behavior, whether it is true public relations or not, is harmful. It does not help anyone understand anything any better. All these practices are worthy of condemnation.

Publicists across America generate an incredible amount of information and other material today. Young journalists are often amazed at the sheer volume of such information that comes into the newsroom, over the transom so to speak. While some of this material is valuable, and provides the initial basis for a useful news story, too much of it clogs up the mass communication system. Hundreds of pages of press releases are generated each day by the agencies of the federal government located in Washington, D.C. Someone in the press has to read all this material and evaluate its newsworthiness. This takes an inordinate amount of time, time which might be better spent chasing a solid story. There is so much of this information it often blinds reporters. The infamous My Lai massacre, exposed in *The New York Times* by reporter Seymour Hersh, was actually first reported in an official U.S. Army press release that the press ignored or did not see for several months.

Press releases are often supplanted by media events as agencies, organizations, and individuals seek to attract attention to themselves or their activities. Interview shows on local radio stations are dominated each day by all the travelling writers and others out promoting books, causes, conferences, and ideas. Politics has been especially clogged up with such public relations activities. Candidates use the press conference or staged rally or speech to both attract the attention of reporters to what they are saying and doing, and distract reporters from other aspects of the campaign, such as where their money is coming from, their record, and other less-flattering news.

The plethora of press releases, staged events, and other "journalistic aids" can sometimes make reporters lazy. Used to such help, when it doesn't exist stories are passed over. Former journalist Ellen Hume notes, in a *New York Times* Op-Ed piece on why the press did not do a better job in anticipating the savings and loan crisis, that journalists have gotten used to having their information pre-digested. Hume quotes Brooks Jackson, a talented former *Wall Street Journal* reporter, who said: "We usually depend on governmental institutions or groups like Common Cause or Ralph Nader or General Motors or somebody to make sense out of all this data for us." But there were no PR people at hand when the savings and loan industry began to unravel. (See pp. 425–427 for a discussion of the impact of public relations on the news.)

Finally, and this is a problem in journalism and not public relations, much of the material that is published and broadcast but has been generated by public relations efforts is never identified as such. The reader or viewer ends up treating the story just like any other story that the newspaper or broadcasting station might have generated on its own. Many small newspapers and broadcasting stations, short of staff, will use such unedited material to fill up their news columns or news shows. But even large and wealthy media use this material in an unidentified fashion. In 1980 the *Columbia Journalism Review* reported that in its study of a single edition of the *Wall Street Journal* it found that 53 news stories had been based upon public relations releases. Thirty-two of these releases were printed almost verbatim, and in 20 instances the stories carried the slug, "By a Wall Street Journal Staffer." Television stations often use film or videotape (See pp. 357–358 for a discussion of VNRs.) for their newscasts that has been produced by the company or government agency it describes and often promotes.

A reader or viewer looks at an advertising message far differently than a news story. The information in the commercial or ad has been generated by the seller of the product or service. Beware! When a press release is printed as a news story it carries the implication, at least, that the newspaper or broadcasting station has checked out this information and found it to be truthful. The reader or viewer is not forewarned. The guard is dropped. Deception is possible. That is why it is dangerous for the press to present such source-generated material as factual, checked-out news stories. It can seriously damage the credibility the reader or viewer may have in the publication or broadcasting station. The press has enough problems with credibility.

When public relations is practiced by the book, few have serious criticisms with the field. In fact, the public relations specialist performs a valuable function to his or her employer or client and to the community. But more often than not PR is not practiced by the book. Even those in the field acknowledge that. After a long and distinguished career as a public relations counselor, John W. Hill retired from the profession with some fairly harsh words for the corporate community that supports most of the public relations practitioners in America today. Hill, founder of the Hill and Knowlton public relations agency, said: "What is deeply needed is not more money spent on communications, but a revised philosophy and a new concept of external relations—of social issues—in the minds of corporate managements in this country. Words alone are useless if not fully supported by policies and performance."

# MATTERS OF LAW

If persons in public relations or public information attempt to facilitate the flow of selected kinds of information, other persons actively work to stifle that flow. These persons usually use the law to try to block what is broadcast or published. The American press is among the most free in the world; most kinds of information can be safely reported. But there are limits to what can be reported, and there are limits placed on the access that reporters and others have to getting certain kinds of information. Newspaper editors and television news directors are not always in complete control over what is published and broadcast. They may have some stories that they can't repeat, and they may be denied access to information needed for other stories. Let's briefly examine how the law shapes the kind of information a mass media consumer receives.

## ☐ Censorship

Legal restraints against the press fall generally into three categories. First, there are numerous government statutes that prohibit the publication, broadcast, or other distribution of certain kinds of material. Here is a brief summary of some kinds of these laws.

**Sedition** statutes: These laws make it a crime to criticize the government under certain circumstances, or advocate violent changes in government. Throughout its history the nation has wrestled with a central problem. In a democracy, where the people are supposedly the rulers, can the government permit the people to change the form of government, to abolish the democracy, through whatever means necessary? In the late eighteenth century the concern was speech and publications that were critical of the government or the leaders. It was thought that such criticism could foment discontent, riot, even revolution. Similar laws have been adopted which prohibit the criticism of the government during wartime or criticism of the war effort itself. Such laws were common in the early twentieth century. By the middle of this century, the nation became more concerned with revolution of a Communist nature, and speech and press that advocated the violent overthrow of the government were prohibited. Such laws still exist today but have been so tightly framed in light of the First Amendment, that the only thing the government can constitutionally prohibit is speech or press that "is directed to inciting or producing imminent lawless action and is likely to incite or produce such actions." The quoted passage is from an important 1969 U.S. Supreme Court ruling, *Brandenburg v. Ohio,* when the high court reversed the convictions of some members of the Ku Klux Klan who had been convicted of attempting to incite a riot.

National security matters: The government has the power to block the publication of any material thought to endanger the national security in one way or another. But the government must prove that such publication or broadcast will in fact harm the nation. The government failed in such an attempt in 1971 when it sought to stop *The New York Times* and the *Washington Post* from publishing a series of documents called The Pentagon Papers. The Pentagon Papers were a history of the war in Vietnam, compiled by the government and classified as secret. But the Supreme Court ruled that the government had failed to show that any of the revelations in these papers would harm the nation. Eight years later, however, a federal court did uphold a ban on the publication of an article in the *Progressive* magazine. The article contained a strong disarmament argument, but included instructions (either quite detailed or very general, depending upon whom you believe) on how to construct a hydrogen bomb. The publication of such material was barred under federal laws regarding information about atomic energy, according to the U.S. District Court. The case was never heard by an appellate court because a small newspaper published the material while the appeal was pending. So the horse was out of the barn. The government dropped its lawsuit.

Obscenity: Federal, state, and local laws prohibit the broadcast of obscene material. The Supreme Court of the United States has provided a fairly detailed definition of obscenity, but the question of what is and what is not obscene remains confusing. Federal laws also bar the broadcast or telecast of indecent material as well. Indecent material is even less well defined than obscenity, so the broadcaster is left guessing, for example, whether it is permissible to telecast uncut R-rated movies. These rules and others limit the broadcast of profanity and the showing of nudity, two concerns which sometimes face the television and radio news reporter.

Broadcast statutes: There is a wide panoply of broadcast regulations which impinge, at least indirectly, on radio and television newscasting. Laws prohibiting staging news events, laws requiring equal treatment of political candidates, laws requiring the identification of the broadcast of sponsored material, and so on.

## ▣ Civil Liability

The press is also limited by laws which give citizens who believed they have been harmed because of some publication or broadcast the right to sue magazines, newspapers, and broadcasting stations. There are many such laws, but two are most commonly cited—libel and invasion of privacy.

**Libel:** The law of libel protects an individual's reputation. If a broadcasting station or newspaper publishes a news story that harms an individual's reputation (and this can include a corporation, which is considered a "person" in the eyes of the law), that individual can seek money damages in court. Because the First Amendment protects the press in libel actions, it is quite difficult for someone suing the press to win. The individual who brings the suit, called the plaintiff, must prove to the court that they have been identified in the article or broadcast in question, that their reputation has been harmed, that the allegations about them are false, that the publication of these allegations was not the result of an innocent error on the part of the reporter or editor, and that the publication or broadcasting station had been careless or negligent. This is no easy chore. And the law makes bringing a successful libel suit even harder for government officials or other persons who have attempted to lead public opinion on an issue. These individuals must show that the defendant newspaper or broadcasting station was more than simply careless; they must show that the defendant exhibited reckless disregard for the truth. Journalists are free to provide fair and accurate reports of what is said in courtrooms, sessions of the legislature, meetings of government agencies, and during a wide range of other public occasions without fear of a libel suit. Similarly they are able to report, using this same privilege, about what they discover in most public documents. Also, the courts have ruled that statements of opinion are generally free from libel suits, so long as they don't imply false facts as well.

The problem for the press today with libel law is not winning cases, for newspapers and broadcasting stations ultimately win most of the libel cases that have been filed against them. The problem is the cost of defending such cases. Hiring an attorney, going to trial, then to appeal—this is very costly. News organizations have paid millions of dollars simply to win a libel suit that was filed against them. This has an impact on the selection of news. Self-censorship is practiced today in newsrooms across the nation. Stories that are libelous are edited or left out altogether. However, so are stories that are technically safe to print but which might prompt a lawsuit from someone angered by the reporting. Several years ago the *Washington Post* published a story about the president of the Mobil Oil Company, William Tavoulareas, and what he had supposedly done to help his son get a foothold in the oil business. Tavoulareas was furious and sued the *Post*. Several years later the newspaper was exonerated in the courts. But it cost the *Post* over $1.2 million to defend itself. Editor Ben Bradlee said this kind of cost was obviously going to affect news judgments in the future. He said when a reporter walks into his office and says, "Ben, I've got a great story—but it is going to cost you $1.2 million to run it," it had better be a fantastic story, or the newspaper simply won't take the chance on running it. And the *Post* is an aggressive, economically sound newspaper. Many other news organizations have neither the resources nor the gumption of this elite publication, so an even higher level of self-censorship is exercised.

Newspapers and broadcasting stations can also be sued for **invasion of privacy.** The legal right to privacy provides citizens with a broad range of protections that include protection from predatory advertising practices and protection from snooping photographers armed with powerful telephoto lenses. The two areas of the law most commonly associated with newsgathering are publication of private facts, and publishing or broadcasting material that places an individual in a false light. The latter aspect of the law, false light, is very similar to libel; many legal authorities argue that it has no real need to exist. It does extend protection to persons for the publication of material that does not harm a reputation, but is merely offensive to a reasonable person.

The private facts area appears to be far more problematic to the press. The law prohibits the publication of private facts about a person. The revelation of these facts must be regarded as offensive by a reasonable person, and be of no legitimate public interest. The number of plaintiffs who have been successful suing the mass media for the publication of private facts is remarkably small. The courts have granted the press a broad protection by ruling that most news stories published in newspapers or broadcast on radio and television have some legitimate public interest. Consequently, while many lawsuits are generated and must be defended, the press rarely loses such suits. Yet many publications, either fearing a suit or for ethical reasons, often limit what they reveal about the private lives of even newsworthy individuals. Most newspapers and broadcasting stations do not publicize the names of rape victims, even though once these names enter the public record they are no longer considered private. And the victims of other kinds of crimes are also often shielded. Concern about invasion of privacy is not a common reason for rejecting a news story, or part of a news story, but more and more journalists are being sensitized to the problems that unwarranted publicity can cause.

## ☐ Denial of Access

Finally, the government has found that one way to keep news out of the press is to block reporters' access to information. What reporters don't know, they can't print. We will focus upon three areas of the law in this category.

Court records: During the 1980s the government tried to block some reporting about the judicial process by attempting to deny reporters access to court proceedings and court records. Ostensibly to protect the right of the defendant to a trial by an unbiased jury or to protect the privacy of a witness, judges sought to close off portions of pretrial hearings and even trials. But the U.S. Supreme Court and several lower federal courts ruled such actions violated the First Amendment to the Constitution. Only in rare instances today, when the government or some other party to a case is able to show certain harm if the proceeding or record is open, and only if there is no other way to prevent this harm, are judges permitted to close judicial proceedings.

Access to government information: Access to records and documents held by the executive branch of the government is governed at the federal level and in all states by what are known as freedom of information laws. These laws define which records are open to public inspection and copying, and which are not. The federal law, for example, exempts from public inspection, documents that have been classified for national security reasons, internal memoranda and departmental papers, trade secrets and financial information provided to the government by banks and other businesses, personnel files and other personal records, records gathered for law enforcement purposes, and several other categories of information. The federal government, especially in the past ten years, has worked hard to restrict access to as much information as possible by interpreting the exempted categories of information in the federal Freedom of Information Act very broadly, giving access to information only when the law clearly requires that such access be provided. There are many important news stories that are never printed because reporters are unable to gain the confirming public records that support their stories.

Military operations: While there has not been a congressional declaration of war since 1941, there has been no shortage of military activity by American armed forces. Press coverage of the war in Vietnam angered many in the military, who argued that the negative picture of the war painted by journalists hurt the war effort and denied the military the support it needed to win. (Interestingly enough, the military establishment itself has recently rejected this allegation. A book, *The Military and the Media, 1962–1968,* published by the U.S. Army Center of Military History, blames the rise of public discontent with the war on President Lyndon Johnson's ill-conceived war strategy, overly optimistic official statements, and mounting U.S. casualties. Author William M. Hammond reported that while the press coverage was not without flaws, "press reports were still often more accurate than public statements of the administration.")

Until the Persian Gulf War in 1991 there had been no overt military censorship of the press since the Korean War. There were general guidelines reporters were asked to follow in covering the Vietnam War, but there was no attempt by the government to enforce these guidelines by screening news stories before they were published or broadcast.

What the government attempted to do when U.S. forces invaded both Grenada and Panama was to limit press access to the war zone. If reporters can't get there, they have nothing to report. When the United States sent troops to Grenada in 1983, no American reporters were permitted to cover the invasion: American journalists already on the island were detained by the military. Reporters were not permitted to view the military operation for nearly 72 hours.

There was anger from not only the press but the public as well after this incident, and in 1984 the Department of Defense established a news **media pool.** The pool contains 12 to 15 reporters selected by the media, and the Pentagon has promised to take pool members along on military operations provided those involved in the pool maintain secrecy until the operation is underway. The pool was mobilized on several occasions over the next five years, most notably for the U.S. air strikes into Libya and the 1989 naval patrol in the Persian Gulf. And it worked fairly well.

But the pool did not function well when United States forces invaded Panama in December of 1989. The 16-member group was activated late on the evening of December 19th and was flown to Panama City. It arrived at a U.S. air base in Panama around 5 A.M., some four hours after the invasion had begun. Once in Panama, however, the pool members were confined to a building housing the U.S. Armed Forces Radio and Television network. "There," wrote AP correspondent and pool member Steven Komarow, "we watched CNN's coverage of the war we should have been covering. . . ." The first briefing came not from a military commander but from a U.S. diplomat who lectured the reporters on the history of Panama. After five hours the reporters were finally taken off the base and permitted to witness part of the military operation. Even then the press was kept away from some important parts of the military operation and had little exposure to soldiers who had actually been involved in the fighting. "We missed what could have been some great stories," wrote Komarow.

Matters moved from bad to worse when the war in the Persian Gulf erupted in August of 1990. The government used the pool system, military escorts, and overt censorship (called a security review by the military) to control the flow of information about the military operation.

The problems began shortly after American forces began to move into the Kingdom of Saudi Arabia, a nation which resists close scrutiny of its anachronistic conventions. The ruling sheikhs announced strict rules regarding press coverage of the U.S. military in their kingdom. Supported by U.S. military commanders, the Saudi leaders announced rules requiring all reporters who sought to cover frontline operations to operate from press pools that were under the constant supervision of military public affairs officers: all stories and videos were to be screened by military officials before being released for publication or broadcast. The number of journalists in Saudi Arabia was limited to one per news organization. The press immediately protested all these requirements; the major news organizations protested the last requirement the most.

Public affairs officers in the Pentagon told reporters that they would work to modify these rules to make things better for the journalists who sought to cover the war. Several weeks later Pentagon spokesperson Pete Williams triumphantly announced victory to the press: the Saudis would accept more than one journalist per news organization. But in order to get this concession, the press would have to live with the pool system, escorts, and censorship. The journalists had been had.

At the height of the conflict, there were about 800 journalists in the theater of operations. Only about 125 of these were ever assigned to the small 12- to 15-person press pools. Most journalists reported the war from Riyadh and Dhahran. Reporters in the pools could ask to visit certain military units, but unit commanders had the right to refuse to receive the reporters. Reporters said brigade and battalion commanders and the enlisted personnel enjoyed seeing the journalists. Division commanders, many who had served in Vietnam, often refused to have reporters in their areas. "Our mere presence raised questions in their minds about our patriotism, loyalty, and common sense," wrote David Lamb of the *Los Angeles Times.* Reporters who tried to travel outside of the pools were detained if they were caught and faced possible revocation of their press credentials. In addition, the desert was an inhospitable place, with few roads. Getting lost was a real possibility and could result (as it did with CBS correspondent Bob Simon and his colleagues) in being captured by the enemy.

Reporters in the pools were accompanied by military officers, who usually stayed with reporters as they questioned army, navy, and air force personnel. "When a reporter has an officer standing over his shoulders at all times, what soldier being interviewed will spill his guts and speak his personal truth?" noted former NBC journalist and White House press secretary Ron Nessen, who covered the Vietnam War.

After a story was written, the military escorts reviewed it, ostensibly on security grounds. Many stories were passed on to unit commanders for review; some stories were sent back to the United States for approval. This frequently would take one to two days or longer. The delay is what most journalists complained about. The censorship was often for petty reasons. A story by a *Detroit Free Press* reporter that described the F-117 Stealth fighter-bomber pilots as being "giddy" after a mission was rejected; the censor changed the adjective to "proud." Another censor objected to *The New York Times's* reporter Malcolm Browne's description of the F-117 as a fighter-bomber; it is a fighter, Browne was told. Of course the Air Force is trying to convince Congress to fund the B-2 Stealth bomber, Browne notes. "Could it be that if the F-117A is also called a bomber, Congressional critics might argue a second Stealth bomber—the B-2—is unnecessary?" he asked. Reporters, anxious to avoid further censorship hassle, would usually accede to government requests for changes simply to get the story on its way.

Even reporters in pools were not allowed to stay with military units for an extended period of time, as they had been in every other war. They were not allowed to fly on bombing missions, as they had done in World War II. The military closed off public access to Dover Air Force Base in Delaware, the point where the bodies of dead American servicemen and women arrive in the United States. In the past, the press had always had access to film the solemn ceremonies as these bodies were returned to U.S. soil. The military also announced that press coverage of medical care given to American wounded after they returned to the United States would be prohibited.

The picture of the war given to the American people by the military was largely of a bloodless conflict—a war of surgical air strikes, bombs dropped with pinpoint accuracy, and little "collateral damage" (the military euphemism for civilian casualties). "The idea was to suggest that hardly any people were involved in modern warfare, only machines. This explains the emphasis at Alliance press briefings on the damage 'our' machines have caused to 'their' machines, and the reluctance of briefing officers to discuss casualties—on either side," noted journalist Phillip Knightley, who wrote a history of military censorship, *The First Casualty.* There is no doubt that the military's effort to control the flow of information was very effective. Even in midsummer 1991, months after the war ended, the American public knew very little about what had happened in the war. Little by little, bits of data dribbled out. Pictures from Iraq revealed the extent to which the civilian population did suffer, but there were still no firm figures on the number of Iraqi dead, military or civilian. News reports revealed that the vaunted Patriot missile did not work as well as the military first suggested, and that problems in the programming of the computer-guided antimissile could have contributed to the failure of the military to destroy the scud missile that hit a U.S. barracks in Dhahran and took many American lives.

As the ground war broke out the military lost some control over reporters and a few went to the front unescorted. ABC's Forrest Sawyer, one of the first reporters in Kuwait City, said "The best and only real reporting I did was outside the press pool." He and most other reporters called the pool system a travesty. "Reporting is about using your own initiative and going out and learning something of value to your public while staying within the bounds of national security," he added.

The government defended the censorship on national security grounds, and public opinion polls suggest that the American people supported the government. In fact the vast majority of reporters support the government when it comes to the national security question. Generally, the press, whether required to or not, has had a strong sense of protecting national security and has only rarely breached security rules. Barry Zorthian, who was the official spokesman for the United States Mission in Saigon from 1964 to 1968, said that out of the hundreds of thousands of stories that were filed about the Vietnam War, there were only five or six instances when security guidelines were broken.

But the censorship in the Gulf, and indeed in most wars, usually goes beyond protecting national security. It has a political purpose as well: to protect the government from embarrassment, and to keep the public behind the war effort. Journalists are troubled by this kind of censorship; the public should be as well. Harsh truth about the reality of war—the death, suffering, and failures, as well as the successes—can be a political liability for the nation's leaders. But as one reporter noted, the public has a right to know about the bombs that miss as well as the ones that hit, about the defeats as well as the victories.

The law, then, as wielded by both citizens and the government, surely defines the amount and kind of information that flows in the society.

# DECIDING WHAT'S NEWS

Whether a story that appears in a newspaper or on the television news has been generated by a public information officer or a press agent or an enterprising reporter, an editor still made the decision that that particular item was newsworthy. How does an editor make this decision? Is there an *Editor's Handbook* that all editors use that carries a specific definition of news? That is probably what many readers and viewers believe, but that is mistaken. News is not a well-defined commodity like a tree or an automobile or an animal. If 100 persons sitting in a room were given the kind of definition of news used by most editors and news directors, and then sent out to find some news, what they returned with would be a disparate array of items. There are differences in the definition of news even among journalists who have worked in the craft for many years.

Various news media define news differently. Television, with its heavy reliance on pictures, tends to define news differently than the printed press. And within the printed press, magazines define news differently than newspapers. And even within the newspaper business, *USA Today* surely defines news somewhat differently than the *Washington Post.* If an assassin attempted to shoot the President, that would certainly be news, right? It would be news to ABC and the *Washington Post* and the *Wenatchee World.* But would it be news to the editors of the *Women's Wear Daily,* or "Entertainment Tonight," or the *Stamp Collector's Monthly?*

Nonjournalists often believe that the selection of news for the day's newspaper or television news broadcast is governed by political or other ideological criteria. And sometimes such factors surely intervene in the definition of news. But more often than not these factors play little role in determining what is or what is not news on a given day. Defining news is far more confusing and far less sinister than that. In the following pages an attempt will be made to explain some of the factors and circumstances that might prompt an editor or a news director to select one item of information over another for a report about what happened on a given day on this small, blue planet.

Professional journalists are trained to do their jobs, either in a college or university journalism program or on the job. As such they share a common set of values and this, in a limited way, sets some, albeit broad, guidelines about what is and what is not news (figure 11-1). For years, teachers of journalism have attempted to provide definitions of news which, it is hoped, will become the basis for editing newspapers, magazines, or broadcast reports. For example, in his *Reporting* textbook, longtime journalism educator Mitchell Charnley defines news in this way: "News is a timely report of facts or opinion of either interest or importance, or both, to a considerable number of people." Charnley's definition of news is as good a place as any to begin our search for the factors and circumstances that editors use to define news in the late twentieth century.

## Timelines

News tends to be something that just happened. Surely timeliness is defined a bit differently by different kinds of news media. A timely story for an all-news radio station is something that happened 20 minutes ago. A timely story for a newsmagazine is something that happened in the past week. Lots of things are important or interesting, but journalists tend to be interested in reporting important or interesting things that happened recently or will happen tomorrow.

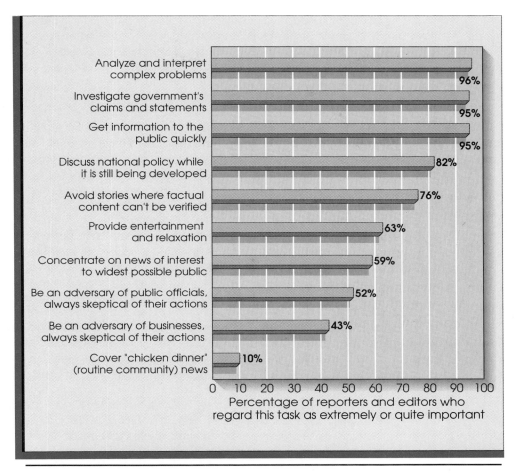

FIGURE 11-1 This chart lists the percentage of reporters and editors who said they believed the journalistic task listed on the left was either extremely important or quite important.
(American Society of Newspaper Editors)

The fact that the U.S. invaded Panama in late 1989 is both interesting and important, but it is hardly newsworthy today. But a court case that was settled today in which a young U.S. soldier was acquitted of murdering a Panamanian citizen during the invasion would be newsworthy, and its reporting would require at least a brief retelling of the story of the invasion. This timely angle is sometimes called a "news peg."

This need for a timely angle or news peg has long been the focus of criticism within the craft of journalism. The need for timeliness has required journalists too often to dwell on event-oriented news, reporting something that just happened. Event-oriented reporting is covered at the expense of issue-oriented news. Let's look at a story from the Pacific Northwest as an example. Logging has long been a major industry in this scenic corner of the United States. Once much of the East and West was covered with timber, but today the great forests remain primarily in this portion of the nation. These forests are being depleted. Men and women can cut down trees far faster than nature can grow them. There has been substantial depletion of the forest land, especially what is called old-growth timber, the huge trees that are a primary source of the large-dimension lumber for beams and other construction needs. The people of the Northwest, including many in the timber industry, have been concerned about this issue for many years. The loss of these trees not only affects employment in the logging industry, but tourism, recreation, and other interests. In addition, the old-growth timber supports a unique ecosystem, which is lost as well when the big trees disappear. But this important issue went largely unreported because it lacked a hard news peg. Enter the spotted owl, a small bird that is on the U.S. government's list of endangered species. The spotted owl survives because of the old-growth ecosystem; when it disappears, the bird will disappear as well. Environmentalists, who sought to save the trees, brought a lawsuit on behalf of the owl. Continued logging of the old-growth timber will result in the extinction of the owl, something federal law is supposed to prevent, they argued. The lawsuit became the news peg needed by the press in the Northwest to begin to explore a wide range of issues associated with forest policies in Oregon and Washington. While the issue is not yet resolved, the debate has been joined, and it is an informed debate because of the extensive news coverage on the issue.

Television and radio are more guilty today of focusing too heavily on event-oriented news than the printed press. Many, but not all, newspapers have greatly improved their coverage of nonevent oriented stories. Yet event-oriented news continues to dominate the news columns. If an editor has two stories to choose from, one that describes the closing of a manufacturing plant that will put 200 workers out into the street and another about changes in manufacturing technology that will, over the next ten years, result in the loss of thousands of jobs, nine out of ten editors will select the first story. It is more immediate, more visible, more timely. Consequently, if the mass media have a blind side, and remember they are our eyes and ears, it is their inability to report or even recognize the impact of change over time. As a result we are often surprised by events that we might have anticipated if issue-oriented reporting, coverage of the nontimely story, was more common.

## ☐ Interesting or Important

An item that is selected as news should be interesting or important. But to whom? The reader or viewer or listener, obviously. Not always.

Reporters and editors don't work in a vacuum. And when a news report is prepared, it may be of interest or importance to one or more of five different constituent groups or individuals. Advertisers and sponsors have ideas about what is interesting and important. Enough has been written in this book for the reader to understand that some stories are published or broadcast because they are important to advertisers, or more important to advertisers than anyone else. In the magazine industry there is even a name for such stories—**complementary copy.** Many magazine advertisers will not buy space unless such stories are also included in the edition. And there are not many newspaper reporters and broadcast journalists who have not prepared a story because a "good advertiser" is interested in it.

Reporters also must think about their editors when they prepare the news. Editors and news directors have biases. A reporter learns quickly that his or her editor likes certain kinds of stories and doesn't like other kinds of stories. If the reporter has a choice among stories, or can choose an angle to emphasize, what the editor likes or doesn't like is an important factor that will be considered.

Some stories are more interesting or important to a particular reporter. Reporters who cover a beat often have a wide variety of potential news stories that might be covered. An environmental reporter, for example, might prefer to cover stories about water problems because he or she thinks these are more important than other kinds of environmental stories, or he or she understands water quality stories better than stories about air pollution or chemical waste dumps. There is only so much time to gather the news, only so much time to broadcast or space to publish environmental news. What the reporter finds most interesting or important can be a critical factor in defining what is or is not news on a given day.

Reporters use news sources to gather information. And news sources play a role in the reporter's selection of news. Very few newspaper stories or broadcast reports

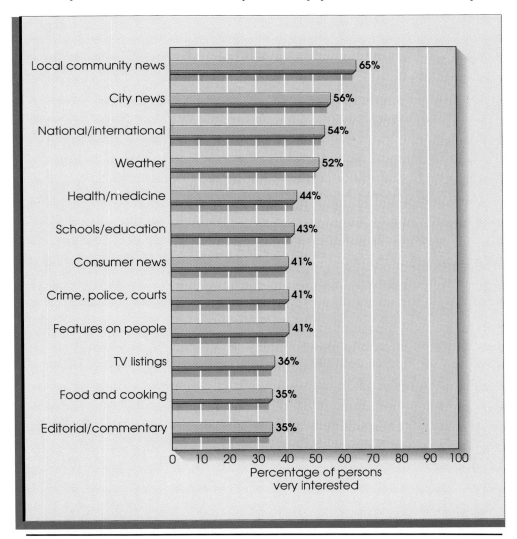

FIGURE 11-2 Percentage of readers who said they were very interested in various kinds of news.
(Belden Associates)

are the result of reporters digging through files, poring over documents, or viewing news events firsthand. The overwhelming majority of stories are based on sources: people who tell the reporter what is going on or what happened. While some of these are one-time sources (the witness to a fire, for example), most sources used by reporters are continuing sources. The reporter will use the source over and over again. This could be an aide to the mayor, for example, or a spokesperson at the police department or a clerk in the county courthouse. The relationship between a reporter and a source is an intricate one, far too complex to detail here. Needless to say, however, it is a relationship in which each member of the relationship needs the other.

An obvious element in this relationship is the need for the reporter to keep the source happy so the stream of news from the source continues to flow. At times, then, the reporter will publish a story that is of interest or importance to the news source, simply to please the source. A fire chief is proud of a new piece of equipment and wants a story about it. A member of Congress is sponsoring a bill to help the elderly and wants the story publicized back home. A university public relations director wants publicity for a new evening degree program. In each of these situations the reporter and his or her editors may feel there is bigger news, more important stories. But to placate the source and to insure that the newspaper or broadcasting station will continue to get cooperation and important news from this source, what is of interest or important to the source becomes a factor in news selection.

Finally, news is what is interesting and important to readers or viewers or listeners (figure 11-2). Application of this criteria sounds simple, but it is not. For example, should the press report news that it believes is of interest to readers and viewers, or should it report news that editors and reporters believe *should be* of interest to readers and viewers? Readers might like one more story on Princess Di and Prince Charles. But they might be better served by a story on the growing disparity among the economic classes in Great Britain. If the press is to serve the reader's needs and interests, how are these needs and interests determined? As noted previously (see pp. 131–132) readership polls and research using focus groups often generate notoriously flawed results. Clearly a medium that totally ignores what its readers or viewers want in its digest of news will soon fail. But many editors and news directors are properly wary of the problems associated with preparing their daily news reports with heavy guidance from polling data. A good editor will try to lead the reader or viewer, to interest them in important news that should be reported.

## □ Time and Space

If a newspaper had an infinite number of pages, if a television news broadcast had an infinite number of minutes, selecting what is and what is not news would be somewhat easier. But there are limits to both the space in a newspaper and minutes in a news program. Broadcast journalists often comment that they don't have the luxury that the print journalist has of adding a couple of additional pages to an edition to make room for more news. But print journalists really don't have that luxury either. The size of the news hole in a newspaper, the space set aside for news, is determined by the amount of advertising carried in that particular edition. The more advertising, the larger the news hole. At some newspapers the size of the news hole is established each day, tied directly to the percentage of advertising in that edition. At other newspapers editors are guaranteed a certain amount of space, regardless of the percentage of advertising. But this guaranteed amount is based upon the percentage of advertising expected in that edition. In either case, it is highly unlikely that the editor can simply add two additional pages to the newspaper to make room for more news. If a major story were to break (i.e., the war in the Persian Gulf) it is more likely that the news hole would be enlarged by eliminating some ads than by adding pages to the newspaper. Because there is more advertising published on Wednesday and Thursday, there is more news published on Wednesday and Thursday. This means that a particular story ("150 Gallons of Waste Oil Seeps into Creek") may be published on a Wednesday or Thursday, but may not make the newspaper on Monday or Tuesday. Broadcasters have the same size (amount of time) news hole each day, so the amount of advertising carried on any particular day is not a factor. Only the very few minutes devoted to news is a limit.

What else is happening on a particular day, when tied to the time and space limitations, is also relevant in news selection. There are heavy news days and there are slow news days. The story about the waste oil spill might be pushed out of the newspaper or the television news broadcast by other, more important news. Similarly, stories that might normally be passed over by the press on a Tuesday or Wednesday, make it into the newspaper or television broadcast on weekends, when little news is generated. Tune in to a radio or television news show on Saturday or Sunday and note the number of stories about auto accidents or boating mishaps or minor crimes. Most of these stories would go into the wastebasket on a weekday when the myriad of government agencies in the community, the courts, the legislative bodies, the schools, are all generating more important news. All three national television networks telecast Sunday interview programs featuring government officials, programs like "Meet the Press" or "Face the Nation" simply to generate news on the weekends. Former President Reagan gave a radio address each Saturday morning for almost eight years while he was in the White House, knowing that what he said would be widely reported because there was little other news to report on Saturdays. The space and time available, then, have a great deal to do with determining the selection of news.

## ☐ The Timing of News

Like all manufactured commodities, newspapers, magazines, and radio and television news broadcasts are generated through a production schedule. Work starts on Monday afternoon to prepare material for publication of the newspaper at noon on Tuesday. Some pages must be filled with news stories before Tuesday morning. So a story that is ready to be published on Monday afternoon has a better chance of getting into the newspaper than one that is not ready to be published until late Tuesday morning. Consider a story on the increasing number of foreclosures on family farm mortgages. Three-hundred-and-fifty column inches of newshole may be open on Monday afternoon when the editor looks at that story. It is a good story, so it is edited and prepared to be published. If the same story appeared on the editor's desk on Tuesday morning when the remaining news hole had shrunk to 80 or 100 column inches, there may be other more important news to crowd out this story. The system, then, is biased toward older news. The earlier the editor gets the story, the better chance it has of being published.

Television faces the same problem. What is to be broadcast on the evening news is planned in advance. Surely, when a major story breaks, a station can interrupt its planned schedule and carry a live report on a breaking story. But this is costly. Prepared news must be discarded. Going live entails added costs as well. So this doesn't happen that often. Consequently, if a television report can be completed—in the can, so to speak—in the early afternoon, it has a better chance of getting on the evening news. Again, a bias toward older news. Political candidates, for example, know this, and schedule their photo opportunities in the morning, so the reporters have plenty of time to edit their videotape and prepare their reports.

There are two other time biases. Scheduled news has a better chance of being telecast or published than unscheduled news. If the editor or the news director knows that a story will occur—a press conference—at 10 A.M., he or she can assign a reporting team to cover the story, and leave room in the newspaper or the television newscast to include this report. What if the story turns out to be a dud? Then it may not be included. But in an era of increasing cost consciousness, news executives are reluctant to abandon a story in which they have invested time and effort, or, in real terms, money.

Finally, there is undoubtedly somewhat of an East Coast bias, especially in television news. This is because of the three-hour time difference between New York and the West Coast. The national television news shows are actually produced while it is still the middle of the afternoon on the West Coast. Therefore, news that happens early in the afternoon in Los Angeles or Seattle is really too late to be included in the network evening news. By the next day the stories are old news. *Los Angeles Times* media reporter David Shaw says the bias goes even deeper. Because the New York media have historically focused on Europe, their neighbors across the Atlantic Ocean, they have been slow to cover the burgeoning economic power of Asia, the growth of the Pacific Rim, and the enormous investment of Japanese money in American enterprise, Shaw notes. Also, since the major national news media are located in New York, when the people who run ABC, CBS, NBC, *The New York Times,* the *Wall Street Journal, Time,* and *Newsweek* read their local news media, they read about what is happening on the East Coast. This influences their choice of a menu of national news. Such major domestic issues as the drought, the taxpayers' revolt of the late 1970s, the tremendous burgeoning of the Hispanic culture in the West and Southwest, did not affect New Yorkers, were not publicized in New York media, and hence were largely absent from the national press as well.

## ◻ The Importance of Others

The use of a news story by a competing news organization, especially a prestigious news organization, will often enhance its value as news to a news editor. Certain publications, like *The New York Times* and the *Washington Post,* and certain television operations, like ABC, CBS, NBC, and CNN, are considered among the elite of America's news organizations. What they consider news is always regarded seriously by news editors in other parts of the nation. This is not always because these organizations are on the cutting edge of news; they frequently are not. They simply have prestige among journalists. In mid-1984, the Pacific News Service distributed to 200 newspapers and broadcasting stations a well-documented story that the Central Intelligence Agency was circulating an assassination manual in Central America. The story was not used by most newspapers. Three months later *The New York Times* ran a front page story on the manual, and suddenly reports began cropping up on television and in many newspapers. "The handling of the CIA manual story underscores the influence of *The New York Times* and the *Washington Post* on the nation's news agenda," noted Gilbert Cranberg in an article in the *Washington Journalism Review*.

The editors of *The New York Times* and the *Post* watch network television news, and vice versa. And news sources know this. When the Reagan State Department wanted to turn its latest policy line into news, it would give an exclusive interview to a *Times* reporter, according to former State Department spokesperson John Hughes. He said he could count on television's follow-up during the day, since TV reporters commonly used *The Times*'s report as their source. Skeptics are urged to watch the evening news programs and compare their contents with the news content of *The Times* and the *Post*. Sometimes even the same feature stories appear. Editors at *The Times* and the *Post* also follow the lead of television on occasion. The elite press, then, helps define what is news.

But what others regard as news works as a factor in news selection in another way as well. **Pack journalism** is a term to describe the manner in which reporters and editors often rush helter-skelter to a news story, just because competing newspapers or broadcasting stations have rushed to a particular story. In such instances the exercise of good judgment by the press, which is more common than critics would suggest, is usually suspended in favor of "getting the story," at all costs. Recall, if you can, the pack of hounds that chase a fox during the hunt, all racing after one another, through the woods, over the streams, in pursuit of what the leader believes is the fox. Rarely, if ever, do you see any of these animals stop to regard whether in fact it is a real fox they are chasing, or whether mindlessly following the pack is the best way of capturing this elusive forest denizen. With a piercing howl, off they go, one after another. Journalists sometimes behave in the same fashion.

Since 1982 police in the Puget Sound region of the state of Washington have been seeking one or more killers in what has become known as the Green River murders. This individual (or individuals) is responsible for the death of as many as 45 young women. By February of 1986, the $2-million-a-year investigation had gathered 600 latent fingerprints, 6,000 pieces of evidence, and 10,000 names of individuals described by the police as "persons of interest." The Seattle press had covered this story consistently and responsibly. The daily newspapers in the region had long ago lost the smell of blood and reported the story as a disturbing and perplexing police investigation. Seattle-Tacoma television stations also had treated the story seriously. The four local commercial television stations with news operations reflect the sophistication of the big city market, but have never reached the heights of hype common in other major markets.

Late in the afternoon on February 6, the police took into custody for questioning yet one more person of interest. KOMO television reporter Roger Nelson previously had received a tip from someone inside the investigation that police were planning to question this individual, but agreed to hold the story until the suspect was taken into custody. At 5 P.M. that afternoon the news came from KOMO that the nation's worst unsolved serial murder case appeared to be coming to an end. The report caught not only the viewers by surprise but most of the rest of the Seattle press corps. What followed was a worst-case example of pack journalism.

Television reporters and production crews descended upon the suspect's neighborhood, beaming live broadcasts back to their stations and to viewers throughout the region. While no reporter mentioned the suspect's name, the address of the house was clearly visible as cameras focused on police and FBI agents searching the home. Neighbors were questioned and their sometimes hysterical references to living next to a killer were telecast. Reporters sought out and reported every possible detail on the suspect's life, many of which he had never revealed (such as a previous criminal record) to even his closest friends. Reports circulated (and most turned out to be false) that the "person of interest" trapped animals in the area in which many of the bodies had been found; that he was known to have mutilated animals; that Portland, Oregon, police had linked him to a string of serial murders in that city. One anchor even reported an unsubstantiated comment by a coworker of the suspect that he (the suspect) had joked about killing a prostitute. Four hours after he was arrested, after passing several lie-detector tests, the suspect was released. No charges were ever filed.

The Seattle television media, and even the newspapers, were left with egg on their faces. A lawsuit was filed by the victim in this case and later settled out of court. It was the scent of the prey, the excitement of the pack, that drove the press (especially TV) in this case to totally uncharacteristic excesses. One television station got out of the gate first, and the rest had to catch up. Each reporter had to top the competition with a little more intimate detail, a little more intimidating comment. The results of pack journalism are not always this bad, but rarely does this kind of journalism produce the quality of information that would be expected if the reporter exercised the judgment and patience required by the craft.

## ▣ Matters of Policy and Taste

The fact that the law often acts as a censor of the press has been previously noted. But there is considerable self-censorship in the press as well—occasions when the press has the news but chooses not to publish it (figure 11-3). Matters of perceived taste frequently impact upon news selection. Editors decide that a story is simply not appropriate to tell. Oftentimes this is a correct decision; there is surely enough tasteless news published or broadcast. But sometimes such a decision is incorrect, and actually deprives the reader or viewer of important information.

Imagine you are a reporter and have discovered a serious threat to the health of hundreds of thousands of people. A serious disease has developed, and it will kill most of those who acquire it. But at the same time, imagine that you can't report this story, because editors or news directors believe that the words you need to use to describe how this disease is transmitted from one human to another will likely offend a great many readers and viewers. This was the plight of the press in the early to mid-1980s as it sought to explain the AIDS epidemic to Americans.

AIDS was first seen in this country in 1979, but the coverage of the disease was slow to develop. The press was still referring to AIDS as a mystery epidemic in 1983, even though in the United States as many as four persons per day were dying of the disease. The press was not alone in its confusion about the problem; doctors and researchers were confused as well. And because of the scarcity of medical knowledge, most reporters were forced to rely on a few official sources. And when these sources were wrong, misinformation spread rapidly. At one point researchers targeted people from Haiti as a high-risk group because they found the disease so prevalent among Haitian immigrants. It must be something in their ethnicity, it was thought. What doctors failed to realize at the time was that the immigrants had lied to researchers when they were questioned about drug use and homosexuality because the Haitian culture has strong taboos against both behaviors.

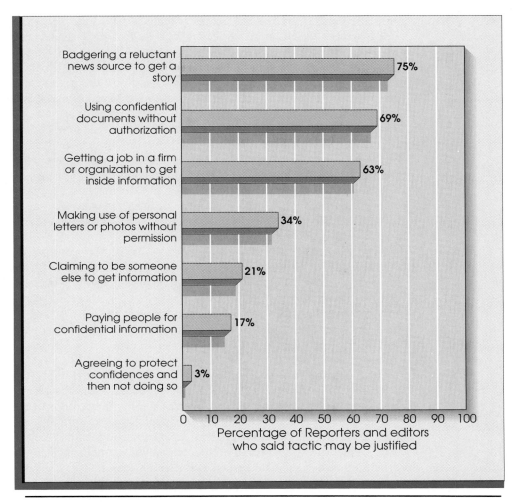

FIGURE 11-3 Percentage of newspaper reporters and editors who said they believed that using certain newsgathering tactics to get a story may be justified in some instances.
(American Society of Newspaper Editors)

In the early 1980s the press reported that AIDS was spread through sexual intimacy, sexual contact, or personal contact. At the same time stories noted that the disease was hitting the homosexual community very hard. Doctors knew that the disease was spread mainly through sexual intercourse, and primarily by anal intercourse as practiced by homosexuals. But journalists did not report that because it was thought that words like "anal intercourse" were not fit for family newspapers or television newscasts.

It wasn't until the fall of 1985 that the honesty in reporting that was needed began to creep into the press. The fact that Rock Hudson was stricken with AIDS was publicized. And with the opening of school, controversy developed in many districts where parents objected to sending their children to school with other kids who had AIDS. This is when the Ryan White story developed, the little boy who was literally run out of town because he had acquired AIDS—through a blood transfusion. On September 9 NBC science/medical reporter Robert Bazell used the term *anal intercourse* during an appearance on the "Today Show" as he admitted that, "We have been squeamish, using words like intimate contact and sexual contact." While this term had been used in a few newspapers, the television appearance seemed to break open a log jam and finally, the press began to report explicitly about the ways in which AIDS is transmitted.

But serious damage had been done. By using vague terms like *personal contact* and *sexual contact* in early reports, the press clearly overstated the ease by which the disease is transmitted. And this generated unwarranted public fears in many cases; at schools for example where parents believed their children were in danger if they were in the same classroom with an AIDS victim. Yet at the same time, the lack of precision in reporting failed to provide readers and viewers, especially homosexuals, with the information they needed badly—that certain sexual practices were extremely dangerous and should be avoided.

Today, at a time when the AIDS crisis seems to be growing, the coverage of the problems seems to be waning. In a report published in the *Washington Journalism Review* in early 1990, John-Manuel Andriote noted that many of the reporters who covered the story during the 1980s say they are burned out and want to move on to other matters. And many of these reporters believe people have tired of hearing about the problem as well. "It's like Sydney Schanberg writing about Cambodia [the Killing Fields]," noted Laurie Garrett, an AIDS reporter at *Newsday*. "People don't want to hear about stacks of skulls anymore."

The decision to use or not use specific language in stories about AIDS is governed by the news policy at a broadcasting station or newspaper. There are generally scores of such policies, mostly unwritten, within news organizations. Policies are used to reduce the total amount of potential news by arbitrarily eliminating some news. For example, even a large-sized daily newspaper cannot publish all the stories about police activity and crime in the community, so guidelines are erected. Robberies that net more than $500 are covered, those that net less are not, for example. If someone is hospitalized because of injuries from an auto accident, a story about the accident is published. If there are no injuries or no hospitalization, no story.

Some news organizations have policies on the mix of news that is published or broadcast. American newspapers tend to publish a small amount of world news. This is not because what is happening in Europe or Africa is not important, but because the editors believe national or local news is more important to readers. Many newspapers have policies about running at least one or two local stories on the front page each day or about the amount of total space allotted to foreign news.

Certain kinds of stories are not reported by some news organizations. Many newspapers and television stations have policies against reporting news about bomb threats. People who plant bombs or threaten to plant bombs feed on such publicity, some believe, and reports about their activities simply encourage more bomb threats. Other news organizations have policies against reporting suicide or at least calling a death a suicide. Some newspapers have a policy of printing the name of every person arrested for prostitution; others have a policy of deleting the name of the person arrested for prostitution but printing the name of the person who was arrested for soliciting the act of prostitution instead. Many of these policies seem arbitrary, and some often don't make sense. Yet they exist and often determine whether a particular story is news or not.

## ☐ The Ease of Getting the Story

The news selection process tends to be biased toward news that is easy to gather and against news that is hard to gather. This is not a generalization that will hold up 100 percent of the time, nor is it meant to indict reporters and editors as being lazy or slothful. It simply reflects human nature. If there are two acceptable ways of doing something, most people will take the easy way.

The beat system of reporting, where journalists are assigned to cover specific kinds of news on a regular basis, is a good example of this generalization. Stories that occur on a reporter's beat are more likely to be reported than stories that occur off the beat. It simply takes more effort for an editor to discover and assign a reporter to cover an off-beat story.

The efforts of public information officers and public relations specialists in making news easier for reporters to obtain have been outlined in the opening section of this chapter. As has been noted, without the assistance of these individuals many important news stories would never be told. Reporters often don't have the time or the inclination to cover all the bases that need to be covered.

For example, Ralph Nader is a kind of public relations practioner without portfolio. In the nearly 35 years that he has been in the public spotlight, he has brought media attention to dozens of important public issues that otherwise would have likely remained undercovered or uncovered. He started with automobile safety, forcing journalists to confront statistics and data that the auto industry had blithely hidden from view. Journalist David Bollier notes in an article in the *Columbia Journalism Review* that in 1988 Nader successfully brought two other important public issues into the national spotlight, automobile insurance reform and congressional pay raises. "Two sleeper issues suddenly became hot national news" because of Nader's activity, Bollier wrote. Media critic Mark Hertsgaard said that Nader "politicizes issues, forcing them into the open." Not all public relations specialists are like Ralph Nader, but many have the capacity to bring media attention to an otherwise clouded issue.

At the same time, too much reliance on public relations specialists or public information officers can wreck havoc on the press. Remember, much (maybe most) of the material generated by public relations practitioners is self-serving drivel, not worthy of anyone's attention. It is purely an effort to serve a paying client or a government agency. When used by the mass media, this information often pushes out more important news. And, if the information that has been generated is not completely accurate or is a one-sided view of a problem, the mass media suffer the loss of credibility in the eyes of readers or viewers.

There is no better way to explore the credibility problem than to examine briefly public relations and the pharmaceutical or drug industry. The prescription drug industry faces a unique problem. It wants to sell to the public the medicines it has developed and manufactured. But members of the public cannot buy such drugs without the permission of a physician. Advertising to the the public, therefore, is generally ineffective and isn't used very often. What the industry tries to do instead is to use the news organizations within the mass media, which have credibility, to spread the word about new products in hopes that patients will then request them from their doctors. Public relations blitzes usually accompany the FDA approval of a new drug.

In 1982 both print and broadcast media prominently heralded the arrival of a new drug which was supposed to cure a severe skin disease called cystic acne. The drug was marketed under the name "Accutane." Almost all drugs have potential side effects, and the makers of Accutane, Hoffman-LaRoche Inc., listed these in the literature distributed about the drug. Most reporters noted the most common likely problem, chapped lips. But few reporters, most of whom were caught up in the public relations euphoria about the medication, noted a more serious possible consequence—birth defects in children born to women who take the drug during pregnancy. In their attempts to verify Hoffman-LaRoche's claims about the drug, reporters contacted medical researchers who had tested Accutane. Their evaluations were universally positive.

The positive press reports paid off for the company; patients, especially women, pushed their doctors hard for prescriptions for the new drug. But about a year later Accutane was again in the news. Young women who used the drug while they were pregnant were giving birth to children with severe deformities, including blindness, deafness, brain injury, defective hearts, and others. By the fall of 1984 there were 25 cases of the birth of deformed Accutane babies. At least 75 other pregnant women chose abortion instead. Many doctors came forth and were critical of the drug. "I really feel the drug has been fantastically overpromoted for the number of patients who should be treated with [Accutane]," Dr. Frank Yoder of Ohio State University told the *Washington Post*. What Dr. Yoder did not say was "that the vehicle for this fantastic overpromotion was the press," notes Jim Sibbison, a writer who documented this story in the *Columbia Journalism Review*.

But what about the "independent" evaluations the reporters had obtained from physicians who had tested Accutane? Reporters had not told readers, and in fact some did not know themselves, that many of these physicians were on the Hoffman-LaRoche payroll as clinical investigators. "The Washington correspondents' approach to reporting FDA news of newly approved prescription drugs is simplicity itself," wrote Sibbison. "They usually wait for company or FDA press releases to be delivered to their offices, make telephone calls for more information, then write the story. The tendency to accept this publicity at face value seems to be deeply ingrained," he added.

There is probably no better (or worse) example of the slavish domination of the press by public relations in our history than the manner in which the National Aeronautics and Space Administration, NASA, used the press for more than 30 years to build support for the nation's space program. The tragic result of this PR blitz was a generally noncritical, unquestioning press which must at least share a portion of the blame for the Challenger disaster that claimed the lives of the seven crew members.

From the inception of the space program in the 1950s NASA, with the cooperation if not support of the press, had focused public attention not upon the important and complicated technical aspects of space travel but upon the astronauts. Americans became almost personally acquainted with the original Mercury astronauts through skillful publicity generated by the government. As such, the press tended to lose focus of the technical elements of the program. And this was unusual, considering the money the nation invested in this program. As generally uncritical as the press has been regarding weapons procurement for the military, those stories that do appear about the development and testing of new aircraft, for example, focus on the attributes of the plane, not the pilots.

NASA suffered severe technical difficulties as the space program began in the 1950s and continued into the 1960s. The first Apollo moon flight was delayed more than six months after a fire broke out in the spacecraft cabin and killed three astronauts during a countdown rehearsal. Tragedy was barely averted three years later in 1970 when Apollo 13 lost all power due to an explosion while more than 200,000 miles from Earth. Still, the press remained generally uncritical and, more important, uncaring. There was no investigative reporting into whether or not NASA was doing its job properly; whether its concept of the space shuttle made sense; whether taxpayers' money was being well spent. Reports on shuttle flights reflected NASA public relations—stories about crew members, experiments that were scheduled to be carried out, and so forth.

The press barely noted technical problems that were arising. Testimony before the Rogers Commission which investigated the Challenger disaster revealed that there was great apprehension within NASA over the faulty performance of the O-rings (the piece of equipment that failed in the accident) on earlier shuttle missions. "TV journalists (along with their print brethren) had missed that story cold," wrote Neil Hickey in *TV Guide*. "It was a story that cried out for exposé, for angry, illuminating, hour-long documentaries at any time in the several years preceding the catastrophe," he added. "We didn't ask more of the tough questions," said reporter Ed Turner of CNN. "Yes, we should have dug harder and deeper into things," noted Dan Rather of CBS. But Rather notes that NASA didn't want the public to know about the trouble they were having with the O-rings. Of course not. Public information specialists in the agency wanted NASA, which must each year seek congressional approval of its budget, to appear to be an efficient, highly skilled operation. But Rather, a veteran of the investigative journalism on "60 Minutes," obviously knows that no government agency, or business, or labor union, wants reporters to find out its problems.

In the months before the Challenger mission NASA was having more and more problems keeping shuttle launch dates as one problem after another seemed to spring up. But the press seemed to ignore those clues; there was little hard-nosed reporting. Reporters simply relayed what they were told by NASA information officers. Network news anchors nightly chided the agency. "Yet another costly, red-faces-all-around space-shuttle launch delay," Rather noted on the day before the Challenger accident. "Once again a flawless liftoff proved to be too much of a challenge for Challenger," noted a reporter on ABC's "World News Tonight." And Tom Brokaw on NBC noted that there was "still another delay in efforts to put the first school teacher [astronaut Christa McAuliffe] into space."

To this day no one has uncovered a single, undisputed answer to the question of why NASA decided to launch the Challenger the day of the accident. Warnings about safety problems were apparently abundant. After the accident, the press was diligent in its efforts to find out what happened. And the American people know a great deal more about shuttle problems today than they did in early 1986. Yet even in 1991, as delay after delay continues to plague launching the shuttle fleet, American journalists seem surprisingly docile in their approach to this multibillion dollar program. There is no doubt that the legion of information officers employed by NASA has helped the press and the public understand essential aspects of the American space program. Without them we all would be less knowledgeable. They have served their agency well. Yet one wonders if they and the press have served the nation as well. For too many reporters, a shuttle launch is not a news story about government but a hi-tech week in the Florida sun.

# THE COST OF NEWS

Anyone who pays attention to the promotional messages published and broadcast for newspapers and especially television news shows might expect that what it costs to cover a story is immaterial to news organizations in the late twentieth century. "If It Happens, We'll Be There." "Give Us Thirty Minutes, We'll Give You the World." "The Only News Source You'll Ever Need." And so on.

But like other businesses, news organizations have news budgets. And whether a story is reported or not may come down to how much it costs to get the news. After the cataclysmic eruption of Mt. St. Helens in Washington state in 1980, the volcano continued to burp small amounts of ash and steam almost on a weekly basis for many months. Each time this happened a Seattle newspaper would fly a photographer down to the volcano and publish a picture of this activity on the front page or the front of the regional news section. When asked how long such coverage would continue, the editor honestly answered, "Until my travel budget runs out." And sure enough, soon after that, though the mountain continued to spurt debris into the sky, the pictures stopped. The budget had been expended.

The economics of newsgathering is a more serious problem today as a bottom line mentality has taken hold in many newspapers and most television news operations. Some newspapers and television news departments have made serious cuts in personnel and expenses, and this has a direct impact on the amount of news that is covered. And if the news isn't covered, it certainly has no chance to be included in the daily news report. Dan Rather recently lamented the diminishing amount of foreign news coverage in American journalism. "Make no mistake, the trend line in American journalism . . . is toward decreasing foreign coverage," he wrote in a *Newsweek* magazine "My Turn" column. The newsman said that more and more people in journalism look at news as strictly a commodity. "There's a lot of talk about generating more product with less investment. As with any commodity, the game is to buy low and sell high. Foreign news is expensive." Rather argues that many news operations use the excuse that the public isn't interested in foreign news to cut back on its coverage. Rather said he disputes this assertion, arguing that what people want is quality journalism, regardless of what it is about.

Newspapers and the television networks have all made substantial cutbacks in overseas personnel in recent years, preferring instead to "parachute" reporters in when stories develop in various parts of the globe. Consequently, Americans rarely get other than crisis-type stories from much of the world. Africa is a good example. All three television networks at one time had bureaus in Kenya. No longer. It was too expensive, reported Joanmarie Kalter in *TV Guide*. When the crisis in the Persian Gulf broke out, American reporters flocked to this part of the world. Previous to that crisis there had been a remarkably small amount of news published or broadcast about this supposed strategic area of the planet. Television, with the tremendous growth of satellite technology, is better equipped now than ever before to cover the world. Paradoxically, the introduction of this equipment is one of the reasons for the cutbacks, according to some. Because the new technology requires more personnel—to edit and send stories from the field—it has made foreign news reports more expensive, writes Kalter.

In the United States, budget problems limit the number of reporters who are assigned to cover even the nation's capital. And that is one of the reasons, according to some observers, that the press totally missed the explosive story of greed and political debasement in the Department of Housing and Urban Development in the Reagan administration. News organizations simply did not have enough staff to routinely cover HUD. "If you had a reporter at HUD and knew the people in the bureaucracy, you're almost bound to have broken that story," said Jack Nelson, head of the *Los Angeles Time*'s 42-member Washington bureau. One publication did uncover the story before the scandal bubbled to the surface, the *Multi-Housing News,* a tabloid-size trade magazine for builders and housing developers. So the story was there; it was simply missed by the reporters, stretched too thin to cover the many, many tentacles of the monstrous federal government.

Most editors and news directors frankly admit to budget limitations, but most will argue they still cover the essential news. But the decision as to what is essential and is not essential for readers and viewers often becomes an economic decision, not a journalistic one.

## ☐ Simplicity Is Best

One of the goals of journalists is to take complicated information, attempt to simplify it as much as possible, and then present it in a manner that an audience of nonexperts can understand. A noble cause. But the need to present easy-to-understand information has manifested itself in an unforeseen way; there is a bias in news reporting toward doing simple rather than complicated stories. Simple stories are far easier to report.

Take a story about the cleanup of a waste dump for example. A tough nut to crack for a reporter who is writing or speaking to an audience that is generally science-illiterate. Instead of the waste dump story, why not report a crime—a murder, for example. Crime is the simplest of news to report. There is a beginning, a middle, and an end to each story; there are good guys and bad guys, the stuff of drama; and there is little technical jargon. Also, a reporter has only a handful of sources with which to cope: police, lawyers, witnesses, victim's family, perhaps the defendant. A story about a waste dump is much tougher. Where do you start? Who do you talk with? How do you explain complicated chemical and biological concepts to readers or viewers? Then there is the economic angle, "experts" disagreeing over the dangers involved, the difficulty in conveying the dangers inherent in what appears to be a piece of land or a pile of steel drums.

Confounding all this is the belief held by a growing number of editors and reporters that people won't read or watch complicated or long stories. "Statistics are dull," is a motto of many in the industry, forgetting that readers pore over column after column of statistics on the sports pages and in the business section.

What it all comes down to is that simple stories seem to be best for many in journalism. And this, as much as anything else, explains why many of the most pressing, important, and complicated stories seemingly go unreported. When the press is forced to cover a complicated story, it sometimes finds it extremely difficult. Review the press coverage, for example, of the nuclear reactor accident at Three Mile Island in Pennsylvania in 1979. When communications professor and former *Newsweek* editor Edwin Diamond examined the press reports on the disaster, he concluded that the press simply didn't measure up to the occasion. (Both the government and the power industry failed, as well, Diamond noted.) Reporters, dependent upon sources for their news, found three sets of experts at the site: spokespersons for the power plant, the state, and the federal government. And each set of

Most people, according to research, found out about the assassination of President John Kennedy from a friend, neighbor or co-worker, not from the mass media. But tens of millions were watching television two days later when accused assassin Lee Harvey Oswald was gunned down in the basement of the Dallas police station by Jack Ruby. Oswald's murder contributed to the generation of various conspiracy theories about the death of the president.
(Compix of United Press International)

experts had its own explanation about what was taking place. In their study of the same coverage Peter Sandman and Michael Pader discovered that the government deliberately underestimated the danger because it thought the press would overestimate the danger. "The prediction was self-fulfilling," they wrote. "Believing that the Nuclear Regulatory Commission was grossly minimizing the threat, the media magnified the commission's public statements on the likelihood and imminence of disaster." By accident, readers and viewers got a roughly accurate picture of what was going on. At the daily press conferences about the disaster fully one-third of the reporters could not understand what the government scientists were saying. "These were the reporters whose recurring nightmare was that the NRC would announce a meltdown in technical language and they [the reporters] wouldn't realize what happened," Sandman and Pader noted. If more reporters had attempted to report upon the complexities of nuclear power prior to the accident, many more qualified journalists would have been prepared to deal with the emergency. But nuclear power is a complex issue, not a sexy topic. Technical stories are one problem; economic stories are another.

The economic story of the decade and one of the most important stories in recent memory was the collapse in the savings and loan industry. The press missed this story. Why? Partly because it was a tough story to cover. Reporter Ellen Hume notes that the story was complicated and boring and failed to interest many mainstream journalists. Regulatory changes—such as accounting tricks and reduced capital requirements—that helped paper over the first phase of the crisis were difficult to explain and never became big news.

Financial stories are particularly hard for television, notes Hume. There are likely to be few memorable sound bites associated with the solvency of thrift institutions, and the story offered little opportunity for pictures. In 1988 the president of NBC news, Michael Gartner, observed that the savings and loan story did not lend itself to images, and without such images, "television can't do facts."

Pictures are the key to television, and that undoubtedly explains why in the autumn of 1988, in the midst of a presidential election campaign, with the savings and loan crisis bubbling just below the surface, scores of U.S. journalists trekked to Barrow, Alaska, 320 miles above the Arctic Circle, to report on the plight of three gray whales trapped in a hole in the ice. The whales had stayed behind to eat more shellfish as the remainder of the pod made its way south for the winter. Normally these three whales would have drowned, as hundreds do each year. "Their plight was a perfectly normal one," an observer noted, "a routine Darwinian cruelty." But television discovered this story, and what happened next is chronicled in Tom Rose's *Freeing the Whales: How the Media Created the World's Greatest Non-Event*. Rose reports that 150 journalists descended upon Barrow, which had only 80 hotel rooms. Rooms were auctioned off each night to the highest bidders. The story lasted for two weeks until Soviet ice breakers, heralding a new era of Soviet-American cooperation, freed the trapped creatures. Total cost of saving these animals: $5.75 million.

Most of the rest of the world thought the story was a hoot, but the American mass media took it seriously. It was the lead story on the network newscasts on several occasions. Why? There were pictures and emotions. Men and women reaching out to help their fellow creatures of the earth. And while it may have been a hardship to report, given temperatures and wind-chill factors of as low as 50 degrees below zero, it was a simple story to tell. Much easier than attempting to explain why whaling by the Soviet and Japanese threatens to exterminate some species of whales.

The penchant of too many in the press to select simple over complex news becomes an increasingly serious problem as the world in which we live becomes more and more complicated. The application of this standard is seen in the selection of a wide variety of news. In reporting the economy the press tends to focus on a handful of economic indicators which are announced by the government or some other agency, rather than exercising enterprise and digging beneath the surface. If the stock market goes up or the stock market goes down, there is always a market analyst available to quote, even though most of these analysts aren't close to the New York Stock Exchange and often know little more than the journalist who asks the question. The dangers in this kind of reporting became acutely clear in the fall of 1987, just before the stock market took a dive. "While experts warned increasingly that the market was overheating and heading for a possible disaster, newspapers and the major network evening news shows—the places where most Americans get their information—provided much the same kind of inconsequential daily coverage as before," wrote John Lawrence, a former assistant managing editor of economic affairs for the *Los Angeles Times* in the *Columbia Journalism Review*. "What was needed over the many months of the bull market was far less of the standard analysis . . . and far more digging into the workings of a market whose players and mechanisms had changed radically in recent years," he added. Lawrence said the most significant changes in the market were the increasing domination of trading by managers of huge pools of money (mutual funds and pension funds), their transformation from investors to speculators, and the impact new speculative games were having on stock prices. This complex story went largely unreported, and the market crash came as a surprise to most Americans.

Journalists have always found a convenient excuse for their preference for simple news; they assert that most Americans are dolts and can't handle anything terribly complicated. This has become a kind of self-fulfilling prophecy as most readers have been conditioned to expect "see Spot run" kind of journalism. However, a talented journalist can take a complicated story and present it in a way that most readers can understand and appreciate. But this takes work. Today, the tendency toward selecting the simple is exacerbated by the desire of most newspaper and broadcast editors to "keep it short." Many environmental journalists complain that there is less attention being paid to environmental problems today than in the 1970s, when the dangers were far less apparent than they are now. Surely when a disaster occurs, the press is there. But publications and broadcast news seem unwilling in the regular coverage of the news to take the time and space needed to present news stories about severe and complicated environmental problems.

# OTHER BIASES IN NEWS SELECTION

Bias, a dirty word in most newsrooms, manifests itself in many ways. We have already noted that reporters and editors have interests that sometimes color their selection of the news, so personal bias exists. There are institutional biases as well. In a recent issue of the *Columbia Journalism Review,* former *Seattle Times* reporter and University of Washington journalism professor Doug Underwood documented that the Boeing Company, the biggest employer in the Puget Sound region, was extended far less critical coverage by the Seattle newspapers than one might expect and the company probably deserved. Newspapers have traditionally protected hometown industries. In the early 1980s when General Motors announced it would close a plant in Flint, Mich., resulting in the loss of 3,600 jobs in a community already suffering from auto industry layoffs, the story was hardly news at all in the *Flint Journal.* The onerous announcement was buried in a long story about the decision of the Buick Division of GM to build a new small car in Flint. Constructing the new small car would create no new jobs, however. Readers had to wade through ten paragraphs of that story before they found out about the massive layoffs, according to Michael Moore in a story in the *Columbia Journalism Review.* For many years the *Tri-City Herald* in eastern Washington state was one of the few newspapers in the nation that reflected a positive attitude about nuclear energy and nuclear weapons production. The huge Hanford Federal Nuclear Reservation provides thousands of jobs for the local community. Headlines like "Radiation Linked to Good Health," and "A-Plants Don't Taint the Environment" were common in the newspaper in the early 1980s.

Large advertisers are also protected in many instances, protected to the point that when the press attempts to give them honest coverage, they scream. Nordstrom, Inc. has been one of the great retail success stories of the 1980s. Beginning decades ago as a shoe store in Seattle, the clothing and footwear retailer now has stores across the nation. The company's hallmarks have been high-quality clothing and shoes for upscale buyers and a deep dedication to service. But in the winter and spring of 1990 editors at Seattle's two daily newspapers began to feel the heat from Nordstrom as they attempted to report on a simmering labor dispute between the company and its retail workers, who complained they were being taken advantage of by the firm. When the Washington Department of Labor and Industry upheld a complaint by the union against the company, this was reported in both the *Seattle Times* and the *Seattle Post Intelligencer,* as were other employee allegations against the company. Nordstrom's response to the charges was given equal press coverage. But the negative publicity was more than the retailer could take, and in March of 1990 Nordstrom announced it was cutting back its advertising in the local newspapers. James Nordstrom charged that the newspapers were showing favoritism to the union and called the newspapers' handling of the labor dispute as "the worst in the nation."

There was a good deal of soul searching by the management of both newspapers who stood by their coverage. *Times* columnist Rick Anderson was so concerned that he went back and looked at several hundred stories published about Nordstrom in his newspaper in recent years. He announced his findings in his column. The reports, he wrote, "amounted to a seemingly endless string of stories about Nordstrom successes, rising stocks and profits, and the release of another line of fashions or fragrances." The continuing positive coverage of the company by both Seattle newspapers was what the company apparently came to expect, he noted. "As Jim Nordstrom said," Anderson concluded, "there's been favoritism. Except, as the record shows, it's been heavily in favor of, not against, Seattle's hallowed retail institution." In recounting this story in the *Columbia Journalism Review,* University of Washington journalism professor Doug Underwood noted that "as long as retailers continue to think of this flattering coverage as 'news,' newspapers should hardly be surprised if the retailers react with alarm whenever reporters start digging into an industry in turmoil."

So biases surely exist. But probably the two most important biases that affect the selection of news are far less obvious. The first is negativism. Ask any editor the number of times a reader or viewer has called and said, "Isn't there any good news to report? Why all the stories about gloom and doom?" Watch the campaign coverage in the next national election. Most observers who study such reporting have shown that the news is not pro-Democrat or pro-Republican. It is generally negative toward both candidates. A study by *Channels* magazine of the 1984 campaign revealed that on television the negative news outweighed the positive news by as much as eight to one.

News usually involves something that has happened that is out of the ordinary, not simply the routine of life. An airplane is expected to pick up passengers, take off, fly to its destination and land safely, and when that happens it is not news. But when a plane crashes it is news. Most people live lives that are uneventful. But when these lives are disturbed, when a person is robbed or harmed by an intruder, or injured in a traffic accident, that is news. If a government of a Third World is stable, it's usually not news. If it is toppled by a coup, it is news. People are supposed to have enough to eat and be disease free; when they are starving or ravaged by an epidemic, that's news. There is a strong bias in the press to select stories that tell of the unusual, the out-of-the-ordinary, and these stories usually bring readers and viewers reports about bad things.

There is one more important bias in the American press, the bias toward reform or change. This is not as evident as the negative bias and may not even exist at a few newspapers and magazines and broadcasting stations. But the reporters and editors in most news organizations tend to reflect the belief that change is better than the status quo, that things should be better and can get better.

Sociologist Herbert Gans studied almost two decades of news coverage by several national newsgathering organizations. Using the messages conveyed by these stories, he constructed what he said he believes are the values inherent in the selection of news by at least these American journalists. These are some of the values he discovered.

1. Ethnocentrism—American news values America and reports the world in terms of our own country.
2. Altruistic democracy—There is a strong implication that political and governmental action should be based upon public interest and service and not self-interest or personal gain.
3. Responsible capitalism—There is an optimistic faith reflected in the news that our economic system works like our political system, that businesses and corporations will compete with one another in order to create prosperity for everyone in the nation.
4. Small-town pastoralism—There is a strong bias in favor of rural, small-town settings. "Stories about city neighborhoods," Gans writes, "judge the neighborhoods by their ability to retain the cohesiveness, friendliness, and slow pace ascribed to small towns. . . ."
5. Individualism—There is a strong sense of working to preserve the freedom of the individual against the encroachments of nation and society.
6. Moderatism—Moderation in all things is valued. Extremism regarding anything is suspect. Gans points out how the press sustains the importance of the middle ground by critically treating persons at both ends of any spectrum of activity or belief. News coverage is usually not kind to atheists or religious fanatics, conspicuous consumers or those who reject materialism, political ideologues or unprincipled politicians, and public officials who follow party lines (hacks) or those who never follow party lines (mavericks).
7. Order—News tends to often focus on political disorder or social disorder. In noting such events as news—i.e., something out of the ordinary—the press is suggesting that order is the favored norm.
8. Leadership—The news tends to focus on leaders; it sometimes creates them. Leaders should be strong but benevolent. Our leaders frequently are pictured as persons who generally will determine what we are and will become.

When put together these factors reflect a strong strain of reformism, or progressivism, a political philosophy that flowered at the end of the nineteenth century via the Progressive political party. This reform spirit has a peculiarly American shading, and while it cannot be said that in its entirety it represents a contemporary American ethos, parts of it are central to our cultural values. Journalists probably reflect this spirit of reformism more than most in society. What is it, after all, that prompts most people to enter journalism? It is not the pay, although a handful of journalists make a lot of money. And it is not the working conditions, because especially in the beginning of their careers, journalists work all hours of the night and day. Some young people go into journalism because they like to write, and they are interested in what is happening around them. But an even larger number seek to become journalists because it represents an opportunity for them to help make a difference, to accomplish something, to change for the better (however they define this) the world around them. This is the same spirit that motivates people to become teachers and social workers, and the values of a journalist tend to be far closer to those kinds of people than to the values of accountants or salespeople or bankers. These values are surely reflected in news selection. These values prompt the journalist to ask the mayor why she hasn't made the police chief hire more Hispanic or African American officers, or ask the corporate president why the company has been slow to control its pollution problems, or ask the school superintendent why the students' test scores are not better. The journalist could have just as easily asked the mayor how she has managed to keep the budget balanced, or ask the corporate president why the company's dividend isn't a bit higher, or ask the school superintendent why the curriculum in the elementary schools is better today than it was 20 years ago. This spirit of reformism does shape the news.

What is news? Tough to say, isn't it? Lots of factors influence what we read or watch or hear in the news. In many instances the public is getting the most important and interesting stories of the day, getting the information we need to maintain control over our environment. But in other instances the news we get is shaped by totally extraneous factors and is really irrelevant to our survival. Readers and viewers need to know this and take the necessary steps to fill in the gaps left by the incomplete news reports.

## BIBLIOGRAPHY

These are some of the materials that were helpful in the preparation of this chapter.

Bollier, David. "Ralph Nader, News Creator," *Columbia Journalism Review,* May/June, 1990.

Brecher, Edward M. "Straight Sex, AIDS, and the Mixed-Up Press," *Columbia Journalism Review,* March/April, 1988.

Carey, Bill. "TV Near-Hysteria Scars Suspect and News Media," *The Los Angeles Times,* April 17, 1986.

"Dangerous Liaisons, Journalists and their Sources," *Columbia Journalism Review,* July/August, 1989.

Diamond, Edwin, and Belletto, Christopher. "The Great Verbal Cover-Up," *Washington Journalism Review,* March, 1986.

Dow, David. "Covering a Whale of a Story," *Washington Journalism Review,* March, 1989.

Gans, Herbert. *Deciding What's News.* New York: Pantheon Books, 1979.

Hickey, Neil. "The Challenger Tragedy: It Exposed TV's Failures as Well as NASA's," *TV Guide,* January 24, 1987.

Hume, Ellen. "Why the Press Blew the S & L Scandal," *The New York Times,* May 24, 1990.

"Inside the Invasion," *Newsweek,* June 25, 1990.

Karp, Walter. "Who Decides What Is News? (Hint: It's Not Journalists)," *Utne Reader,* November/December, 1989.

Katz, Tonnie. "How U.S. Papers Cover Foreign News," *APME News,* August 15, 1989.

Lawrence, John F. "How Street-Smart Is the Press?" *Columbia Journalism Review,* January/February, 1988.

Moore, Michael. "How to Keep 'em Happy in Flint," *Columbia Journalism Review,* September/October, 1985.

Pember, Don R. *Mass Media Law* (5th ed.) Dubuque, Iowa: William C. Brown Co., 1990.

Pride, Mike. "A Grieving Concord Repelled by Media Misbehavior," *presstime,* March, 1986.

Rather, Dan. "The Threat to Foreign News," *Newsweek,* July 17, 1989.

Rose, Tom. *Freeing the Whales,* New York: Birch Lane Press, 1989.

Rubin, David M. "How the News Media Reported on Three Mile Island and Chernobyl," 37 *Journal of Communication* 42, 1989.

Russell, Dick. "The Media and the Environment," *Extra,* May/June, 1988.

Shaw, David. "East Coast Bias Colors the Media," *The Los Angeles Times,* November 17, 1988.

———. "Media Increasingly View World Events Through the Same Eye," *The Oregonian,* September 11, 1989.

———. "Press Turns a Mirror on Itself," *The Los Angeles Times,* June 19, 1988.

———. *Press Watch.* New York: Macmillan Publishing Co., 1984.

Sibbison, Jim. "Pushing New Drugs—Can the Press Kick the Habit?" *Columbia Journalism Review,* July/August, 1985.

Vasquez, Juan. "Panama: Live from the Marriot," *Washington Journalism Review,* March, 1990.

# CHAPTER 12

# MASS MEDIA AND CULTURE

A variety of metaphors have been used thus far to describe the various functions or roles undertaken by the mass media in America. The mass media have been described as an engine that helps run our economy, as a sentry or watchman which alerts us to changes in the environment. In this chapter we will discuss another media function, we will portray mass media as a kind of glue which holds our society together. Or as a mirror which reflects an image of who we are as a society and as individuals in that society.

Both of these metaphors aptly describe the role played by the mass media in generating, sustaining, and reflecting our common culture. Virtually all commentators who have attempted to describe the various roles undertaken by mass communications in contemporary society include such a role. Harold Lasswell described this role as the transmission of our social heritage. When most of humankind lived in small villages, the responsibility of passing down the heritage of the society fell to the elders, who would tell stories to the young about what had taken place in the past, or what they thought had taken place. Mass communications provides this function today, passing on the history and values of a people to one generation after another.

Paul Lazarsfeld and Robert Merton argue that the mass media have the tendency to keep society stable by conferring status (through media recognition) on those who tend to support the values of the society, and exposing those persons who deviate from the societal norms. The police officer who risks his life to stop a robbery becomes a celebrity in the community because of press publicity about his heroic deeds. Meanwhile, the robber must face the embarrassment of a trial, and the publicity that results from the trial will stigmatize the felon as someone who is going to be punished for bad or abnormal behavior. Through these means, the mass media tend to hold the society together by the public reinforcement of its values. There is the assumption, of course, that all parts of society share the same values. That may not be a valid assumption. In some parts of the community, for example, the actions of the police are thought to be repressive, and those who stand up to the police are considered heroic.

The impact of the mass media on society is a subject of great debate, as will be noted later in this chapter. While there is little doubt that the mass communication

One function of the mass media is to pass on from one generation to the next the values and history of the society. PBS's exploration of another time in "Making Sense of the Sixties" explored a recent time that seemed as alien as the distant past to many Americans.
*(Left photo:* © Bob Fitch/*Right photo:* © Ivan Massar)

systems play important roles in shaping, transmitting, and reflecting culture, there is often little agreement on exactly how this is accomplished. Neil Postman, for example, has argued in his book *Amusing Ourselves to Death* that the impact of the medium—television, in this case—has a somewhat greater impact on the society than has been suggested by others. Canadian Marshall McLuhan was the first to popularize the notion of the importance of the medium over the message, arguing that television was a more natural medium for human communication because it involved all the senses, not simply the visual senses required by print media. He argued that our culture was being radically altered by television. Postman's argument is less amorphous. He argues that the manner in which we discover what we know governs what we know. "The concept of truth," he writes, "is intimately linked to the biases of forms of expression." For over 500 years, developed societies used the printed word to discover what they needed to know. "We are now a culture whose information, ideas and epistemology are given form by television, not the printed word," he noted. Because television is primarily an entertainment medium, television has "made entertainment itself the natural format for the representation of all experience. "The problem is not that television presents us with entertaining subject matter but that all subject matter is presented as entertaining," Postman asserts. And he cites television news, the coverage of the political process, even television as a pulpit for an exposition of religion, as examples of his arguments. Postman doesn't explicitly blame the technological medium of television, but the values of those who operate and control the system.

It is also necessary to deal with the matter of intended versus unintended effects when talking about the impact of mass communication on the values in a community. As noted in Chapter 3, the source of the communication and the message transmitted are only part of the communication equation. The receiver of that message is another factor in this process. More than 70 years ago, a campaign was launched to try to abate bigotry by publishing a series of cartoons that reflected bigotry at its worst. The notion was that this exaggeration would reveal the stupidity of such bigotry, and this was undoubtedly the impact the cartoons had on many people. But many bigoted persons enjoyed the cartoons for exactly the opposite reason; the drawings tended to reinforce their bigotry and prejudice.

The mass media also can unintentionally send mixed messages to the audience, and this can result in confusion. In September of 1990, CBS presented a rare, primetime documentary on American education. In it commentators and others "waxed eloquent about the need for inspired principals and dedicated teachers," noted *New York Times* television writer John J. O'Connor. At the same time the three commercial networks were premiering their new fall primetime series, many of which ("Ferris Bueller," "Hull High," "Parker Lewis Can't Lose," and others) focused upon young Americans, including their schooling. "More often than not," O'Connor noted, "the school principals are portrayed as grumbling misfits, the teachers are blithering incompetents. Students who show the slightest interest in their studies are invariably depicted as wimps. The heroes are those who can best foul up the system. . . ." Which set of values did television intend to suggest? What set of role models will the younger members of the audience adopt? O'Connor noted a news story about a group of parents in one school who complained to school officials because the children of Asian immigrants study too much.

It is also important when looking at the mass media as a force in shaping culture to examine its impact both on society and on individuals. We have already noted two societal impacts, the transmission of the heritage of the culture of a people, and the stabilizing function through reinforcement of norms. Mass media also provides a society with a sense of commonality through the exposition of a common language and common customs. Celebrating the Fourth of July is something done by Americans, and no other people. The mass media help generate this celebration. The mass media play a role in integrating new members of the society into the culture. Immigrants, even those who cannot read English, can learn about their new homeland by watching television, listening to music, viewing pictures in newspapers and magazines. Young people are socialized into the society in much the same way. The mass media help hold a people together, permit the members of the society to define what they have in common, or what they should have in common, with others in the society. The mass media can help define the common aspects of a nation. But not without a cost, as we will note later when the impact of a mass culture is evaluated.

Mass communications also have an impact on individuals as they attempt to relate to the society. In his book *Mass-Mediated Culture,* Michael R. Real outlines many of these impacts. Individuals can learn their own identity through what is expressed in the mass media. The media can provide individuals with a frame of reference for their own behavior and the behavior of others, and this assists them in interpreting everyday life. Through the knowledge that they are sharing an experience with others, individuals feel a more cohesive relationship with other people in the society. The mass media can teach people the meaning behind certain experiences

For decades, female roles in primetime television were limited to long-suffering wives and mothers. During the last decade some changes have taken place. Sharon Gless was featured for several years as police detective Chris Cagney on "Cagney and Lacy." In 1991 she played a public defender on "The Trials of Rosie O'Neill."

and help them cope with similar problems. The mass media also permit individuals to escape and relax, "to laugh, get angry, feel affections, or be bored without a feeling of any responsibility or an awareness of any consequence," Real notes. Mass media also permit individuals to experience parts of the culture vicariously. There are many other functions that one may point out as well.

The basic point of all of this is that mass media are powerful elements that insure a certain cohesiveness in a large, differentiated society such as ours. And they assist in defining the sum of this society, its culture, its norms, its expectations, its rules, to individual members of the society. American society would not dissolve if mass media suddenly disappeared, but it would change dramatically. A substitute for the socializing influences of the mass media would have to be found. What would likely occur would be a return to a tribal-like existence. The total society would break down into smaller and smaller groups in which individuals such as priests or shamans could exercise many of the same functions now carried out by the mass media. The national culture would dissolve into thousands of minicultures, and centuries from now these cultures would likely be as different from one another as the U.S. and Ethiopian cultures are today.

# THE GENERATION OF CULTURE

The word *culture* has a multitude of definitions, all the way from the behaviors and beliefs of a particular society or part of a society (i.e., the youth culture or the drug culture) to the act of growing microorganisms (i.e., he is going to prepare a culture from this bacteria), to a set of rules for making objects, or doing things, for knowing the world, for making things. In this section of the chapter, the term *culture* is intended to refer to those aspects of the society represented by the intellectual, inventive, and creative dimensions of a people: their arts, their crafts, their scholarship, the product of any group of people living, working, and playing together. But even this limited definition of culture is not without confusion.

Most scholars have identified at least three kinds of "culture" in American society. There is what is defined as a **folk culture,** the culture of common people, produced by artisans who live in the community in which the culture is consumed. "Generated spontaneously, bound by tradition, and passed on through personal contacts, folk culture reflects the values, attitudes, and daily experiences of the group," wrote scholar Kathleen Turner. A vivid expression of folk culture can be seen by anyone who visits a county fair. The handmade clothing, the embroidered tablecloths, the intricate quilts, the handcrafted furniture are all examples of folk culture or folk art, as are the music and the stories that are told, the dances, and the games. Folk culture is generally regarded as the culture of the past, the culture that existed prior to the mass media. But examples of folk culture abound today, even in urban areas. For all its tastelessness at times, graffiti can be regarded as a kind of folk art practiced by an urban subculture.

Then there is the elite culture, culture with a capital C, the **high culture.** This is generally the culture of the upper classes or highly educated, produced by talented and often well-known artists, and consumed by a select few. This elite culture tends to be molded by aesthetic canons which are applied by professional critics. What is good or bad is determined not necessarily by whether the audience enjoys it, but whether the artists have produced something memorable within the guidelines of these canons. If folk culture is noted for its purity—it springs directly from the people who consume it, elite culture is noted for its complexity, its aesthetic intricacies.

Finally there is **mass culture** or **popular culture**—music, writing, drama, creations, and goods of all kinds with a broad-based appeal. This kind of culture is tied directly to the growth of the mass media, a culture that is generally created by persons other than the consumers of the culture.

Fifteen years ago Donald Dodson argued that there were subtle but important distinctions between popular culture and mass culture, distinctions not recognized by most persons who have written about culture. Dodson argued that *popular culture* is really folk culture "wrought by modern technology and a money economy." The relationship between the artist and the audience is paramount in popular culture. And while entrepreneurs or businesspeople facilitate the transmission of popular culture from the artists to the audience (i.e., record companies, motion picture studios), these businesspeople tend not to influence the cultural artifacts. It is simply folk culture mediated by technology. Dodson used as his example of popular culture the San Francisco rock music scene in the 1960s which generated bands such as the Jefferson Airplane and the Grateful Dead. These bands and many others grew from within the community, playing concerts in dance halls and at parks. The bands did not have business agents or recording contracts. Recordings came later, and the energy and innate purity of this music was transmitted fairly truthfully by phonograph records and tapes. Perhaps a more contemporary example is early rap music, a music of the streets generated largely by urban blacks that expresses their frustrations and hopes, their view of the world. This music moved from the urban cultures that generated it to a much wider audience via records and tapes.

*Mass culture,* on the other hand, while it involves a relationship between the artist and the audience, is generated by the entrepreneurs who control it, Dodson says. It is a wholly manufactured culture designed to take advantage of known public tastes, and the businessperson retains ultimate control over the artistic work. The goal is not artistic purity or the expression of values or traditions or emotions. The goal is the maximization of profit. Dodson cites the creation of the singing group the Monkees in 1965 by two Hollywood producers, Robert Rafelson and Berton Schneider, who sought to duplicate the recent success of the Beatles. The pair advertised for "4 insane boys, age 17–21." Four youths were selected, none of whom had ever worked together before, and three of whom had no musical background. Record producer Don Kirshner produced the musical sound desired and taught the Monkees to fit into it. RCA spent $100,000 promoting the first album, and Screen Gems, which owned the rights to the television series, licensed more than 50 Monkee products. Other recording companies followed suit. Buddah Record's two biggest "bubblegum" groups, the Ohio Express and the 1910 Fruitgum Company, were in reality some studio musicians assembled by record producers. The two groups had the same lead singer, Joey Levine. Contemporary examples of manufactured mass culture include the ingenue Debbie Gibson, who took singing, acting, and dancing lessons before Atlantic Records would sign her, and the vocal duo (or no-vocal duo) Milli Vanilli. Rob Pilatus and Fab Morvan quickly rode to the top of the pop charts in 1989, winning a Grammy award for their first (and only) album. But in 1990 it was revealed the pair had not sung a single note on the recording; other performers sang the songs. During concerts the duo lip-synched to recorded music. Milli Vanilli was the creation of record producer Frank Farian, who called the musical fraud an "art form." The charade fell apart when Rob and Fab announced that they wanted to do some of the singing on the second Milli Vanilli album. These are total entrepreneurial creations, or what Dodson would call representations of mass culture.

Whether it's called mass culture or popular culture, or whether there is a meaningful distinction between the two as Dodson asserts, this kind of culture is controversial among intellectuals. "Whereas folk art is praised for its cultural purity, and elite art is praised for its aesthetic complexity, popular culture attracts a storm of controversy over its value and its effects," wrote Turner. "Do popular culture and the mass media that convey it fulfill real needs for a large number of people, or do they subvert society in a variety of insidious and degrading ways?" she asks, reflecting the debate over this issue that has persisted for almost a century.

Many critics glibly dismiss popular or mass culture. Turner has outlined this position in her monograph, *Mass Media and Popular Culture.* Film critic Dwight MacDonald applies what he calls the law of Raspberry Jam to popular culture; the farther a culture spreads, the thinner it gets. The term *popular culture* is contradictory for MacDonald. Culture that is popular cannot also be the uplifting, enlightening, aesthetic experience of the genuinely cultural.

Social scientist Ernest van den Haag, in an article first published in the 1960s,

Rock duo Milli Vanilli was exposed in 1990 as a fraudulent singing group—performers who mouthed the lyrics sung by others. They followed in the footsteps of what was probably the first producer-manufactured singing group in the nation, The Monkees. The group members performed the songs, but barely. Pictured above are Monkees Peter Tork, Mickey Dolenz, Mike Nesmith, and Davy Jones. Only Nesmith had any musical background and, as it turned out, musical talent.

argued that mass culture has had a negative effect on humankind. Van den Haag argued that because mass culture is produced for the people, rather than produced by the people, life is reduced to largely a spectator sport. We live vicariously the experiences of others, he wrote, and noted the contrast between a young man sitting under a tree on campus playing a guitar and singing, and the same young man listening to a portable radio (or a Walkman in 1990).

The mass appeal needed to make mass culture profitable deindividualizes us, van den Haag asserts. Producers have become the elites by appealing to consumer tastes, and the ability to bestow prestige and income has shifted from the educated and informed elites to the mass. Mass culture appeals to the base instincts in individuals, distracting rather than enlightening them. The amount of mass culture needed to fill the hours of television and radio and the print media is tremendous. Potentially important talent is diverted toward cranking out acceptable material, away from the creation of art. Many contemporary critics of mass culture, for example, have noted the talented composer John Williams, who spends much of his time preparing soundtracks for films like *E.T.* rather than generating serious musical compositions. The same criticism is applied to writers who prepare television screenplays rather than work on serious fiction.

Mass culture, excessively thrust upon the people, tends to isolate people from one another, from themselves, and from real experience, van den Haag asserts. Real life becomes trivial in the face of vicarious experience. Historians who have studied the diaries and personal letters of people who lived even a century ago reveal that real life experience was an exciting dimension of everyday existence. It was a singularly important event when a young person went off to college. The exposure to a totally new environment was remarkable and rewarding. Yet why should young people today be thrilled with leaving home to attend a university? They have been around the world via television. They have been to the moon and back. Van den Haag says that the "total effect of mass culture is to distract people from the lives which are so boring that they generate obsession with escape. Yet because mass culture creates addiction to prefabricated experiences, most people are deprived of the remaining possibilities of autonomous growth and enrichment, and their lives become even more boring and unfilled." The masses turn to the mass media for a tranquilizer, not a challenge. The audience is not galvanized into thought or action but floats along, reassured and pacified.

Mass culture has been criticized as well because it is designed to appeal to the widest possible audience. Whereas America consists of people from a variety of ages, ethnic groups, occupations, and religions, the audience for media marketers is

American history is white history to most persons in the nation. And mass media have done little (outside a relative handful of TV documentaries in recent years) to dispel this myth. The 1989 film *Glory* depicted fairly accurately the role played by black Americans in the Civil War—a role neglected both in history books and in the popular mass media. (© 1989 Tri-Star Pictures, Inc. All rights reserved.)

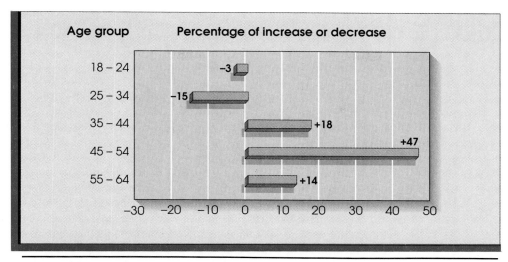

| Age group | Percentage of increase or decrease |
|---|---|
| 18 – 24 | −3 |
| 25 – 34 | −15 |
| 35 – 44 | +18 |
| 45 – 54 | +47 |
| 55 – 64 | +14 |

−30  −20  −10  0  10  20  30  40  50

FIGURE 12-1 Television generally ignores the elderly and creates the image that the nation is largely populated by persons under 40. That is not true, and will be even less true by the year 2000. This chart shows the projected changes in the age of Americans during the last decade of the 20th Century.
*(TV Guide)*

the corporate perception of "everybody," the ultimate average person, notes scholar Kathleen Turner. Historian Oscar Handlin argues that a culture which discounts our socioeconomic, temperamental, and attitudinal differences addresses only "the empty outline of the residual American." As a result, Handlin argues, the average offering of the media is "doomed to irrelevance in the lives of its audience; and the feedback from the consciousness of that irrelevance, without effective countermeasures, dooms the performer and the writer to sterility." Any regular viewer of television, the "massest" of our mass media, can surely support these criticisms. American television is generally a picture of a white, middle to upper middle class, Christian society. It generally ignores the Hispanic, African American, and Asian American cultures, the lower classes, and the non-Christian dimensions of the American experience. (See figure 12-1.)

# THE OTHER SIDE

There are thoughtful observers who challenge this wholesale condemnation of mass or popular culture. Leo Rosten, a writer and editor, asserted in 1963 that most criticism of mass culture and the mass media that produce and transmit it comes from intellectuals who don't understand the media or the people. The deficiencies of the media and what they produce are deficiencies of the masses; he argues, "Most people prefer pinball games [or video games today] to philosophy." Given the limitation of time and space, the "culture" produced by the mass media is more inventive and varied than most people admit. Rosten insists there are good dramas, good comic strips, and good films today, and that the intellectuals usually discover artists in the mass culture long after the public has discovered them.

Other observers of our culture argue that critics dismiss mass culture simply because it is a product of a commercial environment. They point out that high culture has a commercial character of its own that affects the works produced and the creators. And this is undoubtedly true. When selecting a series of plays for a coming season, the artistic director of a repertory theater company must keep in mind that ticket sales will sustain the company through the season. So despite a wish to present avant garde or experimental drama, it is the traditional plays by Arthur Miller, Tennessee Williams, and others that will fill the house. The music director of a symphony faces the same challenge.

Many critics of mass culture say it is derivative; it borrows from other aspects of art; it has nothing new to say. The defenders of mass culture agree that originality is rare in the mass media, but note that originality in anything is rare. There are even instances in which the fine arts borrow from the mass culture: the artistic works of Andy Warhol and Roy Lichtenstein are two examples. Many culturalists argue that the lines between mass culture and high culture and folk culture are often not that clearly drawn. Many artists can work in more than one. Many popular motion picture stars often appear in classical and contemporary drama on the Broadway stage. The late Leonard Bernstein, a serious musician by all measures, generated *West Side Story*, one of the most popular musicals of all time.

To the charge that mass culture provides only escapism, defenders assert that the popular arts are in many ways an expression of daily life as experienced by ordinary people. The attacks on mass culture employ a double standard based not on the content of the culture, but on class differences. "The hard-working physicist who enjoys a paperback detective story is judged to be 'relaxing,' while a similarly hardworking lathe operator who watches the same story being presented on the TV screen is considered to be 'seduced' and 'narcotized,' " wrote Harold Mendelsohn. The difference lies not so much in how that time is spent as in whose time it is.

Kathleen Turner quotes David Manning White as attributing this dual standard to a "mixture of noblesse oblige and polite contempt for anyone outside university circles, or avant-garde literary groups." White adds, whether the music is by the Beatles or Brahms, listening to it is still an individual's choice of ways to fill time that might otherwise be filled by jogging, gardening, cooking, painting, or any of a variety of other available pursuits. For White, disdain for the ways "the masses" choose to occupy their time is "neo-elitist."

In the end both sides ask, which came first, the chicken or the egg? Dwight MacDonald says "the masses, who have been debauched by several generations of this sort of thing, in turn came to demand such trivial and comfortable cultural products." Rosten asks the same question, but in a different way. Was mass culture thrust on a sophisticated public, or was it created in response to demands from an unsophisticated one? Mass culture is not bad, he notes, for a mass society. It fulfills a need and supplies enjoyment for those unable (or unwilling) to appreciate culture at higher levels. Turner concludes that the critics of mass culture argue that the mass media *affect* society in major, manipulative, and insidious ways. Those who defend this culture contend that the mass media *reflect* society, and the popular culture generated is no more or less than what the public wants and deserves.

This debate over high and low culture has endured for nearly a century and is no closer to being resolved today than in 1900. Yet it seems there may be new dimensions to the mass media that raise new questions in this debate. There is general agreement among social scientists that those who attack the mass culture probably overstate the manipulative ability of the mass media. (See Chapter 3.) Many of the arguments about how mass culture debases the audience reflect the now discredited "bullet theory" of media effects. This might suggest that mass culture more likely reflects our society than affects it. But does even mass culture truly reflect American society today? Or have the economic and other imperatives clung to so strongly, especially in network television which is the principal progenitor of our mass culture, forged a content in our culture which reflects little more than what programming minions believe society is all about?

Some say that television is a mirror of American society. But if it is, it is an uncertain mirror at best, one that reflects an ambiguous picture. At worst it reflects fantasy or matter that bears not the slightest resemblance to our values, our concerns, or our standards. To construct a picture of what we are based solely on the picture presented by the mass media, again primarily television, would leave us with both more and less than what we really are. We would see a society not nearly as ethnically or racially diverse as it truly is. We would see a society which is generally Christian (and largely Protestant), and a society in which elemental American values such as education, love, honesty, and hard work are often demeaned. From situation comedies we would get the impression that the American family is troubled, but only with problems that can be resolved in 30 minutes or less. And the children generally know more about solving these problems than the parents. Television drama reveals a society which values violence as a solution to a great many problems. Advertising on television displays a society that views women more as sex objects than anything else, a society in which material goods represent accomplishment and satisfaction, a society that is more concerned about underarm perspiration or bad breath than about starvation, infant mortality, or other substantial human tragedies. Advertising also reveals a people who spend more time talking with one another about the taste of coffee and breakfast cereal, the problem of irregularity, and whether one headache remedy works faster than another than about the schools their children attend, the nation's foreign policy, or environmental problems. Overall television pictures us as a generally happy people with few daily frustrations, or as writer David Susskind has expressed it, "a happy people seeking happy solutions to happy problems."

Emmy-award-winning television writer Loring Mandel argues that television has failed because it does not truly transmit the substance of our culture. Mandell wrote that television programming tells us certain things:

> That American is traditionally anti-intellectual. A lie. That the Good Man is the man who ultimately goes along. A lie. That love is good, sex is better, and that passion doesn't exist. That any means are justifiable. That passivity is wise. That intensity is a spectator sport. That people bleed only from the corner of their mouths, and that instant regeneration of tissue is a fact of violence. And by the purposeful omission of material that is relevant to our contemporary situation the entertainment programmers make reality more foreign to us. By expressing simplistic solutions to all problems, they rob us of the tools of decision. The truth is not in them.

We are lost in Kansas City, Mandel concludes, with a road map for Nashville, and "we're going mad from irrelevance."

Interestingly, Mandel wrote those words more than 20 years ago, but they are as appropriate today as they were then with only a few exceptions. There are some programs now that at least attempt to present a more realistic view of contemporary life, that reveal that solving problems is not simple. But mainstream television has changed little. Most popular situation comedies are simply "I Love Lucy" in color and contemporary dress.

Why doesn't our mass media, again, especially television, do a better job of reflecting the culture of the masses it seeks to please? Why must it perpetually be bland escapism? Is it incapable or only unwilling to provide us with an expression of daily life as experienced by ordinary people? Some of the answers to these questions can be found in an examination of the commercial culture which generates what we watch on television. And that is the next topic.

# MAKING TELEVISION PROGRAMS

Nearly all of American television series are produced in Hollywood by several hundred producers and writers. In 1979 writer Ben Stein interviewed 40 television writers and producers and concluded that one of the reasons that most American television programs look alike is because most of the people who write and produce these shows share similar views. Stein said his interviews revealed that these people had generally the same view of businesspeople (basically bad, evil), crime (usually violent, perpetuated by middle- or upper-class people), the military (bumblers, selfish bureaucrats), small towns (wicked places, narrow, reactionary), the wealthy (cheaters, liars, the lucky few), and the poor (basically good, honest, nice). "Television is what comes out of the Los Angeles community's head, and since Los Angeles is what goes into their heads, Los Angeles is what comes out," Stein wrote.

Stein's study, recounted in his book *View from Sunset Boulevard,* has been correctly criticized for being too narrow, for talking to too few people. Even in 1979 it was hard to lump the work of a writer/producer like Norman Lear ("Maude," "All in the Family") with the work of writer/producer Jack Webb ("Dragnet," "Adam-12"). There is diversity today as well, with such individualistic creators as David Lynch ("Twin Peaks"), Diane English ("Murphy Brown"), Steven Bochco ("L.A. Law"), and Marsha Posner Williams ("Golden Girls," "Babes"). Yet Stein's assertions are correct in important ways. Most television series are generated in Los Angeles, and if they reflect any part of the American culture, they represent the culture that is viewed through the prism of Southern California—a region that is hardly representative of the total United States. The men and women who make most of these television shows shop at the same stores, eat at the same restaurants, attend the same plays, essentially exist in the same cultural environment. It is difficult for them to reach beyond the bounds of this culture to imagine a different environment for the programs they write and produce.

When one thinks of commercial network television the term *art* rarely comes to mind. But the creation of these programs can be as much an art as the creation of a painting or a novel. The operative words in the preceding sentence are "can be." Artistic works tend to be the creation of individuals. While even painters and novelists sometimes seek advice or guidance, the finished product is a creation of a single intellect, a single imagination. At one point in its history, network television would let a Paddy Chayefsky or a John Frankenheimer create a television program largely without interference. But such days are gone. For the most part in the 1990s, television programs are created by groups of people. Not in a formal sense; the screenwriter still prepares the script. But from the time the first draft is prepared until the program finally is telecast, several other individuals have an opportunity to make changes in the script, and most of them take advantage of this opportunity. Just as important, the business aspects of television dominate even the production end of the industry. "Businessmen are fully in charge now," noted producer James L. Brooks ("The Simpsons," "The Mary Tyler Moore Show"). "They will not divorce themselves from the process. They will direct the process, and conduct the process, and you can't lick it," Brooks said.

The process of creating a new television series usually starts with writers trying to sell an idea for a series to a production company. The production company will ultimately have to sell this idea to the network. It is true that some prominent producers and writers who have a successful track record have a relatively easy time getting acceptance for an idea, but that is not the norm for most in the business. Production company executives usually believe they know what the networks are looking for each season, so the writers' ideas are immediately reshaped by executive producers and others who want to enhance the possibility of a sale. Once the producers and the writers come to some kind of agreement, they approach the network to try to get financial support to develop a script for a pilot episode of the program. Most ideas for series stop at this point; the network is not interested. But in those cases where the network is willing to give the go ahead, you can be certain it is not before their own programming people add their "creative suggestions" to the writer's ideas. This creativity by committee continues through the development and completion of the script. Oftentimes even the writer can't recognize his or her original ideas when the script is finally approved for shooting. Writer David Handler related how he and his partner once approached a production company with an idea for a show about three young men who played out their mystery novel fantasies as detectives in a 60-minute adventure/comedy series. The network never approved the script, but before it was finally rejected the series had been reshaped by producers and the network into a 30-minute program about three young men who own a diner in New York and are battling the owner of a slick, jumbo coffee shop for survival while they help people in the neighborhood solve their problems. "Instead of respecting a writer's idea for a show, the networks treat new scripts like raw material, putting them through a sausage grinder until most writers can't even recognize their original idea," wrote writer/producer Richard Levinson.

When a network buys a script, it most often agrees to pay the cost of a **pilot episode;** the introductory episode when all the characters are introduced and where the basic premise of the program is outlined. Again network programming people keep their hands in the pie, suggesting actors and actresses to fill the parts, asking for script changes along the way. Writer/producer David Rintels asserts that the real network interference begins when the producer begins to shoot the script. "That's when they say, okay, but change this character to a female and make her a blonde," Rintels said. More pilot films are ordered than will ever be used, usually three to four times more than are needed to fill out the primetime schedule. How do the networks choose among the pilots? Audience testing is one tool. Ratings when and if the pilot is broadcast is another. Screenings for advertisers is still another method. Frequently the networks base their decisions upon arcane formulas; i.e., there must be X number of car crashes every 12 minutes. Some programmers insist that all new programs must be what are called high-concept shows, ones that can be easily explained in a few lines in the *TV Guide* description.

A proposed program that looks like an existing popular television program or even a successful movie has a much better chance of making it into the network's schedule. The 1990–91 television schedule provides ample evidence of this. Four new television series were based on successful films: "Parenthood," "Uncle Buck," and "Ferris Bueller" kept the same name as the films that spawned them. "Parker Lewis Can't Lose" was a Ferris Bueller clone. And speaking of kids and schools, the success of "Head of the Class" and "Wonder Years" spawned two additional "high school" situation comedies, "Hull High" and "Beverly Hills 90210." In 1989 there were "America's Funniest Home Videos" and "Totally Hidden Videos;" the networks added two new video shows in 1990: "Haywire" and "America's Funniest People." The success of "L.A. Law" generated new interest by the networks in law-oriented shows; "Law and Order," "Against the Law" and "Trials of Rosie O'Neill" joined the primetime schedule. "Golden Girls," an NBC hit about three feisty elderly women who share a home, spawned an imitator, "Babes," a show about three feisty queen-sized women who share an apartment. "Roseanne," featuring comedienne Roseanne Barr, was successful in giving viewers a vision of a working class American home; CBS put its money on "Lenny," featuring comedian Lenny Clarke, another comedy about a working class family. Finally, the success of Angela Lansbury as a murder mystery novelist who is an amateur detective in "Murder She Wrote" prompted CBS to buy into "Over My Dead Body," with Edward Woodward as a murder mystery novelist who is an amateur detective. The fact that many of these programs failed before the year ended is irrelevant; the same pattern of cloning something that has already succeeded will be followed next year, and the following year . "The networks have rules because they have no idea why they are making programs except to make money. Since nobody has a magic formula that tells how to win in the ratings every time, people develop this formula idea," wrote Todd Gitlin in his book, *Inside Prime Time*.

## ▣ The Networks' Role

The networks play the most important role in the creation of programming because in the end, they choose to buy or reject the product. A producer who consistently fails to meet network specifications will die a slow death. Even after a show is scheduled, the network can and does ask for changes if the ratings are not as high as they believe they should be. David Gerber, the producer of "For Love and Honor," a short-lived series highly regarded by many critics, describes what happened after the first few episodes were telecast on NBC. They wanted bigger stories, larger-than-life situations, Gerber said. The stories should be larger, more pronounced, more melodramatic, the producer was told. Network programmers wanted operatic stories. "Operatic—does that mean soap opera?" Well, you could say soap opera, he was told. Gerber, a powerful producer, could have fought but chose instead to change the show. Low ratings finished the program quickly, so Gerber was left without his program or his honor.

What are the specifications for network programming? Leonard Goldberg, once chief of programming for ABC and now a producer, outlined them this way. "When I became head of programming I got a very simple order. I was told that I work for a profit-making organization and my job was to deliver the largest possible audience while spending the smallest possible amount of money. If in the process I could get quality programs, that would be great, but that was not necessarily part of my job," Goldberg added. The networks are in the business of delivering the largest possible audience for the advertiser. So the specifications for a program are simple—the programs that are to be aired are programs that everyone will love.

That sounds facetious, but it is not. Decisions about programming are made in an atmosphere of fear: fear of alienating the audience, fear of alienating the network bosses. Everything starts with a simple proposition—the programming must be a suitable setting for the advertising. If you compare a television program and television advertising to a painting and a frame, the television program is the frame and the advertising is the painting. The program must provide the proper frame for the commercials. An unsuitable frame will distract viewers or alienate them. In the so-called Golden Years of Television, the mid-1950s, serious drama was a staple of the medium. But the drama was unsettling to most advertisers and to many programmers. In their commercials, advertisers were telling viewers that most of life's problems can be solved by buying an advertised product. The dramas suggested that life was far more complicated than that, and happiness was often hard to attain at any price. The Golden Age died. Things haven't changed. Advertisers have consistently failed to support provocative programming such as ABC's "The Day After," a program about nuclear war, and "Playing for Time," a drama set in a Nazi concentration camp. The issues involved are controversial, the message of the drama bleak. Not a good setting for the happy jingles of American television advertising. Usually the network will censor the potentially controversial material even before the advertisers have a chance to get their two cents worth into the discussion. In the late 1980s and early 1990s many producers have had a difficult time trying to include the controversial topic of abortion in their programs. The television movie, *Roe v. Wade,* that focused on the landmark Supreme Court ruling regarding abortion had 17 script rewrites before it was acceptable to NBC. The network tried to prevent the cast, director, screenwriter, and others from giving interviews about the film, fearful that their comments might provoke a controversy. Many scenes were changed because network officials feared they were too "pro choice," or provoked too much sympathy for Jane Roe (Norma McCovey), the woman who sought the abortion in this real life story. Officials at both Fox and NBC asked that script changes be made in episodes of "Parker Lewis Can't Lose" and "Midnight Caller" respectively to delete abortion references. Television is supposed to reflect the culture, and is there any issue more visceral in our culture today than the abortion question? Yet many at the networks feel that there is no "safe" way to reflect this dimension of America, so they seek to avoid mentioning the issue.

Two important programming credos guide the operation of network entertainment television. The first is, attract the largest possible audience for every program. In many instances this means simply to lure the greatest number of warm bodies to the television set. But as television advertising and programming becomes somewhat more sophisticated (in some unusual ways) attracting the largest audience may mean attracting the largest number of persons in a specific demographic group. The elderly, for example, are not generally regarded as "good" viewers for most advertisers, so a show that built a large viewership of older people might not be attracting the best audience for the advertisers. What the network may be seeking is the largest number of women age 25 to 40, for example.

The second credo works in conjunction with the first; offend the fewest number of people. Not attracting an audience in the first place is bad; driving away those viewers who are attracted is worse. So offensive programming is taboo—sort of. Networks are willing to risk offending some viewers if they believe that because of the off-color nature of the program, for example, they are luring in other viewers who might not normally be watching the show. "Married . . . with Children" offended a great many people with its raunchy humor. Protests even resulted. But the

Media watchdog groups like Christian Leaders for Responsible Television and the American Family Association warned advertisers to stay away from the Fox Network's "Married . . . with Children." These groups complained the show was too adult, tasteless, crude, and offensive. But the network stuck with Al and Peg and the rest of the Bundy's, and many viewers appreciated the opportunity to watch this nontraditional (for television) view of the American family.
(Kelly Television Co.)

Fox Network knew that the show attracted a lot of other viewers *because* of its raunchy humor. The risk was worth it. Consequently the networks are willing to endure a certain amount of heat from viewers and others to telecast a spicy made-for-television movie if they think the film will attract a large audience. At the same time the networks will use concerns about "taste" to censor programs in which they have less faith or have invested less money.

One of the schemes used by the networks to try to attract a large audience is the principal of familiarity; give the audience something that has worked before on another show or in the movies. We have discussed this earlier. But there are other devices as well. Let's examine a couple of these before exploring the problems of audience and offensive programming.

### ☐ TV Qs

The television networks and the Hollywood production studios use TV Qs as one means to try to attract the largest possible audience. The people who make television programs are among the many clients for this research that has been developed by Marketing Evaluations, Inc. The TV Q is a popularity poll administered periodically to a sample of 6,000 Americans who are asked to rate as many as 1,500 performers and entertainers. The interview subjects are asked two questions: Do you know who this person is? Do you like this person? The scores on the familiarity and popularity scales are combined and from that a "Performer Q" emerges. Marketing Evaluations polls its clients to find out the names of performers to put on the list. Advertising agencies and motion picture production companies use the TV Q ratings also. In 1990 it cost a client $950 to get a Q rating for a single performer; $70,000 for the entire package. Television networks and filmmakers can select "popular" performers with high TV Q ratings to help attract a larger audience. Marketing Evaluations also rates television shows seven times each year.

The ratings are seriously flawed, according to many critics. Some people say the sample is poorly drawn. Others argue that the persons polled often confuse the performer with the character portrayed on television. Estelle Getty, who plays Sophia on "Golden Girls" usually scores well in the Q ratings. But she argues that most people don't really know her at all; they love the character she plays.

The networks say they don't use the Q ratings to cast television programs, but many producers don't believe that. And they dislike the system. "The reports are blacklists," said producer David Dortort. "It is a subtler, more vicious form than the McCarthy-era blacklists. (See pp. 39 for a discussion of this era.) A producer tells a network he wants this writer or that actor to do such and such a program, but he keeps hearing that the people or the idea are 'unacceptable' . . . they've consulted their data, and that ends it," he added. A bill was recently introduced into the California legislature that would have banned the use of Q ratings, but the measure was defeated after market research firms undertook a massive lobbying effort with the legislators.

Bill Cosby was generally atop the Q ratings in the late 1980s and early 1990s, followed by whomever happened to be popular at the time. Clint Eastwood, who ranked number 2 in 1988, didn't make the top 10 in 1990. While many performers are proud of their high Q ratings, maybe they shouldn't be. Right behind Cosby in the number 2 slot in 1989 were the California Raisins, the Claymation stars of a handful of television commercials.

## ☐ Audience Testing

How can a network know before a show is aired if the audience will like it? Why not show it to a few people and ask their opinion? Such is the theory of audience testing, something previously discussed in the chapter on motion pictures.

Each network uses a different system. All have a single purpose—to get in-depth audience reaction to the pilot film or program. Sometimes the material is screened to a couple of hundred homes on a cable system; researchers follow up the telecast with questions. Or a theater is used, with an audience invited to view a new television series or made-for-television film. Audience Studies Incorporated has operated Preview House on Sunset Boulevard for many years, and it is one of the busiest audience-testing facilities in the nation. It costs a network or anyone else about $9,000 for a basic testing.

Names of potential members of the audience are culled from reverse directories and lists prepared by canvassers who work the shopping malls around Los Angeles. Preview House testers try to get the right mix of age, gender, income, and the like. Participants fill out detailed questionnaires before and after the screening. While the program is being shown, they use an electronic dial that is attached to a computer to register their positive or negative feelings about the program. Each participant sits in an assigned seat so the viewer's positive or negative reaction to various parts of the program can be correlated on a demographic basis; i.e., young women like this section of the program, older men do not. Ushers cruise the aisles during the screening to spot people who are not twisting their dials. They are cut out of the sample electronically. At the end of the session, a drawing is held for a few small prizes.

More elaborate and intimate testing is possible through the use of focus groups. A handful of people sit in a small, informal setting, discussing what they like and don't like about a program. ASI designed a special voice-activated television camera that automatically follows the conversation in the room, recording each word, each expression. A modified lie detector is also used in some situations. The participant's fingers are wrapped with computer sensors covered with Velcro strips. As a program or commercial is screened, the participant emits involuntary reactions that are transmitted by the sensors to a computer. The result is what is known as "a subconscious involuntary response graph."

Does this testing help the networks find potential winners and losers? They like to think so, but some critics disagree. The people who are selected (or actually volunteer) to be in the audience testing groups are not a representative sample of television viewers, some critics argue. The viewing is also artificial. People don't normally watch television in such a setting, and this has the real potential to change their response to what they see. Producers especially find such testing onerous. In addition to echoing the complaints aired above, they assert that it often takes a viewer two or three episodes to get into a television series. The pilot films are crammed with material to establish the characters, setting, and premise, and this can often interfere with attempts to make this first show compelling or funny. There is sufficient evidence to doubt the effectiveness of testing. Many shows that were highly rated in audience testing fail, and fail rather quickly. Two ill-fated series from the mid-1980s named "Manimal" and "Rousters" come to mind. And other shows that tested poorly have gone on to great success. Test data on the number 1 rated show "Hill Street Blues" strongly suggested the show had no chance to succeed. Network officials acknowledge these failures, but argue that the test data is on target more often than not. For network programmers, however, the test data can provide a soft landing if a show they have built into the primetime schedule fails. "It certainly tested well," they can argue as they hastily rearrange the schedule to find something else that might work.

## ☐ Thou Shalt Not Offend

There is little value to a television network in building a huge audience for a television series if the content of the program offends viewers, and they switch channels. Thou shalt not offend is a maxim etched on the walls of the programming offices of all commercial television stations, especially the over-the-air networks. Avoiding program content that might offend is a big task for the television industry in the 1990s. Not that television is especially bold these days, but that so many Americans are offended by so many different things in the 1990s. It is estimated there are more than 250 groups in the nation that monitor television and attempt to exert pressure on the networks to change or remove programs that they find offensive. And these are formal groups. There are hundreds more ad hoc groups, informal church groups, and others who also have a point of view and are eager to express it.

Traditionally, television hasn't done a very good job of resisting pressure on its programming. The medium was barely out of its infancy when the "Red Scare" of the early 1950s descended upon the nation. And while all the mass media knuckled under to the pressure from the conservative, right-wing, anti-Communist witch-hunters, television's collapse before this attack seemed especially craven. Self-appointed vigilante groups published long lists of entertainers and other industry people whom they considered to be at least sympathetic to the Communist cause, and networks used these lists to guide their casting and booking decisions. Sponsors added pressure as well. Ed Sullivan's popular "Toast of the Town" show inadvertently booked dancer Paul Draper, whose name was on one list of "forbidden" performers. The Ford Motor Company, the sponsor of the show, asked Sullivan to issue a public apology, and he did, begging forgiveness for permitting a "performer whose political beliefs are a matter of controversy" on his show. In a press release drafted by Ford, Sullivan announced a truism that turned into an industry creed. "The whole point of the 'Toast of the Town' is to entertain people, not offend them." Draper and scores of other artists were banned from television, and these blacklists lasted well into the 1970s. There are those who argue that some performers are still blacklisted.

Since that time the industry has arrayed a shameful list of instances of blatant censorship. Sexual topics most often come to mind when one thinks of such censorship, and when theatrical movies were an important programming fare, the networks often cut them up so badly it was difficult to recognize the film. An entire subplot of the film *Diary of a Mad Housewife* was eliminated when it was telecast because it included adultery, but without the subplot the remainder of the film made absolutely no sense. Nowadays some film directors maintain a clause in their contracts that requires their approval before a film may be edited for telecasting on television.

But sexual material is not the real problem; the networks eschew controversy of any kind. In the early 1970s one of the networks loved a story idea proposed by producer/writer David Rintels. It was the story of a photographer in Vietnam who captures on film the terror on the face of a cocky young American soldier who meets the enemy for the first time. The young soldier sees the photo and on the next patrol begins to worry whether the photographer will again photograph his fears and anxiety. In searching for the picture-taker the boy becomes worried and careless and is killed. The network loved the story, Rintels said, but wanted to change the locale to Spain, and make the cocky young soldier into a bull fighter. Why? The war in Vietnam was controversial.

CBS censored text rolled at the end of an episode of "WKRP" which focused on the death of 11 young persons at a rock concert in Cincinnati when thousands of ticket holders ran to get close to the stage before the concert began. The producers of the show tried to tell the audience with text that Cincinnati had banned "festival seating" at rock concerts, but no other city had yet followed suit. The network would not allow the producers to mention that no other city had banned festival seating. Too controversial.

In 1982 network censors cut the final scene from the made-for-television movie, *My Body, My Child,* a sensitive teleplay about a middle-aged Catholic woman who must decide whether to get an abortion or give birth to what will certainly be a deformed child. The drama focuses upon the torment and moral conflict the woman must face, and in the final scene she decides an abortion is the only humane alternative. Network officials were fearful of alienating the large and very vocal anti-abortion lobby, so they simply cut the scene and let viewers decide for themselves what the woman should do. Abortion is controversial.

In the spring of 1982 CBS cancelled both "WKRP" and "Lou Grant." Both programs had sagging ratings, but many persons in the industry suggested that the shows were terminated because Howard Hesseman of "WKRP" and Ed Asner of "Lou Grant" both were too politically outspoken in their support of the rebels in El Salvador. Politics is generally considered off limits. So is religion. And when is the last time a program was broadcast that focused on the excesses of advertising or censorship in television?

During the last few months of 1985 network censors at NBC killed several old episodes of "Saturday Night Live," episodes the network originally aired, because they thought the material on drugs was unsuitable for today's audience. NBC censors also forced the producers of a drama about the hijacking of an airplane to change the ending of the story. In the original script the passengers, who overpower the terrorists, "try" the terrorists for killing two passengers and hang them before the plane lands in London. NBC censors said this was too strong, and in the version shown on television the two terrorists die after an accidental shooting. And Harlan Ellison, the creative consultant for CBS's "Twilight Zone" quit the program after the network refused to air an episode he had written in which a bigoted welfare worker tells four small boys—two Hispanic and two black—that Santa Claus doesn't come for black children. Ellison said that the episode was a "tough statement against racism" and that its Christmas setting made it particularly powerful. The network said the program had no value for the Christmas season. They agreed to let Ellison do an anti-bigotry show not pegged to Christmas. The writer's reaction: "What? The dark side of the Easter Bunny? The first time I tried to make a statement head-on, I was stopped."

Television censors are surely sensitive enough. But the multitudes of television monitoring groups "help" the censors by pointing out material that has slipped through the cracks. These groups most frequently protest the manner in which the members of the group are portrayed in a specific television program. Sometimes this pressure is put on programming produced by the news and public affairs divisions of the networks. CBS found itself under the wrath of the powerful National Rifle Association following the broadcast of the documentary, "The Guns of Autumn" that was critical of many hunting practices. More often pressure groups attack entertainment programming where they know the backbones of network executives are considerably more flexible. The problem is not new. The late Rod Serling, someone who believed in the medium as perhaps no other writer, said he worried about the serious problems faced by television writers. "A medium best suited to illumine and dramatize the issues of the times has its product pressed into a mold, lily white, and has its dramatic teeth yanked one by one." People of Italian and Sicilian background didn't like the words Mafia and Cosa Nostra and were successful in getting references to such groups taken out of popular crime shows. The National Gay Task Force protested the portrayal of homosexuals in many television programs and launched a campaign to change these portrayals. The Gray Panthers protested the image of the elderly on television; feminists protested the portrayal of women on "Little House on the Prairie" and "The Waltons." Blacks protested their image on many programs, including "Mr. Dugan," a Norman Lear comedy about a black congressman, a show that never even got on the air. The American Health Care Association protested a segment of "Lou Grant" which exposed the heartless practices of some nursing homes. Jewish groups unleashed a full-scale assault on CBS for permitting the broadcast of a television film about Fania Fenelon, a Jewish survivor of the holocaust in which Vanessa Redgrave, someone quite outspoken in her support for militant Arab causes, played Ms. Fenelon. American Indians successfully blocked and forced revision of the film made of Ruth Beebe Hill's best-selling book, *Hanta Yo.* Suppliers of nuclear power in the nation have been upset about the manner in which the industry has been portrayed in "The Simpsons." The program features the character Homer Simpson, a not-too-hip nuclear power plant worker. The show has included comic jabs at the lack of safety and security at the power plant, and references to "Blinky," a three-eyed fish. Pressure was put on both the Fox Network and the producers of the program to modify that image.

Television, even entertainment television, bears some responsibility for reflecting an accurate picture of the hundreds of subgroups within our culture. But having said that, the question is: What is an accurate picture of these subgroups? Is there a prescribed way, an official way of looking at Catholics or Jews or homosexuals or Hispanics or African Americans or school teachers or the elderly? Surely as a society we hope that all citizens take the time to view these elements of our diverse culture fairly, in an open-minded fashion. We hope people look for the best in all individuals and groups. We want understanding, not hostility. But each individual in the society views others in that society from his or her own perspective, through eyes that are shaded by education or lack of it, experience, and ultimately prejudice. The mass media should not be faulted for presenting controversial views of the elements of our society. But they should be faulted for not presenting enough views of the diverse

The culture transmitted by the mass media in the United States tends to be a reflection of the white culture. Many whites are confused and even angered when the views of persons in other cultures—views which often characterize whites negatively—are presented. Spike Lee's controversial film *Do the Right Thing* is just such an example. Pictured are Lee (right) and Richard Edson, who played the son of the owner of a pizza shop where Lee worked.

elements in our society. American Indians may be understandably upset when a television network attempts to present a view of their culture which they find inaccurate or even distasteful. But the solution to this problem is not to censor this view; it is to present the Native American viewpoint as well. Similarly, the networks should present programming which reflects the way gays and the elderly and African Americans and others view their culture, and the rest of the world. In a small way the film industry does this. Spike Lee's films (*Do the Right Thing* and *Mo' Better Blues*) have been accused of being antiwhite and anti-Semitic. But what Lee has done is present for the first time the African American's view of some aspects of the white and Jewish cultures; we have seen the white view of the black culture for decades.

## ☐ Heating Up in the 1990s

At the end of the 1980s network television attempted to grow up a bit and began offering more adult fare in its programming. It still avoided controversial kinds of programs, but faced with a loss of viewers to cable television and home video movies, the networks decided to loosen up somewhat. Significant deregulation of the broadcasting industry had taken place; the government seemed to be looking the other way. In January 1989 *TV Guide* presented an outline of what was now allowed on network television, and what was still taboo. Sexual behavior could be more explicit, producers being permitted to go about as far as possible without nudity. Even bare bottoms were being tolerated. Language was looser as well with double-entendres about sex and occasional foul language permitted. While the AIDS crisis tended to focus public attention on the dangers of irresponsible sex in the real world, bed-hopping still seemed to be a popular indoor sport on television. The networks were seemingly cutting back on violence, and the portrayal of the use of drugs and alcohol were being toned down.

Elizabeth Jensen of the *New York Daily News* wrote in January of 1989 that the "three networks are slowly but steadily redefining what they will and will not air—and the result this season has been more explicit television." The reason, according to the networks: Public standards are changing. "Our policies reflect the standards and mores of the society as we glean them from sociological studies, the print media and things that go on in day-to-day life," said Christina Hikawa, the East Coast vice-president for broadcast standards for ABC. (Broadcast standards is the network euphemism for censorship.) All three networks announced they had cut back the number of censors from as many as 90 people per network to an average of 30 or 40.

Perhaps the new broadcast standards did reflect the changing public standards, but did not reflect the standards of many of the conservative media-monitor groups that began to howl in protest within months. By April the pressure groups were in action, and the networks were in retreat. A single letter from a 41-year-old Michigan woman to several companies that advertised on Fox's "Married . . . with Children" prompted Procter & Gamble, McDonald's, Kimberly Clark, and other businesses to pull their advertising from the racy situation comedy. Advertisers reacted in a similar fashion when "Saturday Night Live" telecast a sketch filled with raunchy language as a spoof on censorship. The network also took heat for its sexy "Nightingales" series about a group of nurses. Even a scene from Ralph Bakshi's Saturday morning "Mighty Mouse" cartoon was cut after a family in Kentucky complained that the diminutive superhero appeared to be sniffing cocaine when he sniffed a flower petal.

Pressure groups had found that advertisers were even more wary about controversy than the television networks. And so the focus of pressure shifted to network advertisers. Organizations like the American Family Association and Christian Leaders for Responsible Television (CLeaR-TV), two conservative religious groups spearheaded by the Rev. Donald Wildmon of Tupelo, Miss., threaten advertisers with product boycotts if they continue to support programming the organizations don't like. These groups are extremely well-organized and well-financed, and with only a few telephone calls can unleash a barrage of thousands of boycott letters and cards from generally mindless group members who write what and when they are told. And this scares the devil out of the advertisers, despite the fact that a boycott of RCA by an earlier Wildmon group was a dismal failure. CLeaR-TV objects to sex, profanity, and violence—and to the way Christians are sometimes portrayed on television. After General Motors had been battered by a boycott threat, its public relations director John McNulty promised the leaders of CLeaR-TV that the company would keep its advertising out of shows that involve "gratuitous sex, or violence, or anything that reflects badly on some people, such as Christians." Once the threat of the boycott materializes, pressure groups can use less costly measures to work their will. McNulty said that after Pontiac Motor Division advertised on an episode of "Wiseguy" that included a suggestive sexual scene, he got a personal call from the Rev. Wildmon complaining about this sponsorship.

What it comes down to is that groups like this will protest anything that challenges their traditional values, which they believe are the true national values in the United States. Advertisers are attempting to avoid such protests by employing research services such as Advertising Information Services, a company whose employees screen programming for sponsors and warn them about any possible problems. AIS had more than 50 major corporate clients in 1989. Advertisers are now even beginning to insist that programs sold in first-run syndication, which traditionally have not been previewed by the advertisers before broadcast, be screened before they will buy commercial minutes. "It's becoming more and more a condition of sale," said Mike Moore, media director for D'Arcy Masius Benton & Bowles.

In the United States people enjoy the right to protest about anything, including what is telecast on network television. Whether these protests are misguided or on target is solely a matter of personal perspective. But by making an organized attack upon the networks, and more importantly the advertisers, their only source of network revenue, these pressure groups are seriously distorting television's reflection of the nation's culture. America is not generally a promiscuous country, but the national attitudes about sex and profanity are far more mature than what is revealed each night on network television. In fact, the view of sexual behavior that television represents is much like the view represented by immature, adolescent boys. Sex is a continual reference point for most early-teenage American boys; titillation is a way of life. But usually little else happens. TV is much the same way. Many network television series seem to have sex on the brain, but do little else to explore the procreation process. This has brought a protest from, of all groups, Planned Parenthood, which complains that the networks fail to provide viewers with a realistic or responsible view of sexual activity, especially the results of sexual activity. If true, this failure may be at least one of the reasons that a 1990 Kinsey Report revealed that most Americans are woefully uninformed about sex.

In the wake of the new round of protests, the networks backed off from their new philosophy of loosening up standards. NBC reestablished a vice-presidency for broadcast standards and in May of 1991 cut adult scenes from two premiere epi-

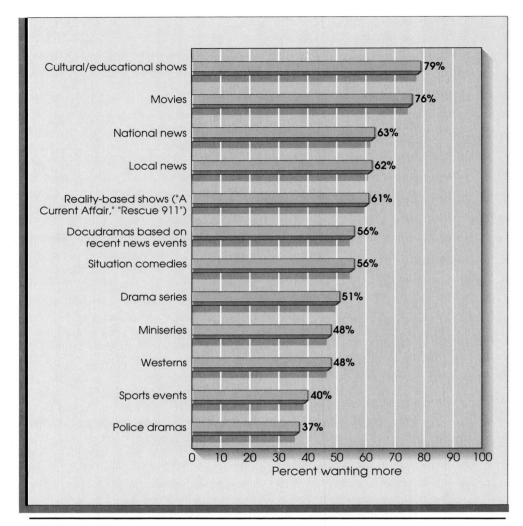

FIGURE 12-2 Network programming decisions usually reflect what advertisers or vocal pressure groups say they want or don't want. *TV Guide* asked viewers in 1990 what kinds of shows they wanted to see more of. The bars on the graph indicate the percentage of respondents who said they wanted more of a specific kind of programming.
*(TV Guide)*

sodes of its new series, "Sisters." Many production companies were told to tone down program content. Producers and network officials are once again going at each other over themes such as AIDS, homosexuality, and abortion.

Any attempt that television may make to reflect the spectrum of American culture is surely hampered by the circumstances under which television programs are created. Whether it is the need to please too many people, the fear of offending a few, or the fact that most television programs are created by a small group of persons living in an unrepresentative corner of the nation, the system works against the medium reflecting honestly and openly what America is all about (figure 12-2).

If television fails to accurately reflect American culture, what does it reflect?

There is a growing feeling among many that the medium reflects a fantasy world that some mistake for the real world, a fantasy world that not only affects the way people in other cultures look at us (for American television is consumed in all corners of the world), but the way that many of us view our own world. The medium walks a fine line between fantasy and reality, and some argue that this line is becoming more and more blurred. Let's examine this matter for a few moments.

## An Unreal World

We live in a world in which reality is imperfect; it doesn't quite measure up to our expectations. Imagine that, to compensate, people began to substitute a mediated or television reality (or fantasy) to fill this gap.

Farfetched, no doubt. But this was the kind of world envisioned by science fiction writer Ray Bradbury in *Fahrenheit 451*. The written word was banned from this futuristic society; only pictures, comic strips, and interactive television were permitted. Television was everywhere, showing citizens their outside world. When a crime occurred, television cameras provided live coverage of the police pursuit of the suspected felon. Pictures showing the capture of the criminal were intended to soothe the audience, to strengthen their notions that government was protecting the safety of the people. But police could not always capture these felons, so actors and actresses stood by to play the role of the criminal, ultimately to be captured. Despite the fact that the robber or murderer remained at large, people believed he or she had been captured. This provided them with the necessary reassurance.

Interestingly, writer Martin Mayer only half-kiddingly suggested something similar to this scenario in his book *Making News*. Mayer points out that many in the television news business feel it is important for the television newscast to find some means of emotionally bonding with the viewers; hence, the emphasis on emotional rather than informative pictures. Former NBC journalist Linda Ellerbee recounted a conversation she once had with NBC news chief Reuven Frank on the importance of pictures that evoke feelings and responses. "What are the best pictures from a plane crash? . . . According to Frank: a stocking hanging from a tree, a doll with a broken face—this, in their way, tell you more than words do," Ellerbee said.

This emphasis on emotional moments, Mayer said, had led the television networks to focus on the crying and grieving relatives of persons held hostage by terrorists, such as the 39 people held captive after the hijacking of the TWA flight 847 in 1985. Mayer speculates, however, that with network news budgets being trimmed, the news divisions will soon realize that it is too expensive and even unnecessary to send camera crews all over the country to the homes of grieving spouses and parents and brothers and sisters. Actors and actresses can be employed for these purposes at a far lower cost. "As the laugh track superseded the studio audience for sitcoms, professionals will replace real hostage families," Mayer notes. The viewers will not know the difference, and the networks will still gain the advantages of the emotional bonding between people watching the telecast and the distraught relatives. Farfetched? The so-called reality-based current affair programs on TV today, where reenactment of real events is common and largely unpublicized, suggests this is not farfetched.

All persons live in two separate worlds, a world of fantasy and a world of reality. Most people move back and forth between these two worlds. A few spend most of their time in the real world and are generally regarded as unimaginative, dull, too serious. Some spend most of their time in the fantasy world and are generally regarded as dreamers, even mentally unstable. Most of the time, most people keep the world of reality and the world of fantasy apart. Today, however, the mass media—especially television—seems to be making it harder and harder to recognize the separation between these two worlds. Through the use of a great many devices, most of which are conventions normally associated with drama, television news is often taking on a fantasy-like quality. On the other hand, through its emphasis on real life programming, and its use of actual news events as the basis for its drama, television is creating a dramatic form with the authenticity of real life. Most of us still are capable of separating the two worlds, but for some, it becomes harder and harder.

This is not necessarily a new phenomenon. In the crudest sense, the news has in the past been communicated through entertainment forms. Balladeers sang of real life; and those who create the myths and legends that abound in all cultures use storytelling to communicate stories that contain at least the essence of real life. This nation was awash in a sea of fake newsreels in the first 40 years of this century; films that purported to show real life but used dramatic reenactments instead. And of course real life has been the basis for plays, novels, and short stories for centuries.

But this mixing of reality and fantasy on television is more serious. There has never been a mass medium so pervasive. And television is a medium that uses pictures, not grainy newsreel film but sparkling clear videotape. Pictures don't lie, we are taught. But that is not true, especially with the development of technology that can alter both still pictures and moving video images in ways undetectable by the untrained human eye. So the blurring of fantasy and reality on television is a matter of some concern, since it clearly affects the way we view what is supposedly a reflection of our culture. Let's first briefly examine television news and explore some of the ways in which it attempts to be more entertaining by adopting the conventions of drama, the conventions of the fantasy world.

## THE CONVENTIONS OF TELEVISION NEWS

Television viewers expect certain things when they watch television news. At the very least they expect to see a faithful representation of what is happening in the world around them. Through the use of pictures and reporters who are trained to synthesize elaborate or complex stories, television news is expected to present an accurate, truthful report of the day's events, or at least as much of what happened as can be included in a relatively brief newscast.

But television, which is an entertainment medium, has never been particularly comfortable with news. Initially news was something undertaken to serve the public interest, almost a charitable function akin to a popular television star making an appearance on a telethon or at a benefit dinner. When it was later discovered that news could actually produce significant revenues for the medium, the powers that be in television were still uncomfortable. If we can make X number of dollars just by reporting on the day's news, can't we increase revenues by enhancing the news, making what took place in the world a little more interesting for the viewers? It must be remembered that much of real life is uninteresting to the people who operate an entertainment industry. So if real life is boring to them, it must be equally boring to the audience. Slowly, always fearful of going too far, television has added one di-

Helicopters are valuable tools for television news departments, taking reporters on a moment's notice to stories miles away. But too often the use of helicopters dictates the news coverage presented by the station: this coverage often runs toward presenting live pictures of unfolding events—both the newsworthy and the non-newsworthy.
(© Gary Harper/KING Television)

mension after another to its news in an effort to give it life, make it more interesting, to draw more viewers.

With the introduction of the electronic newsgathering equipment, television news gained the capability to bring viewers live news, almost at the drop of a hat. A few stories, a very few, demand live coverage. Presidential press conferences, congressional hearings, and a handful of other news stories meet these requirements. The audience is better served in most other instances if the reporter gathers the information, separates the wheat from the chaff (what is news and what isn't), and then reports the synthesis he or she has prepared. This is what viewers expect to see. And so when television brings viewers other kinds of news as it actually happens, unedited, often with little context, it is in a sense attempting to duplicate the storytelling associated with drama.

One memorable example of "going live" with a story was the television coverage in the 1980s of a shoot-out between Los Angeles police and a gang of self-styled revolutionaries named the Symbionese Liberation Army, or the SLA. (This is the group that kidnapped Patty Hearst, an heiress to the Hearst newspaper fortune taken by force from her home in 1974 and who later willingly or unwillingly participated in the criminal activities of the radical group. Hearst was captured (or rescued) by the police in 1976.) As the cameras watched, the police fired round after round into the small frame home, finally setting it afire, killing its occupants. There was little narration, no synthesis. The coverage looked more like scenes from a made-for-television movie than news.

But surely this was television at its best, bringing viewers real life, wasn't it? Not really. Television news is far more capable of bringing viewers real life when reporters assume the traditional role of condensation and summary. Why? Because the camera lies. A television camera, CBS journalist Eric Severeid once said, is like a flashlight in a darkened room. It illuminates one tiny part of the room to the exclusion of all other parts, those parts on either side or above or below the spotlight. And by focusing on "real life," the camera can often bring viewers a seriously distorted view of what is taking place. Imagine there is a garden with a small cesspool. You view this scene via television, which focuses only on the cesspool. What do you see, a garden with a small cesspool, or just a cesspool?

The mass media, and especially television, have the capability of creating distortions or even myths about real life by focusing intensely on one particular event or kind of event. In the mid-1980s many Americans abandoned their plans to visit southern Europe after a series of incidents in which terrorists killed foreign nationals, including U.S. citizens. Stories about plane hijackings and terrorist attacks at airports were common fare in the press. And because these incidents were so heavily covered, the mass media badly overstated the real dangers, made what were really isolated incidents appear to be commonplace. "The cumulative effect of seeing an airliner 1,000 times with a hole in it almost makes it seem as if it happened 1,000 times," wrote communications scholar Neil Postman. When in fact, while this near-hysteria swept the United States, the number of such incidents had actually changed little from previous years. The number of U.S. citizens killed in such attacks was less in 1984–85—during the peak of the news coverage—than during 1974–75, when there was much less publicity about these events. Actually, 41 U.S. citizens died at the hands of terrorists in 1984–85. Seventeen thousand American people were murdered in the United States in 1984 alone. Yet through overemphasis, and by constantly shining its spotlight on a few incidents rather than the entire scene, the mass media distorted these facts. Viewers did not see real life.

Studies have been made comparing the coverage by television about crime in American society and what happens in real life. In other words, what do Americans who experience "real life" primarily through watching television know about crime in the United States? By watching television such a viewer would conclude that most crime in America is violent crime. Stories about violent crime alone make up as much as 20 percent of all the news on some local television newscasts. In fact only 10 percent of all crime is violent. And the emphasis in TV news stories about crime is usually on crime that occurs in "nice neighborhoods," in the suburbs for example. Those who often feel the most vulnerable to crime, the elderly lady who lives next door, for example, are really far less at risk than a young black male in the inner city. In fact, by greatly overemphasizing the dangers of suburban crime, television has inadvertently aided the burgeoning home security industry, which consistently cites statistics on the likelihood of break-ins without adding that most such robberies occur in the poor sections of the inner city, not the suburbs. But television rarely focuses on crime in the inner city. When child abuse became a major news story in the late 1980s, the cameras focused on day care centers and suggested that it was in such facilities that children faced the greatest peril. Reports from the National Center for Child Abuse said that a child was at greatest risk at home, but this fact was not heavily publicized.

The camera lies. By bringing viewers unfiltered live coverage the television can mislead. By focusing on a few aspects of real life, television denies the viewer the needed perspective and can distort reality.

## ☐ Other Dramatic Devices

Television news has adopted many other conventions of drama in an effort to make their newscasts more palatable to what they believe is an uninterested audience. This may come as a shock to young people, but musical themes and interludes have not always been a part of a newscast. Music is more correctly associated with films, to add drama, to highlight comedy. Why did NBC pay Oscar-winning composer John Williams (*E.T.* and others) to write a theme for the NBC news?

The most successful primetime network news program is "60 Minutes," a pioneer in adding the stuff of drama and fantasy to a news program. Reporters and producers pose as people they are not in order to get stories; just as actors and actresses play a role in a television series. "60 Minutes" pioneered the use of the hidden camera to trap the subjects of their news probes. When we normally watch the news, we know that the persons who are being photographed know they are on camera. It is drama when the camera traps the participants and shows us their "real life" as it is being played out. The CBS program also has made great use of the confrontation interview, in which a reporter or someone else confronts a reluctant subject. Sparks fly, tempers flare, conflict ensues. This too is the stuff of drama as opposed to the dispassionate recitation of the day's events by a reporter, the typical news presentation. In drama there are always protagonists and antagonists, good guys and bad guys. Critic Neil Shister noted that "60 Minutes" has brought "theatrics to reportage, made news into mini-morality plays." The "60 Minutes" news crew will swagger into town, like a marshal in the old West, prepared to take out the villain who is polluting a creek, or cheating immigrants, or making improper use of the legal system.

What is real? What is not? Not enough fans of "reality shows" of the 1980s and 1990s asked these questions; viewers often confused re-enactments with real news footage. "Cops" was the Fox Network's entry into the real-life police series sweepstakes. (Kelly Television Co.)

Geraldo Rivera brought more drama to news when he invited the audience to join him in a suspenseful search for Al Capone's vault: news contrived like a dramatic story. A spate of so-called "reality" shows bombarded the syndicated television market in the late 1980s and early 1990s. Footage of real life events is intermingled with re-creations of news on programs with names like "Cops," "Cop Talk," "Rescue 911," "America's Most Wanted," "Unsolved Mysteries," and "A Current Affair." When the newsfilm didn't exist, these programs provided viewers with a dramatic approximation, with emphasis on the word "dramatic." ABC failed to tell its evening news audience that it used fake film to document how an American bureaucrat supposedly passed secrets to a foreign agent. In the summer of 1989 both CBS and NBC announced they too would use re-creations on some of their news programs, including "West 57th," "Yesterday, Today and Tomorrow," and "Saturday Night with Connie Chung." (The *Wall Street Journal* asked, "Who will play Connie Chung?")

Re-creations were used as a part of one of television's most innovative early series, "You Are There." But this was a history program, and if the fact that it was 1588 and Walter Cronkite was supposedly interviewing Philip II of Spain who had just launched the Spanish Armada against England didn't tip off viewers that this was a re-creation, the crude television production (state-of-the-art at the time) made it a dead giveaway. But the re-creations used by television today bear a striking resemblance to news coverage. It is very difficult for viewers to separate fact from fiction, real life from fantasy.

Remember what was said at the beginning of this section. Imagine a world in which many find reality imperfect. Without dramatic footage, television producers believe the viewers will regard the news, real life, as imperfect. And so they generate a reality that is better than real life in many instances.

## ▣ The Dramatic Side

As news pushes visibly into the world of fantasy, drama pushes in the opposite direction, toward the world of reality. Make no mistake, the best dramatic stories, from Greek tragedies through Shakespearian plays to American novels, have been based one way or another on real life. Those who create the best fiction seem to have the skill to distill the very essence of real life into a story of some kind. And this can be immensely effective, both as drama and as a picture of some aspect of the world around us. The plight of the Depression-era dirt farmers from Oklahoma and Texas who were forced to leave their homes and seek work in the West was portrayed by the press and even by documentary filmmakers such as Pare Lorenz in *The Plow that Broke the Plain*. But was there ever as vivid a picture of these refugees as the one painted by John Steinbeck in *The Grapes of Wrath?* Good drama and fiction, then, should express real life.

But in television in the 1990s, the expression of "real life" in drama has caused a blurring of the line between what is real and what is not. This is at least partially the result of several developments which were not a problem when Shakespeare was writing about Henry IV or Richard III, or when Steinbeck was writing about the Joad family.

First of all is the heavy marketing impetus of entertainment television. *The Grapes of Wrath* was not heavily advertised as "being based on a true story," or "real-life fiction." Those who read it and knew something about the plight of the so-

Steven Bochco's "Hill Street Blues" was promoted as a look at real-life police work. Cinema and sound techniques were devised to sustain this video reality. Yet the story lines within the show were often miles away from real-life police work and the criminal justice process.
(NBC Photo)

called Okies recognized it as a fairly accurate reflection of what had happened. But today, to add credibility, to attract more viewers, or for whatever reason, a good deal of television drama is emblazoned with the words "real life." Some television programs have even gone so far as to attempt to duplicate the real world chaos in their settings. In his book *Inside Prime Time* sociologist Todd Gitlin describes how the producers of "Hill Street Blues" purposefully used shaky hand-held cameras, busied up the set with ambient conversations in the background, with performers walking through the set, even between the camera and the principal performers, to suggest the confused nature of a real-life police station. So viewers today, while they know they are watching drama, are nevertheless prompted by settings or promotional messages or other devices to expect at least some dimensions of real life in the programs they view.

One problem exists, however. Television isn't really satisfied with real life, which is imperfect, incomplete, confusing, contradictory. There are often no good solutions to real-life problems. So while the medium tells viewers to expect real life, it changes real life to suit its entertainment needs. When "Lou Grant," a TV series about a large metropolitan newspaper, examined the very real question of whether journalists should be able to shield the names of their confidential news sources, the program copped out in the end, with the source agreeing to have the name revealed. This does happen occasionally in real life. But the program was built on the dramatic premise of whether the right of the reporter to shield the source is more important than the need of society for this bit of information. The ending did little to answer this dilemma.

Or take the case of an NBC made-for-TV movie about the very real plight of unemployed steel workers in the United States. The story was about the closure of a steel mill in the East, but just as easily could have been about an auto plant in the Midwest, or a timber mill in the Northwest. For almost two hours the film poignantly examined the plight of healthy, adult men and women who are suddenly without a job and with little prospect of getting work. The drama realistically explored the difficulties in the industry, of foreign competition, and focused on the slow and painful breakdown of one proud unemployed worker. Surely this vividly presented a critical issue facing the nation. What do we do with these workers? How do we keep these mills open? But NBC could not leave us with a real life problem. In the end the workers in the town got in their cars and headed for the next town, the one just over the next hill, and viewers were left with the distinct impression they would all be back in a few days with new jobs, even better than their old ones. A totally phony ending because television, as an entertainment medium, cannot leave the audience with despair. And millions of viewers, who knew nothing of the plight of these poor workers but what they saw in the film, were told that there really isn't an unemployment problem; there are plenty of jobs, just over the next hill.

Even the real life "Hill Street Blues" often ended up presenting a totally fabricated vision of the criminal justice system. When a judge in one episode released an Hispanic rape suspect because he was informed of his rights as a suspect in English, not Spanish, a female undercover agent from the precinct was sent out to right this legal wrong. In a nearby bar she tricked the suspect into speaking English, and then shot him when he appeared to draw a weapon. "Hill Street Blues" is "real life," and the show presents a "real life" solution to the problem of these liberal judges who free the guilty to rape again. But law professor Alan M. Dershowitz points out that this is not a realistic picture of how the law works. "Nearly every legal premise underlying the dramatic denouement of this episode is wrong," he said. There is simply no legal basis for busting a bailed rape suspect who had fooled a judge into believing that he spoke only Spanish," he wrote in *TV Guide*. Dershowitz adds that such fantasy in "real life" programs frustrates viewers who wonder why their police departments don't act so "efficiently."

Most Americans realize that even real life drama on television is not really a reflection of real life. But many Americans do not. People who have not experienced a variety of aspects of real life are sometimes confused. Reporter Michael Leahy interviewed high school students in the small town of Grants, N.M., in 1986 and found many of them very apprehensive about the notion of living in or even visiting Miami, Florida. "How could you want to go to a place where people get caught in gun battles between pushers?" asked student Tammy Vigil. "Miami is too fast," echoed student Thersea Closs. "You don't have to worry in Grants about rapists just because it's 8 o'clock and dark." Neither student had ever visited Miami; their fearful impressions of the city had been totally shaped by the television series "Miami Vice."

Others who are older, but who rely heavily on television as a companion or for their view of the world, share this unrealistic view of the world. We are entering an age, say many experts, where many Americans are visually literate and verbally illiterate. Television is the dominant form of mass communications; sometimes the only form. These people don't read newspapers, magazines, or books. Many don't even

True-to-life dramas are the stuff of primetime dramatic specials, but rarely do they reach either the dramatic or factual heights of "An Early Frost," the first important television film about AIDS. Solid performances by Ben Gazarra (top), Gena Rowlands, and Aidan Quinn strengthened this program, which won the plaudits of television viewers, critics, and the medical profession. (NBC Photo)

watch television news, except the "reality" based, recreation-filled, tabloid shows. Many of these persons are extremely lonely and find companionship through television. And these are not always the uneducated or the infirm who are confined to their homes. "If the television breaks I panic," said one Manhattan editor in an interview with author Louise Berkowitz, author of *Alone in America*. Another executive in New York used the word "panic" to describe the sensation of facing an evening alone, scanning the television listings and finding nothing to watch. "For a moment," she said, "I forget that I know how to do anything else alone."

Some experts have attributed the success of the multitude of talk shows (Oprah, Donahue, and others) to the fact that passive and shy viewers can watch the programs, believing they are a part of a social situation. But they aren't asked to talk. The view of the world shared by many of these people is skewed heavily towards entertainment television's view of the world. And as we have seen, this is not a realistic view.

Emmy-winning television writer Loring Mandel, in a 1986 article in *Parade* magazine, argues that it is a significant failure of television that it does not transmit the real substance of our culture. And he lists some additional basic misconceptions communicated by the medium:

The shows teach us the world is violent but bloodless. That loss, pain and grief are not consequences of violence. That healing is instantaneous. That children are smarter than adults. That most women are bleeding hearts and most men are self-important. That no problem is so great that it can't be solved in a half-hour. Or an hour. These things are drummed at us. We hear laughter at words that don't evoke laughter and watch anger evoked only by the need for a cliffhanger. We see human relationships built entirely upon false emotions. And we can't easily separate the fantasy from the real.

Heavy television viewers are the persons most seriously confused by this mixture of fantasy and reality in contemporary entertainment television. But all of us become confused at times. When Robert Young portrayed Doctor Marcus Welby on television he received as many as 250,000 letters a year seeking medical advice. The medical profession seemed a bit confused as well, as Young/Welby was often invited to speak to medical societies and at medical school commencement exercises. Arthur Hill had the same experience when he played attorney Owen Marshall for many years. And this is now happening to cast members of the popular "L.A. Law." When television attempted to portray real life journalism on the Lou Grant show, it succeeded in confusing even journalists, who adopted spunky investigative reporter Joe Rossi (played by Robert Walden) and invited him to speak before groups of reporters and editors and to journalism school classes. Ed Asner, who played Lou Grant, was featured in a series of advertisements in American newspapers extolling the virtues of the printed press—something he may or may not know anything about.

Advertisers even take advantage of this confusion. Robert Young was featured in a series of television commercials pitching the benefits of decaffeinated Sanka coffee to persons with frazzled nerves. Or was that Doctor Welby giving us that friendly advice. And who better to remind us about safeguarding our vacation money than a policeman? Actor Karl Malden, who for seasons captured killers and thieves as Lt. Mike Stone on "The Streets of San Francisco," was hired to pitch the value of American Express traveler's checks. He even wore the same kind of dated hat that he wore in the TV series while filming the commercials. Even political leaders can sometimes become confused, it seems. *Newsweek* reported in 1990 that former president Ronald Reagan sent a note to Augusta Lockridge after she was blinded. "Nancy and I are sorry to learn about your illness. Our thoughts and prayers are with you. God bless you." Augusta Lockridge is a fictional character on the soap opera "Santa Barbara."

By stressing that its basis is in real life and by adjusting its picture of real life to meet the needs of an entertainment medium, television drama is perceptibly confusing many persons about what is real, and what is only fantasy.

## ▨ The Docudrama

As if "real life" television dramas don't cause enough confusion for many viewers, the medium has generated a new dramatic form that is even worse—the docudrama. Dramas are advertised or created in such a way as to suggest to viewers that they are based on real life. Docudramas are supposed to BE real life, with actors and actresses playing the parts of the principal characters.

This hybrid documentary/drama format is a highly popular one in the television industry. In 1989–90 docudramas focused on more than a dozen contemporary "events" including the Robert Chambers/Jennifer Levin "preppie murder" in New York City, the search for California's night stalker killer, the life of Rock Hudson, the sordid divorce saga of Roxanne Pulitizer, the story of a young gang of white teenagers who chased a young black man to his death in New York's Howard Beach, the John Walker spy scandal, and the Challenger space shuttle accident. In 1990–91 the trend continued with docudramas about Edmund Perry, the gifted black prep school student who was shot by a policeman in New York City; Charles Stuart, the man who killed his wife in Boston, then pretended they both had been attacked by a young black male; Robert Gale, a U.S. doctor who went to the Soviet Union to treat people hurt in the Chernobyl nuclear disaster; Jerry Levin, the CNN correspondent who was kidnapped by terrorists in Lebanon; and the Pan AM Flight 103 that exploded over Lockerbie, Scotland.

A documentary is a television program or motion picture presentation of factual events or circumstances, according to a well-known dictionary. It is supposed to be real life. Drama is a composition portraying the life of characters by means of dialogue and action and is designed for theatrical performance. It is fictional. A docudrama falls somewhere in between, fiction as fact or fact as fiction. English professor Mark Harris notes, "In practice, the docudrama is a synthetic product having neither the factual or actual air of a documentary nor the unity and interest of drama." While these television stories are heavily promoted as giving viewers "real life" or "the true story" or "what really happened," as a matter of fact there is a tremendous amount of fictional material added. Protests from citizens in Atlanta prompted CBS to precede the broadcast of its "Atlanta Child Murders" docudrama with a disclaimer. But the warning wasn't much help to most viewers. It said, "Some of the events and characters are fictionalized for dramatic purposes," but never revealed what was fact and what was fiction. In the aftermath of the program CBS adopted a 12-page set of guidelines governing the production of docudramas. Former Georgia Governor George Busbee told *TV Guide* that if the guidelines had existed when CBS first saw the script for "Atlanta Child Murders," the show could not have been produced. Daniel Schorr, senior news analyst for National Public Radio, argues in a recent edition of *Channels* magazine, that the docudramas have removed the last remaining inhibitions against the assault on reality. "At best they simplify reality, at worst they pervert it," he wrote.

Why does television broadcast docudramas? They are cheaper to make than a real documentary, which often takes months of research and filming and sometimes simply can't be made at all. The script is thrown together, often with little logic or coherence. "The docudrama is a way to do things without having to do the work that ought to go into them, and yet, however badly done, a docudrama will attract an audience on the grounds of it being true," wrote educator Mark Harris. The networks also enjoy the built-in promotion for the film that was generated when the "event" was in the news.

In some docudramas the names are changed, but viewers are led to believe that the story is what actually happened. More commonly real names are used. But the stories remain heavily fictionalized. A recent docudrama on Anwar Sadat, the martyred Egyptian leader, was so full of errors it enraged the Egyptian people. The story trivialized and confused Sadat's motives for signing the peace treaty with Israel. There were gross errors in costumes, accents, and the portrayal of other real people like former Egyptian president Gamal Nasser and Israeli leader Menachem Begin. Sadat was shown embracing his wife in public, something an American leader might do but something no Egyptian man would ever do. The anger in Egypt was so strong that the nation banned any film or television program produced by Columbia

Too many Americans learn about the past from historical docudramas. Most of these programs tend to be heavy on the drama and light on the "docu," or fact. Gabriel Byrne played "Columbus" in a six-hour miniseries that contained serious historical flaws, but was promoted as a true account.
(CBS Photo)

Pictures, which made "Sadat." In "Atlanta Child Murders" CBS totally manufactured a critical scene—it never happened in real life. The depiction of real life events and people was inaccurate and misleading. Producer Abby Mann contended that Wayne Williams, who was convicted of the crimes, was railroaded, yet even William's attorney was unhappy about the production.

In "Robert Kennedy and His Times" producers included nothing about the American-sponsored invasion of Cuba, the role played by the U.S. government in the 1963 assassination of the president of South Vietnam, and several other negative aspects of Bobby Kennedy's role in government. Media critic David Shaw called the docudrama a sanitized and distorted picture of American foreign policy during a turbulent period when Robert Kennedy was a close advisor to his brother, President John Kennedy. John Seigenthaler complained in a column in *USA Today* that the program made it appear that President John Kennedy was around primarily to help his brother Robert run the federal government. Seigenthaler worked for Robert Kennedy in the Justice Department and was portrayed in the production. He said the show had an "error ridden storyline," including a scene in which "I turn up at a meeting that never occurred and speak a line that contradicts what I thought." Media critic Shaw wrote, "Hollywood takes a controversial contemporary story. . . or marketable name, keeps the real life names and rearranges the facts to suit its artistic and commercial purposes. Voila: the best of all possible worlds—the marquee value of a true story and the dramatic value of 'enhanced' truth."

What is wrong with this blending of fact and fiction? Several things. First some people discover all they know about a subject—like Robert Kennedy's life or the Atlanta child murders—from watching a docudrama. These people are badly misled. Even people who may know more about a topic may alter their truthful perceptions when influenced by a vivid drama which expresses a lie. These kinds of false pictures can result in putting needless strains on society by suggesting that something that is real is not or vice versa. People in Atlanta were properly outraged when the Wayne Williams story was televised and suggested that the young black man had been sacrificed in order to protect the real killer or that police prosecuted Williams to stop public outcries about the crimes. Producer Abby Mann may believe this and has every right in the world to suggest this thesis either in a documentary or a drama. But viewers must be warned they are not seeing real life, not what actually happened, but Abby Mann's view of what happened.

Such programs usually result in ultimately cheapening the characters about whom they are written. In NBC's "Kill Me If You Can," the story of convicted murderer Caryl Chessman's fight to stop his execution, the Chessman played by Alan Alda is not the clever, resourceful Chessman of real life but a fine featured hero, almost a comic book character. And the noble Rosalie Asher, a woman who devoted years of her life to Chessman's defense, is reduced to a pretty face, a romantic interest.

To meet show biz requirements, the real life conflict presented in the docudramas is often greatly oversimplified or enhanced so it becomes a brawl. In the HBO presentation of "Murrow," the conflict between the journalist and CBS became a struggle between bad guys and good guys, between crusading journalists and corporate greed, something that distorted the truth, according to former CBS correspondent Daniel Schorr. "The real conflict—which the television industry has still not resolved—was between a journalistic conception of responsibility to the public and a corporate concept of responsibility to stockholders and a vast and chronically insecure entertainment enterprise to which, after all, journalism is a relatively small and often irritating appendage," Schorr noted. And in "Murrow," he continued, CBS chairman William S. Paley and former network president Frank Stanton are diminished both by the script and the actors who portrayed them. "They appear not only as villains, but as rather uninteresting villains."

Finally, and not unimportantly, the docudramas tend to prey on the families and friends of those real life persons involved in these stories. A substantial number of businesses have developed which rush to the scene of the latest tragedy, attempting to get contracts which will lock up the rights to the story. Competition can be bloody. After 18-month-old Jessica McClure was hauled from a well in Midland, Texas, the townspeople who assisted in rescuing her engaged in a bitter and protracted fight over the TV rights. After Francisco (Chico) Mendes Filho, the leader of the Brazilian rubber tappers union and an outspoken crusader against the destruction of the rain forests, was murdered, no less than eight different film companies fought to get the rights to his story.

"Why do we have to relive this?" asked Mrs. Jane Smith, the widow of Challenger pilot Mike Smith. "Why don't they leave it alone?" Fred Friendly, a Columbia journalism professor and former president of CBS news, said that most such docudramas trample on their subjects' emotions. "I don't care if they cooperate or not. I think you ought to leave these people alone because they've already suffered greatly," he said.

So television has come full circle, from news with dramatic conventions to simulated or re-created news, to real life drama, and to docudramas; and all in the name of giving us more than reality can provide. In the end Americans are going to have to decide which world they want to live in. If we want news and information to be dramatic and entertaining, if we want our drama filled with both real life and simple solutions to tough problems, if we want to learn what is going on in the world through the eyes of a scriptwriter rather than a journalist, then we must realize we are living in a fantasy world, a world that really doesn't exist. So long as we know that, there is no problem. But if we forget that and begin to make decisions about how we live based upon this vision of a fantasy world, then we endanger both ourselves and the other occupants of this planet.

The mass media either affect or reflect the culture of a society. We have suggested that they are more likely to act as a mirror of the people in the nation that they serve. But that is true only if the mass media wish it to be true. This discussion was aimed at arguing that television, the most pervasive, the most visceral of our mass media, doesn't really reflect our society. But if our reliance upon this medium continues to grow, that fact may be immaterial. Television may convince us instead that the fantasy world it offers us each day is the real world. The myth becomes reality.

## BIBLIOGRAPHY

These are some of the materials that have been helpful in the preparation of this chapter.

Bernikow, Louise. "Is TV a Pal—or a Danger—for Lonely People?" *TV Guide,* October 25, 1986. Colling, Maurice. "Tabloid Clones Invade TV," *TV Guide,* November 18, 1989.

Dershowitz, Alan M. "These Cops Are Guilty," *TV Guide,* May 25, 1985.

Diamond, Edwin, et al. "TV and the Hostage Crisis," *TV Guide,* September 21, 1985.

Goldman, Kevin. " TV Network News Is Making Re-Creation a Form of Recreation," *The Wall Street Journal,* October 30, 1989.

Harris, Mark. "Docudramas Unmasked," *TV Guide,* March 4, 1978.

Hurley, Dan. "These Hush-Hush Q Ratings—Fair or Foul?" *TV Guide,* December 10, 1988.

Jensen, Elizabeth. "Taste Test: Networks Are Serving Hot Menus," *The Seattle Times,* January 8, 1989.

Leahy, Michael. "Our Cities Are Big, Bad Places—If You Believe Prime-Time TV," *TV Guide,* May 3, 1986.

Lowry, Dennis T., and Towles, David E. "Prime Time TV Portrayals of Sex, Contraception, and Veneral Disease," 66 *Journalism Quarterly* 347, Summer, 1989.

McManus, Michael. "TV Advertisers Respond to Christian Boycott," *Seattle Post-Intelligencer,* March 10, 1990. Mandel, Loring. "Television Pollutes Us All," *The New York Times,* March 25, 1970.

Mayer, Martin. *Making News.* New York: Doubleday and Co., 1987.

Polskin, Howard. "Does 'Married . . . with Children' Go Too Far?" *TV Guide,* July 29, 1989.

————. TV's Getting Sexier . . . How Far Will It Go?" *TV Guide,* January 7, 1989.

Postman, Neil. *Amusing Ourselves to Death.* New York: Penguin Books, 1985.

Real, Michael. *Mass-Mediated Culture.* Englewood Cliffs, N.J.: Prentice-Hall, Inc., 1977.

Schorr, Daniel. "Harvest of Shame," *Channels,* March, 1986.

Shaw, David. "Danger! Please Don't Mix Fact with Fiction," *TV Guide,* April 20, 1985.

Smith, Sally B. "TV Docudramas: Questions of Ethics," *The New York Times,* February 14, 1985.

"The Trouble with Harry," *Columbia Journalism Review,* January/February, 1990.

Turner, Kathleen J. *Mass Media and Popular Culture.* Chicago: Science Research Associates. 1984.

# CHAPTER 13

# THE POLITICAL FUNCTION: GOVERNMENT AND THE MASS MEDIA

*T*he mass communication system in the United States undertakes many important social functions. Three of these have been discussed in previous chapters: an economic function, an information function, and a cultural function. A fourth function is no less important than the other three—the governmental function.

Ours is a representative democracy made up of a federal government, 50 state governments, and thousands of local governments. These governments serve the nearly 250 million people who live in the United States. This is a system that was created more than 200 years ago with the ratification of the Constitution of the United States.

The Constitution is a rather short document, considering its importance and lasting qualities. Its text is devoted largely to outlining the organization and operation of the United States government. The first ten amendments to this constitution, which were ratified two years after the constitution itself, guarantee basic freedoms to American citizens. And among these freedoms, none is more important than freedom of expression.

Philosophers have long attempted to justify the need for freedom of expression in a society, any society. Many have argued that individuals within a society are not capable of fulfilling themselves as human beings without freedom of speech and freedom of the press. Others have argued that freedom of expression plays a critical role in our search for truth and knowledge—a basic human need. And freedom of expression permits a society to operate more efficiently and peacefully. Those frustrated by the policies of the government may resort to actions against the government if they are not permitted to vent these frustrations through speech and press. And government decisions are more readily accepted by a people when those people have had the opportunity to debate the issues, to express their points of view on the problems. All of these are generally accepted reasons for the maintenance of freedom of expression in a society and in this society in particular. But there is one reason even more important than those listed: our system of government will not operate as it is supposed to without freedom of expression.

In the first place, freedom of expression is the foundation upon which all our other political rights and privileges rest. Our other freedoms, like the freedom to be free from unreasonable police searches, or the freedom to vote, or the freedom from self-incrimination, would be absolutely meaningless if we did not enjoy freedom of expression. If someone denied us the right to vote, how could we protest without freedom of expression? How could we speak out against illegal police actions if there were no freedom of speech? If the government failed to hold scheduled elections, how could the newspapers challenge this action without freedom of the press? The First Amendment, then, which guarantees freedom of speech and press, truly supports all the other constitutional guarantees.

Ours is a representative democracy. Periodically we nominate and elect citizens to manage the affairs of government for us for a short time. Our choice in who is selected to undertake these tasks is heavily dependent upon what we know about those who seek these jobs. The free press is supposed to provide us with this information. And once these persons are selected, the information we acquire about how well they are doing their jobs is primarily provided to us by the press. This latter is what is called the "watchdog" function. If freedom of expression were taken out of our governmental equation, it would not be harder to maintain our representative democracy; it would be impossible.

Most adults today surely realize that what has been just described is an ideal; this is the way the government, and the interplay between government and the mass media, is supposed to work. It doesn't always (usually?) work that way in the 1990s. It should be comforting to realize that it didn't always work that way 200 years ago either. The theory of our democracy has always been just that, a theory. There have been times when reality more closely paralleled the theory than it does today. But there have been times when things were much worse, as well. Both the theory and reality almost died in 1861 when the people of the nation actually went to war against themselves.

Undoubtedly one of the most critical changes that has taken place in the nation in the past 200 years is an important change in the nature of the mass communications system and how it serves the nation. It has already been noted that the founders of the Republic expected the press to play an important role in the functioning of the nation's political system. But the press system they viewed was far different from the one that exists today. Newspapers were political in nature, filled with news of government and political essays. They were small in size and circulated few copies. Almost any citizen could find a printer willing to publish his or her handbill that expounded a new idea, one not found in the press. And these could be easily circulated. The existing system of publication in 1789 seemed completely suitable to serving the political needs of the nation. It is a valid question to ask whether the press of the 1990s is as suitable or at all suitable to meet the needs of our democracy.

The press is not expected to play such an important role in the political process in other nations, those with a different kind of governmental system. The relationship between the press and the government has been explored frequently by scholars who have developed some blueprints or sketches of these relationships. Let's examine these for a few minutes before exploring the role undertaken by the mass media today to fulfill the charge it was implicitly given 200 years ago—the charge of servicing the democratic system.

## SOME PRESS THEORIES

In 1956 three scholars, Fred S. Siebert, Theodore Peterson, and Wilbur Schramm, published a book entitled *Four Theories of the Press*. The title was a misnomer. What the authors presented were four descriptions of how press-government relations might be structured, not testable theories. The four theories in the book are closely tied to nations and to historical periods. A central theory in the volume is the proposition that a mass media system will tend to take on the coloration of the social and political structure of the nation within which it operates. Let's look briefly at each of these so-called theories and then examine other theories that have been proposed more recently.

In an authoritarian state in which the power moves from the top down, where an autocratic ruler like a king or a dictator controls virtually all activity in the nation, the press is highly regulated and operates at the behest of that ruler or government. Samuel Johnson wrote two centuries ago that "Every society has a right to preserve public peace and order, and therefore has a good right to prohibit the propagation of opinions which have a dangerous tendency." This idea is the rationale for the authoritarian press system; the press cannot do anything that rocks the boat.

Authoritarian rulers generally have a very low opinion of the average citizen who cannot (in their eyes) function without some sort of guidance or direction. The state must be strong and regulate virtually all levels of human conduct. The government knows what is best, and grumbling by the press can only bring about dissatisfaction and alienation, something that is not good for either the people or the government.

An authoritarian press is usually privately owned, but operates only with government permission. All material is censored before it is published or broadcast. Journalists are licensed and if they abuse their limited rights the license is revoked. Government critics in the press are usually quickly brought to trial and strong punishment is meted out to deter other potential transgressors. The press gives the people what the rulers want the people to have—no more, no less. The press is permitted to publish or broadcast only as long as it operates in this fashion.

England and much of the rest of the civilized world struggled under an authoritarian press system from the late fifteenth well into the eighteenth century. Authoritarian press systems still exist today in some nations controlled by dictators, primarily in Latin America.

When Seibert, Peterson, and Schramm wrote their book, about a third of all people lived in communist nations. Today communism is a dying political philosophy, but the press system it spawned is still worth examining. The Soviet/communist press system shares many of the attributes of the authoritarian system, but with some important distinctions. Mass media in communist nations are owned and controlled by the communist party and the government. The press is told what it cannot do, as in an authoritarian state. But the mass media are also assigned certain responsibilities as well and must fulfill these responsibilities to retain the support of the party leaders who are also the top leaders of the government. The press is considered an instrument designed to work for the development and the good of the state.

Press functions in the Soviet/communist system include working for revolutionary change, the explanation and interpretation of all events and happenings in terms of the party dogma, and support of party policies. The press generally speaks with a single voice; all media tend to carry the same message. There is little overt censorship; only the party faithful are permitted to work in the mass media and these workers believe in what the party is doing and will follow any guidelines that emerge. Soviet/communist news media like *Pravda* and *Izvestia* in Russia do criticize the government, but usually for failing to efficiently carry out communist party mandates or programs. The press is truly an educational arm and propaganda agent for the party.

Libertarianism arose centuries ago as a response to authoritarianism. Libertarians assume men and women are rational beings capable of intellectual growth and decision making. The needs of the individual are supreme; government is created to serve these needs. Human beings can only fulfill their potential unencumbered by the government. Members of the society can correctly decide what is best only if they are given an opportunity to hear all sides of an issue; truth can be discerned by the individual only when there is a free and open encounter of all ideas. An authoritarian would argue that the common individual is incapable of discovering the truth, what is right and what is wrong. The communist would say that it is not up to the individual, the party must decide what is right and wrong.

Libertarians have a healthy suspicion of government and the press system in a libertarian nation is free-wheeling with few, if any, government controls. A true libertarian—and the label has become misshapen in recent years with the growth of a so-called libertarian political party that rejects many of the traditional tenets of this philosophy—believes in tolerance of all points of view. Who knows what person might have the right answer? A great American trial judge, Learned Hand, once wrote to an equally great Supreme Court justice, Oliver Wendell Holmes, "Opinions are never absolute. If someone disagrees with you kill him for the love of Christ and in the name of God, but always remember that he may be the saint, and you the devil."

The libertarian press system is privately owned and operated. The government has little role to play, save acting as a neutral forum for disputes that arise between citizens and the mass media, like a libel lawsuit. Libertarianism took root in the rough and tumble political climate of eighteenth century America and has generally held fast ever since. It was well suited, not only to our political philosophy, but to our laissez-faire economic notions as well. Critics of the system in this century, however, have argued that while our libertarian press system remains free from government control, it has instead become a captive of our economic system. Advertisers can and do dictate the content of the press today. Usually not in the blatant fashion that one might see in an authoritarian state ("you publish this story at your peril"), but in a more subtle fashion. Advertisers will support those publications and programs that meet their marketing expectations. Publications and programs that fall outside those expectations—whatever they might be—will die. Also, the growing concentration of ownership of the mass media, noted in several places in this text, is a phenomenon which has reduced the likelihood for a diversity of ideas in the press.

In 1947 a small group of scholars and philosophers collectively called the Commission on Freedom of the Press took note of these developments and suggested a new press-government relationship labeled the social responsibility press theory. This theory reflects the argument that a press free from government control is not truly free to serve the political system if it is controlled instead by hostile or uncaring economic interests.

As might be expected in our capitalist nation the social responsibility theory has remained controversial since it emerged in the post-war years. Supporters of this idea call for something they label positive liberty of the press, freedom for something as well as freedom from something. It is well and good that the press be free from the constraints of the government; only then can it fulfill its proper role. But if the press uses this freedom only to fatten the collective purses of the publishers and station owners it is surely not serving society. The mass media have responsibilities: they must provide people with important news and information in a context that is meaningful; they must accurately portray the diversity in our society and the aspirations of all people; and they must provide us with a realistic sense of the fabric of our society. But if the mass media are free, who will make certain these responsibilities are fulfilled? This is the task of government, according to supporters of the social responsibility system. "Government remains the residuary legatee of responsibility for adequate press performance," wrote philosopher William Hocking, one of the architects of this theory. The government should help society get what it needs from the media. It is this proposed role of government that makes the theory controversial.

It must be remembered that the social responsibility theory was fashioned immediately after the Second World War and reflects important social and intellectual currents of that era. First of all, the social responsibility theorists appear to have far less regard for the innate wisdom of the individual than do libertarians. But libertarianism was born in the eighteenth century, an era that highly prized individualism and the rationality of man. The value of the individual had surely diminished in the eyes of many by the twentieth century, the age of collectivism. And social science had cast serious doubts about the rationality of man; the discovery of our subconscious suggested we were often motivated by less than noble goals or even logic.

Governments were to be feared and loathed in the eighteenth century, an era of bloody revolutions. But our opinion of government had changed substantially by the mid-twentieth century. It was government that had brought us out of the Great Depression, that had won the war in Europe and in the Pacific, that had helped us conquer deadly disease. Government was benevolent and should be trusted to serve society. The social responsibility theory views government as a natural ally to the citizen and the obvious power to control the excesses in the private economy that seem to divert the press from its rightful obligations.

Thirty-five years have passed since *The Four Theories of the Press* was first published. Many question the usefulness of these four propositions, arguing that few government/press relationships ever completely and accurately mirror one of the four theories, or, more persuasively, that new forms of government/press relationships have evolved in the past 35 years that do not fall under one of the original theories. William Hachten, a University of Wisconsin scholar, proposed in 1981 changes and additions to the four theories. Hachten accepts the authoritarian and communist theories from Siebert, Peterson, and Schram, but adds three new models—Western, revolutionary, and developmental. The libertarian and social responsibility theories are unified under the Western heading. He argues the two are both Western in origin and represent similar points of view. In the revolutionary theory the press operates outside the traditional press/government relationship to further a revolutionary cause such as toppling a government. Such a theory may be seen in operation in many parts of the so-called Third World and the use of the press by various revolutionary groups in the Middle East provides a good example of Hachten's typology.

The revolutionary model is transitional and soon emerges into Hachten's fifth theory—developmental. This theory is imbued with the ideas of social science researchers such as Daniel Lerner and Lucian Pye who suggest that communication media can be utilized to promote national development in less developed nations. The press has a serious role to play, to work with the government to bring economic and social and political growth to an emerging nation. "The development concept is a view of mass communication from the many nations of the third world where most people are colored, poor, ill nourished, and illiterate, and it reflects resentments against the West where people are mainly Caucasians, affluent, and literate," Hachten wrote.

Still another model has been proposed by Robert G. Picard. Taking note of growing socialistic ideals in parts of Western Europe—especially Scandinavia— Picard proposes a democratic socialist theory. While leaning toward libertarianism, the press in a democratic socialist system is not nearly as concerned with money making or government interference. The role of the press is to provide an avenue for citizens to express their ideas and to fuel the political and social debate over important issues. "Under such an approach, the state takes action to ensure the ability of citizens to use the press and to preserve and promote media plurality," Picard wrote. Ultimately, he said, ownership would be public and not-for-profit, through foundations or nonprofit corporations, journalist-operated cooperatives, and other collective organizations. Such an ownership structure was clearly not envisioned in the earlier social responsibility theory, and this is the most significant difference between the two theories.

The inherent value in any of these theories is its ability to help us visualize and ultimately understand the relationship between a nation's mass media and its government. As such there may well be as many legitimate "theories" as there are nations on this planet.

## INFORMATION NEEDS TODAY

Regardless of what theoretical model the modern American political system mirrors, information remains the lifeblood of that system. To participate intelligently in a democracy today, the citizen probably needs more information than at any time in the past 200 years. The issues that must be decided are more complex, the risks are higher, government has gotten much larger and in some instances more distant, and so forth. It is this imbalance between need for information (although not always demonstrated by the public) and the quantity of information *easily* available that is at least partially responsible for some of the disarray in the U.S. political system (figure 13-1). (The qualifier "easily available" must be included because any person willing to take the time and effort to find out what is going on in government or politics will discover a plethora of printed material in most libraries. But the vast majority of this information is transmitted in a greatly abbreviated fashion or is not transmitted at all by what might be called the mainstream mass media, the typical daily newspaper, television newscasts, even newsmagazines.)

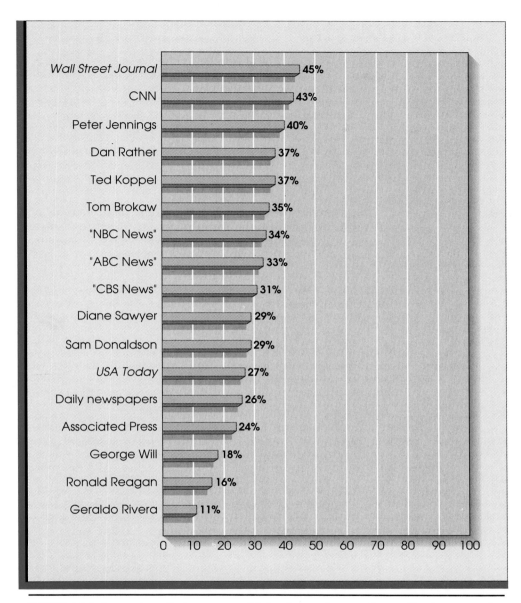

FIGURE 13-1 Even when it does a good job of reporting on the political process, the press faces the problem of low credibility. The chart indicates the percentage of persons who considered various news organizations or personalities to be highly believable. (Gallup Poll, 1989)

By virtually any measure taken by virtually any person, the U.S. political system has some serious problems. Most would agree that more and more of our elected public officials are far more interested in getting re-elected than in governing after they have been elected. The American public is, in most instances, the most politically apathetic body in the free world. The willingness of the people in Eastern Europe to make substantial economic and other sacrifices to gain the right to govern themselves provides a sharp and telling contrast to our own political laziness. In America, as one observer noted, an elected official is someone who gets 51 percent

of the votes cast by the 40 percent of the 60 percent of the eligible voters who registered. The cost of seeking even a modest state or national political office has gotten
so high that only those with wealth or the access to wealth can seriously contemplate
running for office. And because it costs so much to run, this has increased the importance of those special interest groups and other wealthy patrons who can finance the
political aspirations of office-seekers. The problems in the American political system
stem from a great many causes. The behavior of the mass media is only one of those
causes. In fact, however, the mass media could help solve some of these problems if
they exercised more leadership and provided their audiences with a more nutritious
informational diet. But in fact that has not happened; if anything, the mass media
have exacerbated many problems—generated by other forces in the political system.

While there is enough blame to go around, television among all mass media,
must shoulder the majority of this responsibility. It has fundamentally changed the
manner in which candidates for national, state, and even important local office run
their campaigns. While not everything television brings to an election campaign is
bad, there is more bad than good in the way it is being used today by both those in
a campaign and by those who report on the campaign. Perhaps the most serious
consequence of television's greatly enhanced role in the electoral process is that it
has turned this process into a spectator sport. Politics, as it has been traditionally defined, is participation, not just watching.

Neil Postman points out in his book *Amusing Ourselves to Death* that every institution which has attempted to use television for its own purposes has been
changed by television. This is true in education, religion, news, and politics. To use
the medium properly, the institution must adopt the values of television. And, as
Postman argues, "entertainment is the supraideology of all discourse on television."
Or to put it another way, "The problem is not that television presents us with entertaining subject matter but that all subject matter is presented as entertaining."

"The sad lesson after some 30 years of television's participation in national politics is that it is not television which has adapted itself to the norms of politics, but
politics which has adapted itself to the norms of television," wrote former *New York
Times* correspondent and author David Halberstam. "Politics is television, television
is entertainment, and entertainment is politics," he adds. Public television's Robin
McNeil puts it this way: "Television is American politics in the way that television is
American sports."

While television surely is to blame for many of the current problems in our political system, many myths have arisen which blame it for matters for which it likely
has little responsibility. It is said that television has created the politics of symbolism—Jimmy Carter carrying his own suitbag, Ronald Reagan and his fetish for jelly
beans, simple slogans, bumper-sticker philosophy. Television certainly enhances the
ability of any candidate to transmit such symbolism, but political symbols were
around for many years before television existed. Andrew Jackson ("Old Hickory")
used hickory poles as symbols of his candidacy. And William Henry Harrison's "Tip-
pecanoe and Tyler Too" predates television by almost a century. Abe Lincoln was
elected for many reasons; some voters may have been swayed by his rustic, log
cabin, rail-splitter image.

It is also argued that a plain-looking individual can no longer be elected to high
office. If you want to run for the Senate or for Mayor's office in a big city, you'd
better look like Robert Redford or Meryl Streep. A close look at the members of

Congress and other elected officials suggests that this is more myth than reality. What about former New York Mayor Ed Koch?

Finally, television is blamed for negative campaign techniques which appear to be so prominent lately. Again, television can transmit the substance of negative charges more widely and more quickly, but negative campaign tactics are nothing new. In 1804 the President of Yale University warned voters that if Thomas Jefferson were re-elected President, "Our wives and daughters would become the victims of legalized prostitution." Twenty years later the supporters of John Quincy Adams called Andrew Jackson a bigamist, while Jackson supporters charged that while Adams was U.S. envoy to Russia, he pimped for the Czar. And in 1928, when New York Governor Al Smith became the first Catholic to be nominated for the presidency, his opponents used a photograph of him standing in front of the Holland Tunnel in New York City and distributed thousands of small posters saying that this was the underground tunnel to the Vatican through which the College of Cardinals would come to assert papal supremacy over the U.S. government.

The impact television has had on the American political process is somewhat more subtle than those suggested by the myths related above. Nevertheless, television is regarded by most who study politics as the single most important force in the political process of electing a United States president, and certainly among the most important elements in the election of U.S. senators and representatives, state officials, and even big-city mayors. We are going to examine the role played by television from two perspectives. First, the impact of television advertising on the electoral process, and then the impact of television on the journalistic coverage of this process. The focus of our inquiry will be heavily weighted toward the election of the president of the United States. This is but one office in a nation of tens of thousands of political offices. Surely it is the most important office. More than that, however, the problems associated with television and the electoral process are magnified substantially in the race for the presidency. Hence they are more easily seen, and more easily documented. Readers need to be cautioned that the impact of television in other political races may not be as harmful, or may even be positive. History suggests, however, that campaign practices flow down rather than up. And what is common in a national campaign today may well be common in state and local campaigns tomorrow. We already know, for example, that many European political leaders have begun to adopt American techniques of running for office.

## TELEVISION ADVERTISING AND POLITICS

Anyone who remembers Michael Ritche's 1972 film *The Candidate* (which was based on John Tunney's successful campaign for the U.S. Senate in California) remembers the character played by Allen Garfield, the media advisor/campaign manager. For many, this was undoubtedly the first realization of the growing power of these political gurus who today have come to fairly dominate many election campaigns. With the emergence of television advertising as such a dominant aspect of the political campaign, the role of the media advisor has become exaggerated. Many credit Roger Ailes, George Bush's media advisor in 1988, with playing perhaps the most important role in the election of the vice-president to the White House. Ailes, who reportedly cost the Bush campaign $25,000 a month plus nearly $3 million in commissions on advertising, even went so far as to participate in the decision to select Dan Quayle as Bush's running mate.

The media advisor is an artifact of the modern television campaign. Franklin Roosevelt, who first ran for President in 1932, had a campaign manager and a press secretary when he ran for President, but he did not have a **media advisor.** Most media advisors are described disparagingly but accurately as hired guns. They will work for almost any candidate, provided the money is right. Some have predilections for Democrats or Republicans, liberals or conservatives, but generally they don't regard as important the meshing of their political philosophy (if they have one) with the candidate's. The *Columbia Journalism Review* reported in 1989 that one media advisor (who also happened to be a working reporter for a daily newspaper) whose $10,000 proposal to provide consulting services to the Democratic candidate for state attorney general was rejected, turned around and sold the same proposal to the Republican candidate for the same office. Media advisors tend to come from a background in advertising or public relations. They usually have some knowledge about how the mass media operate (deadlines, production schedules), and most regard themselves as amateur psychologists or sociologists who understand mass behavior and attitude change. They tend to also have familiarity with show business techniques and some fundamental insights into the working of public opinion polling. But above all, these people are not embarrassed to be cast in the role of an overt manipulator of public opinion on behalf of a paying client who wants badly to be elected. Do they have any qualms about selling the public a lemon or using their talents to win an election for someone who will be an incompetent governor or mayor? Generally not. When queried about this, media advisor Joe Neopolitan told a reporter that his business was elections and campaigns. He frankly admitted he knew and cared little about government and felt no responsibility at all if his client was elected and turned out to be a turkey.

The media advisor has many tasks, including reshaping the candidate's image when possible. Roger Ailes, who started out as a production assistant in television and moved on to become the producer of "The Mike Douglas Show," pounded away at candidate George Bush in coaching sessions, trying to help the candidate overcome what *Newsweek* called his "squeaky voice, his jerky hand chops, and his clumsy hand waving." He worked to make Bush appear to be more forceful in public and to speak in sound-bites, telling quips and one-liners that can be picked up by television news. Constance Snapp, the Reverend Pat Robertson's media advisor in 1988, worked hard to change her candidate's image from a television evangelist to a Christian businessman. Polling indicated that most voters lumped Robertson into the same pile with Jerry Falwell and Jimmy Swaggart. To separate her candidate from the other evangelists, she worked hard to arrange mainstream, nonreligious appearances for Robertson, urged reporters to call him Mr. Robertson rather than the Reverend Robertson, and to describe him as a Christian businessman, not a television evangelist. The efforts were quite successful, Snapp reported.

But the biggest job for the media advisor is creating or supervising the creation of political advertising for the candidate, the so-called **polispots.** These 30-to-60-second commercials have become the centerpiece of many, if not most, major political campaigns. The ads often define the campaign for the candidate, and even major campaigners like Edward Kennedy have referred audiences and reporters to "my TV ads" when they asked questions about issues and policies.

## ◻ Impact

One of the most interesting questions in modern politics is: do these advertisements work? Do people actually decide to vote for a candidate because of their television spots? The answer to that question, like so many other questions about media effects, is we don't know for certain. It is very hard to measure what factors are considered by a voter when making a decision to choose one candidate rather than another. In many instances voters themselves cannot accurately articulate why they voted for Smith rather than Jones. Researchers suggest that the spots are probably most effective when there is a shortage of other information about a candidate. This is true also with editorial endorsements of candidates by newspapers. The fact that the *Times* said it supports Bush for president is probably far less important than the newspaper's support for Nelson as a candidate for superior court. Voters know very little about who is running for the judicial bench, and a newspaper endorsement can be quite meaningful. Consequently, political spots are quite effective in creating name recognition for candidates, and this has permitted persons who have been active in politics for a very short time to raise their public visibility quite rapidly through the use of such advertising. How many people had even heard of Jimmy Carter prior to 1975? Conversely, these ads are undoubtedly less effective when voters know a great deal about the candidate.

Like all advertising, political spots play an important role in reinforcing preexisting tendencies in voters. They can provide, for example, additional reasons to support a candidate for persons who have already decided to vote for that candidate. Does this mean the advertising is unlikely to change a voter's mind? Yes, unless the voter's decision to support a candidate is based on incomplete or inadequate data. But most communication researchers would acknowledge that if a voter has firmly made up his mind to vote for candidate Jones, advertising for Smith is unlikely to have much of an impact.

Is campaign advertising truthful? Not always, at least in the strictest sense. Government regulations regarding misleading or false advertising are not generally applied to political campaigns. Some find this somewhat troubling. The government is more concerned that an advertisement for a $1.39 tube of toothpaste is truthful than an ad for a candidate for president of the United States. The message about the toothpaste is far less important than the message about the presidential candidate, they argue. But that is exactly why the government keeps its hands off political advertising. The messages are too important (or at least they are presumed to be) to permit government to interfere as an arbiter of truth or falsity.

Most political advertising is substance free, and this, in the end, is more important than whether it is truthful or not. Political advertising, like product advertising, is often designed to exploit emotional rather than intellectual responses in the voters. Candidates seek to achieve a kind of emotional bonding with the voters. Find out what values the voters believe are important, and then communicate the message that the candidate believes those values are important as well. The Bush campaign very effectively bonded with the voters on the emotion of patriotism, the flag and the Pledge of Allegiance being the symbols generated by the campaign. It was also successful in bonding on the emotion of fear using advertising suggesting Michael Dukakis favored releasing violent criminals on weekend furloughs from prison. Little of a candidate's advertising reveals how the candidate stands on more substantive issues or policies. It generally succeeds only in expressing an empathy with the voters' feelings. In the end the spots are probably comparable to one of America's favorite snack foods, Hostess Twinkies. The spots, like Twinkies, are tasty and easily digested. And two or three Twinkies will satisfy an individual's appetite. But they do nothing to satisfy the nutritional needs of the human body. Voters who are beaten over the head with political advertising think they know more about the candidates and the issues than they really do. Their appetite for campaign information is satiated. But they really know little about the important matters.

But whether or not political spots are effective in winning voters to one side or the other is almost immaterial. They have become the salient feature in most major campaigns because they are favored by three important constituencies. First, the candidates and their media advisors love them. The advertisements give the candidates the opportunity to control their image, to be something they aren't. The story is told of candidate Gene Stunkel who ran for Congress in a downstate Illinois district. Stunkel was a small-town businessman who was not used to being on the campaign stump, and his public performance was tentative at best. But a series of advertisements generated by a media advisor pictured Stunkel as a no-nonsense, assertive individual, just the kind of fellow who should be elected to Congress. Stunkel was so pleased with this image that he watched tapes of the advertisements over and over again and attempted to become the man who was pictured in these political spots. By repeatedly showing pictures in political spots of a filthy Boston harbor (which really wasn't Boston harbor), George Bush created the image that he, not Michael Dukakis, was the "environmental" candidate in 1988. Also the candidate packaged in the political spot does not make a slip of the tongue, never says the wrong thing. And this is of considerable importance in an era in which the news media tend to jump on all a candidate's mistakes, minor or otherwise.

Secondly, television networks and stations that run the commercials like them for at least two reasons. The first reason is that they generate considerable income for these networks and stations. Even though the law forces broadcasters to normally charge candidates their lowest rates, there is still so much advertising coming in that it is quite profitable. And there is no need for the broadcasters to *sell* this advertising time, which makes political spots even more profitable for the TV station. During a national election year it is not uncommon for one or more of the presidential candidates to rank as one of the top 25 advertisers during that year. Broadcasters also favor the polispots because they don't interfere with scheduled programming as longer candidate presentations might. When the founders of the Republic scheduled the national elections for the first Tuesday in November little did they realize that the autumn months would become the most important months for television. It is in September and October that the networks and the local television stations introduce their new programming for the year. Programmers at the networks firmly believe that unless a viewer gets hooked on a show early in the fall, he or she will never watch it. So any thought of preempting new (or old) primetime programs for 15- or 30-minute political speeches sends shivers up the spines of television executives. The polispots are perfect, for they can be broadcast like any other commercial, without interfering with the programs.

Finally, and not unimportantly, most viewers prefer the short commercials to longer candidate presentations. Many viewers don't want to watch "boring" political speeches. They don't want their favorite TV programs preempted for a campaign speech. If they think they can be informed on the political campaigns by watching political spots, most TV viewers would just as soon do it that way.

## The Problems with Spots

What's wrong with the political spots? It has been asserted here and elsewhere that the political commercials are not responsible for the growth of symbols over substance in many campaigns. They don't seem to be able to move masses of voters toward one candidate or another in some unnatural way. It is often argued that a candidate can buy the election by running more political spots than an opponent, but most studies reveal that the candidate who spends the most on advertising wins only about 50 percent of the time, what might be expected from chance alone. What then, is the problem?

The most serious problems all revolve around money. The increasing use of television advertising has vastly increased the cost of running for public office. The total campaign expenditures for all the House and Senate races in the nation in 1980 was $239 million. Eight years later this total had jumped to $540 million (figure 13-2). That is a 130 percent increase in less than a decade. And most of this increase can be attributed to television advertising, which usually consumes between 45 and 60 percent of all campaign expenditures.

Prior to the March 8, 1988, "Super Tuesday" primary in the last presidential election, three leading presidential candidates, Bush, Dukakis, and Robert Dole, had each spent more than $16 million on television advertising. Both Bush and Dukakis spent more than $30 million on TV ads in the general election campaign. In 1988 the average cost of winning a seat in the U.S. Senate was $3.7 million; again, more than half of which was spent on television advertising. A week before the 1990 Texas primary election for governor of that state, the candidates had spent more than $25 million, most of which went to television advertising. In all recent presiden-

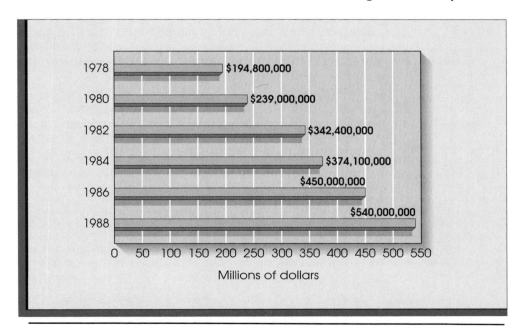

FIGURE 13-2 Total campaign expenditures by election year for U.S. House and Senate races.
(National Association of Broadcasters)

tial elections, serious and well-qualified candidates have run out of money even before one candidate had enough delegates pledged to secure the nomination. Political advertising is now the fastest growing slice of TV advertising, with rates growing four times faster than the Consumer Price Index. In any election, the biggest winners are always the television stations, the advertising agencies, and the media advisors.

The high cost of campaigning surely limits who can run for office. The average person simply cannot contemplate running for a high elective office today; he or she simply does not have sufficient revenue to pay the bills. But the growing expenditures of campaign money on television advertising has also limited other ways in which the candidate might campaign.

With more and more dollars going into television advertising, the candidate is left with less money for traditional means of campaigning, means that often employ people. Door-to-door solicitation, coffee klatches, store fronts, campaign offices, and other traditional campaign devices are falling aside. These other activities have employed campaign volunteers by the thousands in the past. It is true that a candidate can reach more people more cheaply with a television spot than with any other kind of campaign device, but it is also true that telecasting political commercials involves far fewer people in the campaign. It was noted previously, politics is participation, not simply watching. Yet today more and more of national and state political campaigning is played out on the television screen rather than the political rally or the neighborhood meeting or even the partisan parade. Nearly all of us are spectators, just as we are spectators when we watch anything else on television. Is it any wonder that a diminishing number of Americans vote in each national election; spectators aren't supposed to participate. We are not expected to do anything after we have watched an NFL football game or "Roseanne." Why are we expected to take some action after we have watched a televised political campaign?

Finally, when candidates seek to buy television time, they must pay for the time before the spots are run. TV money is what they call "up-front" money. This is one reason why political campaigns start so early and last so long in the United States. Someone who is seeking the presidency must begin to raise money 24 to 36 months before the election if they are to have sufficient funds to buy television time during the critical days preceding the primary elections. The better known a candidate is, the better his or her chances of raising money. Candidates must start campaigns early so they will be known by the time the public starts to get interested in the campaign. If the candidate finds it impossible to raise sufficient funds before big chunks are needed to purchase TV time, he or she often has to borrow money. To whom is the candidate then beholden?

The growing emphasis on television commercials in elections has vastly raised the cost of campaigning, has modified the campaign in such a way as to eliminate many of the traditional people-oriented modes of campaigning in favor of video presentations, and has forced candidates to start campaigning months in advance in order to arrange sufficient funds to buy the needed TV time.

After every election there are always substantial complaints about the growing emphasis on paid television commercials. And proposals are always put forth to change the system. Many argue that broadcasters should be forced to grant blocks of free time to candidates for public office, that those seeking office should not have to buy time. Granting such free time could be made a part of the requirements that must be met to gain a television license, or have a license renewed. Broadcasters obviously oppose this idea, pointing out that the television industry would have lost more than $200 million in revenues in 1988 on just the congressional races alone. And that sounds like a lot, until it is arrayed against the $27 billion in total TV ad revenues earned in 1988. Only three other nations in the world permit paid political advertising during election campaigns: Canada, Japan, and Australia. And only Norway and Sri Lanka do not require television stations to provide free television time for candidates.

When a proposal for free TV time is put forth, the major objections (not including the loss of revenue, which is soft-pedaled by television executives even though it is their biggest objection) usually focus on allotment of time. If the networks and stations had to provide time, how much time would each candidate get? Would the candidate for the Socialist Labor Party get as much time as the candidates for the Democratic and Republican parties? Surely these are difficult problems to solve, but not of a magnitude of landing an astronaut on the moon. And we did that in 1969.

But it is not just the broadcasters who oppose such plans. Incumbent office holders generally oppose such plans as well. It is far easier for an incumbent to raise campaign money than for a challenger to raise campaign money. And each time an incumbent is re-elected, it gets a little easier to raise money. Someone who is seeking an office can promise that if elected he or she can help a campaign contributor. Someone in office can help immediately. Right now the election game for Congress is contested on an uneven playing field, with incumbents generally able to raise far more money for the campaign than the challengers. Again, generally speaking, members of Congress don't want to lose this advantage. It is why more than 90 percent of incumbents are normally re-elected.

The only hope for such campaign reform is for the public to become interested enough in this issue to force their elected representatives to require broadcasters to provide free time for all candidates. But the next election always seems a long way away, and too many Americans seem distracted by other matters to focus on something as esoteric as this.

Other proposals have surfaced as well to try to reform various aspects of the political commercials. The Fairness in Political Advertising Act, introduced but never adopted by Congress, would restrict campaign commercials to showing only the candidate's image and voice, or his or her spokesperson. No staged reproductions, no minisagas, no sweeping panoramas of the American landscape. Supporters of the measure believe it would clean up many of the ads, and by making them less desirable to candidates, reduce the number that are telecast.

Another measure introduced after the 1988 campaign was aimed at reducing the number of negative ads; that is, ads that attack a candidate. Under this provision of this measure, if a negative statement is made about a candidate, such as George Bush's charges that as governor of Massachusetts Michael Dukakis was furloughing prisoners who were murderers and rapists, the negative statement must be made by the opposing candidate personally. That is, Bush would have had to appear in the ads making the charge against Dukakis.

Neither of these measures is likely to be adopted. There are certainly First Amendment considerations in both cases. And those considerations will likely be raised as the objections to the proposals. But remember, the members of Congress now are the candidates who won the last election. The system worked for them. What's the old saying—if it ain't broke, don't fix it.

## ◻ The Press and the Campaign

Television advertising has changed the manner in which candidates campaign for high office in the United States. Surprisingly, it has also changed in subtle but important ways how the news media cover these campaigns. Let's look briefly at how television advertising has worked this magic and then examine other aspects of political news coverage.

The need to raise money to buy television advertising has forced presidential candidates to begin their campaigns 18 to 24 months before the election is held. If the campaign starts then, the press generally thinks it should begin to cover the campaign. So major newspapers and broadcasting networks assign reporters to follow many of these potential candidates around the nation as they give speeches to help build a war chest for the upcoming political battles. Interestingly, this is the time when some of the most meaningful press coverage takes place. The candidates are telling voters about their ideas on the issues and government policies. This is the first time the reporters have heard these speeches, and they find them interesting. They write stories about these speeches, and about other aspects of the candidate's background and credentials. Unfortunately the readers and viewers are not very interested in the campaign at this point and tend to ignore these stories. When the voters become interested, in the midst of the primary races, or even before the general election, the reporters have lost interest in these matters. They have already written dozens of stories about the candidates' position on the issues. They are bored with these stories, and besides, they believe that readers and viewers already know this. As the election grows closer, the press tends to focus on stories that deal less with the issues and more with who is winning.

A few states like Iowa and New Hampshire begin holding presidential primary elections and party caucuses almost ten months before the election. To voters outside these states this seems pretty silly, but to the reporters and candidates these very early elections are terribly important. They are important to the candidates because their success in such elections is directly related to their ability to keep raising money. Win and donations pour in; lose badly and the money spigot begins to run dry. For reporters who have become bored following candidates around the country for more than a year, this early voting is a breath of fresh air. Finally, some drama, some emotion, some winners and losers. Consequently, the national coverage of these early primaries by both television and the printed press vastly overstates their importance to the final selection of a president. And due to the enormous amount of news coverage given these primary elections and caucuses, the public gets an exaggerated view of their importance.

Finally, and perhaps most importantly, because the campaign starts so early and because fundraising by the candidates has become such an important element in the campaign, the news media have been given an extraordinary amount of power in determining the outcome of the final election contest. Most political observers agree that the press has little to say about who wins, but it has a lot to say about who loses.

In the bad old days the political bosses determined who was likely to win or lose because they often controlled the political parties with an iron hand. They could insure a voter turnout; they could insure financial support. But the bosses are gone. Strangely, the press has picked up some of this power.

At the presidential and even the state level major American newspapers and magazines and television networks have a strong ability to determine who is and who is not a legitimate contender for the office. "We don't control anything in presidential primaries," noted political consultant/media advisor David Garth. "In our wacky system, you have Iowa and you have New Hampshire and you have all the other primaries and caucuses, which puts control into the hands of the press," he adds.

There is what some observers call the anointment process, the power of the press to select from the field one or two candidates, and by special exposure make these candidacies seem especially promising by means of a cover story in *Time* magazine, a lead article in *The New York Times Magazine,* a long television interview with Barbara Walters. While such coverage undoubtedly has very little impact upon the average voter, it has significant impact upon people who control the the contribution of large sums of money to a campaign and to persons who may be delegates to the national conventions. Someone who is going to contribute money to a campaign hopes to get something in return; it makes little sense to back a loser. If the editors of *Time* magazine think this candidate is so strong that they are putting his/her picture on the cover, this is someone who has a chance to win it all. And the money men and women like this kind of candidate.

We ask our journalists to use their knowledge and experience to interpret various aspects of the political process. We hope this is done realistically and with sufficient background information. During the primary election season, such interpretation can act as a prism through which we view the election process, and this can be good or bad for some candidates. For example, every candidate whose name is on the ballot in a primary election runs against real candidates and a phantom candidate as well; this phantom's name is "expected." Journalists tell their readers and viewers that Jones will probably win the New Hampshire primary with 47 percent of the vote. Jones wins but only gets 40 percent of the vote. A good victory nevertheless, but not as good as "expected," the press notes. Immediately Jones is on the defensive, trying to explain why—though he won the primary handily—he didn't get as many votes as the journalists thought he would. Jones' stock can plummet. In 1984 in Iowa reporters predicted that Walter Mondale and John Glenn would finish atop the Democratic caucuses. Mondale won 49 percent of the vote, but Glenn didn't do very well. Gary Hart won 16 percent of the vote, hardly a public mandate, but he did much better than "expected." Suddenly Hart was among the frontrunners.

Oftentimes there are legitimate reasons for the successes and failure of a candidate in a primary, reasons that are ignored or get buried in the 25th paragraph of a story. George Bush won the Iowa primary in 1980, smartly outpolling his rival Ronald Reagan. But George Bush had campaigned in Iowa for 10 days; Reagan visited the state only 45 hours. This fact was ignored by most journalists. By setting expectations and evaluating results, journalists have the ability to influence how we view the outcome of primary elections and caucuses. Again, most observers argue that such coverage has minimal impact on the average voter. But this can be very meaningful to those who financially support candidates.

The press can fatally cripple a candidate by ignoring his or her campaign, or declaring he or she has no chance to win. Newspapers and television stations are going to devote only so much time to covering even a presidential election. Reporters and editors must decide, then, which candidates they will cover. Not all candidates will get equal coverage; some will get no coverage at all. The rationale for this selection is usually based on the likelihood that the candidate can win the election.

The candidates who are most likely to win get the most coverage. This makes sense. Except, for a candidate to win the public recognition needed to win an election, the candidate must receive media coverage. To raise money to run a campaign that will expose the candidate's stand on the issues takes money. But a candidate who gets little or no media coverage will win neither public recognition nor financial backing. The decision by a newspaper not to cover a candidate because he can't win becomes a self-fulfilling prophecy. The candidate can't possibly win because the newspaper has chosen to ignore his campaign.

This has been the plight of third-party candidates for decades. But because television has so greatly increased the cost of running for election, third-party candidates suffer even more today. In 1980 the Citizens Party candidate for president was Barry Commoner, a noted environmentalist and educator. In his campaign Commoner was talking about the issues, unlike the major party candidates. But he could not get press coverage. One reporter even asked Commoner whether he was a serious candidate or "just running on the issues." Finally, in frustration, the campaign prepared and broadcast a radio ad that used the word "bullshit" to describe what Commoner said was the empty rhetoric of the campaign. The results were immediate; in two days Commoner and the Citizens Party received more news coverage than it had during the entire campaign. Of course most of the press coverage focused on the radio ad, not on Commoner, his ideas, or the platform of the party.

George McGovern, who was the Democratic presidential nominee in 1972, was surely a long shot when he announced he was a candidate again in 1984. He joined other Democrats as they traveled around America, holding debates on important issues. And McGovern did well in these debates, gaining a positive reaction from the assembled voters. But because he was not among those that journalists regarded as a frontrunner, his performance in the debates got very little press coverage. Consequently he had extreme difficulty raising needed funds and dropped out of the race. At one point one of his aides called Washington columnists Jack Germond and Jules Witcover and asked why they were giving McGovern so little coverage. He said he was told that McGovern could not be treated as a serious candidate because he had raised so little money. These journalists did not understand (or chose to ignore) that political fundraising is closely tied to media coverage.

Paying attention to or ignoring a candidate can have the opposite impact as well. The press can elevate the status of a candidate well beyond realistic public support. The candidacy of Illinois Congressman John Anderson in 1980 was largely a function of his popularity among reporters. Anderson had no real geographic base and no real ideological base for his campaign. He was simply more interesting to many reporters than Jimmy Carter, who, because of the Iranian hostage crisis, had become a drudge, or Ronald Reagan, whose tightly controlled campaign offended many in the press. The press coverage of Anderson enabled him to move from relative obscurity to a national stage in a matter of weeks. The Anderson campaign would have been impossible before TV and before journalists replaced political bosses as arbiters of viable candidates.

Voters should expect the press to take a leadership role in helping citizens establish a political agenda and guide them toward the correct choices in selecting a candidate. This is the editorial function of the mass media. But this is not necessarily the function of reporters asked to cover the political process. Through selective use of time and space, by highlighting one candidate over another, by establishing performance norms, by setting public expectations; a few national newspapers and magazines, and the television networks have attained a more prominent role in the presidential selection process than they perhaps even realize. In a real sense they have become more important than the political parties.

The cost of and emphasis on television advertising has had one additional impact on news coverage of political campaigns. Because advertising time is so expensive and because candidates believe so firmly that visual exposure is the key to a successful campaign, persons running for high office will do almost anything to get free television time. We have all seen news film of candidates pumping gasoline to dramatize the oil crisis or slopping pigs to dramatize the farm crisis. Many media advisors work hard to arrange photo opportunities and put candidates in often ridiculous postures to get free television exposure on the evening news. But in some instances candidates even alter their position on an issue or their normal manner of campaigning, just to nail down time on the 6 o'clock news.

David Halberstam recounts the story of then-President Jimmy Carter, campaigning in Ohio, giving his audience a relatively low-key, quiet but firm, message on his support for arms control. His aides told Halberstam that they hoped this would contrast sharply with the posture of his opponent, Ronald Reagan, who they believed wanted to junk strategic arms limitations. They envisioned Carter's dignified and Presidential talk as the lead item on the evening news. But in talking with network reporters after the speech, Carter aides found the journalists were unimpressed with Carter's low-key approach. Not only wouldn't the President's speech lead the evening news; it might not make it on the program at all. Aides told Carter that he must be more forceful, more aggressive on the issue in his next speech that day. In Philadelphia Carter did just that and undertook a harsher and personal attack on Reagan whom he said represents a threat to the stability of peace in the world. "That's more like it," Halberstam says. "He makes the evening news with that." The desire to win free media time can push candidates to the trivial or the exceptional act that attracts attention. It tends to sharply lower the substantive level of the campaign. Many in the press decry such tactics, but the broadcast industry fails to acknowledge that the entertainment imperative in television news is largely responsible for this diminution in the level of the campaign.

# THE MODERN CAMPAIGN

Reporters who cover the news assume that they are in control of that news coverage. In an election campaign the reporter assigned to a candidate watches and listens to the candidate as the campaign progresses. He or she talks to voters, to political experts, to other reporters, all the time, sifting the wheat from the chaff. Finally, the reporter assembles the story and prepares it for publication and broadcast. You can say or do what you like, the reporter tells the candidate, but I am going to tell my readers or viewers what is going on. This is how it is supposed to work, but especially at the level of a presidential campaign, it doesn't really work this way anymore.

Successful candidates like political advertising spots because they permit them to control the presentation of their image. More and more this philosophy has been applied to all aspects of the campaign. In the modern presidential campaign the candidate's handlers try to totally control the presentation of the candidate's image. They do so by extensively controlling the candidate, the press, and ultimately the candidate's image.

## ◻ Controlling the Candidate

In order to control a candidate's image, the handlers must control the candidate. In the modern campaign the candidate is on a very short leash. Roger Ailes, Bush's media advisor in 1988, said that "There are three things that get covered: visuals, attacks and mistakes. You try to avoid the mistakes and give them as many attacks and visuals as you can."

The rules of the game dictate that media advisers and aides plan a daily message or theme for the candidate. One or two events are scheduled in which the candidate can publicly explore the theme. Handlers then keep the candidate away from the press the remainder of the day. The press is often permitted to look but not talk. Photo opportunities are permitted, but no questions may be asked. The well-handled candidate strictly limits all contact with the press; no ad hoc press conferences. Former vice-president Walter Mondale who ran against Reagan in 1984 noted that during the campaign he held several news conferences every day; Reagan held not one from the convention until election day. "The result: I had great difficulty controlling my message, while Mr. Reagan had complete control. Every night I was responding to tough ones [questions]. Every night he was talking about puppy dogs and picket fences."

George Bush closely followed Reagan's model in 1988. "I have never seen a candidate kept so isolated from the press," said CBS's Bob Schieffer. ABC's Brit Hume added, "The candidate keeps the focus on his message by making sure that's all there is to cover."

Controlling when the candidate meets with the press is only half the battle; the well-managed candidate is also limited in what he or she can say to the press. The ideal comment in the 1990s is a pithy phrase of 10 or 12 words that makes what television news reporters call a "sound bite," those few words by the candidate broadcast with the story. In 1988 the sound bites dominated the campaigns. "Read my lips; no new taxes" was surely the classic, but Democratic vice-presidential candidate Lloyd Bentsen's remark to his opponent Dan Quayle, "You're no Jack Kennedy" ranked very high among political observers as well.

It seems fairly simple for the handlers to control the candidate. But how do they control the press? Generally by controlling the logistics of campaign travel. Reporters follow the candidate in the candidate's plane or a second aircraft. They are kept away from the candidate if they are in the same airplane. And when they land, they are herded, a lot like cattle are herded, from one speaking engagement to the next. When the plane lands, there are usually buses waiting for the reporters to take them to the campaign event. Upon arrival the reporters are kept away from the candidate and herded into a special area set aside for the press. When the candidate finishes the speech or whatever, reporters are quickly put back on the buses. There is no time to talk with spectators or local party officials. "The rules are brutally simple," wrote Joel Swerdlow in the *Washington Journalism Review*. "Buses wait for no one. So reporters had to forget about wandering off into the crowd for interviews. . . If you indulged in such wanderlust you might be left behind in Abilene, Texas, with no commercial flights scheduled to leave until the next day." Imagine calling your editor with that story.

Finally there is the control of the image of the campaign itself. Crowd size, for example. If only a small crowd shows up at the airport to meet the candidate, those people are herded into a narrow roped-off area. The camera platform is erected behind the crowd so video cameras must shoot over the crowd to focus on the candidate. The visual image shows the candidate speaking to what appears to be a tightly packed crowd in front of the speaker's platform. TV viewers automatically assume the crowd extends out on either side of the platform as well.

Timing is important as well. Media advisors make certain the press gets only a single story each day, the one story that the campaign wants told that day. In 1988 George Bush flew into Texas to talk to a crowd of primarily Hispanic immigrants. The message the campaign wanted these people to hear—that the vice-president was in favor of federal aid to education and other federal programs that the poor tend to rely upon—was not a message campaign handlers wanted conservative voters across the nation to hear. How could the candidate control national exposure of this speech? The camera platform was erected in such a way that the cameras would be facing the sun as Bush gave his talk that afternoon. The video was awful, and campaign handlers knew the networks were unlikely to use the picture. To kill the story altogether Vice-President Bush held an impromptu news conference before he boarded his plane where he made an important announcement that was well calculated to grab attention. Which story got on the news that night? Take a guess.

Richard Nixon pioneered this kind of closed campaign. Ronald Reagan's campaign staff perfected it. And George Bush used the model well in 1988. This is likely to be the campaign of the future, because those candidates who were more accessible to the press, who permitted reporters more freedom to talk to the people around the campaign, who failed to follow the "message of the day" strategy (Walter Mondale and Mike Dukakis, for example), lost the election.

What we have talked about is largely television coverage of the campaign. What about the print reporters? Unfortunately, too many of them are being bottled up as well. There is no question that a goodly number of American newspapers provide, on a daily basis, substantial news coverage of the presidential campaign. Those who choose to read newspapers like *The New York Times,* the *Washington Post,* the *Los Angeles Times* and even some smaller daily newspapers can gain a fairly complete picture of the issues in the campaign, where the candidates stand on these issues, and what else is taking place during the campaign. But the campaign coverage in the typical daily newspaper is not that much superior to network television, according to most observers. This is true of state and local campaigns as well.

In the first place, the modern campaign is orchestrated towards the needs of television, not the print media. In years past when reporters crowded on the platform to hear the candidate's speech, it was the print reporters, pen and pad in hand, at the front of the crowd. The cameras were relegated to the back. Today the situation is reversed. Logistically, the campaign is oriented toward the video cameras. For everyone else it is catch-as-catch-can.

The print reporters' editors watch the campaign via television. If a print reporter strays away from the mainstream "message of the day" that is transmitted on the evening television news, the editor will want to know why. The newspaper's coverage is often expected to mirror the coverage on television. In the past that was not as much of a problem. While the network television report was a minute or 50 seconds, the print reporter could file a long story. But as was noted in other parts of this book, long newspaper stories are an endangered species. Be brief; keep it short. Instructions like these push the reporter toward accepting the same kind of news given to television, a simple single theme message from the campaign staff each day. What is replacing the substance formerly transmitted by most newspapers is what Knight-

Ridder political reporter James McCartney has labeled "junk news". This kind of news fairly came to dominate the 1988 campaign. Let's explore modern campaign coverage by looking more closely at the last major presidential campaign, the Bush-Dukakis race of 1988.

## ☐ Bush-Dukakis in 1988

The last presidential campaign was very similar to the campaigns of 1980 and 1984. The Republicans, following traditions established by Richard Nixon in 1968, showed they had a great deal more savvy in operating a national campaign where the goal is winning the White House rather than enlightening the voters. The Democrats, looser and initially more open, failed again.

"Among the tricks employed by Ailes and [James] Baker were tricks perfected by Michael Deaver & Co. in the Reagan campaigns of 1980 and 1984," wrote reporter William Boot in the *Columbia Journalism Review*. The Deaver approach, according to Boot, is "Read my lips: No access. Daily visuals. Simple message. See Dick clap. See Jane cheer. See Dick and Jane vote Republican." Bush's handlers adhered rigidly to this format, keeping reporters so far from the candidate that some of them resorted to megaphones and binoculars. Bush and his staff stayed at a different hotel than the reporters when they traveled. Compare this to 30 years ago when John and Robert Kennedy would socialize with reporters in the hotel bar at the end of a day of campaigning. Bush rode on a separate airplane, and only a pool of two or three reporters was allowed to fly in that aircraft. It didn't really matter; he never talked with the reporters anyway. When reporters had questions for the vice-president, they were referred back to the Washington campaign headquarters. Some reporters say it reminded them of the Vietnam War when more news about the war was coming out the Pentagon rather than the field headquarters in Saigon. "What you have here is a group of prisoners; we are essentially hostages," noted reporter Eric Engberg.

Boot notes that there were some improvements in press coverage in the 1988 campaign over the 1984 edition. The networks seemed to devote a little more time to issues of substance, even though the candidates generally refused to discuss such matters. They painstakingly, if sometimes belatedly, corrected misstatements made by the candidates during the debates, Boot said. "By the end of the race, they were even running point-by-point rebuttals of the more egregiously misleading campaign ads." Strangely, however, these corrections and rebuttals seemed to have little effect on most voters. And this is perhaps one of the most interesting stories of modern campaigning.

The story begins in the mid 1980s when CBS correspondent Lesley Stahl did a painstaking evaluation of Ronald Reagan's public statements and pledges and compared them with his policies as president. In each case she showed portions of the President's previous campaign statements or public appearances and then, while these pictures were being transmitted, told viewers how they differed from the actual policies. She was certain she would get an angry call from the White House after the long segment was broadcast. She did get a call, but it wasn't from an angry staffer. As Michael Deaver later told Bill Moyers in a television interview, the White House was thrilled that CBS had run all those positive images of Reagan. But what about the negative verbal comments Stahl had made? People don't remember those, Deaver said. They only remember the nice pictures.

This same phenomenon occurred in 1988 as television reporters attempted to tell audiences the truth about what was going on as pictures of the staged or choreographed events were shown on the screen. ABC's Brit Hume did this when Bush visited a California Highway Patrol Academy. In his voice-over Hume mocked the contrived proceedings, warning viewers not to believe everything they see and hear from the candidate. "But as an old TV pro," William Boot noted, "he must know that verbal disclaimers of this sort are close to futile." Boot quoted Mark Crispin of Johns Hopkins University. "A visual image is always going to overwhelm a mere voice that accompanies it—the pictures will win out, and that's something that the most adept handlers really understand. I'm afraid not enough TV reporters understand." Michael Deaver understands this. So did Baker and Ailes. Dukakis's handlers weren't as smart. They put their candidate in an oversized tanker's helmet and filmed him riding around in an M-1 tank. The verbal message was simple: Mike Dukakis is for defense. But more people remembered the image of the candidate in the silly-looking hat than remembered the verbal message.

When all was said and done, the bulk of the 1988 campaign coverage, television and print, could be put into one of four categories: stories about character and morality; stories about conflict between or among the candidates; stories about the campaign process, commercials, strategy, and so forth; and stories about who was ahead—the opinion polls.

The morality issue emerged in 1987 when reporters from the *Miami Herald* staked out a Capital Hill townhouse occupied by Senator Gary Hart and reported that he had spent the night there with a woman named Donna Rice. Hart, who was not happily married by all accounts, at first denied the charges. Later pictures of Hart and Rice on a fishing boat surfaced as well, and the candidate dropped out of the race. This seemed to open a door through which reporters had not often passed in earlier campaigns. Most reporters covering John Kennedy's campaign in 1960 knew of his adulterous actions, but this was never mentioned in news accounts of the campaign. The Hart story seemed to slip the leash on some reporters, however, and questions about adultery and drug use and other matters formerly considered private were now asked in public. Journalists had generally been guided by the rule that a candidate's private conduct remains private, unless it has an effect on his public life. But the Hart case put a new spin on this old rule; the candidate's judgment came into play. If a married United States senator who is running for president lacks the good judgment to stay away from other women, then he lacks the judgment to be president.

In the wake of the Hart scandal the press began to more closely scrutinize the private lives of a great many candidates. Many times this was done for good cause; other times reporters seemed to delve into these matters simply because it seemed to be the thing to do. Some observed that journalists were becoming "character cops."

Many observers inside and outside the press applauded this development. They noted that many prominent public officials were playing one role for public consumption but living a somewhat different life. The time had come, these people argued, that such public officials be exposed for this duplicity. The way someone lives a private life surely does have an important bearing on whether they deserve to be elected to public office, they said, because it is likely to affect how they hold this office. Others disagreed. *New York Times* columnist Tom Wicker noted that reporters and editors themselves not unfamiliar with adultery and drug use, were being hypocritical in their eagerness to hold public figures to new standards of morality.

"Freedom of inquiry is too important to be called into question by intrusive, arrogant and sanctimonious prying into private lives and behavior," he said.

## ☐ Zinger versus Zinger

The most notable campaign stories in 1988 as in most recent campaigns were the attacks one candidate made against another during the election campaign. These attacks generated what someone labeled "zingers," one line shots by one candidate against another. The candidates fired the first shot, but the zingers often rebounded for days or weeks as they were repeated over and over again in television news broadcasts and in newspaper stories. One researcher even kept track of which zingers were used most often. Bush placed five in the top ten: his description of Dukakis as a card-carrying member of the A.C.L.U.; "read my lips;" "A thousand points of light;" "About as clean as Boston Harbor;" and his remark that Dukakis thought that a naval exercise was something you find in the Jane Fonda workout book. This last zinger was marvelously crafted, hitting Dukakis not only for his supposed weakness on defense issues, but invoking one of the most hated (to conservatives) of all liberal symbols, Jane Fonda, who in a previous incarnation was an active Vietnam war protester and even visited the enemy capital of Hanoi during the war. Democratic vice-presidential candidate Lloyd Bentsen had two on the top ten list, his remark that his opponent Dan Quayle was "no Jack Kennedy," and his de-

One of the most notable television "moments" during the 1988 presidential campaign was the interview CBS's Dan Rather attempted to conduct with George Bush about the (then) vice-president's role in the Iran-Contra scandal. A heated argument ensued and the broadcast and Dan Rather became the focus of an intense controversy. News coverage of the argument ("Who won?") pushed aside the real story: that Bush had once again failed to answer questions about his role in the scandal.
(CBS Photo)

scription of the massive deficits generated under the Reagan administration as $200 billion in "hot checks." Dukakis had one on the list, his description of Bush as the "Joe Isuzu of American politics," the reference to a lying car salesmen. Ann Richards, who gave the keynote address at the Democratic convention scored with a description of George Bush as someone "born with a silver foot in his mouth." And the old war horse, Ronald Reagan, made the charts with his famous description of the political term *liberal* as "the L. word."

What any of these had to do with the issues facing the nation as the campaign was conducted remains a mystery. But these became not only the sum and substance of the candidates' rhetoric, they became a substantial portion of the news coverage as well. Statements like these generate far more heat than light, but the press is attracted to fire. Such sparks in a campaign have always drawn reporters' attention. But in the past, the distant past albeit, such zingers played an interesting, but minor role in the campaign.

## And They're Coming Around the First Turn

A staple of modern campaign reporting is the voter preference poll. Karlyn Keene, managing editor of *Public Opinion Magazine,* said more than 300 national polls (and probably hundreds more regional and local polls) were taken for news organizations between April 1987 and November 1988. She said during the last two months of the campaign alone, 124 news media polls were made public, compared with only 44 during the similar period in the 1984 election and 99 during all of 1984. Republican campaign chairman Lee Atwater said there were so many polls being taken by the news media, especially in the early primary and caucus states, that the Bush campaign was able to suspend polling and use the data generated by the press.

"While the polls are more accurate than in the past, they are still wrong more often than their sponsors admit," noted Jonathan Alter in a 1988 election wrap-up in *Newsweek.* Alter said it was the sponsorship that was at the heart of the problems. The polls are generated by most news media organizations as marketing devices; they are used for promotional purposes. But good polling costs a lot of money. "Having commissioned expensive polls at least partly for promotional purposes, news organizations felt obliged to play them big," he added.

But that is only one reason the polls are becoming so popular. The polls attempt to create drama where often none really exists. In early September, two months before the election, isn't it exciting to announce that the candidates are neck-and-neck, or one is gaining on the other. This will catch a reader or viewer's eye where a long story on the candidate's position on energy conservation may not. And the polls provide an opportunity for graphics. This used to be an advantage only for television, but with many American newspapers attempting to look more and more like television news, graphics is important on the front page as well. Colorful lines and charts and bar graphs brighten up a newspaper.

Finally, poll stories are simple to do. Again, Jonathan Alter: "Such stories are easier to report than, say, a candidate's remedy for America's trade deficit. Reporters simply go out and lazily round up quotes to fit the poll results—like sports writers after a baseball game. That both degrades the craft of political reporting and lends false authenticity to coverage."

Those who condemn the obsession with voter preference polls argue that many are inaccurate—and they are. The polls said Dole was supposed to win in New

Reports on political popularity polls have been and remain basic fodder in modern campaign reporting. Most of the time, when they are conducted properly, the polls are fairly accurate; but sometimes they are wrong. Most pollsters picked Thomas Dewey to defeat Harry Truman; these polls were so persuasive that the *Chicago Tribune* didn't bother to see how the election really turned out. Truman won rather handily.
(AP/Wide World Photos)

Hampshire in 1988 and he didn't. Al Gore was going to be crushed on Super Tuesday and that didn't happen either. But polling that is well done is correct far more often than it is wrong. The problem is many local news organizations who want to capitalize on the polling frenzy, but don't want to spend the money, conduct sloppy polls that are very misleading.

But there are two other more serious problems with the poll mania. Publishing and broadcasting stories about the polls takes up valuable space that could and should be devoted to stories about the candidates and the issues. Also, the polls divert the focus of news coverage from the proper targets—the candidates—to the voters. What the voters think about the candidates a month before the election is not nearly as important as what the candidates think about the voters.

## ◻ The Story Becomes the Story

In the end, the story which dominated the coverage of the 1988 presidential race was not the candidates or the issues, but the campaign—what the candidates were doing to try to win the election. The media began reporting on itself. *Newsweek* magazine described a scene in Iowa prior to the caucuses where a farmer was being interviewed by a newspaper reporter who was being shot by a still photographer who was being taped by a TV crew, all of which was the subject of a magazine's story on media coverage. "For much of the race," wrote William Boot, "journalists discussed an unprecedented flood of inaccurate charges and misleading television campaign ads in terms of the effectiveness of a candidate's game plan." The polls became a subject of news coverage; not what they revealed, but the fact that so many were being taken. There were stories about strategy, staff shake-ups, media advisors, the way reporters were being handled by the candidate's handlers, and so on. The campaign process became more of an issue than trade deficits, arms control, taxes, or farm policy. When the candidates debated, commentators focused not so much on what was said as how it was said. They talked about whether the candidates seemed nervous or confident or relaxed. Commentators noted that the candidates seemed likable and that they had a mature understanding of camera angles. ("I noticed. . .Dukakis played to the camera," noted ABC's Jim Wooten after the first debate.) After the second debate, Dan Rather reported that there hadn't been many sound bites in Dukakis's answers to the questions. His colleague Bruce Morton responded that that was one of the Democratic candidate's problems, "his message doesn't sound bite as easily." Reporters would talk to other reporters about the candidate's "spin doctors," partisans who besiege reporters on behalf of a candidate after a speech or an event and tell them what it really means. After one debate Lesley Stahl of CBS asked reporter Mark Nelson of the *Dallas Morning News* what the Bush spin doctors were saying.

Admittedly it is difficult for reporters to raise real issues when the candidates themselves are talking about the Pledge of Allegiance to the flag. But that is their job. Elections are surely media events in the late twentieth century, but they must be more than that as well.

## ◻ Who Knows Best?

Ever since Ronald Reagan ran for the presidency there have been those in journalism who have argued that the media advisors who run the modern campaigns (and control the flow of the press coverage of the president as well) know more about how the mass media operate than the mass media do. Journalist Barbara Matusow was one of the first to make this observation in the early 1980s. The Bush campaign of 1988 clearly demonstrated this assertion, as campaign managers used some of the old rules of journalism to marshal positive press coverage for the vice-president.

People who operate political campaigns are aware of the mandate in both television and print journalism today to "keep it short." Indeed, the average length of a network news sound bite, which was 45 seconds in 1976, had dropped to 9 seconds by 1988. Just enough time to say "Read my lips; no new taxes"; and that is what the candidate said.

Reporters are supposed to be objective, so the Bush people knew reporters could not take sides in the GOP attacks on Dukakis. Reporters who often know things are prevented, under such a rule, from repeating them. The rules of objectivity are part of the reason that reporters like to focus more on the campaign process than the campaign issues. The campaign process is one area in which the reporter is permitted to be judgmental. "It is acceptable for reporters to say who is making hay, but not who is making sense," notes Jonathan Alter. So reporters could tell readers and viewers that Dukakis had screwed up during a campaign trip to Nebraska and said the wrong things to farmers, things that would hurt his campaign. But they can't say that he screwed up in his campaign speech, that his plan to solve the nation's deficit problems won't work. Journalists can point out who had the best day campaigning, but not who has the best plan for national defense. A well-organized campaign, like the Bush campaign, will be subject to far fewer press mistakes, and hence have better news coverage.

Reporters are supposed to be fair. The Bush people knew this as well, so when the press began to explore the negative campaigning that was taking place, they presented a picture of both candidates throwing mud at one another. That was true, but the Bush campaign was the most flagrant offender, according to most neutral observers. The balanced news reports, however, made both candidates appear to be equally at fault. This attempt to be objective and fair required reporters to censor themselves in some instances. The Massachusetts criminal furlough program that became the focus of one Bush attack on Dukakis was started by a Republican governor, not Dukakis. But reporters who knew this did not report it—until Dukakis himself said it. And in the early campaign reports on the candidates' advertising, they tended to focus more on its effectiveness (process) rather than whether it was truthful or not (substance.)

In the end, the American people were badly shortchanged by most of the campaign coverage. "They're getting very sophisticated, and they know how to use us," said CBS chief Washington correspondent Bob Schieffer recently. "We never really got to them in this election. It's a very, very hard thing that we haven't sorted out in television, and I don't think the newspapers have either."

## ▨ What to Do?

There is no shortage of ideas of ways to correct the problems with the press coverage of the modern political campaign, especially the presidential race. And most of these suggestions come from journalists themselves, who are quite aware of the shortcomings of their reporting. Each winter after a presidential election, post mortems are held across the nation where journalists talk about the problems of covering such an event. Most all agree that it is incumbent upon the journalists to regain control of the press coverage of the campaign, wresting it away from the candidates. Some have suggested that reporters focus much less on day-to-day coverage and focus on larger issues. The wire services and a handful of pool reporters could follow the candidates around the nation and provide any play-by-play coverage that is required. The majority of journalists assigned to the campaign could focus on issues or talk with voters or more closely examine the candidate's record. Television, it is said, must simply refuse to be a party to staged, message-oriented photo events. Telling voters that these are staged events while the images are being telecast does not ameliorate the impact of the campaign visuals. The networks must simply refuse to use such material. If the candidate wants to get on TV, he or she will have to do something, or say something meaningful. And the press must publish the bulk of its substantive news about the candidates when the voters are interested in the campaign, in the weeks before the election, not 12 months earlier when the campaign begins.

Journalists should also reconsider some of the traditional rules of the craft that were used against them in 1988; abandon or revise those rules that are no longer useful. Fairness in reporting is important, but balance is not always the same thing as fairness, many note. And if fairness is to remain a standard, reporters must remember the need to be fair to readers and viewers as well as the candidates. Reporters should be allowed to make judgments about substance as well as process. This is what the label "news analysis" is designed for.

Polling should not be abandoned, but used more creatively. Polling should be used to find out what is on the voter's mind, not simply who he or she will vote for. A news organization could use polling to discover what the voters believe are the most important issues that will face the next president or senator or whatever. Polling or other research devices can be employed to find out if the voters know the candidates' positions on these issues. This could help focus reporting. If the public has little idea where candidate X stands on the granting of offshore oil leases, a reporter should be assigned to find out, and a story on that should be published for the voters. Polling is a useful device, if it is used in a useful manner.

The press has an obligation in our society to provide the voter with the needed information to make an informed choice on election day, to present a picture of reality upon which the citizen can act, as Walter Lippmann once noted. Few would argue that this obligation is being fulfilled.

# THE PRESIDENT AND THE PRESS

Providing information to voters before an election is one important mission the press is expected to perform. Reporting on the actions of government in between elections is equally important. Government news is still a staple for most newspapers and broadcasting stations, although the focus of this news has changed somewhat in recent years. There is less news on the mundane and routine aspects of government and more emphasis on scandal and other "sexy" government matters. Still, a citizen who carefully uses local newspapers and television and radio news can gain a fair approximation of what the officials in their state and local governments are up to.

Coverage of the national government, while much more intensive in some regards, oftentimes is less complete than coverage of local and state government. This is due in part to the immense size of the federal government. Even the most serious-minded editor is daunted by the sheer size of the bureaucracy. Having said that, however, the press coverage of the national government is still far more unidimensional than it should be or needs to be. News from Washington, D.C., in the 1990s tends to be about the president.

Stories about Congress and the scores of other federal agencies in the nation's capital are surely published and broadcast, but there seems to be fewer and fewer of them each year. A study done in 1976 by Alan P. Balutis on daily New York newspapers revealed that between 1970 and 1974 nearly 75 percent of all national news reported focused on the President. Only 17 percent of the stories were about the Congress. A more recent study of network television news revealed that from 1980 to 1984, 3,545 stories about the Congress were broadcast compared with 7,824 in the preceding five years, a drop of about 55 percent. And when stories about Congress are published or broadcast, they often don't focus on its legislating function. The Center for Media and Public Affairs reported that from January, 1989 through May 1989 the three television networks carried 435 stories on Congress. But of that total 286 had to do with three issues: the pay raise, the nomination of John Tower as Secretary of Defense, and the problems of Speaker Jim Wright. Why are Congress and the other federal agencies so often ignored? It is much easier to cover the President, one man in one place. There are hundreds of stories in the Congress and hundreds more in the federal agencies. Which ones should be covered? Who should be interviewed? It can be a difficult job. Television, at least, requires a steady diet of pictures, color, personalities, and stories that can be told in 90 seconds. Many newspapers today unfortunately follow a similar formula. "Congress dwells on issues that are arcane and often complicated and lumbers through a legislative process that is slow-moving and often dull," notes Greg Schneider in the *Washington Journalism Review*. Legislating is not only dry, wrote Schneider, it is nonvisual. There are few good pictures, short of the infrequent legislative hearing that produces sparks and drama as the congressmen and senators confront hostile witnesses. In addition, covering the White House is probably the preeminent journalistic job in the United States today. While not *every* journalist aspires to this post, to carry both White House press credentials and a press card from a major American news medium is surely regarded as a sign of great success. It is no accident that most network anchor people, weekdays and weekends—Tom Brokaw, Sam Donaldson, Dan Rather, and others—covered the White House at one point in their career.

Covering the White House was not always the choice assignment it is today. An up and coming reporter in 1900 would have likely preferred the police beat over a chance to go to Washington, D.C. and cover William McKinley. It was not until the 1930s, when Franklin Roosevelt was in the White House and the eyes of the nation were focused upon the nation's capital that covering the president became a prestigious assignment. It has been that way ever since and today nearly 1,800 correspondents are accredited White House reporters.

Press relations between the President and the press were informal at best until the development of the presidential news conference. Woodrow Wilson initiated regular meetings with the press during his two-term presidency from 1912 to 1920. The press conference is unique in the world. The British prime minister and her ministers regularly visit Parliament for questioning, but the President of the United States is the only national leader expected to appear regularly before the press to answer questions. Some presidents do this better than others. Harding, Coolidge, and Hoover all found the practice onerous and their press conferences are hardly memorable. Franklin Roosevelt was a master at the game. His success can likely be attributed to his understanding of the importance of the President's relationship with journalists, whom he tended to like. They in turn were fond of him and often protected him from embarrassment. The American press, for example, simply did not publish pictures of the President in his wheel chair or being helped to a speaking podium. Most believed that such pictures would hurt Roosevelt, weaken his important image. Often on Sunday evenings Roosevelt and his wife Eleanor would invite a handful of newspeople for supper at the White House.

But Roosevelt was not a patsy; he could and did scold the press. Two reporters were once made to stand in the corner wearing dunce caps during a news conference after they had published what the President considered to be erroneous stories. And Roosevelt awarded another reporter an Iron Cross, a high German military honor, after publishing a story that the President thought would help the Germans during the Second World War. Truman and Eisenhower were less successful with the press, but both continued regularly scheduled news conferences. Truman once said the regular news conference was important because it permitted him to find out what was on the minds of the people of the nation through the reporters' questions. Eisenhower permitted the press conferences to be filmed, but the White House screened all film before it could be shown publicly.

John Kennedy was the next virtuoso with the press. He, like Roosevelt, was fond of reporters and they liked him as well. But he clearly did not share FDR's understanding of the role of the press in a democracy. At press conferences he was charming and witty and seemed to enjoy sparring with reporters, but he wanted the journalists to be cheerleaders, not watch dogs, and was often swift and sharp in his response to fault-finding by the press. He publicly criticized journalists and frequently called editors to complain. He once very publicly cancelled 22 White House subscriptions to a New York newspaper that angered him with a story. He actively sought to have *The New York Times* remove reporter David Halberstam from Vietnam because the journalist's stories reflected in the early 1960s the growing military involvement of the U.S. in Southeast Asia and the folly of this intervention. *The Times* kept Halberstam in Saigon, refusing to bend to White House pressure.

Lyndon Johnson knew how to use political power but never learned about the power of the mass media, especially television. His relations with most reporters were frayed, and the fact that he led the nation into a very unpopular war complicated matters even more. It was the Nixon administration that is the real watershed in presidential press relations. Richard Nixon was the first American president to fully understand the power of television; he was also the first president to orchestrate from election to resignation a complicated and very successful "media strategy." His press relations were among the stormiest ever. Events that took place during Nixon's five and one-half years in office continue to haunt both journalism and government. The President, the Vice-President, the Attorney General, and several top presidential aides were proven to be indiscreet, dishonest, or even corrupt. Corruption was not new in Washington when Nixon took office. But never had it run so deep; never had an administration handled the problems it created so badly. Press efforts to uncover this scandal and corruption alienated many who served in government. Derision, fear, and even dislike seemed to underscore the relationship between some members of the press and many government officials. But the journalists had been taught this new attitude by the former President himself. "Nixon brought his capacity for suspicion and innate hostility to the Washington press corps and turned that body into a press corps in his own image," wrote David Halberstam in an insightful article in *Esquire* in 1974.

Richard Nixon was elected president using the first sophisticated television campaign, from slick commercials to staged, televised town-hall meetings. His staff carefully controlled press access to the candidate, shielding him from the press and public except at those times when they were in complete control. "Media strategy" was a central part of the election campaign. Nixon went to Washington in 1969 expecting to find the kind of press corps that had existed when he left the nation's capital in 1961, but it had changed. The partnership between press and government which had worked well during the Cold War in the fifties when Nixon was vice-president had ended. Lyndon Johnson had mauled the Washington press corps as he sought to win the war in Vietnam. *New York Times* associate editor Tom Wicker summed up the changes: "In the fifties we had an assumption of infallibility about presidents. By 1965, with the war and the obvious manipulation of Johnson, that had begun to change. By 1967 it was pretty well gone. And by 1968 it had swung the other way; nothing Johnson could say was trusted." Nixon didn't expect or, some say, understand that the press corps had changed. Others say he saw this change immediately and retreated to his media strategy to deal with these suspicious journalists.

Nixon's media relations became a model for future presidents, so it is instructive to study them briefly. Virtually everything Richard Nixon planned to do or did was done with one eye on the mass media. How would people perceive his actions through the media? George Reedy, one of Lyndon Johnson's press secretaries, notes that "Presidents do not have press problems. They have constituent problems. . . . The things that bother the press about a president will ultimately bother the country."

One senses that Nixon understood this only partially. He saw the press as an isolated, hostile agency. He saw reporters' questions not as a reflection of national curiosity or frustration but as a personal attack on Richard Nixon. His press strategy was aimed at driving a wedge between the people and the press, a sort of macabre reinforcement of his own distorted view. If he could convince the people that it was the President and the public against a hostile, nihilistic press, he could take any heat generated by the mass media. It would be politically harmless. To a surprising extent this strategy worked; today we still suffer from this legacy. The press is viewed by many not as an amplification of the voice of the people, not as a representative of the public, but as a separate agency with alien values and extreme power, something to be feared and controled.

Many peripheral factors aided the President in implementing his strategy. The size of the government increased so rapidly in recent times that the press, often unwilling to pay the economic costs required to increase the size of its news staffs, has instead paid a far greater price by permitting government to supply much of the news that it needs. A government called upon to supply news can also hide news. Government press agents, not completely accurately titled "public information officers," developed highly successful strategies at emphasizing positive achievements and covering up embarrassing material.

Since the late 1940s the Cold War has provided a strong excuse for such a cover-up. The nation cannot afford to reveal information that would endanger national security. This sometimes valid excuse has become a cozy sanctuary in which public officials can hide. Nixon used this excuse and many others in the development of his media strategy which had several distinct but complementary elements.

Nixon sought to centralize the control over the flow of information about the government in the White House. When there was good news, it was released by the President. Bad news was revealed by other officials outside the White House. Cabinet members were instructed on what to say on many policies. Nixon also classified great amounts of information as secret or top secret, starting a trend that was interrupted only briefly when Jimmy Carter was in the White House, but which was continued under Presidents Reagan and Bush.

Richard Nixon did not like the printed press because reporters could interpret the President's words, select which quotes to use, and undertake similar journalistic functions. Nixon instead liked to talk directly to the people through television. He frequently made televised addresses to the nation, usually aired in the early evening hours to avoid forcing the networks to preempt their popular primetime programs. His press conferences were also televised, giving him still another chance to talk directly to the people.

Nixon didn't trust the press and trusted the Washington press corps least of all. He believed that he could maintain successful public relations with the heartland of America, the South, the Midwest, and the West, by dealing directly with the press in the regions. He made trips throughout the nation to hold briefings with regional journalists. Sometimes these briefings were used to announce important federal policies, other times simply to permit these regional reporters to hear the President's own words, unfiltered by the Washington press corps. The reporters who regularly covered the White House were generally excluded from these sessions, and often the regional "reporters" who attended these meetings were broadcast station managers and newspaper publishers rather than reporters. Nixon handled their "softball" and sympathetic questions with ease. The administration also flooded the nation's smaller newspapers with "press kits" filled with information about administration policies and programs and the position the President had taken on many issues. Many smaller papers devoured this information, treating readers to all manner of Republican news.

Finally, to compensate for any bad news that was published or broadcast about the President and his administration, Nixon and his staff went to great lengths to convince the American people that the press—especially the Eastern newspapers and the television networks—could not be trusted.

Vice-President Spiro Agnew led these attacks on the press, starting in a November 1969 speech in Des Moines to a highly partisan Republican gathering. From this rigged environment where applause and laughter were programmed by the party the vice-president tore into the national news media. He called them unfriendly and untrustworthy, and said that the coverage of the Vietnam War was biased. News at the three networks is selected by a small group of individuals, Eastern effete snobs, who told nothing but the bad things about America, he said. There was too much power in the hands of a few people—people who did not have to stand for election every four years.

Agnew's speeches were intended to communicate on two levels. The epithets and invectives were aimed as barbs at the press, sharp reactions from an administration feeling itself under siege by the press. But the speeches were designed to speak more subtly to the American public. The message was simple: "Don't believe what you read in your newspapers and see on television. These news media are untrustworthy."

A measure of the success of this campaign to discredit the press can be seen by the fact that millions of people steadfastly refused to believe news reports about the Watergate mess that ultimately toppled the Nixon presidency. Such reports were exaggerated, untrue, one-sided, or hostile. These stories were the final piece of evidence needed by many to accept the truth of Agnew's argument—the press was out to get President Nixon. It was only after months and months of hearings, the revelation of one piece of new evidence after another, that most of the people finally came to see that the press was telling the truth.

Nixon and Agnew left a legacy that continues to damage the credibility of the American press. The press is not without fault itself; it makes plenty of errors. But never before had a President and a vice-president been so specific and unrelenting in their charges against the news media. In his darkest days during the Civil War, Abraham Lincoln did not attack the press which constantly nipped at his heels, demanding that he get on with the war. Wilson did not attempt to characterize as lying and untrustworthy the press that opposed his efforts to build a League of Nations. America is going to have to live with this legacy for some time to come.

## ■ Ford, Carter, and the Press

The relationship between the press and Presidents Gerald Ford and Jimmy Carter was never very good, though it never reached the stormy moments of the Nixon administration. Both, especially Carter, used press strategies developed by Nixon to deal with the mass media. But neither man was as skilled a manipulator as Nixon.

When Gerald Ford became president he inherited a press corps that said it was ready to trust the chief executive again. Nixon had resigned in disgrace. Ford, a long-time member of the House of Representatives, had been appointed vice-president after Spiro Agnew resigned under a cloud of tax fraud. Ford was a nice man, and he came to the White House promising candor and honesty and enjoyed warm relations with the press for many weeks. But his honeymoon with the press began to deteriorate when he pardoned Richard Nixon. News secretary J. F. terHorst was misled by Ford staff members and in turn misled White House reporters about the pardon. Angered, terHorst resigned, and this episode cost Ford the good will of many members of the press corps. Ron Nessen, an NBC White House correspondent, was named to replace terHorst and worked to establish positive press relations for the president. Ford met more often with the press, and Nessen reshaped the presidential press conference in important ways that permitted, among other things, the opportunity for reporters to ask follow-up questions. In the past a reporter asked one question, and then the President moved to the next reporter. Nessen had a few scrapes with White House reporters who often complained that he was late coming to briefings. On one occasion reporters accused the press secretary of lying. All-in-all, however, Ford and Nessen established cordial press relations again in the White House.

Jimmy Carter was never very comfortable with the members of the Washington press corps. He was considered an outsider by many, winning the Presidency after serving a short term as governor of Georgia. He considered himself an outsider and built his campaign on that theme. This alienated many Washington reporters, who are, after all, insiders, part of the establishment that Jimmy Carter ran against. Carter's choice of Jody Powell as press secretary also caused problems. Powell had never been a working reporter, despite being a close and trusted confidant of the President. Powell was also somewhat of an intellectual and was usually more than a match for the White House reporters in the constant battle of wits. But Powell, an outsider himself, was often bewildered by what he found in the nation's capital. In fact, he frequently referred to the "strange and unnatural world of press–government relations."

Carter, like Nixon, attempted to control the flow of information in his administration. He personally announced after several days of hard bargaining at Camp David, that Egypt and Israel had reached an agreement in peace negotiations. In 1979 Carter went to Golden, Colorado, to celebrate Sun Day and announce that his administration would spend an additional $100 million for solar energy research. The announcement was adroitly timed to hit most reporters on deadline, and the story got front-page treatment. It was never widely reported that Carter resisted efforts by his own Department of Energy to budget $400 million rather than $100 million for solar energy research.

When Carter took office in 1977 he promised to hold two news conferences each month. He kept this promise until mid-1979 when problems began to mount, and he simply stopped meeting with reporters regularly. His news conferences were televised at first, but in the second half of his administration he met regularly with visiting editors, outside the reach of the television cameras. Instead he used prepared televised addresses to speak to the nation about energy problems, the Iranian crisis, and the serious inflation that infected the nation's economy. He also held 30 town meetings throughout the nation, going around the Washington press corps much like Richard Nixon.

Carter's press relations hit a low point in the middle of his third year in office and never bounced back. The national economy was in trouble, and the press tended to place much of the blame for these problems on Carter. A few reporters actually seemed happy to see the "outsider" fail. Carter became embittered, according to many reports, and began to believe and say that journalists are addicted to reporting conflict, confusion, and scandal, thereby handicapping the president's capacity to govern. Most presidents are personally liked by the press. Carter was not. Most reporters had little admiration for him; they grew weary of his moralizing and preaching. Some said he treated them like his Sunday school class. Franklin Roosevelt and John Kennedy both lectured reporters as well but were well-loved. The problem was that Carter and most of his staff were not Washingtonians, had little in common with Washingtonians, and didn't seem to like Washington and many Washingtonians.

As the friction developed Carter became more aloof. Any hope of repairing the breach between the President and the press was lost when militant Iranian students took over the American embassy in Iran. Each night television reports brought home the story that the great American military and diplomatic leviathan, led by Jimmy Carter, was unable to free the American citizens held hostage. The President, indeed, the entire administration, appeared impotent. Carter began to hate television, as broadcast journalists nightly reminded the national audience that "this is day 277 of America held hostage." The President and others said that these reports played a major role in Carter's electoral defeat in 1980.

The administration attempted to pressure the press in early 1980. Both the State Department and the White House tried to block a March 2, 1980, segment of "60 Minutes" which outlined the widespread torture and murder of Iranian citizens by the Shah of Iran's secret police. Press secretary Jody Powell called the president of CBS news and asked that the segment be cancelled, arguing that the broadcast could exacerbate the hostage crisis. But the segment was aired nevertheless.

During the 1980 election Carter accused the television networks of unfairly boosting the candidacy of rival Democrat Senator Ted Kennedy. He became even more bitter and banned television cameras from his last two presidential press conferences. He announced that if he was re-elected such a ban would continue during his second term of office. But he wasn't re-elected and soon became a nonperson in the eyes of the Washington press, someone so disregarded that the *Washington Post* believed and published a story that Carter had actually bugged the Blair House quarters of President-elect Reagan and his wife in the days before the inaugural. An apology and retraction were issued a few days later.

## ◼ The Reagan Administration

Ronald Reagan came to the White House with a reputation for being the master media politician, the "great communicator." His performance in office generally lived up to that reputation. His 1980 political campaign had been well run, taking a lesson from the Richard Nixon campaign book. But Reagan had assets that Nixon did not have. He had been an actor and was very comfortable with the media. On election night in November 1980 CBS's Walter Cronkite had Gerald Ford in the studio with him while CBS correspondent Jerry Bowen was with the president-elect at the victorious Reagan headquarters. Cronkite invited Reagan to put on a headset so he could talk directly to Gerald Ford. Without hesitation Reagan took the earphones and microphone and began a conversation. It is not easy to imagine Nixon or Jimmy Carter or Ford responding to Cronkite's request in such a matter-of-fact way. But Reagan grew up in the world of media; he was comfortable with it.

Ronald Reagan is also a very likable person. Reporters speak of his "implacable affability," another asset Nixon never enjoyed. In early 1981 commentator David Brinkley described the new President to his TV audience as "a man who, if you're tuned in that way, would be pleasant to be with outdoors and who could gather up brush, build a little fire, scour out the skillets, and cook a fairly decent burger." An all-American, in other words. Even as Reagan's second term in office reached the midway point and his press relations became somewhat frayed, most reporters still professed a genuine affection for the President.

Reagan also took office with another advantage not shared by Nixon, what appeared to be a free ride from the press, far in excess of the normal honeymoon given a new President. What were the reasons for this free ride? "Chief among them," wrote C.T. Hanson in the *Columbia Journalism Review,* "was a strange process in which the press, echoing the new administration, exaggerated Reagan's popularity and his "mandate," which helped to cow congressional Democrats, whose quiescence in turn made the press more bovine, which in turn made the president seem more unassailable, and so on." The public mandate was never really that strong. Only 27 percent of all eligible voters supported Reagan in the 1980 election. Even Reagan staff members later confessed that the "mandate business" was part of a carefully created illusion. One anonymous White House official told *Los Angeles Times* reporter Jack Nelson, "We were never quite as strong as we gave the impression of being. We pretended that we had a mandate that was very much larger than it was. A tremendous number of people voted against Jimmy Carter, not for Reaganomics." The assassination attempt on the President also extended his honeymoon with the press.

At least six members of the President's staff played a direct role in setting the administration's media policy—James Baker, Michael Deaver, Richard Darman, David Gergen, Edwin Meese, and Larry Speakes (and later Marlin Fitzwater). In his book *On Bended Knee,* Mark Hertsgaard states that this team established a basic news management formula: plan ahead, stay on the offensive, control the flow of information, limit reporters' access to the president, talk about the issues you want to talk about, speak in one voice, and repeat the same message many times. Early morning meetings in the White House were used to establish a single message that the White House wanted to communicate that particular day. " 'What are we going to do today to enhance the image of the President?' was the dominant question," one participant in these meetings told Hertsgaard. Devising the "line of the day" or "the message of the day" was intended to "make sure we're all saying the same thing," according to Michael Deaver. The line of the day was then transmitted by computer to other senior administration officials, who, in turn, handed it down to their press aides. At a 9:15 A.M. briefing, news secretary Larry Speakes would announce the President's schedule for the day, point out specifically which events would be made accessible to network cameras. In this way Michael Deaver and his staff could control what pictures the American people would see on the evening news. Hertsgaard notes that the White House control over network television's portrayal of the President was so pervasive early in the administration that in the words of former "CBS Evening News" senior producer Richard M. Cohen, "Michael Deaver should have been listed as the executive producer on all the political stories we broadcast." The networks permitted this heavy-handed direction because they wanted pictures of this very photogenic president for the evening news, and if they wanted pictures, they had to play by Deaver's rules.

Reagan used television very effectively. Michael Deaver explained that Reagan's effectiveness on TV was why he consistently argued for primetime televised press conferences and speeches; Reagan was "unfiltered" in these appearances. "It isn't Ronald Reagan at 2 o'clock in the afternoon translated by the networks in the evening. It's Ronald Reagan into the home." Deaver noted that every time the President appeared on TV through a speech or a press conference and was able to communicate directly with the American people his popularity in the polls increased.

While Reagan's popularity may have increased after each televised appearance, he found the televised press conference to be an event not altogether to his liking. He had fewer, formal press conferences than any recent President (figure 13-3). Franklin Roosevelt had almost eight press conferences per month. Truman had four, Eisenhower, Kennedy, and Johnson about two per month. Ford and Carter held about one press conference per month, Nixon and Reagan far fewer than one each month. The problem with the formal press conference lies as much with the press conference itself as the president. There is a real advantage to the president to talk

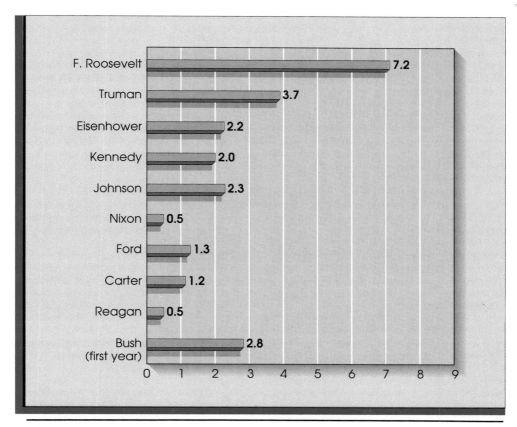

FIGURE 13-3 Average number of news conferences held per month in office by U.S. presidents.
*(The New York Times)*

with reporters to find out what is on people's minds, as Harry Truman would say. But the formal televised press conference has taken on a significance far in excess of its worth. It has become a test, both for the press and the president. The infrequency of the press conferences results in a wide range of questions being posed by reporters who briefly become performers in front of a national television audience. No journalist wants to throw up a "soft-ball" to the president, so the questions are often obtuse, deal with highly detailed matters, or are cosmic in scope. (How can we bring peace to the world?) Since John Kennedy, who relished his exchanges with the press, presidents have come to believe that they have to be all-knowing, NBC commentator John Chancellor pointed out in *TV Guide.* "The press has come to expect the president to be a walking encyclopedia, and if he doesn't know the fine print in Title IV of the Mongoose Protection Act, that is taken as a sign of incompetence."

With the president apparently on trial, his staff goes to great lengths to prepare him for this ordeal. Recent presidents, including Reagan, often spent two days reading briefing books on a wide range of topics to prepare to answer questions. Reagan's staff went so far as to hold rehearsal sessions, where the President stood at the podium and was questioned by staff members, who then evaluated his answers. Each reporter at the press conference is given an assigned seat. President Reagan was given a photo of each reporter, the location of the reporter's seat, and the reporter's name. He memorized first names and at the conference gave the impression of being on a first-name basis with journalists he had never met. But who is to tell; certainly not the reporter who has just been called by his or her first name by the president of the United States during a televised press conference.

Many members of the President's staff feared the live press conferences because of Ronald Reagan's propensity for misstatement. While he did very well at reading prepared remarks, he lacked the quickness of a Kennedy, Nixon, or even Carter to respond to a journalist's inquiries. He was described as the least intellectual of any president in the White House in modern times. He lacked a sense of history; he rarely read books. He frequently lacked the ability to deal with the often aggressive and wide-ranging questions thrown up by reporters. His slips of the tongue became infamous in Washington, but were usually not reported. When they were reported Reagan became angry. At one news conference the President told reporters that he could document his answers to five questions the journalists reported he had mistakenly answered at a previous meeting with the press. He held a piece of paper in his hand that he said proved he was right, but no one was allowed to see the paper and during the remainder of the press conference Reagan made several additional misstatements regarding the history of the war in Vietnam. Sometimes, as when he erroneously said that the South African government had granted civil rights to blacks in that nation, the resulting embarrassment required a presidential correction. But most of the time no correction was issued, in fact, such misstatements were often ignored by reporters. Former Carter press secretary, Jody Powell, briefly a newspaper columnist after Carter's defeat, was invited to attend a presidential briefing at the White House. During a speech at the University of Washington in 1984 Powell related that during the briefing Reagan made a comment that suggested he, the president, could recall nuclear missiles once they were launched. Powell said he was certain that the other reporters in the room would feature that misimpression in their stories, but none did. When he asked his colleagues why they ignored this item, he said he was told—Oh, that's just the President. He makes mistakes like that quite often.

Controlling the flow of information that came out of the White House was a dominant part of the Deaver-Reagan press strategy. The only individual who could seriously disrupt this strategy was Ronald Reagan, so the staff worked hard to keep the President away from situations where Deaver and company were not in control of what the President said. In mid-1982 when Reagan joined the leaders from several Western European nations for an important economic summit meeting in Europe he was the only national leader who did not meet with reporters to answer questions. When at public gatherings or meetings, reporters were prohibited from asking questions. This practice continued even through Reagan's campaign for re-election. During that campaign while Reagan was touring a wildlife refuge in Maryland to show his concern for the environment, reporters shouted a question at the President about his controversial appointment of an individual to an advisory panel on oceans and atmosphere. Larry Speakes, a Reagan press aide, stepped in front of the President to cut off the question, according to Barbara Matusow in an article in the *Washington Journalism Review.* "My guardian says I can't talk," Reagan said. Other White House aides clicked off television lights so pictures could not be taken.

The trip to Maryland was what Presidential aides call a photo opportunity. Questions are not permitted in such situations. Such rules were established to protect the President from himself, according to former aide Lyn Nofziger. "If we just let him go his own way, we'd have a perpetual press conference." Many reporters agree. "If you get the question within earshot, he'll answer it because he is a decent guy," said one veteran wire service reporter in an article in the *Washington Journalism Review.*

But the White House strategy had serious faults for the public if not for the President. Reporters simply didn't have much opportunity to ask the President a direct question. Consequently, the viewers of the evening news were treated (mistreated) to the spectre of what John Chancellor calls "government by cupped ear." Whenever the President walked to a car or his helicopter, reporters, kept yards away by rope barriers, shouted questions to the leader of the free world, questions that could barely be heard over the whine of an aircraft engine or idling automobile motors. The President, who is hard of hearing, cupped his hand over his ear to try to catch the question. When he heard one, he shouted out a one line answer. Many reporters were angered by their treatment; some left their jobs, according to Jane Meyer, a reporter for the *Wall Street Journal.* "What I find absolutely revolting about the whole situation—and it was introduced by President Reagan—is that policy is now communicated by three questions shouted over the roof of a car," says Sara Fritz of the *Los Angeles Times,* 1984 president of the White House Correspondents Association. "I have actually heard reporters yell, 'What about the Middle East?' Is that any way to discuss foreign policy?"

But other journalists place part of the blame on the press. William Greider, *Rolling Stone* magazine's national editor and former assistant managing editor of the *Washington Post* suggests: "The press has a fundamental obligation to report what the president says and does—but that's not the end of its obligation. They are not doing enterprise reporting on Ronald Reagan. They are saying, 'If they [the White House] don't hand it to us, we can't report it.' "

For six years, Reagan's press relations were handled by Larry Speakes, called the chief White House spokesman. When Reagan became president, James Brady was his press secretary, but Brady was seriously wounded when John Hinckley tried to kill the President. Deputy press secretary Larry Speakes took over Brady's duties, but White House director of communications David Gergen was the chief power in the administration. It was an awkward time. Gergen had access to Reagan, but rarely met with the press. Speakes met with the press, but had limited access to the President. No single person was truly responsible for press relations, and confusion was common. Gergen resigned and was replaced in spirit if not title by Michael Deaver, a close Reagan aide. Then Deaver resigned and in January 1985 Reagan named Patrick Buchanan as director of communications. Buchanan was a speech writer for Richard Nixon and remains a doctrinaire conservative ideologue. His appointment was viewed as threatening by many in the press in the 1970s. "I think Buchanan believes the Eastern, liberal media is unfair to conservatives, and he'll make every effort he can to press-bash," said ABC's Sam Donaldson. In early 1987, Buchanan resigned, frustrated by his failure to influence White House policy. During Larry Speakes's final two years as chief White House spokesman he solidified his position in the administration. He attended more important meetings, had good access to the President, and reporters knew that Speakes' words reflected administration policy and ideas. While he had some flare-ups with reporters, usually provoked by complaints from journalists, Speakes seemed to get along well with most of the White House press corps.

When Speakes resigned in 1987 to take a lucrative job on Wall Street, he was replaced by Marlin Fitzwater, who had served for 20 years as a government press officer and, prior to his White House assignment, was press secretary to Vice-President George Bush. Bush retained Fitzwater as the White House spokesperson when he became president in 1989.

A year after his resignation as press secretary, Speakes dropped a bomb on the Washington press corps when he revealed that on two occasions, once in 1983 and once in 1985, he fabricated quotations that were attributed to President Reagan. Speakes made the revelation in a book, *Speaking Out.* It is not unusual for press secretaries to present sentences or even entire speeches as the actual words of public officials after their bosses have reviewed the material in question, according to *New York Times* journalist David Johnston. "In addition, press secretaries routinely paraphrase the boss's thoughts or ideas. Not often, but on occasion, a spokesman will make up a quotation," he wrote. Ron Ziegler, Nixon's former press secretary, said that Speakes had violated White House norms established by custom. "I never thought of doing it," he said. And Ron Nessen, Gerald Ford's press secretary agreed that Speakes had gone beyond accepted practice. "A key part of the job is to accurately reflect the President's views. But Larry just didn't make it up. He created this whole scene in the briefing. It goes way beyond the line," Nessen added.

## ◻ The Bush Presidency

A *Washington Journalism Review* article on the press relations during the first year of George Bush's presidency was titled "Mr. Nice Guy Meets the Press." This is a good general summation of the early years of the Bush administration. The aggressive handlers that surrounded President Reagan for eight years were gone, or at least not nearly as obvious in the Bush White House. The "line of the day" and the intense efforts to package the president for the evening television news programs seemed to be missing. Still, many of the other successful formulae devised by the Reagan administration continued to be applied by members of Bush's staff.

Most observers noted that George Bush was getting on very well with the White

House press corps. His was not a television presidency. In the first year in office he was on television far less often than his predecessor. Several reporters have said he is somewhat uncomfortable with television and the whole apparatus of image making. "He doesn't like that part of the presidency," according to NBC's Jim Miklaszewski. "The Reagan-Bush difference is like night and day," says CBS's Lesley Stahl. "This White House doesn't care if the president gets on the evening news or not." Ironically, some of the television journalists who grumbled about media management by the Reagan White House now miss it. "People who did stories about the cynical, manipulative Reagan presidency are now complaining about the unfocused, unpackaged Bush presidency," noted Gerald F. Seib, the White House correspondent for the *Wall Street Journal.*

There is no question efforts have been made to try to stage events and manage the news, but not nearly to the extent undertaken in the Reagan presidency. But many of these attempts have failed, largely because Bush's people aren't as good at this as were Reagan's handlers. In March of 1989 Bush took a trip to Pennsylvania to dramatize that drugs had even begun to affect the traditional cultures of rural America. Perhaps the most moving meeting held by the President was his meeting with Amish leaders. But Amish religious traditions banned television cameras, and America missed these scenes. On his trip to China, Bush's media managers concocted an unscheduled stop for the President in Tiananmen Square, a terrific photo opportunity. But the stop was not scheduled properly for network television news, and another video opportunity was botched. In September of 1989 the President gave a nationwide address on drugs, and showed viewers a bag of crack which he said had been purchased across the street from the White House. But reporters soon uncovered the fact that the undercover narcotic agents had set up the crack buy near the White House so the President could use the bag as a prop. These examples show that Bush's handlers are at least attempting to orchestrate some press coverage. "They just aren't doing it very well," noted *Washington Post* Outlook section editor David Ignatius.

Stephen M. Studdert, whose title was assistant to the president for special activities and initiatives, was the closest staff equivalent to Michael Deaver in the Bush administration. But Studdert, who had little background in handling the media, was replaced in less than a year by Sig Rogich, a Las Vegas-based public relations consultant and advertising executive. He had worked closely with Roger Ailes during the 1988 Bush campaign.

While some in the press were perhaps frustrated because Bush's staff made their jobs a little more difficult (they had to work harder to get their pictures), the President received high marks from journalists regarding the number of press conferences he held. During the first ten months in office he held 28 press conferences, some televised, most not televised. (Reagan held only 48 in eight years in office.) "Bush himself has said he's amenable to everything, not afraid of the press, and doesn't need a lot of preparation for press conferences," wrote Jack Nelson, the *Los Angeles Times* Washington bureau chief. "The preparations he's had for these [press] conferences have been two or three minutes standing in the hallway before he goes in," Nelson said.

Following the Reagan presidency, a blue ribbon commission at Harvard's John F. Kennedy School of Government studied the presidential press conference and reported it was "in a serious state of disrepair." The press conferences are high on drama and low on content, the report concluded. The dynamics of the live televised event work against substance and for drama. Indeed, television permits the reporters to become performers as well, and this may account for the fact that according to researchers who have studied the press conferences, the length of the average question asked by a journalist grew from 15 words during Franklin Roosevelt's term in office, to close to 150 words today.

By holding more frequent press conferences, President Bush has apparently followed one of the recommendations of the commission report. Other suggestions are that the press conferences be held during the day, not at night, to help de-emphasize the show business elements in the gathering; that reporters attending be limited to regular White House correspondents, with a few seats set aside to be filled by lottery for nonregular White House reporters; that some press conferences be focused on specific issues to permit specialized journalists to ask more pointed questions, and that the 30-minute running time for the press conference be extended. Whether these other suggestions will be followed or not will be determined largely by the president and his media handlers, who may be uncomfortable with greater press exposure to the president.

As noted previously, Bush's press secretary is Marlin Fitzwater. A native Kansan, Fitzwater came to Washington, D.C., in 1965 with a degree in journalism and a short stint as a professional journalist. He has worked as a public affairs officer in a variety of departments. He worked as a deputy press secretary for a short time in the Reagan White House, then worked as Vice-President Bush's press spokesperson before replacing Larry Speakes in 1987. Bush, who had previously been happy with Fitzwater's work, retained him in that post. For the most part, the members of the press corps have praised Fitzwater for his fairness and affability. The atmosphere at press briefings has improved under Fitzwater. "It isn't the lion's den it was under Larry Speakes," said Helen Thomas, the UPI reporter who is the dean of the White House press corps. Thomas has worked with 15 different presidential press secretaries and noted that Fitzwater is "one of the best I've seen because he keeps his incredible cool and patience and sense of humor."

## A FINAL THOUGHT

Long-time Washington reporter Douglass Cater noted: "Amid the disputations between media and government, there is a danger of ignoring the common obligation they share to provide 'a picture of reality on which one can act.' " It was noted earlier that it was the mission of mass media in this country to bring to citizens a picture of reality upon which we can act in evaluating our elected officials, in choosing among those who seek public office, in informing us upon issues that confront the government. There has never been a nation with as much mass media as now exist in the United States. If quantity alone determines the success or failure of the press in accomplishing this mission, we should be the best informed and most knowledgeable citizenry in the world. But as you can see, many elements work against us in this regard. The government and those who seek office attempt to manipulate the coverage they receive by the press, and there are too many lazy journalists who, while decrying this manipulation, appreciate how easy it makes their jobs. Television reporters are often more interested in pictures and mood and emotion than information and ideas and facts. It sometimes seems the best minds inside and outside the media are not working to inform the public, but working in ways to confuse and delude the viewers and readers. We have looked at the most visible tip of the iceberg of the relationship between the press and those who govern us. As previously noted, more often than not the press fulfills its responsibilities in this regard. But, and this is more important, too often they fail us.

## BIBLIOGRAPHY

These are some of the materials that have been helpful in the preparation of this chapter.

Alter, Jonathan. "Nobody Knows What the Hell's Goin On," *Newsweek,* February 1, 1988.

Armstrong, Scott. "Iran-Contra: Was the Press Any Match for All the President's Men?" *Columbia Journalism Review* May/June, 1990.

Barber, James D. "Candidate Reagan and the Sucker Generation," *Columbia Journalism Review,* November/December, 1987.

Boot, William. "Campaign '88: TV Overdoses on the Inside Dope," *Columbia Journalism Review,* January/February, 1989.

"Bush's Media Wizard," *Newsweek,* September 26, 1988."Campaign Coverage Dissected," *presstime,* January, 1989.

"Campaign Coverage Dissectech" *presstime,* January, 1989.

"Chasing the Political Ad Dollar on TV," *Channels,* February, 1988.

Commoner, Barry. "Talking to a Mule," *Columbia Journalism Review,* January/February, 1987.

*Covering Campaign '88.* New York: Gannett Center for Media Studies, 1989.

*Covering the Candidates: Role and Responsibilities of the Press.* Reston, Va: American Press Institute, 1987.

Diamond, Edwin; Marin, Adrian; and Silverman, Robert. "Mr. Nice Guy Meets the Press," *Washington Journalism Review,* January/February, 1990.

Dowd, Maureen. "In Bush's White House, the Secretary Is the One with the White Hat," *The New York Times,* January 18, 1990.

———. "President and the Press: A Clash of 2 Obsessions," *The New York Times,* January 1, 1990.

Gans, Curtis B. "Let's Abolish Paid Political Television Commercials," *The Seattle Times,* April 22, 1979.

Greenfield, Jeff. *The Real Campaign: How the Media Missed the Story of the 1980 Campaign.* New York: Summit Books, 1982.

"The Great TV Shout-Out," *Newsweek,* February 8, 1989.

Halberstam, David. "How Television Failed the American Voter," *Parade,* January 11, 1981.

Hallin, Daniel C. "Whose Campaign Is It, Anyway?" *Columbia Journalism Review,* January/February, 1991.

Hertsgaard, Mark. "Journalists Played Dead for Reagan. Will They Roll Over Again for Bush?" *Washington Journalism Review,* January/February, 1989.

———.*On Bended Knee.* New York: Schocken Books, 1989.

"How the Media Blew It," *Newsweek,* November 21, 1988.

Hoyt, Michael. "Exploring Caucus Country," *Columbia Journalism Review,* January/February, 1988.

Ignatius, David. "The Press and the Presidency," *The Seattle Times,* May 28, 1989.

Johnston, David. "Who's Talking? Putting Words in Official Mouths," *The New York Times,* April 21, 1988.

Judis, John B. "The Hart Affair," *Columbia Journalism Review,* July/August, 1987.

Kalb, Marvin. "TV Election Spoilers," *The New York Times,* November 28, 1988.

Kalter, Joanmarie. "Covering Presidential Campaigns? They're 10% Journalism and 90% Stamina," *TV Guide,* November 12, 1988.

King, Wayne. "Presidential Poll Prompts Repackaging of Robertson, " *The New York Times,* June 23, 1988.

McElwaine, Sandra. "Marlin and the Wolf Pack," *Washington Journalism Review,* June, 1988.

McGinnis, Joe. *The Selling of the President, 1968.* New York: Trident Press, 1969.

McGovern, George. "George McGovern: The Target Talks Back," *Columbia Journalism Review,* July/August, 1984.

Mater, Gene. "Pandora's Box of Free Time Proposals," *Washington Journalism Review,* July/August, 1990.

Mauro, Tony. "It's Not Too Late to Save the Presidential Press Conference," *Washington Journalism Review,* January/February, 1989.

Ornstein, Norman. "What TV News Doesn't Report About Congress and Should," *TV Guide,* October 21, 1989.

Ornstein, Norman, and Robinson, Michael. "The Case of the Disappearing Congress," *TV Guide,* January 11, 1986.

*The People, Press and Politics.* Los Angeles: The Los Angeles Times, 1988.

Picard, Robert G. "Revisions of the Four Theories of the Press Model," *Mass Comm Review,* Winter/Spring, 1982/83.

Pollard, James E. *The President and the Press: Truman to Johnson.* Washington, D.C.: Public Affairs Press, 1964.

"The President and the Press," *Newsweek,* February 6, 1989.

"The President Under Glass," *The New York Times,* October 8, 1988.

*The Press, the Presidency, and the First Hundred Days.* New York: Gannett Center for Media Studies, 1989.

"Refereeing the TV Campaign," *Washington Journalism Review,* January/February, 1991.

Robinson, Michael J., and Ranney, Austin (eds.). *The Mass Media Campaign in 1984.* Washington, D.C.: American Enterprise Institute, 1985.

Siebert, Fred S.; Peterson, Theodore; and Schramm, Wilbur. *Four Theories of the Press.* Urbana: University of Illinois Press, 1956.

Weiss, Philip. "Party Time in Atlanta," *Columbia Journalism Review,* September/October, 1988.

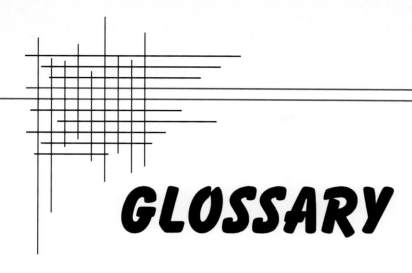

# *GLOSSARY*

**above-the-line costs** money spent on the creative part of a film: script, salaries for performers, etc.

**access to the media** a phrase referring to the proposition that to enjoy full First Amendment rights citizens should be able to use the mass media to express their ideas.

**agenda setting** a phrase referring to the proposition that while the mass media cannot tell us what to think, they can, by choosing what to report, tell us what to think about.

**basic cable** the cable service provided to a subscriber for a flat, monthly fee. Basic cable normally includes a wide range of advertiser-supported channels.

**below-the-line costs** the money actually spent producing a film: sets, travel to locations, film, etc.

**billboards** on-screen graphics during a television news show that feature the name of the news program and the sponsor's logo.

**black lists** lists (generated by various conservative anti-communist interests in the late 1940s and early 1950s) of persons thought to be somehow tied to left-wing or socialist or communist causes and thus not employable in the mass media.

**block booking** an illegal practice by which a film distributor will permit a theater to show a hit picture only if the theater is willing to show other, less popular films as well.

**book ends** a television commercial that is divided into two 15- or 30-second parts and shown before and after another commercial.

**breakout** a magazine publishing process that permits an advertiser to buy space in a limited number of copies of a national magazine: i.e., those copies delivered in a particular city or those copies delivered to persons living in affluent areas.

**bullet theory** a discredited communication theory suggesting that persons could be strongly and directly influenced by mass communication.

**byline** the name of the journalist or writer who wrote the article.

**catalytic hypothesis** the notion that watching violent television programming might provoke a violent response.

**catharsis hypothesis** the notion that watching violent television programming provides an emotional outlet for pent-up frustrations and anger.

**channel** the means of transmitting the message.

**classified advertising** small textual ads carried in newspapers and magazines generally priced by the word or the line.

**Communications Act of 1934** the law that outlines the regulation of American broadcasting.

**complementary copy** non-advertising material published by a magazine in order to satisfy the demands of an advertiser.

**content analysis** the systematic study of the content (words, pictures, nuances, etc.) of any communication.

**counter programming** telecasting programming that is likely to attract viewers not interested in other programs on at the same time: i.e., telecasting an adult comedy when the other networks are telecasting family programs.

**day-parts** segmenting a 24-hour day into parts on the basis of the likely audience watching at that time: i.e., prime time, late night, early morning.

**decode** to convert the words, pictures, or symbols contained in a message into meaningful thoughts or ideas.

**digital audio broadcasting** a system of radio broadcasting which relies on the transmission of the signal in a digital rather than an analog code.

**digital audio tape (DAT)** a system of tape recording and playback that uses a digital code, similar to the system used on compact discs.

**display advertising** large newspaper and magazine ads which feature material (drawings, decorative type, photos, etc.) other than text.

**drive-time** the early morning and late afternoon hours when commuters are listening to their radios as they drive to and from work.

**duopoly rule** rule that no single individual or company can own more than one television station or AM or FM radio station in the same market.

**electronic pagination** electronically laying out the pages of a magazine or newspaper on a computer.

**encode** to put a message into words or pictures so it can be transmitted to the receiver.

**ENG** electronic newsgathering gear (video recorders, editors, etc.) used by television news reporters.

**enhanced underwriting rules** rules that permit public broadcasting stations to use corporate logos, slogans, and expanded messages to acknowledge corporate sponsorship of various programs.

**experimental research** the attempt to study a communication problem by duplicating a real life situation in a controlled environment such as a laboratory.

**feedback** the response from the receiver of a message to the source of the message.

**film rental revenues** those revenues that pass from the exhibitor to the distributor of a film, after the exhibitor has taken out his/her share.

**fin-syn rules (financial interest-syndication rules)** federal rules that define the rights of television networks to own and syndicate programs.

**flexography** a one-step printing process that is a hybrid of both the letter-press and offset printing processes.

**FMX** an enhanced FM stereo radio transmission system that uses a third channel to enhance the sound of the broadcast.

**folk culture** the culture created by a community of people for themselves; it reflects their attitudes and beliefs.

**format** the type of programming a radio station chooses to broadcast: i.e., rock music, talk radio.

**grazing** the practice of using a remote control channel changer to switch among television programs.

**gross participation deal** an agreement that gives certain film performers, writers, and directors a percentage of the total amount of money a film earns, before costs are deducted.

**gross revenues** the total amount of money earned by a film.

**hard news** serious news; news about government, politics, the environment, crime, disasters, etc.

**high culture** culture that is generated by master artisans and is defined by critics and others: elite culture.

**high definition television (HDTV)** digitally transmitted television that has a superior picture and a more rectangular (compared to contemporary television) height-to-width ratio.

**horizontal programming strategy** a strategy in radio to reach a widely differentiated audience with diversified programming.

**hostage film** an independently made film usually funded by a large studio that refuses to distribute the film when it is completed because the studio does not believe it will be successful, and does not want to spend any more money on marketing the film.

**HUTs** homes using television; 93 million plus in the United States in 1991.

**hypodermic needle theory** *see* bullet theory.

**infomercial** a 30- to 60-minute commercial that tries to look like a real television program and is telecast by a television station for a substantial fee.

**invasion of privacy** a civil action that can be brought against a mass medium (or individual) that alleges use of a name for commercial purposes without consent, intrusion into private affairs, or disclosure of private information about a person.

**jet-ink printing** a printing process that permits a magazine publisher to print personalized messages in each individual copy of a magazine.

**joint operating agreement** a legal agreement that permits two newspapers in the same market to combine all their operations except their newsrooms to reduce costs.

**jump** the continuation of a news story from the page on which it starts to another page in the newspaper.

**letterbox format** putting black borders along the top and bottom of a film so it may be seen on a square television screen in the same rectangular height-to-width ratio as it was originally filmed.

**letter-press printing** the original printing process where raised letters are brushed with ink and then rolled against paper to leave a printed impression.

**libel** a civil action that can be brought against a mass medium or individual alleging that a published or broadcast communication has harmed the reputation of an individual.

**linotype** a machine developed in the late 19th century that permitted printers to mechanically set a line of type, instead of having to set each letter into the line by hand.

**marketing mix** the total package of sales, sales promotion, packaging, distribution, and advertising that is designed to move a product from a manufacturer to a buyer.

**marriage mail** combining a variety of direct mail advertisements into a single package to save postal costs.

**mass culture** the contemporary culture of the people, or culture that has been created by professionals and sold to people: i.e., radio, television, movies.

**media advisor** the individual who assists the political candidate in using the mass media, both as an advertising and as a news medium, by planning and directing a targeted media campaign.

**media pool** a small group of reporters who are selected to cover a story and then share the information and video they collect with other members of the press who are not in the pool.

**menus** sets of directions which appear on the computer screen to assist a person using an interactive data base to derive the information that is sought.

**mobile DJs** record spinners who carry their own audio equipment, records, CDs, and tapes to provide dance music for clubs and social events.

**modeling hypothesis** the notion that young people who watch violence on television will try to imitate that violence in real life.

**muckrakers** a small group of investigative journalists who wrote in the early 20th century about corruption in business and government.

**narrowcasting** programming a radio station with a format that will appeal to a very narrow segment of the audience.

**national display advertising** display advertising published by a local newspaper for national brand name goods and services.

**national spot advertising** advertising carried by local radio and television stations for national brand name goods and services.

**network affiliate** a television or radio station that has a contractual agreement to carry programming in its particular market that is provided by a broadcast or television network.

**network compensation** money paid to a network affiliated television station by the network for telecasting the advertising contained in network programs.

**newsbooks** the first newspapers, appearing in 1609.

**nut** a term used to indicate the expenses incurred by a theater operator; this amount is deducted by the theater owner from the gross revenues earned from ticket sales.

**objectivity** a journalistic notion that a reporter should present readers or viewers with only the facts and that personal bias has no place in a story.

**offset printing** the use of printing plates derived from a photographic process; on the press, an ink and water mixture is put on the plate and a roller picks up the images and transfers them to the paper.

**oligopoly** a market situation where there are a small number of producers or providers of most goods and services, and they have considerable power to set prices and establish other market conditions.

**one-to-a-customer rule** a federal regulation stating that a single individual may own either a TV station or an AM/FM combination, but not both, in a single market.

**owned and operated stations** television stations in major markets that are owned and operated by the three major television networks: ABC, CBS and NBC.

**pack journalism** reporters defer their individual judgment about a story and cover it because everyone else is covering it.

**pay cable** those cable channels for which a subscriber must pay a fee in addition to the charge for a basic cable package: i.e., HBO, Showtime.

**payola** the practice of record promoters giving gifts to disc jockeys and station program directors to try to influence them to play certain records over the air.

**pay-per-view television** a cable or other controlled television distribution system that requires users to pay for each program they watch, rather than buying a package of programming on a monthly basis.

**pilot episode** the first episode of a television series that is made to show the network the quality and nature of the program.

**platforming** opening a motion picture in only a handful of theaters with little advertising, with the hope that good critical reviews and word of mouth will generate enough interest in the film that it can be gradually shown in more theaters.

**playlist** a list prepared by a radio station program director or DJ of the songs that can or must be played on the air.

**polispot** a television commercial for a candidate for public office.

**popular culture** the culture of the masses, or contemporary folk culture that has been mediated in some way to reach a wider audience.

**production code** a code that was used by the film industry to censor movies from the 1920s until the mid-1950s.

**product placement** the practice of businesses paying movie producers to display or mention brand name products in a motion picture.

**rating** the score given by A.C. Nielsen and other television rating services to a television program; the percentage of all the homes having television in which a program was seen.

**receiver** the person who accepts the message transmitted by the sender.

**Red Scare** the period from the late 1940s through the early 1950s during which allegations were made that communists had infiltrated the mass media and other industries.

**reference group** persons who are close to us (family members, friends, co-workers, fellow students) and help us to define ourselves and our lives.

**remnant space** advertising space that has not been sold just before a magazine is to be published; it is usually offered to advertisers at a discounted rate.

**retail advertising** newspaper display advertising for local businesses.

**run-of-press (ROP)** ads purchased run of press can be published anywhere in the newspaper, as opposed to a preferred position for which the advertiser must pay extra.

run of station  ads purchased run of station may be telecast or broadcast anytime, as opposed to a time slot adjacent to a particular program, which usually commands a premium price.

sedition  utterances or publications that criticize the government or political leaders, or advocate overthrowing them.

segmentation  building a newscast for a particular segment of the viewing audience: i.e., older people, affluent women.

selective binding  a binding process that permits a magazine publisher to create custom editions of each issue of a magazine for readers with different interests.

selectivity  a theoretical proposition that people view and remember communication differently, depending on their psychological predispositions.

sell through  selling, rather than renting, videocassettes of feature films to customers. Cassettes thought by the video distributor to have high sell-through potential will be priced very low.

share  a score given to a television program by a rating company like A.C. Nielsen; the percentage of those homes in which television was being viewed at the time that a particular program was watched.

simulcasting  a radio station broadcasting the same program over both its AM or FM frequencies.

SNV  satellite news vehicle; an elaborate electronically equipped truck that permits television news reporters to telecast live reports from distant locations, transmitting the pictures and sound via a satellite to the television station.

soft news  not hard news; feature stories, personality columns, gardening tips, recipes, health advice, etc.

station programming cooperative  a system in which all public TV stations have a vote in the selection of programs that the Public Broadcasting Service will telecast each season.

stripping  the practice of local television stations showing reruns of a television series that was originally broadcast weekly now on a daily basis, Monday through Friday.

survey research  the means used by social scientists to try to uncover data by systematically asking questions to a usually randomly selected group of persons.

sweeps  four months each year (November, February, May, and July) when all local television stations are rated to establish advertising rates for the succeeding months.

syndication  selling the rights to broadcast a program to a local television station; normally this is done with reruns, but there is a considerable amount of first run programming that is also being syndicated today.

talk radio  a program format in which a host invites listeners to call in and comment about current issues; the host is often quite outspoken regarding this issue and attempts to generate conflict through the callers' comments.

teletext  an electronic transmission system that carries a limited amount of data to the home via unused parts of a television signal; this data is decoded by a small converter attached to the TV set when the subscriber seeks information contained in the system.

total market coverage  a direct mail service that provides advertisers with complete saturation of a market area, as opposed to using a newspaper which is only delivered to subscribers' homes.

**two-step flow** a communication theory suggesting that some people (called opinion leaders) get information about issues from the mass media, develop ideas and opinions about the issues, and then pass along both the information and their ideas and opinions to others.

**underground press** small, anti-establishment newspapers that developed in the late 1960s and circulated information about the counterculture, drugs, music, etc. to like-minded individuals.

**uses and gratification theory** a theory that people are purposeful in their use of mass media, motivated by individual needs and desires.

**vertical programming strategy** programming a radio station to attract a small segment of the broader audience: *see also* narrowcasting.

**videotex** an interactive electronic data base where subscribers request information stored in computers; data is then transmitted along telephone lines and accessed by the subscriber using a computer or other video terminal.

**VNR** video news release; a video version of a press release, prepared in hopes that it will be telecast during the news as a part of the show.

**wide release** a film distribution strategy where a movie opens in a great number of theaters on the same day, and the opening is accompanied by heavy promotion of the film.

**wire service** a news gathering agency which provides news and other information to clients (like newspapers and broadcasting stations) that pay for this service.

**yellow journalism** sensationalistic journalism that featured exaggerated news stories and graphic pictures; it was practiced by many newspapers at the end of the 19th century in an attempt to lure the masses to their publications.

**zapping** the practice of fast-forwarding through commercials on television programs that have been recorded on a VCR for delayed viewing.

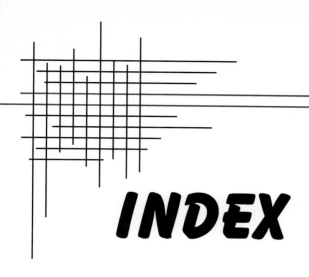

# INDEX